MARXISM AND DOMINATION

Marxism and Domination

A NEO-HEGELIAN, FEMINIST, PSYCHOANALYTIC THEORY OF SEXUAL, POLITICAL, AND TECHNOLOGICAL LIBERATION

Isaac D. Balbus

PRINCETON UNIVERSITY PRESS
PRINCETON, NEW JERSEY

FOR
CAPPY

We must be ready . . . to abandon a path which we have followed for a time, if it seems to be leading to no good end. Only believers, who demand that science should be a substitute for the catechism they have given up, will blame an investigator for developing or even transforming his views.

—FREUD, *Beyond the Pleasure Principle*

Certainly, I shall avoid the company of detractors of a great man. If I happen to agree with them on a . . . point I grow suspicious of myself; and in order to console myself for having seemed to be of their opinion. . . . I feel I must disavow and keep these false friends away from me as much as I can.

—BENJAMIN CONSTANT, "De la Liberté des Anciens Comparée à Celle des Modernes"

What we have to accomplish . . . is [a] relentless criticism of all existing conditions, relentless in the sense that the criticism is not afraid of its findings and just as little afraid of the conflict with the powers that be.

—MARX, Letter to Arnold Ruge, September 1843

Contents

ix

PREFACE

This book has been a long time in the making. It is, in fact, the culmination of a theoretical and political journey that has lasted for more than a decade. As I left graduate school and began to teach at the very end of the 1960s, I (along with many other scholars of my generation) embraced Marxism as the standpoint from which I hoped to make a social-scientific contribution to the emerging radical movements in Western industrial societies with which I increasingly identified. And so, for the better part of the next ten years, I took up the task of developing a critical Marxian analysis of a few of the manifold forms of domination against which these movements are obliged to struggle. But by the latter part of the 1970s I had already become dubious about the merits of this mode of analysis: it was becoming more and more apparent to me that Marxist theory was unable to account for the origins and persistence of domination and that Neo-Marxist efforts to compensate for this inability through the introduction of ostensibly complementary theoretical assumptions succeeded only in undermining the integrity of Marxism by transforming it into eclecticism. I came, in other words, to the conclusion that the roots of domination are not visible from a Marxian standpoint, and thus that this standpoint does not allow for an adequate theoretical contribution to the practical uprooting of domination. It was not, however, until the very end of the decade and the beginning of the next that I was able to elaborate the rudiments of a more satisfactory, alternative theoretical standpoint. In the light of this standpoint, I now see Marxism as an integral part of the very domination it purports, but fails, critically to comprehend. Thus my Marxist journey has come to an end.

This intellectual journey could not have reached an end independently of a personal voyage on which I was simultaneously embarked that gave me the strength to complete the former in the face of the personal and political risks with which it is necessarily associated. The author of a critique of Marxism—even one animated by the most radical impulses—will inevitably be charged with the ''crime'' of providing grist for the mill of professional anti-Marxists as well as other assorted conservative forces, and thus for having ''betrayed'' the Left at the very point when its unity in the face of the resurgence of these forces is absolutely imperative. The epigraphs to this book signal my awareness of this danger and the essentials of my response to those who, like myself, are concerned about it. But I am well aware that this response will not satisfy many Leftists who remain committed to Marxism and thus that I will be sharply criticized, if not condemned, by some of the same intellectuals with whom I have broken theoretical and political bread over the past ten

xi

years or more. Having long ago been alienated from the "straight" academic world, I now risk estrangement from a Leftist academic community with which I have, and have been, identified and that has been no small comfort in the face of the professional isolation accompanying that earlier rupture. Writing this book, then, meant accepting the possibility of finding myself out on a rather lonely limb. I could not have accepted this possibility, and thus could not have written this book, had I not acquired a measure of the individual autonomy that enables one to affirm one's sense of self-worth in spite of the opposition of significant others. And I would have been unable to acquire this autonomy vis-à-vis my contemporary others had I not learned a great deal about, and come to terms with, the ways in which my encounters with my earliest significant others—especially my mother—decisively shaped my sense of self.

There is another way in which this personal odyssey was indispensable to the writing of this book. The re-discovery of the power of my mother over my life left me emotionally open to take seriously and develop further an emerging feminist analysis of the general social significance of maternal power. As I became increasingly aware of the extent to which my own tendencies both to exercise and acquiesce in domination in my relationships with women, friends, and the "world" were rooted in the nature of my relationship with my mother, the plausibility of a theory that locates mother-dominated child rearing as a central source of sexual, political, and techno-logical domination likewise increased. This theory, in turn, enhanced con-siderably my understanding of the roots of domination in my personal life and thus my struggle against it. I anticipate that some will contend that what I take to be a remarkably fruitful oscillation between the personal and the theoretical is but a classic case of the illicit projection of the idiosyncracies of the former on to the latter. I invite anyone who no longer has an unconscious stake in resisting a theory of maternal power to discuss this contention with me.

If the personal journey I have described has been essential to the writing of this book, it could not have been written without the help of those people who made it possible for me to undertake that journey. From my mother I learned the need for intimacy, without which I never would have had a reason to try to learn how to satisfy this need more completely. The unfailing will-ingness of Cappy Silver to help me fulfill this need gave me both the incentive and the strength to pursue the problem of the childhood origins of those tendencies toward domination that inhibited me from fulfilling it. And Jane Ganet-Sigel helped move me to explore this problem in depth. All three know how grateful I am for what they have given.

Many others contributed substantially to the completion of this book. My dear friends and colleagues Ron Bayer, Larry Cohen, Rob Crawford, and

Peter Knauss all read significant segments of the manuscript. Their support for my project encouraged me to sustain it and their questions and comments undoubtedly helped me improve its outcome. The same is true of the comments and questions of a number of other much-appreciated colleagues at Chicago Circle who read individual chapters: Don Bowen, Doris Graber, Waude Kracke, Eric Moskowitz, and Charles Williams. Jean Elshtain and Peter Stillman read the manuscript for Princeton University Press, and were kind enough to make their detailed criticisms and suggestions available to me. Nancy Hartsock's comments on, and enthusiasm for, Chapters Eight and Nine were equally welcome.

Three students were especially helpful in a number of ways: Demir Aytac, Michael Kurz, and Fariba Zarinebaf-Shahr. The Office of Social Science Research and the Department of Political Science at the University of Illinois at Chicago Circle deserve thanks for having funded the typing of a very long manuscript, as does Janet Gorenson for having typed it with such remarkable competence. My editor, Gail Filion, helped me prune my overgrown prose, and Sandy Thatcher, Assistant Director of Princeton University Press, was an important source of support for my project over the past two years.

I have already indicated my indebtedness to Cappy Silver. But she helped me in many more ways than the one to which I have already alluded. She read the entire manuscript, helped me clarify many of my arguments, and prodded me to shorten and simplify many of my overly-long and often convoluted sentences. She was always willing to listen to me talk about my ideas, and never hesitated to encourage me to get back to work on them when I felt I lacked the strength. For all these reasons, and more, this book is lovingly dedicated to her.

Chicago, Illinois
December 1981

Marxism and Domination

INTRODUCTION

Western Marxism is in crisis. In one form or another, and for a variety of different and compelling reasons, serious critical thinkers and actors on the Left are now obliged to pose the question: can a genuinely radical movement in the advanced capitalist societies be Marxist? Is Marxism the essence, merely a necessary part, or in fact an obstacle to such a movement? The purpose of this book is to address and answer this question.

I propose to address this question through the examination and evaluation of the way Marxist and Neo-Marxist thinkers have understood the concerns of what I take to be three of the central liberation movements in the advanced capitalist societies over the past two decades: feminism, ecology, and participatory democracy.[1] These three movements have immeasurably enriched our understanding of the meaning of a "genuinely radical movement" in the advanced capitalist societies. The feminist movement has demonstrated that a genuinely radical movement must address and seek to overcome a sexual division of labor constituted by the domination of men over women—in short, that an anticapitalist movement must also be antipatriarchal. The ecology movement has made us understand that human liberation cannot be purchased at the price of the domination and degradation of our natural environment, and thus that a radical movement against capitalism must embrace a movement against repressive technology as well. Finally, the movement for participatory democracy has made us appreciate that political domination is inherent in centralized, bureaucratic, and even representative forms of governance, and thus that an anticapitalist movement that is committed to democracy must be decentralized, antibureaucratic, and participatory in both its forms and ultimate goals. The liberation movements of the 1960s and the 1970s have demonstrated that a genuinely radical anticapitalist movement must also be a movement against sexual, technological, and political *domination*—in fact, a movement against domination in all its forms—and thus that the genuinely socialist society of the future must be constituted in and through *liberatory* sexual, technological, and political practices in the present.

[1] My focus on these three movements in no way implies a lack of appreciation for, or commitment to, other centrally important liberation struggles of the past two decades—such as those of black and gay people. I do not discuss these struggles in this book because I am far more theoretically prepared to examine the ones that I have included. This difference in theoretical preparation, in turn, partly reflects a difference in my political experience: whereas I have, in one way or another, been personally involved over the past two decades in participatory democratic, feminist, and ecological struggles, I have not been similarly involved in the struggles of blacks and gays. The focus of this—like any other—work, then, is a function of a combination of theoretical and "practical" commitments whose precise structure is peculiar to its author.

3

Each of these movements has confronted Marxist theorists with the challenge of comprehending critically the structure of domination that the movement attacks in order to contribute to the liberation that it envisions. Thus over the past two decades Western Marxism has been reinvigorated through a profusion of original, as well as rediscovered, studies on patriarchy, the state, and the relationship between humans and their natural surround. It is no exaggeration to argue that this undeniable and remarkable renaissance in Marxist scholarship is largely a result of the effort of Marxist thinkers to address the concerns of the liberation movements of these decades. This theoretical effort to demonstrate the sufficiency, or at least the centrality, of Marxist categories for the comprehension of the structures of sexual, political, and technological domination, of course, is simultaneously an effort to persuade us that the feminist, participatory democratic, and ecological movements must be wholly or at least partly Marxist in practice: if Marxist theory is able to explain (or help explain) the origins and persistence of the three structures of domination, it follows that the three movements that are committed to their eradication should be subordinated to (or at least aligned with) a movement against capitalism that is informed by the assumptions of Marxist theory. In essence, Marxist and Neo-Marxist thinkers have attempted to persuade us through their theoretical efforts that the radical questions posed by the liberation movements of the past two decades lend themselves to adequate Marxist theoretical solutions and thus that the answer to the question: "can a genuinely radical movement in the advanced capitalist societies be Marxist?" is "*yes*."

I shall examine these theoretical efforts in order to ascertain whether this answer is correct, and I shall argue that these efforts have proved unsuccessful. Marxist theory does not—and *cannot*—allow for a satisfactory understanding of the roots of sexual, political, and technological domination, and an anticapitalist movement that is informed by the assumptions of this theory will consequently, and necessarily, be unable to uproot them. The radical questions posed by the three liberation movements do not in fact lend themselves to adequate Marxist theoretical solutions and thus a genuinely radical movement in the advanced capitalist societies cannot be Marxist in character. Indeed, I shall demonstrate that, at bottom, the Marxian theoretical—and thus political—project is part of the very problem of domination that such a movement— one that is simultaneously anticapitalist, feminist, participatory democratic, and ecological—must solve, and that the theory and practice of liberation necessarily entails a movement against Marx.

To assess the adequacy of Marxist and Neo-Marxist theories of patriarchy, the state, and repressive technology is to examine and evaluate the extent to which these structures of domination can be illuminated by means of a conceptual system at whose center lies the category of production. Chapter One of this book analyzes Marx's treatment and elaboration of this category. It addresses, in turn, (a) Marx's theory of the primacy of production, or his assumption that labor is *the* medium for the creation and transformation of human needs; (b) his theory of the determining power of the mode of production, or the assumption that, in any given society, the activities or structures through which human needs are fulfilled are best understood as elements of the mode of production of that society; (c) his theory of the determining power of a specifically capitalist mode of production over the ensemble of structures in this society, or his theory of alienation; and (d) his theory of proletarian class struggle, or his analysis of the way in which the capitalist mode of production generates struggles to transform and, ultimately, transcend this alienated mode of production (together with the ensemble of alienated structures that are determined by it) that are undertaken by agents who are defined in terms of their subordinate place within the process of production. This analysis of the constitutive, internally related elements of Marx's conceptual system is intended to lay the foundation for the subsequent examination of the way in which Marxist and Neo-Marxist thinkers have applied this system to the problems of sexual, political, and technological domination. We shall discover in the remaining chapters of Part I and in Part II that their failures are merely specific manifestations of what Chapter One will reveal to be the general, inherent limits of this conceptual system.

The rest of Part I (Chapters Two through Four) is devoted to an analysis of the theoretical efforts of those Marxists who assume that this conceptual system is both a necessary and sufficient means of illuminating the problems of sexual, political, and technological domination and the possibilities for their elimination. The claim of this type of Marxism (to which I will hereafter simply refer as "Marxism," in contrast to "Neo-Marxism"), in other words, is that these forms of domination are wholly a function of the capitalist mode of production and thus that struggles to eliminate them are exhausted by struggles to eliminate this mode of production carried out by agents of production. The practical political corollary to this approach is that the feminist, participatory democratic, and ecological movements should not be autonomous from, but rather subordinate to (or part of) the class struggle. Here I shall argue, as others have before me, that Marxism underestimates dramatically the relative autonomy of the structures of sexual, political, and technological domination from the mode of production; that these structures cannot be grasped exclusively as structures that perform a function on behalf of capitalism; and thus that the effort to undermine the autonomy of the struggles to eliminate these structures and subordinate them to the class struggle is wholly unwarranted. In short, I shall demonstrate that *if* Marxist theory is necessary for the comprehension of the forms of domination and the possibilities for their eradication, it certainly is not sufficient.

5

In Part II (Chapters Five through Seven) I examine those theories, which I will call Neo-Marxist, that are based on the assumption that Marxism is necessary but insufficient and that Marx's attention to production must be supplemented by additional theoretical concerns. Neo-Marxism asserts that the three structures of domination can only in part be understood as constituent, functioning elements of the capitalist mode of production. It follows that struggles to eliminate domination can only in part be grasped as struggles against the mode of production undertaken by agents defined by their place in production. According to this tradition, in other words, patriarchy, the state, and repressive technology are all relatively autonomous from the capitalist mode of production—each possessing an irreducible dynamic of its own—and the struggles to eliminate these forms of domination thus have an autonomous basis and should not be subordinated to, but rather aligned with, the class struggle.

Although it is superior to Marxist theory, I shall argue that Neo-Marxism is unable adequately to illuminate the problems of sexual, political, and technological domination insofar as it fails to develop a coherent synthesis of Marxist theory and the variety of other theories—including psychoanalysis and linguistics—with which it attempts to complement Marxism. This theoretical eclecticism, moreover, characteristically culminates in a covert reassertion of the very primacy of production that the Neo-Marxist insistence on the relative autonomy of the three structures of domination from the mode of production would seem to deny. The practical political corollary to the theoretical eclecticism of Neo-Marxism is that its assertion of the necessary autonomy of the sexual, political, and technological liberation struggles from the class struggle is unaccompanied by any clear conception of the relationship among these struggles and between them and the class struggle. The political consequence of the Neo-Marxist reassertion of the primacy of production is the tacit denial of the autonomy of these liberation struggles from the class struggle and thus the suppression of political eclecticism at the cost of the effective subordination of the former to the requirements of the latter.

This oscillation between eclecticism and orthodoxy is not accidental. It results not from the failings of individual theorists but rather from an inherent yet unacknowledged and thus unclarified tension between the master theoretical assumption of Marxism—the primacy of production—and the assumptions of the supplementary theoretical traditions on which Neo-Marxism is obliged to rely. The absence of a coherent Neo-Marxist synthesis is rooted in the incompatibility between what is held to be the necessary theory and the additional theories that are supposed to make for a sufficient theory. To the extent that these additional theories are essential to illuminate the problems of sexual, political, and technological domination/liberation, the Neo-Marxist claim that Marxism is insufficient but necessary necessarily becomes suspect.

Part III (Chapters Eight through Ten) seeks to transform this suspicion into a case against Marxism. In it I return to the analysis of Marx's concept of production in order to demonstrate that the logic of this category is precisely the logic of the very structures of domination—sexual, technological, and political—that the category purports critically to comprehend. Thus the logic of Marxism is, at bottom, antithetical to the logic of the liberation struggles that strive to supersede these structures. It follows that neither the theory nor the practice of these struggles can be Marxist and that they must, instead, transcend Marxism. The structures of domination, in other words, cannot be grasped as constituent elements of a particular mode of production because the very existence of "production" necessarily implies these structures. Production, I shall demonstrate, is not a universal category that can be used to explain domination but is rather a constituent element of a historically specific *mode of symbolization* that demands critical comprehension. Nor can the liberation struggles be conceptualized or organized as part of or even aligned with the "class struggle," since the class struggle itself is part and parcel of the very mode of symbolization that the liberation struggles are obliged to overcome.

Thus, with the aid of Hegel, Norman O. Brown, and recent feminist transformations of Freudian psychoanalytic thought, I develop a new theory of culture that enables me to conceptualize Marxism as an integral part of the very symbolic structure it claims to surmount. More specifically: production (now understood as technological domination), sexual domination, and political domination are elements of a whole or a totality characterized by an exclusively instrumental mode of symbolizing the relationship between the self and the "natural," sexual, and political others with whom/which it relates—a mode, in short, in which self and other are related as subject to an object. Borrowing, extending, and modifying the argument of Dorothy Dinnerstein, I try to show that this Instrumental mode of symbolization is rooted in and reproduced by the nuclear form of mother-monopolized child rearing.[2] This mode of child rearing, I contend, necessarily engenders an instrumental unconscious symbolization of the world, and thus it must be thoroughly transformed if a new, post-instrumental mode of symbolization is to come into existence.

In the final Chapter of Part III I suggest that the three liberation struggles of the past two decades are, in fact, the embryonic elements of such a new,

[2] The use of the term "mother-monopolized," or "mother-dominated" child rearing should not convey the impression that women have freely chosen disproportionately to assume the responsibilities of nurturing and disciplining infants and young children. To the contrary, they have throughout history been obliged to assume these responsibilities. I emphasize this from the outset in order to forestall the objection that a critique of mother-monopolized child rearing amounts to "blaming the victim."

7

qualitatively transformed mode of symbolization. No longer viewed through the lens of Marxism—where they necessarily assume secondary importance—or Neo-Marxism—where they become more important but nevertheless ultimately unrelated—the struggles to create a liberatory sexuality, technology, and politics display both a centrality and an inner unity constituted by the postinstrumental logic that each embodies. At bottom, the movements against sexual, political, and technological domination are one movement, the movement to transcend the existing Instrumental mode of symbolization and to create authentically reciprocal relationships with our sexual, political, and natural others, relationships within which these others are recognized as subjects in their own right. This struggle for a new culture, I conclude, with Dinnerstein and other feminists, necessarily embraces an effort to inaugurate and consolidate a new form of child rearing—a new mode of introducing human beings to the first, and most significant, others to whom they will relate—in which women and men play an equal part. It is, moreover, a struggle in which we all have an interest and in which we can therefore all participate.

PART I

MARXIST THEORIES
OF DOMINATION

CHAPTER ONE

THE CONCEPT OF PRODUCTION IN MARX

FROM HEGEL TO MARX: THE PRIMACY OF PRODUCTION

The elaboration of the category of production in Marx is inextricably intertwined with his theoretical struggle with Hegel. The very essay—"Critique of the Hegelian Dialectic and Philosophy as a Whole," in the *Economic and Philosophic Manuscripts of 1844*—that announces Marx's definitive philosophical break with his former mentor credits Hegel with discovering, albeit "within the sphere of abstraction," the centrality of labor to the human condition: "The outstanding thing in Hegel's *Phenomenology* . . . is . . . that he . . . grasps the essence of *labour* and comprehends objective man— true, because real man—as the outcome of man's *own labour*."[1] Since Marx himself acknowledges that his discovery of the primacy of production is deeply indebted to Hegel, our discussion of the concept of production in Marx properly begins with Hegel's treatment of this concept in *The Phenomenology of Mind*.

The section on "Self-Consciousness" situates labor within a more general process that Hegel refers to as the struggle for recognition. According to Hegel, the central and enduring human dilemma is the problem of achieving recognition from a world—both natural and social—that is initially encountered as an *other* that is resistant to our will. Humans are born into a world that is alien to them—from which, in other words, they are estranged—and are thus obliged to struggle to surmount this otherness or estrangement if they are ever to feel at home with, i.e., integrated within, this world. This integration, in turn, is only achieved when individuals come to see themselves in nature in general and other human beings in particular, when alienated relationships characterized by an opposition between the subject and the objects to which/whom he or she relates give way to unalienated relationships of reciprocal intersubjectivity. Individual self-consciousness—or what we today might call individual identity—is thus the result of a struggle that begins with opposition and culminates ideally, or in what Hegel calls its "proper"

[1] Karl Marx, "Critique of the Hegelian Dialectic and Philosophy as a Whole," in Robert C. Tucker, ed., *The Marx-Engels Reader*, first ed. (New York: Norton, 1972), pp. 99 and 89 (emphases in the original).

11

form,[2] in unity, i.e., of a dialectic formalized in Hegelian logic as the "unity of opposites." This dialectic of recognition, however, has until Hegel's time not appeared in its "proper" form; human history up to this point has entailed a variety of distorted struggles for recognition whose efforts to annul otherness fail to culminate in reciprocity or unity and thus fail to achieve self-certainty or self-consciousness.

Hegel's famous chapter on "Lordship and Bondage"—his penetrating dissection of the master-slave relationship—is an analysis of one such important historical form of these flawed or repressive struggles for recognition. The master-slave relationship should be understood as a metaphor for that form of the struggle for recognition that is characterized by the domination of one party to a human relationship over the other. In such a relationship, the master attempts to annul the otherness of the slave by treating him or her as an object of control; the resistance of the other is overcome insofar as the other is treated as a thing to be possessed and thus as a mere extension of the self. This effort by the master to achieve recognition through domination, however, is necessarily unsuccessful; the drive for self-consciousness demands that we be recognized by another being that we recognize as human—demands reciprocity—whereas the condition of the slave, or, more generally, the dominated, is precisely his or her *thingness*, his or her lack of humanity.[3] The slave, by definition, cannot give the master the recognition he desires. Thus domination is an inherently inadequate mode of the struggle for recognition.

It is, however, a mode that contains the seeds of its own transformation. The fact that the slave labors for his or her master, while the master merely consumes the fruits of this labor, means that an alternative mode of recognition is open to the former that is foreclosed to the latter. By working on the world and forming objects, the slave gains a sense of mastery or power that enables him to become aware of "having and being a 'mind of his own' ";[4] by making the world an extension of his/her self—a projection of his or her free thought—the slave comes to recognize his/her independent existence notwithstanding the efforts of the master to reduce him or her to the entirely dependent condition of being a mere extension of the master. Thus the paradox of the master-slave dialectic is that recognition culminating in self-consciousness is available to the slave but not the master. The "self-conscious" slave, moreover, will no longer tolerate slavery. It follows that the dominative mode of the struggle for recognition is not only inadequate but also intrinsically unstable, destined to give way to other modes of the struggle for recognition.

Hegel's general point here is that work is a medium for the development

[2] G.W.F. Hegel, *The Phenomenology of Mind*, J. B. Baillie, trans. (New York: Harper & Row, 1967), p. 236.

[3] Charles Taylor, *Hegel* (Cambridge, Eng.: Cambridge University Press, 1975), p. 153.

[4] Hegel, *The Phenomenology of Mind*, p. 239.

12

of human self-consciousness rather than a mere means to physical survival. Human beings can achieve a kind of recognition through labor, or what Hegel calls *objectification*, because labor enables them to transform nature in accordance with their projects and thus to see themselves in their products. It is important for our subsequent discussion to emphasize, however, that for Hegel labor is only one mode of the struggle for recognition; it by no means exhausts the forms through which human beings strive to achieve integration with nature and among themselves. It is not, moreover, a primordial condition, coextensive with human existence itself; in fact, as we have seen, Hegel understands it to emerge out of, and in reaction to, a prior form of the struggle for recognition, the master-slave relationship. The effort to secure recognition through the production of objects is a response to an "improper" or repressive struggle for recognition between two subjects: for Hegel, domination precedes objectification.

Finally, although objectification is an advance over domination, it is neither the final nor an entirely unalienated or adequate mode of recognition. As Hegel makes clear at a later point in the *Phenomenology*, the objectifying consciousness remains divided against, rather than at one with, the world on which it works.[5] Thus objectification is destined to give way to a higher form of recognition that entails a purer or more perfect unification between humans and the world in which they live. What Hegel takes this higher form to be will be described in chapter Eight.

In Marx's hands the concept of labor explodes the limits within which Hegel confines it, the movement from Hegel to Marx is a movement in which one particular mode of a more general struggle for recognition becomes synonymous with that general struggle itself: the struggle for recognition becomes production. Production, in the process, becomes in Marx what it is not in Hegel: primordial, exhaustive, and unalienated.

To begin with, *primordial*. Nothing, for Marx, is historically or logically prior to productive activity. In fact, he boldly announces that humans become human only when and insofar as they begin to produce:

> Men can be distinguished from animals by consciousness, by religion, or anything else you like. They themselves begin to distinguish themselves from animals as soon as they begin to *produce* their means of subsistence, a step which is conditioned by their physical organization. . . . [M]en must be in a position to live in order to be able to "make history." But life involves before everything else eating and drinking, a habitation, clothing and many other things. The first historical act is thus the production of the means to satisfy these needs, the production of material life itself. . . . [T]he satisfaction of the first need (the action

---

[5] *Ibid.*, pp. 579-98.

13

of satisfying, and the instrument of satisfaction which has been acquired) leads to new needs; and this production of new needs is the first historical act.[6]

Human history, in short, begins with productive activity; labor is thus "the first premise of all human existence" both in the sense that it is necessary for the physical reproduction of the human species and in the sense that it engenders the new needs on which the subsequent development of the species depends. Engels even argues that the evolutionary leap from ape to human was itself in large part a function of labor.[7] Marx engages in no such speculation, but merely argues that labor is at the root of the evolution of the human species subsequent to that leap.

Marx's assertion of the primordial character of labor is simultaneously the denial of Hegel's thesis that domination precedes objectification. Insofar as objectification is from the very beginning necessary for the survival of the species, i.e., co-extensive with human existence itself, it follows that there are no prior forms of the struggle for recognition from which objectification can be derived. Intersubjectivity does not, *pace* Hegel, precede objectification, and thus objectification cannot be grasped as a function of a repressive form of intersubjectivity, i.e., of domination. Indeed, Marx will argue that exactly the opposite is the case. Objectification is not the consequence, but rather the source, of intersubjectivity: "*In order to produce*, they enter into definite connections and relations with one another."[8] Thus domination, as one form of intersubjectivity, must be understood as a function of (certain forms of) objectification.

Marx comes to this conclusion because he conceives of production not merely as primordial but also as exhaustive; labor is not only an irreducible form of the struggle for recognition but in fact *the essential form* of this struggle. Thus Marx tells us that "labour [is] the essence of Man" and that "life activity" is "productive life itself."[9] With Hegel, Marx understands that human identity is self-constituted through "transforming activity."[10] Against Hegel, however, this transforming activity is understood as nothing

[6] Karl Marx and Friedrich Engels, *The German Ideology*, in Tucker, *The Marx-Engels Reader*, pp. 114, 119-20, emphasis in the original.

[7] *Ibid.*, p. 119. Frederick Engels, "The Part Played by Labour in the Transition from Ape to Man," in Karl Marx and Frederick Engels, *Selected Works* (New York: International Publishers, 1968), pp. 358-68.

[8] Cited in Jean-Paul Sartre, *Critique of Dialectical Reason* (London: New Left Books, 1976), p. 44, emphasis added.

[9] Marx, "Critique of the Hegelian Dialectic and Philosophy as a Whole," p. 90, and "Estranged Labour," in Tucker, ed., *The Marx-Engels Reader*, p. 61.

[10] Herbert Marcuse, "The Foundations of Historical Materialism," in *Studies in Critical Philosophy* (Boston: Beacon Press, 1973), p. 47.

14

other than labor or objectification: "As individuals express their life, so they are. What they are, therefore, coincides with their production, both with *what* they produce and with *how* they produce."[11] Production, then, is the expression of life itself, *the* mode of human "self-genesis"; "the *entire . . . history of the world* is nothing but the begetting of man through human labour."[12]

This assimilation of the struggle for recognition to the category of production means that the particular structure of the latter becomes the general model for human self-genesis or development:

> We shall, in the first place, have to consider the labour-process independently of the particular form it assumes under given social conditions. . . . Labour is, in the first place, a process in which both man and Nature participate, and in which man of his own accord starts, regulates, and controls the material re-actions between himself and Nature. He opposes himself to Nature as one of her own forces, setting in motion arms and legs, head and hands, the natural forces of his body in order to appropriate Nature's productions in a form adapted to his own wants. By thus acting on the external world and changing it, he at the same time changes his own nature. He develops his slumbering powers and compels them to act in obedience to his sway.[13]

Like Hegel, Marx understands that human nature is not constant but is rather defined and redefined through a process in which humans struggle to negate or surmount the otherness of their environment in order to make it an extension of themselves and thus to recognize themselves within it. Unlike Hegel, however, the "environment" against which they struggle is reduced to nature, and the means of making the environment an extension of themselves in order to achieve recognition are reduced to the production of objects that they can recognize as their own. Human history, in other words, becomes the history of human objectification; the struggle for recognition becomes the struggle to master and transform nature. (As we shall see in Chapter Eight, the model for the struggle for recognition thus becomes a subject-object relationship.)

In Marx's hands, then, labor becomes an ontological category: it is that activity that constitutes the Being of human beings.[14] Put otherwise, production is the one constant, unchanging structure within which human history unfolds and on which the flux of human history depends:

[11] Marx and Engels, *The German Ideology*, p. 114, emphases in the original.

[12] Marx, "Critique of the Hegelian Dialectic and Philosophy as a Whole," p. 99, and "Private Property and Communism," in Tucker, ed., *The Marx-Engels Reader*, p. 78, emphasis in the original.

[13] Karl Marx, *Capital*, Vol. I (New York: International Publishers, 1967), p. 177.

[14] Marcuse, "The Foundations of Historical Materialism," pp. 12, 25.

15

So far therefore as labour is a creator of use-value, is useful labour, it is a *necessary condition, independent of all forms of society, for the existence of the human race; it is an eternal, nature-imposed necessity*, without which there can be no material exchanges between Man and Nature, and therefore no life.[15]

Just as the savage must wrestle with Nature to satisfy his wants, to maintain and reproduce life, so must civilized man, and he *must do so in all social formations and under all possible modes of production*.[16]

These passages from *Capital*, Marx's major late work, make it clear that he conceives of production as a transhistorical, universally applicable theoretical category. Some years earlier, however, in the "General Introduction" to the *Grundrisse*, Marx had warned his readers of the limits of "abstract categories," including the category of labor itself:

[A]ll epochs of production have certain common traits. . . . *Production in general* is an abstraction, but a rational abstraction in so far as it really brings out and fixes the common element and thus saves us repetition. Still, this *general* category . . . is itself segmented many times over and splits into different determinations . . . [therefore] just those things which determine their development, i.e., the elements which are not general and common, must be separated out from the determinations valid for production as such, so that in their unity . . . their essential difference is not forgotten.[17]

What Marx appears to be saying in this rather ungainly passage is that insofar as the general category of production applies to all human societies, this category will not help us to understand that which fundamentally distinguishes one form of society from another. To understand this requires that one move to a lower, less general level of abstraction that focuses on the "essential difference" between one form of production and another. Thus, although "all production is appropriation of nature on the part of an individual within and through a specific form of society,"[18] the specific form of the society will be a function of the specific mode of the appropriation of nature. Thus far the argument merely points to the concept of a "mode of production"— a concept about which we shall have more to say shortly—as the necessary theoretical starting point for the analysis of any specific social formation.

In this same chapter, however, Marx offers an additional caveat regarding the category of production that is more serious, and certainly more perplexing,

---

[15] Marx, *Capital*, Vol. I, pp. 42-43, emphasis added.

[16] Marx, *Capital*, Vol. III, in Tucker, ed., *The Marx-Engels Reader*, p. 320, emphasis added.

[17] Karl Marx, *Grundrisse: Foundations of the Critique of Political Economy* (Middlesex, England: Penguin Books, 1973), p. 85.

[18] *Ibid.*, p. 87.

16

than the admittedly rather commonplace observation that an abstract, general category will necessarily fail to illuminate the differences among the concrete, specific realities to which it equally applies: "[The] example of labour shows strikingly how even the most abstract categories, despite their validity—precisely because of their abstractness—for all epochs, are nevertheless, in the specific character of this abstraction, themselves . . . a product of historic relations, and possess their full validity only for and within these relations."[19] Here Marx appears to be arguing that the category of production is *more applicable* to some historical periods than to others; the problem is not that a transhistorical category is of limited utility in grasping any specific historical period but rather that the category is more useful in grasping some epochs than others. But this argument tends to call into question the transhistorical character of the category itself: what does it mean to say that the category of labor is valid for all epochs but that it is fully valid only for some? How can the category be both historically specific and transhistorical?[20]

I shall return to this ambiguity when I analyze the way in which it resurfaces in Marx's concept of a mode of production. For now, I will merely reiterate that, despite his equivocation in the *Grundrisse*—an equivocation absent in *Capital*—Marx equates the struggle for recognition with production and equates production with the human condition itself. Two profound consequences follow from this twofold equation. First, it follows that all human struggles will be conceptualized as struggles that are ultimately rooted in, and hence about, productive activity: "Thus, according to our conception, *all the conflicts* of history have their origin in the contradiction between the productive forces and the mode of intercourse."[21] Marx, in contrast to Hegel, will deny the claim of those who believe that and act as if there are modes of achieving identity vis-à-vis the world that are autonomous from the process of objectification: "Just as our opinion of an individual is not based on what he thinks of himself, so, we cannot judge . . . a period . . . by its own consciousness; on the contrary this consciousness must be explained rather from the contradictions of material life, from the existing conflict between the social productive forces and the relations of production."[22]

Second, it follows for Marx, also in opposition to Hegel, that it is mean-

[19] *Ibid.*, p. 105.

[20] Jean Baudrillard, *The Mirror of Production* (St. Louis, Mo.: Telos Press, 1975), p. 84.

[21] Cited in T. B. Bottomore, *Karl Marx: Selected Writings on Sociology and Social Philosophy* (New York: McGraw Hill, 1964), p. 247, emphasis added. The "mode of intercourse," as G. A. Cohen has noted, is Marx's early formulation of the concept that he will later capture with the phrase the "relations of production." *Karl Marx's Theory of History: A Defence* (Princeton, N.J.: Princeton University Press, 1978), pp. 142-44. I discuss and evaluate Marx's theory of the "contradiction" between the productive forces and the relations of production in Chapter Four.

[22] Karl Marx, *Preface* to *A Contribution to the Critique of Political Economy*, in Tucker, ed., *The Marx-Engels Reader*, p. 5.

ingless to speak of the transcendence of objectification in favor of "higher" forms of recognition. Given the ontological status of objectification, the transcendence of objectification would be the transcendence of human life itself.[23] Humans are destined forever to struggle for recognition in and through the transformation of nature and thus the transformation of themselves. This destiny, however, is in no sense tragic, since, for Marx, this transformative dialectic is the very condition of human freedom, of the development of the power and the emancipation of the senses of humankind.

The capacity for objectification, to begin with, entails the capacity to shape nature in conformity with a freely chosen plan; humans are not obliged merely to adapt to the constraints of the natural environment but can perpetually transcend these constraints through the objectification of the projects of their imagination. According to Marx, "what distinguishes the worst architect from the best of bees is . . . that the architect raises his structure in imagination before he erects it in reality."[24] Thus, whereas an animal "produces only under the dominion of immediate physical needs . . . man produces even when he is free from physical need and only truly produces in freedom therefrom."[25] This capacity for imaginative production, i.e., for genuine creativity, in turn, implies that humans are "species-beings," that is, beings who are able to relate to the universal or species aspects of the various objects which they confront in the world and thus to grasp their inherent potential. As Marcuse puts it,

> If man can make the species of every being into his object, the general essence of every being can become objective for him: he can possess every being as that which it is in its essence. It is for this reason . . . that he can *relate* freely to every being: he is not limited to the particular actual state of the being and his immediate relationship to it, but he can take the being as it is in its essence beyond its immediate, particular, actual state; he can recognize and grasp the *possibilities* contained in every being; he can exploit, alter, mould, treat and take further ("produce") any being according to its "inherent standard."[26]

The capacity to grasp the inherent potential of the objects of nature enables humans to transform these objects into concrete manifestations of human intention. Human freedom, in fact, is nothing other than this ability to overcome the otherness of nature by making it into an extension of ourselves. "[T]he sensuous world," Marx tells us, "is not a thing given direct from all eternity, remaining ever the same, but the product of industry . . ."; as

---

[23] Marx, "Critique of the Hegelian Dialectic and Philosophy as a Whole," pp. 86-103.

[24] Marx, *Capital*, Vol. I, p. 178.

[25] Marx, "Estranged Labour," p. 62.

[26] Marcuse, "The Foundations of Historical Materialism," pp. 15-16, emphases in the original.

18

laboring beings humans are the active makers of the very world that comes to confront their senses and are, therefore, "free beings[s]."[27] At the same time, since the world they confront is a world they have made, they can recognize themselves in, and thus be integrated within, this world. To put this another way, insofar as humans can best know what they have made, and insofar as they have made their "natural" environment, they can truly come to know the world that they inhabit.[28] Thus Marx concludes that "the celebrated 'unity of man with nature' has always existed in industry."[29]

The human power to transform nature is at the same time, according to Marx, the power to create and develop an infinite variety of human needs and sensibilities. Thus "the forming of the five senses is a *labour* of the entire history of the world";[30] in producing objects and the implements with which to produce them, humans transform the very needs that engendered these productions, creating new and different needs that become the basis for further acts of production. That which feels good, smells good, tastes good, sounds good, and looks good—in short, that which humans desire—is not fixed but is a function of "*what* they produce . . . and *how* they produce."[31] Humans not only make the world, they also make themselves; their freedom is not only the freedom to create a world but also the freedom to create the needs that both anticipate and respond to this world. Consequently it should come as no surprise that Marx defines communism, i.e., the genuinely free society whose existence coincides with the human essence of objectification, as "the complete *emancipation* of all human senses and attributes."[32]

Among the needs that labor produces is what Marx calls "the need of the greatest wealth," namely, the need for "the *other* human being."[33] Production is an inherently social activity, and thus production is, at least in the long run,[34] a socializing activity, one which makes humans aware of their reciprocal

[27] Marx and Engels, *The German Ideology*, p. 134. Marx, "Estranged Labour," p. 61.

[28] Marx nevertheless argues that "the priority of external nature remains unassailed." *The German Ideology*, p. 135. Thus nature exists independently of and is the presupposition for the human labor that transforms it. The capacity to engage in objectification successfully, in other words, is contingent on the adequacy of the human being's understanding of the inherent structure of the objects that constitute his or her "raw material." See Alfred Schmidt, *The Concept of Nature in Marx* (London: New Left Books, 1971), pp. 62-68, 96-98.

[29] Marx and Engels, *The German Ideology*, p. 134.

[30] Marx, "Private Property and Communism," p. 75, emphasis added.

[31] Marx and Engels, *The German Ideology*, p. 114, emphasis in the original.

[32] Marx, "Private Property and Communism," p. 73, emphasis in the original.

[33] *Ibid.*, p. 77, emphasis in the original.

[34] As we shall see, Marx argues that the form within which production is carried out in a capitalist society functions to disguise its social nature. But the duration of this society, in the light of Marx's theory of history, is judged to be the "short run": in the "long run," the inherently social nature of production will prevail and be carried out within a properly social form. See below, pp. 48-54.

interdependencies, which makes them understand that the development of individuality and the development of sociality go hand in hand. Put otherwise, the production and exchange of objects mediates relationships among human beings in the sense that, at least ideally, their production and exchange enable humans to achieve mutual recognition:

> Suppose we had produced things as human beings: in his production each of us would have twice affirmed himself and the other. (1) In my production I would have objectified my individuality and its particularity, and in the course of the activity I would have enjoyed an individual life; in viewing the object I would have experienced the individual joy of knowing my personality as an objective, sensuously perceptible and indubitable power. (2) In your satisfaction and your use of my product I would have the direct and conscious satisfaction that my work satisfied a human need, that it objectified human nature, and that it created an object appropriate to the need of another human being. (3) I would have been the mediator between you and the species and you would have experienced me as a reintegration of your own nature and a necessary part of yourself; I would have been affirmed in your thought as well as your love. (4) In my individual activity, I would have immediately confirmed and realised my true human and social nature.

> Our productions *would be so many mirrors* reflecting our nature.

> What happens so far as I am concerned would also apply to you.[35]

Marx is saying that produced objects not only symbolize the relationship between human beings and nature but also symbolize the relationship of one human being to another; through the objects he or she produces and exchanges, the individual can see his or her connection with the other person, thus overcoming the otherness of that person and achieving genuine reciprocity or integration with him or her. Once again, with Marx the struggle for recognition, in this case the recognition of individuals vis-à-vis other individuals, is understood to be a function of objectification.

Against Hegel, then, Marx concludes that objectification—at least in principle—offers the potential of a struggle for recognition that culminates in a genuinely unalienated or integrated relationship between humans and nature and among human beings themselves. Given a society that properly understands and thus unleashes this potential, human beings will be able to feel at home with the world and at home with themselves; thus his definition of

---

[35] Cited in David McLellan, *Marx Before Marxism* (London: Macmillan, 1970), pp. 178-79, emphasis added.

20

communism as "the *genuine* resolution of the conflict between man and nature and between man and man."[36]

THE CONCEPT OF THE "MODE OF PRODUCTION"

If, as we have seen, "labour is the essence of Man," it follows that the essence of the human condition at any particular time lies in the specific way in which humans labor; if, in short, "life activity" is "productive life itself," the mode of life of a particular people will be a function of their particular mode of production. A necessary corollary to the postulate of the ontological primacy of production, in other words, is the assumption of the analytical or sociological primacy of the concept of the mode of production: this concept becomes the key to unlocking the secrets of any given social formation. Henceforth Marx, and Marxists, will grasp the structures or practices of a particular society as constituent elements of the mode(s) of production of that society.[37]

This formulation, however, poses the problem of what it means to say that a social structure or practice is a "constituent element" of the mode of production. It is clear that the formulation attributes a certain causal primacy to the mode of production. What is unclear is exactly what kind of causality is being implied. The history of Marx-interpretation can in large part be read as a history of different answers to this question. My effort to clarify the concept of the mode of production—which is itself an effort to clarify the foundation on which the theories discussed and evaluated in the first two parts of this book are built—demands that I examine some of these answers and their implications.

The most conventional, and inadequate, answer is that the primacy of the mode of production should be understood as implying mechanical or *linear causality*. This interpretation of Marx's concept, characteristic of most of his orthodox Marxist-Leninist-Stalinist "friends" as well as most of his liberal foes, rests heavily upon a certain reading of what is admittedly the most "mechanistic" of Marx's texts, the famous *Preface* to *A Contribution to the Critique of Political Economy*. In it Marx announces boldly that "the mode of production of material life determines the social, political and intellectual life process in general." According to the reading in question, this passage entails (a) the assumption that social reality is divided into discrete parts or

[36] Marx, "Private Property and Communism," p. 70, emphasis in the original.

[37] Marxists argue that a given society may well be a function of more than one mode of production, but that one mode of production will always predominate over the others. On this point, see Samir Amin, *Accumulation on a World Scale*, Vol. I (New York: Monthly Review Press, 1974), pp. 37-38.

"factors"; (b) the assumption that the behavior of one part, namely the economic part, determines the behavior of all the other parts; and (c) the assumption that the behavior of all the other parts does not determine the behavior of the economic part.[38] Thus the primacy of the mode of production is interpreted according to the model of an economic base determining the noneconomic superstructures in unilinear or unidirectional fashion.

There are many reasons for rejecting this by-now thoroughly discredited interpretation. To begin with, as Bertell Ollman has pointed out, the impression of "automatic dependence" of superstructures on the economic base rests in part on an accident of translation: "English translators have tended to reinforce whatever 'determinist' bias is present in Marx by generally translating *bedingden* (which can mean 'condition' or 'determine') as 'determine'."[39] If "the mode of production of material life" merely "conditions" the "social, political and intellectual life process," then the various superstructures must be conceptualized as relatively autonomous from the base on which they rest. Marx himself, as Harrington has recently emphasized, often commented on this "relative autonomy," as, for example, when he tells us that "In the case of the arts, it is well known that certain periods of their flowering are all out of proportion to the general foundation of society, hence also to the material foundation, the skeletal structure as it were, of its organizations."[40] The introduction of the concept of "relative autonomy," then, demands, at the very least, that we qualify or modify assumption (b) in the model of linear causality.

Second, and more important, the model of linear causality simply does not correspond to the way in which Marx characterizes the relationship between base and superstructures in his own analyses of concrete social formations. In these analyses, as many have pointed out, Marx never merely establishes the dependence of the superstructures on the economic base but rather always examines with great care the way in which the various superstructures, in turn, react on and influence the very base on which they depend.[41] The influence that Marx attributes to superstructural factors, in other words, flies in the face of assumption (c), above, of the model of linear causality, and we can therefore conclude that this model did not serve as a theoretical map for Marx's own empirical investigations. It follows that we cannot plausibly

---

[38] Cited in Bertell Ollman, *Alienation: Marx's Conception of Man in Capitalist Society* (Cambridge, Eng.: Cambridge University Press, 1971), p. 6. See also Michael Harrington, *The Twilight of Capitalism* (New York: Simon & Schuster, 1976), p. 38, and Melvin Rader *Marx's Interpretation of History* (New York: Oxford University Press, 1979), p. 3.

[39] Ollman, *Alienation*, p. 259, n. 23.

[40] Marx, *Grundrisse*, p. 110; Harrington, *The Twilight of Capitalism*, pp. 70-73.

[41] Ollman, *Alienation*, p. 9; Harrington, *The Twilight of Capitalism*, pp. 81-82.

claim that Marx intends us to interpret his general theoretical assertion in the *Preface* according to this model.

Observations such as these have led Marxists to relax assumptions (b) and (c) in order to interpret Marx's assertion of the primacy of the mode of production according to what might be called a model of *modified linear causality*. Thus Engels argues, in an oft-cited passage, that "According to the materialist conception of history, the production and reproduction of social life is the *ultimately* determining element in history. More than that neither Marx nor I have ever asserted. Hence if somebody twists this into saying that the economic element is the *only* determining one, he transforms that proposition into a meaningless, senseless phrase."[42] He emphatically rejects the claim "that because we deny an independent historical development to the various ideological spheres which play a part in history we also deny them an effect upon history."[43] According to this modified base-superstructure model, then, the ultimate or long-run determination of the noneconomic superstructures by the economic base in no way precludes these superstructures from assuming a relative autonomy from this base and, at least in the short or intermediate run, from playing a determining role vis-à-vis this base. Apart from the thorny, perhaps irresolvable difficulty of distinguishing the ultimate or "last instance" from the short or "intermediate run" in such a manner as to render Engels's formulation of *ultimate* determination by the economic base verifiable rather than merely rhetorical, the principal problem with this model is that it retains assumption (a) of the model of linear causality, i.e., the assumption that social reality is segmented into separate, mutually exclusive parts or factors. To speak of the superstructures, notwithstanding their relative autonomy and short-run causal efficacy, as ultimately dependent on an economic base is to continue to invoke an architectural metaphor whose application to social reality is misplaced: whereas it *is* meaningful to speak of the base or foundation of a building antedating, and thus having an existence independent of, the superstructure which is erected on it, it is not meaningful to speak of the economic part of a society antedating or having an existence independent of all the other parts of the society with which it is intertwined. What the model calls the base and what it calls the superstructures "have a simultaneous and mutual existence"[44] that cannot be grasped if we proceed from the assumption that "society" is the addition or result of separate factors. The social whole, in other words, cannot be conceived as the sum total of its parts, since to speak of social parts is already to presuppose a social whole within which these parts are functioning. Thus the effort to conceptualize

[42] Cited in Harrington, *The Twilight of Capitalism*, p. 44, emphasis in the original.

[43] Cited in Ollman, *Alienation*, p. 9.

[44] Harrington, *The Twilight of Capitalism*, p. 62; see also Rader, *Marx's Interpretation of History*, pp. 53-54.

social causality must abandon the *atomistic* model of social reality underlying both the original and modified base-superstructure model.[45]

There is ample evidence to suggest, in fact, that Marx did just this. In *The Poverty of Philosophy* he attacks the essentially linear model of society of Proudhon, arguing that "the production relations of every society *form a whole*" and speaking of society as a "structure . . . in which all relations coexist simultaneously and support one another."[46] In *The German Ideology* he emphasizes that the "mode of production must not be considered simply as being the reproduction of the physical existence of . . . individuals" but rather as "a definite *mode of life*" as a whole.[47] Finally, in his mature methodological introduction to the *Grundrisse*, he characterizes the mode of production as a "totality" and an "organic whole."[48] All these formulations indicate an effort to conceptualize society in wholistic, rather than atomistic fashion and suggest that the famous assertion in the *Preface* of the determining role of the mode of production should be read in the light of this effort.[49] In short, the base-superstructure model, whether modified or original, is not only not adequate, it is not consistent with Marx's own wholistic epistemological commitments.

The most explicit outline of the model that purports to be consistent with these commitments appears in the introduction to the *Grundrisse*. Here the concept of the mode of production denotes that a given society will be conceptualized as a whole or totality each of whose parts or elements perform functions that are themselves aspects or preconditions of the overriding function of production. Broken down into its constituent parts, this conceptuali-

---

[45] For a sustained non-Marxist critique of atomistic models of social reality, see Roberto Unger, *Knowledge and Politics* (New York: The Free Press, 1975).

[46] Karl Marx, *The Poverty of Philosophy* (New York: International Publishers, 1967), pp. 110-11, emphasis added.

[47] Marx and Engels, *The German Ideology*, p. 114, emphasis in the original.

[48] Marx, *Grundrisse*, pp. 99, 100.

[49] For an impressive, although ultimately unpersuasive, argument to the contrary, see G. A. Cohen, *Karl Marx's Theory of History: A Defence*. Cohen contends that Marx's thesis of the primacy of the mode of production entails a causal relationship between an externally, rather than internally, related base and superstructure. But this reading of Marx is purchased at the price of an almost complete neglect of the wholistic epistemological observations cited above as well as the incorporation of these observations into a full-fledged model of an "organic totality" in the introduction to the *Grundrisse*. Rader, *Marx's Interpretation of History*, ch. 2. Cohen's construal of the base-superstructure relationship as a functional relationship, moreover, tends to undermine his thesis of external, rather than internal, causality: functional explanation implies a commitment to the very organic model that Cohen fails to discover in Marx. On this, as well as other, related issues, see Peter Singer, "On Your Marx," *New York Review of Books* (December 20, 1979), pp. 44-47, and Walter L. Adamson's review essay of Cohen's and Rader's books as well as William H. Shaw, *Marx's Theory of History*, in *History and Theory*, 19 (1980), pp. 186-204.

zation entails: (a) the notion that the social whole is present in each of its parts; (b) the notion that the whole that is present in each of its parts is the function of production; (c) the notion that this function is accomplished in and through reciprocal interaction among the parts of the whole; and (d) the notion that, notwithstanding this reciprocal interaction, the part that consists in the activity of material production predominates over the other parts.

(a) The structures or practices of a society are "distinctions within a *unity*,"[50] i.e., they must be understood as parts of an already existing whole. Each part interiorizes or expresses the whole in the sense that each contributes to the performance of a single common function. Put otherwise, the whole is understood to be present within each structure or practice insofar as each structure or practice is grasped as a form or mode of appearance of an underlying, more essential activity.[51] As diverse structures performing a common function, as different forms of appearance of a single, overriding essence, each part of a society implies the other parts, as well as the whole, of that society, much as each part of the human body implies every other part of the body as well as the body in its entirety.

(b) The overriding function to which the diverse structures of a society are understood to contribute is production; the essential activity of which the different social practices are modes of appearance is objectification. Thus the concept of a mode of production is a shorthand way of expressing the axiom that it is the unity established in and through the functional requisites of production that allows us to speak of a society as a "totality" or an "organic whole": the different parts are conceived of as parts of a whole insofar as they are all conceived to be essential for production. To conceive of the unity of a society in the light of production means that other, nonproduction practices will only shine in a borrowed light: political activity, religious activity, intellectual activity, etc., will not be understood on their own terms but rather will be conceptualized as structures that perform the function of production, as forms of appearance of objectification. The corollary to the assumption that production is the essential human activity, in other words, is the assumption that other human activities are inessential and only become important insofar as they are conceived as either surrogates for, or part of, production. I shall return shortly to the ambiguity signaled in the phrase "either surrogates for, or part of."

At this point it is sufficient to emphasize that, with the concept of a mode of production, the "entire life process [of a society] is . . . comprehended by Marx from the perspective of production."[52] Thus, in the introduction to

---

[50] Marx, *Grundrisse*, p. 99, emphasis added.

[51] Ollman, *Alienation*, Ch. 2-3. But see Harrington, *The Twilight of Capitalism*, pp. 71-72, for a qualification of this formulation.

[52] Jurgen Habermas, *Knowledge and Human Interests* (Boston: Beacon Press, 1971), p. 327.

25

the *Grundrisse*, the process of societal reproduction is identified with the cycle of production itself. To understand a society, Marx tells us, is to comprehend it as a "unity of the diverse" aspects or "moments" of the process of production: production (narrowly understood), distribution, exchange, and consumption:

> In production the members of society appropriate (create, shape) the products of nature in accord with human needs; distribution determines the proportion in which the individual shares in the product; exchange delivers the particular products into which the individual desires to convert the portion which distribution has assigned to him; and finally, in consumption, the products become objects of gratification, of individual appropriation.[53]

The anatomy of the social body will be analyzed according to this functional cycle: every social structure or organ will be grasped in the light of the contribution it makes to the functions of production, distribution, exchange, and consumption. Insofar as each of these functions, in turn, is for Marx, and for reasons I shall discuss, a subfunction of the function of production, the structures or organs by means of which the functions of distribution, exchange, and consumption are performed are, at bottom, organs of production.

(c) Although production, distribution, exchange, and consumption are all "moments" or subfunctions of production, they are not "identical, but . . . all form the members of a totality, *distinctions* within a unity." If the general concept of totality implies the unity of the whole, Marx's concept of a "*concrete*" totality implies that this unity is achieved in and through distinctions or differentiations among the various parts of the whole.[54] Just as the over-riding function of the life or survival of the human organism is achieved in and through a number of subfunctions such as digestion, circulation, etc., none of which is identical to any other, so the overriding social function of production requires the subfunctions of production, distribution, exchange, and consumption, each of which is distinct from the other. And just as the survival of the physiological organism is assured by means of the interactions among the various physiological subfunctions, so too the survival of the social organism is achieved in and through the interactions among the functions of production, distribution, exchange, and consumption:

> [I]n its one-sided form, production is itself determined by the other moments. For example, if the market, i.e., the sphere of exchange,

[53] Marx, *Grundrisse*, pp. 101, 88-89.
[54] *Ibid.*, pp. 99, 101, emphases added. See also Karel Kosik, *Dialectics of the Concrete* (Boston: D. Reidel Pub. Co., 1976).

26

expands, then production grows in quantity and the divisions between its different branches become deeper. A change in distribution changes production, e.g., concentration of capital, different distribution of the population between town and country, etc. Finally, the needs of consumption determine production. *Mutual interaction takes place between the different moments. This is the case with every organic whole.*[55]

"Mutual interaction . . . between the different moments" implies, of course, mutual interaction among the various structures through which the four functions are performed. Thus we should expect to find in any given society, reciprocal causation among what are ordinarily thought of as political, religious, ideological, and economic structures. The precise nature of the mutual interaction among these structures and their associated functions, moreover, cannot be determined a priori but only by means of "empirical observation."[56] To conceptualize society as a mode of production, then, is not to take recourse to a "single-factor" model of explanation but rather to view the social whole "as a rich totality of many determinations and relations."[57]

(d) The "mutual interactions" among the various functions and structures, however, take place within a whole in which the function of production, narrowly understood (and the structures through which it is performed), "predominates . . . over the other moments."[58] Although it is true, then, that nonproduction functions and structures will exercise an important influence over production functions and structures, and that the precise nature of the mutual interaction between both sets of functions and structures can only be ascertained by means of empirical observation, we should always expect that the production functions and structures will have disproportionate influence over the others. Thus:

In all forms of society there is one specific kind of production which predominates over the rest, whose relations thus assign rank and influence to the others. It is a general illumination which bathes all the other colours and modifies their particularity. It is a particular ether which determines the specific gravity of every being which has materialized with it.[59]

In *Capital*, Marx makes it clear that the "specific kind of production" to which he refers in the *Grundrisse* is what I have called the subfunction of production:

[55] Marx, *Grundrisse*, pp. 99-100, first emphasis in the original, second added.
[56] Cited in Harrington, *The Twilight of Capitalism*, p. 82.
[57] Marx, *Grundrisse*, p. 100.
[58] *Ibid.*, p. 99.
[59] *Ibid.*, p. 107.

27

In every case it is the immediate relationship of the owner of the conditions of production to the immediate producer—a relationship that always conforms naturally to a specific developmental stage of the manner and mode of labor and thereby to its societal productive power—in which the innermost secret, the hidden basis of the entire societal construction, and therefore of the political forms of sovereignty and dependency relations as well, is found.[60]

However much the functions of distribution, exchange, and consumption, and the structures associated with them, influence the function of (extracting surplus) labor, "in every case" it is this latter function that assigns the former functions and structures their "rank and influence." Thus the conclusion in the *Grundrisse* is that "a definite production thus determines a definite consumption, distribution and exchange as well as *definite relations between these different moments*."[61]

As Michael Harrington and Melvin Rader have pointed out, these passages testify to a somewhat strained effort by Marx to articulate a novel conception of social causality, a conception of "dominant functions" within an organic whole.[62] Against those who maintain that the notion of reciprocal interaction among the parts of a totality is logically incompatible with the notion that some parts exercise disproportionate influence over the others, Harrington suggests that recent developments in non-Marxist systems theory demonstrate precisely the opposite. He cites the work of a contemporary econometrician that consists in distinguishing from among all the interacting functions of an economic "system" those "core" functions without which the system would simply be unable to persist; these functions might be said to predominate over the others, notwithstanding their "mutual interaction." Similarly, both Harrington and Rader argue that our experience with our own bodies confirms the notion of dominant functions within an organic whole characterized by reciprocal interaction: we know that all the functions and associated organs of our body are mutually interrelated, but we also know that there are some functions and organs that we can live without. A hand or a leg can be amputated, a brain or a heart cannot. Thus Harrington concludes and Rader concurs, that "organic wholes, be they human bodies or human societies, can have . . . dominant functions."[63] It would appear, then, that there is nothing logically incoherent about the model of causality embedded in Marx's concept of a mode of production.

[60] Cited in Harrington, *The Twilight of Capitalism*, p. 87.

[61] Marx, *Grundrisse*, p. 99, emphasis in the original.

[62] Harrington, *The Twilight of Capitalism*, p. 69; Rader, *Marx's Interpretation of History*, pp. 75-81.

[63] Harrington, *The Twilight of Capitalism*, p. 69; Rader, *Marx's Interpretation of History*, p. 78.

28

These observations, however, do not end the matter. Although it is undoubtedly the case that *some* organic wholes or systems can be coherently conceptualized as possessing dominant functions, this does not necessarily mean that Marx's particular conception of a mode of production characterized by the dominant function of production is a coherent conception. The abovementioned examples of coherent conceptualizations are instructive, because in both cases the functions/structures that are held to predominate over the other functions/structures with which they ordinarily interpenetrate are clearly more essential to the survival of the system as a whole. The human organism can survive without a hand but not without a brain; thus it makes sense to argue that the structure that is the brain and the functions it performs predominate over the structure that is the hand and the functions it performs. But Marx, as we have seen, claims that production predominates over distribution, exchange, and consumption. Distribution, exchange, and consumption, however, do not stand in relationship to production as the functions of the hand to the functions of the brain; as integral elements of the cycle of production itself, they cannot be dispensed with and are in fact every bit as essential to the mode of production, i.e., the system as a whole, as that particular part of the cycle that is production, properly speaking. Their relationship to the latter, in other words, is not like the relationship of the functions of the hand to the functions of the brain but rather more like that between the functions of the heart and the functions of the brain, both of which are indispensable for the survival of the organism and neither of which can legitimately be claimed to predominate over the other. A properly drawn analogy between the social and the physiological "organic whole" thus leads to the conclusion that production "narrowly understood" is no more a "core function" than the other elements of the production cycle. Harrington's and Rader's argument on behalf of the predominance of production over distribution, exchange, and consumption rests, then, on a misdrawn analogy and is not logically coherent.[64]

Marx himself tried to argue, in the *Grundrisse*, that "production is the real point of departure" of the production-distribution-exchange-consumption cycle, "and hence also the predominant moment." Here the assertion of the predominance of the moment of production rests not on the notion of a core function, but rather on the assumption that production originates and renews each cycle: "it is the act through which the whole process again runs its course." But this argument will not wash either, because, as Marx himself demonstrates elsewhere in the *Introduction*, one could just as easily argue that the process originates and renews itself in consumption: although it is

---

[64] See the exchange between Rader and Peter Singer in *The New York Review of Books* (February 21, 1980).

true that the production of an object creates the need for its consumption, it is equally true that the desire to consume an object serves as the motive for the production of that object.[65] Thus Marx's assertion of the predominance of production over the other elements in the production cycle has the character of an arbitrary assertion.

In fact, it might be argued that the plausibility of this assertion rests entirely on what Habermas calls a "terminological equivocation," that is, on a tendency for Marx—and the reader—to redefine the "moment" of production so that it comes to embrace the process or cycle of production as a whole.[66] Marx, in other words, can only salvage the assertion that production is the dominant function by building into his concept of production the very elements that production is supposed to "determine": thus the proposition "distribution, exchange, and consumption are *determined* by production" becomes the proposition that "distribution, exchange, and consumption *are* production," i.e., the proposition becomes true by definition. And this tautology tells us no more than what the concept of a mode of production told us in the first place, namely, that all activities in a society will be grasped as functions or aspects of production. In sum, despite appearances to the contrary, the proposition that a mode of production is characterized by the dominant function of production contributes no more information than the proposition "a mode of production is a mode of production."

This can be put another way. Since Marx is unable convincingly to demonstrate why the subfunction of production "in every case" or "in all forms of society" predominates over the other subfunctions of the production cycle, the theory of the determination of the "life process in general" by the "mode of production" in no way tells us which particular activity among all those that are conceptualized as functions or aspects of production will be the dominant factor under what conditions. It is completely possible, in other words, that different activities will take on the role of dominant factor in different societies; thus, in practice, the determination exercised by the mode of production may mean something radically different in one form of society than it does in another.

Marx himself alluded to this problem, without being fully aware of its dimensions, when he argued, somewhat cryptically, that the category of production is valid for all epochs but only "fully valid" for some.[67] We are now in a position to appreciate how this equivocation enters into the concept of the mode of production as well: the primacy of production over the rest of life may have a fundamentally different meaning depending on the epoch in question. If, in short, the category of production is valid for all epochs but

[65] Marx, *Grundrisse*, pp. 94, 92-93.

[66] Habermas, *Knowledge and Human Interests*, p. 328.

[67] See above, p. 17.

only fully valid for some, then by the same token we are obliged to say that the theory of the determining role of the mode of production is valid for all epochs but only fully valid for some. Marx, in fact, says as much in the *Introduction* to the *Grundrisse*:

> Bourgeois society is the most developed and the most complex historic organization of production. The categories which express its relations, the comprehension of its structure, thereby also allow insights into the structure and relations of production of all the vanished social formations out of whose ruins and elements it built itself up, whose partly unconquered remnants are carried along with it, whose mere nuances have developed explicit significance within it, etc. *Human anatomy contains a key to the anatomy of the ape.* The intimations of higher development among the subordinate species, however, can be understood only after the higher development is already known. The bourgeois economy thus supplies the key to the ancient, etc. But not at all in the manner of those economists who smudge over all historical differences and see bourgeois relations in all forms of society . . . although it is true . . . that the categories of bourgeois economics possess a truth for all other forms of society, *this is to be taken only with a grain of salt.* They can contain them in a developed, or stunted, or caricatured form, etc., *but always with an essential difference.*[68]

"The categories of bourgeois economics possess a truth for all other forms of society," but "this is to be taken only with a grain of salt"! Marx clearly wants to have it both ways: the concept of a mode of production both is and is not a transhistorical category.[69] On the one hand, he is aware that this concept, like any other, is historically specific; that it expresses a unique truth about one particular form of society, namely bourgeois or capitalist society. On the other hand, he contends that the concept, its historical specificity notwithstanding, provides "the key" to unlock the truth about human societies in general. The assumption that reconciles these apparently contradictory claims is that capitalist society "built itself up" from the "ruins and elements" of the "structure and relations" of earlier societies; there is a structural continuity between the former and the latter—notwithstanding "an essential difference" between them—that parallels the anatomical continuity between humans and apes that exists in the face of *their* "essential difference." Thus bourgeois society is to earlier forms of society as the human is to the ape. And if "human anatomy contains a key to the anatomy of the ape," i.e., if the analysis of human anatomy enables us to grasp the anatomy of the ape

[68] Marx, *Grundrisse*, p. 106, emphases added.
[69] Baudrillard, *The Mirror of Production*, pp. 84-85.

as a less developed version of the former, then it follows that the categories by means of which bourgeois society can be comprehended "allow insights into . . . the vanished social formations" from which they have evolved.

An analogy with natural evolution thus purports to reconcile the tension between the simultaneously transhistorical and historically specific nature of Marx's theory of determination by the mode of production. But this analogy is, to say the very least, extraordinarily problematical. The structural continuity between human and ape perforce implies a demonstrable functional continuity between them: to argue that human anatomical structures are more developed versions of the anatomical structures of apes is also necessarily to assert that the former structures enable their bearers better to perform functions that are also performed by the latter. But it is not at all clear that a comparable functional continuity underlies otherwise essentially different societies, and thus it is not necessarily plausible to contend that one society is a more highly evolved form of the others: what, in short, is the function common to different social organisms that parallels a function such as circulation that is common to different physiological organisms?

Marx's answer, of course, is the function of production. The one constant amid the endless flux of history is precisely the activity of production through which this flux is generated. Thus the assertion that the structures of bourgeois society are more developed versions of the structures of earlier societies amounts to the claim that these structures enable the former society to perform the function of production more effectively than the latter societies. Marx makes this claim explicit in a letter to P. V. Annenkov in which he argues that

Because of this simple fact that every succeeding generation finds itself in possession of the productive forces acquired by the previous generation, which serve it as the raw material for new production, a coherence arises in human history, a history of humanity takes shape which is all the more a history of humanity as the productive forces of man and therefore his social relations have been more developed.[70]

His claim entails two separate assumptions: (a) that all generations throughout history are engaged in the activity of production, and (b) that succeeding generations are generally able to engage in this activity more effectively than preceding generations. Given these assumptions, "a coherence arises in human history," i.e., it becomes possible retrospectively to identify the structures of earlier societies as less developed versions of the structure possessed by bourgeois society. Thus does the concept of determination by the mode

---

[70] Tucker, ed., *The Marx-Engels Reader*, second ed., p. 137.

of production "allow insights into the structure of . . . vanished social formations."

The assumption (b) of a universal tendency for the productive forces to develop can be derived from (a) the assumption of the universality of production plus (c) the assumption of a universal tendency of succeeding generations to learn from the efforts of their predecessors, i.e., the assumption of human rationality.[71] If, for the sake of argument, we grant the plausibility of assumption (c), the truth of assumption (b) depends upon the truth of assumption (a), i.e., it follows that, if production is universal, there will be a general tendency for the powers of production to increase. But is production universal? Is it the case that all generations throughout history have engaged in this activity?

This question surfaces, in different guises, in the course of the effort of contemporary Marxist theorists to apply the concept of determination by the mode of production to "vanished social formations," i.e., to precapitalist societies. These are all societies in which the productive forces are far less "developed" than in capitalist societies and in which a variety of nonproduction activities appear to play a correspondingly far more central role than in the latter. According to Louis Althusser and his followers, this diversity of dominant functions is completely consistent with Marx's theory of the determining role of the mode of production, since "in real history determination in the last instance by the economy is exercised precisely in the permutations of the principal role between the economy, politics, theory, etc."[72] The mode of production is ultimately *determinative*, in other words, precisely because it is responsible for selecting the structure or activity that becomes *dominant* in any given society. This distinction between dominant and determinative, the Althusserians claim, is made by Marx himself in *Capital* in response to the charge that his method applies to capitalist but not precapitalist societies: "It is clear that the Middle Ages could not live on Catholocism nor the ancient world on politics. The way and mode in which they gained their living explains why in one place politics played the decisive role, and in the other, Catholocism."[73]

To begin with, then, determination by the mode of production means something different in different forms of society. Whereas in a capitalist society the economic factor is both determinant and dominant—it is, for reasons that I shall discuss presently, "only under capitalism that economics as such plays the leading social part in its own name"[74]—in all precapitalist societies noneconomic factors—politics, religion, kinship, etc.—assume the

[71] Cohen, *Marx's Theory of History: A Defence*, pp. 152-57.
[72] Louis Althusser, *For Marx* (New York: Pantheon, 1969), p. 213.
[73] Cited in Harrington, *The Twilight of Capitalism*, p. 67.
[74] *Ibid.*, pp. 67-68.

dominant role. At bottom, however, determination by the mode of production is the same in all forms of society, because it is precisely the organization of production that determines which noneconomic factor becomes dominant and why. Thus, for the Althusserians, the apparently decisive influence of the extra-economic in precapitalist societies is ultimately illusory, since the hidden "reason behind this extra-economic reason is [itself] economic."[75]

The Althusserian interpretation relies, then, on the assumption of a trans-historical economic reason that is distinct from the noneconomic "reasons" that are its effects. When Marx argues that "the way and mode in which they gained their living explains why in one place politics played the decisive role and in the other, Catholocism," he takes refuge in the notion that it is possible in all places to distinguish the activity of gaining a living, i.e., production, from the nonproduction activities—political, religious, etc.—that the mode of gaining a living is supposed to explain. But this notion is untenable. As Paul Cardan, Jean Baudrillard, and Marshall Sahlins have all demonstrated,[76] in pre-capitalist societies what Marx calls the activity of "gaining a living" and what I have called "nonproduction" activities are, in fact, inseparably fused. Marx himself recognizes this elsewhere in his writings: according to Lukacs, he argues that in precapitalist societies "economic elements are *inextricably* joined to political and religious factors" and "economic and legal categories are objectively and *substantively so interwoven as to be inseparable.*"[77] As such, it is impossible coherently to argue that the former explain the latter. If, as Marx contends, a capitalist society is, in fact, the first in history in which economic activity is *not* inextricably intertwined with political and/or

---

[75] Andre Glucksmann, "A Ventriloquist Structuralism," *New Left Review*, No. 72 (March-April 1972), p. 80.

[76] Paul Cardan, "Marxisme et theorie revolutionnaire," *Socialism ou barbarie*, No. 39 (March-April 1965), 16-66; Baudrillard, *The Mirror of Production*; Marshall Sahlins, *Culture and Practical Reason* (Chicago: University of Chicago Press, 1976).

[77] Georg Lukacs, *History and Class Consciousness* (Cambridge, Mass.: M.I.T. Press, 1971), pp. 55, 57, emphases in the original. According to Lukacs, "it follows from this that historical materialism cannot be applied in quite the same manner to pre-capitalist social formations as to capitalism. Here we need much more complex and subtle analyses in order to show, on the one hand, what role was played from among all the forces controlling society by the *purely* economic forces in so far as they can be said to have existed in a 'pure' state in the strict sense of the word. And on the other hand to show the impact of these economic forces upon the other institutions of the society. For this reason much greater caution is required when applying historical materialism to earlier societies" (p. 238, emphasis in the original). This appeal for "caution" implies the recognition that the applicability of historical materialism is contingent on the existence of "purely economic forces." But the existence of these forces in precapitalist societies is precisely what Lukacs denies when he argues that economic and non-economic forces are *"inextricably* joined" and *"inseparable"* in those societies. Thus the conclusion he should have drawn is not that "historical materialism cannot be applied in quite the same manner," but rather that it cannot (successfully) be applied at all, to "pre-capitalist social formations."

religious activity,[78] then it is the only society in which "gaining a living" as a distinct activity exists. With his notion of a transhistorical "gaining a living," then, Marx is guilty of doing precisely what he accuses his bourgeois theoretical opponents of doing, i.e., projecting the specific logic of bourgeois society back into the past and thus reading the past entirely in terms of the categories of the present.[79] There is, in short, no transhistorical economic reason. Insofar as the Althusserian explanation for the dominant role of non-economic factors relies on this notion, it is really no explanation at all; their dominance remains an anomoly for a theory that attributes ultimate determinative power to the mode of production.

Maurice Godelier, a Marxist anthropologist, has advanced a different interpretation that purports to avoid the difficulties of the Althusserian. Faced with the dominant role of kinship relations as the organizing principle of "primitive" societies, Godelier concludes that "here relations of kinship serve as relations of production."[80] Whereas for Althusser the mode of production is determinative in that it "selects" the social factor that becomes dominant, for Godelier the determinative power of the mode of production is expressed through the fact that the dominant social factor is always a relation of production. In principle, any social activity can "play a dominant role in the functioning and evolution of a society," but it only does so insofar as it "directly and from within assumes the function of a relation of production."[81] Thus the dominant role of ostensibly noneconomic institutions in precapitalist societies is not an anomaly for the theory of the determinative power of the mode of production once we understand that the institutions that play a dominant role are really "economic" after all.

Godelier's interpretation avoids the difficulty inherent in the Althusserian conception of an economic instance that is forever separate and distinct from the other social "instances" it is held to make dominant; in this sense it is truer to the precapitalist fusion of what we call economic activity and what we call noneconomic activity. This advantage, however, is purchased at an exorbitant price, namely the transformation of Marx's proposition that the mode of production plays the determinative role in a society into a statement that is purely tautological: for Godelier, whatever activity can be demonstrated to predominate over all the other activities in a society becomes, by definition,

[78] See below, pp. 38-40.

[79] Glucksmann, "A Ventriloquist Structuralism," p. 80.

[80] Maurice Godelier, "Infrastructures, Societies and History," *New Left Review*, No. 112 (November-December 1978) p. 87.

[81] *Ibid.*, p. 90. Like the Althusserian interpretation, Godelier's is able to claim textual support from Marx. Thus on one occasion Marx declares that "religion, family, state, law, morality, science, art, etc., are only particular modes of production." Cited in Rader, *Marx's Interpretation of History*, p. 59.

the mode of production! The theory of determination by the mode of production, then, becomes true by definition and does not lend itself to possible falsification. Nor is it a terribly useful tautology, because it in no way helps us to understand which social activities become determinative—and thus function as the mode of production—under what conditions. We are back to where we started, because this was exactly what the theory of the determinative power of the mode of production was supposed to tell us! At bottom, Godelier's interpretation of Marx's thesis is no more helpful than Althusser's.

Althusser's and Godelier's interpretations can be understood as imaginative examples of the only two logically possible—but equally inadequate—solutions to the problem that precapitalist societies pose for Marx's theory of the determinative power of the mode of production. The problem is to reconcile Marx's overriding assumption that production is the essential human activity with the manifestly decisive role that ostensibly nonproduction activities play in these societies. The Althusserian solution maintains that the manifestly decisive role of nonproduction activities is merely apparent, since at bottom it is production activities that account for this decisive role. Faced with Marx's assumption that only production activities are essential, Althusser chooses to emphasize the corollary that nonproduction activities are mere surrogates and therefore ultimately inessential. Godelier's solution, on the other hand, is to argue that nonproduction activities are only ostensibly nonproduction and are at bottom activities of production. Starting from Marx's assumption that only production activities are essential, Godelier opts for the converse proposition that all essential activities are production. Althusser adheres to the distinction between production and nonproduction, but at the cost of ultimately denying the determinative role of the dominant institutions in precapitalist societies; Godelier, in contrast, is able to "see" the determining power of these dominant institutions, but only at the cost of obliterating the distinction between production and nonproduction (and, in the process, inflating Marx's concept of production so that it loses its definitional connection with "objectification" and comes instead to embrace, at least in principle, any human activity whatsoever). Thus Althusser's interpretation culminates in a theory that is wrong and Godelier's in a theory that is true by definition; neither can account for the phenomena for which they purport to account.[82]

Indeed, anyone who proceeds from Marx's assumption that "production is everything" and who confronts the manifest importance of what seem to be nonproduction activities in precapitalist societies will be obliged to con-

---

[82] The same can be said, of course, of the two versions of the theory of class conflict that follow from their respective interpretations of the determinative role of production: the claim that all important conflicts are rooted in production is either wrong (on the narrow, Althusserian meaning of production) or empty of meaning (on the all-encompassing, Godelierian meaning of production) when applied to precapitalist societies.

clude either that "nonproduction is nothing" (i.e., inessential) or that "everything is production." Marx's assumption of the primacy of production, in other words, robs ostensibly nonproduction activities of their autonomous being: whether they are defined as "not-production" and therefore inessential or as "production" and therefore essential they are not theorized on their own terms. Insofar as such activities predominate in precapitalist societies, it is scarcely plausible to maintain that the concept of determination by the mode of production supplies the key to unlock the mysteries of these societies. A capitalist society, however, is an economic society par excellence—a society in which all human activities do appear to be subordinated to the demands of production—and would therefore seem to be a natural "home" for this concept. At first glance, it would appear that the problems that beset the concept of determination by the mode of production when it is applied to precapitalist societies will be absent when it is applied to the reality of a capitalist society.

THE CAPITALIST MODE OF PRODUCTION

"What [individuals] are," Marx has told us, "coincides with their production, both with *what* they produce and with *how* they produce."[83] In a capitalist mode of production, what individuals produce are commodities: "The wealth of those societies in which the capitalist mode of production prevails," the first sentence of volume I of *Capital* announces, "presents itself as 'an immense accumulation of commodities', its unit being a single commodity."[84] A commodity, in turn, is a twofold reality, both a use-value and an exchange-value. As a use-value, it is a qualitatively distinct object that fulfills a qualitatively distinct human need. As an exchange-value, however, it exists and is valued not because it fulfills this need but rather because it can be exchanged for another commodity. The fact that the objects produced through the capitalist mode of production take the form of commodities thus means that they will not be produced unless they can be exchanged and will not be distributed unless they are in fact first exchanged. A society dominated by the capitalist mode of production, in other words, is the first society in history in which the distribution of products depends overwhelmingly on that institution known as the market.[85]

If commodities are what individuals produce in a capitalist mode of production, the process of surplus-value extraction describes how commodities are produced by these individuals in this mode of production. This process

[83] See above, n. 11.
[84] Marx, *Capital*, Vol. I, p. 35.
[85] Karl Polanyi, *The Great Transformation* (Boston: Beacon Press, 1957), esp. Chs. 3-6.

begins when the individual who owns or controls the means of production, i.e., the capitalist, purchases (along with raw material and machinery) the labor-power of the individual, i.e., the worker, who lacks ownership or control of the means of production and is thereby obliged to sell his or her labor-power in order to purchase the commodities that will enable him or her to survive. Thus, in a capitalist mode of production, labor-power becomes a commodity that is bought and sold like any other;[86] for the first time in history the institution of the market comes to extend its sway over industry, over the uniquely human activity which is objectification. Having purchased the labor-power of the worker, the capitalist attempts to set this labor-power in motion in order to produce a commodity whose exchange-value is greater than the exchange-value of the labor-power, the raw materials, and the machinery embodied in the commodity, i.e., in order to produce a surplus-value. Put otherwise, a capitalist society is the first society in history in which goods and services will only be produced if their production yields a profit.

According to Marx, the capacity of the capitalist to extract surplus-value from the sale of the commodities produced by the worker rests on the former's ability to force the worker to work for a period of time that is longer than the period during which the worker would have to work in order to produce the commodities necessary for his or her subsistence and that of his or her family. Since the monetary value of these commodities is the exchange-value of the worker's labor power, we can say that the use-value of the commodity labor-power is to produce a surplus over and above its exchange-value. Thus the source of surplus-value is the difference between the necessary and surplus labor of the worker, and the rate of surplus-value extraction is a function of the magnitude of this difference.[87] Marx's lapidary formulation neatly summarizes what I have said thus far: "The whole capitalist production rests here: that labor is purchased directly, and in the process a portion of this labor is appropriated without compensation, but is then sold in the product. This is the ground of existence, the idea of capital."[88]

The process of surplus-value extraction—and thus the capitalist mode of production—presupposes "nothing less than the institutional separation of society into an economic and political sphere."[89] This separation is implicit in the fundamental premise of this mode of production, namely that the owner of the means of production purchases the labor-power of someone who is

---

[86] Labor-power, according to Marx, is not quite a commodity like any other. Rather it is the only commodity that is "a source not only of value, but of more value than it has itself." *Capital*, Vol. I, p. 193. The unique property of that commodity which is labor-power, in other words, is that it produces surplus-value.

[87] *Ibid.*, pp. 167, 193, Ch. 9.

[88] Cited in Harrington, *The Twilight of Capitalism*, p. 98.

[89] Polanyi, *The Great Transformation*, p. 71.

deprived of control of the means of producing his or her subsistence. On the one hand,

> [L]abor-power can appear on the market as a commodity only if, and so far as, its possessor, the individual whose labour-power it is, offers it for sale, or sells it, as a commodity. In order that he may be able to do this, he must have it at his disposal, must be the untrammeled owner of his capacity for labour, i.e., of his person. He and the owner of money meet in the market, and deal with each other as on the basis of equal rights, with this difference alone, that one is buyer, the other seller; *both therefore equal in the eyes of the law.*[90]

Formal-legal equality, Marx is telling us, is a precondition of the capitalist mode of production. If both capitalist and worker are "equal in the eyes of the law," however, this can only mean that there exists a legal or a political sphere in which rights and obligations are not a function of the drastic economic inequality between the two. Formal-legal equality, in other words, implies the existence of a political arena separate and insulated from the economic arena in the sense that position within the latter is not a formal criterion for participation within the former. This unprecedented structural separation of that which, in all previous modes of production, was inseparably fused, means that

> The authority which the capitalist takes on as the personification of capital in the immediate production process, which he wears as the leader and controller of production, is *essentially different* from the authority on the basis of production with slaves, serfs, etc. On the basis of capitalist production, the mass of the producers confront the social character of their production in the form of a strong, ruling authority and as a hierarchically ordered social mechanism of the labor process—which authority only comes to its bearer as the personification of the conditions of labor as against labor, and not, as in earlier forms of production, as political or theocratic rule.[91]

Thus the "ruling authority" within the capitalist mode of production, in contrast to all previous modes of production, is "self-legitimating" in the sense that "there appears nothing *higher in itself*, nothing legitimate for itself, outside this circle of social production and exchange."[92] The exercise of economic authority, in other words, will not be subordinated to political or moral criteria but rather understood to flow directly from what appears to be an exchange of equivalents between capitalist and worker. The insulation of

[90] Marx, *Capital*, Vol. I, p. 168, emphasis added.
[91] Cited in Harrington, *The Twilight of Capitalism*, p. 97, emphasis added.
[92] Marx, *Grundrisse*, p. 409, emphasis in the original.

39

the economic sphere from political criteria thus goes hand in hand with the insulation of the political sphere from economic criteria. They are in fact two sides of the same coin, the separation of economy and polity in a capitalist mode of production.

This structural separation can also be seen in the other fundamental premise of the capitalist mode of production, namely that the worker is free from, i.e., deprived of, any control over the means of producing that which is necessary for his or her survival and that of his or her family. This "freedom," which for Marx is the real basis of the legal freedom to which I have already alluded, implies the dissolution of those networks of reciprocal obligation that, in all precapitalist societies, precluded labor from becoming a mere "object of commerce" and embedded "the motives and circumstances of productive activities . . . in the general organization of society."[93] Now, for the first time, a "private" economic sphere will be carved out of society that will be largely exempt from the requirement of "public" or communal morality. To put this another, starker way, a capitalist society is the first society in history in which the community as a whole does not guarantee the survival of its individual members and in which, as a consequence, the fear of death becomes the chief animating impulse behind productive activity. Freed from any permanent ties to the land or the community, obliged to transform his or her labor-power into a commodity in order to ensure his or her survival, the worker becomes, in the eyes of the capitalist, a mere factor of production, not fundamentally different from the raw materials and machinery that are also necessary for the production of surplus-value. Indeed, this is what it means for the capitalist to act "rationally"; on pain of extinction he is obliged to treat the worker as a mere means to the end of surplus-value rather than as a fellow member of a human community. The structural separation of the economy and the polity thus inevitably expresses itself in an opposition between the rational and the ethical in bourgeois society.

The amoral character of capitalist production is by no means, for Marx, an unmitigated evil. Freed from ethical and political restraint, the capitalist can bend all his energies to the single-minded pursuit of surplus-value:

> Use-values must . . . never be looked upon as the real aim of the capitalist; neither must the profit on any single transaction. The restless *never-ending* process of profit-making alone is what he aims at. This *boundless* greed after riches, this passionate chase after exchange-value, is common to the capitalist and the miser; but while the miser is merely a capitalist gone mad, the capitalist is a rational miser.[94]

[93] Polanyi, *The Great Transformation*, p. 70.
[94] Marx, *Capital*, Vol. I, pp. 152-53, emphases added.

Since surplus-value, rather than use-values or human needs, is "the chief end and aim of capitalist production"[95] and since the pursuit of surplus-value is "boundless," it follows that capitalist production, in contrast to all previous forms of production, will be limitless in character. It is a mode of production, in other words, that entails a dramatic and persistent expansion or "universalization" of both the power of human beings to control nature and the scope of their social interactions. These are the twin aspects of what Marx refers to as the "civilizing influence" of the capitalist mode of production.[96]

On the one hand, the unlimited nature of the goal of surplus-value extraction dictates that the development of the technological means of fulfilling this goal will likewise proceed without limit: "Modern Industry never looks upon and treats the existing form of a process as final. The technical basis of that industry is therefore revolutionary, while all other modes of production were essentially conservative."[97] This perpetual development of what Marx calls the forces of production, set in motion by the "boundless greed" for surplus value, creates the necessary precondition for a society of abundance in which the heretofore seemingly inescapable brute fact of scarcity and its attendant consequences could be definitively transcended.[98] At the same time, it lays the foundation for a society in which that proportion of an individual's life devoted to necessary labor—the human labor required for the reproduction of that society—will progressively diminish and the proportion of the individual's life that consists in genuine free or "disposable" time will progressively increase.[99] The capitalist's "werewolf hunger" for surplus-value demands that he progressively replace "living labor" with "dead labor"— human beings with machines—and thus opens up the road toward automated production, a realistic destination given a different mode of production in which "labour time" is no longer the "sole measure and source of wealth."[100] Thus capitalism furnishes the material basis for the eventual realization of an age-old dream of humankind: the liberation from burdensome toil.

The same imperative that produces unlimited technological expansion also leads to an unprecedented geographic expansion, and thus "universalization," of human productive activity. This is the second aspect of the "civilizing influence" of capital; the "passionate chase after exchange-value" assumes worldwide dimensions and culminates in the creation of a world market that is, in turn, the precursor of an emerging world society:

[95] *Ibid.*, p. 230.
[96] Marx, *Grundrisse*, p. 409.
[97] Marx, *Capital*, Vol. I, p. 486.
[98] Marx, *Grundrisse*, pp. 540-42; Marx and Engels, *The German Ideology*, p. 125.
[99] Marx, *Grundrisse*, pp. 705-709; *Capital*, Vol. III, p. 320.
[100] Marx, *Grundrisse*, p. 706.

The bourgeoisie has through its exploitation of the world-market given a cosmopolitan character to production and consumption in every country. To the great chagrin of Reactionists, it has drawn from under the feet of industry the national ground on which it stood. All old-established national industries have been destroyed or are daily being destroyed. . . . In place of the old wants, satisfied by the productions of the country, we find new wants, requiring for their satisfaction the products of distant lands and climes. In place of the old local and national seclusion and self sufficiency, we have intercourse in every direction, universal interdependence of nations. And as in material, so also in intellectual production. The intellectual creations of individual nations become common property. National one-sidedness and narrow-mindedness become more and more impossible, and from the numerous national and local literatures, there arises a world literature.[101]

Capitalism, unlike any mode of production before it, provides the material basis for that universal, worldwide human solidarity that is foreshadowed in Marx's concept of species-being.

Thus the liberation of productive activity from political or moral constraints, characteristic of the capitalist mode of production, culminates in the creation of the necessary preconditions for that society of the future—a communist society—in which the human potential for objectification—and thus recognition vis-à-vis nature—and for socialization—and thus recognition vis-à-vis other human beings—will become fully manifest in everyday human existence. These necessary preconditions, however, are at the same time a radical denial of this human potential; the capitalist mode of production, as we shall see, entails a form of objectification and a form of socialization in which individual recognition vis-à-vis nature and vis-à-vis other individuals cannot be successfully achieved. In short, the paradox of the capitalist mode of production is that its unprecedented extension of human power over nature culminates in the creation of a "natural" and a social world within which individuals cannot be integrated and from which they are in fact estranged.

Estranged, to begin with, from nature. The capitalist mode of production, as we have seen, is predicated on a permanent division of labor between an individual who controls but does not produce—the capitalist—and an individual who produces but does not control—the worker. In the ordinary course of events, the worker who sells his or her labor-power to the capitalist is obliged to give up any and all control over the critical decisions concerning the objects he or she will produce. The quality, quantity, and destination of the objects produced by the worker are determined not by the worker but

[101] Karl Marx and Friedrich Engels, *Manifesto of the Communist Party* in Tucker, ed., *The Marx-Engels Reader*, pp. 338-39.

rather by the nonworker, i.e., the capitalist, to whom the worker has sold his or her labor-power. Thus, in a capitalist mode of production, those who produce are separated or alienated from the object of their production; as Marx puts it, "the worker is related to the *product of his labor* as to an *alien object.*"[102]

The production of objects, it will be recalled, is for Marx *the* form of the struggle for recognition vis-à-vis nature; recognition is achieved by making nature an extension of oneself and thus coming to see oneself in nature. Objects, in other words, are the material crystallization of the human relationship with nature. The alienation of the worker from the objects he or she produces thus entails the alienation of the worker from nature; since the objects produced by the worker are not his or her objects, the production of these objects does not enable the worker to make nature an extension of him/herself and does not enable the worker to see him/herself in nature. "[T]he sensuous external world," Marx argues, "more and more ceases to be an object belonging to his labour . . . therefore the greater [his] product, *the less is he himself.*" The struggle for recognition, in other words, is necessarily abortive; it does not culminate in an overcoming of the otherness of nature but rather results in a confrontation between the worker and an "alien objective world" that becomes opaque and thus cannot serve as a source of human identity.[103]

Much the same can be said of the relationship between the capitalist and nature. At best the capitalist is involved in only half of the process of objectification; if the worker forms the object but does not participate in its planning, the capitalist plans the object but does not participate in its formation. As such, he lacks that contact with "the sensuous external world" without which the struggle for recognition cannot culminate in integration. The control that the capitalist exercises over the production of objects, moreover, is radically circumscribed by the fact that all his decisions are subordinated to the overriding imperative to extract surplus-value—an imperative he must heed "on pain of extinction." Marx refers to the capitalist as the "personification of capital";[104] he is not a free agent but must rather submit to the "laws" of an impersonal structure and carry out its imperatives. Strictly speaking, then, the objects over which the capitalist exercises authority belong not to him but to capital, and he is no more in a position to see himself in nature through the objects he "produces" than is the worker. The capitalist is every bit as alienated from nature as the worker.

The division between mental and manual labor constitutive of the capitalist mode of production thus precludes both worker and capitalist from achieving that union between planning and execution that Marx defines as the essence

---

[102] Marx, "Estranged Labour," p. 58, emphases in the original.

[103] *Ibid.*, pp. 58-59, emphasis added.

[104] See above, n. 91.

of the genuine creativity of a species-being. Neither produces an object in conformity with a "freely chosen plan" that corresponds to a need for that object; the worker produces the object in order to secure a wage that will allow him or her to survive, and the capitalist produces the object in order to extract a surplus-value that will allow capital to survive, i.e., to reproduce itself. For both, labor is "not the satisfaction of a need; it is merely a *means* to satisfy needs external to it."[105] A capitalist mode of production thus necessarily breaks the link between what human beings need and the objects they produce; this is simply another way of emphasizing that it is not use-value but rather surplus-value that is "the chief end and aim of capitalist production."

This break in the link between human needs and human objects prepares the way for a curious, deadly inversion in which humans become dominated by the very objects they have produced: "The *alienation* of the worker in his product means not only that his labor becomes an object, an *external* existence, but that it exists *outside him*, independently, as something alien to him, and that it becomes a power of its own confronting him; it means that the life which he has conferred on the object confronts him as something hostile and alien."[106] The object "becomes a power of its own confronting him"; not only is the object not an extension of the self, but the self comes to define itself as an extension of the object. The object is, ideally, a means to the end or need that set in motion the production of the object. Under the capitalist mode of production, however, the object becomes an end in itself and human needs become mere means to the existence of the object. Thus the need to produce, and the manifold needs that, at least in principle, are both the impetus for and the outgrowth of the need to produce, give way to the exclusive and overriding need to consume that which has been produced: "private property has made us so stupid and one-sided that an object is only *ours* . . . when it is directly possessed . . . by us."[107] The capitalist mode of production, Marx is telling us, entails a drastic impoverishment in the scope of human needs: "In place of *all* [the] physical and mental senses there has therefore come the sheer estrangement of *all* these senses—the sense of *having*."[108] The capitalist form of objectification thus betrays the promise of the emancipation of human needs and senses inherent in objectification; its dramatic extension of human power over nature culminates, paradoxically, in a striking reduction in the diversity of human needs, as humans become impotent in the face of the very objects they have produced. The capitalist form of human mastery

---

[105] Marx, "Estranged Labour," p. 60, emphasis in the original.
[106] *Ibid.*, p. 58, emphases in the original.
[107] Marx, "Private Property and Communism," p. 73, emphasis in the original.
[108] *Ibid.*, emphases in the original.

44

over nature results, ironically, in a world of produced objects that becomes a "second nature"[109] that exercises mastery over its human creators.

Under the capitalist mode of production, individuals are unable to see themselves as creative subjects who have engendered objects but come instead to see these objects as subjects on which they are dependent and before which they are obliged passively to submit. Marx refers to this profound reversal in the relationship between subject and object as the "fetishism of commodities":

> There it is a definite social relation between men assumes, in their eyes, the fantastic form of a relation between things. In order, therefore, to find an analogy we must have recourse to the mist-enveloped regions of the religious world. In that world the productions of the human brain appear as independent beings endowed with life, and entering into relation both with one another and the human race. So it is in the world of commodities with the products of men's hands. . . . To them, their own social action takes the form of the action of objects, which rule the producers instead of being ruled by them.[110]

The struggle for recognition vis-à-vis nature in a capitalist mode of production culminates not merely in a lack of development but also in an actual loss of human subjectivity. Fetishism means that individuals cannot see themselves as subjects at all, and thus that they lose their self-consciousness or identity.

The estrangement of the individuals from nature in a capitalist mode of production is paralleled by their estrangement from one another; an abortive struggle for recognition vis-à-vis nature is accompanied by a distorted struggle for recognition vis-à-vis other human beings. To begin with, the "despotism of the workshop" that severs the worker from any control over the objects he or she produces goes hand in hand with "anarchy in the social division of labour," with "independent commodity producers" who produce exclusively in the name of their own "private" interests and establish contact with each other only insofar as it is necessary to exchange their products.[111]

> As a general rule, articles of utility become commodities only because they are products of the labour of private individuals or groups of individuals who carry out their work independently of each other. . . . Since the producers do not come into contact with each other until they exchange their products, the specific social character of each producer's labour does not show itself except in the act of exchange. In other words, the labour of the individual asserts itself as part of the labour of society,

---

[109] Lukacs, *History and Class Consciousness*, p. 128.

[110] Marx, *Capital*, Vol. I, pp. 72, 75.

[111] *Ibid.*, p. 356.

45

only by means of the relations which the act of exchange establishes directly between the products, and indirectly, through them, between the producers. To the latter, therefore, the relations connecting the labour of one individual with that of the rest appear, not as direct social relations between individuals at work, but as what they really are, *material relations between persons and social relations between things*.[112]

The paramount reason for social interaction under such a "private" mode of production is the need to exchange objects. Social intercourse is not engaged in for its own sake but rather becomes a function of the movement of things; thus in a capitalist society the personification of things to which I have already alluded is accompanied by the "thingification" or reification of persons. Persons are valued only insofar as, and to the degree that, they are necessary for the exchange of things; "within the relationship of estranged labour each man views the other in accordance with the standard and the position in which he finds himself as a worker." Thus capitalism "has left remaining no other nexus between man and man than naked self-interest, than callous 'cash payment'."[113] Conceiving of the other as but the means to his or her private end, each individual necessarily becomes mistrustful of and alienated from every other individual.

The reification of human relationships under the capitalist mode of production, in other words, means that the struggle for recognition that individuals engage in cannot culminate in an overcoming of otherness, and guarantees, in fact, that individuals will remain opaque to each other's eyes. The exchange of products does not mediate among human beings in such a way that products become the symbol of their social connections, but rather only of the lack thereof:

> I have produced for myself and not for you, as you have produced for yourself and not for me. You are as little concerned by the result of my production in itself as I am directly concerned by the result of your production. That is, our production is not a production of men for men as such, that is, social production. Thus, as a man none of us is in a position to be able to enjoy the product of another. *We are not present to our mutual products as men*. Thus, neither can our exchange be the mediating movement which confirms that my product is for you, because it is an objectification of your own essence, your need. For what links our production together is not the human essence. Exchange can only set in motion and activate the attitude that each of us has to his own product and thus to the product of another. *Each of us sees in his own*

[112] *Ibid.*, pp. 72-73, emphasis added.

[113] Marx, "Estranged Labour," p. 63. Marx and Engels, *Manifesto of the Communist Party*, p. 337.

product only his own selfish needs objectified, and thus in the product of another he only sees the objectification of another selfish need independent and alien to him.[114]

The exchange of products under a capitalist mode of production necessarily fails to culminate in genuine mutual recognition, and cannot therefore contribute to the development of individual identity or self-consciousness.

But there is more. Not only does the exchange of products fail to mediate properly among human beings; as we have seen, human beings come to mediate between the exchange of products in the sense that their social intercourse is virtually exclusively engendered by the need to exchange them. This means that individuals will see in other individuals only those attributes that are essential for the exchange of products. Since, in a capitalist mode of production, the attribute that is most essential to this purpose is money, individuals will be recognized only insofar as they become representatives of money. Thus Marx argues that "money . . . becomes the *real community*"[115] in a society dominated by the capitalist mode of production, the only communal bond among otherwise isolated individuals. Money, in turn, enables the individual to represent himself or herself as something which he or she is not:

> [W]hat I *am* and *am capable* of is by no means determined by my individuality. I am ugly, but I can buy for myself the most *beautiful* of women. Therefore I am not *ugly*, for the effect of *ugliness*—its deterrent power—is nullified by money . . . I am bad, dishonest, unscrupulous, stupid; but money is honored, and therefore so is its possessor . . . Does not my money therefore transform all my incapacities into their contrary?[116]

To recognize people exclusively through the money they possess is to recognize people as they are not; the struggle for recognition through social relationships under capitalism culminates not only in a failure to overcome mutual otherness but also in a situation characterized by mutual self-deception. The other, and thus the self, cannot be known; individual identity can no more be achieved vis-à-vis other individuals than it can be achieved vis-à-vis nature.

The very mode of production that fosters an unprecedented expansion of human power over nature as well as an extraordinary expansion of the scope

---

[114] Cited in David McLellan, *The Thought of Karl Marx* (New York: Harper & Row, 1971), pp. 112-13; emphases added.

[115] Marx, *Grundrisse*, p. 225, emphasis in the original.

[116] Karl Marx, "The Power of Money in Bourgeois Society," in Tucker, ed., *The Marx-Engels Reader*, p. 81, emphases in the original.

of social intercourse thus precludes either nature or society from being a source of genuine human identity. Individuals are obliged to live within a natural and a social world from which they are estranged, within which they cannot achieve integration. Since, as we have seen, labor is the human essence, the alienation of labor inherent in the capitalist mode of production entails nothing less than "a catastrophe affecting the human essence."[117]

PROLETARIAN CLASS STRUGGLE

If capitalism is a catastrophe for the human essence, it also prepares the way, in dialectical fashion, for its "redemption." Having created universal alienation, it also creates the agent who will eventually eliminate it. In a word, it creates the *proletariat*. If, as Marx argues, an adequate theory of the capitalist mode of production demands that we demonstrate "in the positive understanding of the existing state of things at the same time also the understanding of its negation, of its necessary destruction,"[118] then the adequacy of Marx's theory ultimately rests on the adequacy of his location of the proletariat as the agent that will carry out this negation.

Marx's focus on the proletariat is from the very beginning conditioned by his search for a revolutionary subject capable of transcending the alienation of human beings from their natural and social world that is endemic to the capitalist mode of production. In the 1843 *Introduction* to the *Critique of Hegel's Philosophy of Right*, he argues that in order for human "emancipation" to occur:

A class must be formed which has *radical chains*, a class in civil society which is not a class of civil society, a class which is the dissolution of all classes, a sphere of society which has a universal character because its sufferings are universal, and which does not claim a *particular redress* because the wrong which is done to it is not a *particular wrong* but *wrong in general*. There must be formed a sphere of society which claims no *traditional* status but only a human status, a sphere which is not opposed to particular consequences but is totally opposed to the assumptions of the . . . political system; a sphere, finally, which cannot emancipate itself without emancipating itself from all the other spheres of society, without, therefore, emancipating all these other spheres, which is, in short, a *total loss* of humanity and which can only redeem itself

---

[117] Marcuse, "The Foundations of Historical Materialism," p. 29.
[118] Cited in Glucksmann, "A Ventriloquist Structuralism," p. 92.

48

by a *total redemption of humanity*. This dissolution of society, as a particular class, is the *proletariat*.[119]

Marx's argument here is decidedly teleological: if the goal of human emancipation is to be realized, then there must be someone to realize it. The someone who must realize it, moreover, must be so constituted that its struggle to emancipate itself is necessarily a struggle to emancipate all human beings from the alienation from which they suffer. The mission of liberating humanity from universal alienation demands, in other words, that there be formed a universal class in order to carry out this mission. Having deduced the necessity of a universal class from the function or the *telos* of transcending alienation, Marx concludes that there is, in fact, such a class and that this class is the working class, or the proletariat. Thus the transcendence of alienation and the working class "are related as mission and agent."[120] Marx's definition of the proletariat is inseparable from the function or mission of emancipation that it is supposed to carry out.

In the very next breath Marx announces that "the proletariat is only beginning to form itself . . . as a result of the industrial movement,"[121] i.e., he is fully aware that as of 1843, the industrial working class has barely begun to exist, much less to undertake its vocation of transcending alienation and with it the capitalist mode of production. What then justifies the attribution of this historic vocation to the working class? How does Marx know that his claim that the proletariat is a universal class—a class whose particular interest coincides with the general human interest—is any more valid than the claims of universality made by the bourgeoisie and other former ruling classes that he contests?[122] Depending on what is meant by "liberate itself," the claim on behalf of proletarian universality to the effect that "it cannot liberate itself without . . . destroying *all* the inhuman living conditions of contemporary society"[123] is either an empirically testable hypothesis that demands further support or it is simply true by definition. In the absence of additional arguments, the plausibility of Marx's claim rests entirely on the tendency to build into the notion of "liberate itself" the notion of "general human liberation,"

---

[119] Tucker, ed., *The Marx-Engels Reader*, p. 22, emphases in the original.

[120] Adam Przeworski, "Proletariat into a Class: The Process of Class Formation from Karl Kautsky's *The Class Struggle* to Recent Controversies," *Politics & Society*, 7 (1977), p. 346; see also Shlomo Avineri, *The Social and Political Thought of Karl Marx* (Cambridge, Eng.: Cambridge University Press, 1968), Ch. 2.

[121] Tucker, ed., *The Marx-Engels Reader*, p. 22.

[122] Marx and Engels, *Manifesto of the Communist Party*, p. 344, and *The German Ideology*, p. 138; see also Alvin W. Gouldner, *The Future of Intellectuals and the Rise of the New Class* (New York: Seabury Press, 1979).

[123] Karl Marx, *The Holy Family* in Tucker, ed., *The Marx-Engels Reader*, p. 105, emphasis in the original.

in which case the "theory" of the universality of the proletariat becomes purely tautological. Marx's assertion in *The Holy Family* that:

it is not a matter of what this or that proletarian or even the proletariat as a whole *pictures* at present as its goal. It is a matter of *what the proletariat is in actuality*, and what, in accordance with this *being*, it will be historically compelled to do. Its goal and its historical action are prefigured in the most clear and ineluctable way in its own life-situation as well as in the whole organization of contemporary bourgeois society.[124]

certainly does nothing to detract from the impression of tautology. Instead it merely informs us that the tautology has history on its side, to which we are entitled to respond: how do we know this? In order to rescue his claim of "universality" from tautology and determine if in fact it is any more persuasive than similar claims made on behalf of previous "rising" classes, Marx must specify exactly what it is about "its own life-situation as well as the whole organization of . . . bourgeois society" that prepares the industrial working class to undertake a struggle to liberate itself which is at the same time a struggle to liberate all of humanity. To put this another way, he needs to explain why, at least in the long run, the struggles of the working class (a) cannot be contained within the capitalist mode of production and (b) if they cannot be so contained, why they will not culminate in the creation of a new mode of production in which alienation is also endemic.

Elsewhere in *The Holy Family* Marx argues that the different way in which workers as compared to capitalists experience alienation prepares the former, in contrast and opposition to the latter, for an assault on the capitalist mode of production as a whole:

The possessing class and the proletarian class represent one and the same human self-alienation. But the former feels satisfied and affirmed in this self-alienation, experiences the alienation as a sign *of its own power*, and possesses in it the *appearance* of a human existence. The latter, however, feels destroyed in this alienation, seeing in it its own impotence and the reality of an inhuman existence. To use Hegel's expression, this class is, within depravity, an *indignation* against this depravity, an indignation necessarily aroused in this class by the contradiction between its human *nature* and its life-situation, which is a blatant, outright and all-embracing denial of that very nature.

Within the antagonism as a whole, therefore, private property represents the *conservative* side and the proletariat the *destructive* side. From the

---

[124] *Ibid.*, pp. 105-106, emphases in the original.

former comes action aimed at preserving the antagonism; from the latter, action aimed at its destruction.[125]

As owner and controller of the means of production, the capitalist receives and consumes material and psychic benefits that give him an illusion of power and thus a material and psychological stake in the very system in which he is alienated. Alienated though he be, then, we cannot expect the capitalist to struggle to eliminate the capitalist mode of production; indeed, we should rather expect that he will struggle to the very end to defend it. The worker, on the other hand, receives no such material or psychic compensation for his or her alienation; no illusion of power, but rather the perception of impotence accompanies his or her experience of alienation. Thus we should expect that the worker, in contrast to the capitalist, will be aware of his or her alienation, i.e., of the "contradiction between its human nature and its life-situation," and that he or she will attempt to transcend it.

Thus far the argument remains unpersuasive. Marx has not explained why the worker will not be content to struggle for the material and psychic benefits that he or she presently lacks instead of against the alienating mode of production as a whole, and why this consumption-oriented struggle will not culminate in the same illusion of power and lack of awareness of alienation that these benefits produce in the capitalist. An additional assumption is therefore required, namely that the worker will, at least in the long run, be unable to procure such benefits, i.e., that the capitalist mode of production is structurally incapable of granting them. This, in fact, is precisely the assumption Marx makes in the *Communist Manifesto*, where he develops the thesis of the absolute immiseration of the working class. Starting from the assumption that profits and wages are necessarily inversely related, he deduces the necessity of catastrophic economic crises or breakdowns that culminate in the pauperization of the working class: "The modern labourer . . . instead of rising with the progress of industry, sinks deeper and deeper below the conditions of existence of his own class."[126] Thus the capitalist system will be unable, over the long run, to meet even the most basic subsistence needs of the worker, and the worker's struggle for benefits necessarily pits him or her against the capitalist system as a whole. Marx assumes that there will be a direct, even biological link between the struggle of workers for benefits and the struggle to transcend capitalism and alienation; workers will be obliged to eliminate the capitalist mode of production because their very lives depend on its elimination.

There are two principal problems with this argument. First, even if the thesis of absolute immiseration were correct and workers were "biologically"

[125] *Ibid.*, pp. 104-105, emphases in the original.
[126] Marx and Engels, *Manifesto of the Communist Party*, p. 345.

compelled to struggle against capitalism, this does not necessarily mean that they would be involved in a struggle for an unalienated mode of production, i.e., for communism. Even if it could be demonstrated that the struggle for benefits necessarily explodes the limits of the capitalist mode of production, Marx has not demonstrated how and why a consciousness that is anticapitalist but "consumerist" will be transformed into a consciousness that understands consumption to be an illusory compensation for alienation and is thus not only anticapitalist but genuinely communist. Indeed, if working-class consciousness remained a "consumer-consciousness," we should expect the struggle against capitalism to culminate in another alienated mode of production, since, as we have seen, a consumer-consciousness is, by definition, an alienated consciousness. At the very least, Marx has not accounted for that transformation of consciousness without which the "universality" of the proletariat cannot in fact exist, without which there is no guarantee that the "victory" of the proletariat will not entail the foundation of a new form of human alienation.

Second, as Marx himself later argued, especially in *Capital*, the thesis of absolute immiseration is not in fact correct. This is because the assumption on which it is based, namely that of an inverse relationship between profits and wages, is likewise incorrect. As Martin Nicolaus, Michael Harrington, and many others have shown, Marx demonstrates that under conditions of what he calls the production of "relative surplus value," i.e., where capitalists increase the rate of surplus-value extraction not by lengthening the working day or by lowering wages but rather by decreasing with the aid of modern machinery the proportion of the working day that is devoted to necessary labor as compared to surplus labor, profits and wages are not inversely related.[127] Marx came to recognize that capital accumulation can proceed in the absence of a decline in the living standard of the working class and even in the face of a progressive increase in real wages of the better part of the working class. The long-run fate of the majority of the working class is not absolute immiseration but, notwithstanding periodic crises, gradual and sustained improvement in their level of "benefits."

This recognition, of course, completely undermines the theory of an immediate, biological link between the struggle for benefits and the struggle

[127] Harrington, *The Twilight of Capitalism*, Ch. 5; Martin Nicolaus, "Proletariat and Middle Class in Marx: Hegelian Choreography and the Capitalist Dialectic," in James Weinstein and David W. Eakins, eds., *For a New America* (New York: Vintage Books, 1970), pp. 252-83. Marx does, of course, derive from the progressive substitution of machine for human labor a *tendency* for the *rate* (but not the volume) of profit to fall, but acknowledges at the same time a number of countervailing tendencies that may well, in any given capitalist society, prevent the first tendency from being realized. Thus the actual relationship between profits and wages that prevails in any such society cannot, in fact, be deduced from the "law" of the "increasing organic composition of capital."

against capitalism; if capitalism can in fact grant these benefits, then there is no reason to assume that the struggle to procure them "explodes the limits" of the capitalist mode of production. In short, we cannot deduce a working-class struggle against alienated capitalist production from the existence of a working-class struggle for consumption. In fact, on the basis of the same assumption that Marx makes with respect to the capitalist, namely that benefits produce an illusory sense of power and thus a lack of awareness of alienation, we might well deduce that workers will also develop an illusory sense of power and a lack of awareness of alienation, and thus that they will also oppose struggles to eliminate the capitalist mode of production. The assumption in *The Holy Family* that links "conservatism" to the receipt of benefits turns out to be an extraordinarily "dangerous" one because, once it can be determined that capitalism can provide benefits to workers, one is tempted to conclude that workers as well as capitalists will defend the very system in which they are alienated: if the argument is true for the capitalist, it should also be true for the worker.[128]

On the other hand, if we reject the assumption that benefits received by workers militate against an awareness of alienation and thus against an anticapitalist consciousness, it seems we must reject the assumption as it applies to capitalists as well: if the argument is untrue for workers, it should be untrue for capitalists. We are left either with no reason to expect that workers will be more anticapitalist than capitalists or with no reason to assume that anticapitalist impulses cannot emanate from within the capitalist class itself. In either case, Marx has not been able to demonstrate that the proletariat is the universal class whose struggle to liberate itself is a struggle to liberate humanity.

This problem remains unresolved throughout Marx's writings. It is evident in *Capital*, where, having abandoned the theory of absolute immiseration, Marx nevertheless continues to express confidence in the revolutionary potential of the working class:

Along with the constantly diminishing numbers of the magnates of capital, who usurp and monopolise all the advantages . . . grows the revolt of the working-class, a class always increasing in numbers, and disci-

---

[128] It is of course possible to argue that only benefits above a certain level produce conservatism, and thus that a working class that receives benefits below this level remains potentially revolutionary. This is *not* Marx's argument, however, and it is difficult to imagine how any such "relative deprivation" argument would be consistent with his assumption of dichotomous (class) interests. Such an argument, moreover, is vulnerable to the demonstration that any transition to socialism is likely—at least in the short run—to *increase* the deprivation of benefit-oriented workers and thus that it would be "rational" for them to resist, rather than support, this transition. On this point, see Adam Przeworski, "Material Interests, Class Compromise, and the Transition to Socialism," *Politics & Society*, 10 (1980), pp. 125-53.

plined, united, organised by the very mechanism of the process of capitalist production itself. The monopoly of capital becomes a fetter upon the mode of production, which has sprung up and flourished along with it, and under it. Centralization of the means of production and socialization of labour at last reach a point where they become incompatible with their capitalist integument. The integument is burst asunder. The knell of capitalist private property sounds. The expropriators are expropriated.[129]

Stirring words. But their optimism is not founded on any compelling analysis of the origins or growth of anticapitalist consciousness on the part of those who are to "expropriate the expropriators," i.e., the working class. In fact, just twenty-five pages earlier, Marx had presented a compelling analysis of why, "in the ordinary run of things," we should *not* expect the development of such a consciousness:

> The advance of capitalist production develops a working-class, which by education, tradition, habit, looks upon the conditions of that mode of production as self-evident laws of Nature. The organization of the capitalist process of production, once fully developed, breaks down all resistance. . . . The dull compulsion of economic relations completes the subjection of the labourer to the capitalist. Direct force, outside economic conditions, is of course still used, but only exceptionally. In the ordinary run of things, the labourer can be left to the "natural laws of production," i.e., to his dependence on capital, a dependence springing from, and guaranteed in perpetuity by, the conditions of production themselves.[130]

At the very least there remains an unexplained gap between Marx's stubborn confidence in the ultimately revolutionary nature of working-class consciousness and his own analysis of the way in which the conditions of the capitalist mode of production reproduce, "in perpetuity," a working class that "looks upon the conditions of that mode of production as self-evident laws of Nature." Given this gap, Marx's confidence in the role of the proletariat as a universal class remains rather more an empty *wish* than a plausible expectation.

It is, moreover, a wish that has not been realized in over one hundred years of practice. Marx's theoretical problem, namely that he is unable to offer a convincing or even persuasive explanation for his expectation that the working class will function as a universal class would be of little moment if in fact

[129] Marx, *Capital*, Vol. I, p. 763.

[130] *Ibid.*, p. 737; see also the contradiction between p. 488 and pp. 422-23 on the effects of modern machinery.

the practice of the working class had lived up to this expectation. But it has not, at least not yet. The problem, then, is not so much that Marx fails to provide adequate conceptual foundations for his theory of the revolutionary nature of the proletariat but rather that this theory has not been confirmed by the subsequent history of working-class struggles in Western capitalist societies. More often than not, it would seem, the consciousness and practice of the Western industrial working class has been directed toward the amelioration of its level of consumption rather than the transformation of its mode of production. The "reformist" nature of the working-class movement is, to say the least, an anomaly for a theory that attributes a revolutionary vocation to the working class.

A good part of the history of Marxist thought is the history of the effort to respond to this anomaly in a way that saves the theory. One such response is to deny that the reformist nature of the working-class *movement* disconfirms the theory of the revolutionary nature of the *working class*; that the movement has been reformist is not the fault of the consciousness or spontaneous practice of the working class—which remains "revolutionary"—but rather the consciousness and practice of its nonproletarian leadership. The impulses of the working class are always revolutionary, but they have been effectively held in check, i.e., "betrayed," by their union and party leaders. Thus the elimination of this reformist leadership is the necessary and sufficient condition for the proletariat's resumption of its revolutionary mission.[131] The problem with this response, of course, is that it entirely begs the question of why a revolutionary working class would permit itself consistently to be betrayed by reformist leaders. To explore this question is to call into question the assumption of the "always revolutionary" nature of the consciousness and spontaneous practice of the working class, but this assumption is precisely what this interpretation refuses to call into question. To put this another way, the "spontaneist" response saves the theory of the universality of the proletariat at the price of transforming the theory into a tautology and thus a proposition that is not in principle falsifiable. In the process, the factors that actually influence the level of working-class consciousness and practice remain completely unclarified.

An alternative, and initially more compelling response, acknowledges that the consciousness and practice of the working class has been reformist, but argues that this does not disconfirm Marx's theory because there are good reasons to expect that this consciousness and practice will become revolu-

---

[131] This argument appears in a variety of different historical versions. Trotskyists use it against Stalinists; Council Communists use it against both Trotskyists and Stalinists as well as Leninists in general. For an example of the Council Communist argument, see Stanley Aronowitz, "Left-Wing Communism, The Reply to Lenin," in Dick Howard and Karl E. Klare, *The Unknown Dimension: European Marxism Since Lenin* (New York: Basic Books, 1972), pp. 169-94.

tionary in the future. The nonrevolutionary nature of working-class consciousness up to the present time does not render false the theory that attributes an interest in transcending capitalist alienation to the working class. Rather it means that the working class suffers from "false consciousness" because it does not yet understand its true interest. This interpretation, in contrast to the spontaneist, has the merit of taking the absence of revolutionary working-class consciousness and practice seriously, i.e., as a problem that needs theoretical attention. An account of the determinants of false consciousness, however, could only save the theory of proletarian universality if it could be demonstrated that these determinants can themselves be adequately comprehended in the light of the fundamental assumptions of Marxism. Whether this can be done is, at best, an open question.[132] Even if it could be done, the following, and overriding, problem remains: to argue that working-class consciousness would be revolutionary save for certain obstacles, and that the elimination of these obstacles will, therefore, lead to the development of revolutionary working-class consciousness, is to fall back on precisely what is most problematical in Marx's theory, namely the assumption that, in the absence of "obstacles," there are compelling reasons to expect that the proletariat will function as a universal class. As we have seen, the problem is that Marx presents no such compelling reasons. In the absence of such reasons, a theory of the determinants of false consciousness in no way stands as an adequate theory of the determinants of proletarian universality.

Let me put this another way. If we did not assume that there were compelling reasons for the proletariat to define *its* interest as the interest in transcending capitalist alienation, then there would be no warrant for characterizing its failure to so define its interests as false, and we should rather perhaps conclude that Marx's theory is false. The entire problematic of false consciousness is based on a search for the causes of an absence. That this absence should be a problem worth pursuing, however, rather than a nonproblem, assumes that it is an absence of a presence that is reasonable to expect. But this is precisely what Marx has been unable to demonstrate. This suggests, once again, that it is Marx's theory, rather than working-class consciousness, that must be called into question. Thus the false consciousness response no more saves the theory than does the spontaneist response.

The failure of the working class to develop a revolutionary consciousness and practice, I have been arguing, necessarily calls into question Marx's theory of proletarian universality and thus his theory of the overcoming of capitalist alienation. If the proletariat, moreover, has more often than not been nonrevolutionary, it is also true that nonproletarians have often been

---

[132] A question to which, in the light of the analysis in the rest of Part I and Part II, we will later have to answer "no."

revolutionary. Students, intellectuals, and other nonworkers have regularly played central roles in the drama of anticapitalist action.[133] Their centrality to this drama would also appear to be an anomaly for the theory that the proletariat is *the* universal class.

One characteristic response to this apparent anomaly is that these non-working-class struggles are not in fact anomalous for the theory of the exclusively revolutionary nature of the working class because these struggles are not really revolutionary. At best, so the argument goes, they are peripheral to, at worst diversions from, the class struggle between labor and capital. However frequent and however intense, these "fractional" nonclass struggles are ultimately inessential; their presence, in fact, is merely the symptom of the absence of a fully developed class struggle. One problem with this effort to save the theory of the exclusively revolutionary nature of the working class is that the theory becomes circular: any apparent instance of revolutionary struggle on the part of actors other than the working class that would appear to undermine the theory is redefined so that this struggle becomes nonrevolutionary. In the meantime, the frequency, variety, and intensity of nonclass struggles remains completely unclarified. The purity of the theory is thus purchased at the exorbitant price of a complete divorce from the diverse reality of actual political conflict in capitalist societies.[134]

There is another, equally serious, problem with this line of defense. The defense asserts that examples of revolutionary consciousness that do not derive from the proletarian condition do not falsify the theory that this condition is the exclusive source of revolutionary consciousness because these are not genuine examples of revolutionary consciousness. But the problem is that *the consciousness of Marx and the overwhelming majority of Marxist theorists does not derive from a proletarian source.* Are we to conclude, therefore, that this consciousness is likewise not a "genuine" example of revolutionary consciousness? If so, then what grounds are there for accepting, or even seriously entertaining, the theory that emanates from this consciousness? If not, and we maintain that the Marxist consciousness is genuinely revolutionary in spite of its nonproletarian origins, then what grounds are there for holding that the consciousness of other nonproletarian individuals and groups is necessarily suspect due to its "bourgeois" or "petty bourgeois" origins? When applied to itself, this version of the theory dissolves in contradiction: its content and its origins are hopelessly at odds with each other.[135]

An alternative line of defense purports to avoid these difficulties by arguing that revolutionary struggles undertaken by nonworkers do not disconfirm the

---

[133] Gouldner, *The Future of Intellectuals and the Rise of the New Class.*

[134] Przeworski, "Proletariat into Class," p. 369.

[135] Alvin Gouldner, "Prologue to a Theory of Revolutionary Intellectuals," *Telos*, No. 26 (Winter 1975-76), 3-36.

theory of the exclusively revolutionary nature of the working class because these struggles are really working-class struggles. Students, intellectuals, and other anticapitalist actors are, in fact, part of a vastly expanded working class; their struggles confirm, rather than refute, the theory that the working-class position is *the* source of revolutionary consciousness and action.[136] This interpretation, in contrast to the first, at least has the merit of taking seriously the political conflicts that dominate the landscape of contemporary capitalist societies. In the process, however, the concept of "working class" loses all of its explanatory power. Ostensibly nonproletarian struggles are redefined as "proletarian" as soon as they reveal that they are anticapitalist; the proposition "only the proletariat is revolutionary" is transformed into its converse, "only the revolutionary is a proletariat." The criterion for class membership is no longer an objective position vis-à-vis the means of production but rather simply a certain kind of behavior: to be a member of the proletariat is to behave in a certain way, namely according to the "historic vocation" that Marx and Marxists assign to the proletariat. Once class position is redefined to refer to behavior, however, it is no longer possible to claim that the concept of class position can explain behavior.[137] This version of Marx's theory of the origins of revolutionary consciousness and practice merely redescribes such consciousness and practice as "proletarian," and, having done so, leaves us utterly without any means of locating its origins and thus being able to anticipate or explain it. At the same time, on this behavioral account of what it means to be a member of the proletariat, it is probably true that the great majority of individuals who are workers by virtue of their position vis-à-vis the means of production, would have to be excluded from membership in the proletariat on the grounds that they fail to conform to the criterion of "revolutionary."

Unlike the first, this line of defense attempts to resolve the apparent contradiction between a theory that asserts that the proletarian condition is *the* source of revolutionary consciousness and the fact that this theory has been developed by nonproletarians by arguing that intellectuals are workers and therefore really proletarians after all. Given this expanded concept of proletarian position, the content and the origins of the theory are no longer at odds with each other; the theory is internally consistent when applied to itself. But this consistency is gained only at the cost of an extraordinary inflation of Marx's concept of the proletariat, one that effectively severs its connection to objectification. The meaning of production expands to embrace those activities—including thinking and communicating, the activity of intellectuals—that are ordinarily conceived of as nonproductions. Production comes to mean

---

[136] Serge Mallet, *Essays on the New Working Class* (St. Louis, Mo.: Telos Press, 1976); Alexander Cockburn and Robin Blackburn, eds., *Student Power*, (Middlesex, England: Penguin Books, 1969).

[137] Przeworski, "Proletariat into Class," p. 369.

anything and everything, and the proposition that revolutionary conflicts are rooted in the activity of production thus becomes a meaningless proposition. To put this another way, having redefined the concept of the proletariat to include, at least potentially, virtually everyone, we are not one whit closer to being able to explain which segments of this vastly expanded proletariat are likely to become revolutionary under what conditions. In particular, we have no way of accounting for the disproportionate salience of intellectual "proletarians" within revolutionary, anticapitalist movements. We are thus back to where we began. This line of defense, then, is ultimately no more adequate than the first.

Adam Przeworski has recently attempted to move Marxist theory beyond the impasse of these two interpretations. Unlike the first, he refuses to argue that the nonworking-class struggles that proliferate under capitalism are ultimately unimportant; indeed, he wants to be able to explain them, at least in part, in Marxist terms. Unlike the second, he refuses to argue that these nonworking-class struggles are really struggles undertaken by the working class after all: "students, women, Protestants, consumers are not classes and to the extent to which they appear as collective actors in struggles, these conflicts are not between or among classes."[138] But if these conflicts are not unimportant and they are not "between or among" classes, how is it possible to maintain Marx's proposition that important, i.e., potentially revolutionary, conflicts in a capitalist mode of production are (working-) class conflicts?

Przeworski's answer is that we should understand the class conflict to which this proposition refers to include "struggles *about* class formation as well as struggles *among* organized class forces." Any given struggle is a class struggle precisely insofar as it "has the effect of class organization or disorganization,"[139] i.e., because it necessarily influences the capacity and willingness of the members of the working class to organize themselves as a class united against capital and to struggle on that basis. And any given struggle is important for precisely this reason. Thus Marx's theory is completely consistent with the persistence and importance of the manifold political struggles in a capitalist society that are not undertaken by agents of production.

Przeworski is aware that he has "rescued" Marx's proposition by transforming it into a tautology, but, he argues, it is a useful tautology, a "methodological postulate" that directs us to analyze all conflicts in the light of their effect on (working-) class formation. But why should we allow our analysis to be so directed? Why, for example, should we analyze racial conflict in the light of its effects on class conflict rather than the reverse? Unless it can be persuasively argued that class conflicts are always more important than all other forms of conflict, Przeworski's methodological postulate would ap-

---

[138] *Ibid.*, p. 386.
[139] *Ibid.*, pp. 385, 386.

pear to be completely arbitrary. At this point he offers an answer that he acknowledges to be "rudimentary," and one that I would argue is completely unsatisfactory:

> What is lawful about historical development is the development of the forces of production, specifically, the process of capital accumulation. . . . The assumption of class analysis is . . . that the historical development of capitalist societies is to be understood in terms of the development of the capitalist system of production, more specifically, in terms of the process of the accumulation of capital and all its attendant consequences.[140]

Conflicts rooted in production are thus more important because the forces of production are "lawful." But this is precisely what is at issue: how do we know that they are lawful, that "historical development" is a function of "the development of the capitalist system of production"? To restate the problem, it is true by definition that the historical development of a *capitalist* society is a function of the capitalist system of production, since the adjective "capitalist" defines the society in terms of its system of production. But the decisive question is precisely whether the society should be defined as a capitalist society in the first place or whether it should not perhaps be defined along some dimension other than production which is perhaps as, or more, essential. This, for example, might well be the claim of someone who asserted the autonomy of racial or religious conflicts from production conflicts; if he or she defended the assertion that production conflicts should be studied for their effects on racial or religious conflicts with the argument that the development of a racist or Christian society is a function of the system of race relations or the system of religious relations, he or she would be operating on precisely the same logical level as Przeworski.

Ingenious though it be, Przeworski's reinterpretation of the Marxist theory of (working-) class conflict as *the* source of revolutionary change does not succeed in rescuing the theory from the impasse in which he found it. At bottom, his defense of this theory is merely a restatement of the assumption that a society can best be grasped as a mode of production. And this assumption is precisely what is in question. We have already examined some of the ambiguities in the concept of a mode of production, and thus some of the general problems associated with the effort to grasp a society in the light of this concept. The next six chapters of this book will clarify and specify these problems as they manifest themselves in Marxist and Neo-Marxist theories of sexual, political, and technological domination.

[140] *Ibid.*, pp. 387-89.

CHAPTER TWO

MARXIST THEORIES OF PATRIARCHY

THE FEMINIST MOVEMENT

The latter part of the 1960s was punctuated by a veritable explosion of feminist consciousness and organization in the advanced capitalist societies. The shock waves from this explosion reverberated throughout these societies to the point where none of their parts was exempted from the charge of being male-dominated or patriarchal in character. Unlike a previous generation of twentieth-century American feminists, whose efforts were largely restricted to challenging the legal and political subordination of women, the new generation of feminists questioned, and sought to transcend, the sexual division of labor as a whole and the way in which this division of labor guaranteed the subordination of women to men in every sphere or aspect of contemporary life. The ubiquity of sexism, it was understood, demanded a movement for sexual liberation that was every bit as encompassing as the structure of domination against which it was obliged to struggle.

The feminism of the 1960s and 1970s embraced, as the Suffragist movement of the Progressive era did not, an attack on male domination within the "personal" sphere of everyday life. The traditional division of labor within the family, the sexual objectification of women both within and without the family, the interiorization of this objectification in women who come to see themselves exclusively through the eyes of men, the very definition of what it means to be feminine as compared to masculine—all became grist for the critical mill of the contemporary feminist movement. By describing, and challenging, the way in which male domination manifests itself and is reproduced within our most intimate, even unconscious, activities, feminists demonstrated convincingly that "the personal is the political" and that the liberation of women would require a transformation of the innermost structure of the very male-female relationships that had heretofore been understood to be "beyond politics." The feminist movement of the past two decades was thus an important contribution, as well as essential corrective, to the commitment of the male-dominated New Left to the transformation of everyday life: there can be no human liberation without a transformation of everyday life, but no transformation of everyday life without the elimination of male domination of everyday life.

At the same time, and again in contrast to their Suffragist ancestors, many contemporary feminists were explicitly anticapitalist. Either they understood that the liberation of women could not be achieved in the absence of the elimination of the capitalist mode of production and the creation of a genuinely socialist society, or they had earlier and independently arrived at socialist commitments in the course of their participation in the civil rights and antiwar movements of the 1960s. Whatever the reasons, and for the first time in the twentieth century, large numbers of women who defined themselves as feminists also defined themselves as socialists.[1] They were thus obliged to forge a feminist-socialist, or socialist-feminist, political practice. More precisely, their task was to unite a struggle against patriarchy with a struggle against capitalism that would culminate in the creation of a socialist society that was not characterized by male domination.

New Left feminists understood that the elimination of capitalism and the creation of socialism was a necessary, but certainly not sufficient, condition for the emancipation of women. In this they differed dramatically from their comrades within the Old Left, for whom "socialist revolution" had always been the solution to the problem of the subordinate status of women; for whom, in other words, the struggle for the liberation of women should be subordinated to the struggle for the elimination of capitalism. Unlike the Old Left, whose commitment to the Soviet Union or other state socialist societies prevented them from analyzing, or even recognizing, the pervasive nature of male domination in these societies, New Left feminists were in a position to grapple with, and draw the appropriate consequences from, the fact that patriarchy and "actually existing socialism" went hand in hand. That is, they were in a position to conclude that collective ownership of the means of production and "production for use" in no way guaranteed an end to the subordination of women and thus that an anticapitalist revolution that was not supplemented by an antipatriarchal movement could well culminate in (state) socialist patriarchy.

The feminists' experience with male-dominated New Left movements, moreover, convinced them that male socialists could not be relied on to initiate such an antipatriarchal movement. Indeed, as the "shitworkers" for, and the sexual objects of, the male leftist leaders of the civil rights and antiwar movements, New Left women regularly received striking and enraging confirmation of the way male domination can manifest and reproduce itself in

[1] The historical identification of feminism as a bourgeois movement partly accounts for the persistent reluctance of many socialist women, particularly in Europe, to define themselves as "feminists." See Eileen Manion, review of Elaine Marks and Isabelle de Courtivron, *New French Feminisms: An Anthology* in *Telos*, No. 45 (Fall 1980), pp. 211-15.

the structures and practices of even the men who are committed to a socialist tranformation.[2] Given their "patriarchal attitudes,"[3] a patriarchal culmination of an anticapitalist struggle led by such men was no mere hypothetical possibility but rather a virtual certainty. Women, at least initially, would have to rely on themselves to lead the movement against patriarchy and to guarantee that this movement would not be subordinated to the struggle against capitalism.

Very roughly, this was the political conjuncture that precipitated the renaissance of Marxist theorizing about patriarchy and the possibilities for its elimination to which the analysis in this chapter is devoted. Marxist theorists sought to demonstrate that the relationship between male domination and capitalism can best be illuminated from a Marxist perspective and thus that the New Left feminists' problem of unifying an anticapitalist and an antipatriarchal struggle could only be resolved with the aid of Marxist theoretical guidance. The Marxist theoretical claim, in other words, was that the subordination of women and the possibilities for their liberation can only be adequately understood if we proceed from the assumption of the primacy of production. The rest of this chapter elaborates and assesses this claim.

MARX ON PATRIARCHY

Marx himself could shed little light on the problem of patriarchy. Indeed, he assumed that this problem was rapidly being solved by capitalism itself, i.e., that the development of the capitalist mode of production would undermine the material basis of a male-dominated sexual division of labor both within the family and throughout the society at large. Marx never anticipated the problem that preoccupies contemporary feminists—the problem of how to make an anticapitalist revolution that is also antipatriarchal—because he assumed that the inner logic of capitalism is antipatriarchal.

On the one hand, the capitalist mode of production undermines the family, and thus the traditional site of patriarchal authority, within the working class. By transferring productive activity from the home to the factory and employing women and children, as well as men, in this activity, the "capitalistic mode of exploitation" progressively erodes "the economical basis of parental authority."[4] Capitalism subverts the traditional sexual division of labor within the home by eliminating labor from the home. At the same time, the fact that

---

[2] See the various accounts summarized in Juliet Mitchell, *Woman's Estate* (New York: Pantheon Books, 1971) pp. 84-86.

[3] The title of a book by Eva Figes (New York: Stein and Day, 1970).

[4] Cited in Sheila Rowbotham, *Woman's Consciousness, Man's World* (Middlesex, England: Penguin Books, 1973), p. 103.

63

fathers, mothers, and children spend the great part of their waking hours in debilitating factory labor means that it is no longer really possible to speak of the place where they resuscitate themselves as their home or even to speak of them as constituting a "family." Thus Marx decries the "practical absence of the family among the proletarians," and notes with indignation that:

> The Bourgeois clap-trap about the family and education, about the hallowed co-relation of parent and child, becomes all the more disgusting, the more, by the action of Modern Industry, all family ties among the proletarians are torn asunder, and their children are transformed into simple articles of commerce and instruments of labour.[5]

And so, according to Marx, the despotism of capital within the factory comes to replace the despotism of the father within the home. Factory despotism, in turn, is indifferent to, and destructive of, the sexual division of labor:

> The less the skill and exertion of strength implied in manual labour, in other words, the more modern industry becomes developed, the more is the labour of men superseded by that of women. *Differences of . . . sex have no longer any distinctive social validity for the working class.* All are instruments of labour.[6]

The rule of capital, in short, is impersonal and abstract; it recognizes human beings who labor only insofar as they represent the category "labor-power." Since the introduction of modern machinery into the workplace compensates for the relative physical weakness of women and enables them to perform tasks that were heretofore reserved for men, i.e., enables women as well as men to represent the category "labor-power," it follows that sexual identity will become progressively less relevant as a basis for the division of labor within the workplace. Thus we should expect that it will also become increasingly irrelevant as a determinant of the consciousness of workers, who will necessarily come to think of themselves first and foremost as members of the proletariat rather than as men or women. The development of capitalism fosters class, rather than sexual, consciousness among those who are obliged to sell their labor-power in return for a wage.

It does so as well among the bourgeoisie. If the capitalist mode of production divests the proletarian family of its economic functions and thus renders it superfluous, it simultaneously reduces the family of the bourgeoisie to its economic function and thus transforms it into "a mere money relation." "The bourgeoisie has torn away from the family its sentimental veil. . . . On what

---

[5] Marx and Engels, *Manifesto of the Communist Party*, pp. 349-50.

[6] *Ibid.*, p. 341, emphasis added.

foundation is the . . . bourgeois family based? On capital, on private gain."[7] Here Marx appears to have in mind the tendency for ruling-class marriages to serve as the basis for economic alliances that are mutually beneficial to the contracting parties and their families. Economic self-interest, rather than reciprocal affection, is the tie that binds the bourgeois family together; as such, the relationship between bourgeois men and bourgeois women is an exchange relationship not fundamentally different from the exchange relationships that increasingly come to embrace the entire society. And, as in the case of any exchange relationship, "the individual [within the family] carries his . . . power . . . in his pocket,"[8] i.e., power within the family is a function of money rather than sexual identity.

Thus the reduction of men and women who labor to representatives of labor-power is paralleled by the reduction of men and women who purchase labor-power to "personifications" of capital.[9] Both reductions entail the elimination of a sexual, in favor of a purely economic, basis of the division of labor, and both therefore entail the elimination of patriarchy: "The bourgeoisie, wherever it has got the upper hand, has put an end to all feudal, patriarchal . . . relations. It has pitilessly torn asunder the motley feudal ties that bound man to his 'natural superiors,' and has left remaining no other nexus between man and man than naked self-interest, than callous 'cash payment.' "[10]

It is clear, then, that Marx treats patriarchy as a precapitalist structure that is an element of a precapitalist mode of production. Given the assumption of the primacy of production, it follows that the triumph of the capitalist mode of production over the feudal mode of production brings about the end of patriarchy; the transformation from precapitalist modes of production to the capitalist mode of production is a transformation from male domination to the domination of capital. Curiously enough, Marx's prognosis for patriarchy is not fundamentally different from that of the contemporary Liberal or "bourgeois" feminist who operates under the assumption that male domination can be eliminated within the framework of the capitalist mode of production. Despite their obvious differences, both Marx and the Liberal feminist agree that patriarchy is not endemic to capitalism, that capitalism is in fact ultimately inconsistent with patriarchy, and that the solution to the problem of patriarchy is therefore to be found in the development of capitalism itself.

The persistence of patriarchy in the face of one hundred years of capitalist development calls into question all of these assumptions. Capitalism has altered, but certainly not destroyed, the proletarian family; although women have been drawn into the paid labor-force, their entry has not been nearly as

[7] *Ibid.*, pp. 338, 349.

[8] Marx, *Grundrisse*, p. 157.

[9] Marx, *Capital*, Vol. I, p. 10.

[10] Marx and Engels, *Manifesto of the Communist Party*, p. 337.

65

uniform or rapid as Marx anticipated. Nor, moreover, have working women been liberated from their traditional role within the family. Sexual identity remains a centrally important criterion for the exercise of authority within the working-class family. At the same time, sexual identity, contrary to Marx's expectations, is far from becoming irrelevant as a basis for the division of labor within the workplace: the introduction of modern machinery notwith-standing, job segregation on the basis of sex is as prevalent now as it ever was, with women typically assigned to tasks that are analogous to those tasks they have traditionally performed, and still perform, within the family.[11] Laboring men and women alike may be viewed by their employers as mere "instruments of labor," but the way these instruments are used and the level of remuneration for their use depends decisively on their sex. Nor can it be plausibly argued that sexual identity is irrelevant as a basis for the division of labor and authority within the capitalist class. On the one hand, it is upperclass men who dominate the commanding heights of the corporate hier-archies. On the other hand, it is the women who are married to these men who mix them their martinis when they get home and who follow them from city to city when they get their promotions.

Contrary to Marx's expectations, then, the development of the capitalist mode of production has not significantly undermined a male-dominated di-vision of labor; patriarchy remains alive and well despite Marx's prediction of its early demise. Thus it has fallen to Marxists after Marx to develop, where Marx did not, a theory of the relationship between patriarchy and capitalism that could account for the persistence of the former without un-dermining the assumption of the primacy of the latter.

Contemporary Marxist Theories of Patriarchy

Faced with the coexistence of patriarchy and capitalism, contemporary Marxist theorists have sought to demonstrate the way in which the persistence of the former is necessary for the reproduction of the latter. Patriarchy—or a male-dominated sexual division of labor—antedates the capitalist mode of production, and, in this sense, Marx was correct to describe it as a "precap-italist" relation. Marx failed, however, to understand the important ways in which this relation "was retained and maintained by the new mode of pro-duction,"[12] and thus he was unable to grasp the way in which this precapitalist relation assumes a specifically capitalist form and thus becomes, in its spec-ificity, a capitalist relation. Rather than undermining the material basis of the

---

[11] Rowbotham, *Woman's Consciousness, Man's World*, p. 87; Mitchell, *Woman's Estate*, p. 144.

[12] Mitchell, *Woman's Estate*, p. 113.

patriarchal division of labor, capitalism adapts this division of labor to its own purposes and serves as its new material basis. To understand patriarchy as an historically specific, rather than abstract, phenomenon, in other words, is to grasp it as a structure that performs functions on behalf of the capitalist mode of production. Thus the fate of patriarchy has become inextricably intertwined with the fate of capitalism.

The capitalist mode of production, to begin with, effects a profound separation between the point of production and the point of consumption, or between workplace and home. The emergence of industrial capitalism is coextensive with the concentration of productive labor, i.e., labor that produces surplus-value, in factories that are structurally separate and geographically distant from the home. Industrial capitalism thus divests the family of economic functions that were formerly carried out in the home; no longer the site of productive labor, the home becomes a place of preparation for and recuperation from this labor. A situation in which one structure performs a number of interrelated functions is replaced by a situation in which two structures perform discrete functions. Another, less euphemistic way of saying this is that capitalism ruptures the unity of work and life.[13]

This capitalist division of labor between workplace and home is established within the framework of a preexisting sexual division of labor that assigns child-rearing responsibilities exclusively to women. Given these child-rearing responsibilities, which demand the presence of women within the home, the separation of workplace from home effected by industrial capitalism simultaneously entails the exclusion of women from the workplace. Exclusion from productive labor is thus the characteristic form that patriarchy assumes under developed capitalism. Whereas in precapitalist as well as early capitalist societies women raised children *and* engaged in productive labor along with men, in industrial capitalist societies their exclusion from the latter relegates them to the role of "mothers." Or, in Eli Zaretsky's words, "the housewife emerged, alongside the proletariat—the two characteristic laborers of developed capitalist society."[14] The superimposition of the capitalist division of labor on the preexisting patriarchal sexual division of labor results in the creation of a sphere of work that is encoded as "male" and a sphere of the home that is encoded as "female." Since it is wage labor that produces "value" in a capitalist society, women's labor within the home will not be valued, or will be valued less than that of men. The subordination of women is thus both the precondition and the result of their exclusion from productive

---

[13] Marx, "Estranged Labour," p. 60; Eli Zaretsky, "Capitalism, the Family, and Personal Life," *Socialist Revolution*, Nos. 13-14 (January-April 1973), pp. 66-125, and No. 15 (May-June 1973), pp. 19-70.

[14] Zaretsky, "Capitalism, the Family, and Personal Life," p. 114.

labor; capitalism both feeds off, and reproduces in a new form, the domination of men over women.[15]

The specific form that patriarchy assumes under capitalism, in turn, performs decisively important functions for the reproduction of this mode of production. For the sake of convenience, these functions can be grouped under two major headings, "economic" and "ideological."

Economic Functions of Patriarchy

The division of labor that assigns women to "unproductive" labor in the home enables capitalists to benefit from this socially necessary labor without having to pay for it. Housework and child rearing are essential for the reproduction of the wage-labor force. The fact that these activities are performed by women, without remuneration, in the home means that the capitalist's contribution to the reproduction of the labor-power of his workers is far less than it would otherwise have to be. Given that "domestic labor . . . is enormous if quantified in terms of productive labor,"[16] the fact that it is not so quantified under the capitalist form of patriarchy entails an enormous saving for the capitalist class, which is able to extract a far greater volume of surplus-value than would be possible if its wage-costs included housework and child rearing. As Margaret Benston puts it, "the wages of a man buy the labor of two people."[17] Alternatively, it might be argued that the fact that women perform unpaid labor essential for the subsistence of the worker and his family means that the wage paid to the worker is far below the subsistence level.[18] From either perspective it is clear that the result is that the patriarchal division of labor functions to maximize capitalist profits. Its elimination would therefore produce a drastic reduction in profits and thus threaten to undermine the capitalist mode of production as a whole. (Marxist-feminist theorists differ with respect to the question of the seriousness of this threat; I shall return to this question shortly.)

Marxist-feminists also emphasize the role women play as a "reserve army" of labor. When the capitalist economy expands and the demand for labor increases, large numbers of women are readily available for employment in productive labor. Because their employment is viewed by their employer, and

[15] *Ibid, passim.* Margaret Benston, "The Political Economy of Women's Liberation," in Leslie B. Tanner, ed., *Voices From Women's Liberation* (New York: Mentor, 1970), pp. 277-92.

[16] Juliet Mitchell, "Women: The Longest Revolution," cited in Benston, "The Political Economy of Women's Liberation," p. 282.

[17] "The Political Economy of Women's Liberation," p. 285.

[18] Jean Gardiner, "Women's Domestic Labor," in Zeilah Eisenstein, ed., *Capitalist Patriarchy and the Case for Socialist Feminism* (New York: Monthly Review Press, 1979), p. 83.

often by themselves, as merely temporary and supplementary to that of their husbands, women typically find themselves ghetto-ized within the lowest paying sectors of the labor force. "Under capitalism, the family system . . . provides a mechanism for the superexploitation of women as wage workers,"[19] i.e., it enables capitalists to extract surplus-value at a far higher rate than would otherwise be possible. At the same time, because they often view their employment as temporary and as secondary to their obligations within the home, women are typically less wage-militant and organizable than their male counterparts. For this they earn the distrust and even enmity of male workers, who perceive the presence of women within the labor force as an obstacle to the growth of unions and the augmentation of their wages.[20] The patriarchal division of labor thus produces disunity rather than solidarity within the working class; this "ideological" function of patriarchy will be discussed in greater detail below.

When the economy contracts, and the demand for labor decreases, women can be expelled from the labor force "with fewer social consequences than any other component of the reserve army of labor."[21] Because of the "temporary" and "supplementary" nature of their employment, unemployment among women is often not even recognized as such; rather they are merely returning, following a brief interlude, to their "natural" work within the home. Consequently, lay-offs of female workers are likely to engender less resentment and fewer protests than lay-offs of male workers. The patriarchal division of labor that assigns women to the home permits the capitalist system to tolerate a far higher level of unemployment than would otherwise be possible; thus capitalists can maintain levels of profit during periods of contraction without having to pay an exorbitant political price.

Finally, the fact that women, whether they are engaged in productive labor or not, are responsible for the home means that they are ideally suited to perform the consumer functions so essential to advanced capitalist societies. Marxists from Baran and Sweezy to Marcuse have emphasized the extent to which the reproduction of these societies depends on the infinite expansion of needs that can only be satisfied through commodities. The ideology and practice of "consumerism" matches the quality and quantity of human needs to those which the capitalist mode of production is capable of satisfying.[22] The division of labor that assigns women primarily to the home enables this function to be performed by "specialists" in consumption. On the one hand,

[19] *Women's Liberation and the Socialist Revolution* (New York: Pathfinder Press, 1979), p. 23.

[20] Rowbotham, *Woman's Consciousness, Man's World*, pp. 94-96.

[21] *Women's Liberation and the Socialist Revolution*, p. 24.

[22] Paul A. Baran and Paul M. Sweezy, *Monopoly Capital* (New York: Monthly Review Press, 1966); Herbert Marcuse, *One-Dimensional Man* (Boston, Beacon Press, 1964).

69

if they are not employed, or employed only part-time, women, it is alleged, have far more time than male wage workers to plan and execute the consumption of commodities, i.e., to shop. On the other hand, whether they have no paying job or one which is typically unrewarding, women are likely to compensate for the absence of creativity within the sphere of production by making "consumption a 'creative' activity and a means of self-expression."[23] To put this another way, women, or so it is argued, are particularly likely to fall victim to the fetishism of commodities. Whichever way we put it, what is clear is that patriarchy creates a situation in which millions of human beings have the time and the emotional energy to devote themselves to procuring the goods that the system can deliver, thus submitting to and reproducing the "comfortable unfreedom"[24] on which the stability of advanced capitalist societies depends.

Ideological Functions of Patriarchy

These economic functions by no means exhaust the contribution that patriarchy makes to capitalism. The male-dominated sexual division of labor also helps create the ideological preconditions for the persistence of the capitalist mode of production, fostering the development of a consciousness among workers that is predisposed to acquiesce rather than resist. Patriarchy, in other words, is an essential determinant of false, rather than socialist, consciousness within the working class.

The structure of the family, to begin with, enables it to function as both a source and satisfier of needs that cannot be satisfied within the alienated capitalist workplace. The division of labor that dictates that the home will not be a site of wage labor also determines that it will be a preserve of "expressive," rather than "instrumental" values; freed from primary responsibility for wage labor, women can be socialized into nurturing roles that enable them to provide the emotional warmth and comfort that is absent within the male world of "work." This nurturance, in turn, makes alienation within the workplace easier to bear; without it, the workplace might well become intolerable.[25] The family, in short, is a "haven in a heartless world"[26] that functions to make this world more endurable and thus helps to reproduce it.

Marxist-feminists also argue that "the family system is a repressive and

---

[23] Batya Weinbaum and Amy Bridges, "The Other Side of the Paycheck," in Eisenstein, ed., *Capitalist Patriarchy and the Case for Socialist Feminism*, p. 198.

[24] The term is Marcuse's, in *One-Dimensional Man*, p. 1.

[25] Nancy Chodorow, "Mothering, Male Dominance and Capitalism," in Eisenstein, *Capitalist Patriarchy and the Case for Socialist Feminism*, pp. 95-98; Talcott Parsons and Robert F. Bales, *Family, Socialization and Interaction Process* (Glencoe, Ill.: Free Press, 1955).

[26] Christopher Lasch, *Haven in a Heartless World* (New York: Basic Books, 1977).

conservatising institution that reproduces within itself the hierarchical, authoritarian relationships of the capitalist workplace."[27] Here they echo Wilhelm Reich, for whom the sexual repression enforced by the patriarchal family produces an identification with parental authority that provides the libidinal basis for subsequent acquiescence to the capitalist boss and the capitalist state.[28] Unlike Reich, however, contemporary Marxist-feminists emphasize the disproportionate burden that women bear in carrying out the task of authoritarian socialization:

> Profits depend more and more on the efficient organization of work and on the "self-discipline" of the workers rather than simply on speedups and other direct forms of increasing the exploitation of the workers. The family is therefore important both to shoulder the burden of the cost of higher education, and to carry out the repressive socialization of children. The family must raise children who have internalized hierarchical social relations, who will discipline themselves and work efficiently without constant supervision. . . . Women are responsible for implementing most of this socialization.[29]

Women, after all, have exclusive or primary responsibility for child care; they are thus the first authority figure the child encounters. As such, they play a decisive role in inculcating that form of the authoritarian personality which is essential for the reproduction of the advanced capitalist system. In this way the "hand that rocks the cradle" helps the capitalist to "rule the world."

Finally, and as I have already suggested, Marxist-feminists emphasize the way in which patriarchy divides the working class, militating against the development of a unified socialist consciousness. If, as Engels argued, within the working-class family the husband "is the bourgeois [and] the wife represents the proletariat,"[30] i.e., if there is a domination-subjection relationship based on sexual identity, then there is a structural basis for hostility, rather than solidarity, within the working class. If the male worker views his wife as inferior, he cannot see her as a "comrade"; indeed, he is probably more likely to vent his rage on her than on his capitalist boss. On the other hand, since the woman is oppressed by her husband, she has good reason to view him as an "oppressor," as part of the problem rather than part of the solution. This sexually based opposition within the family is reinforced by a sexual

---

[27] *Women's Liberation and the Socialist Revolution*, p. 20.

[28] Wilhelm Reich, *The Mass Psychology of Fascism* (New York: Farrar, Straus & Giroux, 1970); see also Chapter Six, below.

[29] Peggy Morton, "A Woman's Work Is Never Done," cited in Mitchell, *Woman's Estate*, p. 152.

[30] Frederick Engels, "The Origin of the Family, Private Property and the State," in Karl Marx and Frederick Engels, *Selected Works* (New York: International Publishers, 1968), p. 510.

71

division of labor that assigns women to the lowest paying, least unionized jobs. In both arenas, patriarchy cuts across the class cleavage in such a way as to make it difficult, if not impossible, for a consciousness of the primacy of this cleavage to emerge within the working class.

Marxist theorists thus argue that patriarchy performs indispensable functions for the capitalist mode of production. This argument purports to demonstrate that it is capitalism that provides the "material basis" for patriarchy, and thus to justify the conclusion that the elimination of capitalism and the creation of socialism entails the destruction of the material basis of patriarchy. It follows that "women's liberation is part of the historic struggle of the working class against capitalism," and that "support for building an independent feminist movement is part of the strategy of the revolutionary working class."[31] Thus the so-called "independent" feminist movement must ultimately be linked with, and subordinated to, socialist forms of organization that represent the one social agent with an overriding interest in the revolutionary transformation of the capitalist mode of production, namely the proletariat. It is now time to evaluate this conclusion and the entire Marxist argument on which it is based.

The demonstration that patriarchy presently performs essential functions for capitalism does not prove that patriarchy is an inherent requirement of capitalism. Proof of this thesis would demand a convincing demonstration that alternative structures could not be elaborated that would perform the same functions. This objection, of course, can be raised against any "functionalist" argument. What makes it particularly relevant to the present argument is that Marxist-feminists themselves have entertained the question of whether the sexual division of labor that assigns exclusive or primary responsibility for the home to women could be eliminated without undermining the stability of contemporary capitalism. Juliet Mitchell and Jean Gardiner, among others, have emphasized that the dramatic expansion in women's participation in the paid labor force in most Western capitalist societies since World War II has already created a variety of pressures for the transformation of this division of labor, including demands for state-supported day care centers, wages for housework, and conversion of housework into a public industry.[32] Gardiner argues that there is no inherent reason why these demands for the socialization of domestic labor cannot be met by the capitalist system, at least during periods of expansion when there is a need for more women workers and for an increase in the level of consumption among the working class.[33] Sheila Rowbotham maintains, on the other hand, that although the socialization of

[31] *Women's Liberation and the Socialist Revolution*, pp. 85, 64.

[32] Mitchell, *Woman's Estate*, p. 55; Juliet Mitchell, *Psychoanalysis and Feminism* (New York: Vintage, 1975), p. 411; Gardiner, "Women's Domestic Labor," pp. 173-89.

[33] Gardiner, "Women's Domestic Labor," pp. 184, 188.

domestic labor "is not inconceivable, the economic and social cost would mean a capitalism which was fundamentally different from any system known now and would probably be extremely destructive to its own continuation."[34] Other Marxist-feminists have simply concluded that the elimination of women's domestic responsibilities under capitalism is impossible, but their conclusion usually rests on little more than the reiteration that the prevailing sexual division of labor performs indispensable functions on behalf of capitalism, and thus begs precisely the question of the possibility of alternative structures that might perform the same functions.[35]

If a reformed capitalism could accommodate an elimination of the sexual division of labor, then this would refute the Marxist-feminist theory that the destruction of capitalism and the creation of socialism is the necessary precondition for the elimination of patriarchy. On the other hand, even if it were possible to demonstrate that capitalism cannot, for all practical purposes, dispense with patriarchy, this would in no way support the conclusion that the elimination of capitalism and the creation of socialism is the sufficient condition for the liberation of women. This conclusion would only follow if it were possible to prove that the capitalist mode of production is not merely a material basis, but *the* material basis of patriarchy. This is precisely what Marxist theorists of patriarchy have not proved.

Nor can it be proved, since it flies in the face of the reality of contemporary state socialist societies. The persistence of a male-dominated sexual division of labor in these societies immediately undermines the theory that capitalism is the exclusive source of patriarchy in the contemporary world. The sexual division of labor in the Soviet Union, for example, is not essentially different from that which prevails in Western capitalist societies. Although the official census of the Soviet Union reports that "90 per cent of all urban women between the ages of 16 and 54 hold jobs outside the home . . . the average Soviet woman spends four to seven hours a day on housework."[36] Woman's "double day" persists under state socialism; notwithstanding their high rates of participation in the paid labor force, they retain virtually exclusive responsibility for the functions of child rearing and housework within the home. (This fact alone tends to undermine the thesis that the subordination of women is primarily a result of their exclusion from wage labor, as well as the corollary that, in Engels's words, "the first premise for the emancipation of women is the reintroducton of the entire female sex into public industry."[37]) As in the case of capitalist societies, moreover, women wage earners in the Soviet Union

---

[34] Rowbotham, *Woman's Consciousness, Man's World*, p. 82.
[35] Benston, "The Political Economy of Women's Liberation," p. 288.
[36] *Women's Liberation and the Socialist Revolution*, p. 58.
[37] Cited in Benston, "The Political Economy of Women's Liberation," p. 283.

73

are concentrated disproportionately in less-skilled, lower-paying, less responsible jobs, and in traditional female sectors of production and services. For example, 43.6 per cent of all women still work in agriculture, while another quarter are employed in the textile industry. Eighty per cent of all primary and secondary school teachers, and 100 per cent of all preschool teachers, are women. In 1970 only 6.6 per cent of all industrial enterprises were headed by women. According to 1966 statistics, average women's wages in the Soviet Union were 69.3 per cent of men's.[38]

Thus the sexual division of labor persists, both within the Soviet family and within the Soviet workplace. Nor is the situation any different in the Eastern European state socialist societies.[39] Those state socialist societies that have acknowledged the problem of the persistence of patriarchy, moreover, have not been able to eliminate it. Despite the recent introduction of a Family Code that obliges Cuban men to share the burdens of housework, Cuban women regularly depart from the paid labor force because they find that, in the absence of sufficient public restaurants, day care, and laundry facilities, they cannot fulfill what are considered their household obligations. Acknowledgment of the problem of patriarchy in Cuba, moreover, is often mixed with official support for the traditional sexual division of labor: Resolution 40, issued by the Cuban Ministry of Labor in 1978, excludes women from some 300 types of jobs, at least in part on the grounds that they are too "frail" to perform them.[40] The situation in China is not fundamentally different. Despite dramatic advances in the condition of women since prerevolutionary days, "domestic production inside the home is typically defined as women's work," "women are the first to be laid off when employment drops," "are concentrated in the low-wage neighborhood 'housewife' industries," and "are likely to encounter residual sex-typing on the job."[41] The description of sex-typing as "residual," it must be added, is obviously far too sanguine in the light of the apparent reversals in the fortunes of Chinese women since the demise of the Cultural Revolution.[42]

Thus the roots of patriarchy are deeply embedded in the soil of state socialist

[38] *Women's Liberation and the Socialist Revolution*, p. 59.

[39] *Ibid.*, pp. 59-61.

[40] Carolee Bergelsdorf and Alice Hageman, "Emerging from Underdevelopment," in Eisenstein, ed., *Capitalist Patriarchy and the Case for Socialist Feminism*, pp. 271-95.

[41] Judith Stacey, "When Patriarchy Kowtows," in Eisenstein, ed., *Capitalist Patriarchy and the Case for Socialist Feminism*, pp. 326-27.

[42] For a recent example of the post-Maoist reassertion of the traditional patriarchal division of labor in China, see "Comrade Lonelyhearts," *Newsweek* (December 29, 1980), p. 27. See also Vera Schwarcz, "Ruminations of a Feminist in China," *Quest: A Feminist Quarterly*, V, No. 3 (1981), pp. 27-40.

societies, and for this reason alone it would appear that the Marxist theory that locates the capitalist mode of production as the material basis of patriarchy is woefully inadequate. The effort to rescue this theory with the claim that state socialist societies are really capitalist societies, after all, ultimately proves unsuccessful. On the one hand, if—with Marx—we define a "capitalist society" as one dominated by a mode of production in which labor-power becomes a commodity and is set in motion on behalf of the overriding imperative of surplus-value production, then it is clear that state socialist societies are not, in fact, capitalist societies: there is neither a market in labor-power nor the predominance of profit among the criteria that determine its disposition in the Soviet Union and its satellites.[43] Interpreted strictly, then, the claim that such societies are capitalist societies can easily be refuted empirically. If, on the other hand, we expand the meaning of "capitalist society" to embrace state socialist conditions, then we inflate the concept of a capitalist mode of production to the point where it becomes virtually identical to any industrial mode of production in which patriarchy exists, in which case the "theory" that capitalism is the material basis of patriarchy becomes nonfalsifiable.

On the other hand, Juliet Mitchell's effort to save the theory with the argument that patriarchy persists in state socialist societies as a mere residue or survival from their capitalist past fails to explain how an inheritance from capitalism can be so systematically interwoven into the very fabric of a socialist society, and assumes as true by definition precisely what needs to be demonstrated, namely, that the oppression of women is not intrinsic to the socialist system.[44] To put this another way: if we deny that the ubiquity of patriarchy under state socialism demonstrates that the former is intrinsic to the latter, then we cannot with consistency claim that the pervasiveness of patriarchy under capitalism proves that patriarchy is an inherent requirement of capitalism. Alternatively, if we assume that the presence of patriarchal structures within capitalist societies is not the presence of a precapitalist survival but rather of structures that perform specifically capitalist functions, then by the same token we should assume that the presence of essentially similar structures within state socialist societies is the presence of structures that perform specifically state socialist functions.

Thus the logic that leads to the conclusion that capitalism is a material basis of patriarchy necessarily culminates in the conclusion that state socialism is also a material basis of patriarchy, and the Marxist effort to demonstrate that capitalism is *the* contemporary material basis of patriarchy must therefore be judged a failure. Since the destruction of capitalism and the creation of

[43] Michael Goldfield and Melvin Rothenberg, *The Myth of Capitalism Reborn* (San Francisco: Soviet Union Study Project, 1980).

[44] Mitchell, *Woman's Estate*, p. 95.

75

state socialism do not guarantee the eradication of the structural basis of patriarchy, there can be no warrant for the argument that the feminist movement must ultimately be subordinated to an anticapitalist, pro-socialist struggle led by the working class and its representatives. Rather, if socialism is a necessary but insufficient condition for the elimination of patriarchy, it follows that an antipatriarchal movement must retain its autonomy during the period of the transition to socialism as well as throughout the entire period of socialist construction. This autonomy would be the only possible guarantee of continued struggle against the material basis of patriarchy under socialism and thus of the creation of a socialist society that was not characterized by male domination.

If a successful assault on patriarchy demands a feminist movement that is autonomous from the class struggle, then the Marxist insistence that the former should be subordinated to the latter necessarily functions to reproduce the very patriarchy to which Marxism is ostensibly committed to eliminating. And if the political consequence of the theory of the determining power of the mode of production and the ontology of objectification on which it is based is the reproduction of male domination, is it too much to suggest that this theory and that ontology are inherently patriarchal? Is it not possible, in other words, that the definition of production as *the* distinctively human activity participates in the characteristically male denigration of the nonproduction activities to which women have historically been disproportionately consigned? From this perspective, the Marxist theory of the primacy of production can be grasped as yet another theory that serves to legitimate a sexual division of labor that encodes women's activities within the home as less valuable than men's work outside it. I shall return to this issue in Part III.

Thus far I have been arguing that patriarchy cannot adequately be understood if it is exclusively conceptualized as a structure that functions on behalf of the capitalist mode of production. Now I want to argue that it cannot be adequately understood if it is exclusively conceptualized as a structure performing functions on behalf of *any* mode of production. To conceptualize it in this way is to treat patriarchy as a determined, derivative phenomenon and thus to be unable to appreciate the way in which it plays a determining, constitutive role vis-à-vis the mode of production. The assumption that the mode of production molds patriarchy in order to suit its own purposes neglects the possibility that patriarchy molds the mode of production in order to serve *its* purposes. If it is true that patriarchy is a structure that performs capitalist functions, it is equally true that capitalism can be understood as a structure that performs patriarchal functions. If the specific form that male domination assumes is a function of capitalist reproduction requirements, the specific form that capitalism assumes is a function of the reproduction requirements of male domination.

76

More specifically, it is possible to understand both the extent and the nature of women's participation in the capitalist labor force only if we assume that the development of the latter is conditioned by the imperatives of a male-dominated sexual division of labor. As Eisenstein has emphasized, "deference to patriarchal hierarchy and control is shown in the very fact that the search for cheap labor has not led to a full integration of women into . . . the labor force."[45] A purely economic explanation would lead to the expectation that, given the relative cheapness of female labor, female participation in the labor force should be not only equal to, but greater than, male participation; the fact that female participation is dramatically lower than male, despite its relative cheapness, suggests that we must look not to the interest in maximum surplus-value extraction (profitability), i.e., not to the very motor of the development of the capitalist mode of production, but rather to an extra-economic interest for an adequate explanation. Nor can this interest be defined as the long-run interest of capitalists in fomenting division within the working class and thus contributing to the reproduction of the capitalist mode of production. As Heidi Hartmann has pointed out, although it is true that capitalists have reaped certain benefits from sexual segregation within the labor force, it is also the case that "male *workers* have been instrumental in limiting the participation of women in the labor market."[46] Hartmann shows that the history of American unions, for example, is in many ways a history of male efforts to restrict the entry of women into the skilled trades. The effort to rescue an economic explanation with the argument that women's entry into these trades threatened the economic interests of male workers will not wash:

> That male workers viewed the employment of women as a threat to their jobs is not surprising, given an economic system where competition among workers was characteristic. That women were paid lower wages exacerbated this threat. But why their response was to exclude women rather than to organize them is explained not by capitalism, but by patriarchal relations between men and women: men wanted to assure that women would continue to perform the appropriate tasks at home.[47]

The kind of work done by women who gain entry to the labor force is also decisively conditioned by the need to maintain the male-dominated division of labor of a patriarchal society. Women, it has often been noted, are concentrated in precisely those jobs that are most similar to the "jobs" they do within the home; as teachers, secretaries, nurses, social workers, etc., they perform those "helping" or "nurturing" functions that they perform without

[45] Eisenstein, ed., *Capitalist Patriarchy and the Case for Socialist Feminism*, pp. 29-30.
[46] "Capitalism, Patriarchy, and Job Segregation," in *ibid.*, p. 229, emphasis added.
[47] *Ibid.*, p. 219.

pay within the family.[48] The division of labor within the family, which assigns men instrumental roles and orientations and women expressive roles and orientations is reproduced within the workplace insofar as women who do gain access to it typically are assigned the more expressive tasks. (As I have already suggested, this is also the case in state socialist societies, where women are concentrated in traditional forms of women's labor and where domestic work whether socialized or not, has remained the preserve of women.) Similarly, the division of labor that transforms women into objects of male sexual enjoyment prevails within the workplace, dictating that women regularly face sexual harassment from their male employers and fellow-workers and that their economic survival depends on their ability to behave in ways that are considered feminine in contrast to their masculine counterparts.[49] Thus, as Juliet Mitchell has acknowledged, "the *family* structure dominates even at the scene of work (or behind the scenes determines it)."[50] From this perspective, relationships within the workplace are as much a microcosm of relationships within the family as relationships within the family are a microcosm of relationships within the workplace; if it is true that, within the family, the husband "is the bourgeois [and] the wife . . . the proletariat," it is equally true that, within the workplace, the capitalist is often the father or the sexual predator and the worker is often the mother or the sexual prey.[51]

Thus the conclusion is inescapable that "patriarchy, far from being vanquished by capitalism, is still very virile; it shapes the form modern capitalism takes, just as the development of capitalism has transformed patriarchal institutions."[52] Because patriarchy plays a determining, rather than merely determined role, it is impossible to maintain that, with the superimposition of the capitalist mode of production on a male-dominated sexual division of labor, this mode of production simply becomes the new material basis of patriarchy. Whereas Marx erred in assuming that the material basis of patriarchy lies in precapitalist modes of production, and that capitalism would therefore destroy patriarchy, contemporary Marxists err in assuming that *the* material basis of patriarchy is to be found in capitalism, and that socialism will therefore destroy patriarchy. Both err in assuming that the material basis of patriarchy lies elsewhere, namely, in the mode of production. Neither is able to understand that, if patriarchy plays a determining role vis-à-vis the

[48] Rowbotham, *Woman's Consciousness, Man's World*, pp. 87, 89.

[49] Catherine A. Mackinnon, *Sexual Harassment of Working Women* (New Haven, Conn.: Yale University Press, 1979).

[50] Mitchell, *Woman's Estate*, p. 126, emphasis in the original.

[51] Batya Weinbaum, *The Curious Courtship of Women's Liberation and Socialism* (Boston: South End Press, 1978); Michael Albert and Robin Hahnel, *Unorthodox Marxism* (Boston: South End Press, 1978), Chs. 5-6.

[52] Hartmann, "Capitalism, Patriarchy, and Job Segregation," p. 208.

mode of production, this can only be because it carries its material basis within itself and that it retains it prior to, during, and subsequent to the epoch of the capitalist mode of production.

(This does not mean, as we shall see in a subsequent chapter, that patriarchy is a universal, permanent structure of human civilization. I emphasize this now in anticipation of the characteristic Marxist conclusion that if someone argues that a structure is not a function of the mode of production she must be arguing, in reactionary fashion, that this structure is inevitable rather than historically contingent. This conclusion, it should be clear, merely follows for someone who accepts the assumption that the field of social determination is exhausted by the mode of production. It is precisely this assumption that is in question, both in this chapter and throughout this book. There is an alternative to the "either/or" of a conception of social determination by the mode of production versus a "metaphysical" conception of "natural" determination, one which I shall introduce in Part III under the heading of determination by the *mode of symbolization*. It is the Marxist, moreover, who runs the risk of treating patriarchy as an unexplained, indeed, inexplicable phenomenon. If patriarchy persists across a number of different modes of production, then it cannot be understood to be a function of a particular mode of production. But the assumption of the primacy of production would appear to foreclose the possibility of any alternative explanation of its social origins, persistence, and possible transformation. Thus talk of its elimination takes on the character of an empty, "utopian" wish, and patriarchy becomes a theoretical inevitability.)

Let me try to put this another way. Although the capitalist mode of production generates its own reproduction requirements, in and of itself it does not determine the sexual identity of the individuals who are obliged to fulfill these requirements. That capitalism requires a reserve army of labor, private reproducers of labor-power, authoritarian socializers, and "expressive" nurturers, does not mean that capitalism requires that women monopolize these tasks. That they become the preserve of women is a function not of the capitalist mode of production but rather of the way in which this mode of production is obliged to adapt to a preexisting and persisting sexual division of labor in which men dominate women. It is patriarchy, not capitalism, that determines the sexual identity of those who perform the various functions that capitalism demands, and, for this reason, it is precisely patriarchy that remains completely unexplained after an analysis of capitalist functions has been completed.[53] Thus all the contemporary Marxist theories of patriarchy

[53] After completing this chapter I discovered that Heidi Hartmann makes an essentially identical point in "The Unhappy Marriage of Marxism and Feminism: Toward a More Progressive Union," in Lydia Sargent, ed., *Women and Revolution* (Boston: South End Press, 1981), pp. 10-11.

I have reviewed beg the very question that any adequate theory of patriarchy must address, i.e., why is there a male-dominated sexual division of labor?

There is, to be fair, a traditional Marxist answer to this question. I refer to Engels's analysis of the origins of patriarchy in *The Origin of the Family, Private Property and the State*. This analysis links the subjugation of women to the emergence of class society and the first forms of private property, and thus purports to demonstrate the ultimately economic basis of the patriarchal system. According to Engels, who relied on the by-now thoroughly discredited anthropological speculations of Bachofen and Morgan,[54] the earliest human societies were primitive communist societies in which the absence of monogamy and the presence of matrilineal descent precluded the domination of men over women: women did not "belong" to particular men, and women, not men, controlled the inheritance of wealth. Under these conditions, the division of labor

> was a pure and simple outgrowth of nature; it existed only between the two sexes. The men went to war, hunted, fished, provided the raw material for food and the tools necessary for these pursuits. The women cared for the house, and prepared food and clothing; they cooked, weaved, and sewed. Each was master in his or her field of activity: the men in the forest, the women in the house.[55]

Primitive communist matriarchy, however, was not destined to persist. Advances in productive techniques, and the transition from hunting and gathering to agriculture in particular, led to the development of a "surplus" or an amount of wealth over and above what it was possible for the primitive community immediately to consume. Thus men, who, according to the "natural" division of labor, were responsible for procuring food, now had an incentive to transform what they procured into their private property and to "overthrow the traditional order of inheritance in favor of [their] children." This was done by transforming women into the sexual property of men, i.e., through the institution of monogamous marriage; "monogamy," according to Engels, "arose out of the concentration of considerable wealth in the hands of one person—and that a man—and out of a desire to bequeath this wealth to this man's children and no one else's." Monogamy thus entails "the overthrow of mother-right . . . [and] the *world historic defeat of the female sex*. The man seized the reins in the house . . . , the woman was degraded [to] the slave of the man's lust, a mere instrument for breeding children."[56] Monogamy, in short, inaugurates patriarchy, which is thus understood as a

---

[54] See the relevant essays in Michelle Zimbalist Rosaldo and Louise Lamphere, *Woman, Culture and Society* (Stanford, Calif.: Stanford University Press, 1974).

[55] Engels, "The Origin of the Family, Private Property and the State," p. 577.

[56] *Ibid.*, pp. 495, 511, 496 (emphasis in the original).

structure of male domination over women that functions to guarantee and reproduce male ownership of private property. The demonstration that patriarchy is in the service of private property, together with the demonstration that private property is the result of the development of the forces of production vindicate the assumption that patriarchy is best understood in the light of the category of production.

Engels's account, however, raises as many questions as it answers and is, in fact, fatally flawed. Even if we accept what almost all contemporary anthropologists dispute, namely that there were primitive matriarchies,[57] a moment's reflection should demonstrate that Engels's explanation for the transition from matriarchy to patriarchy is not internally consistent. He argues that men's imposition of monogamous marriage on women is the cause of their subsequent subordination; the fact that women submitted to an imposition that was obviously inconsistent with their interests, however, can only be explained if we assume that women were already subordinate to men, and thus that monogamy was the result rather than the cause of women's subordination. But if monogamy was the result of women's prior subordination, then the transition from nonmonogamous communist society to monogamous class society cannot be understood as the "overthrow of mother right . . . [and] the world-historic defeat of the female sex," since this overthrow and this defeat must have already occurred. On the other hand, if women's subordination antedated the emergence of monogamous, class society, then it must have existed in primitive communist society. But, if it existed in primitive communist society, then: (a) Engels's description of this society as nonpatriarchal is wrong, and (b) his claim that patriarchy emerges as a device to preserve (male) private property is untenable.

Similarly, Engels's argument that the desire of men to exclude women from property ownership was the impetus for the imposition of monogamy is inconsistent with his claim that "the first class antagonism which appears in history coincides with the development of the antagonism between man and woman in monogamian marriage."[58] If men were already motivated by a desire to assert their superiority vis-à-vis women, then there must have existed a structural antagonism between men and women prior to the emergence of the institution of monogamy that is supposed to inaugurate this antagonism. Engels himself offers evidence that supports this interpretation, although he does not recognize it as such. He describes the "pairing family," in contrast to the earlier "group marriages," within primitive society as a situation in which "one man lives with one woman, yet in such a manner that polygamy and occasional infidelity remain *men's privileges* . . . ; at the

---

[57] See note 54.

[58] Engels, "The Origin of the Family, Private Property and the State," p. 503.

same time, the strictest fidelity is demanded of the woman during the period of cohabitation, adultery on her part being cruelly punished.''[59] Here Engels acknowledges that primitive communist societies were characterized by male ''privilege,'' yet he refuses to draw the appropriate conclusion, namely that these societies, far from being matriarchal, were characterized by a structural antagonism between dominant men and subordinate women.[60] If this is the case, then, if by ''class'' we mean, as Engels appears to mean, any structurally based antagonism, we would have to argue that so-called ''classless'' primitive communist societies were not really classless at all. On the other hand, if we restrict the meaning of class to economically based antagonisms, then we would be obliged to conclude that sexually based antagonisms antedated the emergence of class antagonisms. In either case, Engels's argument falls apart.[61]

Engels's description of the division of labor between the sexes under primitive communism also provides possible support for the conclusion that this division of labor was already patriarchal. That men procured food while women prepared it, that men were free to roam on the hunt whereas women were confined to the home, may not on its face constitute evidence of male domination. What is certain is that anyone who ignores this evidence on the grounds that this division of labor is ''a pure and simple outgrowth of nature'' merely takes for granted, in typically patriarchal fashion, precisely what must

[59] *Ibid.*, pp. 487-88, emphasis added.

[60] Rather he argues that women themselves brought about the transition to the pairing marriage (and the male privilege that accompanied it) because they ''longed for the right to chastity.'' *Ibid.*, p. 492. See also Mark Poster, *Critical Theory of the Family* (New York: The Seabury Press, 1978), p. 44.

[61] This collapse in the unity of Engels's argument is presaged in his very methodological starting point. He tells us that ''According to the materialistic conception, the determining factor in history is, in the final instance, the production and reproduction of immediate life. This, again, is of a two-fold character: on the one side, the production of the means of existence, of food, clothing and shelter and the tools necessary for that production; on the other side, the production of human beings themselves, the propagation of the species. The social organization under which the people of a particular historical epoch and a particular country live is determined by both kinds of production; by the stage of the development of labor on the one hand and of the family on the other.'' (Cited in Eisenstein, ed., *Capitalist Patriarchy and the Case for Socialist Feminism*, p. 15.)

Notice that Engels substitutes for Marx's monism of production a dualism of production (the sphere of labor) and reproduction (the sphere of the family), which he tries, in vain, to paper over by referring to both as ''production.'' His argument that ''social organization . . . is determined by *both* kinds of production'' constitutes a tacit admission that reproductive structures cannot be deduced, but rather are at least partly autonomous, from production structures and thus a denial that the family can adequately be grasped as a constituent element of a mode of production. As Eisenstein notes, these conclusions, however, are repressed through the categorization of antagonisms between men and women as ''class'' antagonisms, which effectively subsumes the relations of reproduction under the relations of production. *Ibid.*, p. 13.

be explained, namely a culturally defined sexual division of labor. Once again, Engels's account begs precisely those questions that are most important.[62]

Thus Engels's economic explanation for patriarchy is really no explanation at all, since it presupposes the very male-dominated sexual division of labor that it purports to explain. The same is true of Wilhelm Reich's theory of "the imposition of sexual morality," which is in its essentials a variation on the theme developed by Engels.[63] Indeed, I would argue that any exclusively economic explanation of patriarchy is necessarily circular and therefore question-begging. The assumption that an interest in the control of property generates an interest in the subordination of women requires the additional assumption of an interest in exclusively male control of property; this assumption, in turn, entails the assumption that a male-dominated sexual division of labor, i.e., patriarchy, already exists. Alternatively, if these additional assumptions are not made, then there is no way to move from the assumption of an interest in control of property to an interest in the subordination of women. Thus it is impossible to deduce domination based on sex from domination based on property. A theory that proceeds from the assumption of the primacy of production is no more able to account for the origins of patriarchy than it is able to account for its contemporary persistence.

---

[62] Similar questions can be raised concerning Engels's contention that private property resulted from the emergence of a surplus generated from the development of the forces of production. Why should the mere existence of a surplus necessarily result in differential appropriation of this surplus, unless we assume that primitives were already motivated by characteristically bourgeois desires for "more"? Even if we grant that the production of a surplus resulted in the emergence of classes, why did this surplus arise in the first place? To attribute it to new productive techniques only begs the question of why these techniques were permitted to develop in the context of a primitive society whose basic structures were designed to prevent the emergence of a surplus. For these problems see Jean Baudrillard, *The Mirror of Production* (St. Louis, Mo.: Telos Press, 1975), and Pierre Clastres, *Society Against the State* (New York: Urizen, 1977).

[63] Wilheim Reich, *Sex-Pol* (New York: Vintage Books, 1972), pp. 104-249. Reich attributes the onset of patriarchy in primitive society to "alterations in the circulation of the [marriage] dowry by which the chief could accumulate vast amounts of property" and which gave him an interest in insuring his line of inheritance. He fails entirely even to pose the prior question of why the chief was male in the first place. Poster, *Critical Theory of the Family*, p. 48, and below, Chapter Six.

CHAPTER THREE

MARXIST THEORIES OF THE STATE

THE MOVEMENT FOR PARTICIPATORY DEMOCRACY

The past two decades in the advanced capitalist societies have been marked by the emergence of a socialist Left that is anti-statist in character. In large part, this anti-statism is precisely what distinguishes this New Left from the Old Left of the Second and Third Internationals. The Old Left had always posed the alternative between capitalism and socialism as above all a choice between the irrationality of the market and the rationality of a centrally planned economy, or between private ownership and state or collective ownership of the means of production. Much of the "newness" of the New Left consists in its refusal any longer to pose the problem of capitalism versus socialism in this manner, in its rejection of the assumption that the opposition between them can be adequately captured in the distinction between market and plan or between private and state ownership of the means of production. State ownership and central planning of the means of production, New Leftists have argued, is in principle every bit as compatible with the exclusion of workers in particular and citizens in general from participation in the decisions that shape their lives as is private ownership of the means of production and the market; production "for use" is not necessarily any more democratic than production for profit. A genuinely socialist society must be a genuinely democratic society, one in which the division of labor between rulers and ruled both inside and outside the sphere of production is superseded by direct and equal participation in collective decision making by all those who are affected by these decisions. The choice between capitalism and socialism, then, is properly understood as one between a society in which democracy is entirely absent within the workplace and merely indirect and attenuated within the state and a society in which all spheres of collective life are characterized by the maximum possible amount of *participatory democracy*.

The New Left's repudiation of statism as a socialist goal was matched by a thorough distaste for statist means of reaching this goal. The Old Left, in spite of its internal divisions, was united in its conception of the transition from capitalism to socialism as a process of statification. Although Social Democrats argued that this transition could be achieved with the aid of the existing and until-now capitalist state, and Marxist-Leninists insisted that it could not be accomplished without the "smashing" of this state and its replacement by a new and different one, i.e., the dictatorship of the proletariat, both agreed that a sustained and profound strengthening of the state was the sine qua non of socialist transformation.[1] Consistent with its commitment to participatorily democratic ends, the New Left rejected this statist conception of socialist means: neither the centralization of the hierarchical bourgeois state nor the centralization of the hierarchical vanguard party could unleash a process that would culminate in the decentralized, nonhierarchical society of the future. Instead, such a process requires decentralized, nonhierarchical forms of struggle that anticipate, however imperfectly, the organizational forms of the future socialist society. The struggle against capitalism, in other words, cannot be severed from the struggle for socialism; the elimination of the social relations that reproduce the "old" human being can only be accomplished in and through the creation of social relations that engender the "new" human being. From Berkeley to Paris, from the movements for student power in the universities to the movements for self-management in both factories and communities, New Leftists demonstrated that the goal of a participatorily democratic socialist society demands a participatorily democratic anticapitalist movement.

The emergence of this anti-statist vision of socialist means and ends was conditioned by the experience of, and reaction against, political domination in the industrial societies of both the East and the West. On the one hand, Khrushschev's revelations of Stalinist "deformations" at the 20th Congress of the C.P.S.U. meant that it was no longer possible to deny or ignore the reality of state repression in so-called "state socialist" societies. However incomplete and self-serving, these revelations constituted a telling admission that state ownership of the means of production and political domination could be, and in fact were, inextricably intertwined at the very center of the international socialist movement. Thus the New Left, in contrast to the Old, was in a position to draw the conclusion that a genuine commitment to socialism not only did not require uncritical support of the Soviet Union and its client states but demanded a stance toward what is sometimes called "actually existing socialism" that was every bit as uncompromisingly critical as the stance that the Left had always maintained vis-à-vis capitalism. The statist road to socialism was therefore no longer credible as a model for the socialist transformation of the advanced capitalist societies. Instead, the increasing awareness of the systematic nature of political domination in the East encouraged the understanding that an anticapitalist revolution that was not antistatist in its goals and forms could well culminate in the reproduction of

---

[1] Nicos Poulantzas, *State, Power, Socialism* (London: New Left Books, 1978), pp. 251-55.

85

such domination in the West. In short, the discovery of the absence of democracy under state socialism was a decisively important impetus for the redefinition of the socialist project in the West as a movement for participatory democracy.

On the other hand, this redefinition was also encouraged by the increasingly central role of the state in the advanced capitalist societies themselves. The full-blown emergence, following World War II, of state-regulated capitalism in the United States and Europe was paralleled by a dramatic decline in the effectiveness of representative democratic mechanisms and institutions in these societies; the increasing preeminence of the administrative branch of the state seemed to be the inexorable result of the assumption of critical economic functions by a state whose expenditures now accounted for between a third and over a half (depending on the country) of the gross national product.[2] Insofar as the great bulk of these expenditures were social-welfare-related, moreover, the growing interdependence of state and economy necessarily entailed an expanding administrative penetration and colonization of areas of everyday life that were formerly exempt from direct state interference.[3] Thus, at the very point at which the tentacles of the state were encircling a larger and larger proportion of the social body, representative mechanisms for holding the state accountable to the members of this body were progressively "withering away." The culmination of this twofold development was an unprecedented bureaucratization of everyday life in the advanced capitalist societies. Thus it is not surprising that the heart of the New Left was a movement of students initially directed against the bureaucratization of state and state-supported university education that quickly blossomed into a general assault against bureaucratization as such.[4]

Everyday experience with increasingly pervasive political domination in the advanced capitalist societies and heightened awareness of systematic political domination under state socialism combined to precipitate a practical critique of bureaucracy in general and the state in particular. This practical critique of the state, in turn, pointed to the necessity for a critical theory that was able simultaneously to account for the nature and persistence of this object and to clarify the liberatory political alternative in whose name the struggle against it was being undertaken. Thus the stage was set for a remarkable renaissance of the heretofore largely undeveloped Marxist theory of politics, i.e., for a sustained effort on the part of Marxists to demonstrate that the problem of political domination and its transcendence is, at bottom, a problem of the mode of production and its transformation.

[2] Alan Wolfe, *The Limits of Legitimacy* (New York: The Free Press, 1977), pp. 174-75, 257.

[3] Morris Janowitz, *The Last Half-Century: Societal Change and Politics in America* (Chicago: University of Chicago Press, 1978), pp. 140-41; Ira Katznelson, "Considerations on Social Democracy in the United States," *Comparative Politics*, No. 11 (October 1978), pp. 77-99.

[4] Cockburn and Blackburn, eds., *Student Power, passim*.

CONTEMPORARY MARXIST THEORIES OF THE CAPITALIST STATE

Well over a century ago Marx and Engels formulated their famous thesis that "the modern state is but a committee for managing the common affairs of the whole bourgeoisie."[5] It is no great exaggeration to argue that for over a century thereafter, Western Marxist analysis of the state amounted to little more than ritualized invocations of this classical thesis that the state serves the interest of the capitalist class.[6] The latter part of the 1960s, however, marked the beginning of a period characterized by a remarkable resurgence of Marxist theorizing about the state. By the middle of the next decade this theorizing had developed to the point where a number of clearly defined and distinct Marxist approaches to the state could be identified.[7] Each of these approaches was constituted by a different and, at least at first glance, incompatible interpretation of Marx's famous dictum concerning the (capitalist) class character of the state.[8]

Instrumental Theories

As the name implies, Instrumental Marxist theories translate the proposition that "the modern state is but a committee for managing the common affairs of the whole bourgeoisie" into the proposition that the state is but an instrument or tool of the capitalist class. The metaphor of a "tool" implies that a set of subjects or individuals consciously wields the state in order to achieve their purposes. Under this interpretation, the statement, "the state serves the interest of the capitalist class" is equivalent to "the state does what powerful members of the capitalist class want it to do." One should therefore expect a more or less direct, one-to-one relationship between capitalist demands and public policy.

The effort to demonstrate this causal connection, and thus to verify the hypothesis that the state serves the interest of the capitalist class, typically embraces the following types of evidence:

(a) Information concerning the class background of the incumbents of positions of state authority. Thus Instrumental theorists such as Domhoff and

---

[5] Marx and Engels, *Manifesto of the Communist Party*, p. 337.

[6] The great exception to this generalization was the work of Antonio Gramsci. See his *Prison Notebooks* (New York: International Publishers, 1971).

[7] David A. Gold, Clarence Y. Lo, and Erik Olin Wright, "Recent Developments in Marxist Theories of the Capitalist State," *Monthly Review*, 27 (October-November 1975), pp. 29-43, 36-51.

[8] What follows does not purport to be an exhaustive account of Marxist theorizing about the state over the past decade. One glaring omission is the lack of any discussion of recent Marxist efforts to theorize about the impact of the international economic crisis on the state. I would nevertheless maintain that any such discussion would have to confront the theoretical issues that I raise.

Miliband have convincingly demonstrated the disproportionate presence within the state of individuals recruited from the "higher circles" of the capitalist class; the commanding heights of the legislative, executive, and judicial branches of the state in all Western capitalist societies are overwhelmingly peopled by individuals drawn from the upper class.[9] Under the assumption that officials with upper-class backgrounds will pursue policies consistent with the interests of the class from which they have been recruited, these data, it is argued, provide powerful support for the proposition that the state serves the interests of the capitalist class.

(b) Information concerning the disproportionate pressure that members of the capitalist class outside of the state are able to bring to bear on the state. Here an equally convincing effort has been undertaken to demonstrate that capitalist interests have: (1) a far greater chance of being effectively organized and (2) a far greater chance of being taken seriously than any other interests within the society as a whole. On the one hand, superior financial resources and control over the organs of popular opinion provide the capitalist class with a near-monopoly on the channels of communication that flow from society to the state. On the other hand, the dependence of state officials on capitalist financial support as well as their dependence on "business confidence," i.e., their fear of investment strikes, means that capitalist demands that are addressed to these officials are far more likely to receive a receptive hearing than the demands of any other classes or groups within the society.[10] Whereas most Instrumental theorists have been content to detail the sources of this "potential power" and have not studied the actual processes through which it becomes manifest in concrete instances of policy making within the state,[11] one prominent group known as the theorists of "corporate liberalism" has been able to demonstrate that, contrary to conventional wisdom, powerful members of the capitalist class were a critical source of inspiration and support for state policies in the early decades of the twentieth-century in the United States that helped to mold the basic contours of contemporary welfare-state capitalism.[12]

The combination of superior internal and external strength thus leaves members of the capitalist class, in contrast to those of any other class, in a position to enforce their will through the state. The state, in short, will do what capitalists want it to do because the state is both directly (internally)

---

[9] Ralph Miliband, *The State in Capitalist Society* (New York: Basic Books, 1969); G. William Domhoff, *Who Rules America?* Englewood Cliffs, N.J.: Prentice Hall, 1967).

[10] Miliband, *The State in Capitalist Society.*

[11] Nelson Polsby, *Community Power and Political Theory* (New Haven, Conn.: Yale University Press, 1963); Robert A. Dahl, "A Critique of the Ruling Elite Model," *American Political Science Review*, 52 (June 1958), pp. 463-69.

[12] James Weinstein, *The Corporate Ideal in the Liberal State* (Boston: Beacon Press, 1968).

and indirectly (externally) controlled by capitalists. Consequently, the conclusion appears inescapable that the state serves the interest of the capitalist class, or, to put it another way, that the capitalist class is the *ruling class* in a capitalist society.

This appearance notwithstanding, a number of telling objections can be raised against the Instrumental version of the Marxist theory of the state. If the hypothesis that the state serves the interests of the capitalist class means that the state always does the bidding of powerful members of this class, then it is not difficult to find empirical evidence to the contrary. Although it is undoubtedly true that some state policies have received the support of, and have even been initiated by, leading members of the capitalist class, it is equally true that many crucially important state policies in Western capitalist societies have been initiated and maintained in the face of powerful, and sometimes even unanimous, opposition on the part of the members of this class. The labor policies of the American New Deal, for example, come immediately to mind. And the New Deal is only one example among many others of periods of capitalist state activity in the West that run counter to the expressed preferences of the leaders of the corporate sector.[13] In short, a wealth of historical evidence can be brought to bear that refutes a strict interpretation of the theory that the state is a mere instrument or tool of the capitalist class.

In the face of this evidence, Instrumentalists have typically sought to qualify this proposition in order to save it. The capitalist class, they argue, is always able to enforce its will with respect to genuinely *important* policies; when it loses we can be certain that the issue was not, from its perspective, of any great consequence. Apart from the implausibility of the assertion that a set of policies such as the New Deal was "unimportant" and the failure to explain why the energies of so many capitalists would have been mobilized to oppose policies that they deemed to be "unimportant," the problem with this type of argument, as many have noted, is that it forestalls any effort to test the original hypothesis: the evidence is interpreted in such a manner that any policy on which the capitalist class did not prevail becomes, by definition, unimportant, so that the hypothesis becomes nonfalsifiable in principle.[14] Alternatively, Instrumentalists argue that those state policies that are enacted in the face of the opposition of the capitalist class are always implemented

---

[13] Claus Offe, "Structural Problems of the Capitalist State. Class Rule and the Political System: On the Selectiveness of Political Institutions," in Klaus von Beyme, *German Political Studies*, Vol. I (Beverly Hills: Sage Publications, 1974), pp. 31-57. See also Theda Skocpol, "Political Response to Capitalist Crisis: Neo-Marxist Theories of the State and the Case of the New Deal," *Politics & Society*, 10, No. 2 (1980), pp. 125-153.

[14] Polsby, *Community Power and Political Theory*; Isaac Balbus, "Ruling Elite Theory vs. Marxist Class Analysis," *Monthly Review*, 23 (May 1971), pp. 36-46.

89

in such a way that they are denuded of their original anticapitalist content and thus never fundamentally threaten the interests of that class.[15] Here, too, the problem of nonfalsifiability rears its head: in the absence of an independent specification of the "fundamental" interests of the capitalist class, there is a strong temptation to conclude that every instance of policy enactment that controverts the will of the capitalist class is, by definition, a policy that is implemented in an unthreatening manner. Even if this problem could be avoided, we would still be left entirely in the dark as to why the policy opposed by the ruling class was enacted in the first place. In sum, however compelling the Instrumentalist theory appears at first glance, further reflection reveals that it lacks explanatory power.

Further reflection reveals that the theory also lacks logical coherence. Even if it were possible to demonstrate what the theory asserts, that the state regularly does what powerful members of the capitalist class want it to do, this would not necessarily constitute proof that the state serves the interest of the capitalist class. Marx and Engels argued, it will be recalled, that the state serves "the *common* interest of the *whole* bourgeoisie"; these adjectives, which I have emphasized, alert us to the possibility, even the likelihood, that the class interest of capitalists is fundamentally different from what happens to be the will or desire of even the most powerful set of capitalists at any particular time. Given the structure of the capitalist mode of production, every individual capitalist is obliged to pursue, in single-minded fashion, the short-run goal of maximum profit and to be unconcerned with the consequences of his action for the mode of production as a whole, or what might be called his long-run interest. At the same time, given the competing relationships among various fractions of the capitalist class, e.g., monopoly capital versus competitive capital, domestic versus international capital, etc., state policies that respond to the preferences of one sector of the capitalist class are likely to encounter the opposition of other sectors of the capitalist class. For both reasons, it is highly improbable, if not impossible, that capitalists outside the state would be able to articulate, let alone organize, a unified class will that would be subsequently imposed on the state. Given this disjuncture between the preferences of individual capitalists and their class interest, a successful effort to demonstrate a direct causal link between a particular state policy and a particular capitalist preference would not only fail to confirm but would in fact tend to disconfirm the theory that the state serves the interest of the capitalist class. If, in other words, the state simply did the bidding of individual capitalists, or even of a given fraction of the capitalist class, it would simply be unable to do what has to be done to reproduce the mode of production as a whole and would thus be unable to serve the interests of capital as a class.

---

[15] Balbus, "Ruling Elite Theory vs. Marxist Class Analysis."

Conversely, it follows that the ability of the state to do this is predicated on its *not* being a mere tool of capitalist subjects, on its possession of a form or structure that renders it autonomous in important measure from their preferences.[16]

This suggests that an analysis of the internal structure of the state would be central to any adequate theory of the state. Instrumentalism, however, does not encourage this analysis: to conceive of the state as a mere instrument of the will of dominant social actors is to fail even to pose the problem of the specific form of the state and the way in which this form articulates with the overall requirements of the mode of production of which these actors are a part.[17] The theory that the state merely does what capitalists want it to do completely begs the question of "why this state rather than any other?"— why, for example, would capitalists employ a liberal democratic rather than monarchical state?—because it neglects entirely the problem of the way in which the specificity of the state structure constrains the intentions and behavior of those who operate within it. To put this another way, the assumption underlying Instrumental Marxist theories that the social class from which state authorities have been recruited will be the overriding determinant of the way in which they behave ignores the fact that state authority is exercised according to certain internal decision-rules that oblige *anyone* to act in a certain way, irrespective of his or her class background.[18] It follows that the class character of the state cannot be demonstrated by merely ascertaining the class backgrounds of the incumbents of state authority positions. The political, in other words, cannot be directly and mechanically reduced to the economic; the state is not merely an instrumental phenomenon, but plays, by virtue of its internal structure, a constitutive role of its own.

The attribution of a purely derivative status to the state indicates that Instrumentalism remains on the terrain of the very model of linear causality that Marx himself repudiated in the "General Introduction" to the *Grundrisse* as incapable of grasping the organic unity of social life.[19] To conceive of the state as a tool wielded by (capitalist) individuals is to conceptualize these individuals as separate from and prior to the state; first we have the class-based desires of individuals, and then we have the implementation of these

[16] Offe, "Structural Problems of the Capitalist State"; Nicos Poulantzas, "The Problem of the Capitalist State," in Robin Blackburn, ed., *Ideology in Social Science* (New York: Vintage Books, 1973), pp. 238-53. In his more recent work Ralph Miliband has recognized the validity of this point, without, however, appearing to appreciate the extent to which it vitiates his earlier work. See "Poulantzas and the Capitalist State," *New Left Review*, No. 82 (November-December 1973), p. 84.

[17] Isaac Balbus, "Commodity Form and Legal Form: An Essay on the 'Relative Autonomy' of the Law," *Law & Society Review* 11 (Winter 1977), pp. 571-88.

[18] Poulantzas, "The Problem of the Capitalist State."

[19] See above, Chapter One.

91

desires through the state. Thus the Instrumentalist approach divides society up into allegedly discrete parts and then attempts to demonstrate the causal primacy of one part over the others. In the process, it utterly fails to recognize that state and individuals, polity and economy, are coexistent and co-determining from the very beginning,[20] elements of an organic whole whose atomization is a form of conceptual violence. To put this another way, since the Instrumentalist approach conceives the class content of the state as having been *imposed on* the state by the will of capitalist subjects, it is obliged to conceptualize the state as the "state in capitalist society"—the title of Ralph Miliband's major work—rather than as an intrinsically capitalist state.[21] Instrumentalism thus rests on the epistemological grounds of the very society—the atomistic, alienated bourgeois society—that it purports to transcend.

Instrumentalism remains on the same political grounds as well: a segmental or partial epistemology necessarily culminates in a theory of only partial social transformation. Since it understands the state's capitalist class bias to be a function of the intentions of capitalists both within and outside the state, Instrumentalism leads to the political conclusion that the class bias of this same state could be reversed if different individuals with different intentions came to control it. The inevitable corollary to the conceptualization of the state as a neutral form that only receives its class content from the "outside," so to speak, is a political strategy that relies on the existing state as a potential ally in the struggle for socialism; as a tool of anti-, instead of pro-capitalist intentions, the same state—an internally untransformed state—can come to serve the interest of the working class. A commitment to the existing representative-bureaucratic state rather than its participatory democratic transformation is thus the implicit political agenda of the Instrumental approach.[22] If Instrumentalism offers an inadequate explanation of the behavior of the capitalist state, and thus fails adequately to illuminate the struggles that the advocates of participatory democracy are obliged to mount against this state, it also entails a statist and therefore inadequate conception of the transition to socialism that in no way serves as a guide for the construction of the liberatory politics of the future. For both reasons, the Instrumental version of the Marxist theory of the state must be rejected. The search for an adequate

[20] *Ibid.*; see also Poulantzas, *State, Power, Socialism*, Part One.

[21] Offe, "Structural Problems of the Capitalist State," p. 31.

[22] The *fact* that some Instrumentalists, such as Miliband, seem to have repudiated a statist conception of the transition to socialism does not deny the logical connection between Instrumentalism and statism, since it can be demonstrated that they have done so at the cost of failing consistently to adhere to their own Instrumentalist commitments and, in fact, introducing extraneous and ultimately contradictory theoretical assumptions. Ralph Miliband, *Marxism and Politics* (Oxford: Oxford University Press, 1977), pp. 72-73; Balbus, "Ruling Elite Theory vs. Marxist Class Analysis."

theory of political domination and the possibilities for political liberation thus requires the examination of alternative Marxist formulations.

Structuralist Theories

The Structuralist version of the Marxist theory of the state, as its name implies, conceives of the state not as an instrument that responds to the will of capitalist subjects, but rather as a structure to which these subjects must subordinate their will and which functions, in spite of or rather precisely because of this subordination, to reproduce the capitalist mode of production and thus serve their class interests. According to this interpretation, the state serves the interests of the capitalist class insofar as it does *not* merely do what powerful capitalists want it to do. Given the disjuncture between the preferences of a short-sighted and internally divided capitalist class and the interests of the class as a whole, the service the state performs on behalf of the capitalist class requires that it regularly undertake activities that controvert the intentions of even the most powerful of capitalists. In order to be able to undertake such activities, the structure of the state must be relatively impervious to demands and pressures that emanate from these individuals. In contrast to Instrumentalism, then, the Structuralist approach is sensitive to, and attempts to elaborate the significance of, the adjectives in Marx and Engels's classical formulation in *The Communist Manifesto*; to enforce the common interests of the whole bourgeoisie, the state cannot be a tool of, but must be autonomous from, the will of the members of this class.

Structuralist writers like Nicos Poulantzas—at least in his earlier works— argue that the state functions to reproduce the capitalist mode of production and thus secure capitalist class interests by acting as a "factor of unity in [the] social formation."[23] The potential for disunity is inherent in the capitalist mode of production. On the one hand, divergent preferences and competitive relationships among the members of the capitalist class guarantee that capitalists will be either unwilling or unable to undertake activities necessary to provide the framework and policies for "healthy" capital accumulation. Thus the state must create this framework and these policies if the necessary level of intracapitalist class unity is to be achieved, and it will be able to forge this unity only if it is able to retain its autonomy vis-à-vis the parochial interests of the competing capitalist fractions. On the other hand, the working class is also a potential source of societal disunity, and its acquiescence must be secured in order to guarantee that this potential does not become manifest in the form of class conflict that threatens the reproduction of the mode of

[23] Cited in Gold, *et al.* "Recent Developments in Marxist Theories of the Capitalist State," p. 37.

production. Since capitalists, however, are dominated by the drive to maximize profits, they can hardly be relied on to undertake activities that secure the acquiescence of the working class. Thus, once again, the task of forging unity, this time interclass unity, falls to the state. The internal structure of the Liberal state, in fact, is ideally suited to the performance of this function. By encoding members of the working class as individual citizens who are formally, i.e., legally, equal, the Liberal state simultaneously atomizes or "declassifies" the members of the working class and recomposes them as members of an overarching political community to which they owe allegiance.[24] This crucial function, of course, could not be performed if the state were an obvious creature of the capitalist class.

Thus, according to the Structuralist interpretation, the state plays a constitutive, rather than merely instrumental, role: it does what capitalists themselves cannot do, i.e., it creates the conditions for "unity" without which the mode of production could not be reproduced. Structuralism, then, at least has the merit of offering an answer to the question of "why *this* state, rather than any other?" At the same time, it has the advantage of appearing far more consistent with historical reality than Instrumentalism. As we saw, the undeniable fact that the expansion of the state has often proceeded in the face of opposition from the capitalist class constitutes a refutation of, or at least a serious problem for, the Instrumentalist hypothesis. Such evidence, it should be clear, in no way calls into question, and in fact is anticipated by, the Structuralist hypothesis: "proof" of this hypothesis lies in the functions that the state performs, not in any correspondence between state actions and capitalist intentions. And one would be hard-pressed to deny that the expansion of the state has been "functional" for the capitalist mode of production.

At the same time, evidence of declining upper-class representation within the state, which undermines the Instrumentalist thesis, creates no problems for the Structuralist theorist, for whom the social class background of the incumbents of state authority is virtually irrelevant as a criterion of capitalist class rule:

> The direct participation of members of the capitalist class in the state apparatus and in the government, even where it exists, is not the important side of the matter . . . The relation between the bourgeois class and the state is an *objective relation*. This means that if the *functions* of the state . . . and the *interests* of the dominant class . . . coincide, it is by reason of the system itself: the direct participation of members of the ruling

[24] Nicos Poulantzas, *Pouvoir politique et classes sociales*, Vol. I (Paris: Maspero, 1971), pp. 138-39; Balbus, "Commodity Form and Legal Form: An Essay on the 'Relative Autonomy' of the Law."

94

class in the state apparatus is not the *cause*, but the *effect*, and moreover a chance and contingent one, of this objective coincidence.[25]

Thus Structuralism, in contrast to Instrumentalism, does not encourage a search for data whose relationship to the proposition that the state serves the interest of the capitalist class is tenuous at best.

Structuralism also avoids the epistemological atomism of the Instrumental approach. Structuralist theorists are not obliged to conceive of society as divided into separate parts in order to establish the priority of one part over the other. Instead, the conceptualization of the state as a structure that performs functions on behalf of a system offers a means of understanding the way in which the whole called the capitalist mode of production is present within the part that is called the state. Thus it becomes possible to understand the state as an intrinsically capitalist state.

Finally, this epistemological wholism has the merit of culminating in a wholistic conception of the transition to socialism. If the form of the state is intrinsically capitalist, then it cannot serve as an instrument of anticapitalist struggle, but must instead be "smashed" or transcended, along with the rest of the capitalist mode of production of which it is an element. The political corollary to the Structuralist approach, in other words, is an insistence on the creation of alternative centers of ("popular") power, or on what is commonly referred to as a "dual power" conception of the transition to socialism. At least at first glance, the Structuralist position appears far more consistent with the participatory democratic commitment to "de-statification" as an essential element of the transition to socialism than the Instrumental approach.

Despite its advantages over Instrumentalism, the Structuralist approach to the state poses as many problems as it resolves. To begin with, its virtue of accommodating a far wider range of actual state activity than the Instrumentalist approach is simultaneously the vice of assimilating any conceivable state activity whatsoever: since the demonstration of the capitalist class character of the state does not require the demonstration of a causal relation between state activity and capitalist intentions, but rather demands that state activity merely be shown to perform indispensable functions for the capitalist mode of production, virtually any state activity can be held to be consistent with the capitalist class character of the state on the grounds that this activity constitutes such an indispensable function. Thus Structuralist theorists of the state typically fail to tell us which state activity would not be consistent with

---

[25] Poulantzas, "The Problem of the Capitalist State," p. 245. Poulantzas even argues in this essay that direct ruling-class participation tends to make it *more* difficult for the state to perform its function of securing the acquiescence of the working class. This argument, however, tends to undermine his general thesis of the irrelevance of the social class of officials to the question of the class character of the state.

the proposition that the state serves the interest of the capitalist class, so that their version of this proposition tends to assume the character of a hypothesis which is, in principle, nonfalsifiable. When Poulantzas argues that "if the *functions* of the state . . . and the *interests* of the dominant class . . . coincide, it is by reason of the system itself," he fails to acknowledge that the coincidence of state functions and capitalist interests is not so much "by reason of the system" as it is by reason of his own definition. The reconciliation that Poulantzas effects between his emphasis on the constitutive role of the state and Marx's theory of its ultimately derivative status is purely verbal: the state is defined as functioning to reproduce capitalist class interests and any conceivable instance of state activity is interpreted in this light.

Faced with the charge that his hypothesis is nonfalsifiable and thus not a genuine hypothesis at all, Poulantzas responded, in 1973, that a successful socialist revolution achieved with the aid of the existing state would, in fact, serve as a disconfirmation of his theory.[26] The clear implication, in other words, is that any state activity short of state-supported revolution is consistent with the thesis that the state serves the interest of the capitalist class. Indeed, in his last book Poulantzas argues that "all measures taken by the capitalist State, even those imposed by the popular masses, are in the last analysis inserted in a pro-capitalist strategy or are compatible with the expanded reproduction of capital."[27]

This response to the charge of nonfalsifiability is woefully inadequate. It is, in fact, more than a little disingenuous. As we have seen, the political corollary to the epistemological wholism of Structuralism is that the state should be smashed, i.e., a total repudiation of the "reformist" thesis that it is both possible and desirable to use the existing state to achieve fundamentally anticapitalist, pro-socialist, reforms. Thus we can presume that Structuralist Marxists who are aware of the political corollary of their epistemological position will strive to prevent the reformist strategy from being adopted. But the point is that the one instance of possible falsification to which Poulantzas points—socialist revolution with the aid of the existing state—could in fact only occur if this vehemently opposed strategy were adopted! To appeal to a future situation as a potential instance of falsification of a theory that is a situation that the theorist is committed to preventing from coming into being is hardly to provide an adequate response to those for whom the sine qua non of a scientific theory is its commitment to falsifiability. To put this another way, if the Structuralist thesis that the state, by virtue of its structure, always serves the interest of the capitalist class were wrong, then there would be no (Marxist) justification for the argument that the state must always be smashed;

[26] Poulantzas made this argument in the course of a conference at Monterossa al Mare, Italy, which I was fortunate enough to attend.

[27] Poulantzas, *State, Power, Socialism*, p. 185.

but, given this argument and the political consequences that flow from it, there is no way to determine whether the Structuralist thesis is in fact wrong. It would appear, then, that the Structuralist approach is able to sustain the basic Marxist thesis that the state serves the interest of the capitalist class only by transforming this thesis into a nonfalsifiable statement that is true by definition.[28]

As Claus Offe has pointed out, this problem of circularity could be avoided only if it were possible to specify those mechanisms internal to the state— which Offe calls "selection mechanisms"—which mediate between the functional requisites of the capitalist mode of production and the policies of the state in order to guarantee that these policies fulfill those requisites.[29] But, apart from their argument that the form of the Liberal state atomizes the working class and thus militates against conflicts that threaten the reproduction of the mode of production, this is precisely what Structuralist theorists of the state typically fail to do. It is one thing to argue that the autonomy of the state from the will of capitalists is the condition that allows these policies to escape their will and thus that the policies can, in principle, serve capitalist class interests, but it is another to explain why these interests and no others are served. The autonomy of the state from the preferences of members of the capitalist class, in other words, is the necessary but not the sufficient condition for the state being able to reproduce their class interests and their class interests alone. Offe emphasizes that "one can speak of a 'capitalist state' . . . only when it has been successfully proved that the system of political institutions displays its own class-specific selectivity corresponding to the interests of the accumulation of capital."[30] But this is exactly what Structuralist theorists have not done.

It is not clear, moreover, how this can be done. As we have seen, the Structuralist position admits of, indeed anticipates, the possibility that state actions that controvert the preferences of capitalists and at least partly respond to the demands of the members of the working class nonetheless serve the interests of capitalists as a class, and not the interests of the working class. The interests of capitalists as a class, we have also seen, entail that which is necessary to reproduce the capitalist mode of production. What justifies the imputation of this interest to capitalists and not to workers, whose conscious-

[28] In his latest book, Miliband has appropriated the Structuralist conception of the "relative autonomy" of the state, with the same result: "Relative autonomy . . . consists in the degree of freedom which the State . . . has in determining how best to serve what those who hold power conceive to be the 'national interest,' and which *in fact* involves the service of the interest of the ruling class." (Miliband, *Marxism and Politics*, p. 83, emphasis added.) What Miliband takes to be a matter of fact is, of course, really a matter of his own definition.

[29] Offe, "Structural Problems of the Capitalist State."

[30] *Ibid.*, p. 36.

97

ness, after all, may in fact be every bit as "bourgeois" as the consciousness of capitalists? What, indeed, allows Marx to speak of the state as securing the common interests of the whole bourgeoisie rather than the common interest of everyone?

To begin with, this judgment is linked to a specific understanding of human interests or human nature that culminates in the conclusion that capitalism is an alienated society that is per se inconsistent with anyone's human interests or nature. In the first instance, it is this understanding that permits Marxist theorists to speak of welfare-state reforms that respond to the perceived interest of the working class as being inconsistent with their class interests; insofar as these reforms promote the acquiescence of the working class to the (alienated) capitalist mode of production, they militate against that flowering of the human potential the necessary ground for which is an entirely new, and different, mode of production. Up to this point, however, the argument could just as well lead to the conclusion that such reforms are inconsistent with the objective interests of capitalists, for they, too, are understood by Marx to be alienated from their human nature under capitalism. What, then, justifies the conclusion that such reforms are inconsistent with the interests of the working class, but consistent with the interest of the capitalist class?

This conclusion can only be justified within the framework of Marx's theory of the proletariat as the exclusively revolutionary agent in a capitalist society. According to this theory, as we have seen, although workers are in a position ultimately to understand and act on their objective human interests, capitalists are not and can instead be expected to struggle to the very end to preserve the systemic source of their own alienation.[31] It is this asymmetry that allows Marx and Marxists to maintain that the reproduction of the capitalist mode of production is in the interest of capital as a class but not in the interest of the working class; the theory emphasizes the incompatibility between capitalism and the interests of the working class because only the working class is deemed to be the audience of the theory.

This means that the hypothesis of the (capitalist) class character of the state can be verified only through the revolutionary action of the working class; if this class functions as a genuinely revolutionary agent, we can conclude that its members have accepted the truth of that hypothesis. Thus the question of the truth of the Marxist theory of the state is inseparable from the question of the truth of the Marxist theory of the proletariat as *the* revolutionary agent. The Structuralist interpretation points beyond itself, in a manner that Poulantzas and his colleagues have not clarified, to a question that transcends the Structuralist framework. The fundamental, virtually defining assumption of this approach, as we saw, is that the class character of the state is an "objective

---

[31] See above, Chapter One.

relation,'' i.e., that it exists independently of the intentions of the actors within the capitalist system. But now it should be clear that proof of the class character of the state is intimately bound up with the character of the intentions—the consciousness and practice—of the working class. The Structuralist effort to establish the class nature of the state without reference to human intentionality must be judged a failure.

If the adequacy of the Marxist theory of the state is inseparable from the adequacy of Marx's theory of the revolutionary nature of the working class, then the Marxist theory of the state must be judged inadequate. In Chapter One I demonstrated that Marx simply failed to present compelling reasons for his expectation that the working class would come to function in a revolutionary manner.[32] On the one hand, the theory that links the proletarian condition to an utter absence of material and psychic benefits, i.e., the theory of absolute immiseration introduced in the *Holy Family* and more fully elaborated in the *Communist Manifesto*, was later repudiated by Marx himself in *Capital* and has been undermined by the subsequent history of working-class struggles in Western capitalist societies. On the other hand, even if it were possible to demonstrate that the rupture of this link (and thus the absence of an anticapitalist working-class consciousness) is only temporary, i.e., that capitalism will ultimately prove to be incapable of satisfying the consumption-oriented demands of the working class, Marx (and Marxists) nowhere demonstrate how and why a consciousness that is anticapitalist but consumerist will be transformed into a consciousness that understands the preoccupation with consumption to be an illusory compensation for alienation within production and is thus not only anticapitalist but genuinely socialist as well.[33] For both reasons, Marx's confidence in the role of the proletariat as a necessarily revolutionary agent is misplaced. Thus it is difficult to see how the thesis that the state serves the interest of the capitalist class but not the interest of the working class can be sustained. This thesis, once again, presupposes that the working class is the privileged audience of the theory, and it is precisely this presupposition that the nonrevolutionary nature of the working class calls into question. At the same time, the presence of members of nonproletarian classes, and the capitalist class in particular, within revolutionary socialist movements also undermines this presupposition. Indeed, the theory of the exclusively proletarian origins of revolutionary needs is belied from the outset by the fact that the author of this theory fails to share these origins.[34] In short, both the absence of socialist consciousness among the working class and the presence of socialist consciousness among nonworkers oblige us to reject the notion of the proletariat as *the* revolutionary subject,

[32] See above, Chapter One, pp. 48-54.

[33] Agnes Heller, *The Theory of Need in Marx* (New York: St. Martin's Press, 1976), Ch. 4.

[34] Gouldner, ''Prologue to a Theory of Revolutionary Intellectuals.''

99

and with it the theory that the state serves exclusively the interests of the capitalist class.[35]

Alternatively, it would be possible to sever the Marxist theory of the state from the theory of proletarian revolution by continuing to maintain the proposition that the state functions to reproduce the capitalist mode of production while abandoning the thesis that this function is in the interest of the capitalist class but not in the interest of the working class. The cost of this conceptual surgery, of course, would be the rupture of the traditional link between theory and practice: now that the proletariat were no longer the privileged audience of the theory, the raison-d'être for the theory of the state would be, at best, unclear. Nor is it clear exactly what would be gained. Even if it were possible to demonstrate that the internal structure of the state enables it to perform the function of reproducing the capitalist mode of production, this demonstration would in no way enlighten us as to why, in any given capitalist society, one particular state policy is enacted rather than any number of others that might equally be understood to have "positive" reproductive consequences. The reformulated Structuralist approach, in other words, *might* help us understand the parameters within which public policy operates, but leaves us totally in the dark with respect to the changing details of actual policy making. Similarly, the generic proposition that the state in all capitalist societies functions to reproduce the mode of production fails utterly to inform us why the activities of the state are far more extensive in some capitalist societies than others. Both of these unanswered questions point beyond the limits of Structuralism and its militant anti-intentionality: to explain the nature and scope of state activities, both within a given capitalist society and across different capitalist societies, requires precisely that attention to the intentions and strategies of various social actors that the constitutive assumption of Structuralism fore-

---

[35] To put this even more strongly: insofar as the intelligibility of the Marxist theory that the state represents the interests of the capitalist class presupposes Marx's theory of the proletariat as the exclusively revolutionary subject, the former theory must be judged as metaphysical as the latter. The latter theory entails, I would argue, a projection of the needs of the theorist onto the working class which is repressed in favor of the conception that the theorist merely represents the needs of the working class. A representational conception of his own discourse thus underlies, and is homologous with, Marx's representational conception of the state: according to Marx's understanding, his theory is to the working class as the state is to the capitalist class (except for the fact that the need of the working class for those "who have raised themselves to the level of comprehending theoretically [its] historical movement as a whole" (Marx and Engels, *Manifesto of the Communist Party*, p. 343) is understood to be temporary in comparison to the permanent need of the capitalist class for the state to represent its interests as a whole). And, in both cases, the representational problematic masks the autonomous, constitutive role of that which is held to play the role of mere representative. We should not be surprised to find, then, that the problem of developing a more adequate, non-representational theory of the state and the problem of developing a more adequate, non-representational theory of discourse are two sides of the same coin.

100

closes from the very outset. If, moreover, the intentions and strategies that are the very stuff of actual policy making are not class-based, but rather originate elsewhere, then the claim that the dynamics of politics are generated by the mode of production cannot be sustained. I shall return to this point when I discuss class-conflict theories of the state.

A final word on the Structuralist approach, this time concerning its political implications. Although, as I have suggested, the wholism of Structuralism is compatible with the commitment of the participatory democrat to a totalistic transformation of all structures of domination, its objectivism is not consistent with this commitment. The argument that individual intentionality is merely an effect of structures of which human beings are obliged to remain, in any mode of production, the mere "supports" ultimately prevents one from being able to distinguish between human domination and human liberation.[36] It is precisely this distinction that is central to any theory of a liberatory politics for the future society and the transition thereto.

"Derivation" Theories

As the name implies, Derivation theorists seek to derive or deduce the form and function of the state from the structure of the capitalist mode of production itself. According to this interpretation, what makes the state a capitalist state is neither that it responds to the preferences of capitalists nor that it performs reproductive functions, but rather the fact that its structure is but the political form assumed by "the basic relation . . . in capitalist society, the capital relation."[37] The state, in other words, is an intrinsically capitalist state because the state *is* capital in its political form. The proof of the class character of the state requires the demonstration neither that it is an instrument of capitalist intentions nor that it performs exclusively capitalist functions.[38] It consists, rather, in the identification of an essential identity or homology between the form of economic exchange and the form of political "exchange" in a capitalist mode of production.

Elsewhere, I have identified and elaborated such an homology between the commodity form and the legal form. The formality of the law, I demonstrated, allows it to function as a universal political equivalent that perfectly parallels

[36] Louis Althusser, *Reading Capital* (London: New Left Books, 1970), p. 180. Michael H. Best and William E. Connolly, "Politics and Subjects: The Limits of Structural Marxism," *Socialist Review*, No. 48 (November-December 1979), pp. 75-99.

[37] John Holloway and Sol Picciotto, *State and Capital: A Marxist Debate* (Austin: University of Texas Press, 1978), p. 14.

[38] Derivationists point out that "in so far as the state is derived from the need to fulfill a function which cannot be fulfilled by private capital, the state's ability to perform this function is already presupposed," thus echoing my criticism of the circular nature of Poulantzas' argument. *Ibid.*, p. 21.

101

the role of money as a universal economic equivalent in a capitalist mode of production: just as the commodity form "replaces" use-value and concrete labor with the abstractions of exchange-value and undifferentiated labor-power, the legal form "replaces" the multiplicity of concrete needs with the abstraction of equal "rights" and the socially differentiated individual with the abstraction of the juridical subject or legal person.[39] Thus I concluded that the logic of the legal form *is* the logic of the commodity form as the latter expresses itself in the political sphere, i.e., that the legal form is a specifically capitalist form.

Apart from the fact that its level of abstraction no more enables it to grasp the dynamics of actual policy making than does the Structuralist approach, the principal, and, to my mind, fatal difficulty with state derivation theories (including, I now understand, my own) is that their assertion of the ultimate causal primacy of the mode of production is arbitrary and, therefore, unconvincing. It is one thing to argue, for example, that an homology exists between the legal form and the commodity form; it is quite another to assert that this demonstrates that the logic of the legal form is but the political expression of the logic of the commodity form. One could, in fact, argue with equal justification exactly the reverse, namely that the logic of the commodity form is but the economic expression of the logic of the legal form, and that the commodity is, in this sense, a specifically legal form. Although this formulation undoubtedly strikes us as somewhat odd, this is only because we are accustomed to proceeding from the assumption that political domination is a function of the mode of production rather than from the assumption that the mode of production is a function of political domination. The point is that the mere identification of an homology between political forms and production forms in no way enables us to determine which of these assumptions is the correct starting point.

This dilemma is merely a contemporary version of an inherent ambiguity in the concept of a mode of production. I suggested in Chapter One that Marx's effort to establish the determination of "the life process in general" by the mode of production waivered between an essentially arbitrary assertion of the primacy of the "moment" or subfunction of material production over the subfunctions of distribution, exchange, and consumption and an exercise in tautology by means of which the moment of material production is redefined to embrace the production cycle as a whole.[40] The same can be said for the effort of the Derivationists: their claim to have "derived" political forms from the mode of production entails either the arbitrary assertion that the

[39] Balbus, "Commodity Form and Legal Form: An Essay on the 'Relative Autonomy' of the Law"; E. B. Pashukanis, "The General Theory of Law and Marxism," in Hugh W. Babb, ed., *Soviet Legal Philosophy* (Cambridge, Mass.: Harvard University Press, 1951).

[40] Habermas, *Knowledge and Human Interests*, p. 328.

102

subfunction of distribution derives from the subfunction of material production (rather than the reverse) or else the redefinition of distribution in terms of production so that the theory of determination by the mode of production becomes true by definition.

The only way in which it is possible to extricate oneself from this dilemma, it seems to me, is to determine whether the hypothesis of determination of the mode of distribution (including the mode of politics) by the mode of production is warranted in the light of historical and comparative empirical analysis. For example, if, as Marx himself suggests at certain points, it could be demonstrated that legal and other political forms were the historical preconditions for the rise of the capitalist mode of production,[41] then one could scarcely argue that these forms *derived from* the capitalist mode of production. As Mihaly Vajda has recently emphasized,

> Marx had forgotten—when he discovered the fact of capitalist exploitation—that a political power was already in place as the separation of civil society and the state occurred, that the great political struggles of the bourgeoisie aimed at nothing else than the demolition of the state bureaucracy in order to win freedom (i.e., freedom of competition). State power has a continuity in history and for that very reason is still today essentially different in many respects in different countries. It expressed a different kind of organization of society than the class organization of bourgeois society.[42]

The standard Marxist response to this type of historical argument is the invocation of the distinction between "genetic" and "structural" priority, i.e., the argument that forms which are historically prior to the capitalist mode of production nevertheless become specifically capitalistic by virtue of the way the mode of production transforms and makes use of them.[43] But, once again, the assumption that it is the mode of production that transforms and makes use of these forms, rather than the reverse, is arbitrary and can only be justified in the light of empirical investigation.

Similarly, evidence that political forms essentially identical to so-called capitalist political forms exist in societies dominated by a noncapitalist mode of production likewise tends to undermine the claim that these forms can be derived from the capitalist mode of production. The proliferation of bureaucratic domination in state socialist societies, for example, calls into question,

---

[41] Marx, *Capital*, Vol. I, p. 169; Margaret A. Fay, "Review of *State and Capital*," *Kapitalistate*, No. 7 (1978), pp. 130-52; Alvin W. Gouldner, *The Two Marxisms: Contradictions and Anomalies in the Development of Theory* (New York: Seabury, 1980), pp. 355-59.

[42] Mihaly Vajda, "The State and Socialism," *Social Research*, Vol. 45 (Winter 1978), pp. 859-60.

[43] Marx, *Grundrisse*, p. 107; Poulantzas, *State, Power, Socialism*, pp. 39-43.

at the very least, the Marxist hypothesis that bureaucracy, as one particular mode of distribution, is determined by the mode of production. The characteristic effort to rescue this hypothesis through the reconceptualization of these societies as capitalist societies effectively transforms into a nonfalsifiable proposition and is thus necessarily a failure.[44] Nor is it helpful to allude, as did Poulantzas in his last book, to "capitalist aspects" of the relations of production of state socialist societies as the determinants of political domination in these societies.[45] On the one hand, the ubiquity of political domination in these societies can scarcely be comprehended as a result of a mere survival of capitalist relations within a predominantly noncapitalist society. On the other hand, if these "aspects" are central to the existing mode of production then they can hardly be considered "capitalist" without an unjustifiable expansion of this concept and the attendant problem to which I have just referred.

The effort of the Derivationists and others to link political domination exclusively to the capitalist mode of production, finally, is bound to dishearten participatory democrats who are committed to the eradication of political domination in all forms of society. Definitionally to preclude the possible emergence of political domination under socialism is scarcely to be prepared to recognize, let alone combat, its existence in the course of socialist construction. Thus the political corollary of the Derivationist theory of the state is no more acceptable than that of the alternative interpretations we have already examined.

Class-Struggle Theories

The tendency of Structuralist and Derivationist theories of the state to abstract from the intentionality of social actors and thus from the dynamics of actual state activity has recently led a number of Marxist theorists to emphasize class struggle as a, or perhaps even *the*, crucial determinant of what the state does. Poulantzas acknowledges that, in his earlier work, "I did not sufficiently emphasize the primacy of class struggle as compared with the State apparatus," and therefore defines the state in his last work as "the condensation of a class relationship of forces."[46] Erik Olin Wright argues that the extent of the divergence between state policies that are "functionally compatible" with the reproduction of the capitalist mode of production and those policies that fall within the "structural limitations" established by the state is, above all, a function of the nature and level of the class struggle

---

[44] See above, Chapter Two.

[45] Poulantzas, *State, Power, Socialism*, p. 24.

[46] Nicos Poulantzas, "The Capitalist State: A Reply to Miliband and Laclau," *New Left Review*, No. 95 (January-February 1976), p. 74, and *State, Power, Socialism*, p. 119.

104

between capital and labor: the more widespread and intense this struggle is, the greater the chance that policies will be enacted by the state that are not compatible with the reproduction requirements of the mode of production.[47] Similarly, Wright and his colleagues Esping-Anderson and Friedland have asserted that "the problem facing advanced capitalist social formations is how can the capitalist state be structured so as to be able to perform functions dictated by economic contradictions given the actual or potential existence of a politically organized working class?"[48] Finally, in an attempt to explain the differential scope and strength of state welfare policies across different Western capitalist societies, Ira Katznelson has developed the notion of a "social democratic surplus," which is determined by the precise nature of class conflict in these societies. "The level of social democracy," he informs us, "is the sum of the reproductive minimum about which there is broad communal consensus, and the results of current contentious factional group and class conflicts."[49]

Each of these formulations can be understood as an effort to achieve a synthesis between the militant anti-intentionality of Structuralist objectivism and the adamantly antistructural tendencies of Instrumentalist voluntarism. The state, it is argued, does exercise a structural determination over the policies that emerge from it, but, at the same time, the structure of, and thus the determination exercised by, the state is itself, at least in part, a result of class struggle. Alternatively, what the state does is understood to be a function of class conflict, but class conflict is itself decisively shaped by the structure and functions of the state. Thus, as Katznelson has emphasized, the state is both "a distinctive 'product' *and* determinant of class reproduction requirements and class conflict."[50]

There are two major problems with this reformulation of the Marxist theory of the state. First, it amounts to little more than a statement of, rather than a genuine solution to, the problem of how to synthesize the objectivism of Structuralism and the voluntarism of Instrumentalism. To argue that "structure" and "struggle" are dialectically interrelated is hardly to develop a theory that specifies the precise nature of this interrelationship. Does class conflict determine political outcomes only within the structural limits established by the state in response to system reproduction requirements, or does it alter these structural limits and system requirements themselves? If the latter, then how far are we from a voluntarist position that attributes state outcomes to the organized intentions of social actors, i.e., what becomes of the notion of

[47] Erik Olin Wright, *Class, Crisis and the State* (London: New Left Books, 1978), Ch. 5.

[48] Gosta Esping-Anderson, *et al.*, "Modes of Class Struggle and the Capitalist State," *Kapitalistate*, Nos. 4-5 (Summer 1976), p. 186.

[49] Katznelson, "Considerations on Social Democracy in the United States," p. 87.

[50] *Ibid.*, p. 85.

structural determination? If, in other words, the state is a mere "condensation of a class relationship of forces," it would appear that the capacity of the state to enforce exclusively capitalist class interests will depend entirely on the strength of capitalist as compared to working-class "forces." Have we not then abandoned the concept of the state as an intrinsically capitalist state, and are we not back to the Instrumentalist position? On the other hand, if class struggle determines political outcomes only within structural limits, then how is it possible to maintain that this struggle and thus human intentionality is a crucial determinant of state action? Have we not returned to the position of the Structuralist, for whom all conscious choice takes place within the framework of an "unconscious" structure that establishes the parameters of choice from beginning to end? In the absence of convincing answers to these and other related questions, the proposed synthesis runs the risk of degenerating into a covert reassertion of the primacy of one of the two terms from which the synthesis is supposed to arise. (In the case of Katznelson's effort, for example, the purported synthesis between structural and intentional determination tends to evaporate in favor of the [unacknowledged] primacy of the latter. Insofar as the reproduction requirements of the capitalist mode of production ["reproduction minimum"] are a matter of a "communal consensus," i.e., are intersubjectively rather than "objectively" determined, and, insofar as this consensus is itself the result of prior "group and class conflicts," it would appear that the concept of "structure" is ultimately reduced to that of an effect of intentions with little or no long-run independent determinative power.)

Even more importantly, this reformulation rests on the ultimately arbitrary assertion that the struggles that in large part determine what the state does are *class* struggles. Once we assume that state activity is largely a result of struggles, then the only way we can defend the proposition that the mode of production determines state activity is to argue that these struggles are exclusively rooted in conflicts of interest that stem from differential relationships to the mode of production. Conversely, if the basis for these struggles lies elsewhere, i.e., not in a relationship to production, then it would be impossible to argue that the mode of production determines the activity of the state. Thus Katznelson's formulation that "the level of social democracy . . . is the sum of the reproduction minimum . . . and the results of current . . . group *and* class conflicts" (emphasis added) begs precisely that question—group *or* class—which must be answered in order to determine whether the emphasis on struggle is or is not consistent with the Marxist thesis of determination by the mode of production.

In fact, as I have already suggested, class struggle remains more of a wish than an empirical reality in the advanced capitalist societies. On the one hand, those economic conflicts that are rooted in production are as likely, or, depending on the society in question, more likely to be relatively narrow interest-group conflicts than genuine class conflicts. The assimilation of these interest-group conflicts to the category of class conflicts, moreover, would mean the assimilation of the Marxist theory of the state to Pluralist theories of the "group bases of politics"[51] and thus the loss of any distinctive Marxist theory of politics. Second, many contemporary economic conflicts are rooted not in the mode of production, but rather in the mode of distribution. As Janowitz and Offe have both argued, one central consequence of the expansion of the welfare state has been that the relationship of the individual to the state institutions of welfare is an increasingly decisive determinant of his or her income and thus that occupation, i.e., relationship to the means of production, is no longer the exclusive, or perhaps even the principal, determinant of the individual's life-chances.[52] The wage, in other words, is no longer the over-riding mechanism of distribution in advanced capitalist societies. Under these conditions, it is no longer possible to maintain, with Marx, that "the structure of distribution is completely determined by the structure of production."[53] (The contemporary Marxist thesis that state welfare expenditures are "social wages," it should be added, fails to salvage the theory of the determination of distribution by production. This determination could only be established if it could be demonstrated that the state distribution of the "social wage" was reducible to the reproduction requirements of the mode of production. As Piven and Cloward have shown, at least for the United States, the expansion and contraction of welfare expenditures is not reducible to these reproduction requirements, unless we were to so expand the meaning of "reproduction requirements" that they embrace everything that political authorities must do in order to respond to the claims that various classes and groups make on the state.[54] In this case, however, the proposition that production determines distribution becomes true by definition.) Thus we should expect to, and do, find that many economic conflicts that affect what the state does are rooted in interests that derive from the relationship of individuals to the mode of state distribution rather than to the means of production. Finally, many of the conflicts that shape the activities of the state are simply noneconomic in character; the attempt to assimilate these conflicts, e.g., religious, racial, and ethnic conflicts, to the category of class conflicts utterly deprives the concept of class of any distinctive meaning. For all these reasons, the claims of the

[51] Earl Latham, *The Group Basis of Politics* (Ithaca, N.Y.: Cornell University Press, 1952).

[52] Janowitz, *The Last Half-Century*, Ch. 5; Claus Offe, "Political Authority and Class Structures—An Analysis of Late Capitalist Societies," *International Journal of Sociology*, 2 (Spring 1972), pp. 73-108.

[53] Marx, *Grundrisse*, p. 95.

[54] Frances Fox Piven and Richard A. Cloward, *Regulating the Poor* (New York: Vintage Books, 1972).

"struggle" theorists that state-determining conflicts are class conflicts is either empirically unfounded or else a mere exercise in definition.[55] Thus the class struggle version of the Marxist theory of the state is no more successful than any other version in demonstrating that the nature of politics in societies with a capitalist mode of production is a function of this mode of production.

Nor does it imply a satisfactory model of liberatory politics for the socialist society of the future or the transition thereto. Insofar as the class struggle approach aspires to a synthesis of the Instrumentalist and Structuralist theories of the state, we should not be surprised to discover that its political corollary embodies elements of both, yet rejects the extremes of each, of these theories. Thus Poulantzas, for example, recently posed the problem of the transition to socialism not as the choice between employing the existing state versus utterly smashing it and replacing it with a completely different state, but rather as the question:

> How is it possible radically to transform the State in such a manner that the extension and deepening of political freedoms and the institutions of representative democracy . . . are combined with the unfurling of forms of direct democracy and the mushrooming of self-management bodies?[56]

The goal, in other words, is to make use of the best of the existing state and replace the worst with a new state form characterized by participatory democracy. The means by which this goal is to be achieved is thus properly understood as a combination of struggle within and a struggle outside the existing state.[57]

The political position that follows from the class struggle approach is certainly more promising than that which emerges from the alternative approaches we have already reviewed. It is, however, beset by one serious problem. It merely states, rather than resolves, the problem of how to coordinate the relationship between the organs of representative democracy and the organs of participatory democracy in the socialist society of the future as well as the relationship between the internal and the external political struggles that are to culminate in the creation of this society. Insofar as it can be argued, with a good deal of justification, that such problems of coordination can be effectively resolved only in practice, it might be objected that the failure of the theory to resolve the problem of coordination is really no problem at all. The practical resolution of this problem, however, must be guided by certain principles that establish priorities among conflicting goals and conflicting

---

[55] See above, Chapter One, and Nicos Mouzelis, "Reductionism in Marxist Theory," *Telos*, No. 45 (Fall 1980), pp. 180-83.

[56] Poulantzas, *State, Power, Socialism*, p. 256.

[57] Nicos Poulantzas, "The State and the Transition to Socialism," *Socialist Review*, No. 38 (March-April 1978), pp. 9-36.

strategies designed to reach these goals, e.g., principles that establish the relative importance of representative as compared to participatory democracy and thus the relative importance of their respective strategies. But these principles are precisely what the theory fails to elaborate.

Nor is it clear that it would be possible to elaborate such principles on the terrain of this, or any other, Marxist theory of the state. The commitment of Poulantzas and other Marxists to participatory or, for that matter, representative democracy has the flavor of an ad hoc commitment rather than one grounded in the basic assumptions of the theory from which they proceed. It is not clear, in other words, how a principled commitment to a combination of participatory and representative democracy, or, for that matter, to either one of them, flows from the assumption that, at bottom, political life is determined by the mode of production. At the very least, we would have to pose the question of whether it is possible to develop an adequate conception of a liberatory politics—a politics for the future, socialist society and the transition thereto—on the foundation of a theory for which the realm of politics is, ultimately, a derivative realm. In the next section I shall argue that the answer to this question is "no."

Marxism as an Obstacle to a Theory of Liberatory Politics

The Absence of a Theory of Liberatory Politics in Marx

It is well known that Marx and Engels argue that the state emerges historically on the foundation of class-divided modes of production and that the state is thus destined to disappear in the classless, socialist mode of production of the future.[58] The state—any state—is an inherent realm of domination. In this section I shall demonstrate that this concept of the state as domination exhausts Marx's concept of politics, i.e., that Marx does not theorize about the possibility of a liberatory politics because for him the activity of politics is, by definition, an activity of domination. Politics betokens an absence of human liberation, one that can only be remedied with an absence of politics. There is, in short, no theory of a liberatory politics in Marx—no principled conception of politics for the future socialist society—because, for Marx, "liberation" (or "socialism") and "politics" is a contradiction in terms.

That political power is for Marx a power of domination emerges clearly in the following oft-cited passages from his work:

---

[58] Marx and Engels, *The German Ideology*, pp. 124-25, 164; Engels, *The Origin of the Family, Private Property and the State*, pp. 586-89.

The working class, in the course of its development, will substitute for the old civil society an association which will exclude classes and their antagonism, and there will be *no more political power* properly so-called, since political power is precisely the expression of antagonism in civil society.[59]

When in the course of development, class distinctions have disappeared, and all production has been concentrated in the hands of a vast association of the whole nation, *the public power will lose its political character. Political power*, properly so-called, is merely the *organized power of one class for oppressing another*.[60]

Although these words were written in 1846 and 1848, respectively, their theme, as Ralph Miliband has correctly noted, echoes throughout Marx's political writings.[61] Not just the state, but political power as such begins and ends with class antagonism and oppression. Since these passages refer, however, to political power rather than simply to "politics," it is possible to argue that, strictly speaking, they do not in and of themselves demonstrate conclusively that Marx links the emergence of politics to the emergence of classes and thus understands that the elimination of the latter will produce the elimination of the former. It could be argued, in other words, that the origin and elimination of political power is not synonymous with the origin and elimination of politics insofar as Marx employs a concept of politics that is broader than his concept of power. This interpretation, however, will not stand up. When Marx says "the public power will lose its political character," it is clear that, for him, "power" is in fact a broader concept than "politics," and thus that he does not envision the elimination of power and the creation of a politics without power in the future, communist society. Rather for Marx "political power" and "politics" are synonymous concepts, and thus the argument about the class-linked destiny of political power is an argument about the class-linked nature of politics *tout court*. That the "political" as well as "political power" has a decidedly negative connotation for Marx is also confirmed in his 1874 marginal notes to his copy of Bakunin's *Statism and Anarchy*, where he argues that "when class rule has disappeared, there will no longer be any state in the present *political* sense of the word."[62] Summarizing the relationship between Marx's theory of politics and his theory of alienation, Meszaros writes that "politics . . . must be conceived as an activity whose ultimate end is *its own annulment* by means of fulfilling its

[59] Marx, *The Poverty of Philosophy*, p. 174, emphasis added.

[60] Marx and Engels, *Manifesto of the Communist Party*, p. 352, emphases added.

[61] Miliband, *Marxism and Politics*, p. 11.

[62] David McLellan, *Karl Marx: Selected Writings* (Oxford: Oxford University Press, 1977), p. 563, emphasis added.

determinate function as a necessary stage in the complex process of positive transcendence,''[63] i.e., politics remains wholly within the realm of alienation. Thus we are entitled to conclude that, for Marx, the disalienated, communist society of the future will be an a-political society.

Yet perhaps we have arrived at this conclusion rather too hastily. Might it not be argued that, although what Marx calls politics is necessarily for him a realm of domination and alienation, he nevertheless has in mind certain social activities that *we* would consider political, yet that do not partake of domination and alienation and thus are to persist in the future society? Have we not made too much of what for Marx is simply a question of definition? After all, in the passage from the *Communist Manifesto*, quoted above, he clearly implies that "public power" will persist under communism, and in the *Critique of the Gotha Program* he suggests that at least some "social functions . . . that are analogous to present state functions" will "remain in existence."[64] Could not this "power" and these "functions" embrace what we might consider liberatory political activity? And, if so, would it not be wrong to conclude that, for Marx, the existence of politics is inseparably linked to the existence of class domination and alienation, and that the class-less, unalienated society will be an a-political one?

In fact, as I shall show, Marx's argument against politics is an argument against any and all social activity that might reasonably be construed to embrace the scope of a liberatory politics. According to Marx, the only public "power" and "functions" that are to outlive classes, alienation, and domination and thus persist in the future society are purely administrative in nature. The best-known passage that makes this argument comes not from Marx, but from Engels:

> As soon as there is no longer any social class to be held in subjection; as soon as class rule, and the individual struggle for existence based on our present anarchy of production . . . are removed, nothing more remains to be repressed, and a special repressive force, a state, is no longer necessary . . . State interference in social relations becomes, in one domain after another, superfluous, and then dies out of itself; *the government of persons is replaced by the administration of things.*[65]

In this case, however, Engels's argument is perfectly consistent with that of Marx. In 1872 Marx writes:

[63] Istvan Meszaros, *Marx's Theory of Alienation* (London: Merlin Press, 1970), p. 160, emphasis in the original.

[64] Tucker, *The Marx-Engels Reader*, p. 395.

[65] Friedrich Engels, *Socialism: Utopian and Scientific*, in Tucker, *The Marx-Engels Reader*, p. 635, emphasis added.

111

What all socialists understand by anarchism is this: as soon as the goal of the proletarian movement, the abolition of classes, shall have been reached, the power of the state, whose function it is to keep the great majority of producers beneath the yoke of a small minority of exploiters, will disappear and *government functions will be transformed into simple administrative functions.*[66]

Similarly, in his marginal notes to *Statism and Anarchy*, Marx argues that:

[A]s soon as the [general] functions have ceased to be political, then there exists (1) no governmental function; (2) the distribution of general functions has become a business matter [!] which *does not afford any room for domination*; (3) the election has none of its present political character.[67]

In other words, when with the advent of communism, general functions have ceased to be political and have become purely administrative, the elections that regulate the distribution of these purely administrative functions likewise become purely "business" or administrative, rather than political matters. This passage, like the two immediately preceding it, underscores the point that for Marx life in the fully developed communist society is bereft of politics but replete with administration. Thus Bertell Ollman concludes that, in Marx's vision, "the work of administration, more properly of coordination, is the only function in communism which is analogous to the duties of a modern state."[68]

But what then of Marx's praise for the obviously political forms and functions of the Paris Commune? Did not these remarkably decentralized and participatory forms and functions constitute what Marx might have considered the basis for a truly liberatory politics, a concrete embodiment of a principled vision of socialist politics? And does not Marx's praise for these forms and functions contradict the contention that communist society will be an a-political society characterized exclusively by administration? Once we recall that, according to Marx in *The Civil War in France*, the commune presaged not the fully developed communist society but rather simply the "dictatorship of the proletariat," and that the dictatorship of the proletariat is, like any other state, a form of class rule or domination, we understand why the answer to these last two questions must be "no." According to Marx, again in his marginal notes to *Statism and Anarchy:*

[A]s long as the other classes, and in particular the capitalist class, still exist, as long as the proletariat is still struggling with it (because with

---

[66] Cited in David McLellan, *The Thought of Karl Marx: An Introduction* (New York: Harper & Row, 1974), p. 184, emphasis added.

[67] McLellan, *Karl Marx: Selected Writings*, p. 563, emphasis added.

[68] Bertell Ollman, *Social and Sexual Revolution* (Boston: South End Press, 1979), p. 82.

112

the proletariat's conquest of governmental power its enemies and the old organization of society have not yet disappeared), it must use coercive means, hence governmental means; it is still a class and the economic conditions on which the class struggle and the existence of classes depend, have not yet disappeared and must be removed by force, or transformed and their process of transformation speeded up by force.[69]

The democratic elements of the Commune, and ideally of the dictatorship of the proletariat, in other words, in no way contradict the fact that this political form, like any other, is a "coercive" one, the rule of one class over another. That this form will be the first in history to embrace the rule of the majority over the minority makes no difference in this context; Marx should be read as simply arguing that democracy and decentralization make the best of a bad situation: the necessity of politics. His commitment to democratic politics, in other words, remains strategic or instrumental in character: "the dictatorship of the proletariat," Poulantzas acknowledges, "was a notion of applied strategy."[70]

Thus Marx's writings on the Commune reinforce the general point I have been making: for Marx, politics is only necessary insofar as, and as long as, classes, alienation, and domination continue to exist. When they exist no longer, politics will be superseded by pure administration. Neither Marx's analysis of the Commune in practice nor the dictatorship of the proletariat in theory can be interpreted as an argument for a truly liberatory politics; they in no way controvert, but rather merely reaffirm, the assertion that, for Marx, the good society is an a-political society. Marx himself had said as much many years earlier, in 1844, when he wrote that socialism requires the "political act" of revolution only insofar as the "overthrow and dissolution" of the capitalist order is necessary, and that, as soon as "organizing activity begins, where its own aim and spirit emerge, there socialism throws the political hull away."[71]

The conclusion is inescapable that both Marx and Engels conceived of the

[69] McLellan, *Karl Marx: Selected Writings*, p. 561.

[70] Nicos Poulantzas, "Towards a Democratic Socialism," *New Left Review*, No. 109 (May-June 1978), p. 79. We should not be surprised, then, to discover that the specific content that Marx gives to this notion varies dramatically over the course of his writings. The "participatory" commune model was, of course, a radical reformulation of the "centralized state" model of the dictatorship of the proletariat that Marx and Engels proposed over twenty years earlier in the *Communist Manifesto*. A few short months after his eulogy to the commune in *The Civil War in France*, Marx appears to return to his earlier "statist" model, and a full decade after his eulogy he calls into question the availability of the Commune as a political model by arguing that it "was in no sense socialist." Gouldner, *The Two Marxisms*, pp. 351-52.

[71] Cited in James Miller, review of Ralph Miliband's *Marxism and Politics, Telos*, No. 36 (Summer 1978), p. 189. Miller also argues that there is no theory of liberatory politics in Marx, but does not attempt to demonstrate, as I shall, that an adequate version of such a theory cannot be derived from Marxist assumptions.

113

transformation from capitalist alienation to communist disalienation as a momentous either/or: *either* a repressive, alienated political society *or* a liberatory, unalienated administrative society that dispenses entirely with politics. In the face of this either/or, there is simply no conceptual space for the existence of a liberatory politics in the socialist society of the future.

What accounts for this lack of conceptual space? What makes it possible for Marx to argue that a communist society will be able to substitute administration for politics? In *Capital*, Marx describes administration as "the work of general supervision and direction," which he likens to the activity of the conductor of an orchestra.[72] For Marx, the members of communist society are analogous to the members of an orchestra, all playing their respective parts in order to create the best possible social "symphony" as a whole. The analogy implies, in other words, that communism will be characterized by a fundamental agreement or consensus on ends that will obviate the need for mechanisms designed for the resolution of conflict over ends and reduce the problem exclusively to one of efficiently coordinating the means necessary to reach these ends.[73] The only "general functions" that are to persist in the society of the future are those that can be encapsulated by the logic of instrumental rationality, in which "the characteristic operation of mind is the choice of means to the attainment of given ends,"[74] an operation of mind that presupposes that the problem of ends has already been solved.

The implicit assumption of consensus underlying Marx's vision of the a-political society has been made explicit by Bertell Ollman in the course of his recent effort to establish the plausibility of this vision:

> Legislatures are political expressions of the principle of majority rule which, in turn, is based on the assumption that on important matters people's opinions are bound to clash. . . . But the people of communism are *agreed on all the subjects which could possibly come before a parliament*. Where *interests merge and decisions are unanimous* it is not necessary to go through the formality of counting hands. Furthermore, all *really major decisions*, those bearing on the structure of communism itself, *have already been taken* by this time. People have what they want,

[72] Cited in Ollman, *Social and Sexual Revolution*, p. 78.

[73] It is perhaps worth pointing out that this analogy rests on a misunderstanding of the relationship between the conductor and the members of an orchestra. The fact that all the members are (in principle) committed to the goal of the best possible performance in no way precludes the possibility that they will have fundamentally different interpretations of what this goal entails and that these different interpretations will serve as the basis for conflict among them. Thus the function of the conductor cannot be reduced to the "technical" one of coordination but also necessarily embraces the resolution of conflict as well. The lesson that Marx should have drawn, but does not draw, from this analogy, then, is that a purely administrative solution to a collective problem is impossible.

[74] Unger, *Knowledge and Politics*, p. 153.

114

that is, communism, and there is nothing for a legislature, whose main function is to make changes, to change.[75]

Thus legislatures in particular and mechanisms for the expression and resolution of conflict in general become superfluous in a society in which, according to Ollman's account of Marx's logic, everyone shares the same social
goals and there is "no clash of basic interests."[76] Here, as usual, Ollman
scrupulously follows Marx, for whom communism signals the end to "antagonism in civil society" and the "*genuine* resolution of the conflict between
man and nature and between man and man."[77]

The absence of politics in the communist society of the future is predicated,
then, on the assumption that this ·society will be one "in which there are no
conflicting demands and the wants of all fit together . . . into a harmonious
plan of activity."[78] It will be a society, in short, in which everyone receives
according to his or her needs and contributes according to his or her abilities,
a society that thereby renders superfluous an authoritative determination of
what its members should receive and what they should contribute. Such a
society will be "beyond justice," i.e., beyond politics, precisely because it
"has eliminated the occasions when the appeal to the principles of right and
justice is necessary."[79] But how is a society in which everyone receives
according to his or her needs possible, what guarantees that the satisfaction
of one person's needs will be consistent with the satisfaction of everyone
else's? And how is a society in which contribution is proportionate to ability
possible, what ensures that the ability of individuals to contribute will be
commensurate with the needs on behalf of which their energies are set in
motion?

I shall deal below only with the first of these questions: the question of
"to each according to his needs."[80] Marx's answer to this question is that
harmonious distribution according to need is possible "after the productive

[75] Ollman, *Social and Sexual Revolution*, pp. 80-81, emphases added.

[76] *Ibid.*, p. 77.

[77] Cited in Miliband, *Marxism and Politics*, p. 11. Marx, "Private Property and Communism,"
p. 70, emphasis in the original.

[78] John Rawls, *A Theory of Justice* (Cambridge, Mass.: Harvard University Press, 1971), p.
281.

[79] *Ibid.*, p. 286. Compare Cornelius Castoriadis, for whom Marx's "solution" to the problems
of justice amounts to "a suppression of the condition under which the problems themselves exist
. . . [a] way of resolving the question of justice (that is to say, of *politics*) [that] create[s]
conditions under which this question is no longer posed." "From Marx to Aristotle, From
Aristotle to Us," *Social Research*, 45 (Winter 1978), p. 723.

[80] The two principles are, for Marx, but two sides of the same coin. Since " 'need' is always
attached to 'power' in Marx's writings as the means through which man becomes aware of the
latter's existence" (Ollman, *Alienation*, p. 78), the principle of distribution according to need
and the principle of contribution according to capacity (power) are, at bottom, the same principle.
Thus the analysis of one will necessarily reveal all the problems entailed in the other.

forces have . . . increased . . . and all the springs of cooperative wealth flow more abundantly,'' i.e., once an economy of abundance has been achieved.[81] "In communism," as Ollman puts it, "all material goods have become as abundant as water is today . . . the community stores are replete with everything a communist person could possibly want."[82] Under these conditions the satisfaction of one person's needs cannot be achieved at the expense of the satisfaction of anyone else's needs; one person's gain can no longer be another's loss. Thus, "in an economy of superabundance where everyone has all that he needs and wants, the question of distributive justice no longer arises."[83] The conquest of scarcity obviates the necessity of politics.

But is the conquest of scarcity really possible in a society such as the one Marx envisions, a society predicated on the unfettered and continuous development of the productive forces? The level of abundance, as Sahlins has emphasized, is not determined by the sheer quantity of goods and services these forces engender but rather by the relationship between these use-values and the needs to which they respond/give rise.[84] Unless it can be demonstrated that needs will not outrun use-values, there is no reason to assume that the conquest of scarcity is possible, no matter how developed the forces of production. Marx alludes to this problem in *Capital*, where he points out that "with [Man's] development this realm of physical necessity expands as a result of his wants," and he tries, but fails, to resolve it in his very next breath when he adds "but, at the same time, the forces of production which satisfy these wants also increase."[85] Since he goes on to argue that the "realm of necessity" will progressively contract, while the "realm of freedom" or genuinely free time will progressively expand, he must be assuming that the development of the forces of production will not only keep pace with, but actually surpass, the development of human wants. But why should this be the case? If, as Marx argues elsewhere, human production is distinctively human precisely because every act of production creates new needs in the process of satisfying old ones, should we not rather conclude that the reverse will be the case, that individuals will perpetually experience wants that cannot be satisfied without the further development of the productive forces?[86] It

---

[81] Marx, *Critique of the Gotha Program*, in Tucker, *The Marx-Engels Reader*, p. 388. The unprecedented development of the productive forces is, according to Marx, the "absolutely necessary practical premise [of Communism], because without it *want* is generalized and with want the struggle for necessities and all the old filthy business would necessarily be reproduced." Cited in Murray Bookchin, *Post-Scarcity Anarchism* (Berkeley: Ramparts Press, 1971), p. 89.

[82] Ollman, *Social and Sexual Revolution*, pp. 74-75.

[83] Nicholas Rescher, *Distributive Justice* (New York: Bobbs-Merril, 1966), p. 107.

[84] Marshall Sahlins, "La Première société d'abondance," *Les Temps modernes*, 268 (October 1968), pp. 641-80.

[85] Tucker, *The Marx-Engels Reader*, p. 320.

[86] *The German Ideology*, p. 120. Norman O. Brown, *Life Against Death* (New York: Vintage Books, 1954), pp. 18, 259.

would appear, then, that a society predicated on the unfettered and continuous development of these forces cannot "conquer," but must rather be dominated by, scarcity.[87] If scarcity engenders the "filthy business" of competition and conflict, which precludes the implementation of the principle of distribution according to need, it follows that a society based on a perpetually expanding technological dynamic cannot, *pace* Marx, distribute its products according to this principle. To the contrary: such a society must have recourse to "principles of right and justice," i.e., to politics, as the condition of its very possibility.[88]

The converse of the proposition that a technologically unlimited society cannot overcome scarcity and thus cannot distribute its product according to need is that the overcoming of scarcity and the possibility of distribution according to need can only be realized in a society that deliberately limits the development of its productive forces. Thus Sahlins has argued that "primitive" hunting and gathering societies were the first real "societies of abundance" precisely because their material needs were so radically limited that they were able to satisfy them in a minimum amount of time, leaving by far the better part of their waking hours available for a variety of nonworking social interactions.[89] Similarly, Whitebook has recently reminded us that the ability of Athenian citizens to participate directly and extensively in the affairs of the *polis* was predicated not only on the fact that production was undertaken by slaves but also on the fact that it was undertaken on behalf of material needs that were, compared to those of "modern" societies, drastically limited.[90] In both cases—indeed, perhaps in the case of all precapitalist societies—the development of needs and the productive forces that engender/fulfill them was radically constrained by a collective "decision" to pursue certain needs and productive techniques and to exclude other needs and techniques. (Marx himself realizes this, without appreciating the extent to which it undermines his conception of human nature as a dialectic of self-constitution through objectification, when he argues, in *Capital* that "the technical basis

[87] Ernest Mandel tries to defend the notion of the conquest of scarcity (and thus the "withering away" of the state) under communism with the argument that "basic needs" are limited and "stable" and are thus amenable to relatively easy satisfaction, satisfaction that enables communist men and women increasingly to experience nonmaterial or "cultural" needs. The first part of this argument runs directly contrary to what we have just identified as the argument of Marx. The second is simply a *non sequitur*: that material needs may be progressively supplanted by nonmaterial ones says nothing about whether this latter category of needs will be experienced as "scarce" and thus, on both Marx's and Mandel's assumptions, give rise to conflicts of interest. Ernest Mandel, *Marxist Economic Theory*, Vol. II (New York: Monthly Review Press, 1968), pp. 660-64. See also Heller, *The Theory of Need in Marx*.

[88] See the appendix to Chapter Three.

[89] Sahlins, *La Première société d'abondance*.

[90] Joel Whitebook, "Pre-Market Economics: The Aristotelian Perspective," *Dialectical Anthropology*, 3 (August 1978), pp. 197-220.

of [modern] industry is . . . revolutionary, while all other modes of production were essentially conservative."[91] What he fails to realize, however, is that the "conservative" nature of precapitalist modes of production is not the result of an inability to "master" nature, but rather of an unwillingness to attempt to do so.)[92] What we retrospectively identify as precapitalist "economies" were, in Polanyi's terms, "embedded" in a political and moral "matrix" that determined the legitimate ends on behalf of which "economic" activity could be undertaken. Any future society that sought to overcome scarcity would similarly be obliged to discriminate between legitimate and illegitimate needs and to establish priorities among the former, i.e., would have to re-embed the economy within a political matrix. The problem of transcending scarcity obliges us to pose the problem of limiting needs, and the problem of limiting needs demands that we pose the problem—the imminently political problem—of "the needs and capacities that a society ought to create."[93]

From this perspective, the Marxian principle of "to each according to his needs" begs the prior, essential question of "which needs?" The argument that "basic needs" must be satisfied equally obscures the fact that a people must first determine what its "basic needs" should be. Marx tells us in volume III of *Capital* that a good society will minimize the time and energy that its members devote to the satisfaction of basic needs (the "realm of necessity") and thereby maximizes the time and energy they have for the pursuit of needs that transcend "mundane considerations" (the realm of freedom).[94] But whether such a society will be a good society depends entirely on the quality of the needs it has "decided" to pursue.[95] He tells us that the "associated producers" must "rationally regulate" the realm of necessity in order to bring it under their "common control," and he thereby subordinates "association" and "community" to the instrumental imperative of administering "necessity," forgetting (or, better, never realizing) that what counts as "necessity"—basic needs—must first be communally established.[96] He wants the economic realm of necessity to constitute the foundation for a collective enterprise that is purely administrative, and thus fails to understand that this economic realm must itself be collectively, i.e., politically, constituted. The irreducibility of

[91] Marx, *Capital* Vol. I, p. 486.

[92] Baudrillard, *The Mirror of Production*, Chs. 3-4.

[93] Castoriadis, "From Marx to Aristotle, From Aristotle to Us," p. 725.

[94] Tucker, *The Marx-Engels Reader*, pp. 319-20.

[95] Marx once poses to himself the "question about the system of needs . . . at what point is this to be dealt with" (*Grundrisse*, p. 528), but nowhere addresses himself to its answer. See Marshall Sahlins, *Culture and Practical Reason* (Chicago: University of Chicago Press, 1976), pp. 148, 151, 169.

[96] Albrecht Wellmer, *Critical Theory of Society* (New York: Herder and Herder, 1971), p. 117.

118

politics, then, consists not only in the fact that the "automatic" regulation or distribution of needs is impossible but also, and even more fundamentally, in the fact that politics is necessarily involved in their very creation.

I have argued that Marx's vision of a completely consensual society that dispenses with politics is a hopelessly utopian vision. That this vision is not only utopian but also dangerous becomes clear if we consider for a moment another contemporary mode of thought that partakes of this conception, namely the so-called "technocracy thesis." According to this thesis, democratic political decision-making or conflict resolution mechanisms have become or should become obsolete in the advanced industrial or postindustrial societies, and are being or should be replaced by exclusively technical mechanisms of system management. This argument is normally predicated on a conception of "the end of ideology," i.e., the notion that all fundamental problems of ends have already been solved so that the problems that remain are problems of means that admit of a purely technical or instrumental solution. In short, the essence of the technocracy thesis is that, under conditions of contemporary industrial societies, rationality is or should become increasingly exhausted by the logic of instrumental rationality; thus those mechanisms for political decision making or conflict resolution predicated on another, noninstrumental rationality have become or are becoming superfluous at best and harmful at worst, and are being or should be replaced by mechanisms that will respond effectively to the exclusively instrumental "steering" problems that remain to be solved.[97]

Marxists have correctly exposed the ideological nature of this thesis, arguing persuasively that it mystifies the fact that decisively important political choices remain endemic to capitalism—above all, the choice of capitalism or socialism—and that this mystification, in turn, contributes to the depoliticization of the population on which the reproduction of capitalism increasingly rests.[98] Yet it should be clear by now that Marx does for the future communist society precisely what the technocracy thesis does for capitalist society! Although they differ in their assessment of exactly when politics and conflict come to an end, their basic logic is identical: politics and conflict come to an end once a certain level of technological development has been reached. It is not unfair to say, then, that Marx projects a technocratic vision of the future society that can be subjected to precisely the same critique that Marxists typically address to contemporary exponents of the technocracy thesis. Marx's vision of the purely administrative nature of "general functions" under communism mystifies the fact that decisively important political choices will persist, even

[97] Jurgen Habermas, *Legitimation Crisis* (Boston: Beacon Press, 1975), Part III.

[98] Ike Balbus, "Politics as Sports: An Interpretation of the Political Ascendency of the Sports Metaphor in America," in Leon N. Lindberg et al., eds., *Stress and Contradiction in Modern Capitalism* (Lexington: Lexington Books, 1975), pp. 321-36.

in that society, and thereby contributes to a depoliticization of the population of this society. Because the vision is premised on the assumption that political choices have become superfluous, it necessarily functions to insulate those that remain—and must remain—from democratic critique and control. Just as the technocracy thesis can be and has been employed to legitimate the degeneration of democratic political forms and activities under conditions of advanced capitalism, so too Marx's thesis of the a-political society can be used to legitimate the "withering away" of democracy under communism.

His theory, in other words, is speechless at best and conciliatory at worst before the problem of the emergence, or the reemergence, of political domination in communist society. Insofar as politics, as we have seen, is inescapable in this society, like any other, so too is the danger of political domination. The inevitable persistence of conflicts over ends necessarily entails the possibility that force or other forms of domination will be employed in order to resolve these conflicts. Thus, contrary to Marx, "the distribution of general functions" will *always* "afford room for domination." Whether domination will come to occupy this room remains an open question, but what is certain is that a theory which refuses to recognize politics in the future society is scarcely in a position to recognize, let alone prepare for, this danger.[99] The absence of a theory of politics for the future society necessarily entails the absence of a critique of political domination in this society.

At the same time, the absence of a theory of liberatory politics also implies the absence of principled guidelines for the political forms appropriate for the struggle against capitalism, i.e., for the transition to socialism. It follows from the principle that ends and means are inextricably intertwined that the forms of political struggle against capitalism must anticipate, however partially or imperfectly, the forms of politics to be created under socialism. The question of anticapitalist practice, in other words, should not be conceived

[99] That Marx anticipates that the administrators of communist society will be elected, and that, according to Richard N. Hunt's *The Political Ideas of Marx and Engels* (Pittsburgh: Pittsburgh University Press, 1974) and Mandel's *Marxist Economic Theory*, he also implies that they should be subject to the immediate recall of the citizens and that all citizens, through rotation, will eventually perform administrative functions, does not really speak to the question of this danger. As we have seen, Marx recommends these procedures precisely because "the [general] functions have ceased to be political" and there is no longer "any room for domination"; they are not intended as safeguards against the possibility of domination but as mechanisms for a routine or business-like distribution of purely administrative functions. Whatever Marx's intentions, moreover, the fact is that these procedures cannot preclude the emergence of administrative domination. The definition of an inescapably political problem as a technical problem is itself the problem, as this definition, once accepted, encourages the electors to defer to the greater technical expertise of the "representatives." It was Bakunin, not Marx, who anticipated and appreciated this problem of domination based on a (professed) monopoly of knowledge. See John Clark, "Marx, Bakunin and the Problem of Social Transformation," *Telos*, No. 42 (Winter 1979-80), pp. 80-97, and Albert and Hahnel, *Unorthodox Marxism*, p. 267.

as a purely instrumental, strategic one, but rather one that can only be answered in the light of an analysis of the political practice appropriate to a genuinely socialist society. Without such an analysis of specifically socialist political ends, there can be no adequate conception of anticapitalist political means. Under these conditions, anticapitalist practice is likely either to degenerate into the unprincipled search for the most efficient means to achieve anticapitalist ends (as in the case of Stalinism) or to be guided by principles that are not specifically socialist, i.e., not grounded in the assumptions of the theory but, rather, borrowed from other theories and thus ad hoc in character (as in the case of Eurocommunist appeals to the virtues of representative democracy and "pluralism").[100] To return to our earlier discussion, there is no way to establish the validity of a "reformist," "dual power," or "combination" conception of the transition to socialism without a principled theory of socialist politics—a theory of liberatory politics—but Marx offers no such theory.

Marxist Conceptions of Socialist Politics after Marx

That Marx himself offers no such theory does not demonstrate that this theory cannot be erected on Marxist foundations. Surely, however, it is no accident that 100 years after Marx wrote, it remains possible for two recent students of the subject to conclude that "no orthodox Marxist has been able to come up with a convincing theory of the socialist state or even of socialist organisations,"[101] and that "if by 'socialism' we mean what Marx used to call the higher stage of communist society, the question of the political superstructure that will be adequate to it is raised neither in theory nor in practice."[102] That there is an absence of a principled theory of socialist politics not only in Marx but in Marxism as a whole immediately suggests the plausibility of my claim that such a theory cannot be derived from the constitutive assumption of Marxism, i.e., the primacy of production. It is now time to substantiate this claim by examining briefly two radically different Marxist approaches that proceed from this assumption yet repudiate Marx's a-political vision of a completely harmonious, conflict-free communist society.

Consider first the thoughts of Chairman Mao. Abandoning Marx's naive, perhaps eschatological vision of the end of conflict under communism, Mao emphasizes the inevitable persistence of "contradictions," albeit "nonantag-

---

[100] See, for example, Santiago Carillo, *"Eurocommunism" and the State* (London: Lawrence and Wishart, 1971), Chs. 4, 6.

[101] Victor M. Perez-Diaz, *State, Bureaucracy and Civil Society* (London: Macmillan Press Ltd., 1978), p. 113.

[102] Arghiri Emmanuel, "The State in the Transition Period," *New Left Review*, Nos. 113-114 (January-April 1979), p. 111. As I will argue below, the very way in which Emmanuel formulates the problem—a political *superstructure* appropriate for socialism—is part of the problem itself.

121

onistic'' in nature, in this society. (That these contradictions will be ''non-antagonistic'' follows definitionally from the assumption that communism is a classless society and the assumption that only class conflicts are ''antagonistic.'' Whether this is a ''useful'' definition is something the now-defeated partisans of the Cultural Revolution might well wish to contemplate.) Given the assumption of the primacy of production, it follows, for Mao, that ''the basic contradictions in socialist society are still those between the relations of production and the productive forces,''[103] i.e., that conflict among ends that is rooted in production is ineradicable. Given the ineradicability of such conflict, organizational mechanisms for the resolution of conflict, that is, political institutions, will necessarily be central to, rather than absent in, the fully developed socialist society of the future. A theory of politics for this society is thus not foreclosed by, but is rather consistent with, Mao's Marxist assumption of the primacy of production.

But what kind of political theory would this be? If politics is understood as an activity that takes place outside production—as Mao understands it—then, on the assumption of the primacy of production, politics will necessarily be conceived as a mere ''superstructure'' that is dependent on or subordinate to the realm of production. As a means to an end outside itself, as an instrument in the service of prepolitical, economic needs, the political institution must (barring recourse to a presocialist concept of presocial ''individual rights'') be evaluated in purely instrumental terms. That is, it will be evaluated exclusively according to its effectiveness as a mechanism for the resolution of production-based conflicts. Political forms, on this conception of the ''political,'' admit of purely relative, rather than principled judgments. It should come as no surprise, then, that Mao informs us that: ''Democracy seems to be an end, but it is in fact only a means. Marxism teaches that democracy is part of the superstructure and belongs to the realm of politics. That is to say, in the last analysis, it serves the economic base. Both Democracy and freedom are relative, not absolute.''[104] Thus Mao demonstrates that when politics is understood as a nonproduction activity, a principled theory of socialist politics cannot in fact be deduced from the assumption of the primacy of production.

Like the Maoist tradition, the Council Communist tradition abandons Marx's vision of a consensual society, and with it his theory of the replacement of politics with administration. Unlike Mao, however, Council Communist thinkers are committed to a principled theory of participatory democracy for the communist society of the future. Thinkers like Anton Pannekoek and Herman Gorter argued that federations of workers councils would provide the institutional framework for a workers' self-management that is conceived as both

[103] Stuart R. Schram, *The Political Thought of Mao Tse-Tung* (New York: Praeger, 1963), p. 240.
[104] *Ibid.*, p. 239.

the means and the end of revolutionary struggle.[105] As the identification of self-management with *workers'* self-management implies, however, this principled commitment to participatory democracy was purchased at the price of the collapse of the distinction between politics and production, and thus of a drastic reduction in the scope of democratic decision making. In short, a noninstrumental theory of participatory politics is consistent with the assumption of the primacy of production only on the condition that politics is identified with production and the meaning of democracy is reduced to workplace democracy.

This reduction is unsatisfactory: a theory of workplace democracy cannot in fact stand as an adequate theory of liberatory politics for the future society. The Council Communist emphasis on the point of production as *the* unit of self-management follows necessarily from the Marxian theory that production is *the* activity through which human needs and capacities develop and unfold. But this chapter has demonstrated that this theory cannot be sustained. Neither the needs of political actors in contemporary capitalist societies nor the needs of political actors in the genuinely socialist societies of the future can legitimately be interpreted as originating exclusively in the mode of production of these societies. Neither (the need for) political domination nor (the need for) political liberation is merely a function of production. It follows that self-government cannot be reduced to what Marx always called "the self-government of the producers": if human needs are constituted in activities other than production, then human beings require self-management in all the institutions in which these activities are performed.[106] The assumption of the primacy of production obfuscates this requirement and leads to what is, at best, a decidedly partial theory of participatory democratic politics. It follows, finally, that a more complete theory of participatory democratic politics demands that we abandon this assumption.

The Maoist and Councilist approaches are the only logically possible solutions to the problem of politics that can be derived from the assumption of the primacy of production. If production is defined as the essential activity, then politics will inevitably be reduced to production, either in the sense that it will be deemed less essential than production (Mao) or in the sense that it will be identified with production (Councilist). The inevitable result is either an unprincipled, instrumental theory of politics that extends beyond the realm of production or a principled theory of politics that is restricted to production. In short, neither Mao nor the Council Communists—nor, indeed, the Marxist

[105] Richard Gombin, *The Radical Tradition* (New York: St. Martin's Press, 1978), pp. 81-118; Stanley Aronowitz, "Left-Wing Communism: The Reply to Lenin," in Dick Howard and Karl E. Klare, eds., *The Unknown Dimension* (New York: Basic Books, 1972), pp. 169-94.

[106] Bookchin, *Post-Scarcity Anarchism*, pp. 146-47; Albert and Hahnel, *Unorthodox Marxism*, Ch. 7.

123

tradition as a whole—is able to develop a principled theory of politics that extends beyond the realm of production. Thus the search for this theory entails the examination of other theoretical traditions.

APPENDIX TO CHAPTER THREE

The argument that the conquest of scarcity eliminates conflict is often accompanied by other, equally unpersuasive, arguments in favor of the obsolescence of politics under communism. One is that the individuals in this society will no longer be self-interested but will rather identify their individual interests with the interests of the entire society; solidarity eliminates the possibility of conflict and thus the necessity for mechanisms of conflict-resolution. The problem with this argument, on the one hand, is that Marx and Marxists typically maintain that the creation of solidarity is contingent on the elimination of scarcity, in which case the argument is necessarily as weak as the "conquest of scarcity" argument with which it is inseparably intertwined. On the other hand, it is not in fact the case that the existence of solidarity precludes the possibility of conflict. Even if we were to assume that each member of communist society, insofar as he or she were no longer self-interested, willingly devoted him/herself to the general interest, we should regularly expect (as in the case of the members of "our" orchestra) to encounter divergent interpretations of exactly what this interest entails. Thus the necessity for principles and mechanisms of conflict-regulation would remain. This, of course, is precisely the problem that Rousseau tried to paper over with his assertion that the general will is "always right."

Another, somewhat different argument is that under communism each producer will necessarily discover that his or her self-interest is identical to the self-interest of every other producer. Since, according to Marx, true wealth is nothing but "disposable time" (cited in Heller, *The Theory of Need in Marx*, p. 127), it follows that each producer will strive for the reduction of labor time, which, in turn, demands the "maximum of rationalization" of the labor-process. The overriding shared interest in this rationalization thus eliminates the possibility of conflict. But this interest is not the exclusive interest of the producers, and it is doubtful that it can legitimately be described as "overriding." On the one hand, it is obliged to compete with their need for material use-values, which need, *ceteris paribus*, may well incline them (or some of them) to work *longer*. On the other hand, Marx tells us in the *Critique of the Gotha Program* that under communism labor "has become life's prime want" (Tucker, *The Marx-Engels Reader*, p. 388), which seems to suggest that the producers will find even "necessary" labor too rewarding

124

merely to strive, in single-minded fashion, for its progressive diminution. For both reasons, it is impossible to demonstrate that there will necessarily be a convergence of self-interest that obviates the possibility of conflicting goals and thus the necessity of principles and mechanisms to resolve them.

After completing this chapter, I discovered that similar objections to Marx's thesis of the obsolescence of politics under communism have been made in Carmen Sirianni, "Production and Power in a Classless Society: A Critical Analysis of the Utopian Dimension of Marxist Theory," *Socialist Review*, 59 (September-October 1981), p. 54. See also erratum, *Socialist Review*, 61 (January-February 1982), p. 6.

CHAPTER FOUR

MARXIST THEORIES OF
REPRESSIVE TECHNOLOGY

THE ECOLOGY MOVEMENT

The 1960s and 1970s will be remembered as a period during which ecology became a mass movement in the advanced capitalist societies of the West. Prior to this time, concern for the preservation of the natural environment had largely been the preoccupation of the members of a "leisure class" whose liberation from industrial production afforded them the time and energy to decry the effects of this production on a nature that they alone were in a position to enjoy. Until the 1960s, moreover, environmentalism was something of an ideological aberration, running as it did against the grain of a conventional wisdom that equated progress with a growing material abundance whose only possible foundation was the unlimited exploitation of whatever natural resources happened to be available. Suddenly, in the late 1960s and early 1970s, large numbers of people of all descriptions came, for the first time in the history of the capitalist West, to call this "wisdom" into question and to mobilize themselves on behalf of the heretofore unthinkable proposition that there were, and should be, "limits to growth."[1] And so ecology became a major political movement of the 1970s, insinuating itself through the fissures of an increasingly discredited ideology of growth and embodying an entirely different conception of the appropriate relationship between human beings and their natural surround.

The devastating effect of decades of capitalist growth on this surround was, of course, a principal precipitant of this movement. The hegemony of the ideology of growth was bound to be challenged once it became apparent that this growth had turned American and European rivers into sewers, air into smog, and food into a threat to, rather than a source of, life itself. Beaches desecrated by oil-spills and hills ravaged by strip-mining helped transform thousands of people into "friends of the earth." Growing awareness of the risks of radiation encouraged increasing resistance to nuclear power as well

[1] The title of an influential, and controversial environmentalist manifesto, Donella H. Meadows, *et al.* (New York: Universe, 1972).

126

as the commitment to replace it with the power of the sun. A reaction against the poisonous chemicals used in processed foods stimulated the demand for simpler, more "natural" foods. Large-scale ugliness provoked many to conclude, with E. F. Schumacher, that "small is beautiful."[2] The demand to set limits to growth was at least in part a response to the increasingly intolerable burdens that the normal, everyday operations of a capitalist mode of production impose on our "spaceship earth."

There are those who would argue that this demand nevertheless helps to sustain the operations of this mode of production: the ideology of inherent limits to growth both obfuscates and legitimates the specifically capitalist limits to growth that have forcefully reasserted themselves throughout the past decade. It is certainly true that the demand to "think small" and lower our material expectations is conveniently consonant with the current inability of many Western capitalist societies to fulfill these expectations; the antigrowth ideology of the ecology movement has been used as a means of propping up the legitimacy of a mode of production that is currently in the midst of a prolonged period of decline.[3] But this short-run convergence of capitalist interests and environmentalism in no way exhausts the ideological significance of the latter, and merely obscures a fundamental incompatibility between them. In the long run, a system predicated on the assumption of unlimited expansion can only be hindered by a movement that is dedicated to the proposition that there are inherent limits to growth. A movement that asserts that production must respect the claims of nature must ultimately become an obstacle to a system in which production respects the claims of profit alone. The "friends of the earth" cannot forever be friends of a mode of production for which the land is but a "factor of production," "raw material" for human exploitation. For all these reasons, and many others, ecology is truly a "subversive science";[4] those who practice it do so on the basis of needs that capitalism is structurally incapable of satisfying.

Many environmentalists, like Barry Commoner, have come to understand this and have therefore argued that an ecological perspective demands an explicitly anticapitalist perspective.[5] Thinkers who have sought to draw out the implications of an ecological awareness for a theory of the good society are well aware that this society cannot be capitalist.[6] Those who have labored

[2] *Small is Beautiful* (New York: Harper & Row, 1973).

[3] For a discussion of this issue, see Hans Magnus Enzenberger, "A Critique of Political Ecology," in Alexander Cockburn and James Ridgeway, eds., *Political Ecology* (New York: Times Books, 1979).

[4] Paul Shepard and Daniel McKinley, eds., *The Subversive Science* (New York: Scribner's, 1969).

[5] Barry Commoner, *The Closing Circle* (New York: Bantam Books, 1974).

[6] See, for example, William Ophuls, *Ecology and the Politics of Scarcity* (San Francisco: W. H. Freeman and Company, 1977).

127

to create decentralized "alternative technologies" that respond to the demands of the ecosphere understand that their efforts are directed against a corporate order whose large-scale, centralized technologies do not. In short, many of the theorists and practitioners of ecology are already ardent anticapitalists.

Unlike their colleagues within the anticapitalist Old Left, however, they conceive of the elimination of capitalism as the necessary, but certainly not the sufficient, condition for the elimination of environmental degradation. As we shall see, the persistence of pollution and other forms of ecologically unsound practice within the state socialist societies obliges ecologists to conclude that collective ownership of the means of production and "production for use" no more guarantees an end to the domination of nature than it automatically produces the elimination of patriarchy or bureaucracy. In fact, they argue that a socialism committed to the overriding goal of growth through large-scale, energy-depleting technologies will, in all likelihood, be every bit as destructive to the environment as capitalism.[7] The environmentalists have taught us, in other words, that an ecologically sound socialism cannot be constructed on the same technological base as capitalism and, consequently, that the transition from capitalism to socialism must entail a transformation in the quality or form—and not merely the quantity or application—of the tools and machines with which productive activity is undertaken. An adequate theory of the domination of nature and the possibilities for its "liberation" thus demands a compelling explanation of the origins and persistence of repressive technology as well as a persuasive vision of an alternative, liberatory technology and the conditions for its realization. We shall now see whether Marxist theory satisfies these demands.

MARX'S THEORY OF TECHNOLOGY

Embracing both the tools with which humans labor and the associated way in which this labor is organized, technology, according to Marx, "discloses man's mode of dealing with Nature, the process of production by which he sustains his life, and thereby also lays bare the mode of formation of his social relations, and of the mental conceptions that flow from them."[8] Technology is then, in the broadest sense, synonymous with production. It follows that Marx's theory of human development through productive activity is nothing other than a general theory of technological development, and that his theory of determination by the mode of production asserts the primacy of the specific mode or form of technology that predominates within any par-

---

[7] Commoner, *The Closing Circle*, pp. 278-79; Ophuls, *Ecology and the Politics of Scarcity*, p. 204.

[8] Marx, *Capital*, Vol. I, p. 372.

ticular society or historical epoch. Thus his analysis of the capitalist mode of production is simultaneously an analysis of the form of technology that predominates within a specifically capitalist society or, alternatively, of the specifically capitalist form of technology (I shall return to the ambiguity signalled by these "alternative" formulations shortly).

In the most general sense, then, our discussion in Chapter One of Marx's treatment of production, mode of production, and capitalist mode of production was an implicit discussion of his theory of technology, and our analysis of the ambiguities, even contradictions, within Marx's treatment of production constituted an indirect analysis of the ambiguities and contradictions in this theory of technology. We saw, for example, that Marx conceives the capitalist mode of production as both the acme of human alienation and the material basis of its transcendence, and that his theory of proletarian revolution fails to resolve this persistent ambivalence in which labor under capitalism is simultaneously conceived as a source of human enslavement and a source of genuinely "radical" needs. We should not be surprised to discover that Marx's treatment of technology under capitalism is similarly ambivalent, and that this ambivalence is likewise never resolved. It is now time to make this explicit. Marx wavers between a conception of technology under capitalism as inherently repressive and a conception of technology under capitalism as potentially liberatory, and he never overcomes the opposition between these antithetical conceptions. Despite his and subsequent Marxist efforts to synthesize these conceptions, there remain two inconsistent Marxist theories of technology and capitalism. Neither, I shall argue, satisfies the demands of an adequate theory.

The "Optimistic" Theory: The Primacy of the Forces of Production

A mode of production, we have seen, entails a characteristic form of appropriating surplus labor, which "conforms naturally to a specific development of the manner and mode of labor and thereby to its societal productive power."[9] Although his terminology is never completely consistent,[10] Marx generally refers to the mode of appropriation or effective ownership as the "social relations of production" and the "manner and mode of labor" as the "forces of production." Thus a mode of production entails a "correspondence between the forces of production (technical equipment and organization of

[9] See above, Chapter One, n. 60.

[10] Ollman, *Alienation*, Ch. 1; Anthony Giddens, *The Class Structure of the Advanced Societies* (New York: Harper Torchbooks, 1975), Ch. 2; Ramesh Mishra, "Technology and Social Structure in Marx's Theory: An Exploratory Analysis," *Science & Society*, Vol. 43, (Summer 1979), p. 135.

labor) and the social relations . . . of production."[11] This correspondence, however, is inherently unstable and, in fact, embodies a contradiction that acts as the motor of historical development. Thus the famous *Preface* to the *Critique of Political Economy* announces that: "At a certain stage of their development, the material productive forces of society come into conflict with the existing relations of production . . . within which they have been at work hitherto. From forms of development of the productive forces these relations turn into their fetters. Then begins an epoch of social revolution."[12]

Here we have the schematic outline of Marx's "optimistic" theory of technology. Within the contradictory unity that is a mode of production, the forces of production play the progressive role, while the social relations of production play the conservative role. The former embody humanity's future, the latter humanity's past. It is the forces of production, in other words, that are the seeds of the new mode of production that germinate within the existing mode of production. The social relations of production, on the other hand, inevitably come to function as a constraint or "fetter" on the growth of these seeds and thus on the new order that they anticipate. Within this contradiction, however, it is the forces of production that are ultimately determinant, for, in the long run, they shatter the social relations of production that can no longer contain them. The transition from one mode of production to another is thus, at bottom, a result of continuous technological development, and the succession of modes of production is for this reason deemed "progressive."[13] In short, the assumption that the forces of production embody the potential for human development and the assumption that the forces of production ultimately determine human history lead inexorably to the conclusion that human history is a history of human development.

It is not my intention to evaluate this scheme as a general theory of technology, although it should be clear that its claim to transhistorical applicability is every bit as problematical as that of the general conception of a mode of production, of which it is an elaboration. My purpose is, rather, to describe and evaluate the way in which Marx applies this scheme to the specific case of the role of technology under capitalism and in the transition to socialism. The specific form of the contradiction between the forces of production and the social relations of production characteristic of a capitalist mode of production, Marx tells us, is the contradiction between the increasingly social character of technology and the purely private mode of appropriating its fruits. Thus socialism, as the definitive resolution of this contradiction, will be

[11] Daniel Bell, *The Coming of Post-Industrial Society* (New York: Basic Books, 1973), p. 72; Marx, *Preface* to *A Contribution to the Critique of Political Economy*, p. 4.

[12] *Ibid.*; see also Marx and Engels, *The German Ideology*, p. 160.

[13] Marx, *Preface* to *A Contribution to the Critique of Political Economy*, p. 5; see also Chapter One, above.

understood as the substitution of a properly social mode of appropriation for the private capitalist mode of appropriation and thus the restoration of a fundamental harmony between the social relations and the forces of production.

On the one hand, capitalist social relations of production encourage, as we saw in Chapter One, an unprecedented growth in the forces of production; the unlimited aim of surplus-value extraction sets in motion a seemingly unlimited process of technological development and thus an unparalleled expansion in human control over the natural environment:

> The bourgeoisie, during its rule of scarce one hundred years, has created more massive and more colossal productive forces than have all preceding generations together. Subjection of Nature's forces to man, machinery, application of chemistry to industry and agriculture, steam-navigation, railways, electric telegraphs, clearing of whole continents for cultivation, canalisation of rivers, whole populations conjured out of the ground— what earlier century had even a presentiment that such productive forces slumbered in the lap of social labour?[14]

The capitalist mode of production "raises the productiveness of labor to an extraordinary degree." It does so with the aid of the machine, which is, according to Marx, "its characteristic instrument [force] of production." As the "substitution of natural forces for human force," machine technology entails "the conscious application of science, instead of rule of thumb," to the process of production. Machine production is thus far more rational than previous forms of production: "The varied, apparently unconnected, and petrified forms of the industrial processes now resolved themselves into so many conscious applications of natural science to the attainment of given useful effects."[15] The capitalist mode of production, in short, is the first mode of production in history to enlist science as a force of production. Capitalism unites, in unprecedented fashion, theoretical knowledge of nature with the practical need to control and transform it, and for this reason, "it has been the first to show what man's activity can bring about."[16]

The unparalleled rationality of machine production is the basis for its incomparable efficiency: the application of natural scientific means to the ends of human production enables—at least in principle—an ever-expanding range of human ends to be achieved with an ever-receding expenditure of human energy. In the language of contemporary systems theory, the machine technology that develops under capitalism is capable of maximizing "output" and minimizing (human) "input." Therein lies its potential perpetually to

[14] Marx and Engels, *Manifesto of the Communist Party*, p. 339.
[15] Marx, *Capital*, Vol. I, pp. 387, 384, 386, 486.
[16] Marx and Engels, *Manifesto of the Communist Party*, p. 338.

augment "real wealth," which, for Marx, is nothing other than the ratio of output to input:

[T]o the degree that large industry develops, the creation of real wealth comes to depend less on labour time and on the amount of labour employed than on the power of the agencies set in motion during labour time, whose 'powerful effectiveness' is itself in turn out of all proportion to the direct labour time spent on their production, but depends rather on the general state of science and on the progress of technology, or the application of this science to production. . . . Real wealth manifests itself, rather—and large industry reveals this—in the monstrous disproportion between the labour time applied, and its product.[17]

Maximum output: the machine technology that develops under capitalism, as we have already seen, lays the foundation for a society of abundance in which there is so much to "go around" that, for the first time in history, the principle of "to each according to his needs" can regulate the distribution of the products of human labor.[18] The machine can abolish scarcity, and with it the competitive struggle for human survival that has been its inescapable product. The development in human productivity that the machine makes possible is the "absolutely necessary practical premise [of communism] . . . because without it *want* is generalized and with want the struggle for necessities and all the old filthy business would necessarily be reproduced."[19] The machine, source of unprecedented human mastery over nature, is thus at the same time the precondition for the heretofore impossible human mastery of human life itself.

Minimum input: the machine technology that develops under capitalism is capable of progressively reducing the amount of time that humans devote to material production, to the point where the age-old dream of liberation from burdensome toil can become a practical reality. On the one hand, this technology can maximize "disposable time outside that needed in direct production," thus making possible "the artistic, scientific, etc. development of the individuals in the time set free."[20] It is the machine, in other words, that will eventually enable "society [to] regulate the general production and thus make it possible for me to do one thing today and another tomorrow, to hunt in the morning, fish in the afternoon, rear cattle in the evening, criticise after dinner, just as I have a mind, without ever becoming hunter, fisherman, shepherd or critic."[21] Automated production promises the abolition of the

[17] Marx, *Grundrisse*, pp. 704-705.
[18] Marx, *Critique of the Gotha Program*, p. 388.
[19] Cited in Bookchin, *Post-Scarcity Anarchism*, p. 89.
[20] Marx, *Grundrisse*, p. 706.
[21] Marx and Engels, *The German Ideology*, p. 124.

division of labor within society and thus makes possible the "free development of individualities" which this division of labor necessarily obstructs.[22]

On the other hand, machine technology promises the elimination of the "despotic division of labor within the workshop" and thus can ensure that whatever remaining time that humans are obliged to devote to "direct production" is spent under the least debilitating, least degrading conditions possible. The productiveness of the machine, we have seen, is based not on labor-time but rather on "the general state of science and . . . on the application of this science to production." In principle, then, the operation of the machine is not predicated on "the theft of alien labour time" or on "command over surplus labour time" but rather on scientific knowledge, which can become the possession of all who work. Machine technology undermines the basis for the division within the workplace between mental and manual labor, and thus between those who rule and those who are ruled. Aristotle, whom Marx refers to as "the greatest thinker of antiquity," understood that

> If every tool, when summoned, or even of its own accord, could do the work that befits it, just as the creations of Daedalus moved of themselves, or the tripods of Hephaestos went of their own accord to their sacred work, if the weavers' shuttles were to weave of themselves, then there would be no need either of apprentices for the master workers, or of slaves for the lords.[23]

Modern machinery has the potential to transform Aristotle's fantasy into reality. It makes workers' control over production a practical possibility for the first time in history.

The liberatory promise of modern machinery, however, is systematically betrayed by the repressive social relations of the capitalist mode of production within which this machinery is confined. These social relations of production guarantee, in fact, that the result of the application of machines to the labor process is not maximum output and minimum input for all but, rather, maximum output and minimum input for the few (capitalists) and minimum output and maximum input for the many (workers). Thus, to begin with, the fact that production is undertaken for the private profit of the capitalist determines that abundance is a condition that applies to his situation alone and that poverty, not plenty, will be the situation of the great majority of human beings. Capitalist social relations dictate that the ability to procure use-values is a function of the exchange-value one possesses. At the same time, they determine that the exchange-value that the capitalist receives from the sale of goods produced by workers but controlled and distributed by him will be

[22] Marx, *Grundrisse*, p. 706.

[23] Marx, *Capital*, Vol. I, p. 408; the previous citations in this paragraph from Marx, *Grundrisse*, pp. 706, 707, and *Capital*, Vol. I, p. 356.

133

far greater than the exchange-value that the worker receives from the sale of his or her labor power to the capitalist. The inevitable result of capitalist relations of production is thus many use-values for the few (capitalists) and few use-values for the many (workers). At the same time the fact that machinery is set in motion by the capitalist for the purpose of maximizing surplus-value creates "the economic paradox, that the most powerful instrument for shortening labour-time, becomes the most unfailing means for placing every moment of the labourer's time . . . at the disposal of capital."[24] Not liberation from burdensome toil, but rather an increase in its intensity and/or its duration, is what modern industry brings the workers. Under capitalism, liberation from toil is the prerogative of the capitalist.

The contradiction between machinery and profit, moreover, is not merely moral. It also entails a fundamental structural incompatibility that is destined to shatter their temporary correspondence. Capitalists will invest in machinery, and productivity will consequently increase, only if they estimate that the eventual result of this investment will be the sale of goods or services at what they deem to be an adequate profit, i.e., only if they believe they will be able to "realize" their capital at a sufficiently high rate. Because they cannot know in advance what the demand for their goods and services will be, and because their own drive for maximum surplus-value obliges them to keep wages low and thus limit the purchasing power of the mass of consumers, there is a permanent likelihood that they will regularly overestimate their ability to realize their capital and thus that they will invest in machinery that they set in motion to produce goods and services that cannot in fact be sold. Thus what Marx calls "the epidemic of over-production" is endemic to the capitalist mode of production.[25]

> The productive forces . . . no longer tend to further the development of the conditions of bourgeois property; on the contrary, they have become too powerful for these conditions, by which they are fettered, and so soon as they overcome these fetters, they bring disorder into the whole of bourgeois society, endanger the existence of bourgeois property.[26]

The capitalists' response to overproduction, in turn, typically involves the "enforced destruction of a mass of productive forces."[27] Faced with declining profits, capitalists are obliged to reduce their costs of production by laying off workers and "disinvesting" in machinery, i.e., cutting back on their orders for new machines and letting the existing machines lay idle and rust. Economic crises in the forms of recessions are thus the periodic expression

[24] Marx, *Capital*, Vol. I, p. 408.
[25] Marx and Engels, *Manifesto of the Communist Party*, p. 340.
[26] *Ibid.*
[27] *Ibid.*; see also *Grundrisse*, pp. 749-50.

of the contradiction between the forces of production and the social relations of production in a capitalist mode of production.[28]

The cycle of overproduction-recession demonstrates that "beyond a certain point, the development of the powers of production becomes a barrier for capital" and "hence [that] the capital relation [becomes] a barrier for the development of the productive powers of labour."[29] The forces of production and the social relations of production, in other words, are mutually restrictive: each threatens the development of the other. The struggle between the forces and social relations of production, however, is not a perpetual stand-off: in the long run, the forces of production overpower the social relations of production and call forth the social relations of production they require. In the *Grundrisse*, Marx tells us that a certain point will be reached where:

> capital, i.e. wage labour, enters into the same relation toward the development . . . of the forces of production as the guild system, serfdom, slavery, and is necessarily stripped off as a fetter. The last form of servitude assumed by human activity, that of wage labour on one side, capital on the other, is thereby cast off like a skin.[30]

and, as we saw in Chapter One, in *Capital* he similarly foresees a time when:

> The monopoly of capital becomes a fetter upon the mode of production, which has sprung up and flourished along with, and under it. Centralisation of the means of production and socialization of labour at last reach a point where they become incompatible with their capitalist integument. The integument is burst asunder. The knell of capitalist private property sounds. The expropriators are expropriated.[31]

None of this of course happens automatically; the "expropriation of the expropriators" is the work of the proletariat. The "integument" will be "burst asunder," capitalist social relations will be "stripped off as a fetter," only insofar as this is willed by the working class. This will, however, is inscribed in the growth of the forces of production themselves: "with this . . . grows the revolt of the working class . . . , always increasing in numbers, and disciplined, united, organized by the very mechanism of the process of cap-

---

[28] Recessions are not the only expression of the contradiction between the forces and the social relations of production. Another is the difficulty, indeed absurdity, of continuing to make labor-time the measure of value when modern machinery progressively divorces productivity from human labor-time. Thus "Capital itself is the moving contradiction, [in] that it presses to reduce labour time to a minimum, while it posits labour time, on the other side, as sole measure and source of wealth." *Grundrisse*, p. 706.

[29] Marx, *Grundrisse*, p. 749.

[30] *Ibid.*

[31] Marx, *Capital*, Vol. I, p. 763.

italist production itself."[32] In the end, then, the proletariat merely executes the sentence on capital that has been pronounced by the forces of production.

It will also fall to the working class to establish the social relations of production that the burgeoning forces of production demand and thus to unleash fully the liberatory potential of the latter. The abolition of wage-labor and the introduction of control over the process of production by the "associated producers" themselves will enable humans to begin "rationally regulating their interchange with Nature, bringing it under their common control, instead of being ruled by it . . .; and achieving this with the least expenditure of energy and under conditions most favorable to, and worthy of, their human nature."[33] Socialist relations of production eliminate all fetters on the forces of production and thus pave the way for a prodigious increase in their development and the abundance that results from this development. At the same time, the abolition of wage-labor severs the link between human labor and human survival and thus dramatically accelerates the automation of the production process, the consequence of which is the progressive decrease in the length of the working day and increase in the availability of genuine free time. Machine technology thus makes possible both the rational regulation of the "realm of necessity" and the continual expansion of the "true realm of freedom" that can "blossom forth only with the realm of necessity as its basis."[34] Socialism is thus the realization of the liberatory promise of modern technology that capitalism betrays.

We are now in a position to question the "optimistic" theory of technology that we have just summarized. This theory, we have seen, asserts the primacy of the forces of production over the social relations of production in the sense that the former come, at least in the long run, to subvert and transform the latter. This primacy, however, is predicated on the assumption of the purely instrumental nature of the forces of production, i.e., on the assumption that the same modern machinery can produce radically different results depending on the nature of the purposes of those who control it. According to this conception, it is not the form of this machine technology (or the science of which it is the elaboration), but rather simply the goal on behalf of which it is set in motion that is specifically capitalist. Since the structure of modern machinery is not understood as intrinsically capitalist, it is possible to envision this structure as a potential obstacle to, and transformer of, the capitalist social relations within which it develops and is initially confined. If, on the other hand, this structure were infused from the very beginning with the logic of capitalist social relations, then we should not expect it to perform, even in the long run, a subversive function vis-à-vis these relations. Similarly, it

[32] *Ibid.*
[33] Marx, *Capital*, Vol. III, p. 320.
[34] *Ibid.*

follows from the instrumental conception that the same technology that serves repressive purposes under capitalism can serve liberatory purposes under socialism, and that it is therefore possible to comprehend the transition from capitalism to socialism as one that rests on a fundamental, unbroken technological continuity. If we were to assume, to the contrary, that there was an internal, rather than purely external, correspondence between the forces and social relations of production, i.e., if we were to argue that the machine technology that develops within the context of capitalist social relations interiorizes the logic of these relations, then we would have to conclude that this technology is per se repressive, and that the socialist project demands the construction of an alternative technology. Under these circumstances, in other words, the transition from capitalism to socialism would require a radical rupture of technological continuity, and socialism could not be conceptualized as the practical realization of the developmental logic of the forces of production.

The history of capitalist societies since Marx demonstrates the inadequacy of his purely instrumental conception. This has been a history of relative harmony, rather than fundamental inconsistency, between the forces and social relations of production. Despite periodic cycles of overproduction-recession, capitalist social relations have not been an insurmountable barrier to the development of modern technology and have, instead, been compatible with a growth in the forces of production that has been far more persistent and dramatic than Marx ever anticipated. Thus, on the one hand, the past one hundred years have witnessed a remarkable rise in the living standards of the mass of working people in capitalist societies; capitalist social relations have not prevented the forces of production from "delivering the goods" to the point where "comfortable repression," rather than absolute deprivation, is the fate of the better part of the Western working class. On the other hand, capitalist social relations have not impeded a progressive reduction in "disposable time," but rather have permitted the forces of production to develop to the point where the question of how to spend leisure time and how to "profit" from early retirement are among the most pressing questions that confront a large segment of the population. Thus the very promise of machine technology—material abundance and liberation from work—that Marx believed unrealizable in and, therefore, subversive of capitalism, has become the program of advanced capitalist societies themselves! In short, capitalist social relations have not been an unbearable fetter on the forces of production, and the forces of production have not been an insuperable obstacle to the persistence of capitalist relations of production. Over the long run, the forces of production have not played a subversive role vis-à-vis these relations, and there is no reason to expect that they will necessarily come to play such a

137

role in the future.[35] All this suggests that Marx's "optimistic," instrumental theory of technology has been undermined by the very development of capitalism itself.

Nor is this theory any better able to comprehend the role of technology under state socialism. According to the theory, the machine technology that develops within capitalism can, and must, be utilized in the construction of socialism. Indeed, it was this theory on which Lenin relied when he announced that socialism equals "Soviet power plus electrification" and when he urged that the "positive" side of Taylorism be adopted within Soviet industry.[36] Lenin believed, with the "optimistic" Marx, that the machine technology developed under capitalism could have liberatory rather than repressive consequences if this technology were controlled by those with specifically socialist rather than capitalist goals. But the entire history of state socialism disputes this contention. The use of unchanging technological means has not in fact been consistent with changed, that is, socialist goals. Machine technology has not eliminated the division between mental and manual labor, and workers in the Soviet Union and Eastern European state socialist societies remain every bit as divorced from genuine control over the means of production as their comrades in the West. Interestingly enough, the only state socialist society that made a serious effort to undermine the division between mental and manual labor and to install a measure of genuine worker's control was the one society that did not unambiguously embrace large-scale, centralized machine technologies and that did, in fact, attempt to develop a variety of alternative technologies. Now, however, we are witnessing in China a simultaneous introduction of Western technology and dismantling of worker's control and the assault on the division of labor. The present Chinese situation strikingly confirms the general proposition that state socialist reliance on the advanced technologies originally developed under capitalism has been subversive, rather than supportive, of the liberatory goals of these societies.

The fact that these technologies are set in motion on behalf of ostensibly socialist, rather than capitalist, ends has not prevented them from wreaking every bit as much havoc on the environment as they do in capitalist societies. Ophuls has concluded that, "With the sole exception of problems related to the mass use of private automobiles, which has not yet reached a significant level, Soviet pollution problems are in almost all respects identical with those found throughout the industrialized world."[37] Similarly, Barry Commoner has noted that:

[35] See Appendix A, Chapter Four.

[36] Rainer Traub, "Lenin and Taylor: The Fate of 'Scientific Management' in the (Early) Soviet Union," *Telos*, No. 37 (Fall 1978), pp. 82-92.

[37] Ophuls, *Ecology and the Politics of Scarcity*, p. 204.

138

environmental pollution in the Soviet Union is following about the same course that it has taken in capitalist countries. . . . In general, the modern technologies of the Soviet Union appear to be as counterecological as those introduced in to the United States economy. . . . [I]n the U.S.S.R.'s socialist system, the drive for "plan fulfillment", like the profit-motivated drive for productivity in the . . . private enterprise system, takes its toll on the ecosystem.[38]

State socialist technology is thus as repressive to the nature around it as it is to the human beings within it. It is, of course, always possible to argue that these societies are not really socialist societies and that, consequently, the repressiveness of their technologies does not refute the instrumentalist hypothesis that the industrial technology that initially develops under capitalism can have liberatory, rather than repressive, consequences under socialism. The problem with this line of argument is that it rescues the instrumentalist hypothesis at the cost of transforming it into a mere tautology. Any industrial society with a repressive technology will be defined as nonsocialist; thus no empirical evidence can be brought to bear on the proposition that existing industrial technology will be nonrepressive under socialism, and the proposition is really nothing other than an exercise in definition. To make the "nonrepressive use of contemporary industrial technology" part of the very definition of socialism, moreover, is to preclude rather than encourage the investigation of the possibility that at least part of the failure of past and present efforts to create a liberatory form of socialism results from their reliance on precisely this contemporary technology.

Finally, even if we grant that state socialist societies are not socialist societies, it remains the case, for reasons alluded to in Chapter Two, that they cannot legitimately be considered capitalist societies either. Thus, if the existence of repressive technologies in these societies does not disconfirm the thesis of nonrepressive large-scale technology under socialism, it does refute the hypothesis that capitalist relations of production are exclusively responsible for the repressiveness of contemporary industrial technology. Once we grant that this technology is equally repressive in the context of two different social relations of production, we must become skeptical of the explanatory power of an instrumental theory that attributes the repressiveness of an otherwise neutral technology exclusively to the social relations of production on behalf of which this technology is set in motion.

Thus the development of technology under both capitalism and state socialism tends to call into question the instrumentalist thesis of the potentially

[38] Commoner, *The Closing Circle*, pp. 278-79. For a more recent first-hand account, see *The Destruction of Nature in the Soviet Union* by Boris Komorov (White Plains, N.Y.: M. E. Sharpe, 1980).

139

liberatory character of contemporary industrial technology. It does not, and cannot, refute this thesis outright; evidence of what has been the case in the past and present can never itself prove that the case might not be radically different in the future. That machine technology has been able to flourish in the context of repressive capitalist social relations and that the consequences of this technology remain repressive under state socialist social relations does not demonstrate the sheer impossibility of putting this technology to liberatory use. Such a demonstration, in other words, requires a logical rather than merely empirical argument. This logical argument might run as follows: The assumption of the structural neutrality of the technology that develops under capitalism is inconsistent with the epistemological wholism of Marx, i.e., with the assumption that each part of capitalist society interiorizes the structure of the whole, and implies the very atomistic epistemology that Marx rejects. If Marx understands capitalism as an alienated totality, then how is it possible to argue that the structure of technology, and of the science that underlies it is entirely unalienated? The force of Marx's wholism, in other words, obliges us to argue that the form, and not merely the application, of contemporary technology is at least partly alienated. But, once we admit this, the vision of an entirely liberatory use of this technology is no longer credible. Alternatively, if we argue that science and technology escape capitalist alienation, then we must entertain the possibility that other practices and activities undertaken in a capitalist society may be similarly unalienated, and we run the risk of completely undermining Marx's theory of the pervasiveness of alienation under capitalism and thus of the pervasiveness of the social change necessary for the elimination of alienation. To put this another way: the proposition that the form of science and technology are uniquely untainted by capitalist alienation could only be justified if the objects of scientific and technological practice were naturally rather than culturally constituted; but Marx himself argues, in *The German Ideology*, that the objects of scientific practice are no less culturally constituted than any other: "Even this 'pure' natural science [physics and chemistry] is provided with its aim, as with its material, only through trade and industry, through the sensuous activity of men."[39] Thus Marx's resolutely socio-historical conception of human practice would appear to foreclose the possibility of a naturalistic justification for the thesis of an unalienated science and, consequently, for the instrumental theory of the potentially liberatory use of contemporary industrial technology. Conversely, if Marx's instrumentalist theory of technology is right, then it would appear that his general conception of human practice is wrong. Turn and twist as she might, the defender of Marx's "optimistic" theory of technology is unable to establish its consistency with the rest of his conceptual system.

[39] Tucker, *The Marx-Engels Reader*, p. 135.

Thus this conceptual system points to the necessity of an alternative theory of technology.

The "Pessimistic" Theory: The Primacy of the Social Relations of Production

I have already suggested that an alternative theory is, in fact, present within the body of Marx's writings. Indeed, much of his own analysis of the development of technology under capitalism constitutes an implicit repudiation of the very instrumental theory we have just reviewed. Whereas the optimistic theory asserts the primacy of the forces of production over capitalist social relations of production and thus conceives socialism as written into the very logic of an ineluctable technological progress, the "pessimistic" theory upholds the primacy of capitalist social relations over the forces of production and thus points to the conclusion that the construction of socialism cannot rely on, but rather demands a qualitative break with, the logic of technological progress under capitalism. According to this conception, in other words, the possibility of socialism cannot be grounded in the development of technology under capitalism since this technology is an intrinsically capitalist technology; thus the construction of alternative, socialist relations of production requires a parallel and simultaneous elaboration of an alternative technology.

This theory, in contrast to the first, never receives explicit formulation by Marx. It is, rather, implicit in his analysis, particularly in volume I of *Capital*, of the history of technological innovation under capitalism. Marx emphasizes that technological innovation was not an important precondition of the capitalist mode of production. This mode of production is founded not on the development of precapitalist forces of production but rather on a violent transformation of property relationships that Marx refers to as "primitive accumulation," i.e., "the historical process of divorcing the producer from the means of production."[40] Primitive accumulation, in other words, is the process through which peasants are expropriated from their land and transformed into landless proletarians who have only their labor to sell, and it is a process in which "conquest, enslavement, robbery, murder, briefly *force*, plays the great part."[41] It is a process, moreover, that leaves the existing means of production largely intact. Thus it is violence, rather than technique, that shatters feudal relations of production and replaces them with capitalist relations of production. Marx's own outline of the transition from feudalism to capitalism constitutes a denial of the primacy of the forces of production in this "epoch of social revolution" and thus an implicit repudiation of the

---

[40] Marx, *Capital*, Vol. I, p. 714.
[41] *Ibid.*, emphasis added.

general theory of technology announced in the *Preface* to the *Critique of Political Economy*.[42]

Since primitive accumulation shatters the property relations but not the technology of feudalism, it follows that the capitalist mode of production inherits a "manner and mode of labor" that is not immediately suited to its purposes. The subsequent development of this mode of production, Marx shows us, can be read as a history of the way in which capitalist social relations transform the preexisting techniques and organization of labor until they engender the forces of production they require. It is the drive for surplus-value that determines, from the very start, both the pace and the form of technological development under capitalism. Thus factory production, which is the characteristic innovation of the first period of capitalist development (which Marx refers to as "manufacture"), is not based on any significant prior technological innovation but relies originally on a technology that "is hardly to be distinguished . . . from the handicraft trades of the [feudal] guilds, otherwise than by the great number of workmen simultaneously employed by one and the same individual capital. The workshop of the medieval master handicraftsman is simply enlarged."[43] The factory is introduced, in short, not because technological development requires it but because continued artisan control over their craft was inconsistent with the effort of capitalists to extract maximum surplus-value from their labor. Stephen Marglin, following in the footsteps of Marx, has demonstrated that the concentration of artisanal production in factories was a result of the desire of capitalists to:

1) control and market the weaver's total production which, if not physically controlled in the factories, would have been partly embezzled;

2) maximize the input of work, i.e., compel the weavers to work longer hours at greater speed than they would have done had they remained the owners of their tools;

[42] For a recent denial of this conclusion and an effort to establish the consistency of Marx's account of the transition of feudalism to capitalism with the theory of the primacy of the forces of production outlined in the *Preface*, see Cohen, *Karl Marx's Theory of History: A Defence*, pp. 175-80. This effort, I would argue, is vitiated by a tendency to construe this theory so broadly that it comes true by definition. For example, Cohen argues that the fact that Marx denies that significant technological advances preceded the emergence of capitalist relations of production in no way demonstrates the inapplicability of his general thesis that social relations of production are transformed, and revolutions occur, when they act as fetters on the developing forces of production, because "not all fettering is of forces which already exist" (p. 177). The theory of the primacy of the forces of production is interpreted to entail the possibility that social relations of production change in anticipation of technological changes that have not yet occurred; thus Cohen rescues this theory only by taking refuge in teleology.

[43] Marx, *Capital*, Vol. I, p. 322.

3) take control of all technological innovation so as to use it for the sake of capital accumulation and not for purposes of more immediate interest;

4) organize production in such a way that the cycle of production could not dispense with the capitalist's function.[44]

Thus the factory is not the expression of an autonomous logic of scientific and technological development but instead the expression of the specific demands of capitalist relations of production. It is not a technical necessity but rather a necessity for profit. It "bears the imprint of capitalist relations of production,"[45] and as such should be considered a specifically capitalist form of the organization of labor.

The factory of the manufacturing period, however, is an imperfect form of capitalist labor organization. Although it "splits up . . . particular handicraft[s] into [their] various detail operations" and, in the process, "converts the labourer into a crippled monstrosity" whose "productive activity [is] a mere appendage of the capitalist's workshop," it is nevertheless still based on the "preponderating influence of . . . skilled" labor.[46] Thus "capital is constantly compelled to wrestle with the insubordination of the workmen," and, during the manufacturing period, "capital failed to become master of the whole disposable working-time of the . . . labourers."[47] The effort to overcome the resistance of skilled workers to exclusively capitalist control of the labor process, in turn, becomes a central impetus to the introduction of technological innovations designed to "de-skill" the labor force. It leads, in particular, to the introduction of modern machinery into the labor process.

Modern machinery "replaces the tool as the main instrument of labor" and thus "undermines the skill of the laborer as the foundation of production."[48] According to Marx:

the life-long speciality of *handling* one and the same tool, now becomes the life-long speciality of *serving* one and the same machine. . . . In handicrafts and manufacture, the workman makes use of a tool, in the factory, the machine makes use of him . . . In manufacture the workmen are parts of a living mechanism. In the factory [based on machinery] we

[44] This is Andre Gorz's summary of Marglin's research in the former's "Technical Intelligence and the Capitalist Division of Labor," *Telos*, No. 12 (Spring 1972), p. 32. Marglin's by now classic essay is entitled "What Do Bosses Do? The Origins and Functions of Hierarchy in Capitalist Production" and appeared in the *Review of Radical Political Economics*, 6 (Summer 1974), pp. 33-60.

[45] Gorz, "Technical Intelligence and the Capitalist Division of Labor," p. 32.

[46] Marx, *Capital*, Vol. I, pp. 338, 360-61, 367.

[47] *Ibid.*, pp. 367-68.

[48] Mishra, "Technology and Social Structure in Marx's Theory: An Exploratory Analysis," p. 142.

have a lifeless mechanism independent of the workman, who becomes its mere living appendage.[49]

The effect of the introduction of modern machinery into the labor process is the growth of the worker's dependence on the capitalist and the gradual elimination of the worker's resistance to his authority that plagued the capitalist during the manufacturing period. Machinery completes "the subjection of labour to capital" that was only partial, or "formal," during the manufacturing period, and thus helps to pave the way for a working class that "looks upon the conditions of [the capitalist] mode of production as self-evident laws of Nature."[50]

This account of the origins and functions of modern machinery consistently upholds the primacy of the social relations of production over the forces of production. It is the capitalist's effort to maximize surplus-value in the face of the workers' resistance to this effort that determines the process of technological development. The industrial revolution does not bring about capitalism; capitalism helps bring about the industrial revolution.[51] Like the factory itself, modern machinery is introduced into the labor process not because it is per se more efficient, but because, according to Marx, it is the most efficient "means for producing surplus-value."[52] Or, to put this another way, we can say, with Andre Gorz, that "capitalism uses the most efficient production technology only so far as the latter is compatible with maximum control and exploitation."[53] Thus machine technology can be considered an elaboration of "science" only insofar as science has itself become "subservient to capital."[54]

According to this account, moreover, the imperatives of capitalist relations of production are present within the very structure of machine technology itself. The relationship between the social relations and forces of production, in other words, is one of internal, rather than merely external correspondence. The assembly line, for example, insofar as it simultaneously isolates workers from each other and divests them of any control over the labor process, is an intrinsically capitalist technology, a concrete manifestation of capitalist re-

[49] Marx, *Capital*, Vol. I, p. 422, emphases added.

[50] Cited in Goran Therborn, *Science, Class and Society* (London: New Left Books, 1976), p. 359. Marx, *Capital*, Vol. I, p. 737.

[51] Mishra, "Technology and Social Structure in Marx's Theory," p. 147. As Mishra points out, the assumption of the primacy of the social relations of production is implicit in the very notion of a capitalist mode of production whose existence is continuous despite the technological discontinuity between the "manufacturing" and the "modern machinery" periods. If primacy were attributed to the forces of production, then these would not be two periods of capitalist development but, rather, two distinct modes of production (p. 148).

[52] Marx, *Capital*, Vol. I, p. 371.

[53] Gorz, "Technical Intelligence and the Capitalist Division of Labor," p. 31.

[54] Marx and Engels, *The German Ideology*, p. 149; see also Marx, *Capital*, Vol. I, pp. 436-37.

144

lations of production. Thus Charles Walker and Robert Guest found, in their study of over a thousand production line workers, that each worker typically "had 'verbal interaction' with only eight or ten other workers. Each worker tended to have almost no communication . . . with workers as close as three work stations away, a distance of no more than forty or so feet."[55] A technology that assigns workers to separate posts and obliges them to stay there inevitably engenders isolation, rather than communication, among those who are subject to it and is thus intrinsically inconsistent with a genuinely socialized mode of production. And, as Harry Braverman has exhaustively demonstrated, the assembly line is only one example of an entire array of industrial technologies introduced under capitalism that are necessarily incompatible with workers' control of their own productive activity.[56]

Marx's "second" theory of technology thus conceives of technology under capitalism not as a tool whose effect depends on the purposes on behalf of which it is set in motion but rather as a structure that imposes certain effects irrespective of the intentions of those who attempt to utilize it. As a structure that responds exclusively to the imperatives of capitalist relations of production, moreover, its effects are inevitably repressive. On this account, we cannot say that the liberatory promise of the technology that develops under capitalism is betrayed by capitalist relations of production because, strictly speaking, this technology contains no liberatory promise: it is not how the machines are used but how they are made that constitutes the heart of the problem.

It follows that we cannot rely on this technology to provide a solution. We should not expect capitalist relations of production to be "burst asunder" by the forces of production because the latter interiorize the logic of, and thus cannot fundamentally threaten, the former. If we insist on speaking of a "contradiction" between the forces and social relations of production, we will have to acknowledge that this contradiction, to borrow a phrase from Mao, is "nonantagonistic," i.e., that it is regularly resolved within the framework of the capitalist mode of production itself. At any rate, we cannot in any case rely on this "contradiction" to culminate in socialism, since socialism requires the complete transformation of the very technology that at present constitutes one term of the "contradiction." As Gorz has suggested, the conclusion to be drawn from Marx's pessimistic theory of capitalist technology is that "any attempt to change the relations of production will be doomed unless a radical change is made in the very nature of the productive

---

[55] This summary of Walker and Guest's findings is reported in Richard Edwards, *Contested Terrain: The Transformation of the Workplace in the Twentieth Century* (New York: Basic Books, 1979), pp. 121-22.

[56] *Labor and Monopoly Capital: The Degradation of Work in the Twentieth Century* (New York: Monthly Review Press, 1974), *passim*.

145

forces, and not only in the way in which and the purpose for which they are used.''[57] To put this another way, the only condition that will make it possible to speak of a genuine, or ''antagonistic'' contradiction between capitalist social relations of production and the forces of production is the conscious creation of an alternative technology that is free from the imperatives of capitalist domination and is consistent with the requirements of socialist relations of production. Socialism runs not with, but against, the grain of the project of technology development under capitalism, and therefore requires a new and different technological project. This much—the necessity of a radical technological discontinuity in the transition from capitalism to socialism—can be inferred from Marx's second theory of technology. More than this he does not tell us.

Marx's pessimistic theory is, in certain respects, more satisfactory than his optimistic theory. To begin with, it appears to be far more consistent with the realities of contemporary capitalist societies in which, as I have suggested, technological development has for the most part been not subversive, but rather supportive, of the hegemony of capitalist relations of production. The application of modern machinery to the process of production has enabled capitalists to extract surplus-value from this process at a rate consistent with a long-run increase (notwithstanding the contemporary decline) in the standard of living of the working class, and has thus functioned to break the link between the struggle for material subsistence and the struggle for socialism. At the same time, mechanization has encouraged a progressive reduction in the portion of life devoted to wage-labor, creating in the process the promise of increased leisure and earlier retirement that undoubtedly makes the alienation experienced in wage-labor more bearable. This ''liberation'' from work, finally, has not been a liberation from capital: capitalist relations of production have ''colonized'' the week-end and the retirement years, transforming them into the bases of profitable industries in which the structure and values of the capitalist workplace are reproduced rather than subverted. Thus, precisely as Marx's second theory would lead one to expect, capitalist relations of production have successfully bent the forces of production to conform to the ends inherent in these relations.

At the same time, Marx's structural theory of technology is far more consistent with the repressiveness of technology in state socialist societies than is his instrumental theory. The fact that the utilization of essentially identical production techniques and modes of labor organization in those societies[58] has culminated in the reproduction of the inequality and environmental degradation characteristic of capitalist societies is a striking confir-

[57] Gorz, ''Technical Intelligence and the Capitalist Division of Labor,'' p. 27.
[58] Braverman, *Labor and Monopoly Capital*, p. 22.

146

mation of Marx's conception of the way in which the imperatives of domination are built into the very structure of this technology. The abortive effort of these societies to realize the liberatory promises of socialism thus confirms the Marxian thesis that the construction of a genuinely socialist society cannot be based on the technology developed under capitalism but demands, rather, the construction of a qualitatively different, alternative technology.

The second theory, however, is not without its problems. If the experience of state socialist societies confirms Marx's thesis of the inherent repressiveness of the technology that develops under capitalism, it tends to undermine his thesis that this technology is an inherently *capitalist* technology. The assumption that the social relations of production are present within the forces of production leads to the conclusion that societies constituted by different relations of production should have different forces of production. This conclusion, however, flies in the face of the reality of state socialism, which is constituted by different relations of production yet the same forces of production. How is it possible to maintain that the technology that develops under capitalism is intrinsically capitalist, in the sense that it interiorizes the logic of capitalist property relations, when this same technology is systematically coupled with state socialist property relationships? If technology always interiorizes the relations of production within which it develops, then we should expect different, rather than essentially identical, technology under state socialism. Conversely, since we find similar, rather than different technology in this mode of production, it appears that we are obliged to conclude that the thesis that the forces of production always interiorize the logic of the social relations of production is wrong, and that we must grant the forces of production at least a certain measure of independence vis-à-vis the relations of production.

There are three possible ways to try to avoid this conclusion, none of which is successful. First, as we have seen in previous chapters, it is always possible to argue that state socialist societies are in fact capitalist societies; i.e., that their relations of production are identical to those of Western capitalist societies, and thus that the identity of their technologies confirms the Marxian theory of the primacy of the relations of production over the forces of production. As I have suggested at a number of earlier points, the problem with this effort to save the theory is that, if by ''capitalist relations of production'' we mean, as Marx meant, ''production of commodities for the purpose of surplus-value extraction,'' then the argument that state socialist societies are really capitalist societies is clearly wrong. If, on the other hand, by ''capitalist social relations of production'' we mean ''any industrial society in which those who labor lack control over the means of production,'' then the proposition that repressive technology is an intrinsically capitalist technology becomes true by definition.

147

Alternatively, one might attempt to rescue the theory that different social relations of production yield different forces of production by arguing that the technology that has developed under state socialist relations of production is, despite its appearances, fundamentally different from the technology that has developed under capitalism, by virtue of the different purposes on behalf of which it is set in motion. An assembly line operated on behalf of the goal of private profit, it might be argued, is not the same "animal" as an assembly line operated on behalf of the goal of plan-fulfillment. The problem with this type of response is that it merely redefines the forces of production to include the social relations of production, so that the hypothesis of an essential correspondence between the two becomes nothing more than pure tautology. It is, moreover, a tautology that is peculiarly insensitive to the experience of the worker, who no doubt continues to find his or her encounter with the assembly line debilitating and degrading in spite of the theory that tells him or her that this line is somehow fundamentally different from the one that the capitalist worker is obliged to encounter: to the worker, "speedup" is undoubtedly experienced as "speedup" irrespective of its underlying rationale.

Finally, the argument has been made that state socialist societies have thus far been unable, for a variety of reasons, to construct their own technologies, and that they have therefore been obliged to rely on specifically capitalist technologies to achieve their purposes. The presence of essentially identical technology under state socialism is thus a capitalist "survival" that the regime will eventually eliminate in favor of a form of technology that genuinely corresponds to its relations of production; the present lack of correspondence between the forces and social relations of production merely indicates that state socialism societies are transitional modes of production destined for further transformation. But when a survival endures for fifty or more years, shows absolutely no signs of passing away, and, in fact, is the regularly and exclusively preferred mode, we are entitled to be skeptical. Despite the fact that he adopts a version of this survivals argument, Braverman himself notes that "one would be hard put to demonstrate that any of the successive Soviet leaderships *has ever claimed that such an attempt* [to create an alternative technology] *should be made at this stage of Soviet history.*"[59] The definition of state socialist societies as transitional modes of production, in other words, is merely a corollary of the definition of a mode of production in terms of a correspondence, rather than divergence, between its forces and social relations of production, and demonstrates precisely that such a definition of a mode of production is unable to comprehend the systematic persistence of state socialist societies.

Try as she might, the defender of Marx's second theory is simply unable

---

[59] *Ibid.*, emphasis in the original.

148

to render this theory consistent with the realities of the state socialist experience. These realities suggest that, contrary to Marx, the forces of production are not merely the creature of the social relations of production but that they possess an at least partly autonomous logic of development. This conclusion takes us partway back to Marx's instrumental theory. Coupled with the insistence that the logic of technological development has heretofore been repressive, however, it brings us perilously close to the conclusion of those theorists of the technological society from Weber to Ellul who have argued that there is an inherent, identical logic underlying industrial production *as such* and that this logic is repressive.[60] If we argue that the technology that has developed under both capitalism and state socialism is intrinsically repressive, but we grant that this technology has developed relatively independently of the relations of production of these two societies, then the conclusion appears inescapable that no transformation in the social relations of production, no matter how fundamental, will be able to eliminate repressive technology and that "unfreedom" is inherent in any modernized society. This, indeed, is precisely the conclusion that Engels draws in his polemic against anarchism in "On Authority":

> If man, by dint of his knowledge and inventive genius has subdued the forces of nature, the latter avenge themselves upon him by subjecting him, in so far as he employs them, to a *veritable despotism independent of all social organization.* Wanting to abolish authority in large-scale industry is tantamount to wanting to abolish industry itself, to destroy the power loom in order to return to the spinning wheel . . . At least with regard to the hours of work, one may write upon the portals of these factories: "Leave, ye that enter in, all autonomy behind!"[61]

Engels's notion of the inherent despotism of machine technology is ordinarily dismissed as inconsistent with the thinking of Marx.[62] But perhaps Engels is not so far from Marx as it would appear. Indeed, I am suggesting that his conclusion is perfectly consistent with the conclusion that follows from at least one effort to reformulate Marx's theory in order to make it square with contemporary reality.

There are, it seems to me, only two other reformulations of the theory that would enable one to avoid Engels's conclusion. The first would entail the rejection not only of the thesis that the forces of production are the mere creatures of the social relations of production but also the argument that these forces as they have developed under capitalism are inherently repressive. In

[60] Jacques Ellul, *The Technological Society* (New York: Knopf, 1964), *passim.*

[61] Friedrich Engels, "On Authority," in Tucker, *The Marx-Engels Reader*, p. 663, emphasis added.

[62] *Ibid.*, p. 662.

this case, it would be possible simultaneously to uphold their independence vis-à-vis the relations of production and to avoid the conclusion that any form of industrial society, even the future genuinely socialist society, will possess a repressive technology. But now, of course, we are back, full-circle, to the instrumental theory in its entirety, with all the attendant problems, even contradictions, that we have already reviewed.

The other alternative would be to abandon the assumption that underlies both Marx's instrumental and structural theories, i.e., the assumption that "the bourgeois relations of production are the last antagonistic form of the social process of production."[63] This would lead us to reject the either/or of "capitalist, repressive technological society" versus "socialist, nonrepressive technological society" and to acknowledge that there are noncapitalist or supracapitalist industrial sources of repressive technology which nevertheless do not exhaust all technological possibilities. Because Marx's thought is constituted by that either/or, he is unable to conceive of this alternative. He is obliged to confound what, I would argue, is the correct claim that the technology that develops under capitalism is repressive with what, I would argue, is the incorrect claim that this technology is intrinsically and exclusively capitalist, because for him a capitalist society is the only possible repressive industrial society. Since for Marx the alternative of capitalism versus socialism exhausts the possibilities for technologically advanced societies, those who accept this definition of the alternatives but acknowledge that technology is repressive under state socialism are obliged to conclude, with Engels, that technology will be repressive in any modern society.

If, on the other hand, we reject the assumption that capitalism is the "last" repressive, or class-based, industrial society, then we can acknowledge the inherent repressiveness of technology under capitalism without having to argue that this technology is intrinsically and exclusively capitalist. We can agree, for example, with Gorz and Marglin's argument that domination is inherent in the very structure of the factory, and in the form of the assembly line itself, without having to leap to the unwarranted conclusion that this domination is nothing but the presence of specifically capitalist relations of production within these technologies. At the same time, since capitalism and state socialism would now be understood to be merely two species of the genus "repressive industrial society" that in no way exhaust the possibilities of technologically advanced societies, we would be able to resist the conclusion that, because repressive technology is not exclusively capitalist, any advanced technology is per se repressive. We could, in other words, give full weight to the facts that the logic of technological development is essentially identical across both capitalist and state socialist modes of production, and that this logic is consequently not a function of the specific relations of production of either,

---

[63] Marx, *Preface* to *A Contribution to the Critique of Political Economy*, p. 5.

without being obliged to conclude that this repressive logic is the only one possible.

Let me try to put this yet another way. Marx wants to treat the repressiveness of technology as an historically contingent, rather than inevitable, phenomenon. His theory of history, however, demands that he conceptualize this contingency as exclusively capitalist in nature. Because repressive technology is not, in fact, an exclusively capitalist phenomenon, Marx's effort to demonstrate that it is an historically contingent rather than inevitable phenomenon is a failure. The pessimistic theorists of the "technological society," on the other hand, leap from the fact that technology is repressive in both capitalist and state socialist industrial societies to the unwarranted conclusion that it must be repressive in any modern society. They assume, in other words, that because repressive technology is common to the history of both capitalism and state socialism it is not an historical but rather a natural phenomenon. There is, then, an underlying assumption that unites both Marx and the theorists of the technological society, despite their obvious differences, namely the assumption that the history of capitalist and socialist societies exhausts the possible history of modern societies. Both theories lack a concept of a repressive industrial society that is broader than the concept of a capitalist society but narrower than the concept of a modern society as such. And this is precisely the concept that is needed, if we want to comprehend, as Marx cannot, the supracapitalist sources of repressive technology as well as to envision, as the pessimistic theorists of the technological society cannot, the possibility of a genuinely liberatory technological society of the future. I have already suggested that this concept cannot be squared with Marx's theory of history, which must therefore be abandoned. In Chapter Eight I shall argue, moreover, that it also cannot be squared with the theory of human nature that underlies his theory of history, and that this theory of human nature likewise must be abandoned.

All the objections I have raised against Marx's structural theory of technology can of course also be voiced against the implicit theory of science that underlies it. If the technology that develops under capitalism is both inherently repressive and intrinsically capitalist, then it would appear to follow that this would also be true of the natural sciences of which this technology is a practical elaboration. Indeed, we have already seen that Marx argues that science "becomes subservient to capital" and that natural scientific activity is an alienated activity insofar as it is "provided with its aim, as with its material . . . through [capitalist] industry," i.e., the natural sciences interiorize the logic of capitalist relations of production and must therefore be understood as specifically capitalist sciences.[64] But these same sciences—with the same

[64] Marx and Engels, *The German Ideology*, pp. 149, 135. Kostas Axelos, *Alienation, Praxis, and Techne in the Thought of Karl Marx* (Austin: University of Texas Press, 1976), pp. 209-12.

aim and material—are practiced in contemporary state socialist societies. Thus Marx's structural theory of the peculiarly capitalist character of these sciences must be rejected.[65] For those who remain within the framework of Marx's conception of history, however, there are only two possible, and equally inadequate, alternatives to this theory.[66] On the one hand, the observation that state socialist societies practice the same natural sciences practiced in capitalist societies can lead to the conclusion that there is nothing inherently repressive or alienated about these sciences—can lead us back, in other words, to Marx's optimistic, instrumental theory of science and technology and all its attendant problems. On the other hand, this observation can lead to the conclusion that the natural sciences are repressive or alienated in both of the modes of production that exhaust the possibilities for a modern, scientifically advanced society and that the natural sciences are, therefore, *inevitably* repressive or alienated—a conclusion that echoes that of the "pessimistic" critics of modernity for whom there is an inescapable opposition between scientific reason and human freedom. In order to avoid either of these unsatisfactory alternatives, we require a concept of an alienated or repressive science that is broader than the concept of a specifically capitalist science but narrower than the concept of scientific reason itself, but this concept, once again, is foreclosed by Marx's basic assumption. I shall address this problem again in Chapters Seven and Eight.

There is a final, and related, problem with Marx's structural theory of technology. This theory, as we have seen, culminates in the conclusion that technological discontinuity, rather than continuity, underlies the transition from capitalism to socialism, and thus, contrary to the argument in the *Preface*, that "the productive forces developing in the womb of bourgeois society" do *not* "create the material conditions for the solution of [the] antagonism" of class society. The Marx of the second theory tells us, in other words, that the construction of an alternative technology is an essential part of the socialist solution, but tells us nothing about what material conditions will make that construction, and thus this solution, possible. His vision of an alternative technology is completely ungrounded in any analysis of the actual dynamic of technological development under capitalism that might help us locate the actual sources of a liberatory technology within this society. Indeed, strictly speaking, we should not expect to find any, since, according to *this* Marx, this dynamic is entirely determined by repressive social relations of production

---

[65] See Appendix B, Chapter Four.

[66] Only two possible alternatives, that is, if we exclude the efforts to reconceptualize state socialist societies as capitalist societies or the domination that exists in these societies as mere capitalist survivals, both of which, I have already demonstrated, are unsatisfactory alternatives.

that engender the forces of production they require.[67] If the Marx of the optimistic theory fails completely to understand the necessity for an alternative technology and uncritically relies on the technology of capitalism to provide the solution, the Marx of the pessimistic theory understands the necessity for an alternative technology as part of the solution but is completely unable to demonstrate its possibility. His vision of an alternative technology remains, therefore, a vague utopian "ought" that is mechanically juxtaposed to an alienated "is."

This problem, moreover, like the others we have reviewed, cannot be remedied through an effort to combine elements of the structural theory with elements of the instrumental theory. The basic assumption of the structural theory is that the form of technology that develops under capitalism is repressive because this form is determined by capitalist relations of production. The basic assumption of the instrumental theory is that the form of technology that develops under capitalism is not repressive because this form escapes determination by capitalist relations of production. Consequently, neither enables us to envision the emergence of a liberatory technology in the context of a capitalist society whose technology is predominantly repressive. Nor is it possible to combine them in such a manner as to be able to envision this possibility. The common assumption that unites these otherwise divergent theories is that the criterion for the repressiveness of technology is the extent of its determination by capitalist relations of production. Thus any theory of technology that is based on this common assumption will necessarily make freedom from determination by capitalist relations of production the criterion for a liberatory technology. But, as we have seen, this is a completely inadequate criterion, because technology may be and, in fact, is repressive even though it escapes determination by specifically capitalist relations of production. To put this another way, a theory that is capable of making an adequate distinction between liberatory and repressive technology must be based precisely on that concept of repressive technology that is broader than capitalist technology, but narrower than modern technology as such, which is foreign to both of Marx's theories and absent from his work as a whole.

---

[67] The theory of the primacy of capitalist relations of production thus treats capitalism as a closed system that tends toward equilibrium. The effort to overcome this impression of closure with the argument that, although "within the . . . limits of capitalism . . . , technology . . . *is produced by* the social relation represented by capital . . . Marx did, of course, give a position of primacy to the 'means of production' in social evolution" (Braverman, *Labor and Monopoly Capital*, pp. 20, 18, emphasis in the original) will simply not do. To argue that the social relations of production are determinant within the structure of the capitalist mode of production but that the forces of production determine "social evolution," i.e., the historical transformation of one mode of production to another, is to invoke precisely that distinction between structure and history, synchrony and diachrony, that the "dialectical" nature of Marx's thought is supposed to deny.

CONTEMPORARY MARXIST THEORIES OF ENVIRONMENTAL DEGRADATION

Contemporary Marxist treatment of the destructive impact of technology on the environment inherits, and suffers from, the absence of an adequate concept of repressive technology. By and large, Marxists who have dealt with the question of environmental degradation have merely applied Marx's criterion for the general repressiveness of technology to the specific problem of the technological repression of nature, with the result that their analyses of this specific problem reproduce all the deficiencies of Marx's general analysis. More specifically, they have assumed that it is the (capitalist) social relations of production that are responsible for the manifold, and dangerous, disturbances to the environment that ecologists over the past two decades have identified, and have therefore prescribed a transformation of these relations of production as the appropriate remedy for these disturbances. In the process, they have necessarily overlooked those determinants of environmental degradation that are not a function of a specific mode of production and thus those that will inevitably outlive the transformation in the relations of production they recommend.

The bulk of recent Marxist writing on the ecological problem is devoted to debunking "mainstream" efforts that fail to appreciate that this problem is determined by the mode of production. As Enzenberger has noted, "the Left has [mainly] seen its task to be to face the problem in terms of an ideological critique."[68] The nature of this critique varies according to whether it proceeds from an instrumental or structural conception of the determinative power of the mode of production.

Instrumental theorists, who are mainly orthodox Marxist-Leninists, have simply repudiated the central tenets of the environmental movement. They have argued, against the "neo-Malthusians" in this movement, that "over-population" does not result from any law of the inevitable tendency for the world's population to grow at a faster rate than the resources available to satisfy its needs, but rather simply from an inequitable global distribution of resources that itself is merely the inevitable consequence of the internationalization of capitalist relations of production.[69] Thus demands for "zero population growth" or even "limits to growth" merely deflect attention from the real source of ecological scarcity—capitalist relations of production—and thus from the task of social transformation without which the problem of "over-population" cannot be resolved. At the same time, such demands obfuscate, in reactionary fashion, the virtually unlimited potential of contemporary technology to satisfy human needs:

[68] Enzenberger, "A Critique of Political Ecology," p. 378.
[69] See, for example, Yevgeny Fyodorov, "Against the Limits to Growth," *New Scientist*, 57 (February 22, 1973), pp. 431-32.

Taking the history of human society as a whole, the per capita production of food (except for a short period in the 1960s) and of the various materials and power needed by man, has increased steadily. And if all the technologies known to man today were in use, then this production could be increased enormously. We believe that the ability to satisfy Man's essential needs has always increased and is increasing faster than the size of the population . . . there are no grounds whatsoever for assuming that this process will not continue in the future.[70]

Thus "there is no need for special measures to limit the world's population either now or in the near future."[71] As Fidel Castro has argued, theorists of population control fail to understand that *"we shall never be too numerous* however many of us there are, if only we all together place our efforts and our intelligence at the service of mankind, a mankind which will be freed from the exploitation of man by man."[72]

Thus Instrumental Marxists have responded to the unrestrained pessimism of the Neo-Malthusians with an equally unbridled technological optimism. They have argued, correctly, that the so-called natural law of the inevitable tendency for the growth of human needs to outrun the human capacity to satisfy these needs abstracts entirely from the social determinants of this gap and thus from the social transformations that can contribute to its elimination. In arguing that global capitalist relations of production are entirely responsible for this gap, however, they have merely replaced one "metaphysical" law with another, namely the law of the inevitable tendency of the growth in the human capacity to satisfy human needs to outrun the growth of these needs. If the Neo-Malthusian law is metaphysical because it abstracts entirely from the limits that the relations of production impose on the capacity of humans to satisfy their needs, the Instrumental Marxist law is metaphysical because it ignores totally the limits that nature, or the ecosystem, imposes on this capacity, and would continue to impose irrespective of transformations in the mode of production. The basic assumption underlying the Instrumental Marxist response to the Neo-Malthusians is the entirely unfounded one that "nature as such presents no obstacles that cannot be overcome by appropriate social arrangements and the wonders of scientific-technological productivity."[73]

This assumption also underlies the Instrumental Marxist critique of that tendency within the ecology movement that concentrates on modern industrial technology as the chief source of environmental problems and thus prescribes a variety of alternative technologies as their remedy. The pollution of air and

[70] *Ibid.*, p. 432.
[71] *Ibid.*
[72] Cited in Enzenberger, "A Critique of Political Ecology," p. 384.
[73] Ophuls, *Ecology and the Politics of Scarcity*, p. 204.

155

water, which has become "a serious threat to mankind," is not the inevitable result of contemporary technology but rather the result of "existing trends in the capitalist world . . . [that] can and must be changed." In fact, "almost all the fundamental scientific problems and technical problems related to eliminating industrial pollution or at least reducing it to a very small magnitude, have been solved [!]" Thus not alternative technology, but more rational use of existing technology (including pollution-control technology) is the solution to the problem of pollution.[74] This solution, Instrumental Marxists admit, would not eliminate the emission of industrial heat and thus the danger of a continuing increase in the temperature of the earth, but this danger, in turn, can be eliminated "by regulating the cloud cover of the planet." Although "it is difficult today to see how this could be done," history tells us that "fundamentally new possibilities for satisfying the needs of mankind regularly arise," and we can therefore be confident that the appropriate technological solution will be developed.[75]

Instrumental Marxists are thus proponents of what has been called the "technological fix." Just as the "junkie's" solution to the problem of the effects of his or her drug addiction is increasing doses of the same drug, so the technological optimist's solution to the problem of the destructive effects of large-scale technology on the environment is increasing doses of large-

---

[74] Thus the one full-scale Marxist study of industrial pollution of which I am aware concludes that "Rational planning is the path out of our crisis but it is a path which will remain closed until the social and economic obstacles which block it are removed. The major obstacles are bureaucracy and the capitalist system of private property with its relentless drive for profit. Their removal is the necessary first step towards a decent and healthy world. Socially rational planning will be impossible until the working people control the means of production on a global scale." Harry Rothman, *Murderous Providence* (London: Rupert Hart-Davis, 1972), pp. 337-38.

If "socially rational planning" means "using only those technologies whose effects on the environment are benign," then it is not clear why worker participation in planning will guarantee "socially rational planning." If, on the other hand, "socially rational planning" simply means "worker participation in planning," then it is not clear why "socially rational planning" will entail the exclusive use of benign technologies. Rothman seems to assume that worker's control of production will enable production to be undertaken on behalf of genuinely common goals, but production on behalf of common goals in no way guarantees that the means employed to achieve these goals will not be destructive to the environment. Conversely, a theory that attributes environmental pollution to the way in which private property and bureaucracy preclude the possibility of production on behalf of common goals will be inadequate. The explanation that relies on private property and the explanation that relies on bureaucracy, moreover, tend to undermine each other. Rothman attributes pollution in capitalist societies to private property and pollution in state socialist societies to bureaucracy. But the admission that "the distortion of planning by bureaucracy" is the basic reason for pollution under state socialism (p. 254) leaves open the possibility that bureaucracy may also be a determinant of pollution in capitalist societies and thus the possibility that pollution in these societies is not exclusively a function of capitalist relations of production.

[75] Fyodorov, "Against the Limits to Growth," p. 432.

scale technology. Moreover, just as the drug addict ignores the fact that his or her system imposes inherent limits on this "solution," so the technological addict is blind to the possibility that some of his technological disturbances are irreversible and thus necessarily and permanently destructive to the eco-system. And, just as the more enlightened junkie searches desperately for the one new drug that will produce only the effects he or she desires and not the dangerous effects he or she seeks to avoid, so the technological optimist who is aware of the problem of the necessarily destructive effects of old technol-ogies heralds the exclusively benign effects of the new. Thus a Polish Marxist theorist has recently argued that, whereas the nineteenth-century "dynamic" machine (e.g., the locomotive, the furnace, the electric turbine, the internal combustion engine) "killed nature," the twentieth-century cybernetic or "di-alectical machine," the machine of the so-called "second industrial revolu-tion," "coexists with nature which it has managed to domesticate." The cybernetic machine, "of which the atomic pile and computer are examples," is no mere "mechanism" but rather "accomplishes a reconciliation of mech-anism with the life environment and develops some features of a living crea-ture." The most advanced information technologies incorporate "organicity," "a complexity of structure which re-enacts the imitation of the concreteness of nature . . . the product of technology becomes a replica of the dialectic of nature." Thus, whereas the dynamic machine was "opposed to nature," the "new machine attempts to place itself inside nature" and will eventually operate in harmony with, rather than destructive opposition to, nature. What-ever destructiveness is currently associated with the new machines is merely transitional, "a matter of 'getting fitted in' the schemes of nature." This "fit," which, for reasons that are left unclear, can be achieved in "communist civilization alone," will eliminate the harmful effects of modern technology that have heretofore plagued the history of industrial societies.[76]

According to this conception, then, there is no need for alternative tech-nologies that respect the demands of nature because the technologies that have most recently developed under capitalism already conform to these demands; their structure is an imitation of the structure of nature itself. It is precisely this assumption, however, that must be questioned. Might it not be argued that the alleged identity of the structure of cybernetic machines and the structure of nature is merely the result of a conceptual operation that projects the structure of these machines onto nature and then "discovers" that these machines are a miraculous "imitation" of nature? If this is the case, would not the "nature" in which "the new machine attempts to place itself" be a nature that has already been defined to conform to the requirements

[76] Janusz Kuczynski, "Man, Technological Praxis and Nature in Dialectical Synthesis," in George F. McLean, ed., *Man and Nature* (Calcutta: Oxford University Press, 1978), pp. 58-71.

of this machine, in which case the problem of the so-called "fit" between machine and nature is nothing but the problem of the elaboration of the utterly untrammeled technological domination of nature? Is it not possible that the conformity between human action and the action of nature is procured definitionally, the "action of nature" having been conceived, from the very beginning, according to a certain model of human action? What I am suggesting, in other words, is that an extraordinary anthropocentrism underlies the extreme technological optimism of the Instrumental Marxist: the argument that there are no inherent natural obstacles to human technological development is ultimately based on a conception of the requirements of nature that is nothing other than an illicit extrapolation from the (present) requirements of human beings. Only a nonanthropocentric understanding of the requirements of nature can provide the standards to evaluate the repressiveness of contemporary technology to nature, but Instrumental Marxists have no such understanding of the requirements of nature.

Marxists who conceptualize the relationship between technology and capitalist relations of production in structural, rather than instrumental, terms are more sympathetic to the ecologists' demands for limits to growth and alternative technologies. Their efforts at demystification purport to demonstrate not that these technological transformations are unnecessary but rather that they are impossible in the absence of the elimination of capitalist relations of production. Thus, for example, Enzenberger does not reject the ecologists' hypothesis that the industrial technology that develops under capitalism is inherently and irreversibly destructive of the natural environment, but argues that the development of an alternative, genuinely nonrepressive technology presupposes an elimination of the capitalist mode of production. "A general social definition of the ecological problem," he tells us, "would have to start from the mode of production." The capitalist mode of production has always generated, and will always generate, want alongside plenty, destructiveness along with productive power. Thus the present ecological "crisis is inseparable from the conditions of existence systematically determined by the mode of production," and no amount of technological tinkering will be able to reverse the inevitable tendency for the technology that develops under capitalism to "threaten all the natural bases of human life." The ecologist who correctly understands that an alternative technology is necessary for human survival must therefore also come to understand that "socialism . . . has become a question of survival." As ecological crises and the inability of capitalist systems to surmount them become increasingly manifest, mass "ecological rebellions" can, depending "on the degree of politicization and organization achieved by then," be transformed into struggles for socialism.[77]

[77] Enzenberger, "A Critique of Political Ecology," pp. 371-93.

158

There are two principal problems with the Structural Marxist critique of mainstream "political ecology," problems that parallel those of Marx's general structural theory of technology. First, its insistence that capitalist social relations are uniquely responsible for the ecological crisis is belied by the manifestations of this crisis in societies with state socialist relations of production. If state socialist relations of production coincide with technologies that are as destructive of the natural environment as those that prevail under capitalist relations of production, then—unless, once again, we redefine state socialism as merely another form of "capitalism"—"a general social definition of the ecological problem" cannot "start from," but rather transcends, "the mode of production." If the ecological crisis is identical across two different modes of production, then we cannot claim that the source of this crisis lies in one particular mode of production. Thus, if the elimination of capitalism and the creation of socialism is the necssary condition, it is certainly not the sufficient condition, for the societal-wide construction of an alternative technology that respects the demands of nature. It follows that the transition to socialism will culminate in an ecologically sound technology only if an ecological movement retains its autonomy and strength throughout this entire transition.

Second, the Structural Marxist critique suffers from the fact that it recognizes the necessity, but not the practical possibility, of the elaboration of an alternative technology in the context of capitalist relations of production. On the one hand, the assumption that capitalist relations of production are embedded in existing technologies leads to the understanding that the struggle to eliminate these relations of production necessarily and ultimately entails an effort to create alternative technologies. The Structural Marxist concludes, where the Instrumental Marxist does not, that a revolutionary technological practice is an integral part of the political practice necessary for the elimination of capitalism. On the other hand, the assumption that technological development is a function of the development of the relations of production completely obscures, even denies, the possibility of the emergence of a revolutionary technological practice within the context of these relations of production. Instead, this assumption leads to the tendency to dismiss contemporary efforts to elaborate an alternative technology as mere "tinkering" and to the conclusion that a transformation of capitalist relations of production is a precondition of significant technological change. And so the Structural Marxist argument moves in a circle.

To break this circle, we need to develop a criterion that would enable us to distinguish technologies that emerge under capitalism that are destructive of nature from those that are not. Then, and only then, would we be in a position to distinguish those technological innovations that involve repressive "tinkering" from those that embody a genuinely liberatory promise. The

159

ability to develop such a criterion, however, is predicated on a nonanthropocentric understanding of the requirements of nature. This understanding, however, is as alien to Structural Marxists as it is to their Instrumental counterparts. Marxist knowledge of the structure of human practice does not yield knowledge of the structure of the ecosystem as a whole; thus the commitment of Structural Marxists to technologies that respect the requirements of this ecosystem is ungrounded in any knowledge that derives from the theory to which they adhere, i.e., it has an ad hoc character. The theoretical grounding of this commitment, then, demands that Marxists learn from ecologists. In short, the "science" of Marxism does not subsume, but must rather be enlightened by, the science of ecology.

APPENDIX A

It is always possible to argue that it is only by virtue of the "imperialist" exploitation of Third World countries that Western capitalist societies have thus far been able to "resolve" the contradiction between their forces and social relations of production and that (a) this resolution merely internationalizes the explosive contradiction between technological development and its capitalist integument in the form of permanent underdevelopment in Third World countries and the anti-imperialist "national liberation" struggles to which it gives rise, and (b) these Third World struggles will eventually eliminate the imperialist exploitation that has heretofore enabled Western capitalist societies to forestall the explosiveness of their internal contradictions and thus, over the long run, capitalist relations of production will prove, after all, to be an unbearable fetter on the forces of production in these societies as well. An adequate response to this argument is beyond the scope of this chapter. But it would necessarily entail an extensive elaboration of the following essential points: (a) The internationalization of the contradiction between the forces and social relations of production may well result in Third World anti-imperialist struggles, but these struggles are not, strictly speaking, proletarian and they do not typically culminate in the creation of a new mode of production that is socialist in Marx's sense of the word. Thus it is impossible to argue that the sentence on capitalism pronounced by the forces of production is executed by the proletariat, or that socialism is inscribed in the very development of these forces, in these societies. The internalization of the capitalist mode of production does not merely displace its contradictions but also demands a fundamental reconceptualization of Marx's theory of the way in which they are overcome throughout a major part of the globe. Given the internal relations among the various parts of Marx's conceptual system, this

160

reconceptualization of the nature of revolution and revolutionary agent in this part of the globe would necessarily entail a reconceptualization of Marx's underlying theory of human nature as well; (b) Even if we grant, for the sake of argument, the highly debatable premises that Western exploitation of Third World countries has thus far been the principal mechanism for the nullification of the explosiveness of the contradiction between the forces and social relations of production in the West and that no other mechanism could perform this function, it does not follow that successful Third World liberation struggles resulting in some version of a state socialist mode of production will eliminate Western capitalist exploitation of the countries that have adopted this mode of production and thus eliminate the ability of Western capitalist societies to render their internal contradictions nonexplosive through imperialist exploitation. The recent efforts of the Chinese leadership to attract Western capital indicate that at least certain state socialist societies are likely to remain available as markets for Western capital, i.e., as outlets that enable Western capitalist societies to dampen chronic crises of "overproduction." Thus the explosion of the internationalized contradiction between the forces and social relations of production in the form of successful Third World revolutions does not necessarily culminate over the long run in the detonation of the contradiction between the forces and social relations of production internal to Western capitalist societies.

APPENDIX B

If Marx's general indictment of science is correct, however, it has implications for his own science. If scientific rationality under capitalism is an alienated rationality, and if Marx claims the status of science for his own rationality, then how is it possible to avoid the charge that Marx's rationality is as alienated as any other? If Marx is right about science, it appears that he must be wrong about everything else. One conventional Marxist response to this version of "Mannheim's paradox" is that Marx's thought escapes alienation because it expresses the revolutionary aspirations of a class, namely the proletariat, which is in the process of creating an unalienated society, a class which according to Marx, is "in civil society . . . [but] . . . not a class of civil society" (*Contribution to the Critique of Hegel's "Philosophy of Right": Introduction*, in Tucker, *The Marx-Engels Reader*, p. 22). It is the universality of the strivings of the proletariat, in other words, that guarantees the universality, or the truth, of Marx's theory. Yet, in the absence of genuinely socialist consciousness among the working class, the "universality" and "revolutionary aspirations" of the proletariat are simply a projection of the theory:

161

the claim that the theory is true because it expresses the unalienated needs of the proletariat degenerates into a hopeless circularity in which the theory merely justifies itself by itself. (See Dick Howard, *The Marxian Legacy* [New York: Urizen, 1978], Chs. 9-10).

Another characteristic Marxist effort to escape Mannheim's paradox entails an appeal to the criterion of practice as the ultimate determinant of the truth of Marx's theory. Marx himself argued, in the Second Thesis on Feuerbach, that "Men must prove the truth . . . in practice" (Tucker, *The Marx-Engels Reader*, p. 108). There are two versions of this appeal to practice. The first points, in orthodox Marxist-Leninist fashion, to the allegedly successful socialist revolutions ostensibly guided by Marx's theory as proof of the truth of this theory. The problem with this line of argument, to begin with, is that the claim that these revolutions were guided by Marx's theory is unwarranted in the light of the fact that virtually all of them occurred in underdeveloped or only partly capitalist societies, i.e., precisely those societies which, according to Marx, would prove infertile soil for the development of socialism. These revolutions, in other words, were made in opposition to, rather than conformity with, Marx's basic principle that an advanced technology is the necessary precondition for socialist revolution—thus Gramsci's famous description of the Russian Revolution as a revolution "against *Capital*"—and their fate cannot therefore be taken as a genuine test of Marx's theory. If it were taken as such a test, moreover, then the fact that virtually all of these revolutions have culminated in societies which are a far cry from Marx's vision of socialism and in which, in fact, workers are every bit as excluded from control over production as they are under capitalism, hardly supports the contention that the truth of Marx's theory has been proven "in practice."

The second appeal to the criterion of practice is more subtle. It acknowledges that genuinely successful socialist revolutions have not yet occurred, but argues that Marx's thought has already significantly contributed to the transformation of consciousness without which these revolutions would be impossible, that it will continue to contribute to this transformation of consciousness, and thus that it is indispensable to the successful socialist revolutions that will in fact eventually occur. The truth of Marx's theory, in other words, will *ultimately* be demonstrated in a socialist revolution that would have been impossible without the aid of Marx's theory. This type of argument, however, permanently postpones any possible test of the theory, since it declares that the theory must be judged not in the light of present but rather future realities. It is of course true that we cannot infer from the absence of authentic socialist revolutions thus far that Marx's theory has been falsified, since it is always possible that they may occur in the future. But any theory that purports to contribute to this eventuality should be able to help us understand why it has not yet come into being; any adequate theory of revolutionary possibilities must be able critically to comprehend the present obstacles to this revolution without whose elimination this revolution will *never* come about. Statist and patriarchal authoritarianism, for example, militate against the development of that socialist consciousness without which no successful socialist revolution is possible. A theory whose ultimate truth claim rests on the contribution it makes to this revolution must be able to provide an adequate account of both political and sexual domination. But, as I have argued, Marx's theory fails to provide such an account, which entitles us to conclude that it is not a sufficient revolutionary theory, that it does not and *cannot* make an adequate contribution to that practice on which it relies for its eventual verification.

In subsequent chapters I shall argue that Marx's central explanatory category partakes of the same logic as the structures of domination it purports but fails to comprehend, and that his theory is not only insufficient for but, in fact, an obstacle to a genuinely liberatory socialist practice. At any rate, even at this point we are in a position to conclude that the appeal to practice as the criterion of the truth of Marx's conceptual categories in no way extricates these categories from the contradiction in which they are enmeshed. There remains an unresolved contradiction between his critique of science as alienated and the fact that this critique is made in the name of science.

CONCLUSION TO PART I

In Chapter One we saw that Marx's commitment to the ontological primacy of production entails the assertion of the analytical primacy of the concept of the mode of production: the assumption that objectification is both *the* primordial and essential medium through which the human struggle for recognition takes place necessarily leads to the assumption that the character of other, non-objectifying human activities is, in the last analysis, a function of the form of objectification. Thus domination—as one particular form of such activities—is ultimately determined by the mode of production.

The analysis in Chapters Two through Four demonstrated that this thesis is inadequate. None of the structures of domination against which the liberation movements of the 1960s and 1970s have struggled can be illuminated sufficiently in the light of the theory of the determining power of the mode of production. If this theory is interpreted to entail the proposition that patriarchy, the state, and repressive technology are functions of a specifically capitalist mode of production, then the presence of these structures in both pre- and postcapitalist societies appears to warrant the conclusion that this theory is incorrect. We have examined, and found wanting, a number of characteristically Marxist efforts to resist this conclusion:

(1) One argument is that these structures are specifically capitalist, notwithstanding their precapitalist existence, because their present and future operation is wholly determined by the dynamics of the specifically capitalist mode of production of which they have become a constituent part. The problem with this argument, as we have seen, is twofold. First, it is *not* in fact the case that the operation of these structures can be accounted for in terms of the functional requisites of the capitalist mode of production; these structures shape in important ways the very mode of production that shapes them. The analysis of the operation of patriarchy, the state, and repressive technology in the context of contemporary capitalist society demonstrates conclusively not only that their development cannot be reduced to the logic of development of the mode of production of this society but also that the development of the latter is itself profoundly influenced by the operation of these structures. Second, the argument that reduces the present and future development of patriarchy, the state, and repressive technology to the logic of development of a specifically capitalist mode of production is also undermined by the fact that these structures continue to develop in postcapitalist, i.e., state socialist modes of production. It is, therefore, typically accompanied by a second argument.

164

(2) This argument is that these structures do *not*, in fact, "develop" in "postcapitalist" modes of production either because (a) state socialist societies are not actually characterized by "postcapitalist" modes of production at all, but are instead, really capitalist societies or (b) these structures are merely capitalist "survivals," i.e., they do not develop within, but are rather destined to be eliminated by, state socialist societies that are in transition to socialism. Both contentions seek to demonstrate that the presence of patriarchy, the state, or repressive technology in state socialist societies does not in fact refute the Marxist theory that their development is a function of a specifically capitalist mode of production. As we have seen, however, both the reconceptualization of state socialist societies as capitalist societies and the reconceptualization of these structures of domination as capitalist survivals succeed in rescuing this theory only at the prohibitive cost of transforming it into a mere tautology.

The conclusion is inescapable that patriarchy, the state, and repressive technology are not functions of, but rather relatively autonomous from the capitalist mode of production. There are some Marxists who acknowledge this relative autonomy but who nevertheless maintain that it is completely consistent with Marx's theory of the determining power of the mode of production. This theory, they argue or imply, should be interpreted to mean not that the structures of domination are a function of a specifically capitalist mode of production but rather that they owe their existence to what all modes of production have thus far had in common, e.g., class division, scarcity, etc. Thus Engels argued that patriarchy is, at bottom, a function of an interest in the accumulation of private property that prevails in all heretofore existing modes of production and both Marx and Engels maintained that political domination (for them, "political power") owes its existence to class conflict, which is itself ultimately a function of scarcity. The analysis over the course of the past three chapters has revealed that there are, however, two insurmountable difficulties with this version of the Marxist theory of the determining power of the mode of production. First, the effort to explain the three structures of domination in terms of features common to all modes of production that have thus far existed leaves entirely unexplained the specific form that these structures assume during any particular historical epoch, and the present epoch in particular. Second, it is not at all clear that factors such as class division and scarcity antedate the structures they are held to explain. The class division on which Engels relies in order to explain the emergence of patriarchy would appear to presuppose the very patriarchy for which it ostensibly accounts, and the scarcity that explains the class conflict that gives rise to the emergence of the state cannot in fact be verified in state-less societies. Thus the effort to rescue the theory of the determining power of the mode of production that interprets this theory in "genetic" fashion, i.e.,

165

as giving an account of the origins of the three structures of domination, fails because this version (a) does not and cannot explain their present operation and (b) is inadequate as an account of origins in the first place.

In short, no interpretation of the Marxist theory enables us legitimately to conclude that patriarchy, the state, and repressive technology are determined by the mode of production. It follows that a transformation of the (present) mode of production will not guarantee the elimination of these structures of domination. Thus Marxism cannot be understood as a sufficient theory of domination, and a political practice that is guided exclusively by its theoretical principles will necessarily entail an unsuccessful assault on the practices of domination. The commitment to eliminate domination demands, then, that the assumption of the primacy of the mode of production be abandoned, and with it the underlying ontological assumption that the human struggle for recognition is exhausted in objectification. An adequate theory of domination and the possibilities for its elimination must proceed, instead, from the Hegelian assumption that there are media other than objectification within which authentic struggles for human recognition take place, media whose investigation can shed additional light on both the sources and the limits of domination. Part Two of this book examines a number of such investigations and considers the way in which their exponents have attempted to reconcile them with those that follow from a Marxist focus on the centrality of the medium of objectification. It is devoted, in other words, to the analysis and evaluation of neo-Marxist efforts critically to comprehend patriarchy, the state, and repressive technology that proceed from the assumption that the concept of "production" is a necessary, but insufficient theoretical starting point, efforts that entail, therefore, a purported "integration" or "synthesis" of this concept with alternative conceptions of the human condition. The failure of these efforts will oblige us to quesion the assumption from which they proceed, i.e., to question not only the sufficiency, but also the very necessity, of Marxism itself.

PART II

NEO-MARXIST THEORIES
OF DOMINATION

CHAPTER FIVE

NEO-MARXIST THEORIES OF PATRIARCHY

INTRODUCTION

In Chapter Two we saw that neither Marx nor the Marxist tradition is able to develop an adequate understanding of patriarchy. According to this tradition, the domination of men over women is, at bottom, a function of the mode of production; the opposition or antagonism between the sexes is rooted in the antagonistic form within which human beings perform their labor. Any effort to demonstrate this proposition, I argued, fails because it presupposes the very sexual opposition it purports to explain. The Marxist tradition begs precisely that question that must be answered by an adequate theory of patriarchy: how and why is the sexual difference between men and women transformed into a hierarchical opposition in which men are in the dominant and women in the subordinate position? The exploration of this question demands the examination of alternative theoretical traditions.

To pose the problem of the transformation of sexual difference into sexual opposition is to ask why the struggle for recognition between man and woman culminates not in a reciprocity that overcomes otherness but rather in a situation in which woman becomes the subordinate "other" of man.[1] Patriarchy can be described as that condition in which men define women as inferior and women are obliged to conform to this definition; men will recognize women only insofar as they are less than men, i.e., less than fully human, and women are constrained to recognize themselves as they are recognized by men. An adequate understanding of patriarchy thus requires a theory of the struggle for sexual recognition that can account for the repressive form that this struggle has assumed throughout history. It requires an approach that—unlike the Marxist approach—treats the formation of sexual identity as problematical and therefore worthy of independent theoretical attention. It is, of course, in Freud and the tradition that bears his name that this attention is both most original and sustained. Thus Marxists who are also feminists have turned to Freud for the illumination of the problem of patriarchy that Marx does not, and cannot, provide.

---

[1] The theme of women as man's "other" was first developed by Simone de Beauvoir in *The Second Sex* (London: Jonathan Cape, 1960).

The feminist appropriation of Freud has been a selective appropriation. Freud not only attempts to explain why the struggle for sexual recognition has heretofore assumed a patriarchal form but also purports to demonstrate that things could never be otherwise, that civilization is inherently patriarchal. The feminist theoretical task has been to historicize Freud's theory of patriarchy, i.e., to demonstrate that the conditions that produce a patriarchal form of the struggle for sexual recognition are not universal or inevitable but, rather, historically contingent and to argue that the elimination of these conditions will make possible a nonrepressive, nonpatriarchal struggle for sexual recognition. In this task of historicization, feminist theorists have relied on Marx; they will use Marx to introduce the history from which Freud abstracts and thus to suspend his equation of civilization and patriarchy. The outcome will be a theory of patriarchy that can be described as Freudo-Marxist.

I shall argue that the Freudo-Marxist theory of patriarchy is ultimately incoherent. But I am getting ahead of myself. Let me first turn to Freud's theory of the struggle for sexual recognition, and then to the way in which this theory has been appropriated by a number of Marxist-feminists who have given it serious attention.

FREUD ON THE STRUGGLE FOR SEXUAL RECOGNITION

Every great thinker takes as a problem what others have taken for granted. In the case of Freud, the problem is the formation of sexual identity. Prior to Freud, no one questioned that there were women and there were men, and that they were different; sexual difference either was indistinguishable or followed naturally, from biological difference. Since Freud, we know that biological difference and sexual difference are of a fundamentally different order and that there is nothing "natural," or automatic, about the movement from the former to the latter; that physiologically male humans and physiologically female humans become "men" and "women" with predominantly heterosexual orientations and "masculine" and "feminine" character traits is not the work of biology but rather the product of human culture. Sexual identity is socially, not biologically constituted. Freud, as much as Marx, accepts the fundamental Hegelian proposition that the self is constituted through its conflictual interactions with the other. Unlike Marx, Hegel, or anyone else before him, however, Freud is aware that this intersubjective constitution of the self embraces even the creation of the very sexual identity of the self. The reproduction requirements of the human species may dictate that males become "men" who desire "women" and that females become "women" who desire "men," but these outcomes are not given with the birth of male and female children and only emerge, in fact, as the product of a complex,

170

protracted, and precarious struggle between these children and the significant others with whom they interact. Between the order of biology and the order of sexual identity Freud uncovers a vast, previously unexplored continent: the human struggle for sexual recognition.

The uncovering of this continent led Freud to a number of profoundly important discoveries. The first of these was the existence of infantile sexuality. Exploding the myth of childhood "innocence," Freud reveals that the infant enters the world with an array of erotic or sexual impulses that demand satisfaction. These impulses are neither genitally specific nor oriented exclusively toward the opposite sex; "polymorphous perversity" and bisexuality are the original or "natural" sexual condition of the human infant. The formation of a "masculine" and "feminine" heterosexual identity is thus not only a work of culture, it is a work of culture that goes against nature, that transforms the initially undifferentiated sexual orientations of the infant and replaces it with a sexual orientation that is differentiated according to gender, and the opposite gender at that. As such, the cultural constitution of sexual identity is indelibly marked by repression: the entry of the infant into the human order is synonymous with the infant's involuntary submission to a radical transformation of his or her sexual orientation. The formation of the sexual identity of the child entails nothing less than a struggle against the infant's body, a struggle which, as we shall see, inevitably leaves its mark on its mind as well. At this point we can simply reiterate that, for Freud, "humanization" and "repression" are inextricably intertwined or, in his words, that "our civilization is, generally speaking, founded on the suppression of instincts."[2] To speak of civilization is necessarily to speak of its "discontents."

The chief agents of this process of the suppression of infantile sexuality are the parents of the child. The child's struggle for sexual recognition is a one-sided struggle with his or her parents; they are the others against whom the separate sexual identity of the child is formed. Thus the "hallowed co-relation of parent and child"[3] is an eminently sexual relation: the intimate and prolonged contact between the infant and its mother determines that the mother becomes the first and most important object of the bisexual drives of the child. The transformation of these drives into heterosexual ones thus begins with the parental enforcement of the taboo on incest; the infant learns that he or she cannot possess the mother and that he or she must therefore alter the object of his or her sexual drives. The male child is forced to give up his desire for his mother in return for the knowledge that one day he will be able to possess someone like his mother, i.e., a woman. The female child, on the

---

[2] Sigmund Freud, " 'Civilized' Sexual Morality and Modern Nervousness," in *Collected Papers*, Vol. II (London: Hogarth Press, 1950), p. 82.

[3] Marx and Engels, *Manifesto of the Communist Party*, p. 349.

171

other hand, is obliged to repudiate entirely her sexual desire for a woman and to transfer this desire first to her father and then to someone like him, i.e., a man. I will consider Freud's elaboration of this difference between male and female sexual development presently. For now it is important to emphasize that, according to Freud, for both children it is the father (or, as we shall see, the symbol of his authority) that enforces the prohibition on incest. Because it is this prohibition that makes civilization possible, Freud concludes that civilization is inherently patriarchal: the Law of the Father is the condition of its possibility. The child's submission to the authority of the father thus signals his or her transcendence of the purely natural order of attachment to the mother and his or her entry into the order of culture. Submission to, and interiorization of, patriarchal authority is inseparable from the formation of the sexual identity of the child. The child will receive recognition of his or her sexual identity only insofar as he or she incorporates the paternal other within him/herself and conforms to his Law.

The child's experience of this struggle and its outcome is unconscious. The successful repression of his or her bisexual drives removes them from conscious awareness; the child remembers neither his or her desire for union with the mother nor the ruthless suppression of this desire that culminates in his or her heterosexual identification. Both this desire and the method of its suppression, however, live in the unconscious of the individual. From Freud we learn that repressed libidinal impulses are never entirely eliminated but rather persist as unconscious determinants of the behavior of the individual. The human self is thus an intrinsically divided self, fatally split between a conscious ego and an unconscious id that serves as the repository of suppressed polymorphous perverse and bisexual drives. The continuing power of these drives manifests itself in a variety of neurotic, or even psychotic symptoms and demonstrates that the ego is not master of its own house. Instead, it is obliged to rely on the superego, i.e., the internalized representative of the authority of the father, to exercise an unconscious censorship of those id-impulses that threaten the gender-specific organization of sexual identity. The rule of the superego produces an individual who is dominated by "tradition and . . . all the time-resisting judgments of value which have propagated themselves . . . from generation to generation."[4] The individual with an effective superego, in other words, is an individual who has incorporated his or her father within him/herself and thus continues to act according to the father's demands. As Marcuse puts it, "the superego . . . enforces not only the demands of reality but also those of a past reality. . . . Adherence to a *status quo ante* is implanted in the instinctual structure."[5] The individual

[4] Sigmund Freud, *New Introductory Lectures on Psychoanalysis* (New York: Norton, 1965), p. 67.

[5] Herbert Marcuse, *Eros and Civilization* (Boston: Beacon Press, 1955), p. 30.

172

carries the parent within him or her throughout life and thus the adult always remains, in part, a child.

The individual permanently bears the marks of its one-sided struggle for sexual recognition with its parents. This struggle, in fact, will be the decisive determinant of the subsequent emotional development of the individual; to state Freud's thesis in its most extreme form, the personality of the individual is but the residue of the particular way in which his or her parents have waged the universal struggle to repress his or her initial sexual orientation and replace it with an exclusively heterosexual identity. Freud's claim, in other words, is not only that the intersubjective constitution of the self includes the formation of a sexual self but that the formation of this sexual self is the principal process through which the entire self is constructed. Since the sexual self is constituted in childood, normally by the age of five or six, it follows that the self as a whole is likewise established and fixed at a very early age. Thus the individual's past dominates over his or her present; human life is, in this sense, inherently conservative. The human being is, according to Freud, "the sole being at the mercy of his childhood."[6]

This much is true for all individuals whether they are born male or female. But if both sexes are "at the mercy of [their] childhood," they are so in a fundamentally different way. The different way in which they are dominated by their childhood, in turn, determines that females will become "women" and males "men" and that women will be dominated by men. The reproduction of patriarchy is thus the inevitable outcome of the struggle for sexual recognition. To understand why this is so requires a more detailed examination of Freud's account of the two sexes' differential passage through what he calls the oedipal stage of this struggle.[7]

The male child's oedipal journey is relatively simple, far more so than that of the female. As he reaches the phallic stage of the organization of his sexual impulses, the male child's "pre-oedipal" and undifferentiated attachment to his mother is transformed into a specific desire to possess her with his penis. Simultaneously he learns, however, that it is his father who is able, by virtue of his superior "equipment," to monopolize the phallic possession of the mother; the child thus comes to experience his father as a rival and wishes to take his place, i.e., to kill him. The male child's hatred of his father, then, is merely the other side of the coin of his love for his mother. The little boy, of course, stands no chance of actually taking the place of his far more

---

[6] Paul Ricoeur, *Freud and Philosophy* (New Haven, Conn.: Yale University Press, 1970), p. 468.

[7] The following reconstruction is based on Juliet Mitchell, *Psychoanalysis and Feminism* (New York: Vintage Books, 1974); Nancy Chodorow, *The Reproduction of Mothering* (Berkeley: University of California Press, 1978); Eli Zaretsky, "Male Supremacy and the Unconscious," *Socialist Revolution*, Nos. 21-22 (January 1975), pp. 7-55.

powerful father. On the contrary, the superior power of his father obliges the boy to renounce his desire for his mother out of fear of the consequences of failing to do so.

More specifically, the consequence that the little boy dreads is his "castration," the possibility that he will be punished with the loss of his penis. The threat of castration thus inaugurates the male child's passage through the oedipal stage. This threat can be translated as the injunction to give up his desire for, and identification with, the mother or else risk becoming like her, i.e., losing his phallus and thus becoming a woman. The symbolic equation of "woman" and "absence of phallus" (or of "man" and "phallus") determines that henceforth the male child's desire to retain his phallus will be experienced (unconsciously, of course) as a desire not to be a woman. To put this another way, he learns to view women as castrated and, therefore, inferior. The oedipal complex of the male child is a classic example of a double-bind: his drives impel him to desire his mother, but his father compels him not to desire his mother. This complex is "resolved," i.e., he escapes his double-bind, when he agrees to give up his desire for his mother in return for the assurance that one day he too, like his father, will be able to possess a woman. Although he cannot have his mother without becoming like her, he can eventually possess her representative on the condition that he becomes like his father. He learns, in other words, that he will get what he wants if he becomes a "man."

Identification with his former rival is thus the way out of the oedipal impasse that confronts the male child. As I have already suggested, this identification entails the internalization of the father's prohibitions in the form of the superego. Because the father is so powerful, and so frightening, his internalization produces a particularly harsh superego, leaving the male child with a highly developed conscience. This conscience, in turn, serves as the basis of the sense of justice and social obligation without which civilization would be impossible. At the same time, the male child's powerful superego enables him to sublimate his sexual energies in the form of labor that is equally indispensable for civilization. Becoming a man means learning to defer his desire for a woman; masculinity entails the capacity to postpone gratification. Since labor is, as Hegel put it, "desire restrained and checked, evanescence delayed and postponed,"[8] it follows that masculinity entails the capacity to labor. Man's dominant place in the world of culture and work is thus inscribed in the solution to the oedipal dilemma of his childhood.

It is otherwise with the female child. The mother is also the female child's first love-object, and, as in the case of the little boy, the little girl when she reaches the genital stage wants to be the phallus for the mother. Like the

[8] *The Phenomenology of Mind*, p. 238.

male child, moreover, the female child's accession to the order of heterosexuality requires that she renounce this desire for the mother. But here the
symmetry ends. The male child's renunciation of his desire for the mother
culminates in the guarantee that he will ultimately possess someone like her;
his heterosexual development does not oblige him to alter the sexual identity
of his eventual love-object, and thus he experiences an underlying continuity
between this love-object and his initial one. The girl child, however, can
experience no such continuity. Because her first love object is of the same
sex as she, the demands of heterosexual development oblige her not merely
to give up her mother but also anyone who is like her mother as an eventual
love-object. Unlike the little boy, the little girl is forced to undergo a radical
transformation in the choice of love-objects; to become a "woman" she will
have to learn to transfer her erotic impulses from the female to the male of
the species. For this reason alone, her path to "womanhood" is more difficult
and precarious than her brother's route to "manhood."

The girl's turn toward men is facilitated by her relationship with her father;
this relationship is as essential to her transition to heterosexuality as the boy's
relationship to his father is to his. But the nature of the two relationships is
entirely different. For the boy, this relationship involves an identification with
the father that signals his exit from the oedipal stage. For the girl, in contrast,
this relationship involves the transfer of her sexual love from the mother to
the father and thus her entry into the oedipal situation. The girl only becomes
a "woman," according to Freud, insofar as she comes to desire her father,
while the boy only becomes a "man" to the extent that he stops desiring his
mother. Whereas the boy's break with his mother-fixation is contingent on
the repression of any sexual love for a parent, the girl's overcoming of her
mother-attachment is predicated on a transfer of sexual love from one parent
to another. Unlike the case of the boy, then, the path of the girl to womanhood
does not require that she ever leave the oedipal stage and, according to Freud,
women never entirely do. To put this another way, they never really leave
their family.

In a moment I will consider Freud's account of the consequences of what
might be called this permanent "oedipalization" of women. Whatever the
consequences of this sexual turn toward the father, however, it is first necessary to understand its cause. What compels the little girl to shift her sexual
attention from her mother to her father? Since, as we have seen, Freud rejects
the thesis of a natural or innate predisposition to heterosexuality, only a
cultural, or symbolic explanation will suffice. Freud finds one in the female
child's experience of castration. Just at that point when she desires to be the
phallus for her mother, the little girl discovers that she lacks one. Not having
what her little brother has, she experiences this lack as castration and as a
mark of her inferiority. Her attitude toward her mother turns to one of contempt

175

when she discovers that her mother also lacks the phallus. At the same time, she blames her mother for not having given her one. This mixture of contempt for and anger at her mother—Freud's infamous concept of "penis envy"— leads her to reject her mother as a love-object and turn instead toward her father, who possesses the phallus and can therefore give her one. In his later writings Freud came to understand that this overcoming of the girl's mother-attachment is never complete and that the girl's love for her father and subsequent love for her husband builds on the ambivalent pre-oedipal attachment of the girl to her mother, that "behind every girl's love for the father, there lurks her love for the mother; for every 'normal' woman who chooses her husband on the acceptable model of her father, the difficulties that ensue are just as likely to echo those that arose with the love and hate for the mother."[9] Yet Freud never abandoned the view that the girl turns toward her father, and then to men generally, because of "penis envy." Nor did he alter his conception that this desire for the phallus becomes, by virtue of an unconscious symbolic equation "penis = child," the desire to be given a child, first by her father and then by her husband, and that the girl's transition to heterosexual "womanhood" therefore entails a transformation from "active" clitoral to "passive" vaginal sexuality.

Having transferred her erotic impulses from her mother to her father, the daughter comes to regard her mother as a sexual rival. The nature of this oedipal rivalry, however, is by no means as intense or consequential as that between father and son. On the one hand, the girl has nothing to fear, since she is already castrated; on the other hand, the mother is not very frightening since she too is castrated, and thus lacks power. To put this another way, the rivalry between daughter and mother is mitigated by their mutual identification with their "common feminine inferiority," so nothing compels the girl to give up her father as a love-object. Instead she "comes to rest in the oedipus complex."[10] Her permanent oedipalization and her interiorization of a sense of inferiority are merely two sides of the same coin. The turn to the father is predicated on an acceptance of castration; the acceptance of castration, in turn, is based on the acceptance of the equation "phallus = power" and the deduction that girls are inferior because of their lack thereof. To become a "woman" is necessarily to recognize that one is lacking and that the only way to overcome this lack is to accept what a "man" alone is able to give.

All the conventional traits of femininity can, according to Freud, be deduced from the girl's oedipal situation. Most obviously, her supposedly natural propensity toward mothering and nurturing is but the consequence of her

[9] Mitchell, *Psychoanalysis and Feminism*, p. 111; see also Chodorow, *The Reproduction of Mothering*, pp. 92, 115.

[10] Chodorow, *The Reproduction of Mothering*, p. 113. Zaretsky, "Male Supremacy and the Unconscious," p. 23.

effort to compensate for her lack through the wish to receive a child (especially a male child) and hence the symbolic equivalent of the phallus. Similarly, the proverbial passivity of women results from the fact that her transition from mother-attachment to oedipal father-love is a transition from an active desire to love her mother to a passive desire to be loved by her father; she wants to *get from* him what she could not *give to* her, and this receptive orientation to her father will become—because of her permanent oedipalization—her orientation to the world as a whole. Her much despised "vanity" is also a compensation for her absence of a phallus; she tries to transform her entire body into a substitute for the sexual object she lacks. In short, "mothering," "passivity," and "vanity" are simply three different but related responses to the terrible "wound" of castration.

Other characteristically feminine traits follow from the particular nature of the oedipal drama of the female child. The girl, in contrast to the boy, is not compelled to give up her mother through the father's threat of castration but does so because she comes to recognize that she is already castrated. In order to become a "woman," in other words, she "does not have to internalize, to the same degree [as the boy] a powerful and punitive father [and] her own superego . . . will, of necessity be weaker."[11] According to Freud, the relatively undeveloped superego of the woman accounts for her tendency to be rather more emotional than rational; since women are not under the control of an effective superego, their feelings tend to be "closer to the surface." At the same time, a weak superego means a limited capacity for sublimation and thus both an undeveloped sense of social justice and capacity for work. Women are as emotionally ill-prepared for the "public" world of culture, politics, and production as they are well-prepared for the "private" world of the family. "Predisposed from infancy to seek their fate within the family, through loving a man and having a child,"[12] women become the willing accomplices of the patriarchal division of labor.

Whatever its limits, Freud's theory provides an account of precisely that reality that the Marxist approach fails to uncover, namely the process through which woman becomes the subordinate other of man. In the course of the struggle for sexual recognition, both the boy and the girl are obliged to interiorize the equation "phallus = power" and to learn to draw the appropriate conclusion, i.e., that the sex that possesses the phallus has power and the one that lacks it does not. Thus do men come to define women as inferior and women come to interiorize this definition. Freud offers us, then, a way of understanding the psychic roots, and thus the tenacity, of contemporary patriarchy that is lacking in Marx. At the same time, Freud's claim that the

[11] Mitchell, *Psychoanalysis and Feminism*, p. 99.
[12] Zaretsky, "Male Supremacy and the Unconscious," p. 24.

oedipal struggle for sexual recognition is coextensive with civilization enables him to shed light on the problem of why all modes of production have thus far been patriarchal and thus purports to remedy the inability of the Marxist concept of the mode of production to illuminate this problem.

THE MARXIST-FEMINIST APPROPRIATION OF FREUD

If Freud's assumption of the universality of the oedipus complex enables him to illuminate the pervasiveness of patriarchy, it also forecloses him or anyone else who accepts this assumption from theorizing about the possibility of its eventual demise. Thus the assumption is necessarily inconsistent with the feminist project, and feminists have called it into question. More precisely, they have sought to determine the historical specificity of the oedipus complex in order to be able to account for why civilization has been patriarchal in the past but why it need not be so in the future. The feminist reaction to Freud, then, has produced a variety of efforts to "historicize" his theory. In this chapter I will consider only those efforts that rely on Marxist categories. I will not examine, however, those historicizations that simply reduce the applicability of the oedipus complex to the conditions of the capitalist mode of production (or one particular period thereof), since they merely reproduce the inability of those efforts I have already reviewed to comprehend patriarchy as phenomenon that transcends these conditions. Rather I will restrict myself to a summary and evaluation of those Marxist-Feminist theories that proceed from the assumption that Freud's theory of the oedipus complex entails a generally acceptable description of the psychological reproduction of patriarchy in both precapitalist and capitalist modes of production but that the applicability of the theory can and will be nullified in the future through a transformation of those social conditions that are common to these past and present modes of production.

Juliet Mitchell's Psychoanalysis and Feminism

If patriarchy reproduces itself through the internalization of the equation "phallus = power," then the claim that patriarchy is universal amounts to the assertion of the universality of this equation. Freud never adequately defends this assertion; he never explains convincingly why the phallus assumes such a privileged position, why it everywhere signifies the presence of power, why, in his words, "for both sexes, only one kind of genital, namely the male, comes into account." Faced with this question, Freud takes refuge either in biology or in mythology. On the one hand, he implies that only the male genital "comes into account" or becomes the privileged signifier because

178

it is larger, or more visible, than that of the female; thus, in his infamous phrase, "anatomy is destiny."[13] This explanation, insofar as it relies on the assumption of a natural identity between a signifier and the concept it signifies, is of course completely inconsistent with Freud's general insistence that sexual meaning or significance is, like any other, symbolically or culturally rather than naturalistically constituted. To put this another way, the argument that the penis becomes the signifier of power because it is more visible begs the question as to why visibility is valorized in the first place.[14] Freud's biologistic explanation is thus really no explanation at all.

Freud supplements his biologistic argument with a "theory" of the patriarchal beginnings of human civilization. Starting from the assumption that "ontogeny recapitulates phylogeny," i.e., that the development of each child recapitulates the historical development of the human species as a whole, he hypothesizes an actual drama coincident with the origins of human society of which the child's oedipal complex may be understood to be the psychic reenactment. Prior to civilization, Freud speculates, there was only the "primal horde" ruled arbitrarily by the father, who monopolized all the women in the community. Civilization was inaugurated when the sons, jealous of the father's sexual privileges and anxious to take his place, banded together first to kill the father and then to create laws and institutions that would enable them henceforth to enjoy women in the security of individual patriarchal families. Civilization thus reproduces the original patriarchal despotism in a new form, substituting the rule of many fathers for the rule of one. Each child's oedipus complex and its patriarchal resolution merely reenacts the "archaic heritage" of this primal murder and its patriarchal outcome.[15] The universality of oedipus is given in the fact that the child's humanization necessarily reproduces the patriarchal foundations of human civilization itself.

This defense of the universality of patriarchy, as many have pointed out, is surely no more satisfying than the first. To begin with, it rests on the extraordinarily problematical assumption that the "memory traces of the experiences of former generations"[16] are somehow preserved in the psychic formation of the members of each new generation. Second, Freud himself acknowledges that the theory of the primal horde itself is purely speculative and, like any hypothesis of social origins, it is of course unverifiable. Finally, the assumption of a precivilized condition that is transcended when beings who are presocial but nevertheless human determine through rational agreement that civilized institutions would be consistent with their respective interests obviously partakes too much of seventeenth- through nineteenth-cen-

[13] Cited in Chodorow, *The Reproduction of Mothering*, pp. 145, 141.

[14] Luce Irigaray, *Speculum: De L'Autre Femme* (Paris: Les Editions de Minuit, 1974).

[15] Marcuse, *Eros and Civilization*, p. 51.

[16] Sigmund Freud, *Moses and Monotheism* (New York: Knopf, 1949), p. 157.

179

tury "social contract" theory to be taken as anything but a myth that illuminates the way in which men in a bourgeois society project their patriarchal present back into the past.

The weakness of these two arguments has left Freud's theory of the oedipus complex vulnerable to the by-now conventional objection that it merely reflects the particular realities of his particular epoch.[17] This objection, according to Juliet Mitchell, throws the baby out with the bath water; in its haste to demonstrate that society need not be patriarchal in the future, it discards precisely that concept that enables us to understand why it has always been patriarchal in the past. Thus she conceives her task as twofold. First, she attempts to establish a more secure foundation for Freud's contention that the oedipus complex has been coextensive with human civilization; in this effort she relies on cultural anthropology, particularly the work of Lévi-Strauss. Second, she tries to make the case that, contrary to Freud, the oedipus complex, and along with it patriarchy, need not be coextensive with human civilization in the future. Here Marx is her ally.

Mitchell appropriates Lévi-Strauss's analysis of kinship structures in order to demonstrate that the oedipus complex is but the inevitable interiorization of their universal logic. This logic, according to Lévi-Strauss, is cultural rather than natural; the laws of kinship do not express biological facts but instead transform them in the service of specifically social ends. Thus the incest taboo that everywhere regulates the biological event of procreation simultaneously establishes the transcendence of biology; the function of this taboo, is not, contrary to conventional wisdom, the prohibition of genetically dangerous matings but is, rather, the creation of social solidarity on a basis wider than that of the immediate biological unit. By forbidding sexual unions within this group, the incest taboo obliges individuals to establish sexual unions outside this group. It guarantees, in other words, that the biological requirement of procreation will be harnessed to a desire for extended sociality and thus engenders the relationships among biological "families" without which a specifically human society would be impossible.

Underlying the bewildering diversity of particular kinship systems, then, is the universal requirement that the members of "one family . . . give up one of its members to another family."[18] A kinship system can thus be understood as a series of reciprocal exchanges of persons that knit together the groups among which the exchanges are conducted. According to Lévi-Strauss, it is everywhere the case that the persons who are exchanged are women and that the persons who do the exchanging are men: "The total relationship of exchange which constitutes marriage is not established between

[17] Betty Friedan, *The Feminine Mystique* (New York: Norton, 1963), pp. 103-25.
[18] Mitchell, *Psychoanalysis and Feminism*, p. 370.

180

a man and a woman, but between two groups of men, and the woman figures only as one of the objects in the exchange."[19] An exhaustive study of kinship systems reveals that it is always men that give away their daughters, or their sisters, to other men; never are women found, not even in matrilineal societies, to have comparable rights of bestowal. Mitchell concurs: "the legally controlled exchange of women is the primary factor that distinguishes mankind from all other primates, from a cultural standpoint."[20] This fact enables us to understand the universality of woman's past and present oppression. To say that women everywhere figure as objects of exchange among men is to say that they are obliged to serve as the means through which a specifically male social bond is formed, the "words" by means of which men communicate to other men. Kinship is thus inherently patriarchal. But kinship is synonymous with human culture itself. It would appear, then, that her reliance on Lévi-Strauss obliges Mitchell to conclude not only that patriarchy has always existed but also that it will always exist in the future, that it is coextensive with human society itself. I will return to this problem shortly.

According to Mitchell, Freud's theory of the oedipus complex is nothing other than an explanation of how each child comes to assimilate the patriarchal law of the exchange of women. "It is *not* about the nuclear family" but rather about "man's entry into culture itself."[21] It describes the insertion of the child into a system of exchange that dictates that men are the exchangers and women the exchanged. The resolution of the male child's oedipus complex signals that he has come to accept the role of exchanger. He gives up his incestuous desires and thus retains his phallus, "the symbolic token which can later be exchanged for a woman;"[22] he unconsciously affirms, in other words, that because he is a "man," like his father, he will eventually have the same right to the possession of a woman that his father has now. Every male child learns, then, that his possession of a phallus will enable him to participate in the exchange of women that is constitutive of patriarchal culture. The entry of the female child into her oedipal stage, in contrast, marks her unconscious acceptance of her role as object of exchange. She rejects her mother and begins to desire her father when she discovers that he alone possesses a phallus; her desire for a child, first from him and then later from another man, is merely a disguised desire for the phallus that she necessarily lacks. Becoming a "woman" thus means coming to desire that which she does not have but what must instead be given to her. It means that she is prepared emotionally to receive the phallus that only the man is in a position

[19] Cited in Gayle Rubin, "The Traffic in Women," in Rayna Reiter, ed., *Toward an Anthropology of Woman* (New York: Monthly Review Press, 1975), p. 175.

[20] Mitchell, *Psychoanalysis and Feminism*, p. 372.

[21] *Ibid.*, p. 377, emphasis in the original.

[22] Rubin, "The Traffic in Women," p. 193.

to exchange and that he will exchange, at least temporarily (in intercourse) or symbolically (through a baby), for control over her body. In learning to be a woman, in short, she develops an unconscious need to serve as the object of a process of exchange that is controlled by men.

Thus Mitchell concludes that Freud's psychoanalysis describes the way in which the universal laws of patriarchal culture are reproduced in the unconscious of the individuals who are obliged to submit to them. The oedipus complex and its consequences are the inevitable psychological correlates of the exchange of women. If this is so, then the fact that male children develop "masculine" traits that prepare them for the world of work and culture while female children develop "feminine" traits that consign them to the world of the family would appear to be coterminous with the very existence of kinship, and hence society, itself. Once again, we seem to be back to the equation of patriarchy and civilization. Mitchell's own argument appears to lead inexorably to a conclusion that she must, as a feminist, at all costs resist. In order to resist this conclusion, she advances the outlines of a theory of the obsolescence of kinship or, in her words, of "the social non-necessity at this stage of development of the laws instituted by patriarchy."[23] This part of her argument is confusing, and, I shall argue, confused. To make sense of it, we shall have to listen very closely to what she says.

The persistence of patriarchy across different modes of production, Mitchell states, demonstrates that the kinship system and the mode of production are "two autonomous areas." They are, however, "interdependent" in that the mode of production determines the specific form in which the universal patriarchal culture will be expressed. In the case of the capitalist mode of production, "the kinship system that defines patriarchy is forced into the straightjacket of the nuclear family." This happens because "the dominant class, the bourgeoisie, needs the reproduction of its labour force. The so-called biological nuclear family is the bourgeoisie's answer to the problem of reproduction."[24]

Paradoxically, the capitalist mode of production determines that the universal laws of patriarchal culture will be expressed in the specific form of the nuclear family precisely at that point when it also determines that these universal laws have become "redundant." To begin with, capitalism divests

[23] Mitchell, *Psychoanalysis and Feminism*, p. 414.

[24] *Ibid.*, pp. 412, 379. This argument, which links the emergence of the conjugal nuclear family to the reproduction requirements of the industrial capitalist labor force, is undermined by the considerable evidence that supports the contention that (a) the nuclear family first developed among the professional classes and the gentry prior to the onset of industrialization and (b) the nuclear family did not develop among the working class until well after the onset of industrialization. See Lawrence Stone, *The Family, Sex and Marriage in England: 1500-1800* (New York: Harper & Row, 1977), pp. 449-50, and Poster, *Critical Theory of the Family*, pp. 46-47.

kinship structures of the economic, political, and religious functions they once performed; "as the productivity of labour develops . . . societies increasingly become dominated not by sex-ties (kinship) but by class conflicts." Thus the "biological [nuclear] family . . . asserts itself in the absence of prominent kinship structures." If not for this family, these already "residual" structures could be eliminated entirely, because "the complexity of capitalist society makes archaic the kinship structures and incest taboos for the majority of people . . . the capitalist economy implies that for the masses the demands of exogamy and the social taboo on incest are irrelevant." In what sense does the capitalist economy imply the irrelevance of kinship? Here Mitchell is particularly vague, but because she refers at a number of points to the "social conditions of work under capitalism that make potentially redundant the laws of patriarchal culture," we can infer that she means to say that the capitalist mode of production is the first mode of production whose labor process assembles and unites large numbers of people in cooperative activity and thus the first that need not rely on the incest taboo and exogamy in order to ensure a social solidarity that is wider than the basic biological unit.[25] She also appears to argue that the exchange of women is "already redundant (except in the upper classes)" because the "daughters of working-class families [are] of little value for exchange," but this, strictly speaking, is an argument about the loss of kinship's economic function that merely repeats her contention that kinship has become residual and does not speak to the possibility of its overall redundancy. Similarly, she contends that "under capitalism, the mass of mankind . . . working socially together *en masse* . . . would be unlikely, *were it not for the preservation of the family*, to come into proximity with their kin." But this argument for the irrelevance of the incest taboo presupposes that the elimination of genetic dangers is, after all, an important function of this taboo, which is precisely what she, following Lévi-Strauss, had earlier denied. And, she appears once again to deny this when she adds, in the same breath, that "if they did [come into proximity with their kin], it wouldn't matter."[26] Thus the only case she makes for the irrelevance of kinship that is consistent with her earlier emphasis on social solidarity as the function of kinship is the argument that this function is now performed by the inherently social mode of the capitalist labor process itself.

It is difficult to know what to make of this claim. It is certainly true that the capitalist labor process brings large numbers of people into daily contact with each other and that the exchange of the products of this process creates a vast network of reciprocal interdependencies. It is not clear, however, that

[25] *Ibid.*, pp. 414, 378-80, 409, 412. I have also relied on Elizabeth Long's review of *Psychoanalysis and Feminism* in *Telos*, No. 20 (Summer 1974), pp. 183-89, in order to help me make sense of this part of Mitchell's argument.

[26] Mitchell, *Psychoanalysis and Feminism*, pp. 379-80.

this is sufficient to generate the solidarity without which the society as a whole could not exist. On the one hand, the alienated nature of the capitalist labor process, Marx tells us, produces a worker who ''no longer feels himself to be freely active in any but his animal functions—eating, drinking, procreating, or at most in his dwelling and in dressing up,''[27] i.e., it produces a person who tries to satisfy his or her need for sociality not through contact with those with whom he or she works but rather within the shelter and privacy of the family. Thus, from a Marxist perspective, it is certainly just as plausible to argue that the social nature of the capitalist labor process reinforces the function of the kinship system as it is to argue that it makes it redundant. On the other hand, the interdependencies engendered by the exchange of products are based exclusively on self-interest, and self-interest is not necessarily a sufficient foundation for the intergenerational persistence of social institutions. In a way, the issue that Mitchell raises is simply a new version of the old question of whether what Durkheim called organic solidarity—or consciousness of interest—can ever entirely replace what he called mechanical solidarity—or consciousness of kind—as the basis of social stability. Interestingly enough, those who argue that mechanical solidarity can never be completely eliminated, even under capitalism, typically locate the kinship system or the family as a, if not *the*, crucial structure through which the shared values on which the persistence of the society is held to depend are internalized and reproduced.[28] Mitchell, in contrast, merely assumes, without demonstrating, that capitalism can dispense with mechanical solidarity and thus that it can dispense with kinship. Alternatively, it may be that she assumes that the capitalist labor process will eventually engender a new kind of mechanical solidarity, i.e., a class consciousness that transcends privatism and self-interest, but this would amount to an argument for the possibility of the redundancy of kinship under socialism, or the transition thereto, not under capitalism. In either case, her claim that there is a ''contradiction between patriarchal law and the social organization of work'' under capitalism remains unsubstantiated.[29]

This claim is particularly problematical in the light of Mitchell's contention that this contradiction is ''held in check by the nuclear family.'' Here too it is not easy to figure out exactly what she has in mind. On the one hand, she argues, as we have seen, that the nuclear family is the specific form within which patriarchal law is expressed in a capitalist mode of production. If this is so, then the assertion of a contradiction between capitalism and patriarchy amounts to the thesis of a contradiction between capitalism and the nuclear

[27] Marx, ''Estranged Labour,'' p. 60.

[28] See, for example, Talcott Parsons and Edward A. Shills, eds., *Toward a General Theory of Action* (New York: Harper & Row, 1962).

[29] Mitchell, *Psychoanalysis and Feminism*, p. 413.

184

family. How, then, is it possible to speak of this contradiction being "held in check by the nuclear family" without denying that there is a contradiction in the first place? How can the nuclear family be both the vehicle for the expression of one of the terms to a contradiction and the means through which this contradiction is forestalled? Mitchell argues that "in industrial society, if the family were not preserved, the prohibition on incest together with the . . . exchange of women would be unnecessary";[30] but this is merely to advance the tautology that patriarchy would be unnecessary except for the fact that it exists. Her formulation, in other words, begs the question as to why the (nuclear) family is preserved. Earlier, she had answered that this family exists in order to fulfill the specifically capitalist interest in the reproduction of the labor-force, i.e., that the nuclear family is a structure that functions to reproduce the capitalist mode of production. But if patriarchy now owes its existence only to the nuclear family, and the nuclear family owes its existence exclusively to capitalism, the conclusion is inescapable that patriarchy now has no other "material basis" than capitalism. This conclusion, however, not only flies in the face of the reality of patriarchy under state socialism (a reality of which Mitchell is aware) but is also completely inconsistent with her general assumption that the kinship system and the mode of production are "two autonomous areas." If they really are autonomous, then the kinship system can never be understood merely as a structure that functions to reproduce a mode of production. But if this is so, then the nuclear family cannot be grasped exclusively as a capitalist reproductive mechanism, in which case it becomes impossible to argue that patriarchy would be redundant if not for the requirements of capitalism.

Mitchell wants to have it both ways. In order to account for the universality of patriarchy in the past and present, she affirms the autonomy of the kinship system from the mode of production. But because she accepts Freud and Lévi-Strauss's assumption of the inherently patriarchal nature of the kinship system, the only way in which she can argue for the elimination of patriarchy in the future is to argue for the elimination of *any* kinship system. This argument necessarily denies the very autonomy of this system from the mode of production that she elsewhere affirms. The alternative, of course, would be to affirm consistently the autonomy of the kinship system but to deny that it is inherently patriarchal and to develop a theory of the conditions under which it can become nonpatriarchal. But this alternative is one that Mitchell is unwilling to pursue. Instead, she is trapped in the entirely untenable position of arguing that at one time kinship was autonomous but that it is no longer once a certain mode of production comes into existence. This position echoes Engels's formulation, which she cites at the outset of her argument for the

[30] *Ibid.*, p. 380.

185

present redundancy of the kinship system, to the effect that "the less the development of labor, and the more limited its volume of production . . . the more preponderatingly does the social order appear to be dominated by ties of sex."[31] We saw in Chapter Two that Engels argued, in dualistic fashion, that social institutions are conditioned by two kinds of production: "by the . . . development of labor, on the one hand, and of the family, on the other."[32] The formulation that Mitchell cites, which is the sentence that immediately follows this argument in the *Origins of the Family*, attempts to resolve this dualism with the proposition that there is an inverse relationship between the development of labor and the importance of kinship. But this proposition ultimately denies the autonomy of kinship from production, since it asserts that the relative autonomy of this system from the mode of production is itself determined by the development of production (in the strict sense of "labor"). That Mitchell endorses this proposition demonstrates that the Marxist thesis of "ultimate" determination by the economic underlies, and thus undermines, her assumption of the autonomy of the kinship system from the mode of production. Her "final" position is thus merely a variant of the Althusserian problematic of dominance versus determination in the last instance that preserves all the contradictions (discussed in Chapter One) of this problematic.

These contradictions come back to haunt Mitchell's political conclusions. On the one hand she argues that the autonomy of patriarchy from capitalism dictates that "a specific struggle against patriarchy—a cultural revolution— is requisite" and that this feminist struggle of women should maintain its autonomy from the working-class movement for socialism as well as retain its raison d'être even after "a socialist economy is achieved."[33] This vision of two parallel movements, neither of which has priority over the other, suffers from a serious practical problem. The description of these movements as "parallel" obscures the fact that their actual relationship is necessarily antagonistic. The definition of the movement for socialism as a working-class movement is predicated on the assumption that an individual's stance toward socialism is determined, in the last analysis, by his or her position vis-à-vis the means of production. On this assumption, then, those who own or control the means of production—be they male or female—are defined as opponents, rather than supporters, of socialism. "Bourgeois" women are thus understood as the enemies of a working-class movement for socialism. The definition of the feminist movement as an anti-patriarchal revolution, on the other hand, is based on the assumption that an individual's sex or "sexual politics"— and not his or her relationship to the means of production—determines his or her ultimate willingness to support this movement. On this assumption,

[31] *Ibid.*, p. 378.
[32] See above, Chapter Two, n. 61.
[33] Mitchell, *Psychoanalysis and Feminism*, pp. 414-15.

working-class men, or at least working-class men who oppress women, are defined as the oppressors against which the feminist movement must struggle, while bourgeois women will be understood as part of the natural constituency of this movement. Thus the enemies of one movement (the oppressors) are the friends of the other (the oppressed). Faced with this reality, what—to coin a phrase—is a working-class woman to do? Is she to consider the bourgeois "member" of her sex an "exploiter" or a "sister"? Mitchell's political vision of the feminist struggle against patriarchy and the working-class struggle against socialism as two parallel and equally important struggles in no way resolves, but rather entirely ignores, this profound political dilemma. The resolution of this dilemma, it would appear, demands that a priority be established between the two movements, but Mitchell specifically disclaims the need for one.[34] The elaboration of a criterion that would enable us to establish such a priority, moreover, is precluded by the assumption of two autonomous, equally fundamental forms of oppression—kinship system and mode of production—that underlies her political vision. The result of Mitchell's theoretical eclecticism, then, is a political eclecticism that is unable to illuminate the relationship between the two movements to which she seeks to contribute.

On the other hand, it is not at all clear what the antipatriarchal, "cultural revolution" led by women entails, or what it could possibly entail. It surely cannot involve a struggle to transform the kinship system since, as we have seen, for Mitchell any such system is patriarchal and thus the elimination of patriarchy requires not the transformation but rather the elimination of this system. It would appear, then, that the feminist cultural revolution must be waged against the kinship system and its oedipal internalization. But Mitchell has told us that the nuclear family is the last stand of the kinship system, and that the nuclear family is maintained in order to serve the needs of the capitalist mode of production. This suggests that the feminist cultural revolution should be waged against the capitalist mode of production, but this, of course, is precisely the function of the working-class movement from which, Mitchell has insisted, the feminist movement must be autonomous. Thus, despite her commitment to two autonomous movements, the logic of Mitchell's argument appears either to deprive the feminist movement of any function whatsoever or else to resubmerge it within the working-class movement. To put this another way, the political function of her assumption of the ultimate determinative power of production compels the conclusion that the feminist movement should be subordinated to the working-class movement for socialism. Mitchell rejects this political conclusion, but it is "written into" the premises

---

[34] *Ibid.*, p. 414.

of the Marxist theory she appropriates in order to accomplish her historicization of Freud and Lévi-Strauss.

To conclude: the failure of Mitchell's political conclusions is the inevitable corollary of the failure of her theoretical effort to synthesize Marx and Freud. Her explicit commitment to two autonomous movements flows from her Freudian (and Lévi-Straussian) assumption of the irreducibility of kinship, and her failure to clarify the relationship between these two movements parallels her inability to reconcile this assumption with Marx's assumption of the primacy of production. Her implicit argument for the subordination of one movement to the other signals that her effort to reconcile the assumption of the irreducibility of kinship with the assumption of the primacy of production gives way to the Marxist reassertion of the primacy of production. She wants both Marx and Freud, but, in the end, she is left only with Marx. And the Marx she winds up with is no better than the one whose limits obliged her to turn to Freud in the first place.

Gayle Rubin's "The Traffic in Women"

Like Juliet Mitchell, Gayle Rubin argues that "one can read Freud's essays on femininity as descriptions of how a group is prepared psychologically, at a tender age, to live with its oppression," and that Lévi-Strauss's analysis of kinship systems can be read as a demonstration of the pervasiveness of the oppression of which Freud studies the psychological effects. Rubin's analysis of the way the oedipal drama of male and female children reproduces patriarchal relationships between men and women and the sense in which this drama is but the interiorization of the rules governing the exchange of women is, in fact, perfectly congruent with that of Mitchell. So too is her conclusion that Freud's and Lévi-Strauss's work "enables us to isolate sex and gender from 'mode of production' " and that the autonomy of the former system from the latter "suggests a conception of the women's movement as analogous to, rather than isomorphic with, the working-class movement, each addressing a different source of human discontent."[35]

Unlike Mitchell, however, Rubin refuses to accept the thesis that the exchange of women is the only possible form of kinship, or "sex-gender," system, as well as the corollary that the oedipus complex is the inevitable psychological complement of this system. She is aware that the acceptance of this thesis leads to the impossible political task of eliminating kinship, and thus culture as a whole. Starting from the assumption that both Freud and Lévi-Strauss have described a form of kinship that has been universal or near-universal ("It is even debatable that 'exchange of women' adequately de-

[35] Rubin, "The Traffic in Women," pp. 196, 203.

scribes all of the empirical evidence of kinship systems'') but need not exist in the future, she calls not for the elimination of, but rather "a revolution in" kinship.[36] In contrast to Mitchell, she is not obliged to turn to the Marxist magic wand of "determination-in-the-last-instance by the economic" in order to make disappear what appears immutable. The revolution she has in mind does not entail the abolition of the family but rather a "reorganization"[37] that would eliminate mother-monopolized child care and thus the common root of both the male and female child's oedipus complex:

> If the sexual division of labor were such that adults of both sexes cared for children equally, primary object choice would be bisexual. If heterosexuality were not obligatory, this early love would not have to be suppressed, and the penis would not be overvalued . . . the entire Oedipal drama would be a relic.[38]

In a subsequent chapter I will examine in detail the writings of feminists who have developed this point and made it central to their analysis of patriarchy and the possibilities for its transcendence. Rubin does not. She acknowledges that "it would be nice to be able to conclude . . . with the implications [of this point] for feminism and gay liberation," but proposes, instead, that the "next step on the agenda" must be "a Marxian analysis of sex/gender systems." One wonders whether this recourse to Marx bespeaks a kind of failure of nerve; at any rate it merely assumes, without argument, that the elaboration of the possibilities for the elimination of patriarchy cannot be undertaken without the aid of Marx, without the prior development of a "political economy of sex." (In Chapter Nine I shall argue that not only is Marx's aid unnecessary for the elaboration of the feminist project, but that his basic assumptions are inconsistent with this project and that the latter must, therefore, be elaborated in opposition to Marx.) In fact, her own analysis tends to undermine this assumption. The most support that she is able to offer for it is the observation that "there is an economics and politics to sex/gender systems"—that material wealth and power are exchanged and accumulated in and through the exchange of women. But she had earlier argued that this

---

[36] *Ibid.*, pp. 176, 199. Rubin is not entirely consistent on this point. In one part of her essay she argues "if there were no gender, the entire oedipal drama would be a relic" (p. 199), but earlier she defines a "sex-gender system" as a "set of arrangements by which a society transforms biological sexuality into products of human activity, and in which these transformed sexual needs are satisfied" (p. 159), i.e., she maintains that a sex-gender system is coextensive with humanity. If this is so, then it is not possible to speculate about the elimination of "gender." But perhaps such speculation is meant to refer only to the elimination of gender as the basis for a societal division of labor rather than the elimination of the more general, indeed universal, phenomenon of the culturalization of sexual differences.

[37] Rubin, "The Traffic in Women," p. 204.

[38] *Ibid.*, p. 199.

is no longer the case with the sex/gender system that is specific to contemporary, capitalist societies: this system "has been stripped of its functions—political, economic, educational and organizational" and "now . . . only organizes and reproduces itself."[39] This suggests that the possibility and necessity of a political economy of sex that exists for precapitalist societies is absent in capitalist societies. If this is so, then it remains a complete mystery why the elaboration of present and future antipatriarchal possibilities requires a turn to Marx and must await the development of a political economic analysis of sex.

Be that as it may, Rubin is intent on demonstrating that a Marxian analysis of sex/gender systems is possible. In order to do this, she attempts to persuade us that the recognition of the centrality of kinship is completely consistent with the fundamental theoretical categories of Marx and, in particular, the assumption of the primacy of production. Thus she states:

> A kinship system is an imposition of social ends upon a part of the natural world. It is therefore "production" in the most general sense of the term: a moulding, a transformation of objects (in this case people) to and by a subjective purpose. . . . It has its own relations of production, distribution, and exchange, which include certain "property rights" in people.[40]

This argument redefines "production" so broadly that it can be used to refer to any human activity whatsoever; thus Marx's proposition that production plays the determinative role in any society can be translated into the proposition that whatever human activity is found to be determinative in a particular society is production! Rubin's formulation is merely a version of Godelier's effort to reconcile Marx's thesis of the primacy of production with the manifest importance of kinship in precapitalist societies through the re-definition of relations of kinship as relations of production, and it entails all the difficulties of this effort that we examined in Chapter One. On the one hand, it reduces Marx's theory of determination by the mode of production to a tautology. On the other hand, it is not a very illuminating tautology at that, because it simply begs the question of what kind of production becomes dominant under what conditions. To put this another way, Rubin's "discovery" that a kinship system is, after all, a mode of production obliges her to redefine the autonomy of the kinship system from the mode of production as the autonomy of one mode of production from another mode of production and in no way illuminates the relationship between the two. Her failure to

[39] *Ibid.*, pp. 204, 205, 199.
[40] *Ibid.*, pp. 176-77.

190

clarify the relationship between the two "analogous" political struggles—the feminist struggle and the working-class struggle—to which she is committed is as inscribed in her theoretical premises as it is in those of Mitchell.

Like Mitchell, Rubin wants both Marx and Freud. Unlike Mitchell, however, she does not ultimately throw Freud away. Rather she retains both Freud and Marx, but at the cost of redefining Marx so broadly that he loses his identity and becomes virtually indistinguishable from Freud or, for that matter, from anyone else. Her Freudo-Marxist synthesis is no more successful than that of Juliet Mitchell.

Eli Zaretsky's "Male Supremacy and the Unconscious"

Zaretsky will have none of the ambiguity that plagues the work of Mitchell and Rubin. Boldly he reasserts the primacy of production as understood by Marx. "Production, the human struggle to master nature, is in part a struggle to master our internal nature, our minds and instinctual needs: this struggle is the object of psychoanalysis." The object of psychoanalysis is thus constituted by material production: the unconscious is the product of the "permanent struggle of men and women against an unyielding nature."[41] It follows that the form of the unconscious is a function of the form of labor.

Thus Zaretsky rejects Freud's and Mitchell's thesis of the primordial nature of the patriarchal unconscious. This unconscious has not always existed, but was created by a certain form of production: "Like the oedipus complex itself, patriarchy has been shaped historically by the changing forms of the compulsion to labor." More specifically, Zaretsky endorses as plausible Engels's "hypothesis that patriarchy arose with the decline of household-centered and communal economies."[42] He thus ignores all the ambiguities and contradictions in Engels's account that we examined in Chapter Two.

The form of "social production" of which patriarchy is an "aspect," Zaretsky tells us, is the direct appropriation of use-values and the "limited development of productive forces" that dominates in precapitalist societies and still characterizes the family within a capitalist society. The "limited development" of the productive forces of precapitalist societies dictated "the submission of the entire society to the forces of nature." Unable to master external nature, these societies produced individuals who were unable to master their internal nature as well. The oedipalized unconscious that Freud discovered is not eternal but merely the unconscious that is generated by this precapitalist inability to master external and internal nature: "Freud's theory

---

[41] Zaretsky, "Male Supremacy and the Unconscious," pp. 37-38, 35.
[42] Ibid., p. 35.

speaks to the fetishized and inverted forms in which the struggle to create and maintain use-values was understood." Since, "within the modern family a world of use-values, laden with fetishized religious and symbolic meanings, still persists in apparent isolation from the capitalist economy," the oedipalized unconscious and thus male supremacy continue to be reproduced within contemporary capitalist societies.[43]

If the problem of patriarchy is, ultimately, "limited development" of the forces of production, then we should expect that the solution to this problem can be found in unlimited development of the forces of production, i.e., the creation of a socialist mode of production:

> [P]atriarchy is rooted in the division of labor in the family, the responsibility of women for housework and child-rearing, and the associated bias in favor of heterosexuality. *These problems concern the organization of production.*[44]

Zaretsky implies that a reorganization of production under socialism, which presumably includes the socialization of housework and child care and thus the elimination of the production of these use-values within the family (once again, we are back to Engels), will eliminate the oedipus complex and the patriarchal division of labor that it both reflects and reproduces. The struggle to eliminate patriarchy is part of the broader struggle to realize socialism.

Zaretsky does not hesitate to draw the appropriate conclusion: the feminist movement must be subordinated to a working-class movement on behalf of socialism. He tells us that "a feminist movement will be necessary long into the period of socialism." (One wonders why, since he has already told us that socialism is the solution to the problem of patriarchy. Perhaps it is because he believes that a socialist society will inevitably be faced with certain patriarchal survivals from its precapitalist and capitalist past.) But there can be no talk of two parallel or analogous movements:

> The difference between a feminist movement and a socialist movement is that the former must struggle for the liberation of women, with all the limitations and advantages implied in representing a *special interest*, while the latter must struggle to transform the *entire society*, in all its complexity.[45]

If the socialist movement is a "struggle to transform the entire society," then it follows that it is a movement against patriarchy. But if it is a movement against patriarchy, it makes a separate feminist movement redundant. Zar-

[43] *Ibid.*, pp. 36, 39-40.
[44] *Ibid.*, p. 52, emphasis added.
[45] *Ibid.*, p. 51, emphases added.

192

etsky's "feminist movement . . . that must struggle for the liberation of women" can exist only as a "special interest" that is subsumed under the working-class movement and the universal interest it is alleged to represent. The elimination of an autonomous feminist movement is the political conclusion that follows inescapably from Zaretsky's unambiguous reassertion of the primacy of production.

The price that Zaretsky pays for the elimination of the ambiguity found in Mitchell and Rubin is the recapitulation of almost all the inadequacies of the Marxist theories of patriarchy we reviewed in Chapter Two. Engels's theories of the economic origins of patriarchy and the economic basis for its elimination are resurrected, in warmed-over fashion, with near-total disregard for the logical and empirical problems that they entail. At the same time, Zaretsky's own account is not even internally consistent: the argument that the limited development of the forces of production is the basis of patriarchy directly contradicts his endorsement of Engels's thesis of the absence of patriarchy under "primitive communism," the societies of "limited" productive forces par excellence. And, if the case of primitive communist societies demonstrates that limited productive forces is not the problem, then it also suggests that unlimited development of the productive forces, i.e., socialism, is not in itself the solution.

One suspects, moreover, that Zaretsky introduces Freud only for the purpose of domesticating him. The assumption that underlies Zaretsky's entire argument is, as we have seen, that there is a one-to-one relationship between the mastery of external and the mastery of internal nature. This may be an assumption of Marx (in fact, we saw in Chapter Four that it is, but that it is inconsistent with other of his assumptions), but it is not Freud's and it is, in fact, the very opposite of Freud's assumption. For Freud, as I suggested at the outset of this chapter, mastery over external nature is inevitably accompanied by repression and thus by neurosis and unhappiness, i.e., by the absence of the mastery of internal nature. Zaretsky merely assumes that Marx is right and Freud is wrong. Freud then becomes a mere adjunct of Marx, someone who testifies that the determinative power of the mode of production runs even deeper than Marx imagined. Freud simply describes the unconscious, psychological effects of that which Marx correctly locates as the cause. To risk a patriarchal, but in this case perhaps appropriate metaphor, Zaretsky's Freudian unconscious is but the child of Marx's production. We cannot even say that his "synthesis of Marx and Freud is a failure" because, in truth, he has not even attempted to develop such a synthesis. He has merely subsumed Freud under Marx. And the result is a theory of patriarchy that is no more satisfactory than the theories of those Marxists who never thought Freud was necessary in the first place.

193

FREUDO-MARXIST THEORIES OF PATRIARCHY AND THE POLITICS OF POSTPONEMENT

The Freudo-Marxist theories of patriarchy that we have reviewed can be understood as responses to the radical feminist insistence that the elimination of male domination should be the overriding political commitment of women and thus that the transformation of the present sex/gender system is the task to which their primary energies ought directly and immediately to be devoted. The message these theories convey is that the radical feminists are both right and wrong. Right, because Freud demonstrates that male domination is not a mere function of the mode of production but is inherent in a sex/gender system that prevails in many different modes of production; the radical feminist understands, correctly, that a socialist transformation of the mode of production that does not include a transformation of this system will simply reproduce, rather than eliminate, the domination of men over women. Wrong, however, because Marx "demonstrates" that the possibility of the elimination of the patriarchal sex/gender system is given only with the development of a certain level of production and thus that the struggle to eliminate the former is ultimately dependent on the struggle to reach the latter. The radical feminist insistence on the immediate transformation of the existing mode of child rearing and the male-female relationships that flow from it fails to appreciate that the elimination of capitalism and the creation of socialism is the prerequisite of this very transformation. Thus the radical feminist must abandon her direct approach and recognize that the "broader" socialist movement is the only possible vehicle through which she will ultimately get what she wants. Even if this were not true—even if it were possible to eliminate the patriarchal sex/gender system without first eliminating the capitalist mode of production— the only way in which the radical feminist can escape the onus of parochialism is to commit at least some of her energies to the struggle for a socialist mode of production, which, according to Freudo-Marxists, is every bit as much (if not more) in the universal human interest as the struggle to eliminate patriarchy. In either case the message from the Freudo-Marxists is: "give up your exclusive commitment to the transformation of male-female relationships and join the movement to transform the mode of production."

Freudo-Marxist theories of patriarchy thus function to at least partly displace the terrain of women's struggles from the world of the family to the world of work. In so doing, however, the theories encourage women to struggle on the very terrain on which, according to these same theories, women are least equipped to succeed. According to the Freud that these theories endorse, as we have seen, the "normal" woman reared within the patriarchal family is emotionally oriented to the family and the relationships within it and ill-prepared psychologically for the "public" arena; lacking the aggressiveness

194

of her male "comrade" and accustomed to measuring herself by his standard, she is likely to defer to him and follow his lead. The assumptions of the Freudo-Marxist theorists lead us to anticipate that women will be followers, rather than leaders, in the very socialist movements in which these theorists encourage their participation; the Freudian part of their theory tells us, in other words, that male domination will be reproduced in the very organizations that are, according to the Marxist part of their theory, ultimately essential for the elimination of male domination. Thus we cannot be confident that a Marxist socialist movement will *ever* make the transformation of the sex/gender or child-rearing system a central practical, rather than merely rhetorical, priority. Instead, we should expect that such movements will regularly and permanently postpone this transformation, since they will be led by men and men will unconsciously, if not consciously, oppose it. This expectation, as Batya Weinbaum has shown, has in fact been strikingly, and tragically, confirmed in the case of all the successful "socialist" movements she examines.[46]

In Chapter Two I suggested that the Marxist assumption of the primacy of production functions to reproduce, rather than undermine, the patriarchal division of labor. If the political consequence of the continuing centrality of

[46] *The Curious Courtship of Socialism and Women's Liberation*, Chs. 6-8. I have personally witnessed this dialectic of postponement within a variety of American New Left settings. During the early 1970s I was a member of a collective that organized and, at least initially, directed an alternative educational and cultural center in New York City that was explicitly committed to both libertarian socialist and feminist goals. The participation of women both within the collective and throughout the organization as a whole did not prevent men from playing a clearly dominant role. (Interestingly enough, some of the more vocal women were clearly the most "male-identified" and among the least sympathetic to feminist demands; it was as if their long struggle to succeed on a male terrain had required such a heavy investment in the norms that govern this terrain that any challenge to these norms provoked a defensive, even hostile reaction on their part.) The result was that the demands of women (and a handful of male supporters) to focus the energies of the organization on the problem of male-female relationships and the system of child rearing that underlies them were rarely taken seriously and never effectively implemented. Thus the problem of child care for the parents of participants never became a major priority and was largely left to women to resolve in whatever ways they could. Similarly, the demand of a number of women on the collective for a general meeting of all women members that would not be open to men and that would enable the women to share the difficulties they experienced in participating in a male-dominated institution encountered the prolonged and derisive resistance of a number of the male Marxist "heavies" on the collective. Such exclusivity, it was argued, was yet another example of the effort "to divide the Left." "Next week," speculated one particularly prominent Marxist ostensibly and publicly committed to feminist goals, "it will be the Dominicans that demand a closed meeting." Here we have a classic example of resistance to a challenge to male domination that is rationalized in the name of Marxist assumptions that relegate women's needs to the status of a special interest. Does this not suggest that the Marxist assertion of the universality of the proletariat and the struggle it wages is as ideological as the universalistic claims of former rising classes that Marx unmasks?

195

production to Freudo-Marxist theories of patriarchy is also a contribution to the reproduction of the very male domination they seek to transcend, the conclusion would appear to be warranted that not only Marxism but Neo-Marxism as well is an obstacle to the feminist project. Just when women are demanding of men: "Join our world and help us remake the family," is it not Neo-Marxism that allows men to respond: "Remake the family, yes, but first—or also—join *our* world and help us remake the mode of production," and does not this response (and the acquiescence of women to it) set in motion a process that enables men permanently to evade that demand? I shall return to this question of the inherently patriarchal character of both Marxism and Neo-Marxism in Chapter Nine. At this point I merely want to emphasize that the feminist project demands a theory that, in contrast to Marxism, does not short-circuit the analysis of the family in favor of the analysis of an elsewhere of which the family is held ultimately to be a mere expression. The possibilities for a nonpatriarchal sex/gender system, in other words, must be located within rather than outside the existing sex/gender system; an adequate critical theory of the patriarchal family must encourage a direct and immediate effort to transform this family. We have seen that Freud's psychoanalytic theory forecloses, rather than encourages, this effort by virtue of his (patriarchal) assumption that the patriarchal family is the only possible family form, and that this led Freudo-Marxists to try to find an opening with Marx. But all Marx offers is a detour that leads to a dead-end. The alternative, we shall see, is a psychoanalytic theory that insists on the irreducibility of the family but that dispenses with the patriarchal assumptions of Freud. A psychoanalysis, if you like, of the power of the Mother.

Chapter Six

Neo-Marxist Theories of the State

Freudo-Marxist Theories of the State

Freud on the Nature of Political Domination

Just as feminists were obliged to attempt to supplement a Marxist approach to patriarchy with theoretical insights derived from Freud, so the partisans of participatory democracy have found it necessary to turn to Freud in order to illuminate the pervasiveness and persistence of the political domination for which Marxist theory does not and (I argued in Chapter Three) cannot account. As in the case of the Marxist-Feminists, this turn to Freud the political theorist has been highly selective and entails an effort to relativize or historicize his theory of political domination in order to reopen and clarify the possibilities for the liberation it forecloses. Once again, it is the thought of Marx on which this historicization will be based. The first half of this chapter deals, then, with Freudo-Marxist theories of political domination and the problem of whether this hyphenated construction signals an accomplished reality or merely an unrealized, or even unrealizable, expectation.

Freud's theory of political domination grows out of, and in a sense is simply an extrapolation from, his theory of patriarchy. The assumption that justifies this extrapolation is that "sociology . . . cannot be anything but applied psychology."[1] Psychology, for Freud, and as we have seen, is the study of the unconscious effects of the individual's early encounter with his or her parents, or of the unconscious presence of the family within the individual and the way in which this presence determines his or her behavior. If sociology is merely "applied psychology," then for Freud society is merely the family writ large; social organization is but an extended form of familial organization. To be more specific, "Freud attempts to show that participation in any social organization—church or army, authoritarian or democratic group, bureaucratized or primitive group . . . —is little more than an extension of the patriarchal nuclear family."[2]

Family relationships, we have seen, are erotic or libidinal relationships.

[1] Freud, *New Introductory Lectures on Psychoanalysis*, p. 179.
[2] Poster, *Critical Theory of the Family*, p. 32.

197

The claim that social or political relationships are, at bottom, an extension of family relationships amounts to the claim that social or political relationships are likewise erotic in nature. The body politic, as the metaphor implies but was never fully recognized until Freud, is a specifically sexual body; the ties that bind the members of the public world of politics are as libidinally rooted as those that bind the members of the private world of the family. Were this not the case, no social group could long endure; "without any addition of libido . . . tolerance does not persist longer than the immediate advantage gained from other people's collaboration."[3] Thus Freud emphatically rejects the Classical Liberal assumption that self-interest or a rational calculus of mutual advantage is the foundation of the social group, and he argues instead that social solidarity is predicated precisely on a transcendence of self-interest or what in this context he calls "narcissism":

> [I]ntolerance vanishes, temporarily or permanently, as a result of the formation of a group. . . . So long as a group formation persists or so far as it extends, individuals in the group behave as if they were uniform, tolerate other people's peculiarities, put themselves on an equal level with them, and have no feeling of aversion toward them. Such a limitation of narcissism can, according to our theoretical views, only be produced by one factor, a libidinal tie with other people.

> [I]n the development of mankind as a whole, just as in individuals, love alone acts as the civilizing factor in the sense that it brings a change from egoism to altruism . . . [T]he essence of a group formation consists in new kinds of libidinal ties among the members of the group.[4]

The libidinal ties that "cathect" the members of a group to one another, however, are not primordial but are rooted in a prior and more powerful libidinal tie that binds each of them to the leader of the group; the mutual identification that characterizes the relationships among the individuals of a group is a function of a more profound, unconscious identification between all these individuals and their leader(s). Thus Freud defines a group as "a number of individuals who have substituted one and the same object for their ego ideal [superego] and have consequently identified themselves with one another in their ego."[5] Social solidarity, in other words, is a precipitate of authority; to understand what holds a group together is, ultimately, to understand the mechanism that binds the followers to their leader. The study of

[3] Sigmund Freud, *Group Psychology and the Analysis of the Ego* (London: Hogarth Press, 1949), p. 57.

[4] *Ibid.*, pp. 56-58.

[5] *Ibid.*, p. 80.

198

society can thus be reduced to the study of authority. To put this another way, Freud defines society as coextensive with political domination.

The identification between followers and leader on which the social group depends is, in turn, and as Freud's definition of the group suggests, the product of the original identification within the family between children and their father. The child, or rather the male child, internalizes his father's prohibition on the expression of his sexual impulses in the form of a superego that effectively and unconsciously wards off these threatening impulses; the formation of the superego signals that the child has incorporated the father within him and thus that the external repression of his sexuality has given way to the internal or self-repression of this sexuality. Freud explicitly compares the repressive role of the superego to the role of the state:

> Our mind, that precious instrument by whose means we maintain ourselves alive, is no peacefully self-contained unity. It is rather to be compared with a modern State in which a mob, eager for enjoyment and destruction, has to be held down forcibly by a prudent superior class.[6]

> This new mental agency continues to carry on the functions which have hitherto been performed by the corresponding people in the external world: it observes the ego, gives it orders, corrects it and threatens it with punishments, exactly like the parents whose place it has taken. We call this agency the superego and are aware of it, in its judicial functions, as our conscience.[7]

Every "normal" individual, Freud is telling us, is his own judge and policeman; every adult carries the state within him in the form of the unconscious presence of his father.

If the superego is the internal representative of the authority of the father within the family, political authority is merely the external representative of, or substitute for, the superego. The relationship between followers and their leader is a sublimated or "aim-inhibited" version of the libidinal relationship between themselves and their father; the acquiescence of the masses to political authority is rooted in their unconscious need for paternal authority:

> The leader of the group is . . . the dreaded primal father; the group . . . wishes to be governed by unrestricted force; it has an extreme passion for authority . . . a thirst for obedience.[8]

---

[6] Cited in Richard Lichtman, "Marx and Freud, Part Two," *Socialist Revolution*, No. 33 (May-June 1977), p. 76.

[7] Sigmund Freud, *An Outline of Psychoanalysis* (New York: Norton, 1949), p. 121.

[8] Freud, *Group Psychology and the Analysis of the Ego*, pp. 99-100.

199

Why the great man should rise to significance at all we have no doubt whatever. We know that the great majority of people have a strong need for authority which they can admire, to which they can submit, and which dominates and even ill-treats them. We have learned from the psychology of the individual whence comes this need of the masses. It is the longing for the father that lives in each of us from his childhood days.[9]

The persistence and pervasiveness of political domination is, then, merely a corollary of the ubiquity of the patriarchal unconscious; mass acquiescence to, even affirmation of, the state is but the consequence of the sexual repression, carried out by the father, without which civilization would be impossible. Freud's theory proposes a novel solution to the classical problem of the origins of political obligation. The transformation of "might" into "right," with which political philosophers have been preoccupied, is but the unconscious and "automatic" result of a prior transformation of the "might" of the child's father into the "right" of the child's superego. The individual affirms the legitimacy of the rule of those who are stronger because he has already affirmed the legitimacy of the authority of his father with the formation of his superego and has, in the process, developed an unconscious stake in his own domination. The individual, in short, is "everywhere in chains" of his own—or rather his family's—making.

Whether this theory constitutes a genuine solution to the problem of why people obey political authority is, of course, problematical. I shall argue later that it does not. For now, I simply want to point out first, that Freud has merely displaced the traditional locus of the problem from the state to the family; whether he has developed an adequate solution to the problem of the transformation of might into right depends upon the adequacy of his explanation of the child's identification with his father. Freud himself was never satisfied with this explanation—he says that "we are far from having exhausted the problem of identification" and that "I myself am far from satisfied with these remarks on identification"[10]—and thus he notifies us that his "solution" is, at best, provisional.

Second, it should be clear that this solution is, strictly speaking, only applicable to the problem of why *men* obey political authority. Freud argues that the female child develops a superego that is much weaker than that of the male child; it follows that we cannot argue that a woman's acquiescence to political authority is but the externalization of a prior internalization of the father in the form of a powerful superego. On Freud's own account of the

---

[9] Cited in Lichtman, "Marx and Freud, Part Two," p. 75.

[10] Freud, *Group Psychology and the Analysis of the Ego*, p. 66, and *New Introductory Lectures on Psychoanalysis*, p. 63.

differences between the male and female child's resolution of the oedipus complex, in other words, the state cannot be a representative of the father for a woman in the same sense, or to the same extent, that it is for a man. Yet this account of sexual difference is nowhere present in Freud's theory of political domination. Instead, and in patriarchal fashion, he writes as if all human beings were men. In defense of Freud, it might be argued that this theoretical exclusion of women from the field of politics simply parallels their practical exclusion from this field; that Freud writes about male politics in the guise of writing about politics in general is merely symptomatic of the reality that politics in patriarchal societies has, after all, been a virtually exclusively male preserve. The problem, however, is that Freud's formulation, as we have seen, forecloses the possibility of fundamentally transforming this reality in the future.

These qualifications notwithstanding, Freud's conclusion is that political authority expresses the universal Law of the Father. Resistance to political authority, moreover, is, according to Freud, every bit as much an expression of this law as is acquiescence. Rebellion against the state is merely a rebellion against the father that bears witness to his continuing presence and power; like any "denial," it preserves the very longing for the father that it appears to negate.[11] The persistence of this longing is evident in the fact that revolutions that purport to eliminate political domination regularly reinstate it in a new form; the inevitable transformation of the political liberators into yet another ruling group affirms the power of the father, from which there is no escape. The "identification of those who revolt with the power against which they revolt" accounts for the "element of *self-defeat*" that has been present in every "betrayed revolution."[12] The universal tendency for political revolutions to reproduce the very domination they have sworn to eliminate is, for Freud, empirical confirmation of the theoretical postulate of the inevitability of political domination.

Wilhelm Reich's Theory of the Authoritarian Character Structure

Wilhelm Reich was one of the first Marxists to examine critically Freud's theory of political domination. The period during which he examined it— Reich's "Marxist period"—runs roughly from the middle of the 1920s to the middle of the 1930s, beginning with a manifest decline in the militancy of the European proletarian movement and culminating in the utter devastation of this movement under German fascism. This was the political context for Reich's selective appropriation of the work of Freud. Contrary to Marx's

---

[11] Poster, *Critical Theory of the Family*, p. 38.
[12] Marcuse, *Eros and Civilization*, pp. 82-83, emphasis in the original.

expectations, the industrial working class had not only failed to develop a genuinely socialist consciousness but, at least in Germany, had come to acquiesce in, or even affirm, a form of domination that was the very antithesis of this consciousness. Thus, for example, "the votes cast by the workers made up approximately 3,000,000 of the 6,400,000 votes received by the National Socialists in 1930."[13] Fascism, in short, was a mass movement. The overriding question to which Reich sought an answer was: how was this possible?

Like other Marxists, Reich argues that the absence or even repudiation of socialist consciousness among the working class entails a failure on the part of the members of this class to recognize that socialism corresponds to their objective interests. With Marx, in other words, he assumes that revolutionary needs develop within the sphere of labor and thus that the proletariat, i.e., the class that labors, is *the* revolutionary agent within societies that are dominated by the capitalist mode of production. Unlike other Marxists of his time, however, he argues that the reiteration of this and other related assumptions of Marx in no way elucidates the present impasse, or even reversal, of the socialist movement. Thus the Third International's definition of fascism as merely the open dictatorship of the leading elements of monopoly capital failed to pose the problem of why this dictatorship was able to rely on mass support. To the extent that orthodox communist theoreticians ever addressed themselves to this question, their answer was hopelessly inadequate. Blame was laid on the reformist, Social-Democratic leadership of the workers' movement for having initiated a "betrayal" of the masses that culminated in their "befogging" under fascism. In the process, the question of why the masses would allow themselves to be "betrayed" by their leaders and "befogged" by fascism was left begging.[14] Similarly, the Left, or Council Communist argument that "the belief in parties [in general, and not just Social-Democratic parties] is the main reason for the impotence of the working class"[15] failed entirely to raise the question of the origins and persistence of this belief.

According to Reich, all of the existing Marxist explanations begged precisely the question that had to be answered, namely, why would the masses embrace their own domination? Why did they not only fail to recognize their objective interest in socialism but also come to act "against their own interest in carrying Hitler to power"?[16] Why, in short, did the working class behave so irrationally? To answer this question, Reich believed, it was necessary to

[13] Wilhelm Reich, *The Mass Psychology of Fascism* (New York: Farrar, Straus & Giroux, 1970), p. 13.

[14] *Ibid.*, pp. 8, 22-24.

[15] Anton Pannekoek, cited in Aronowitz, "Left-Wing Communism: The Reply to Lenin," p. 182.

[16] Wilhelm Reich, *Sex-Pol* (New York: Vintage Books, 1972), p. 283.

202

supplement Marxism with a theory of the determinants of human irrationality. It was necessary, in other words, to turn to Freud.

Reich relies on Freud in order to demonstrate that the members of the working class fail to recognize their interest in socialism because they have an unconscious, libidinally rooted stake in the very social order that socialism purports to eliminate. They will adhere to ideologies and participate in movements that run counter to their objective interests, i.e., they will be victims of "false consciousness," insofar as these ideologies and movements both express and reinforce psychic needs that likewise run counter to their objective interests and bind them to the status quo. Thus, although their consciousness is "false," it has a material base: it is anchored in their instinctual apparatus. This apparatus Reich calls "character structure," which he defines as the "ideological mooring of the dominant economic system in the psychic structure of the members of the oppressed class."[17] The bourgeoisie, Reich tells us, exercises hegemony not only over the conscious but also over the unconscious, life of the masses:

> In a class society, the ruling class secures its position with the aid of education and the institutions of the family, by making its ideologies the ruling ideologies of all members of the society. But it is not merely a matter of imposing ideologies, attitudes, and concepts on members of society. Rather, it is a matter of a deep-reaching process in each new generation, of the formation of a psychic structure which corresponds to the existing social order in all strata of the population.[18]

If we learn from Marx that "the ruling ideas are everywhere the ideas of the ruling class," we learn from Reich's Marxist reading of Freud that "the ruling drives are everywhere the drives of the ruling class."

More specifically, Reich argues that the "ruling" character structure in which the false consciousness of the masses is anchored is an authoritarian character structure. By this he means that the modal personality type in a capitalist society is characterized by an overriding need for order.[19] The person with an authoritarian character structure can find satisfaction only in a situation that is under control; this is a person with a correspondingly profound fear of change or disorder, of a situation that is not predictable. Such a person prizes instrumental activity rather than activity undertaken for its own sake,

---

[17] *Ibid.*, p. 246.

[18] Wilhelm Reich, *Character Analysis* (New York: Farrar, Straus & Giroux, 1972), p. xxii.

[19] Reich occasionally argues that the character structure of the industrial worker is generally less authoritarian than that of the petit bourgeois, or lower-middle class individual, but, as Poster has demonstrated, his argument is unpersuasive. It is, moreover, contradicted by his other arguments that affirm unambiguously the bourgeois nature of the consciousness and drives of the working class. Poster, *Critical Theory of the Family*, pp. 51-52.

203

possessing or accumulating over experiencing, and duty or morality over pleasure—in short, postponed over immediate gratification.

This authoritarian character structure, in turn, predisposes the individual to support authoritarian ideologies and movements that likewise prize duty over pleasure and order over freedom. The individual with an authoritarian character structure, Reich argues, is the individual whose unconscious needs dove-tail perfectly with the authoritarian structure of bourgeois society that is made explicit and carried to its logical extension by the fascist movement. The authoritarian character structure is thus the "mass psychological" basis of the state in general and the fascist state in particular. It is, at the same time, the psychological basis of a profound fear of, and "incapacity for," what Reich calls the "self-administration of life," i.e., socialism.[20] Thus, socialism threatens, while fascism expresses and reproduces, the prevailing psychic needs of the masses: working-class support for fascism, and repudiation of socialism, is rooted in an unconscious need for order that is simultaneously an unconscious fear of freedom. The masses embraced Hitler because "Hitler stirred the deepest roots of their emotional being."[21]

If the authoritarian character structure is the mass psychological basis of the state in general, how can this concept explain the emergence of the fascist state in particular? Reich's problem as a Marxist is to link the phenomenon of fascism to capitalism. In order to do so he is obliged to argue, as we shall see in greater detail below, that it is capitalism that generates the authoritarian character structure and thus that this character structure is the mass psychological basis for all the state forms, including liberal-democratic ones, that capitalism adopts. But liberal-democratic capitalist states, although not without their authoritarian features, are surely different from fascist capitalist states. How can the same concept account for these two very different states? Alternatively, if the concept applies to both of them, can it really illuminate either of them? Reich does not seem to be aware of this problem, but his account of the emergence of fascism in Germany suggests a possible response. This account emphasizes the extent to which the economic crisis exacerbated the emotional insecurities of the masses, reinforcing their profound, unconscious fear of change.[22] This seems to imply that, for Reich, the authoritarian character structure is the necessary, but not sufficient, determinant of the fascist state; all capitalist states rely on this psychological structure, but the fascist state in particular only emerges with the addition of another factor, namely, economic crisis. (Reich also argues that "*disappointment in Social Democracy, accompanied by the contradiction between wretchedness and conservative thinking, must lead to fascism* if there are no revolutionary

[20] Reich, *The Mass Psychology of Fascism*, p. 331.

[21] Reich, *Sex-Pol*, p. 284.

[22] Reich, *The Mass Psychology of Fascism*, pp. 42-46.

204

organizations."[23] But "disappointment in Social Democracy" presupposes a prior commitment to Social Democracy which, according to Reich, is itself a product of "conservative thinking," as well as the withdrawal of this commitment in the face of the inability of Social Democracy to resolve the economic crisis. And the absence of revolutionary organizations has already been explained as an inevitable result of the authoritarian character structure. Thus we are back to the conclusion that "wretchedness" and "conservative thinking," i.e., economic crisis and the authoritarian character structure, are the two determinants of fascism.)

This response, however, is not convincing. On the one hand, during the same period severe economic crises occurred in capitalist societies that did not adopt a fascist state; this fact alone would seem to disconfirm Reich's hypothesis that the combination of the authoritarian character structure and economic crisis leads to fascism. On the other hand, and as we shall see, the theory that Reich relies on to explain the emergence of a fascist consolidation of capitalism is precisely the same as the theory he relies on to account for the emergence of a socialist transcendence of capitalism. Reich will argue that economic crises can undermine the solidity of the authoritarian character structure and thus help generate rebellions against the existing order. He acknowledges, then, that the effect of economic crises need not be the same as, and may in fact be diametrically opposed to, the effect he hypothesizes in order to account for fascism. For both reasons, his theory of the mass psychological basis of fascism remains unpersuasive.

Like Freud, Reich links the development of the authoritarian character structure to the repression of infantile and childhood sexuality. "Sexual inhibition," he states:

> changes the structure [consciousness] of economically suppressed man in such a way that he acts, feels, and thinks contrary to his own material interests . . . the sexually repressed person affirms even the sexual order which restricts his gratification and makes him ill, and he wards off any system that might correspond to his needs.[24]

If sexual repression is responsible for the authoritarian character structure, then the internal obstacles to the development of a socialist consciousness are implanted at a very early age, long before the individual ever gets to the workplace and is exposed to those processes which, according to Marx, would help generate this consciousness. Reich's appropriation of Freud leads to a partial shift of focus from the factory to the family as the decisive capitalist reproductive mechanism. Indeed, Reich argues that the "bourgeois family

---

[23] *Ibid.*, p. 73, emphasis in the original.
[24] *Ibid.*, p. 32, and Reich, *Sex-Pol*, p. 245.

becomes the most important ideological workshop of capitalism through the sexual repression it carries out.''[25]

Reich's account of the process that links this repression to the authoritarian character structure and then to acquiescence to political domination is not entirely clear. In fact, he offers a number of versions of this process. One such version relies on Freud's theory of identification with the father through the formation of the superego: ''the conflict that originally takes place between the child's desires and the parent's suppression of these desires later becomes the conflict between instinct and morality *within* the person.'' On this account, the authoritarian character structure entails an internalization of the father, and adhesion to authoritarian ideologies and movements can be understood, with Freud, as the expression of an unconscious longing for the father. As such, and as in the case of Freud, this account properly applies only to men, although Reich does not acknowledge this. At other points Reich relies not on Freud's theory of identification but rather on a considerably vaguer theory of ''adaptation'': ''the family is the authoritarian state in miniature, to which the child must learn to adapt himself as a preparation for the general adjustment required of him later.'' Here the emphasis appears to be on a structural ''fit'' between the family and the authoritarian state that guarantees that (but does not explain how) the character structure necessary for the latter will be produced within the former. Elsewhere Reich argues that the ''damming up'' of sexual energy results in a ''biophysical rigidity of the organism'' and a ''mechanical mechanism'' that culminates in ''Hitlerism.''[26]

Unlike his first ''Freudian'' version, these last two versions of Reich's theory are applicable to both men and women. They are so, however, precisely because they are so general that they approach vacuity. They tell us no more about the problem of the political consequences of sexual difference than does the Freudian version. At the same time, moreover, neither the functionalist nor the bioenergetic account entails any reference to the unconscious; thus they both dispense with a specifically psychoanalytic explanation of the origins of political domination.

Whatever its ambiguities, however, Reich's analysis stands as a necessary corrective to the analyses of those Marxists who, in Sartre's words:

> are concerned only with adults . . . [and] would believe that we are born at the age when we earn our first wages . . . who have forgotten their own childhoods . . . [and act] as if men experienced their alienation . . . first in their own work, whereas, in actuality, each one lives it first, as a child, in his parents' work.[27]

[25] Reich, *Sex-Pol*, p. 230.
[26] Reich, *The Mass Psychology of Fascism*, pp. 27 (emphasis in the original), 30, 322, 349.
[27] Jean-Paul Sartre, *Search for a Method* (New York: Knopf, 1963), p. 62.

Yet even this critique of Marxism entails an appeal to its authority, namely the assumption that the alienation that we "live" as a child is the alienation that our parents have experienced in their work, i.e., the assumption that sexual repression and its attendant political consequences are ultimately a function of the mode of production. Is this in fact the case? Reich will try to demonstrate that it is, and that Freud's thesis that sexual repression and the political domination that results from it are coextensive with human civilization is wrong. This historicization of Freud, however, will pose at least as many problems as it resolves.

We have seen that Reich refers to the authoritarian family as the "bourgeois family" and that he conceptualizes it as an "ideological workshop of capitalism." He also argues that the family is "a factory for authoritarian ideologies" and that "within the family the father holds the same position that his boss holds toward him in the production process,"[28] i.e., that both the function and the form of the family are analogous to production in a capitalist society. Finally, he attempts to situate the family within the classical Marxist "base-superstructure" schema, arguing that the family mediates between the "two terminal points—the economic structure of society at the one end, the ideological superstructure at the other."[29] These formulations all point to the conclusion that the "social order" to which the authoritarian family corresponds is a specifically capitalist social order, and thus that sexual repression and its political consequences are specifically capitalist phenomena.

And yet Reich equivocates. In the midst of a discussion of authoritarian ideology, he argues that "capitalism, or rather patriarchy" is its "socioeconomic basis."[30] "Capitalism, or rather patriarchy": this casual, almost off-handed terminological equivocation points, despite itself, to a contradiction that threatens to undermine Reich's entire enterprise. Patriarchy, we have seen, antedates capitalism by thousands of years. If patriarchy is the social order to which sexual repression and authoritarian politics corresponds, then it is impossible to link these phenomena exclusively to capitalism. The fascist state, for example, could no longer be understood as a specifically capitalist state. Indeed, Reich appears to acknowledge this when he argues, in *The Mass Psychology*, that the patriarchal family on which fascism rests has endured in essentially the same form for "thousands of years."[31] Reich's analysis of authoritarian rule in the Soviet Union, moreover, similarly weakens the links he wants to forge between political domination and capitalism. The Soviet Union, he tells us, degenerated from the dictatorship *of* the proletariat

---

[28] Wilhelm Reich, *The Sexual Revolution* (New York: Farrar, Straus, & Giroux, 1970), p. 208 and *The Mass Psychology of Fascism*, p. 53.

[29] Reich, *Sex-Pol*, p. 45.

[30] Reich, *The Mass Psychology of Fascism*, p. 56.

[31] Cited in Poster, *Critical Theory of the Family*, p. 51.

to the dictatorship *over* the proletariat because the patriarchal family, source of the masses' "authority-craving," was never successfully transformed. Thus it would seem that patriarchy not only antedates capitalism but can outlive it as well. Reich draws back from this conclusion; in an effort to reforge the links that his own analysis appears to have shattered, he describes the Soviet Union as "State Capitalist."[32] But, as we have seen, the redefinition of the Soviet Union as a capitalist society so expands the meaning of capitalism that it becomes equivalent to any form of (modern) domination, in which case the theory that political domination owes its existence to capitalism becomes true by definition.

These considerations point to the conclusion that patriarchy, not capitalism, is the crucial determinant of sexual repression and political domination and thus would appear to undermine Reich's effort to develop a Marxist historicization of Freud. Patriarchy, after all, spans many different modes of production; how, then, is it possible to reconcile its causal power with Marx's thesis of the determinative effect of the mode of production? We have already examined this problem, and a number of (unsuccessful) efforts to resolve it, in Chapters Two and Five. Reich adopts a variation of Engels's solution to the problem. Engels, it will be recalled, argues that patriarchal class society was preceded by matriarchal, primitive communist society, and that the transition from the latter to the former was a result of the development of private property and the desire to ensure its inheritance. Thus, although patriarchy cuts across different modes of production, it owes its existence to a development in production and will therefore also owe its eventual demise to the development of production.

Reich accepts the essentials of Engels's account and supplements them with an interpretation of Malinowski's analysis of the sexual and economic life of the Trobriand Islanders. According to Reich, this analysis confirms the existence of "primitive communist" matriarchies in which sexual repression and political domination are absent, and thus refutes Freud's thesis that these phenomena are coextensive with human civilization itself. The assumption that underlies Freud's thesis is that "since society does not have sufficient . . . supplies to maintain its members without their working, it must . . . divert their energies from sexual activity to work."[33] This diversion, moreover, must be enforced, "for what motive would induce man to put his sexual energy to other uses if by any disposal of it he could obtain fully satisfying pleasure?"[34] Thus labor and sexual gratification stand in inverse relationship to one another, and, consequently, "our civilization is, generally speaking,

---

[32] Reich, *The Mass Psychology of Fascism*, pp. 216, 277-78, and Ch. 9, *passim*.

[33] Cited in Zaretsky, "Male Supremacy and the Unconscious," p. 27.

[34] Sigmund Freud, "The Most Prevalent Form of Degradation in Erotic Life," *Collected Papers*, Vol. IV, p. 216.

founded on the suppression of instincts.''[35] Reich argues that the case of the Trobriand Islanders indicates that Freud fundamentally miscalculated the relationship between work and sexual satisfaction. The encouragement and proliferation of childhood heterosexuality and the absence of the oedipus complex and its attendant neuroses among adults in this society demonstrates that uninhibited sexuality and psychological health can flourish along with the labor necessary to sustain a culture. Thus ''sexual gratification does not stand in contradiction to the sublimation of sexual drives in the performance of work.'' Reich agrees with Freud that ''labor power . . . is essentially a sublimated sexual energy,'' but denies that a repressive sublimation that restricts sexual fulfillment is inherent in the exercise of this power. (Quite to the contrary: he even suggests that repressive sublimation can lead to a ''disturbance in working capacity.'')[36] Instead, the sublimation of sexual energy necessary for labor demands a repressive restriction of the possibilities for sexual expression and happiness only in those societies characterized by a repressive organization of this labor, i.e., in class societies.

Reich believes that this proposition is also confirmed by Malinowski's analysis. The ''destructive effects'' of the ''marriage dowry'' on the matriarchal organization of Trobriand society vindicates Engels's thesis that an interest in the accumulation of property inaugurates the transition from matriarchy to patriarchy:

[A]lterations in the circulation of the dowry . . . was the decisive step in the change to patriarchy. Once dowries flowed to the chief it became of absolute significance to him to insure his line of inheritance. Needing to be certain of his male heirs, the chief instituted a strict control of women and hence monogamous, patriarchal marriage began.[37]

Reich even claims that this proves that it ''is only the private enterprise[!] form of society which has an interest in sexual repression.''[38] This claim, of course, entails a gross inflation of the concept of ''private enterprise.'' Even if we ignore this problem and allow the concept to stand as a synonym for a ''society organized on the basis of a dominant class interest,'' it is not difficult to show that Reich's ''demonstration'' that this interest generates patriarchy is fatally flawed. In fact, like the Engels hypothesis of which it is a variation, Reich's ''explanation'' of patriarchy presupposes the very phenomenon for which it purports to give an account. The argument that the circulation of dowries to the chief generates an economic interest in the subordination of

[35] Freud, '' 'Civilized' Sexual Morality and Modern Nervousness,'' p. 82.

[36] Reich, *Sex-Pol*, pp. 241, 236.

[37] This summary of Reich's theory of the role of the marriage dowry, which he develops in *The Imposition of Sexual Morality*, is by Poster, *Critical Theory of the Family*, p. 48.

[38] Reich, *Sex-Pol*, p. 237.

women and the installation of patriarchy begs precisely the question that would have to be answered by any adequate account of the origins of patriarchy, namely, why in the first place, is the chief a man? The fact that political power is a "masculine" phenomenon in Trobriand society, in other words, necessarily calls into question the assumption that this, or any similarly organized, society is matriarchal.

Another, related problem is that it is difficult to square Reich's thesis that primitive communist "matriarchies" are without sexual repression with Malinowski's finding that homosexuality is held in contempt by the Trobrianders. Reich assumes that homosexuality is a "pervasion," and argues that its absence is yet another indication of healthy, unrepressed sexuality among the Trobrianders.[39] The rejection of the assumption of the neurotic nature of homosexuality, of course, would lead to an entirely different conclusion: its absence would be an indication of a compulsory heterosexuality that radically restricts the possibilities for the free flowering of human sexual expression. It is, moreover, difficult to understand why we should not reject the assumption since the claim that homosexuality is "unnatural" would appear to be entirely inconsistent with Freud's own insistence on the bisexual "nature" of the infant and the specifically cultural constitution of its subsequent sexual identity.[40]

Similarly, there is, at the very least, a tension between Reich's assertion of the absence of sexual repression in matriarchal societies and the anthropological evidence he cites of "cruel rites of puberty" (including clitoral mutilation) in some of these societies that are apparently designed to suppress adolescent sexuality. Here he argues that when these measures occur the society is already in "transition" to patriarchy, but this argument, of course, transforms the empirical question of the relationship of patriarchy and sexual repression into a pure exercise in definition.[41]

All these problems oblige us to conclude that Reich has not in fact vindicated the Marxist thesis of the economic origins of patriarchy and the sexual repression and political domination that flow from it. To the contrary, his own evidence suggests either that patriarchy is a primordial condition or that

[39] *Ibid.*, pp. 126-30.

[40] Freud's position on homosexuality, in contrast to that of Reich, is ambivalent. On the one hand, he argues that it is not, in itself, a perversion and even implies, at one point, that it is no more problematical than exclusive heterosexuality. On the other hand, he describes it as an inversion, classifies it under the more general heading of the "sexual aberrations," and argues that it results from an "arrest of sexual development." See his "Three Essays on the Theory of Sexuality," *Standard Edition of the Complete Psychological Works* (hereafter, *SE*), Vol. VII (London: Hogarth Press and Institute of Psycho-analysis, 1953), pp. 135-72, as well as the discussion in Ronald Bayer, *Homosexuality and American Psychiatry: The Politics of Diagnosis* (New York: Basic Books, 1981), pp. 21-27.

[41] Reich, *Sex-Pol*, p. 169.

matriarchies were characterized by sexual repression. In either case, he does not develop an account of the origins of sexual repression and authoritarianism that compellingly refutes Freud's thesis that these phenomena are coextensive with civilization itself, and his effort to develop a Marxist historicization of Freud must therefore be judged a failure.

The problems in Reich's theory of the origins of sexual repression and political domination resurface in his analysis of the prospects for their elimination. The assumption that these phenomena have a socioeconomic basis leads inexorably to the conclusion that a socioeconomic transformation is the condition for their abolition: "the abolition of the commodity economy necessarily brings about the elimination of sexual morality [i.e., repression] and replaces it on a scientifically higher and more secure level with . . . support for sexual activity . . . the social revolution will eliminate sexual oppression."[42] Only the elimination of capitalism and the creation of socialism, in short, will make it possible to eliminate sexual repression and its consequences. But Reich has already said that sexual repression is a, perhaps even the, decisively important capitalist reproductive mechanism, i.e., that the persistence of capitalism depends upon the suppression of sexuality, in which case it would seem that capitalism cannot be eliminated without a prior or at least simultaneous elimination of sexual repression. At first glance, Reich appears to be trapped in a vicious circle. We need to examine his analysis more closely in order to determine if he is able to extricate himself from it.

If an authoritarian character structure is the chief obstacle to the development of that working-class consciousness without which socialist revolution cannot occur, it follows that the struggle to transform this character structure is a necessary part of the struggle for socialism. Indeed, precisely this assumption was the basis for Reich's practical political activity. From 1930 until 1933 he organized and worked in "sex-pol" clinics in Germany which were designed to counteract the psychic effects of sexual repression and authoritarian socialization and thus to contribute to the development of working-class consciousness. Adolescent and young workers were encouraged both to become more aware of their at least partly repressed sexual needs and of the connection between the repression of these needs and the requirements of capitalism. This twofold awareness, Reich believed, would lead to the development of what might be called a libidinally rooted class consciousness on their part. Thus could sexual drives be harnessed in support of the struggle for the one society in which sexuality would truly flourish, i.e., a socialist society.

Reich claims that his clinics attracted thousands of workers, both male and female, many of whom became adherents of socialism. However successful

---

[42] *Ibid.*, pp. 242, 248.

211

in practice, however, Reich's effort would have to be judged utopian or impossible in the light of his own theory of the tenacity of a character structure that has been formed in early childhood. Does not this theory suggest that an authoritarian character structure has been irreversibly shaped long before the period of adolescence has been reached? Did not Reich attempt to undo in his clinics what his own theory says cannot be undone (short of prolonged individual therapy, which Reich explicitly distinguishes from the "sex-economic mass hygiene" practiced in his clinics[43])?

It follows from Reich's theory of the crucial role that the family plays in the suppression of infantile and childhood sexuality and thus in the formation of the authoritarian character structure that a successful struggle to transform this character structure would have to focus directly on the transformation of the family. It also follows that efforts to undermine the authoritarian character structure that are undertaken outside the family and after the period of childhood, as in the sex-pol clinics, would be productive only if they were able to build on the struggles of children within the family to resist sexual repression. It would be possible for Reich, or anyone else, to mobilize the sexual energy of adolescents and young adults and channel it in an anticapitalist direction only if at least some of this energy remained unrepressed and unsublimated despite the authoritarian repression to which it was subjected during childhood. But this suggests that the sexual repression and its authoritarian consequences must not be as pervasive or total as Reich sometimes claims, and that contradictory tendencies can be located within the process of reproducing the authoritarian character structure that provide the basis for resistance as well as acquiescence.

Indeed, Reich argues that these contradictory tendencies do exist, that the same process that produces weakness and dependence in the child can often produce a spirit of sexual rebellion and anti-authoritarianism:

> Sexual repression has the effect of making young people submissive to adults in a characterological sense, but, at the same time, it brings about their sexual rebellion. This rebellion becomes a powerful force in the social movement when it becomes conscious and finds a nexus within the proletarian movement undermining capitalism.[44]

This formulation, however, explains too much and thus too little. If sexual repression explains both submission and rebellion, can it really explain either one of them? If the process of sexual repression works the way in which Reich (in at least one version) describes it, producing first an identification with the authority of the father and then an identification with the authority

---

[43] Reich, *The Mass Psychology of Fascism*, pp. 186-87.
[44] Reich, *Sex-Pol*, p. 246.

212

of the state, this would appear to preclude the possibility of sexual rebellion against the father and, in turn, the state. (Reich, in fact, argues in *The Mass Psychology* that, in contrast to the suppression of material needs, which "incites to rebellion," the suppression of sexual needs, inasmuch as it results in a "moral defense," "prevents rebellion against *both* forms of suppression."[45]) On the other hand, if sexual rebellion results from the suppression of the child's sexuality, then this could only mean that the process of authoritarian socialization must have broken down; either the child's identification with the father or his or her subsequent identification with state authority would have to be incomplete. Sexual rebellion entails an unwillingness to postpone sexual gratification; this unwillingness, in turn, presupposes that, repression notwithstanding, there remains unsublimated sexual energy that seeks a direct rather than indirect outlet. But, if this is regularly the case, how can Reich claim that, in general, capitalism produces the character structure that conforms to its ideological requirements? The problem is that Reich fails to illuminate the specific conditions under which the process of dual identification will fail to "take," and thus we are left in the dark as to when we should expect submission and when we should anticipate rebellion. To put this another way, Reich wants to argue, in dialectical fashion, that the process of sexual repression is a contradictory process that contains the seeds of its own destruction, but he fails completely to specify precisely where these seeds lie.

Perhaps aware of the inadequacy of his formulation to this point, Reich offers in the next breath an alternative explanation that links the sexual rebellion of youth to economic crises:

> That the contradictions of sexual repression are seeking a resolution is apparent in the sexual crisis which has enveloped the capitalist countries with a steadily increasing strength since approximately the turn of the century. It fluctuates in its intensity according to the economic crises on which it is directly dependent. (There is an increase in the divorce rate in periods of economic crises). The worsening of the material position of the masses not only loosens the marital and familial binds of sexuality, it stimulates a revolt related to sexual need, along with the revolt stemming from the need for food.[46]

There are a number of problems with this argument. First, the assumption of a direct, one-to-one relationship between a decline in the stability of the economy and a decline in the stability of the family and the character structure it engenders is contradicted by Reich's own analysis of the tremendous "stay-

[45] Reich, *The Mass Psychology of Fascism*, p. 31.
[46] Reich, *Sex-Pol*, pp. 246-47.

ing power'' of character structure, i.e., how character structure accounts for the persistence of ideologies long after the material conditions that generated them have been fundamentally transformed.[47] Second, and as we have seen, Reich himself argues elsewhere that this same combination of the authoritarian family and economic crisis tends to produce not sexual rebellion but rather an intensification of authoritarianism; his crisis theory of sexual rebellion is, in fact, virtually indistinguishable from his crisis theory of fascism. Finally, even if we grant that economic crises can sometimes generate sexual rebellion, we learn from Marx in volume III of *Capital* that capitalist economic crises are temporary phenomena, as much the beginning of a renewal of economic growth as they are the end of a period of economic stagnation.[48] It follows (on the assumption of a one-to-one relationship between economic change and psychic change) that the weakening of authoritarian socialization and the sexual rebellion that results from this weakening are likely to be temporary as well. Up to this point, then, Reich has been unable to account for the permanent possibility of increasing sexual rebelliousness, but this is precisely what he needs to account for in order to make his case that sexual needs are a reliable source of long-term anticapitalist struggle.

Reich offers one final argument in support of this case. The process of sexual rebellion, he tells us, is:

> accelerated by the growing concentration of the masses in larger and larger collective organizations, which promote the breakdown of the institutions of marriage and the family. This is similar to the manner in which capitalist rationalization of the production process tends toward the economic destruction of the family. A new contradiction is produced here between the economic dissolution of the family in the masses and the necessity, from the standpoint of capital and the church, of maintaining the ideology of marriage and having it permanently reproduced in the new generations.[49]

Here the argument is that the imperatives of capitalist production render the family progressively more obsolete and thus undermine the "factory" for authoritarian ideologies on which the persistence of this form of production ultimately depends. The problem with this thesis, however, is that the institutions of marriage and the family have proved far more hardy over the past fifty years than Reich anticipated; despite the loss of its directly productive functions, and notwithstanding high divorce rates, we would be hard-pressed

[47] *Ibid.*, p. 244.

[48] *Capital*, Vol. III (Moscow: Foreign Languages Publishing House, 1959), p. 250; see also Karl Marx, *Theories of Surplus Value*, Vol. II (London: Laurence & Wishart, 1969), pp. 496-97.

[49] Reich, *Sex-Pol*, p. 247.

214

to argue that the family has completely broken down. In one sense, in fact, exactly the reverse has occurred. Contrary to Reich's expectations, the development of capitalism has produced not the "growing concentration of the masses in larger and larger collective organizations" but, rather, their growing concentration within the *family*. The increasing geographic distance between the workplace and the home and the progressive destruction of work-related social institutions (such as bars and clubs) have transformed the family into the principal or even exclusive arena of social life outside the workplace.[50] Thus it is possible to argue that the salience of the family as a locus of socialization has increased, rather than decreased, with the development of capitalism (even though this argument would have to be tempered by the understanding of the way in which this socialization is subjected to the influence of the media and professional expertise). At any rate, Reich's hypothesis of the growing obsolescence of the family is certainly no more persuasive than the one that we reviewed, and criticized, in the preceding chapter. His theory of the origins of sexual rebellion, and thus his case for a libidinally based socialist revolution, remains unconvincing.

This case remains unconvincing for other reasons as well. Even if it were possible to demonstrate the necessary existence of sexual rebelliousness, it does not necessarily follow that this rebelliousness will generate an anticapitalist political response. This follows only if we assume, as Reich does, that capitalism requires sexual repression and thus that "rebellious" sexual needs simply cannot be satisfied within the limits of a capitalist society. At the very least, the development of sexuality under capitalism over the past fifty years would tend to call this assumption into question. On the one hand, it would be impossible to deny that there has been a dramatic reduction in at least *some* kinds of sexual repression: the striking increase in the frequency of sexual relations prior to and outside of monogamous marriage, the breakdown in exclusive heterosexuality, the assertion of women's claims to sexual pleasure, the production and dissemination of sexual information and paraphernalia, the increased availability of legal abortions, etc., all indicate a significant relaxation of sexual taboos since the time that Reich wrote. On the other hand, it is equally undeniable that this upsurge in the expression of unsublimated sexuality has not been accompanied by a corresponding upsurge in anticapitalist consciousness among the masses: capitalist society seems as, or even more, secure than ever. As Marcuse argues, advanced capitalist societies are characterized by a pronounced de-sublimation of sexual energy, but this de-sublimation is repressive, rather than liberatory, insofar as it in no way threatens, but rather merely reinforces, the persistence of these societies. Capitalism

[50] Richard Sennett, *The Uses of Disorder* (New York: Vintage Books, 1971); Zaretsky, "Capitalism, the Family, and Personal Life."

215

has, in effect, coopted sexual rebellion by transforming sexuality into a product that is packaged, merchandised, and sold like any other. In short, when *Hustler* and *Family Circle* compete for our attention at the local supermarket, we have to wonder about any thesis that asserts the incompatibility of sexuality, the family, and capitalism. At least at first glance, the development of capitalism would appear to have falsified Reich's theory of the necessity of sexual repression under capitalism.

Someone interested in saving Reich's theory might argue that the sexual developments to which I have alluded do not constitute a genuine sexual liberation: sexual repression continues to exist despite these developments, and thus there remains a fundamental incompatibility between capitalism and sexual liberation. There remains as well a potential for a genuine sexual rebellion that, in contrast to the present "phony" one, *can* become the basis for an anticapitalist consciousness and movement. This is a legitimate response, but the distinction it draws between a "true" and "false" sexual liberation entails an appeal to a qualitative, rather than purely quantitative, criterion of sexual satisfaction. And this qualitative criterion is precisely what is lacking in Reich.

Reich's term for genuine sexual satisfaction is "orgasmic potency," which he defines as "the capacity to surrender to the flow of biological energy without any inhibition, the capacity for complete discharge of all dammed-up sexual excitation."[51] Sexual desire is energy that produces tension; sexual repression is a blocking or damming-up of energy such that there is no release of tension; and sexual liberation—"orgasmic potency"—is the maximum release of tension. Reich is committed, in other words, to an energistic model of sexuality that appears to allow for an exclusively quantitative, "more-or-less" criterion of sexual fulfillment. At any rate, the energistic model abstracts completely from the social relationship within which human sexuality takes place and thus from the very context to which we would have to refer in developing an adequate qualitative criterion. Given this abstraction and the purely quantitative criterion of sexual satisfaction with which it is associated Reich would be hard-pressed to argue that the past fifty years have not been characterized by sexual liberation, and thus he would have to conclude that his theory of the incompatibility of capitalism and sexual liberation was wrong. Alternatively, if he continued to insist that no genuine sexual liberation has taken place, and that his theory has not, in fact, been disconfirmed, he would be obliged to abandon his energistic model of sexuality and to develop a qualitative, "social" concept of sexual fulfillment. In either case, the unity of Reich's theoretical system would be rent asunder.

The mere demonstration that sexuality is still repressed, moreover, would not be sufficient to vindicate Reich's theory of political domination and the

---

[51] Wilhelm Reich, *The Function of the Orgasm* (London: Panther, 1968), p. 114.

216

prospects for its elimination. As we have seen, to the extent that this theory relies on Freud, it attributes political domination not to sexual repression in general but rather to a specific form of repression that produces an individual who identifies first with the paternal source of this repression and later with the political "substitutes" for this paternal source. The theory of the authoritarian character structure and its political consequences thus presupposes a powerful father against whom the child must struggle in order to form his or her separate identity. It would appear, however, that the transformation from competitive to welfare-state capitalism has invalidated this presupposition. On the one hand, bureaucratically determined work requirements have rendered the father progressively less involved in family life in general and the socialization of children in particular, and, on the other hand, the socialization of children increasingly falls under the direct or indirect influence of the state and the mass media.[52] The result, as it has been so often argued, is a drastic decline in the authority of the father within the family.[53]

If this argument is correct, then it follows that the conditions for the development of an authoritarian character structure no longer exist. The transformation of the father from patriarch to "pal" eliminates the possibility of the internalization of paternal authority and prevents the superego from forming in the way in which Freud and Reich describe. Herbert Marcuse has argued that the individual who emerges from this "fatherless" family lacks a strong superego and thus the internalized morality of his or her nineteenth-century and early twentieth-century bourgeois counterpart.[54] (Interestingly enough, Marcuse characterizes this transformation as a loss of individual autonomy that leaves the individual increasingly vulnerable to mass manipulation. The patriarchal family that is for Reich a bastion of authoritarianism is, for Marcuse, the guardian of individual autonomy.) Christopher Lasch disputes the thesis of the "decline of the superego," arguing instead that a "new kind of superego" is created during "the pre-Oedipal stage of psychic development," but he agrees that the modal personality type in contemporary capitalist societies bears little, if any resemblance to the "anal-compulsive" personality that Freud and Reich describe. Instead, according to Lasch, the individual that typically emerges from the new family is a "narcissistic personality" that craves the approval of other people but is utterly unable to establish intimate relationships with them.[55]

I shall return to these issues in subsequent chapters. At this point it is

[52] Herbert Marcuse, "The Obsolescence of the Freudian Concept of Man," in *Five Lectures* (Boston: Beacon Press, 1970), pp. 46-47.

[53] *Ibid.*; Christopher Lasch, *The Culture of Narcissism* (New York: Norton, 1978), Ch. 2; Alexander Mitscherlich, *Society Without the Father* (New York: Schocken Books, 1970).

[54] Marcuse, "The Obsolescence of the Freudian Concept of Man" and *One-Dimensional Man* (Boston: Beacon Press, 1964), Ch. 3.

[55] Lasch, *The Culture of Narcissism*, pp. 178-79, 37, Ch. 2 *passim*.

sufficient to emphasize that if the authoritarian character structure is no longer the dominant personality type in contemporary capitalist societies then, contrary to Reich, it is not possible to maintain that the persistence of capitalism and the state on which it relies depends on the reproduction of this type of character structure. If Reich's theory were correct, the erosion of this character structure should have been accompanied by the erosion of support for the state and the emergence of a serious and sustained challenge to the capitalist system as a whole. But this has not occurred. This suggests that political domination has other mass-psychological origins than the one that Reich, following Freud, is able to locate. Only when these origins have been uncovered will we be in a position adequately to clarify the prospects for the elimination of political domination.

Finally, we should not be surprised to discover that Reich's analysis of the possibilities for the transcendence of political domination is unaccompanied by any analysis of the nature of political liberation. For Reich, in fact, political liberation is a contradiction in terms: " 'power' always means the subjugation of others." From Freud he borrows the assumption of the intrinsically "irrational nature" of politics; from Marx he borrows the assumption that politics is the "antithesis of work" and arises only because of the irrational organization of work. It follows that the rational organization of work will make it possible to dispense with politics.

This is so because work is a "natural process," one of the "practical functions of life, which obey their own laws." A society that is based on the liberation of work, which Reich calls "work-democracy," is therefore a society that needs no laws other than those that emerge spontaneously and organically from the work process itself. Labor, when it is performed by individuals unencumbered by either sexual or class oppression, is a self-regulating activity: work-democracy "would be the first time that *work* got control of social problems."[56] Reich's "sex-economic" language cannot conceal the fact that he has merely dressed up Marx's and Engels's technocratic thesis of the transformation of politics into administration in new clothing. And, for all the reasons discussed in Chapter Three, this thesis is every bit as problematical in new garb as it was in the original.

The adoption of this implausible thesis is the inevitable result of Reich's effort to use Marx in order to historicize Freud. Freud contends, as we have seen, that political domination is inherent in human civilization. Marx disputes this contention, and tries to make the case that political domination is specific to class civilization alone and will be eliminated in the socialist civilization of the future. His case does not rest on the assumption that a liberatory politics is possible under socialism but rather on the assumption that politics as such

[56] Reich, *The Mass Psychology of Fascism*, pp. 327, 367, 314-15, 368 (emphasis in the original).

will be unnecessary or obsolete in this society. The shared understanding that underlies the opposition between Marx and Freud and that unites them profoundly in spite of this opposition is that the realm of politics is everywhere a realm of domination. Thus a theory of a liberatory politics is foreclosed from the outset by the assumptions of both thinkers on whom Reich relies. It follows that there cannot be a Freudo-Marxist theory of political liberation, and that the elaboration of such a theory necessarily entails a movement beyond both Marx and Freud.

HABERMAS'S COMMUNICATIONS THEORY OF POLITICS

The work of Jurgen Habermas points in this direction. Unlike Marx and Freud, Habermas insists that an adequate theory of political domination implies a satisfactory theory of political emancipation. The effort to elaborate this theory, in turn, demands that he undertake what he calls a ''reconstruction'' of the ''historical materialism'' that presently precludes it. This reconstruction will abandon Marx's assumption of the primacy of production in favor of the assumption of the centrality of both production and communication to the human condition. The adequacy of Habermas's theory of politics will depend, at bottom, on the adequacy of his understanding of the relationship between (what he takes to be) these two irreducible dimensions of human existence.

According to Habermas, Marx's concept of a mode of production unjustifiably collapses these two dimensions into the single dimension of labor. For Marx, as we have seen, a mode of production is also a ''definite mode of life''; the particular form in which human beings relate to nature in the production of their material existence necessarily entails a particular way in which human beings relate to each other (and conceive of this relationship). Intersubjectivity, or human communication, is thus a function of objectification. It is precisely this claim that Habermas contests. He begins by rendering objectification as ''instrumental'' or ''purposive-rational'' action and defining it as action designed to establish and extend human control over the environment through the exploitation of ''technical rules.'' As such, purposive-rational action is distinct from ''communicative action,'' or ''symbolic interaction,'' which is governed by ''norms'' that enable human beings to understand one another.[57] The logical status of this distinction is not entirely clear. On the one hand, Habermas argues that it is an analytical, rather than empirical distinction, i.e., that any given human activity may partake to varying degrees of both ''ideal-types'' of action. On the other hand, he

[57] Jurgen Habermas, *Toward a Rational Society* (Boston: Beacon Press, 1970), pp. 91-92.

219

contends that the particular activity that consists in relating to nature in order to secure "self-preservation through social labor" is exhausted by the logic of instrumental action: "Nature does not conform to the categories under which the subject apprehends it in the unresisting way in which a subject can conform to the understanding of another subject on the basis of reciprocal recognition."[58] In other words, for Habermas "our relation to nature . . . can *only* be one of *instrumental control*."[59] Thus the possibility of a "communicative" relationship with nature is foreclosed from the very outset. But this foreclosure, it would appear, is inconsistent with Habermas's insistence on the analytical nature of the distinction between instrumental and communicative action: if any given human activity can partake to varying degrees of both types of action, then it is not at all clear why a "self-preserving" relationship with nature that is predominantly noninstrumental could not be achieved.

I shall return to this question in the next chapter as well as in Part III. At this point it is sufficient to note that the distinction that Habermas draws between instrumental and communicative action leads him to translate Marx's theory of the determinative power of the mode of production into the proposition that the norms that govern human communication are derived from the technical rules that organize material production. Or, in Habermas's words, Marx's assertion is that "morality is an institutional framework . . . for processes of production."[60]

The analysis in this and the preceding chapters has shown that this assertion is unfounded. The persistence of patriarchal and authoritarian "morality" across different modes of production demonstrates that the repressiveness of communicative norms cannot be derived exclusively from a particular set of rules for the organization of material production. Conversely, the absence of proletarian socialist morality, i.e., class consciousness, among the working class in the technologically advanced capitalist societies demonstrates that the development of liberatory norms does not follow automatically from the technical mastery of nature. Growing human mastery over nature is not necessarily accompanied by a growth in the ability of humans to master their social relationships; the rationalization of human communication cannot be

---

[58] *Ibid.*, p. 87, and Jurgen Habermas, *Knowledge and Human Interests* (Boston: Beacon Press, 1971), p. 33.

[59] Joel Whitebook, "The Problem of Nature in Haberman," *Telos*, No. 40 (Summer 1979), p. 55, second emphasis in the original. See also Vincent DiNorcia, "From Critical Theory to Critical Ecology," *Telos*, No. 22 (Winter 1974-75), pp. 85-95, and Thomas McCarthy, *The Critical Theory of Jurgen Habermas* (Cambridge, Massachusetts: M.I.T. Press, 1978), pp. 23-36.

[60] Habermas, *Knowledge and Human Interests*, p. 57.

reduced to the "rationalization" of the forces of production. Habermas concurs:

> [T]o set free the technical forces of production . . . is not identical with the development of norms which could fulfill the dialectic of moral relationships in an interaction free of domination, on the basis of a reciprocity allowed to have its full and noncoercive scope. *Liberation from hunger and misery* does not necessarily converge with *liberation from servitude and degradation*, for there is no automatic developmental relation between labor and interaction.[61]

If the solution to the problem of purposive-rational action does not yield the solution to the problem of communicative action, then this latter problem must be thought out in its own terms. The autonomy of interaction from labor, in other words, demands a theory of politics that is irreducible to a theory of production, a theory in which the meaning of political domination/liberation is derived from an analysis of the logic of communicative action rather than the logic of purposive-rational action. Thus Habermas turns to what he calls a theory of "communicative competence" as the foundation for the theory of politics that is missing in Marx.

Habermas claims that the criteria for a liberatory politics can be derived from an analysis of the presuppositions of human speech. Every act of speech both presupposes and anticipates an *ideal speech situation* that implies, in turn, a model of a society in which political domination is absent. In what sense is this the case? To begin with, according to Habermas, "every speech, even that of intentional deception, is oriented towards the idea of truth."[62] To engage in speech is necessarily to advance propositions that claim to be valid or correct. Ordinary speech typically rests on a "background consensus" with regard to the validity of these propositions. When this consensus breaks down—when a disagreement arises—the parties to the disagreement can either break off communication or transform the nature of this communication into an explicit effort to determine the truthfulness of the disputed claim. To the extent that they adopt the second alternative, they agree to participate in (what Habermas calls) a "discourse" in which all communicative motives except the commitment to truth are suspended. To put this another way, if the disputants did not assume that they shared this overriding commitment it would, according to Habermas, make no sense for them to continue talking to each other. At the same time, the very act of participating in a discourse designed to (re-)establish an agreement about the truth of a disputed claim

---

[61] Habermas, *Theory and Practice* (Boston: Beacon Press, 1973), p. 169, emphases in the original.

[62] Jurgen Habermas, "Toward a Theory of Communicative Competence," in Hans Peter Dreitzel, *Recent Sociology*, No. 2 (New York: Macmillan, 1970), p. 144.

"carries with it the supposition that a genuine agreement is possible."[63] If, in short, we did not assume that it is possible to distinguish an authentic consensus from a false consensus, there would be no point in participating in a discourse designed to achieve consensus in the first place. Thus speech points inexorably to the notion of truth and the notion of truth necessarily implies a genuine consensus.

But what is a genuine consensus? How do we know if the agreement that issues from any given discourse is justified? In order to answer this question it would appear that we must abandon the terrain of speech and introduce a noncommunicative criterion of truth; conversely, if we remain on this terrain it seems as if we are left without any truth-criterion whatsoever and are thus condemned to a hopeless relativism. In either case the effort to derive normative standards from the structure of human communication has apparently proved abortive. According to Habermas, however, this conclusion is unwarranted: these standards are, in fact, immanent to the very logic of discourse itself. The analysis of this logic reveals that the commitment to truth that motivates the participants necessarily entails a willingness to submit only to "the force of the better argument" and thus an unwillingness to countenance as "genuine" any consensus that rests on any other form of force or constraint, i.e., on domination. Discourse thus implies a commitment to a model of communication free from constraint, to an "ideal speech situation" in which "for all participants there is a symmetrical distribution of chances to select and employ speech acts . . . an effective equality of chances to assume dialogue roles." In an ideal speech situation:

> all participants must have the same chance to initiate and perpetuate discourse, to put forward, call into question, and give reasons for or against statements, explanations, interpretations, and justifications. Furthermore, they must have the same chance to express attitudes, feelings, intentions and the like. . . . In other words, the conditions of the ideal speech situation must insure not only unlimited discussion but also discussion which is free from all constraints of domination, whether their source be conscious strategic behavior or communication barriers secured in ideology and neurosis.[64]

Any consensus that results from a discourse that violates the conditions of the ideal speech situation must be considered false. Conversely, a consensus may be considered genuine when the discourse from which it issues approximates these conditions of "pure communication."

---

[63] Habermas, *Legitimation Crisis* (Boston: Beacon Press, 1975), p. xvi. My account of Habermas's theory relies heavily on the summary that Thomas McCarthy provides in the introduction to this work, as well as in *The Critical Theory of Jurgen Habermas*, Ch. 4.

[64] Habermas, *Legitimation Crisis*, p. xvii.

222

Habermas is well aware that the assumption of an ideal speech situation is "counterfactual," i.e., that "the conditions of actual speech are rarely, if ever, those of the ideal speech situation."[65] In contemporary capitalist as well as state socialist societies, elite monopolization of the means of communication precludes the "symmetry among participants" and the "universal interchangeability of dialogue roles" that this norm demands. Communicative competence may entail a commitment to an ideal speech situation, but "on the strength of communicative competence we can by no means really produce the ideal speech situation independent of the empirical structures of the social system to which we belong."[66] Precisely because of its counterfactual status, the commitment to an ideal speech situation points beyond the existing "factual" order and anticipates an "ideal form of life" whose social structures would, in contrast to those of the present form of life, be consistent with the requirements of ideal speech. The commitment to a liberatory politics is inscribed in the very nature of human speech: speech implies truth, truth implies consensus, consensus implies an ideal speech situation, and an ideal speech situation implies a political order in which domination is absent. Thus "the truth of statements is linked in the last analysis to the intention of the good and true life."[67]

This linguistic reformulation of the "good and true life" does not yield a description of the specific forms of political decision making that are appropriate to this life. According to Habermas, in fact, "democratization cannot mean an a priori preference for a specific type of organization, for example, for so-called direct democracy." But the link he establishes between political emancipation and the conditions of ideal speech establishes, it seems to me, a generalized presumption in favor of those arrangements that secure the "maximum feasible participation" of all citizens in the formulation and disposition of the issues that affect their life chances. Thus, according to Habermas, "it is a question of finding arrangements which can ground the presumption that the basic institutions of the society and the basic political decisions would meet with the unforced agreement of all those involved, if they could participate, as free and equal, in discursive will formation."[68] In the absence of regular opportunities for "all those involved" actually to participate in "discursive will formation" it is difficult, perhaps even impossible, to see how this presumption could be grounded. Habermas may not exclude representative democratic arrangements on a priori grounds, but the logic of his entire analysis points to the insufficiency of these arrangements. Politics is the realm of communication, and communication is that process

---

[65] McCarthy, *The Critical Theory of Jurgen Habermas*, p. 309.

[66] Habermas, "Toward a Theory of Communicative Competence," p. 144.

[67] Cited in McCarthy, *The Critical Theory of Jurgen Habermas*, p. 307

[68] *Communication and the Evolution of Society*, p. 186.

within which human needs are intersubjectively formed and articulated. It follows that, for Habermas, politics is an authentic realm of need-creation and not merely a realm within which (prepolitical) needs are expressed or rep -resented. It follows, finally, that an ideal politics cannot be merely representative but must also be participatory in character.

Thus Habermas's analysis of the logic of communicative competence culminates in a participatory political standard against which any given political order can be compared and found wanting. But he is aware that there is something "peculiarly abstract" about this standard:

> Every general theory of justification remains peculiarly abstract in relation to the historical forms of . . . domination. If one brings standards of discursive justification to bear on traditional societies, one behaves in an historically 'unjust' manner. Is there an alternative to this historical injustice of general theories, on the one hand, and the standardlessness of mere historical understanding, on the other?[69]

Habermas's question is simply a reformulation of the classical problem of developing a normative standard that is historically grounded and therefore effective rather than merely utopian. He wants to demonstrate, in other words, the historical conditions under which a (communicative) standard that is supposed to be implicit in the human condition itself becomes more or less realizable in practice. This was Marx's problem as well: he sought to demonstrate both that labor is definitive of the human condition and that there are specific historical conditions for its effective (unalienated) realization. Marx's solution to this problem of overcoming the tension between the claim that labor is universal and the claim that it has not yet been realized in its essential form was an evolutionary theory that enabled him to "read" history as the progressive unfolding of the universal in the context of the particular. Similarly, Habermas attempts to reconcile the assertion of the universality of his ideal speech standard with its heretofore ubiquitous "counterfactual" status with an evolutionary theory of communicative competence: "the only promising program I can see is a theory that . . . clarifies the historically observable sequence of different levels of justification [of political structures] and reconstructs it as a developmental-logical nexus."[70] In short, Habermas will try to do for communication what Marx has done for labor (although, as the emphasis on "reconstruction" implies, he will dispense with the overtones of historical inevitability that plagued Marx's theory).

It follows from Habermas's earlier insistence on the autonomy of interaction from labor that the developmental logic of communicative competence is not

[69] *Ibid.*, p. 205.
[70] *Ibid.*

reducible to that of production: "normative structures do not simply follow the path of development of reproductive processes [labor] . . . but have an internal history."[71] In fact, the two developments "follow rationally reconstructible patterns that are logically independent of one another."[72] Thus we cannot look to Marx or Marxism for the foundations of a "rational reconstruction" of the logic of normative or communicative development, but must look elsewhere. Habermas finds these foundations in the cognitive developmental psychology of Jean Piaget and his followers.

Only the essentials of Habermas's admittedly "very tentative" appropriation of developmental psychology need concern us here. This psychology is based on the assumption that individual cognitive (Piaget), moral (Kohlberg), and ego (Loevinger) development "runs through an irreversible series of discrete and increasingly complex stages of development; no stage can be skipped over, and each higher stage implies the preceding stage in the sense of a rationally reconstructible pattern of development."[73] Thus, for example, Piaget distinguishes between the preoperational, concrete-operational, and formal-operational stages of cognitive development and Kohlberg distinguishes between the preconventional, conventional, and postconventional (principled) levels of moral development. Whether cognitive or moral learning takes place depends in part on environmental stimuli, but their claim is that *if* it does take place it will *necessarily* pass through these ascending stages. The basic assumption, in other words, is that environmental stimuli are mediated by an invariant sequence of internal structures that itself determines the impact of these stimuli on the individual's learning process. Mental development is, in this sense, both influenced by and relatively autonomous from its "material," or environmental preconditions.

Habermas first attempts to establish a correlation between the findings of the developmental psychologists and his own analysis of communicative competence. He demonstrates that their notions of cognitive and moral development can be translated into the terms of his communications theory and that the highest stages of these developments generally correspond to the capacity to enter into discourse and the ideal speech situation that it presupposes-anticipates.[74] This allows him to maintain that his theory of communicative competence is empirically confirmed by the findings of the devel-

[71] *Communication and the Evolution of Society*, p. xxi.

[72] *Legitimation Crisis*, p. 11.

[73] *Communication and the Evolution of Society*, pp. 157, 73-74.

[74] Actually, this step in Habermas's appropriation of the developmentalists is somewhat more complicated than I have suggested. It entails not merely a translation of their theories into the terms of his communications approach, but rather also a demonstration of the way in which this translation necessarily modifies these theories. Thus he argues that the analysis of communicative competence demonstrates that there is a stage of moral development higher than the one Kohlberg claims is the "final" stage. *Communication and the Evolution of Society*, pp. 87-90.

225

opmental psychologists; the capacity to enter into rational discourse is no mere "ought" but is, rather, the demonstrable culmination of the ontogenesis of the consciousness of the individuals the developmentalists have studied.

Habermas then attempts to establish a parallel between the ontogenetic level and the phylogenetic level of human mental development, i.e., he argues that the historical evolution of "world-views" follows a "rationally reconstructible pattern" that is "homologous" to the pattern Piaget and Kohlberg reconstructed for the cognitive and moral development of the individual. He is aware of, and even details, all the pitfalls of the assumption that ontogeny and phylogeny "recapitulate" one another. He nevertheless locates an allegedly invariant sequence of levels of social integration that runs from "neolithic" societies to "early civilizations" to "developed civilizations" to the "modern age" and that parallels ontogenetic development in the sense that the sequence of social integration involves the internalization of increasingly abstract and universalistic principles.[75] Thus only when the last stage is reached do we find a societal learning capacity that corresponds to the "self-reflective" individual learning capacity that communicative competence entails. To put this another way, it would appear that Habermas's conclusion is that the norm of ideal speech becomes potentially politically efficacious only when a society has reached the "modern," universalistic stage of social integration; the counterfactual status of the ideal-speech situation only effectively anticipates a new "form of life," a society without domination, when the socialization of individuals has come to depend on collective norms or world-views that are already in tension with the dominant social structures that currently preclude the institutionalization of (approximations to) ideal speech.

This conclusion, however, initiates as many problems as it resolves. In the first place, it appears to render superfluous the political functions of the supposition of an ideal speech situation. If the counterfactual status of ideal speech assumes an anticipatory political role only in a society whose culture is already dissonant with the existing structures of power, then it would seem that the effective contradiction is between this culture and these structures and that nothing of an explanatory nature is gained by the supposition of a universal, distinctively human communicative competence. Has Habermas really added anything to the by-now familiar thesis that there is a potentially explosive contradiction between the culture and the class structure of contemporary capitalism,[76] except another normative standard that tells us how this contradiction *ought* to be resolved but in no way clarifies the practical possibility of this wished-for resolution?

The supposition of a universally human communicative competence that

---

[75] *Ibid.*, pp. 99, 102-103, 110-11, 157-58; see also pp. 111-16.

[76] See, for example, Daniel Bell, *The Cultural Contradictions of Capitalism* (New York: Basic Books, 1976). For Habermas's formulation of this thesis, see *Legitimation Crisis*, pp. 75-92.

effectively exists only in modern societies, moreover, smacks of cultural imperialism. Does not his formulation relegate primitive, indeed all premodern societies to the status of less-than-fully-rational, less-than-fully-human societies, and is this not yet another example of a characteristically Western ethnocentrism?[77] To put this another way, is there not something viciously circular—in both the logical and political sense—about an effort to establish the "underdeveloped" rationality of premodern societies that relies on a general standard of rationality that (at least it can be argued) is nothing other than the highest stage of the particular form of rationality that predominates in modern societies?

I shall return to these issues in Part III. Our problem now is the rather more specific one of whether Habermas is able successfully to join his communications theory of culture to Marx's theory of production. Habermas's theory is, in a sense, merely an elaboration of his initial assumption that "there is no automatic developmental relation between labor and interaction."[78] "Still," he tells us in his very next sentence, "there is a connection between the two dimensions."[79] It is this connection that he must spell out if his effort is to stand as a "reconstruction of historical materialism" in any meaningful sense of the term. Indeed, he argues that a satisfactory theory of social evolution demands that his communications theory "be linked convincingly with the precisely rendered fundamental assumptions of historical materialism."[80] It is time to examine and evaluate his effort to forge this link.

Habermas opens the space for a re-insertion of historical materialism by drawing a "distinction . . . between the logic of development of normative structures and the dynamics of this development." Just as the actual dynamics of the child's cognitive and moral learning process cannot be deduced from the internal developmental structures alone but is, rather, a function of an interaction between these structures and the environmental stimuli to which the child is subjected, so the empirical dynamics of social evolution is the result of a dialectic between the developmental levels of social integration and extranormative environmental determinants. Habermas's claim, in other words, is that if a particular society is to evolve it must pass through the sequence that runs from its present stage to the higher stages of social integration that he describes; whether it will in fact so evolve and, if so, when, "depends on *contingent* boundary conditions and on learning processes that

---

[77] For a discussion of this issue, see McCarthy, *The Critical Theory of Jurgen Habermas*, pp. 317-325.

[78] See above, n. 61.

[79] Habermas, *Theory and Practice*, p. 169.

[80] *Ibid.*, p. 12.

can be investigated empirically.''[81] In short, ''the mechanisms which cause developmental advances in the normative structures are independent of the *logic* of their development.''[82]

The ''boundary conditions'' that function as ''mechanisms which cause developmental advances'' are, according to Habermas, ultimately economic conditions: ''In its developmental *dynamics*, the change of normative structures remains dependent on evolutionary challenges posed by unresolved, economically conditioned, system problems and on learning problems that are a response to them.''[83] Here Habermas reasserts the determinative power of the mode of production: it poses the problems to which a change in normative structures represents a possible solution. Because the actual evolution of culture is, in this sense, dependent on the evolution of production, ''culture remains a superstructural phenomenon, even if it seems to play a more prominent role in the transition to new developmental levels than many Marxists have heretofore supposed.'' Habermas is convinced that his communications theory of culture is consistent with the fundamental Marxist assumption of the centrality of labor to the human condition: ''the analysis of developmental dynamics is 'materialist' insofar as it makes reference to crisis-producing systems problems in the domain of production and reproduction.''[84]

Indeed, at least at first glance Habermas's ''reconstruction'' appears to be merely a reformulation of earlier versions of historical materialism that assumed that ''the development of productive forces can be understood as a problem generating mechanism that *triggers but does not bring about* the overthrow of relations of production and an evolutionary renewal of the mode of production.'' But Habermas specifically repudiates this version as empirically indefensible. The hypothesis of the independent, catalytic role of the development of the forces of production is refuted by the fact that ''the great endogenous, evolutionary advances that led to the first [state] civilizations or to the rise of European capitalism were not conditioned but followed by significant development of productive forces.'' Indeed, Habermas argues that the development of the forces of production is entirely dependent on a prior change in normative structures, i.e., an evolutionary advance in the cultural and political domain: ''only when a new institutional [i.e., political] framework has emerged can the as-yet unresolved systems problems be treated with the help of the accumulated cognitive potential; from this there *results* an increase in productive forces.''[85]

---

[81] *Communication and the Evolution of Society*, pp. xxii, 140 (emphasis in the original).

[82] *Legitimation Crisis*, pp. 12-13, emphasis in the original.

[83] *Communication and the Evolution of Society*, p. 98, emphasis in the original.

[84] *Ibid.*, and p. 123.

[85] *Ibid.*, pp. 146, 147, emphases in the original.

228

But this means that the reference that Habermas's theory makes to "crisis-producing problems in the domain of production"—a reference that purportedly secures the materialist status of this theory—cannot be a reference to problems that result from the development of the forces of production. What, then, is the ultimately economic source of the evolutionary challenges to which a change in normative structures is a possible response? According to Habermas, there can be no general answer to this question: the economic bases of "systems problems" are precisely the "*contingent* boundary conditions" to which he has earlier referred, i.e., they are specific to time and place. Thus his account of the transition from "neolithic" (or primitive) to early state societies makes reference to "ecologically conditioned problems of land scarcity and population density or problems having to do with an unequal distribution of wealth," but other evolutionary "advances" may well have been triggered by entirely different economic problems: "whether and how problems that overburden the structurally limited capacity of a society arise is contingent."[86]

We are thus left with a notion of the dependence of culture and its political institutionalization on an economic base that is defined so broadly that it embraces virtually any conceivable environmental condition and will in fact entail radically different conditions depending on the particular time and place. This notion hardly amounts to a vindication of Marx's theory of the determinative power of the mode of production, except if "production" is defined so broadly that it loses any distinctive meaning and becomes equivalent to any material boundary condition whatsoever. And this does not end the matter. Whether any given society responds to the evolutionary challenge posed by economic problems with a successful cultural solution likewise depends, according to Habermas, on contingent conditions.[87] More specifically, a developmental advance in world-views (and their subsequent institutionalization) is contingent on individual "learning processes in the domain of moral-practical consciousness" whose results (somehow) "gain entrance into the interpretive system of the society." These learning processes, which, it should be recalled, are fundamentally different from those that take place in the domain of purposive-rational, or economic, action, function as "pacemakers" of social evolution.[88] Thus the impact of the already contingent economic base on the cultural-political superstructure is mediated by yet another, and this time noneconomic, contingency: the transition from one world-view and its institutionalization to another, i.e., from one level of social integration to another, depends upon an (unclarified) learning process that is originally triggered by an economically based problem, but that may or may not suc-

[86] *Ibid.*, p. 162. McCarthy, *The Critical Theory of Jurgen Habermas*, p. 255.

[87] McCarthy, *The Critical Theory of Jurgen Habermas*, p. 255.

[88] Habermas, *Communication and the Evolution of Society*, p. 160.

cessfully take place. The Marxist thesis of the determinative power of the mode of production is thus stretched so broadly that it becomes indistinguishable from virtually any investigation of the relationship between the cultural/political realm and its environmental preconditions.

Habermas had argued that an adequate theory of social evolution requires that his communication theory "be linked convincingly with the precisely rendered fundamental assumptions of historical materialism."[89] It should now be clear that this link is purchased at the price of the reduction of these assumptions to the level of banality. His sustained effort to reconcile the Marxist thesis of the ultimately superstructural role of culture with the empirical reality that it plays a far "more prominent role" in history "than many Marxists have heretofore supposed" culminates in a Marxism that is emptied of all meaning. His reconstruction of historical materialism is, in fact, and against his own intentions, its effective dissolution.

This dissolution signals Habermas's ultimate failure historically to ground his notion of political emancipation and the theory of communicative competence from which it derives. He was faced with the problem of specifying the conditions under which the implicit commitment to an ideal speech situation becomes politically efficacious, i.e., when it is transformed from an impotent "ought" to an anticipatory norm that can actually motivate individuals to transcend the structures of political domination that currently violate it. In order to solve this problem he turned first to cognitive developmental psychology and then to a synthesis between it and the fundamental assumptions of Marxism. The encounter with developmental psychology yielded the conclusion that the political efficacy of the norm of ideal speech is a function of the preexisting stage of social integration or level of world-view that the society in question has attained. The Marx synthesis, on the other hand, culminated in the conclusion that the level of world-view attained is not a direct function of economic problems but rather of "moral-practical" individual learning processes of which economic problems are merely the stimulus. Thus the political efficacy of the norm underlying communicative action depends on the level of "social-cognitive" development, and the level of social-cognitive development depends upon a learning process that takes place "in the dimension of . . . communicative action."[90] Habermas's argument moves in a circle; at the end of it we are not one whit closer to a solution to the problem of the conditions for the practical realization of the ideal speech situation than we were at the beginning.

It is clear that Habermas's reconceptualization of a genuinely socialist society as the *telos* of human speech itself necessarily leads to a repudiation

[89] See above, n. 80.
[90] *Communication and the Evolution of Society*, pp. 97-98.

230

of the Marxist location of the proletariat as *the* revolutionary agent under capitalism and to a re-opening of the question of the specific audience to which critical theory is addressed. It even suggests, as many have noted, that everyone becomes a potential addressee, a potentially revolutionary agent, because everyone is presumed to share a commitment to ideal speech.[91] In and of itself, this redefinition and broadening of the audience of critical theory is not the problem. The problem is, rather, that Habermas fails utterly to specify the conditions under which *anyone* would be motivated to struggle to put the ideal of pure speech into practice:

> [I]t must be asked whether such a theory sheds any light on what leads human beings to overcome forms of distortive communication and work toward the conditions required for ideal speech. What seems to be lacking here is any illumination on the problem of human . . . motivation.[92]

This illumination is absent because Habermas's analysis abstracts almost entirely from what might be called the psychodynamics of human communication.[93] His conception of an ideal speech situation does make reference to the "insertion of drive potentials into a communicative structure of action" and, as we have seen, he specifically argues that the insertion of neurotic drives into communicative structures necessarily produces distorted, rather than ideal, communication.[94] He seems to be aware, in other words, that there are unconscious motivational determinants of the effective capacity of individuals to enter into reciprocal, undistorted communication with one another.[95] But this awareness is unaccompanied by any effort to specify the nature of these motivational determinants. Thus in his most recent work he gives us absolutely no idea of whether they are present in the modern societies that have ostensibly developed the collective cognitive capacities for ideal speech.[96]

[91] McCarthy, *The Critical Theory of Jurgen Habermas*, pp. 383-86.

[92] Richard J. Bernstein, *The Restructuring of Social and Political Theory* (Philadelphia: University of Pennsylvania Press, 1978), pp. 223-24.

[93] McCarthy, *The Critical Theory of Jurgen Habermas*, p. 352.

[94] *Legitimation Crisis*, pp. 89 and xvii.

[95] This awareness is also manifest in his discussion of Kohlberg, where he points out that an inadequate motivational structure may cause an individual to "fall back in his moral actions . . . below the threshold of his interactive competence." *Communication and the Evolution of Society*, pp. 91-92.

[96] Habermas alludes to this problem in *Legitimation Crisis* with the admission that "I neglect . . . the important sociological question, whether—and if so how—cultural patterns are reflected in personality structures through agencies of socialization and practices of childrearing" (76). Elsewhere in the work he does say that "it can be argued that fundamental convictions of communicative ethics . . . are today already determining typical socialization processes among several strata, that is, they have achieved motive-forming power" (90). This argument rests, in turn, on the assumptions that the probability of what Habermas calls an "unconventional outcome of the adolescent crisis" (90) is steadily increasing, i.e., that adolescents are increasingly unable

231

As we have seen, it can be argued that the dominant personality types in the capitalist form of these societies lack the motivation to participate in undistorted communication. On the one hand, the authoritarian personality has an unconscious need both to dominate and be dominated, and thus is an unlikely candidate for participation in communicative interaction in which domination is absent. On the other hand, "the narcissistic personality is a depoliticized individual . . . bent on private gratification" who "treat[s] the public world with cynicism"[97] and thus can scarcely be expected to display the trust in the intentions of others essential for the ideal speech situation. This suggests that a radical reconstruction of individual personality and the family system that reproduces it is a necessary precondition for a widespread motivation to put the norm of ideal speech into political practice. In the absence of a profound transformation in the psychosexual basis of communicative interaction, in other words, we have absolutely no reason to believe that this interaction will be anything other than repressive or distorted. But Habermas fails to develop a theory of these psychosexual bases and thus can tell us nothing about the prospects for such a transformation.

Finally, the very way in which Habermas defines human communication reflects this neglect of its psychosexual dimension. The presupposition underlying the entire theory of communicative competence, as we have seen, is that intersubjectively secured truth or understanding is the essential function of human communication: "in action oriented to understanding, language

---

to "work out [a] definition of identity" (90) without "the explicit testing of tradition" (91), and that communicative ethics are the only ones that can withstand this testing. Even if we grant the plausibility of these assumptions and thus the plausibility of the argument that rests on them, it by no means follows from the fact that communicative ethics "have achieved motive-forming power" that individuals will be motivated to enter into ideal speech situations and to create the conditions that will make this entry possible. This would follow only if it were the case that child-rearing practices in particular and socialization in general did not result in the formation of other motives that discourage entry into these situations, and this is precisely the question that Habermas entirely neglects. He does argue that withdrawal as well as protest, can result from an unconventional resolution of adolescent crisis; he is aware, in other words that adherence to a communicative ethics is a necessary but insufficient condition for the willingness to struggle on behalf of a society that materializes the possibility of ideal speech. But nowhere does Habermas discuss the sufficient conditions, and in his latest book, *Communication and the Evolution of Society*, the entire problem of the motivational bases for the individual realization of collective cognitive potential is simply dropped. The failure of Habermas to address this problem is particularly striking in the light of the fact that, a little more than a decade ago, he argued that communicative action "is increasingly supplanted by conditioned behavior" and that the "increase in *adaptive behavior* is . . . only the obverse of the dissolution of the sphere of linguistically mediated interaction by the structure of purposive-rational action." *Toward a Rational Society*, p. 107, emphasis in the original.

[97] Seyla Ben Habbib, review of Habermas's *Communication and the Evolution of Society*, *Telos*, No. 40 (Summer 1979), p. 187.

finds the use for which it is fundamentally designed."[98] This is the assumption that justifies his focus on speech and the exclusion of "nonverbalized actions and bodily expressions" from his analysis of communicative action.[99] It also underlies his description of the ideal speech situation as a situation in which "all motives except that of the cooperative search for truth are excluded," i.e., as a situation ideally suited to reaching mutual understanding.[100] In short, Habermas's theory of politics rests on a characteristically "cognitivist" conception of language as above all a vehicle of human rationality.

His theory therefore rests on an inadequate conception of language. Habermas fails to understand that humans speak to each other not merely in order to reach a mutual understanding but also because, as Hegel would have it, they desire the recognition of the other. According to Hegel, "to desire to speak is to desire not satiety, but the discourse of the Other, to desire the desire moving that alien discourse and to want to bask in the recognition that comes from being spoken to and from experiencing the desire of the other in the words he speaks."[101] Habermas forgets that the struggle for recognition necessarily traverses the channels of communicative interaction, and that these channels are, therefore, inevitably filled wth currents of passion as well as reason. It follows that ideal or "pure" human communication cannot properly be conceived as a dispassionate search for truth; viewed from the perspective of an "empassioned" or "embodied" theory of communication, Habermas's ideal speech situation looks anything but ideal. The same would have to be said for the vision of political emancipation that is based on this situation. If we want to derive a notion of a liberatory politics from a theory of communication, it will have to be from a theory which, in contrast to Habermas's, does justice to the passionate nature of this process. But this is a matter for another chapter.

[98] Cited in McCarthy, *The Critical Theory of Jurgen Habermas*, pp. 287-88.

[99] *Communication and the Evolution of Society*, p. 1.

[100] *Legitimation Crisis*, p. 108.

[101] Garth Jackson Gilan, "Toward a Critical Conception of Semiotics," *Cultural Hermeneutics*, 3 (July 1976), p. 420.

CHAPTER SEVEN

NEO-MARXIST THEORIES OF REPRESSIVE TECHNOLOGY

In Chapter Four I argued that neither Marx nor the Marxist tradition is able to develop an adequate theory of the origins and persistence of environmental degradation and thus of the possibilities for its elimination. Such a theory, I suggested, demands a nonanthropocentric conception of the requirements of nature, i.e., demands precisely what is absent in Marx and those who theorize in his name. A satisfactory theory of repressive technology requires a standard of evaluation that is derived not from the analysis of the structure of human action but rather from an understanding of the structure of the ecosystem of which human action is merely an element. At the same time, this theory must be able to explain the existence of technologies that violate this standard with a category that is broader than "capitalism" but narrower than "technology" as such. In this chapter I examine the efforts of two contemporary Neo-Marxists—Herbert Marcuse and Anthony Wilden—to develop a theory that satisfies these requirements yet remains consistent with the basic intentions of Marxism.

HERBERT MARCUSE'S THEORY OF TECHNOLOGICAL RATIONALITY

Marcuse's critical theory of technological rationality is shaped decisively by his encounter with Freud's speculations concerning the instinctual basis of human destructiveness. Freud's account of the libidinal origins of the human drive to dominate nature, Marcuse argues, provides the necessary starting point for a comprehension of the persistence and pervasiveness of repressive technology that is beyond the grasp of a Marxism that, in overly restrictive fashion, locates the capitalist mode of production as the exclusive source of this technology. Only when the libidinal roots of repressive technology are thoroughly understood, he reasons, will human beings be in a position to uproot this technology and create an alternative one that is consistent with, rather than antagonistic to, the requirements of the natural "environment." His vision of a liberatory technology, in turn, is nourished by a notion of libidinal or instinctual restructuring that he derives from Freud. This derivation from Freud, however, is at the same time a movement against Freud, since the libidinal restructuring that can be deduced from his theory as the necessary condition for a liberatory technology is, according to Freud, impossible. Thus Marcuse's task will be to demonstrate the possibility of the libidinal and technological transformation that Freud denies. In this task he will look to Marx as his ally.

Freud on the Domination of Nature

In *Civilization and its Discontents* Freud ventures the alarming hypothesis that human destructiveness toward nature is a manifestation of an instinct for death; "the drive to master nature . . . is the result of an extroversion of the death instinct, the desire to die being transformed into the desire to kill, destroy, or dominate."[1] Somewhat earlier, in *Beyond the Pleasure Principle*, he had first "discovered" the death instinct in the context of an effort to account for the otherwise perplexing tendency of his subjects to relive the emotionally painful experiences of childhood in the present instead of being able to remember them as occurrences in the past. This compulsion to repeat what is painful, Freud reasons, cannot be explained by the pleasure principle— or Eros—that he had heretofore assumed to govern the behavior of the human organism, but must be explained by a drive that overrides, or is beyond, this principle. This drive must be understood as "*an urge inherent in organic life to restore an earlier state of things* which the living entity has been obliged to abandon under the pressure of external disturbing forces . . . or, to put it another way, the expression of the inertia inherent in organic life."[2] If the organism is governed by the principle of inertia, however, this can only mean that it seeks to "return to the quiescence of the inorganic world," i.e., that is strives toward death. Thus Freud concludes that life is but a long "detour to death."[3]

Henceforth Freud will interpret individual psychological development as the result of a profound and perpetual struggle within the individual between the death instinct and its great antagonist, the sexual (or life) instincts. The sexual instincts counteract the tendency toward individual self-destruction by impelling the individual to unite with other individuals; the inertia of the organism is offset by a libidinally based movement toward other organisms. The desire for the other resists the desire for death: the sexual instincts are "the true life instincts . . . [which] operate against the purpose of the other

[1] Norman O. Brown, *Life Against Death* (New York: Vintage Books, 1959), p. 102.

[2] Sigmund Freud, *Beyond the Pleasure Principle*, *SE* Vol. XVIII, p. 36, emphasis in the original.

[3] Cited in Marcuse, *Eros and Civilization*, pp. 23, 25.

235

instincts, which lead . . . to death." Thus Eros delays the "descent towards death," ensuring that the "detour to death" which is life will last as long as possible.[4]

Civilization and its Discontents extends this theory of individual development to the development of human culture as a whole. Culture, or civilization, is nothing but the struggle between life and death, between Eros and Thanatos, a "battle of the giants" whose outcome is anything but clear.[5] Eros makes social life possible by creating the libidinal basis for a social solidarity that transcends the egotism of the individual. At the same time, it supplies the energy for the labor without which a society cannot survive: civilization "obtains a great part of the mental energy it needs by subtracting it from sexuality."[6] The labor that serves life, however, simultaneously serves death; if labor is a sublimation of Eros, it is also a sublimation of Thanatos. In labor "the death instinct would . . . seem to express itself . . . as an instinct of destruction directed against the external world . . .";[7] work diverts destructiveness from the ego to external objects and thus channels the death instinct toward the domination of nature.

From one perspective, this diversion of Thanatos toward nature can be considered a victory for Eros. Labor harnesses the aggressive drives of human beings to the struggle for human survival: "The instinct of destruction, when tempered and harnessed (as it were, inhibited in its aim) and directed towards objects, is compelled to provide the ego with satisfaction of its needs and with power over nature."[8] Thus labor makes death serve the interests of life; the energies of death are obliged to fuel the process of technological development on which the progress of civilization depends.

From another perspective, however, this progress in cultural life is but a descent toward cultural death. Labor involves the sublimation of the sexual instincts, and sublimation entails a subtraction (of energy) from these instincts. Paradoxically, then, the very labor that Eros calls forth necessarily weakens Eros. This weakening of Eros, in turn, increases the power of Thanatos: "After sublimation the erotic component no longer has the power to bind the whole of the destructiveness that was combined with it, and this is released in the form of an inclination to aggression and destruction."[9] In this sense labor can be understood as a victory for death; it unleashes a destructiveness toward nature that knows no bounds and thus threatens the very survival of

---

[4] Sigmund Freud, *Beyond the Pleasure Principle*, p. 40, and *The Ego and the Id*, *SE*, Vol. XIX, p. 47.

[5] Cited in Ricoeur, *Freud and Philosophy*, p. 305.

[6] Sigmund Freud, *Civilization and its Discontents* (London: Hogarth Press, 1949), p. 74.

[7] Cited in Ricoeur *Freud and Philosophy*, p. 296.

[8] Freud, *Civilization and its Discontents*, p. 101.

[9] Freud, *The Ego and the Id*, pp. 54-55.

the planet itself. The progress of civilization is bound up with the ultimate destruction of civilization. The mastery of nature comes, in the end, to defeat "Man."

From either perspective, nature is the loser. Whether the domination of nature culminates in human life or death, it remains the case that nature is dominated. The individual who labors, Freud is telling us, is the individual who hates nature, who relates to it as the mere "raw material" for his aggressive manipulation. The degradation of the environment is thus inseparable from the labor that makes civilization possible. Human technology is repressive per se.

Marcuse's Critical Appropriation of Freud

Marcuse attempts to annul Freud's equation of civilization and the domination of nature by demonstrating that the instinctual organization that Freud correctly locates as the basis of this domination is peculiar to certain forms of human culture rather than inherent in human culture as such. This instinctual organization, according to Freud, and as we have seen, is demanded by the labor without which any civilization would be impossible: labor entails the sublimation of Eros, and the sublimation of Eros is inseparable from the extroversion of the death instinct toward the natural world. Like Reich, Marcuse argues that this repressive instinctual organization is not intrinsic to all forms of human labor but is specific to alienated labor, i.e., labor that is set in motion in order to secure and reproduce the domination of one group of human beings over another. Whereas Freud had deduced "desexualized" labor from the "brute fact of scarcity"—"since society does not have sufficient . . . supplies to maintain its members without their working, it must . . . divert their sexual energies from sexual activity to work"[10]—Marcuse insists that this deduction:

> is fallacious in so far as it applies to the brute *fact* of scarcity what actually is the consequence of a specific *organization* of scarcity, and of a specific existential attitude enforced by this organization. The prevalent scarcity has, throughout civilization (although in very different modes), been organized in such a way that it has not been distributed collectively in accordance with individual needs, nor has the procurement of goods for the satisfaction of needs been organized with the objective of best satisfying the developing needs of the individuals. Instead, the *distribution* of scarcity as well as the effort of overcoming it, the mode of work, have been *imposed* upon individuals—first by mere violence, subsequently by a more rational utilization of power. However, no matter

[10] See above, Chapter Six, n. 33.

how useful this rationality was for the progress of the whole, it remained the rationality of *domination*, and the gradual conquest of scarcity was inextricably bound up with and shaped by the interest of domination.[11]

Freud conflates the sublimation inherent in the labor essential for any civilized form of human association with the repressive sublimation specific to the labor "shaped by the interest of domination," the modification of the human instinctual apparatus that the universal struggle against scarcity demands with the drastic restructuring of this apparatus that the hierarchical organization of scarcity requires. Put otherwise, Freud confuses "basic repression"—the "considerable degree and scope of repressive control over the instincts" that "any form of the reality principle demands"—with "surplus repression," or the "*additional* controls over and above those indispensable for civilized human association . . . arising from the specific institutions of domination."[12]

Marcuse believes that this distinction between basic and surplus repression opens the way for an historical specification of the human drive toward mastery over nature and thus for a conceptualization of its ultimate elimination. Only the surplus repression of the sexual instincts that the interest in domination requires, he reasons, weakens these instincts to the point where they can no longer bind the death instincts and these instincts assume, therefore, the form of destructive impulses vis-à-vis the natural world. More specifically, the extroversion of the death instinct in the guise of "constructive technological destruction" is specific to that stage of human history in which the domination of human being over human being is regulated by the "performance principle," i.e., by the near-total mobilization of the human body and mind "as instruments of alienated labor."[13] Under the repressive rule of the performance principle, contemporary civilization—both capitalist and state socialist—enforces an unprecedented "desexualization of the body: the libido becomes concentrated in one part of the body [the genitals], leaving most of the rest free for use as the instrument of labor." It is not labor as such but only alienated labor that demands that weakening of the libido on which the destructive manifestation of the death instinct depends. It follows that the "qualitative change in the development of sexuality [that] must necessarily alter the manifestations of the death instinct" is contingent on the elimination of alienated labor.[14] The transcendence of this form of labor makes possible a desublimation of sexual energy—an eroticization of the entire human body—and thus a strengthening of the life instincts that effectively precludes the destructive expression of the death instinct in the form of the domination of

[11] Marcuse, *Eros and Civilization*, p. 33, emphases in the original.
[12] *Ibid.*, p. 34, emphasis in the original.
[13] *Ibid.*, pp. 79, 42.
[14] *Ibid.*, pp. 44, 126.

238

nature. Thus the liberation of labor will entail the liberation of nature; the end to the domination of human being over human being will mean the end of the domination of human beings over nature.

I will examine Marcuse's analysis of the prospects for this twofold liberation presently. At this point it suffices to point out certain ambiguities in the way he poses the problem that will return to haunt whatever specific solution—or solutions—he envisions. Insofar as Marcuse subordinates the domination of nature to the existence of alienated labor, he devotes his energy to the elaboration of a theory of the possible overcoming of alienated labor. But—irrespective of its particular content—such a theory of the end of alienated labor will be only as convincing as a theory of its origins. This theory of origins, however, is precisely what is lacking in Marcuse (as well as Marx). Marcuse assumes that, but does not explain why, domination takes the specific form of alienated labor in contemporary civilization. If alienated labor is but one form of the more general phenomenon of the hierarchial "organization of scarcity"—if the performance principle is only one of a number of repressive reality principles that make up the history of humanity—then an explanation of this particular mode of domination would have to be derived from, or at least subsumed under, a more general theory of the domination of humans over their fellow human beings. No such theory, however, is to be found in Marcuse's writings: he tells us that "the gradual conquest of scarcity was inextricably bound up with and shaped by the interest of domination," but fails to say why this should have been the case. The adverb "inextricably" implies a necessary, rather than contingent, relationship between the conquest of scarcity and domination, but the precise nature of this necessity remains unclarified.

Marcuse's critique of Freud's effort to link nonlibidinal labor directly to scarcity precludes his arguing that domination flows inexorably from this "brute fact" itself. But if domination is not inherent in scarcity, in what sense is it inextricably bound up with the conquest of scarcity? Should we perhaps read this claim to imply that it is not scarcity, but rather the effort to *conquer* scarcity, that gives rise to the domination of humans by humans? The problem with this formulation, however, is that the metaphor of the conquest of scarcity implies the very domination of nature for which the theory of social domination is supposed to account: the domination of humans over nature results from the domination of humans over humans, but the domination of humans over humans results from the domination of humans over nature. And so the argument moves in a circle. I shall return to this and related problems. The point I want to underscore now is that Marcuse fails to develop a coherent theory of the origins of social domination/alienated labor. For this reason his analysis of the possibilities for the elimination of alienated labor is bound to remain less than wholly convincing.

239

Whatever its ambiguities, Marcuse's critical appropriation of Freud clearly entails a repudiation of Freud's thesis of the inherently repressive nature of all human technology in favor of the thesis of the intrinsically repressive character of the technology of "contemporary civilization," i.e., of industrial societies regulated by the "performance principle." Marcuse's defense of this latter thesis does not rest exclusively on Freud's analysis of the destructive instinctual organization that this principle demands. He is aware that a compelling indictment of contemporary technology necessitates a critique of the science or form of reason of which this technology is an application. In the absence of such a critique, for example, it might be possible for someone to accept Freud's account of the destructive tendencies of the instincts but to argue that these tendencies are, or at least can be, held in check by a non-destructive reason, and thus to call into question the thesis of the inherently repressive nature of technology under the performance principle. In order to counter this type of argument, Marcuse will have to demonstrate that contemporary reason itself is intrinsically repressive or destructive. He will try to show, in other words, that the destructive manifestations of the death instinct are present in the very reason that is called on to keep this instinct in check.

This demonstration relies, in part, on Max Scheler's theory of modern science as *Herrschaftswissen*, that is, as "knowledge for the sake of domination."[15] With Scheler, Marcuse argues that modern science presupposes and originates with a profound reconceptualization of nature and its relationship to human beings. From classical Greek through medieval thought, nature was conceived in teleological terms, that is, as infused with value or purpose. Conceptualized as an end in itself, nature could not become a mere means for human ends; to the contrary, the good life was defined as the life that was led in conformity with what were assumed to be the requirements of nature. The relationship between human beings and nature was understood in ethical terms; the physical sciences were subsumed under an overarching metaphysical or religious world-view.

Enlightenment thought, beginning with Francis Bacon in the seventeenth century, carries out the project of the eradication of the teleological conception of the world, of the "disenchantment" of nature. Nature will no longer be understood as a purposeful whole; stripped of value, it becomes "value-free"; divested of subjectivity, it becomes a pure object. This transformation in the concept of nature entailed a reconceptualization of its relationship to human beings: a value-free world is a world prepared for subjection exclusively to human values; the de-subjectification or "objectification" of nature paves the way for its domination by the human subject. No longer conceived as an end

---

[15] See William Leiss, *The Domination of Nature*, (New York: George Braziller, 1972), p. 105.

in itself, nature ceases to be a limit that human beings must respect and becomes instead a mere field for unlimited human action, raw material for human intervention and manipulation. Thus the "positive sciences" detach themselves from the ethical or religious framework within which they were formerly constrained. The disenchantment of nature sets the stage for the "inquisition of Nature" that scientific research, according to Bacon, carries out.[16]

Prior to any particular analysis that it may undertake, then, the modern scientific ego is already "a subject against an object":

> Nature is *a priori* experienced by an organism bent to domination and therefore experienced as susceptible to mastery and control . . . The science of nature develops under the *technological a priori* which projects nature as potential instrument, stuff of control and organization.[17]

Marcuse locates this technological a priori in the very ideal of pure knowledge that animates modern science: the representation of nature in the form of mathematical equations. This quantitative representation presupposes that nature is divested of its quality; the concrete and otherwise incommensurable entities of the natural world are conceptualized abstractly as fungible "matter" so that it becomes possible to express their relationships in mathematical terms. This "formalization" of nature is, according to Marcuse, at the same time its "functionalization": science projects nature as "mere form" and thus enables it to "be bent to practically all [human] ends." The knowledge of nature that this "pure" science yields is not knowledge as such; rather it is instrumental knowledge, i.e., knowledge that yields the possibility of prediction and control. The nature that modern science discloses is not nature "in itself" but only nature as it becomes a "possible object of man's manipulation." Scientific reason, in short, is not the only possible reason; it is, rather, a "specific historical project."[18]

Scientific reason, in turn, tends to become totalitarian. Marcuse develops a version of Husserl's theory of the way in which "Galilean science" veils, and thus comes to dominate, the very *Lebenswelt* (lifeworld) from which it emerges. As we have seen, the practice of science is rooted in a specific experiential need or value, namely the need to master the natural environment. The abstractness of scientific practice, however, conceals its connection to this concrete need of the *Lebenswelt*; the mathematical idealization of nature is confounded with the structure of nature as such, and the practice that moves within the idealized horizon claims to be value-free—the only possible source of objective knowledge—insofar as its only goal is to penetrate this structure.

---

[16] *Ibid.*, p. 55.

[17] *Ibid.*, pp. 99-100; Marcuse, *One-Dimensional Man*, p. 153, emphasis in the original.

[18] Marcuse, *One-Dimensional Man*, pp. 157, 155, 124.

Husserl points out that "the actor in this drama (the scientist) never appears in the process of scientific investigation";[19] according to the (fetishized) self-understanding of the positive sciences, it is precisely the (alleged) absence of ties between the scientist and the subjectivity of his or her *Lebenswelt* that assures the objectivity of his or her practice. Since objectivity is defined in opposition to the *Lebenswelt*, the values and modes of experiencing the world that predominate there will be denigrated as "unscientific" and "merely subjective." A fetishized science undermines the integrity of all world-views other than the one on which it is based (but which it does not even recognize); thus one value—the value of the domination of nature—comes to establish hegemony over all other possible values. The technological *a priori* of modern science eventually "circumscribes an entire culture; it projects a historical totality—a 'world.' "[20]

Marcuse thus grasps modern science as a conceptual structure that necessarily performs repressive functions: it engenders the domination of nature as well as its own domination over alternative modes of understanding, and relating to, nature. As such, his analysis entails a complete rejection of the Instrumental Marxist thesis that a structurally unchanged science, and the technology to which it gives rise, could become a vehicle for liberation if it were freed from the control of the dominant interests it serves.[21] At the same time, Marcuse's analysis calls into question the Structural Marxist thesis that the repressiveness of science and technology results from the presence within them of specifically capitalist relations of production. Modern science, according to Marcuse, is not a specifically capitalist science. It is, rather, a form of reason that predominates in both capitalist and state socialist societies, i.e., in "advanced industrial societies" in general.[22] It follows that the elimination of capitalist relations of production is not a sufficient condition for the creation of a liberatory science and technology.

[19] This formulation is William Leiss's in *The Domination of Nature*, p. 132.

[20] Marcuse, *One-Dimensional Man*, p. 154.

[21] This rejection of Instrumental Marxism in *Eros and Civilization* and *One-Dimensional Man* is itself rejected somewhat later in *An Essay on Liberation*: "Is it still necessary to state that not technology, not technique, not the machine are the engines of repression, but the presence in them, of the masters who determine their number, their life span, their place in life, and the need for them? Is it still necessary to repeat that science and technology are the great vehicles of liberation, and that it is only their use and restriction in the repressive society which makes them into vehicles of domination?" (Boston: Beacon Press, 1969), p. 12.

Since Marcuse returns to the anti-instrumental position three years later with the publication of *Counter-Revolution and Revolt*, I conclude that the above passage runs counter to the basic thrust of twenty years of his writings on the subject of science and technology. For an alternative interpretation, see Leiss, *The Domination of Nature*, Appendix, and for an analysis of the unpersuasiveness of this interpretation, see Robert D'Amico's review of *The Domination of Nature* in *Telos*, No. 15 (Spring 1973), pp. 142-47.

[22] Marcuse, *One-Dimensional Man*, p. xvi.

In Chapter Four I argued that an adequate conception of repressive science and technology must be (a) broader than capitalist science and technology but (b) narrower than science and technology as such. Marcuse's conception clearly satisfies the first of these criteria. But does it satisfy the second, i.e., does it entail a coherent vision of an alternative, nonrepressive science and technology? To put the question another way, does Marcuse's critique of the dominant Western reason disclose the possibility of another, superior reason, in whose behalf the critique is carried out, or is the critique merely an irrational repudiation of reason itself? Marcuse denies, of course, that his critique is an assault on science or reason per se, and argues on behalf of a "new idea of reason" or a new science "which would arrive at essentially different concepts of nature and establish essentially different facts," and thus make possible an entirely new technology.[23] But what would be the conceptual structure of this new liberatory science, and how would it be different from the repressive science that it supersedes?

In *One-Dimensional Man* Marcuse proposes the idea of an aesthetic science in which "the function of Reason . . . converges with the function of *Art*." Under this condition, the commitment of art to the "pacification of existence" would no longer function as an impotent protest against the aggressive, instrumental logic of the scientific enterprise but would, rather, come to infuse the very logic of this enterprise. This new science, in turn, would make possible a new technology whose construction would proceed under the influence of aesthetic categories and commitments: "technics . . . itself [becomes] the instrumentality of pacification, organon of the 'art of life'." This fusion of art and technics "alters the relationship between technology and its primary object, Nature," substituting a liberating mastery for a repressive one and "reducing the ferocity of man against Nature." But the concept of mastery remains intact: "Pacification presupposes mastery of Nature, which is and remains the object opposed to the developing subject."[24] In *One-Dimensional Man*, the reconceptualization of the human relationship to nature implicit in the new, aesthetic science does not transcend the framework of a "subject against an object" that is, according to Marcuse, the very presupposition of the existing science. Contrary to Marcuse, then, it does not appear as if his new science could "arrive at essentially different concepts of nature." One wonders, therefore, whether Marcuse's distinction between a liberating and a repressive mastery of nature is merely an ideological formulation and obfuscation of the distinction between a benevolent and a tyrannical despotism. Marcuse's protestations to the contrary notwithstanding, his new science

[23] *Ibid.*, pp. 167, 227-28.
[24] *Ibid.*, pp. 238 (emphasis in the original), 236, 240.

remains as bound to the conceptual universe of domination as the old science he condemns.

Marcuse appears to recognize this in *Counter-Revolution and Revolt*. In this later work he specifically repudiates the thesis that a liberatory science can remain within a conceptual framework in which nature is defined as an object opposed to a human subject. "This notion of nature is a *historical* a priori, pertaining to a specific form of society." Contrary to the argument in *One-Dimensional Man*, the conception of nature as an object confronted by a subject is not inherent in reason or science as such but rather only in a particular form of science, and a repressive form at that: nature is not ontologically an object but is merely so conceived by humans whose sensibilities have been shaped and stunted by the imperatives of an unfree society. In contrast, in a genuinely free society, human beings will recognize "nature as a *subject* in its own right—a subject with which to live in a common . . . universe." Thus Marcuse no longer speaks of the "liberating mastery" over nature but rather of the "liberation of nature" itself. Under this latter condition, the human struggle with nature could "subside and make room for peace, tranquility, fulfillment." The notion of nature as "value-free matter" that becomes the object of unlimited human exploitation would give way to the idea of nature "as a *cosmos* with its own potentialities," potentialities that human beings will strive to respect and enhance.[25] An instrumental relationship in which nature exists exclusively for the sake of human beings will be transcended in favor of a reciprocal relationship in which humans acknowledge the claims of nature and come to understand that the fulfillment of *their* nature depends on the fulfillment of these claims as well.

Marcuse denies that this new, receptive stance toward nature is incompatible with scientific objectivity. (The latter *is* inconsistent, he argues, with a teleological conception of nature, that is, with a notion of a nature ruled by an overarching purpose or plan. But no such purpose or plan is implicit in the conception of "nature as subject" that he proposes, and thus his conception cannot be ruled out on the grounds that it violates the "postulate of objectivity."[26]) To the contrary, this "very different a priori" would lead not to a repudiation of science but rather to the creation of a fundamentally different science. It is at this point, however, that Marcuse's analysis becomes extremely vague. He tells us that, under the impact of this new a priori, "the development of the scientific concepts may be grounded in an experience of nature as a totality of life to be protected and 'cultivated,' and technology

---

[25] Marcuse, *Counter-Revolution and Revolt* (Boston: Beacon Press, 1972), pp. 61, 60, 69, all emphases in the original.

[26] *Ibid.*, p. 66.

would apply this science to the reconstruction of the environment of life."[27] But more than this he does not say.

We have already seen that, for Marcuse, the formalization of nature inherent in contemporary science presupposes a conception of nature as an object of manipulation by a human subject. Now we have learned that this conception is per se inconsistent with the liberation of nature. It would appear, then, that we are entitled to conclude that a liberatory science cannot be based on the formalization of nature but must instead embody an entirely different conceptual structure. But what would this conceptual structure look like? If, for example, a liberatory physics could not make use of the abstract concept of mass, what would be the more concrete concept that it would employ? The logic of Marcuse's argument seems to point to some notion of a "qualitative physics," but this notion was specifically repudiated in *One-Dimensional Man*.[28] Nor is it taken up again in *Counter-Revolution and Revolt*. The question of the conceptual structure of the new, liberatory science remains unanswered.

And necessarily so. The problem of the transformation of science (and technology) cannot be resolved independently of the problem of the transformation of human instinctual needs; the new rationality implies a "new sensibility."[29] We have seen that the prevailing scientific rationality is rooted in the strength of destructive libidinal impulses within the individual psyche. It follows that the emergence of the new science on which the liberation of nature depends is contingent on a "decisive change in the instinctual structure: the weakening of primary aggressiveness."[30] We have also seen that, according to Marcuse's reading of Freud, the strength of "primary aggressiveness" is proportionate to the repressive sublimation of the sexual, or life instincts: the hypothesis is that a desublimation of Eros will lead to a decline in the power of Thanatos. Thus the liberation of the nature outside us is contingent on the liberation of the nature within us; the question of the prospects for a new, liberatory science takes us back to the question of the prospects for sexual liberation.

This sexual liberation, in turn, depends upon the elimination of alienated labor, on the eradication of the performance principle: since the repressive sublimation of Eros is rooted in repressive work, it follows, as we have already learned, that a desublimation or liberation of Eros demands the transcendence of repressive work. Marcuse argues that this transcendence of the performance principle is now a "realizable historical possibility" due to the very achievements of this principle itself:

[27] *Ibid.*, p. 61.
[28] Page 166.
[29] Marcuse, *An Essay on Liberation*, p. 37.
[30] Marcuse, *Counter-Revolution and Revolt*, p. 75.

245

The repressive reality principle becomes superfluous in the same measure that civilization approaches a level at which the elimination of a mode of life that previously necessitated instinctual repression has become a realizable historical possibility. The achievements of repressive progress herald the abolition of the repressive principle of progress itself. It becomes possible to envisage a state in which there is no productivity resulting from and conditioning renunciation and no alienated labor: a state in which the growing mechanization of labor enables an ever larger part of the instinctual energy that had to be withdrawn for alienated labor to return to its original form, in other words, to be changed back into energy of the life instincts.[31]

Technological rationality as the basis for the solution to the problem of technological rationality? Indeed, Marcuse advances the apparently paradoxical proposition that "the completion of the technological project involves a break with the prevailing technological rationality."[32] Let us examine carefully his effort to unfold, or rather to unravel, this paradox. Marcuse will, in fact, propose two incompatible solutions to the problem of overcoming alienated labor, neither of which is satisfactory.

Marcuse's first solution is a version of the one that Marx poses in volume III of *Capital*: the elimination of alienated labor is linked to the progressive automation of the production necessary for the satisfaction of all "vital needs" and thus to the elimination of human labor from the sphere of necessary labor.[33] The assumption underlying this solution is that "the realm of freedom actually begins only where labour which is determined by necessity and mundane considerations ceases; thus in the very nature of things it lies beyond the sphere of actual material production."[34] Labor that is "determined by necessity," i.e., that procures the "necessities of life," is thus inherently a realm of unfreedom: since "human existence in this realm is determined by objectives and functions that are not its own and do not allow the free play of human faculties and desires . . . , it can never be a realm of freedom and gratification."[35] If human necessary labor is intrinsically unfree, or alienated, it follows that the only possible solution to the problem of overcoming alienation is the overcoming of human necessary labor. And this, argues Marcuse, is precisely what automation makes possible: the progressive substitution of machine for human labor in the realm of necessity guarantees that the increasing satisfaction of "basic human needs" will proceed on the basis of

---

[31] Herbert Marcuse, *Five Lectures* (Boston: Beacon Press, 1970), p. 39.

[32] Marcuse, *One-Dimensional Man*, p. 231.

[33] *Ibid.*, p. 16, and *Eros and Civilization*, p. 178.

[34] Tucker, *The Marx-Engels Reader*, p. 320.

[35] Marcuse, *Eros and Civilization*, pp. 178, 142.

246

the "reduction of labor time to a minimum." The historic achievement of the technology of the performance principle is the virtual elimination of the necessity of human performance in the production of socially necessary goods and services, i.e., the creation of the basis for a human life "without toil."[36]

The progressive contraction of the realm of necessity made possible by automated labor is, at the same time, the progressive expansion of the "realm of freedom": automation "can release time and energy for the free play of human faculties *outside* the realm of alienated labor."[37] Outside this latter realm, as Marx puts it, "begins that development of human energy which is an end in itself, the true realm of freedom."[38] Freed from the constraint of having to work in order to survive, individuals would be able to engage in a wide variety of playful or "unproductive" activities. Since their bodies would no longer be mobilized as instruments of alienated labor, they would no longer have to suffer from the repressive sublimation of their sexual energies:

> In this case, the quantum of instinctual energy still to be diverted into necessary labor . . . would be so small that a large area of repressive constraints and modifications, no longer sustained by external forces, would collapse. Consequently, the antagonistic relation between pleasure principle and reality principle would be altered in favor of the former. Eros, the life instincts, would be released to an unprecedented degree.[39]

This unprecedented release of Eros, in turn, undermines the destructive expression of Thanatos. The death instinct is not eliminated, but its aggressive manifestations are minimized and "the conflict between life and death is . . . reduced." Since the basic objective of the death instinct, according to Marcuse, "is not the termination of life but of pain—the absence of tension," and since the expansion of Eros entails a dramatic reduction in the pain or tension that individuals experience, "Eros would, as it were, absorb the objective of the death instinct," and "pleasure principle and Nirvana principle [would] then converge."[40] Under these conditions, humans would no longer be driven to dominate nature, and a new, qualitatively different science and technology would develop. This science and technology, in contrast to the one that it supersedes, "would be free for trans-utilitarian ends, and free for the 'art of living' " that characterize the expanding realm of freedom.[41]

The realm of freedom, with its transformed instinctual organization and science and technology, "can [however] blossom forth only with the realm

---

[36] *Ibid.*, p. 138.
[37] *Ibid.*, p. 142, emphasis in the original.
[38] Tucker, *The Marx-Engels Reader*, p. 320.
[39] Marcuse, *Eros and Civilization*, p. 139. See also *Five Lectures*, p. 40.
[40] Marcuse, *Eros and Civilization*, pp. 214-15.
[41] Marcuse, *One-Dimensional Man*, p. 231.

of necessity as its basis.''[42] Because at least some human participation in the realm of necessity remains essential, there remains the problem of the principles that are to guide the organization of human energies within this realm. Marcuse, following Marx in *Capital*, argues that

> The optimum in this realm is . . . to be defined by standards of *rationality rather than freedom*—namely, to organize production and distribution in such a manner that the least time is spent for making all necessities available to all members of society. Necessary labor is a system of essentially inhuman, mechanical and routine activities; in such a system, individuality cannot be a value and end in itself. Reasonably, the system of societal labor would be organized rather with a view toward saving time and space for the development of individuality *outside* the inevitably repressive work-world.[43]

A standard of "rationality rather than freedom," organization "with a view toward saving time and space"—it would appear that Marcuse is arguing that the realm of necessity is a realm in which technological rationality—the rationality of the performance principle—will inevitably prevail. Indeed, this argument is made explicit at the end of *One-Dimensional Man*:

> Here [in the realm of necessity] technological rationality, stripped of its exploitative features, is the sole standard and guide in planning and developing the available resources for all. Self-determination in the production and distribution of vital goods and services would be wasteful. The job is a technical one, and as a truly technical job, it makes for the reduction of physical and mental toil. In this realm, centralized control is rational if it establishes the preconditions for meaningful self-determination. The latter can then become effective in its own realm [the realm of freedom].[44]

Marcuse's first effort to solve the problem of alienated labor and the domination of nature that results from it culminates, then, in a vision of a society in which technological rationality and a post-technological rationality prevail in different realms of life and are able to coexist simultaneously and harmoniously. But this notion of a happy coexistence of two entirely antithetical forms of rationality, it seems to me, is extraordinarily problematical. Marcuse

---

[42] Tucker, *The Marx-Engels Reader*, p. 320.

[43] Marcuse, *Eros and Civilization*, p. 178, first emphasis added. Here Marcuse echoes Marx, for whom the development of any society "depends on economization of time. Economy of time, to this all economy ultimately reduces itself. . . . Thus economy of time . . . remains the first economic law on the basis of communal [communist] production. It becomes law, there, to an even higher degree." *Grundrisse*, p. 173.

[44] Marcuse, *One-Dimensional Man*, pp. 251-52.

248

has already told us that technological rationality implies the domination (or the "repressive mastery") of nature, i.e., that the technologies that embody this rationality will necessarily be destructive of the natural environment. To rely on the completion of technological rationality within the realm of necessity to provide the material preconditions for a break with technological rationality in the realm of freedom is to depend on technologies that destroy nature in order to achieve its liberation, which would appear, at best, to be an extremely risky proposition! Similarly, Marcuse has demonstrated that technological rationality rests on an individual instinctual organization that is characterized by the repressive sublimation of Eros and the release of the destructive manifestations of Thanatos. It follows that the realm of necessity in the future society will require the participation of individuals with repressive character structures. Are we to imagine that these individuals will be able to alter these structures at will as they pass from this realm to the realm of freedom? The repressive sublimation that underlies the sphere of technological rationality (however reduced in scope) would appear to preclude the emergence of the liberatory desublimation on which the sphere of post-technological rationality is supposed to be based.

Marcuse's own theory of the repressive desublimation that characterizes contemporary advanced industrial societies undermines the assumption that a reduction in the scope of repressive sublimation (and technological rationality) gives rise to sexual liberation (and post-technological rationality). According to this theory, the mechanization and partial automation of labor in these societies has already permitted a "sweeping desublimation" of sexual energy and a significant liberalization of sexual morality. This desublimation, however, has been "controlled" in such a manner that the sexual energy it releases is necessarily re-integrated into the sphere of the performance principle, i.e., sexuality becomes a commodity that is produced, packaged, and marketed like any other. Thus the sexual desublimation in advanced industrial societies is repressive insofar as it merely reinforces, rather than challenges, the hegemony of technological rationality. Under these conditions, "desublimation [is] compatible with the growth of unsublimated as well as sublimated forms of aggressiveness [which are] rampant throughout contemporary industrial society."[45]

If the technologically produced contraction of the realm of necessity in these societies has proved compatible with the persistence of a repressive and aggressive instinctual organization, what guarantees that the further contraction of this realm will be conducive to a liberatory transformation of this instinctual organization in the society of the future? If, in short, repressive desublimation is a "by-product of the social controls of technological reality"

---

[45] *Ibid.*, pp. 72, 77-78.

today, why should it not continue to be a "by-product" of this reality tomorrow? Marcuse argues, of course, that there will be a qualitative difference between today and tomorrow. The transition from contemporary one-dimensional industrial societies to the unalienated industrial society of the future "can only be the result of qualitative social change" that eliminates the economic and political obstacles to the further development of automation,[46] and thus to the unfolding of the liberatory potential of technology, that are intrinsic to both capitalist and state socialist societies. This economic and political change, however, presupposes instinctual change:

> These causes [of domination] are economic-political, but since they have shaped the very instincts and needs, no economic and political changes will bring this historic continuum to a stop unless they are carried through by men who are physiologically and psychologically able to experience things, and each other, outside the context of violence and exploitation.[47]

Instinctual change is thus a prerequisite of the economic and political transformation that is, itself, a precondition to the further automation of necessary labor. Marcuse's answer to the dilemma we have posed, then, is that the contraction of the realm of necessity in the future society will, in contrast to the present society, take place under the guidance of what he calls the "new sensibility" and that this contraction will have, therefore, liberatory rather than repressive consequences.

This answer enmeshes Marcuse in another dilemma, which he himself characterizes as the " 'vicious circle' of freedom and liberation":[48] in order to persuade us that the consequences of the completion of technological rationality in the future society will be liberatory rather than repressive he takes recourse to the prior existence of a new sensibility which, according to his own analysis, can only be the result of the completion of this rationality. In order to convince us that desublimation in the future will not be repressive, he assumes that a non-repressive desublimation will have already taken place, and thus he inadvertently suggests that it will not be necessary in the future! Alternatively, if we argue that the new sensibility already exists, prior to the transition to the new society, i.e., within the existing, "one-dimensional" society, how is it possible to maintain that the desublimation that takes place within this latter society is entirely repressive? As Marcuse puts it, "transcendence beyond the established conditions . . . presupposes transcendence *within* these conditions."[49] This paradox, of course, is not merely Marcuse's but that of any thinker who assumes that individual change results from social

---

[46] *Ibid.*, p. 72 and Marcuse, *Eros and Civilization*, p. viii.

[47] Marcuse, *An Essay on Liberation*, p. 25.

[48] Marcuse, *One-Dimensional Man*, p. 223.

[49] *Ibid.*, emphasis in the original.

change but also understands that social change will not occur unless individuals change. However, even if it were possible to resolve this paradox, e.g., to demonstrate that the existing repressive society allows for a partial nonrepressive desublimation that establishes the preconditions for the transition to the future liberatory society in which complete nonrepressive desublimation would alone be possible, Marcuse would be faced with the following problem. If the individuals who will enter the realm of necessity of the future society already have transformed, even incompletely transformed, sensibilities, what guarantees that they will willingly submit to the rule of technological rationality, i.e., the "rational" expression of the "old" sensibility, that will, according to Marcuse, necessarily prevail in that realm? Earlier I argued that if the individuals of the future society are psychologically prepared for the (technological) realm of necessity, then they will not be prepared for the (post-technological) realm of freedom. Now I am suggesting that if they are psychologically prepared for the realm of freedom, they will not tolerate the requirements of the realm of necessity. Marcuse wants to, but cannot, have it both ways.

If Marcuse's vision of a society divided between technological and post-technological rationality is untenable, so too is his—and Marx's—distinction between the two human realms to which these rationalities correspond. As we have seen, the distinction between the realm of necessity and the realm of freedom is a distinction between human activity that is necessary to fulfill basic or vital needs and human activity that is undertaken as an end in itself. Only after their basic needs have been satisfied can individuals exercise genuine self-determination; the more quickly and efficiently these needs can be satisfied, the more time and energy individuals will have for this exercise. Thus a "non-repressive order is essentially an order of *abundance*" in which "all basic needs can be satisfied with a minimum expenditure of physical and mental energy in a minimum of time."[50] The entire argument presupposes, then, that it is possible unambiguously to determine the basic needs of the members of a society. But Marcuse, like Marx, is well aware that an individual's basic needs are not a physiological or psychological constant but are culturally and historically constituted: individuals in fundamentally different societies will have fundamentally different basic needs and, even within one society, an individual's basic needs will change over time.[51] It follows that for any society and at any time the technological satisfaction of basic needs must be preceded by a cultural definition of these needs. Because this cultural

[50] Marcuse, *Eros and Civilization*, p. 177, emphasis in the original. Marcuse's insistence that "the conquest of scarcity" (p. 138) overcomes repression or domination is inconsistent with his earlier critique of Freud's effort to link repressive, alienated labor to the "brute fact" of scarcity (p. 33).

[51] Marcuse, *One-Dimensional Man*, p. 241.

251

definition constitutes the meaning of basic needs, it cannot itself be classified as falling either within the realm of necessity or the realm of freedom. It does not fall within the realm of necessity because it constitutes this realm, and it does not fall within the realm of freedom because, for Marcuse as well as Marx, this realm only begins beyond the realm of necessity. Thus Marcuse's (and Marx's) distinction between necessity and freedom is a wholly inadequate starting point for the comprehension of the process through which human needs are defined.[52] It does not provide an adequate criterion for the evaluation of this process in any given society. The maxim: do everything possible to minimize the amount of time and energy that humans devote to the realm of necessity and maximize the time and energy available for the realm of freedom cannot tell us how to organize a process that transcends the distinction between these two realms.

That the cultural constitution of basic needs transcends the distinction between necessity and freedom, moreover, suggests that this distinction itself is not primordial or ontological but presupposes and grows out of a particular historical mode of this cultural constitution. To understand why this is the case, imagine a society in which the need for activity undertaken for its own sake was experienced as every bit as vital as the need to fill one's stomach. In this case, the need for freedom or self-determination would have to be understood as part of the realm of necessity, which is to say that the distinction between the realm of necessity and the realm of freedom would break down. This suggests that this distinction only makes sense within a society in which the need for self-determination is *not* experienced as a vital need, i.e., to an alienated society. It is, therefore, an entirely inadequate framework within which to theorize about the possible overcoming of alienation.

Marcuse's second "solution" to the problem of overcoming alienated labor does not completely abandon, but merely modifies, this framework. In "The End of Utopia," he suggests that

> decisive elements of the Marxian concept of socialism . . . belong to a now obsolete stage in the development of the forces of production. This obsolescence is expressed most clearly . . . in the distinction between the realm of freedom and the realm of necessity according to which the realm of freedom can be conceived of and can exist only beyond the realm of necessity. This division implies that the realm of necessity remains so in the sense of a realm of alienated labor, which means, as Marx says, that the only thing that can happen within it is for labor to be organized as rationally as possible and reduced as much as possible. But it remains labor in and of the realm of necessity and thereby unfree.

[52] See above, Chapter Three, and Albrecht Wellmer, *The Critical Theory of Society*, pp. 116-18.

252

I believe that one of the new possibilities, which gives an indication of the qualitative difference between the free and the unfree society, is that of *letting the realm of freedom appear within the realm of necessity—in labor and not only beyond labor.*[53]

But what does it mean to let "the realm of freedom appear within the realm of necessity—in labor and not only beyond labor"? According to Marcuse, it means that in the future, genuinely unalienated society "even socially necessary labor can be organized in harmony with the liberated, genuine needs of men."[54] Here Marcuse rejects emphatically his earlier assertion that the activity of "material production . . . can never be a realm of freedom and gratification"[55] and argues instead that it must become such a realm if alienation is to be overcome. His focus shifts from an emphasis on the quantity to an emphasis on the quality of necessary labor: "the quantitative reduction of necessary labor could turn into quality (freedom) not in proportion to the reduction but rather to the transformation of the working day."[56] The transformation of labor that Marcuse now envisions is one in which work would be "accompanied by a reactivation of . . . eroticism." Under these conditions of eroticized or libidinal labor, repressive sublimation would be unnecessary and labor "would tend to become gratifying in itself without losing its *work* content"; "socially useful work [would be] at the same time the transparent satisfaction of an individual need."[57] To speak of the possibility of erotic work, however, is necessarily to deny the fundamental assumption of Marx—with which Marcuse was, in *One-Dimensional Man*, in complete accord—to the effect that "labor cannot become play."[58] Indeed, Marcuse now credits Fourier, the very thinker to whom Marx's sober caveat was addressed, for "not shrink[ing] back in fear, as Marx still did, from speaking of a possible society in which work becomes play."[59]

This vision of a society in which work becomes play avoids many of the dilemmas that plagued Marcuse's first solution to the problem of transcending alienated labor. Rather than a society divided between two different, and antithetical, forms of rationality and instinctual organization, he offers a model in which a single rationality and instinctual organization pervade the entire society: since the technological rationality and repressive sublimation of the performance principle are entirely overcome, it is no longer necessary to

[53] Marcuse, *Five Lectures*, pp. 62-63, emphasis added. For a similar formulation, see *An Essay on Liberation*, pp. 20-21.

[54] Marcuse, *Five Lectures*, p. 68.

[55] Marcuse, *Eros and Civilization*, p. 142.

[56] Marcuse, *An Essay on Liberation*, p. 21.

[57] Marcuse, *Eros and Civilization*, pp. 196 (emphasis in the original), 192.

[58] Marcuse, *One-Dimensional Man*, p. 240. Marx, *Grundrisse*, p. 712.

[59] Marcuse, *Five Lectures*, p. 68.

attempt the impossible task of rendering them compatible with the post-technological rationality and nonrepressive desublimation with which they are, by definition, incompatible. His new formulation, however, avoids the dilemmas inherent in this task only at the cost of introducing a number of different, equally irresolvable problems.

Once Marcuse argues that work can become play, he calls into question an assumption to which he nonetheless continues to adhere, namely, that the possibility of overcoming alienated labor is linked to a certain level of technological development. On the one hand, he says that "it is the purpose and not the content which marks an activity as play or work" and that "a transformation in the instinctual structure would entail a change in the instinctual value of the human activity *regardless of its content*."[60] Thus it would appear that what would otherwise be considered the same task will be alienating or liberating depending on the purpose or instinctual impulse that motivates it. But, if this is so, then it is no longer clear why liberation should any longer be linked to the progress of mechanization or automation, since this progress determines the quantity of human tasks that remain necessary rather than their quality, i.e., rather than the purpose or instinctual impulse that motivates them. The notion that work can become play, in other words, implies that the possibility of overcoming of alienation varies independently of the quantitative growth in the forces of production. On the other hand, Marcuse continues to link this possibility to an advanced level of technological development. The proposition that "the quantitative reduction of necessary labor could turn into quality (freedom) not in proportion to the reduction but rather to the transformation of the working day" simultaneously denies the existence of a one-to-one relationship between the level of technological development and disalienation and asserts that the increase in the former is a necessary precondition for the latter. Similarly, the argument that Marx's thesis that the realm of freedom only exists beyond the realm of necessity "belongs to a now obsolete stage in the development of the forces of production" implies that the truth of the contrary proposition that "freedom can appear within the realm of necessity" is contingent on the attainment of a new, higher stage in the development of these forces. Marcuse appears to be suggesting that there exists a certain minimum threshold of technological development that must be reached before the qualitative transformation in work that he envisions can become possible, i.e., that a certain level of mechanization and automation is the necessary but not sufficient condition for the transcendence of alienated labor. But, once again, the thesis that the transformation of work into play is entirely indifferent to the content of the work would appear to deny that a given level of technological development is even a necessary condition for

[60] Marcuse, *Eros and Civilization*, p. 196, emphasis in the original.

254

this transcendence. Moreover, even if it were possible to demonstrate that this latter proposition is, after all, consistent with the former, it would remain the case that Marcuse nowhere specifies what this minimally necessary threshold level of technological development would be. Nor, finally, is he able to account, without circularity, for the emergence of the sufficient conditions for the transformation of work into play: if the instinctual restructuring that underlies this transformation cannot itself be derived from the necessary threshold level of technological growth, then the concrete possibilities for this transformation remain unclarified.

Let me restate this problem in a somewhat different manner. Marcuse denies the ultimate validity of Marx's distinction between work and play yet he continues to uphold Marx's distinction between the realm of freedom and the realm of necessity: the emergence of erotic labor signals the appearance of freedom "within the realm of necessity," the organization of "socially necessary labor . . . in harmony with the liberated genuine needs of men." In order to be consistent, and as I have already intimated, should he not rather argue that the emergence of erotic labor abolishes the distinction between the realm of freedom and the realm of necessity, between socially necessary and surplus labor? Should he not recognize that the very concept of necessity (or scarcity) is an expression of the logic of a society governed by the performance principle, and thus an entirely inappropriate starting point for the theorization of its transcendence? Yet Marcuse fails to draw this conclusion, apparently because he is unwilling to question the fundamental Marxist proposition that only an advanced level of technological development makes possible the overcoming of necessity or scarcity on which the existence of socialism depends. But does not Marcuse's argument that work should become play imply that this concept of socialism itself must be transcended?

Marcuse's dilemma is that the concepts of Marx that he rejects are, in Bertell Ollman's words, "internally related" to those that he accepts.[61] One cannot reject Marx's thesis that work is fundamentally different from play without undermining Marx's *entire* conceptual edifice. I have tried to demonstrate, for example, that the distinction between work and play is homologous with the distinction between necessity and freedom, and that calling the former into question necessarily discredits the intelligibility of the latter. Similarly, the rejection of the distinction between necessity and freedom implies a repudiation of the thesis that a certain quantitative development of the forces of production is a necessary precondition to socialism. But the repudiation of this thesis, in turn, undermines Marx's argument that a capitalist mode of production is more "progressive" than those that preceded it because it supplies socialism with its material basis, i.e., it calls into question Marx's

---

[61] Ollman, *Alienation*, Part I.

entire conception of (Western) history as a progress of human rationality. The argument that links the transcendence of alienated labor to the transformation of work into play entails the argument that the problem of the transcendence of alienation cannot be resolved theoretically within the overall conceptual framework of Marx. Marcuse simply cannot have it both ways.

Remember that Marcuse proposed the transcendence of alienated labor as the solution to the problem of overcoming the domination or degradation of nature. Now we have learned from him that the transcendence of alienated labor demands the transformation of work into play. It follows that, for Marcuse, a society that does not dominate nature must be a society in which work becomes play. But Marx has told us that work cannot become play, and thus that a society in which work becomes play is an impossibility. Marx's concept of labor, in other words, leads him to conclude that what Marcuse argues is the precondition for the elimination of the domination of nature is entirely unrealizable. Is not Marcuse obliged, therefore, to conclude that Marx's concept of labor is inconsistent with the liberation of nature, i.e., that it presupposes the domination of nature? Indeed, Marcuse appears to come to this very conclusion in *Counter-Revolution and Revolt*, when he argues that "Marx's notion of a human appropriation of nature [through labor] retains something of the *hubris* of domination. 'Appropriation', no matter how human, remains appropriation of a (living) object by a subject."[62] Does this not suggest that Marcuse is arguing that the structure of what Marx calls labor is incompatible with the recognition of "nature as a *subject* in its own right"[63] that the liberation of nature demands? But, if this is the case, in what possible sense can Marcuse's "second" theory of repressive technology and its transcendence claim to be consistent with the basic intentions or assumptions of Marxism?

Marcuse's theory, it would appear, should rather be understood as a challenge to Marx's ontology of labor or productive activity. To argue, against Marx, that work can become play is to argue that a structure of human action that Marx treats as constitutive of human history as a whole is merely one form that human action assumes within certain historical epochs, a form that will be transcended in the future. It follows that this transcendence cannot be theorized on the basis of the conceptual foundations of the ontology of labor. If, in other words, the liberation of nature demands not merely a transformation in the mode of production but rather an elimination of "production" (as understood by Marx) itself, then we should not expect that developments in the mode of production will provide the basis for the liberation of nature. But, as we have seen, Marcuse's residual Marxist commitments prevent him

---

[62] Marcuse, *Counter-Revolution and Revolt*, pp. 68-69, emphasis in the original.
[63] *Ibid.*, p. 60, emphasis in the original.

from looking anywhere else. Thus his theory of the liberation of nature through the transformation of work into play remains utopian, i.e., ungrounded in any analysis of the possible sources of this transformation in contemporary industrial societies.

In his last two essays on the problem of the domination of nature—"Nature and Revolution" in *Counter-Revolution and Revolt* and "Marxism and Feminism"—Marcuse suggests that the performance principle is a "male principle" and that the overcoming of this principle would entail the transformation of "patriarchal culture," the " 'femalization' of the male."[64] He intimates that, but does not explain how, the domination of nature is rooted in the structure of contemporary patriarchy and concludes that the possibility of the liberation of nature is linked to the elimination of this structure. Because patriarchy is rooted in a certain form of the family or mode of child rearing, we are entitled to infer that the liberation of nature presupposes a transformation in the existing mode of child rearing. Marcuse, however, does not draw this inference, and thus his last published works do not explore this possible source of the liberation of nature. His speculations point to the necessity of a theory of the relationship between patriarchal child rearing and the domination of nature but this is a theory that he himself fails to develop. I shall propose such a theory in a subsequent chapter.

ANTHONY WILDEN'S THEORY OF DIGITAL COMMUNICATION

Like Marcuse, Anthony Wilden argues that the domination and degradation of nature is built into the very epistemological premise of Western civilization. This premise, according to Wilden, is that the relationship between humans and nature entails a hierarchical opposition between two separate entities; nature is conceived as an object that exists merely for the sake of the human subject. This dichotomous or "digital" mode of thought sunders the "symbiotic whole" that is the "natural ecosystem," converting the "analog" or "more-or-less" differences between the living subsystems of this ecosystem into an "imaginary" opposition between the human and the nonhuman. Put otherwise, Western thought reifies the boundary between the human organism and its environment, transforming what is always a conventional or fictional line drawn in accordance with certain human purposes into what appears to be a real barrier dividing "man" from "nature." Nature, in the process, becomes the other of "man": it is defined as that which "man" is not, i.e., it is divested of subjectivity and reduced to the status of a pure object. Conceived as a pure object, nature no longer has anything to say to us: human

---

[64] Marcuse, *Counter-Revolution and Revolt*, pp. 74-75.

communication with nature thus assumes a one-sided or asymmetrical, rather than complementary or reciprocal, form. In the language of the cybernetic theory of which Wilden is so fond, the network of communication that links all the subsystems of the ecosystem is short-circuited by the tendency of the human subsystem to define itself as a closed system and thus to ignore or refuse to process the information it receives from the other subsystems on which it depends. The human subsystem, unlike every other subsystem of the ecosystem, is unable to regulate itself by means of "negative feedback," that is, it refuses to readjust its ends and means in the light of their impact on the various "natural" subsystems whose survival is, ultimately, essential for the survival of the human subsystem as well. Instead, human communication with nature is governed exclusively by "positive feedback," i.e., by a growing discrepancy between the pursuit of human goals and the long-range survival goal of the ecosystem as a whole. In short, the communication between Western human beings and the ecosystem to which they belong is pathological; the epistemology of the Enlightenment is an "epistemology of biosocial imperialism." Since human life is merely a subsystem of the ecosystem as a whole, the epistemology that imperils this ecosystem necessarily imperils human life as well: "any culture that systematically turns difference into unmediated opposition is eventually doomed"; "the system which disposes of its environment disposes of itself."[65]

It follows that the survival of the ecosystem and the human part thereof depends on the elaboration of an alternative epistemology on which the construction of an alternative technology would ultimately be based. This alternative epistemology, of course, is already prefigured in Wilden's cybernetic, ecosystemic perspective, in the light of which the prevailing epistemology is judged and found wanting. Wilden does not claim that this perspective embodies a completely satisfactory epistemology; nor does he address himself to the problem of its technological applications. Instead, he merely, and modestly, proposes that it "points us in the right direction."[66] The cybernetic assumption that, in Gregory Bateson's words, "all behavior is communication"[67] enables us to conceptualize the ecosystem as a vast network of information that circulates among all the subsystems of this system. The relationship between human beings and nature can thus be reconceptualized as an exchange of communication between one subsystem and all the other subsystems of the ecosystem; the notion of an opposition between a communicating subject and a noncommunicative object gives way to a notion of a communicative whole of which human communication is merely one part. Because all living systems

[65] Anthony Wilden, *System and Structure: Essays in Communication and Exchange* (London: Tavistock Publications, 1972), pp. 210, 220, 207.

[66] *Ibid.*, p. 226.

[67] *Ibid.*, p. 203.

are systems of communication, the difference between the human system and nonhuman systems can no longer be conceived, in dichotomous or digital terms, as the presence-absence of communication, but must rather be understood, in analog terms, as a function of the "level of complexity" of their communication. Since all communications systems are "goal-seeking" systems, it follows that the distinction between human and "natural" systems cannot be drawn between a purposeful subject and purposeless objects but must instead be based on the relative "semiotic freedom" or flexibility of their goal-seeking processes.[68] The cybernetic perspective thus makes it possible to conceptualize the difference between humans and the rest of the natural world as a difference within a unity. As such, it simultaneously transcends the Enlightenment epistemology that transforms this difference into an "Imaginary opposition" and a Romantic "nature philosophy" that denies this difference in favor of an unmediated identity.

Wilden contends that his nonanthropocentric, ecosystemic perspective is consistent with the basic assumptions of Marx; indeed, he even claims that it is "a version of the Marxian model" itself. He credits Marx with having long ago discovered that "the system which disposes of its environment disposes of itself," and cites, without reproducing, a passage from *Grundrisse*, as the proof of this discovery.[69] In contrast to Wilden, I will let this passage speak for itself:

Thus on the one hand production which is founded on capital creates universal industry—i.e., surplus labour, value-producing labour; on the other hand it creates a system of general exploitation of natural human attributes, a system of general profitability, whose vehicles seem to be just as much science, as all the physical and intellectual characteristics. There is nothing which can escape . . . from this cycle of social production and exchange. Thus capital first creates bourgeois society and the universal appropriation of nature and of social relationships themselves by the members of society. Hence *the great civilizing influence of capital*, its production of a stage of society compared with which all earlier stages appear to be merely *local progress* and idolatry of nature. Nature becomes for the first time simply an object for mankind, purely a matter of utility; it ceases to be recognized as a power in its own right; and the theoretical knowledge of its independent laws appears only as a stratagem designed to subdue it to human requirements, whether as the object of consumption or as the means of production. Pursuing this tendency, capital has pushed beyond national boundaries and prejudices, beyond the deification of nature and the inherited, self-sufficient satisfaction of existing needs

[68] *Ibid.*, pp. 203, 431.
[69] *Ibid.*, pp. xviii, 207.

confined within well-defined bounds, and the reproduction of this traditional way of life. It is destructive of all this, and permanently revolutionary, tearing down all obstacles that impede the development of productive forces, the expansion of needs, the diversity of production and the exploitation and exchange of natural and intellectual forces.

But because capital sets up any such boundary as a limitation, and is thus *ideally* over and beyond it, it does not in any way follow that it has *really* surmounted it, and since any such limitation contradicts its vocation, capitalist production moves in contradictions which are constantly overcome, only to be, again, constantly reestablished. Still more so. The universality towards which it is perpetually driving finds limitations in its own nature, which at a certain stage of its development will make it appear as itself the greatest barrier to this tendency, leading thus to its own self-destruction.[70]

This passage clearly says something very different from—indeed, exactly the opposite of—what Wilden tries to make it say. To begin with, Marx heralds the process through which nature is reduced to a mere "object for mankind" and a pure "matter of utility" as the "great civilizing influence of capital"; he applauds, rather than bemoans, the development and spread of "theoretical knowledge . . . designed to subdue [nature] to human requirements." Rather than Wilden's critic of the domination of nature, Marx appears, in this passage, as its enthusiastic proponent. Second, Marx tells us that the self-destruction of capitalism will result, not from its domination or mastery of nature, but rather from certain internally imposed limits to its ability fully to achieve this universal mastery. And, if it is capitalism's ultimately limited nature that leads to its self-destruction, the clear implication is that socialism will overcome this limitation and attain the complete mastery of nature that capitalism is unable to attain. All in all, hardly convincing evidence for the proposition that Marx discovered that "the system which disposes of its environment disposes of itself"! To the contrary: the epistemological premise that underlies Marx's argument in this passage not only militates against the discovery of the solution to the problem of a self-destructive Western culture, it is, in fact, precisely the expression of this problem itself.

Wilden appears to recognize Marx's complicity in this problem when he refers, much later in his book, to the "ethnocentrism about supposedly 'backward' ["primitive"] . . . peoples which is so evident in Marx." This recognition of Marx's denigration of "primitive" cultures, however, sits rather uneasily with Wilden's claim that Marx theorized within a cybernetic, or

---

[70] Karl Marx, *The Grundrisse*, David McLellan ed. and trans. (New York: Harper & Row, 1971), pp. 94-95, all emphases except the first in the original.

ecosystemic perspective. If this was the perspective that shaped Marx's thinking, we would be hard pressed to explain how he would have been able to judge as "inferior" primitive cultures, many of which, according to Wilden, are (in contrast to modern Western cultures) "controlled by an ecological cybernetics." Similarly, Wilden criticizes the Marxist anthropologist Emmanuel Terray for developing and applying a model of "human production" that has an "ethnocentric ideology" as "its source," and suggests that this ideology is "possibly derived directly from Marx . . . but certainly characteristic of western culture."[71] But, if Marx is "possibly" responsible for an ethnocentric model of human production, then how is it possible to argue that Marx's model of human production is definitely an example of a nonethnocentric, ecosystemic perspective? Wilden himself suggests, against his own intentions, that Marx's basic assumptions are incompatible, rather than consistent, with this perspective.

Both Marcuse and Wilden, then, fail to develop an adequate Neo-Marxist theory of repressive technology. Both argue that an adequate theory of repressive technology must be based on a conceptualization of the relationship between humans and the natural world that transcends the epistemological premises of the Western Enlightenment, but both suggest, either intentionally or unintentionally, that such a conceptualization is inconsistent with the fundamental assumptions of Marx. Thus they demonstrate, despite themselves, that the synthesis of Marxian and ecological thought to which they aspire is impossible. Even more: they intimate that Marx's central category, the category of "production," expresses the domination of nature and thus must itself be transcended if a theory of a liberatory technology is to be elaborated. More generally, they intimate that Marx's thought is part of the problem of domination rather than part of the solution to this problem. These intimations provide the inspiration for the thesis that I shall develop in the concluding part of this book.

[71] Wilden, *System and Structure*, pp. 385, 368, 388.

CONCLUSION TO PART II

The theories examined in Part II all proceeded from the assumption that the logic of sexual, political, and technological domination cannot immediately be reduced to the logic of a particular form or mode of production and that the illumination of these structures of domination requires, therefore, that Marx's attention to production be supplemented by a focus on other, perhaps equally central, dimensions of the human condition. Thus Neo-Marxists have located and explored the dimensions of human sexuality and human communication in an effort to shed additional light on the problems of patriarchy, the state, and environmental degradation. Insofar as these efforts have been undertaken by Neo-*Marxists*, they have all been committed to the proposition that their theories of sexuality and/or communication must ultimately be harmonized, or synthesized, with Marx's theory of production. The universal failure of these theorists to achieve this synthesis suggests that the Neo-Marxist project is far more problematical than its exponents have been aware.

On the one hand, the Marx-Freud syntheses are all based on the assumption that (a) the sex-gender or kinship system immediately accounts for patriarchy, the state, and the domination of nature, but that (b) this determining effect of the kinship system is, in the final analysis, a function of developments within the sphere of material production. (Rubin's effort is an exception because she maintains the ultimate irreducibility of the sex-gender system to the system of material production and is thus reduced to developing a synthesis of Freud and Marx that merely entails the redefinition of kinship as a form of production.) For Mitchell and Zaretsky, patriarchy is reproduced unconsciously within the family, but this family form, in turn, is rendered increasingly superfluous by the development of material production. For Reich, political domination is reproduced unconsciously by a certain (patriarchal) family form, but this family form is progressively and necessarily undermined by the logic of capitalist development itself. For Marcuse, finally, the drive to dominate nature is unconsciously rooted in the repressive organization of sexuality, which organization ultimately owes its existence to a form of labor to be transcended in the future. I have demonstrated, however, that none of these thinkers demonstrates convincingly that the organization of sexuality that accounts for the structure of domination in question is, in fact, ultimately a function of a certain stage or level of development of material production, and, consequently, that none persuades us that the prospects for the elimination of this structure hinge on tendencies at work within that realm. In the end, their efforts to forge a synthesis between Marx and Freud prove unsuccessful.

The ultimate failure of these Marx-Freud syntheses suggests that they were,

262

perhaps, abortive from the very beginning. In their haste to demonstrate that a reorganization of production entails a reorganization of sexuality (and thus the elimination of the structure(s) of domination), none of the Neo-Marxists (with the partial, ambiguous exception of Marcuse) recognizes, let alone explores, the possibility that the reorganization of sexuality might, rather, entail the elimination of "production" itself. As Freudians, they are all committed to the proposition that objectification involves a sublimation of sexual energy; as such, objectification is not primordial or irreducible but rather must itself be explained as an outcome of the organization of sexuality. On the basis of this proposition, it is only possible to argue, with Marx, that objectification is a universal human structure—an "eternal, nature-imposed necessity . . . independent of all forms of society"—if we also argue that the sexual organization of which it is an outgrowth is likewise universal—which is exactly what Freud asserts but the Neo-Marxists deny. To put this the other way around, if we argue that the organization of sexual energy is historically contingent, then we cannot maintain simultaneously the Freudian proposition that objectification is a sublimation of sexuality and the Marxian proposition that objectification is a primordial, universal structure of the human condition. A theory based on the assumption of the primacy of sexuality cannot supplement, but rather must ultimately undermine, a theory predicated on the assumption of the primacy of production.

Similarly, we have seen that both Habermas and Wilden reconceptualize the structures of domination with which they are concerned as repressive modes of communication. According to Habermas, political domination cannot be adequately conceptualized as a function of a mode of production because the developmental logic of communicative action is distinct from the developmental logic of production. The autonomy of the logic of interaction from the logic of purposive-rational action, however, does not preclude developments within the latter sphere from influencing the actual dynamics of the development of the former, and, for this reason, Habermas claims that his theory of communication is consistent with the historical materialism of Marx. Yet Habermas so attenuates the conceptual links between objectification and communication that his synthesis in no way illuminates the way in which a transformation in the organization of the former might contribute to the liberation of the latter. Even more importantly, Habermas does not explore, but arbitrarily rules out, the possibility that a liberatory transformation of the mode of communication might entail a simultaneous transcendence of objectification itself through a transformation of its communicative or symbolic presuppositions. This possibility is definitionally excluded from the very outset by the assumption that the relationship that labor establishes between human and nature is devoid of communicative presuppositions and is governed exclusively by invariant technical rules. However, if—as Habermas argues—

the distinction between labor and interaction is purely analytical, in the sense that any given empirical act is likely to partake of both of these pure types of action, then it would seem impossible to argue that *any* actual human activity is devoid of communicative presuppositions, in which case it would likewise appear to be impossible to preclude a priori the possibility that a transformation in the mode of communication might fundamentally alter the way in which humans relate to the natural world.

It is precisely this possibility that Wilden envisions. In contrast to Habermas, he conceptualizes communication to include the "material" exchange between humans and their natural environment and thus anticipates that a transformation of the mode of communication will entail a qualitative change in the structure of this material exchange. He implies that the "Western" way of acting on the world will be transcended along with its purely "digital" communicative presuppositions in favor of a fundamentally different mode of acting on the world that materializes a fundamentally different, nondigital or "ecosystemic" epistemology. Wilden's claim that this theory of communication is consistent with Marx rests, however, on the entirely unsubstantiated assertion that Marx's concept of objectification is consistent with Wilden's ecosystemic perspective. If this assertion cannot be substantiated, then we would have to conclude that "production" is a material part of the very repressive mode of communication that guarantees the domination of nature and thus that the elimination of this domination demands the elimination of production.

This, in fact, is what I shall argue in Chapter Eight. I shall demonstrate that objectification entails the domination of nature because it presupposes the very digital epistemology that guarantees this domination. "Production," then, is not an ontological category—not a universal condition of human existence—but an element of an historically contingent, repressive mode of communication, or what I would prefer to call a mode of symbolization, that must be transcended if the domination of nature is to be overcome. This argument leans heavily on Hegel's notion of a post-objectifying stage of the human struggle for recognition, but it also takes Hegel to task for failing materially or libidinally to ground this notion and thus for ultimately mystifying the possibilities for its practical realization. Consequently I devote the final part of the chapter to a discussion of the merits and the limits of Norman O. Brown's psychoanalytically inspired theory of the instinctual prerequisites of a post-objectifying stance toward nonhuman nature. This theory, as we shall see, links the modern compulsion to engage in objectification to the inability to accept death—the unconscious, symbolic equivalent of which is separation from the mother—but ultimately falls short of illuminating the possibility of overcoming this compulsion insofar as it fails entirely to pose the problem of the transformations in the mode of child rearing that would in fact enable us to accept death as well as its unconscious equivalent.

In Chapter Nine I turn, therefore, to the problem of the relationship between the mode of child rearing and the mode of symbolizing, and relating to, nonhuman nature. Here I undertake an historicization of Dorothy Dinnerstein's analysis of the effects of mother-monopolized child rearing in order to demonstrate that the contemporary, "nuclear" form thereof generates an unconscious need of the self to relate instrumentally not only to its "natural" but also to its sexual and political others. The domination of nature, present-day patriarchy, and contemporary political domination are all constituent elements of an instrumental mode of symbolization, a mode of symbolizing the relationship between self and other that is umbilically tied to the specific way in which the self interiorizes its relationship to its first significant other, namely its mother. It follows that the overcoming of the instrumental mode of symbolization and the creation of new, postinstrumental relations between the self and its natural, sexual, and political others is contingent on the elimination of mother-monopolized child rearing. As we shall see, this theory of the relationship of the mode of symbolization to the mode of child rearing entails an effort to clarify the relationship of those two dimensions of the human condition—communication and sexuality—that Neo-Marxism uncovers but ultimately obscures.

PART III

BEYOND MARXISM

CHAPTER EIGHT

PRODUCTION AND THE INSTRUMENTAL MODE OF SYMBOLIZATION

We saw in Chapter Seven that Marx praises the "civilizing influence of capital" through which "Nature becomes for the first time simply an object for mankind, purely a matter of utility."[1] Here Marx uncritically endorses a conception in which nature figures as a mere object that exists for the sake of the human subject, a pure means for the realization of exclusively human ends. Is this praise for an instrumental relationship between humans and their natural world merely an isolated exception to an otherwise fundamentally different conception of this relationship, or does it follow necessarily from the very center of Marx's conceptual system itself, i.e., the ontology of production? In the first part of this chapter I shall demonstrate that an instrumental conception of the relationship between humans and nature is not an exception to, but rather inherent in, Marx's concept of production. Indeed, I shall argue that this concept not only "retains something of" what Marcuse calls the "hubris of domination"[2] but is the ultimate possible expression of this hubris. It follows that a critical theory of domination cannot be based on, but must rather "deconstruct," this concept: if production does not entail an adequate starting point for the solution to the problem of domination because it is part of this very problem, then production must itself be explained in the light of an alternative concept that does not imply an inherently instrumental relationship between humans and their surrounding world. The remaining parts of this chapter are devoted to the elaboration of this concept and thus the foundation on which such an explanation must be constructed.

PRODUCTION AS THE DOMINATION OF NATURE

Let us return to Marx's analysis—summarized in Chapter One—of the universal structure of production, i.e., of the "labour-process [considered] independently of the particular form it assumes under given social condi-

---

[1] Marx, *Grundrisse*, McLellan ed., p. 94.
[2] Marcuse, *Counter-Revolution and Revolt*, pp. 68-69.

tions,''[3] this time in order to emphasize the relationship between humans and nature that this analysis implies. According to Marx:

> Labour is, in the first place, a process in which both Man and Nature participate, and in which man of his own accord starts, regulates, and controls the material reactions between himself and Nature. He opposes himself to Nature as one of her own forces, setting in motion arms and legs, head and hands, the natural forces of his body in order to appropriate Nature's productions in a form adopted to his wants. By thus acting on the external world and changing it, he at the same time changes his own nature. He develops his slumbering powers and compels them to act in obedience to his sway.[4]

To say that the human being "opposes himself to Nature as *one of her own forces*" is, to begin with, to affirm that "man is a part of nature."[5] As a part of nature, human beings have needs that are not fundamentally different from those of other living things; as a "natural being," the human "is a *suffering*, conditioned and limited creature, like animals and plants," as dependent for survival on external natural objects as the plant is on the sun.[6] Insofar as the human being is part of, rather than outside of, "the system of nature," even the distinctively human, or "species," power of objectification may be considered one of nature's powers. Thus Marx describes "human labor power" in the *Critique of the Gotha Program* as a "force of nature" itself.[7]

The peculiarity of this distinctively human "force of nature," however, is that it necessarily becomes the *opponent* of all the other, nonhuman forces of nature: the human being "*opposes himself to Nature* as one of her own forces." Insofar as nature's own "productions" are insufficient for, and may in fact be inconsistent with, human life, humans are obliged to "appropriate [these] productions in a form adopted to [their] wants," i.e., human life demands that nature be brought under human control. Human opposition to nonhuman nature is thus conceived by Marx as a universal requirement of human survival itself: "Just as the savage must *wrestle* with Nature to satisfy his wants, to maintain and reproduce life, so must civilized man, and he must do so in all social formations and under all possible modes of production."[8] Nature will stand forever as the great adversary against which humanity must

---

[3] Marx, *Capital*, Vol. I, p. 177.

[4] *Ibid.*

[5] Marx, "Estranged Labour," p. 61.

[6] Marx, "Critique of the Hegelian Dialectic and Philosophy as a Whole," p. 93, emphasis in the original.

[7] Tucker, *The Marx-Engels Reader*, p. 382.

[8] Marx, *Capital*, Vol. III, p. 320, emphasis added.

struggle, the recalcitrant object that must be bent to the overriding purposes of the human subject.

To conceive nature as that which must be bent or transformed by human beings is to conceptualize it as the raw material or the instrument of human labor. This conception of nature is expressed throughout all of Marx's writing. In four separate works spanning more than thirty years Marx defines nature as:

The primary source of all instruments and subjects of labour

the primordial instrument [of labour]

his [the human being's] original tool house . . . a universal instrument [of labour] . . . a field of employment for his activity

the material on which his labor is manifested . . . from which and by means of which it produces[9]

According to Marx, then, nature only exists "for us" insofar as it can be worked on by us: Nature is matter that receives the stamp of human form.[10] The completion of nature lies outside itself, i.e., in the human use to which it will be put; "Marx saw the as yet unmediated part of nature as only relevent from the point of view of its possible future modification."[11] Nature, in short, is an object that awaits the intervention of a human subject.

To say this is to say that nature has no intrinsic worth, no dignity of its own: "nature, taken abstractly, for itself—nature fixed in isolation from man—is *nothing* for man."[12] Considered independently of its role as a productive force, in other words, nature is without value:

The material of nature alone, in so far as *no* human labor is embedded in it, in so far as it is mere material and exists independently of human labour, has no value, since value is only embodied labour.[13]

[T]he earth in general and all forces of nature have no value because [they] do not present the objectification which comes from work.[14]

---

[9] Tucker, *The Marx-Engels Reader*, second ed., p. 526 (*Critique of the Gotha Program*); p. 264 (*Grundrisse*); p. 346 (*Capital*, Vol. I); p. 72 ("Estranged Labour").

[10] Marx, *Capital*, Vol. I, p. 180, and Schmidt, *The Concept of Nature in Marx*, pp. 76-77.

[11] Schmidt, *The Concept of Nature in Marx*, p. 200.

[12] Marx, "Critique of the Hegelian Dialectic and Philosophy as a Whole," p. 102, emphasis in the original.

[13] Cited in Schmidt, *The Concept of Nature in Marx*, p. 30, emphasis in the original.

[14] Cited in Hannah Arendt, *The Human Condition* (Chicago: The University of Chicago Press, 1958), p. 156. I have taken the liberty of correcting Arendt's mistranslation of "vergegenstand" as "reification."

Through labor humans bestow value on an otherwise value-less nature. Since nature is value-free, it makes no normative claims on the humans who confront it; they are free to make of it what they will, according to their own purposes. As conceived by Marx, the relationship between humans and nature is devoid of ethical significance and is therefore to be evaluated exclusively in instrumental terms, i.e., according to the extent to which the relationship is conducive to the fulfillment of the human purposes that engendered it. Humans are obliged, of course, to acquire "theoretical knowledge of [nature's] independent laws," but this knowledge is merely part of an overall "stratagem designed to subdue it to human requirements."[15] Knowledge of nature is but a means to the overriding end of its effective transformation: one learns the "purposes" of nature the better to make nature a mere extension of human purposes; we discover nature's "independent laws" not in order to respect, but rather in order to undermine, its independence from our existence. Thus Marx, following Bacon, counsels us to obey nature in order to command her.[16] He does not flinch from telling us that insofar as "his labor becomes the source of use values, therefore also of wealth . . . man from the beginning behaves toward nature . . . as an owner, treats her as belonging to him."[17] The relationship between humans and nonhuman nature is thus inevitably and appropriately a relationship characterized by the domination of the former over the latter.

The domination of nature entails its effective transformation: "by . . . acting on the external world" humans are, at the same time, "changing it." Each transformation of nature, in turn, "develops [their] slumbering powers" vis-à-vis nature, setting the stage for increasingly profound and extensive transformations in the future. Human history is thus understood as a perpetual and increasingly successful struggle to transcend natural limits, the progressive substitution of a humanly created environment for the purely "natural" one that preceded it. Thus, for Marx, the domination of nature is also its humanization: "though and because of [Man's] production, nature appears as *his* world and his reality . . . he contemplates himself in a world that he has created."[18]

Marx's "nature," then, is as much a product of human labor as it is its instrument. As product, it is what humans have already made; as instrument or raw material, it is what they will yet make. In either case, nature has no significance for Marx apart from the cycle of human making or production

[15] Marx, *Grundrisse*, McLellan ed., p. 94; see also *Capital*, Vol. I, p. 179.

[16] Leiss, *The Domination of Nature*, pp. 58-59.

[17] Marx, *Critique of the Gotha Program*, p. 383.

[18] Marx, "Estranged Labour," p. 62, emphasis in the original. See also *The German Ideology*, p. 135, where Marx goes so far as to argue that labor is "the basis of the whole sensuous world as it now exists."

to which he subordinates it. In Marx's thought, nature figures exclusively as "a constituent element of human practice."[19] As such, it is but a mirror of human intentions: everywhere man looks, he sees only himself, either what he will do or has done. Marx's anthropocentrism knows no limits: Man, he tells us is "the sovereign of nature."[20]

If the human struggle is a struggle to surmount natural limits, then the most human society—for Marx, a communist society—will be one in which the human power to transcend these limits is most fully developed:

> Communism distinguishes itself from all previous movements by overturning the basis of all previous relations of production and interaction and consciously treating, for the first time, all naturally embedded presuppositions as creations of previous human beings, stripping them of their embeddedness in nature and subjecting them to the power of the associated individuals.[21]

Under communism individuals will recognize "for the first time" what Marx already "knows," namely that nature is but a means to exclusively human ends. Thus everyday communist existence will be characterized by that complete subjection of nature to the "power of the associated individuals" which Marx treats as definitive of the human essence. Put otherwise, communism will entail an unprecedented control over nature, or what Marx describes as "the advent of real mastery over . . . the forces of nature."[22]

Communism will entail as well the advent of genuine human freedom. The subjugation of nature is the liberation of man:

> [W]hen the limited bourgeois form is stripped away, what is wealth other than the universality of individual needs, capacities, pleasures, productive forces, etc., created through universal exchange? The full development of human mastery over the forces of nature, those of so-called nature as well as of humanity's own nature? The absolute working-out of his creative potentialities, with no presuppositions other than the previous historic development, which makes this totality of development, i.e., the development of all human powers as such the end in itself, not as measured on a *predetermined* yardstick? Where he does not reproduce himself in one specificity, but produces his totality? Strives not to remain something he has become, but is in the absolute movement of becoming?[23]

---

[19] Schmidt, *The Concept of Nature in Marx*, p. 30.

[20] Marx, "The British Rule in India," in Tucker, *The Marx-Engels Reader*, p. 582.

[21] Cited in Jeremy Shapiro, "The Slime of History," in John O'Neil, ed., *On Critical Theory* (New York: The Seabury Press, 1976), p. 148.

[22] Marx, *Grundrisse*, p. 110.

[23] *Ibid.*, p. 488, emphasis in the original.

Human freedom and embeddedness in nature are inversely related. Embeddedness, i.e., absence of "the full development of human mastery" over nature, leaves human beings dependent on something outside themselves. As that which cannot (yet) be controlled, nature under conditions of embeddedness is a limit that must be respected, a predetermined standard to which the individual must submit. The individual who respects nature, in turn, cannot make the development of all his or her powers "the end in itself" and is thus unable to participate in "the absolute movement of becoming." Conversely, the overcoming of embeddedness and the "full development of mastery" over nature signal the elimination of any "natural" standard on which the individual is dependent and thus the fact that "man becomes the measure of all things." Liberated from "natural" limits, and answerable only to themselves, humans are no longer constrained to remain that which they have already become but are able to become whatever they choose to become. Whereas in previous societies "the past dominates the present, in communist society, the present dominates the past."[24]

At the same time that Marx treats communism as the effective domination of human beings over nature, he also envisions it as the practical resolution of the conflict between them. Thus in the *Economic-Philosophic Manuscripts* he speaks of communism as "the *genuine* resolution of the conflict between man and nature" and even describes this society as "the consummated oneness in substance of man and nature—the true resurrection of nature."[25] Language such as this has led a number of interpreters to argue that Marx repudiates the Enlightenment conception of a purely instrumental relationship between humans and nature in favor of a conception of a harmonious, reciprocal relationship in which humans respect and even strive to enhance the potentialities of nature; on this interpretation, communism as Marx envisions it entails a unity between humans and their natural surroundings that cannot be conceptualized within the framework of a paradigm in which nature is a pure object that makes no claims against a dominating subject.[26] The problem with this interpretation—apart from the fact that it flies in the face of virtually everything else that Marx says about this relationship—is that the unity or "oneness" between human beings and nature that Marx envisions is in no way predicated on, and is in fact inconsistent with, any reciprocity between them. Thus he says in *The German Ideology* that "the celebrated 'unity of man with nature' has always existed in industry and has existed in varying

[24] Marx and Engels, *Manifesto of the Communist Party*, p. 347.

[25] Marx, "Private Property and Communism," pp. 70-71, emphasis in the original.

[26] Ernst Bloch is perhaps the foremost advocate of this interpretation. See David Gross, "Ernst Bloch: The Dialectics of Hope," in Howard and Klare, *The Unknown Dimension*, pp. 107-30. For a critique of Bloch's interpretation, see Jurgen Habermas, "Ernst Bloch—A Marxist Romantic," *Salmagundi*, Nos. 10-11 (Fall-Winter 1969-70), pp. 311-24.

forms in every epoch according to the lesser or greater development of industry.''[27] For Marx, in other words, some form of unity between humans and nature is inherent in objectification—it is manifest in every human product, which is nothing if not a ''co-mingling'' of the natural and the human, ''Nature's material adapted by a change of form to the wants of man''[28]— and thus ''unity'' in no way presupposes the assumption of a nonobjectifying human stance vis-à-vis nature. The more perfect form of this unity that Marx envisions under communism will be the result not of the transcendence, but rather of the perfection, of the human power of objectification: as Charles Taylor has argued, for Marx ''Man is one with nature because and to the extent to which he has made it over as his expression.''[29] Habermas agrees with Taylor that the unity that Marx envisions ''can only come about through the activity of a subject [and] remains . . . imposed on nature by the subject.''[30] To put this another way: the ''genuine resolution of the conflict between man and nature'' of which Marx speaks is achieved through the victory of the former over the latter; the situation that Marx describes, misleadingly, as the ''true resurrection of nature'' entails nothing other than its complete ''subjugation . . . to a design freely created by man.''[31]

That Marx's concept of the ''resurrection of nature'' is merely another name for its effective domination is amply demonstrated in Jeremy Shapiro's recent effort to explain the sense in which this concept is consistent with Marx's concept of the overcoming of embeddedness. The overcoming of embeddedness, he tells us, ''ends the conflict of nature with itself'' and thus ''is at the same time'' its ''resurrection.''[32] In what sense, to begin with, does embeddedness entail the ''conflict of nature with itself'' such that the overcoming of embeddedness can be plausibly described as the end to this conflict? Embeddedness, as we have seen, refers to limited or incomplete human control over nature; to describe embeddedness as the ''conflict of nature with itself'' is to equate this conflict with the incomplete or unresolved conflict between the human and the nonhuman parts of nature in the broadest possible sense of the term. This means, in turn, that the ''end'' of the conflict of nature with itself can only refer to the complete subjugation of the nonhuman part of nature to the human part of nature. It follows that the emergence of a nature that is no longer rent with strife—the ''resurrected'' nature to which

[27] Marx and Engels, *The German Ideology*, p. 134.

[28] Marx, *Capital*, Vol. I, p. 180.

[29] Taylor, *Hegel*, p. 550.

[30] Habermas, *Knowledge and Human Interests*, p. 32.

[31] Taylor, *Hegel*, p. 550. Axelos concurs: ''The 'resurrection of nature' means . . . the total abolition of nature, the complete technification of what is 'natural.' '' *Alienation, Praxis and Techne in the Thought of Karl Marx*, p. 245.

[32] Shapiro, ''The Slime of History,'' p. 149.

Shapiro, following Marx, refers—is nothing other than the emergence of a thoroughly "humanized," i.e., dominated (nonhuman) nature.[33] As Habermas has argued, any "resurrection of nature" that does not entail its effective domination "cannot be logically conceived within [Marx's] materialism."[34] Far from being a critic, Marx is an unabashed proponent—perhaps *the* proponent—of what Wilden calls the "epistemology of biosocial imperialism" of the Western Enlightenment.[35] An "ecological" Marxism, *pace* Agger and Ophuls, is simply, and necessarily, a contradiction in terms.[36]

Thus even under communism nature remains, for Marx, a pure object of control rather than a subject in its own right with which human subjects enter into a communicative relationship. Speaking in this case for Marx, Habermas states that "Nature does not conform to the categories under which the subject apprehends it in the unresisting way in which a subject can conform to the understanding of another subject on the basis of reciprocal recognition,"[37] i.e., there can be no possibility of genuine reciprocity or communication between humans and nonhuman nature. It follows that, as Schmidt summarizes Marx's position, "The exploitation of nature will not cease in the future, but man's encroachments into nature will be rationalized, so that their remoter consequences will remain capable of control. In this way, nature will be robbed step by step of the possibility of revenging itself on men for their victories over it."[38]

Marx's commitment to the domination of nature manifests itself clearly in the contempt he expresses for any conception that attributes subjectivity to nature. Thus he mocks the sentimentality of the "true socialist" who speaks of "gay flowers . . . tall and stately oaks . . . their satisfaction, their happiness in life, their growth and their blossoming" and who tells us that the "infinite multitude of tiny creatures in the meadow . . . forest birds . . . a mettlesome troop of young horses . . . neither know nor desire any other happiness than that which lies for them in the expressions and the enjoyment of their lives," accusing him of ascribing "to *nature* itself the mental expression of a pious wish [for happiness]" and engaging in "ingenuous philosophical mystification."[39] His scorn for any romantic cult of nature is even more strikingly evident in his critique of Daumer's *The Religion of the New Age* in which he castigates the "effeminate[!] resignation" of a

[33] Joel Whitebook, "The Problem of Nature in Habermas," *Telos*, No. 40 (Summer 1979), p. 59.

[34] Habermas, *Knowledge and Human Interests*, pp. 32-33.

[35] Wilden, *System and Structure*, p. 210.

[36] Ben Agger, *Western Marxism: An Introduction* (Santa Monica: Goodyear, 1979), Ch. 7; Ophuls, *Ecology and the Politics of Scarcity*, pp. 206-207.

[37] Habermas, *Knowledge and Human Interests*, p. 33.

[38] Schmidt, *The Concept of Nature in Marx*, pp. 155-56.

[39] Cited in *Ibid.*, pp. 129-30, emphasis in the original.

276

cult of nature . . . limited to the Sunday walks of an inhabitant of a small provincial town who childishly wonders at the cuckoo laying its eggs in another bird's nest, at tears being designed to keep the surface of the eyes moist, and so on, and finally trembles with reverence as he recites Klopstock's *Ode to Spring* to his children. There is no question, of course, of modern sciences, which, with modern industry, have revolutionized the whole of nature and put an end to man's childish attitude towards nature as well as other forms of childishness. . . . For the rest, it would be desirable that Bavaria's sluggish peasant economy, the ground on which priests and Daumers likewise grow, should at last be plowed up by modern cultivation and modern machines.[40]

The romanticization of nature, in short, is simply inconsistent with modern science and industry and is thus revealed as mere childishness that will necessarily be outgrown.

Marx's denigration of the tendency of some of his contemporaries to attribute subjectivity to nature is paralleled by his devaluation of those cultures in the past in which the attribution of subjectivity to nature is the "normal" mode of human consciousness. We have already seen that in *Grundrisse* he disdainfully describes such practice as "nature-idolatry."[41] Elsewhere in that work he refers to the "limited" and "childish world of antiquity."[42] The metaphor of the child, in fact, dominates Marx's descriptions of "primitive" societies. In three separate passages in volume I of *Capital* he implies that the primitive is to the modern as the infant is to the adult:

[T]hey ["primitive" societies] are founded . . . on the immature development of man individually, who has not yet severed the umbilical cord that unites him with his fellowmen in a primitive tribal community. . . . They can arise and exist only when the development of the productive power of labor has not risen beyond a low stage, and when, therefore, the social relations within the sphere of material life, between man and man, and between man and nature, are correspondingly narrow. This narrowness is reflected in the ancient worship of Nature.

[I]n those ["primitive"] cases, each individual has no more torn himself off from the navel-string of his tribe or community than each bee has freed itself from connexion with the hive.

Where [in tropical "primitive" societies] Nature is too lavish, she "keeps

[40] Marx and Engels, review of G. Fr. Daumer's *The Religion of the New Age*, in *K. Marx and F. Engels on Religion* (Moscow: Foreign Languages Publishing House, 1957), p. 94.

[41] Marx, *Grundrisse*, McLellan Ed., p. 94.

[42] Marx, *Grundrisse*, p. 488.

him in hand, like a child in leading strings." She does not impose upon him any necessity to develop himself.[43]

Some twenty years earlier, in *The German Ideology*, Marx had spoken, with equal if not even greater scorn, of "tribal consciousness" as "sheep-like" or "mere herd-consciousness." This is a consciousness of a nature "with which man's relations are purely animal": a nonobjectifying conception of nature is "a purely animal consciousness of nature (natural religion)."[44]

Marx's denigration of the "childishness" and "animality" of primitive and other nonobjectifying precapitalist cultures follows inexorably from his "ontologization" of objectification. If human being is a Being of objectification, then the members of nonobjectifying cultures will be deemed to be less than fully human. Faced with the conflict between his concept and the reality of primitive peoples, Marx resolves this conflict, in characteristically ethnocentric fashion, by finding these people rather than his concept wanting.[45] Throughout his life Marx castigates the tendency of bourgeois thinkers to mask the explanatory poverty of their fundamental concepts with an evolutionary assumption that enables these members of "the latest form [to] regard the previous ones as steps leading up to itself."[46] But this, it should be clear, is precisely the tendency to which Marx himself falls prey: for Marx, primitive societies, as the name implies, are immature social forms that must be transcended if "mankind [is to] fulfill its destiny."[47] Thus Marx's Western Enlightenment assumption of the domination of nature legitimates the Western domination of those cultures that do not dominate nature; the epistemology of "biosocial imperialism" justifies cultural imperialism practiced against those people who refuse this epistemology.

The struggle against both biosocial and cultural imperialism thus demands that we historicize, rather than ontologize, the concept of objectification. The conflict between Marx's concept on the one hand and both the ecosystem and those people who respect its demands on the other must be resolved in favor of the latter and against the former. The preservation of the ecosystem as well as the human need for a nonobjectifying relationship with its nonhuman elements require, in other words, that we do to/for Marx's constitutive concept what Marx did to/for the central concepts of the bourgeois thinkers he confronts: explain its origins in order to reveal its historical limits. The first step in this critical journey will entail a movement from Marx back to Hegel.

[43] Marx, *Capital*, Vol. I, pp. 79, 334, 513.

[44] Tucker, *The Marx-Engels Reader*, p. 122.

[45] On this point see Baudrillard, *The Mirror of Production*, and Sahlins, *Culture and Practical Reason*.

[46] Marx, *Grundrisse*, p. 106.

[47] Marx, "The British Rule in India," p. 582.

278

FROM MARX TO HEGEL

A reliance on Hegel for the historicization of Marxism appears paradoxical in the light of Marx's claim to have accomplished the definitive historicization of Hegel. According to Marx, Hegel's equation of objectification with alienation effectively transforms alienation into a permanent, unsurpassable phenomenon and therefore must itself be surpassed if the historical limits of alienation are to become visible. Thus we saw in Chapter One that Marx argues that it is not objectification per se but rather only the capitalist form thereof that precludes the integration of humans with their world and among themselves, and that a transformation of the form of objectification—the creation of a socialist mode of production—will enable them to achieve this integration. But now we have seen that objectification—whether capitalist or socialist—necessarily entails the domination of nature and thus that it is inconsistent with the needs of the ecosystem and those who seek an integrated, nondominating relationship with its nonhuman elements. The elimination of domination thus demands not merely a transformation of the mode of objectification but rather the transcendence of objectification *as such*. It follows that the struggle to eliminate domination cannot be understood as a struggle to democratize control over objectification led by those who engage in this activity; a successful conclusion to what Marxists call the proletarian class struggle necessarily culminates in the reproduction, rather than the overcoming, of the domination of nature. The recognition that even a thoroughly democratized objectification entails domination encourages us to examine in a fresh light Hegel's equation of objectification and alienation. It also obliges us to take seriously his claim—dismissed by Marx—that objectification is merely one form of human consciousness that must and will be transcended by a fundamentally different and superior, nonobjectifying form.

In Chapter One we saw that Hegel maintained that the struggle for recognition that occurs in objectification cannot culminate in genuine integration between humans and their world; the objectifying consciousness, although an advance over previous stages of human consciousness, remains an alienated consciousness that does not feel at home with the surroundings on which it depends. We are now in a position to understand why, according to Hegel, this must be the case. For the objectifying or "Enlightenment" consciousness, Hegel tells us in the *Phenomenology*, nature is mere matter devoid of any subjectivity; the objectifying subject defines the natural environment as a pure object and thus experiences no identity or commonality with the world with which he or she is obliged to relate. Conceived as "Man's" absolute other, nature is necessarily denuded of any qualities that might enable human beings to see something of themselves in it. The objectifying consciousness is thus estranged from the very beginning from the natural world on which it depends.

279

Divested of subjectivity or purpose, nature can have no intrinsic significance for the human being, but rather exists exclusively as a vehicle for human purposes: an objectified nature's "being-in-itself descends to the level of empty appearance as a reality opposed to the active [human] consciousness."[48] The "Enlightened" person "walks the earth as in a garden planted for him" in which "everything exists to pleasure and delight him."[49] No longer conceived as an end-in-itself, nature becomes a pure means for human ends: "In [objectifying] *practice* man relates to nature as to something immediate and external. He himself is in this relation an immediately external and hence sensuous individual, who has however the right to conduct himself towards natural objects as their *purpose*."[50] Nature, in other words, only exists for the objectifying consciousness insofar as it is *useful* to it; an instrumental relationship utterly devoid of reciprocity is the only relationship that is possible with a reality on which we are obliged to depend but with which we experience no commonality.

In using nature, the Enlightened consciousness strives to annul its otherness in order to make it an extension of itself. Since this self sees nothing in unmodified nature that resembles itself, the only way in which it succeeds in seeing itself in nature is through the imposition of its own stamp on nature; nature must be made other than what it is so that humans can recognize themselves in it. "The practical approach to Nature," Hegel says, "is determined by appetite, which is self-seeking; need impels us to use Nature for our own advantage, to wear her out, to wear her down, in short, to annihilate her."[51] Hegel does not make it explicit, but it is not difficult to detect a significant parallel between his analysis of the inherently flawed nature of the recognition struggle between master and slave and his analysis of the shortcomings of the recognition struggle that occurs in objectification. Just as the master desires but cannot achieve recognition from the slave because the latter does not appear to the former as an autonomous independent self capable of granting recognition, so too the objectifying consciousness is obliged to seek recognition from a nature that lacks the independence to provide it; in both cases the independent subjectivity that is the *sine qua non* of authentic recognition is eliminated from the outset by the very consciousness that wants this recognition. To put this another way, the only type of recognition that can be achieved vis-à-vis a thoroughly subjugated, "annihilated" nature is the recognition of the self that we have imposed on it. As Marx would have it, "through . . . production [objectification] nature appears as *his* world and

---

[48] Cited in Schmidt, *The Concept of Nature in Marx*, p. 115.

[49] Hegel, *The Phenomenology of Mind*, p. 579.

[50] Cited in Schmidt, *The Concept of Nature in Marx*, p. 99, emphases in the original.

[51] A. V. Miller, *Hegel's Philosophy of Nature* (Oxford: The Clarendon Press, 1970), p. 5.

his reality . . . he contemplates himself in a world that he has created."[52] What Marx takes to be *the* authentic form of recognition, then, is in Hegel's eyes but a narcissistic form of self-contemplation that lacks the reciprocity that genuine recognition demands. Objectification fails to effect any real identification between humans and nature but only establishes the identification of humans with their mirror image.

The Enlightenment relationship with nature is thus fated to oscillate perpetually between opposition and identity. Humans confront an alien, threatening opponent and struggle to defeat it and rob it of its independent existence. But this struggle is always unsuccessful, since the goal of the complete subjugation of nature inevitably eludes those who pursue it. In a passage that can only be described as a remarkably prescient anticipation of a contemporary ecological consciousness, Hegel emphasizes that:

> The necessities and the wit of man have found an endless variety of ways of using and mastering Nature . . . Whatever forces Nature lets loose against man—cold, wild beasts, water, fire—he knows means to counter them; indeed, he takes these means from Nature and uses them against herself. The cunning of his reason enables him to preserve and maintain himself in the face of the forces of Nature, by sheltering behind other products of Nature, and letting these suffer her destructive attacks. *Nature herself, however, in her universal aspect, he cannot overcome in this way, nor can he turn her to his own purposes.*[53]

Every successful effort to master a given part of nature, Hegel implies, has consequences for another part of nature that present human beings with yet another occasion to attempt to master it. Thus the effort to subjugate nature can never eliminate its hostile, threatening character; the struggle to eliminate nature's independent existence (and thus to transcend opposition in favor of narcissistic identity) inevitably gives rise to new and different challenges to the human need for mastery (and thus, reestablishes opposition). Nature as a whole, Hegel warns us, cannot be effectively and definitively dominated: the struggle to dominate nature is a ceaseless, ultimately Sysiphean struggle that precludes human beings from ever being at peace with their world. The struggle for recognition that objectification entails not only fails to conform to the proper "notion" of recognition but is also necessarily self-defeating. For both reasons—ultimately the *same* reason, given Hegel's assumption of the ultimate identity of the desireable and the possible—it is destined to be surpassed in favor of a higher form of human consciousness.

The inauthentic and self-defeating nature of the recognition struggle that

---

[52] Marx, "Estranged Labour," p. 62.

[53] Miller, *Hegel's Philosophy of Nature*, p. 5, emphasis added.

takes place in objectification can also be illuminated through an analysis of the material product in which objectification culminates. It will be recalled that, for Marx, this product, as a melding together of nature's matter and human purpose, entails an effective overcoming of that opposition between subject and object which initiates the activity of objectification. According to Hegel, however, this is not the case; the product that emerges from objectification does not effect a genuine reconciliation between human and nature but is "internally flawed": "Only an *externally* impressed form has arisen on the basis of the existing material, and it is also a contingent characteristic by reason of the limited content of the purpose. The goal attained is therefore only an Object, which again becomes the means or the material for other purposes, and so on until *infinity*."[54]

Since the struggle to dominate nature is never-ending, it follows that a material product will not be treated as an end in itself but will always be available to serve as a means for the further transformation of nature. Any product of the objectifying consciousness will thus be viewed as a mere link in an endless chain of additional objectifications: fertilizer is produced in order to make the land fertile; the land is made fertile in order to grow grain; grain is grown in order to make bread; bread is made in order that we can live. Under these conditions of what Hegel calls "bad infinity" we experience an infinite regress in which there is no final, stable order of things with which we can identify.[55] In short, a nature that is divested of intrinsic significance can only yield products that are devoid of symbolic significance, utilitarian objects that are unfit to serve as a source of authentic individual identity. Hegel's teaching is that an instrumental relationship between humans and their natural world cannot but engender an instrumental relationship between humans and the world of objects they have produced.

Finally, Hegel tells us that this instrumental mode necessarily extends its sway over the relationship between humans and their fellow humans: "as everything is useful for man, man is likewise useful too, and his characteristic function consists in making himself a member of the human herd. . . . He makes use of others and is himself made use of."[56] Conceiving the world in utilitarian fashion, the objectifying consciousness cannot but establish utilitarian relationships within that part of the world that consists in his or her social relationships. The subject that conceptualizes the world as an object is bound to treat the human inhabitants of this world as objects as well: like nature, he "knows them in so far as he can manipulate them."[57] The En-

---

[54] Cited in Schmidt, *The Concept of Nature in Marx*, pp. 106-107, emphases in the original.

[55] Taylor, *Hegel*, pp. 324, 181, 323.

[56] Hegel, *The Phenomenology of Mind*, pp. 579-80.

[57] Max Horkheimer and Theodor W. Adorno, *Dialectic of the Enlightenment* (New York: Herder and Herder, 1972), p. 9.

lightenment thus inevitably culminates in the Terror of the French Revolution in particular and the untrammeled effort to *re-make* human beings in general.[58] The logic of objectification necessarily invades the relationships among human beings. Totalitarian or technocratic politics is the corollary of a totalitarian stance toward nature; the domination of humans over nature cannot but give rise to the domination of humans over themselves.[59] A century before Freud and a century and a half before Horkheimer and Adorno, Hegel succeeds in specifying the fateful "Dialectic of the Englightenment." Against Marx, he teaches that a noninstrumental relationship among human beings cannot be based on an instrumental relationship between human beings and nature; with extraordinary foresight he points out what it has taken us almost two centuries to learn and what Marxists and Neo-Marxists have yet to learn, namely that the unlimited development of the "forces of production" not only does not yield but is in fact an obstacle to the solution to the problem of the relationship of human being to human being. Whereas Neo-Marxists are prepared to accept the proposition that the instrumentally rational exploitation of nature is not a sufficient condition for the elimination of instrumental, exploitative relation- ships among human beings, they continue to maintain that it is a necessary condition for their elimination and thus are obliged to treat what is, in fact, part of the problem as if it were part of the solution. For example, and as we have seen, Mitchell acknowledges that the unlimited growth of the forces of production does not in itself eliminate patriarchal sexual domination, and Habermas argues that this growth is not sufficient for the elimination of political domination, but both assume that an advanced development of what they take to be the transhistorical, distinctively human power of objectification is the *sine qua non* for the creation of a world in which unalienated, liberatory social relationships prevail. They and all other Neo-Marxists thus fail to grasp what Hegel understands so well, namely that the alienation of humans from their natural world that this "development" entails is inextricably intertwined with the alienation of human beings from one another.

From Hegel we learn, then, that objectification is but one part of a cognitive whole or totality that embraces an instrumental relationship between humans and nature, humans and their products, and humans and their fellow humans.

[58] Hegel, *The Phenomenology of Mind*, pp. 598-610; Taylor, *Hegel*, pp. 184-86.

[59] Here Hegel appears to argue that contemporary intersubjective domination owes its existence to objectification. In Chapter One we saw that Hegel argues that objectification is itself a response to a preexisting form of intersubjective domination, i.e., the master-slave relationship. Whatever the ambiguities in Hegel's argument, my argument is that intersubjective domination is both phylogenetically and ontogenetically prior to objectification. Phylogenetically prior: the domi- nation of nature is a relatively recent cultural development, while sexual and political domination are not. Ontogenetically prior: the predisposition of the individual to dominate nature is rooted in the structure of the intersubjective relationship between the child and his or her parents. This argument is developed in the next chapter.

283

This instrumental mode of consciousness—or what I would prefer, in order to avoid the impression that it is merely inside the head, to call an instrumental *mode of symbolization*[60]—is, moreover, an intrinsically alienated mode within which humans cannot achieve integration with their world, their products, and themselves. Human "integration," i.e., an end to alienation, thus demands the transcendence of this mode in favor of a postobjectifying, noninstrumental mode of symbolization.

The broad outlines of such a vision can in fact be found in Hegel's writings. It emerges as an explicit synthesis of the Instrumental and what might be described as a Romantic or primitive mode of symbolization. The Instrumental mode, as we have seen, upholds the rational freedom of the human being at the price of the loss of any sense of unity or identity between this being and nature; the difference between the human and the nonhuman part of nature is transformed into an absolute, hierarchical opposition between the two. The Romantic mode, on the other hand, at least according to Hegel, asserts the oneness or integration between humans and nature at the cost of the denigration of that capacity for rational freedom which is the distinctively human capacity; the difference between the human and nonhuman parts of nature is denied in favor of a vision of their unmediated and immediate identity.[61] Thus neither the Instrumental nor the Romantic mode is able to combine identity and difference, to forge a synthesis between a vision of "expressive unity" with nature on the one hand and the "aspiration to rational autonomy" on the other.[62] This synthesis is precisely what Hegel seeks to express in that mode of symbolization he calls "Absolute Knowledge" (in the *Phenomenology*) or the "Absolute Idea" (in the *Science of Logic*).

On the one hand, Absolute knowledge repudiates the notion of nature as a pure object set over against an exclusively human subject, recognizing instead that there is subjectivity or purposefulness throughout the natural world. Absolute Knowledge transcends the "finite-teleological" standpoint

[60] The term "mode of symbolization" is borrowed from Jean-Joseph Goux, *Freud, Marx, Economie et Symbolique* (Paris: Editions du Seuil, 1973). Like Goux, I use the term in order to grasp the logic of "a social formation in all its aspects" (p. 20), i.e., in order to conceptualize a social whole that is present in each of its parts. Unlike Goux, however, I reject the formulation that this mode of symbolization is "conditioned in the last instance by the economic process" (p. 272), a formulation that rescues Marxist orthodoxy at the cost of an untenable theoretical eclecticism. By now it should be clear that a structurally separate economic process is specific to capitalist society and that Goux's formulation thus conflates the logic of the mode of symbolization of this particular society with the concept of the mode of symbolization in general. To put this another way: the concept of ultimate determination by the mode of production implies an instrumental mode of symbolization and is therefore unserviceable as a theoretical standard for the critical analysis of this mode of symbolization.

[61] Miller, *Hegel's Philosophy of Nature*, pp. 8-9.

[62] Taylor, *Hegel*, p. 545.

284

or the standpoint of "external" teleology for which nature is mere matter that receives its form exclusivey from the (human) outside in favor of the standpoint of genuine or "internal" teleology for which every being of nature has its own distinctive end or form within itself and must therefore be grasped as "free in [its] own peculiar vital activity."[63] Absolute Knowledge is thus able, in contrast to the Instrumental mode, to recognize commonality between the human and nonhuman parts of nature. Unlike the Primitive mode, on the other hand, it refuses to homogenize the different types or levels of subjectivity throughout nature, recognizing to the contrary that the types of teleology characteristic of inorganic, organic, and human nature are different in kind. The purposefulness or "freedom" of the stone is different from that of the plant, and the freedom of the plant is different from that of the human being. Absolute knowledge understands, in fact, that only humans are capable of "self-consciousness"—the capacity to reflect on, be critical of, and transform purposive activity—and thus repudiates any vision of an unmediated, "intuitive" unity with nonhuman nature that is purchased at the price of the sacrifice of human reason.[64] Unlike either of the elements of which it is a synthesis, then, Absolute Knowledge is able to recognize difference within unity; it can acknowledge that "all substance is subject" without insisting that all subjects are identical. It is thus able to find a home or a place for humans within nature that is a properly human place.

It follows from what we have said thus far that, within the mode of symbolization which is Absolute Knowledge, the relationship between humans and nature is no longer instrumental or utilitarian. Humans relate to nature not only in terms of their own purposes but also in terms of the different purposes inherent in *its* various entities; nature for the postobjectifying consciousness is no longer a pure means to exclusively human ends but become an end in itself. Put otherwise, nature regains the intrinsic significance that it lost within the Instrumental mode of symbolization; human interaction with nature once again becomes a meaningful experience. Thus humans will no longer be obliged to strive for meaning through the obliteration or annihilation of nature. Since nature is no longer defined as an alien, recalcitrant other, humans can recognize themselves in it without suffering the compulsion to make it into something other than what it is, namely a mirror image of the human self. The Promethian, ultimately self-defeating struggle to dominate nature gives way to a genuine reconciliation between humans and their world; narcissistic and therefore inauthentic human recognition is surpassed by the experience of authentic identification with the whole of which human reality is only a part. At the same time, however, this integration is not a "primitive"

[63] Miller, *Hegel's Philosophy of Nature*, p. 6; Taylor, *Hegel*, pp. 322-25.
[64] Miller, *Hegel's Philosophy of Nature*, p. 9.

unity in which the human part is dominated by the nonhuman part or even merely submerged within the whole. The postobjectifying consciousness, in other words, does not subordinate its purposes to the purposes of the manifold natural entities with which it interacts, but recognizes that it has purposes or needs that are different from those of the rest of nature and that these distinctive needs have a legitimate claim to satisfaction. This new form of consciousness thus does not dispense with, but rather depends on, the uniquely human tools or inventions that are required to fulfill these needs. Unlike the tools of the objectifying consciousness, however, they are also constructed with the claims of the nonhuman parts of nature in mind:

> the cognition which comprehends [Absolute Knowledge] is the middle term in which universality does not remain on *this* side, in *me*, over against the individuality of the objects: on the contrary, while it stands in negative relation to things and assimilates them to itself, it equally finds individuality in them and does not encroach upon their independence, or interfere with their free self-determination.[65]

Neither instrumental reason nor mere intuition or feeling but rather a new form of noninstrumental, empathic reason will guide the interactions between humans and the world on which they depend.

The language with which it is articulated should not prevent us from recognizing that Hegel's notion of Absolute Knowledge as the ultimate stage of human consciousness embodies the essentials of what I described in the previous chapter as an "ecosystemic perspective" on the relationship between humans and their natural surroundings. As such, it is far in advance of the very Marxism that purports to transcend Hegel; the movement from Hegel to Marx entails a reversion from a postobjectifying to an objectifying or Instrumental mode of symbolization and thus an historical regression. Hegel's vision, not Marx's, speaks to those of us today who are convinced that human liberation cannot be purchased at the price of the domination of nature (but who are also convinced that it cannot be achieved at the expense of reason). Indeed, it directly anticipates the contemporary theoretical efforts of those for whom this conviction is a necessary starting point. Thus the distance between Hegel's vision (as we have thus far described it) of a totality pervaded by subjectivity but characterized by different types thereof and Wilden's cybernetic model of nature as a vast network of communication among entities whose communicative capacities are characterized by different levels of "semiotic freedom" is more terminological than anything else. Similarly, Hegel's notion of a new, noninstrumental and empathic reason that respects the "individuality" of natural objects and does "not encroach upon their

---

[65] *Ibid.*, p. 12, emphases in the original.

independence'' clearly presages Marcuse's vision of a liberatory science and technology that embodies a ''new sensibility'' that enables human beings to recognize ''nature as a *subject* in its own right'' whose potentialities humans will strive to respect and enhance.[66] Hegel's concept of Absolute Knowledge is thus an indispensable starting point for a solution to the problem of the relationship between humans and nature.

So too is it a necessary starting point for a solution to the problems of the relationship between humans and their products and between humans and their fellow humans. Just as an objectifying or instrumental relationship between humans and nature is part of a whole that entails instrumental relations between humans and their products and among human beings themselves, so a postobjectifying, noninstrumental relationship to nature is but one of the elements of a totality that embraces noninstrumental human relationships with their products and among themselves. As in the case of the first relationship, Hegel's vision of these latter two relationships entails a synthesis of Enlightenment and primitive conceptions. For the Enlightenment consciousness products are but means to externally imposed ends; as objects inserted into an infinite chain of objectifications they necessarily lack symbolic significance. For the primitive consciousness, on the other hand, objects assume an eminently symbolic importance. Twentieth-century anthropologists report that objects in these societies function primarily as ''gifts'' (often endowed with magical properties) by means of which obligations to both nonhuman nature and other human beings are fulfilled; they are the vehicles through which individuals identify with a stable, indeed immutable, natural and social order of which they are merely the subordinate, transient, and replaceable elements.[67] Primitive products are thus a symbol not of the individual's power to collaborate with, but rather of the individual's *dependence* on his or her ''natural'' and social others.

Under Absolute Knowledge, products reassume the symbolic significance that they lack for the consciousness of the Enlightenment. Thus we will come to experience a meaningful relationship with our products as a corollary to the meaningful relationship we have established with the nature out of which they are fashioned; just as we no longer merely ''use'' nature, so too we no longer conceive of our products as merely ''useful.'' Since these products are no longer understood as a mere melange of human purpose and alien, formless matter but rather as a synthesis of human purpose and ''natural'' matter infused with its own form or purpose—''purposeful'' matter with which we purposeful beings can identify—they come to represent an authentic, rather

[66] Marcuse, *Counter-Revolution and Revolt*, p. 60.

[67] Marcel Mauss, ''Essai sur le Don,'' in *Sociologie et Anthropologie* (Paris: Presses Universitaires de France, 1950), pp. 145-279. See also Norman O. Brown, *Life Against Death*, Ch. 15.

287

than spurious "unity of subjective and objective."[68] As such, the symbolic significance that these objects assume is necessarily different from their significance for primitive consciousness: as symbols of a genuine reconciliation between individuals and their world (and not the domination of the latter over the former) they serve simultaneously to express the individual's connections with this world and to signify his or her unique presence within it. They affirm the individual's powers of collaboration with, rather than subordination to, the natural and social world on which he or she depends.

It should already be clear that Hegel's vision of a postobjectified relationship among human beings embodies elements of both the Instrumental and pre-Instrumental conceptions of this relationship yet repudiates the extremes of each. We have seen that the Instrumental mode symbolizes human beings as but the means to each others' ends. To put this another way, it prizes individuality or difference among human beings at the expense of any unity or identity among them. The primitive mode, in contrast, and at least according to Hegel, values unity or oneness and cannot tolerate individuality or difference; it thus submerges the individual within the whole or under the domination of those who are deemed to be its incarnation. Valorizing intimacy and denigrating autonomy, the primitive mode of symbolization is the antithesis of an Instrumental conception in which autonomy is upheld and intimacy denied. Hegel's vision overcomes this antithesis by simultaneously esteeming intimacy and autonomy, identity and difference; he understands, in other words, that sociality and individuality are not opposites but rather that each necessarily complements the other. He therefore envisions noninstrumental relationships that maximize individuality as the appropriate form of human relationships. This vision, of course, is not fundamentally different from that of Marx. The difference, as we have seen, is that Marx believes, wrongly, that this vision can be realized—indeed, can only be realized—on the basis of an instrumental relationship between humans and nature, whereas Hegel understands, correctly, that an instrumental relationship between humans and nature precludes the realization of a noninstrumental relationship among human beings.

Table 1 conveniently summarizes Hegel's analysis of the relationship between humans and nature, their products, and themselves in what I have called the Instrumental, pre-Instrumental, and post-Instrumental modes of symbolization.

I have characterized Hegel's vision of a post-Instrumental, postobjectifying mode of symbolization as one in which human beings are able to achieve identification with the subjects of nonhuman nature without sacrificing the rationality that is the distinctive mark of their own subjectivity. But this does

---

[68] Cited in Schmidt, *The Concept of Nature in Marx*, p. 104.

TABLE 1

Mode of Symbolization	Object of Symbolization			
	Nature	*Products*	*Humans*	*The Other (in General)*
Instrumental	Dominated Object	Utilitarian Objects	Autonomy Without Community	Difference Without Unity
Pre-Instrumental	Dominating Subject	Symbols of Obligation	Community Without Autonomy	Unity Without Difference
Post-Instrumental	Collaborative Subject	Symbols of Both Individual Embeddedness and Individual Power	Community and Autonomy	Unity and Difference

not end the matter. According to Hegel, the capacity of human beings to achieve this identification without that sacrifice is predicated on their recognition that both nonhuman subjectivities and their own are emanations of a cosmic subjectivity (the World Spirit) that underlies all of nature, including the human part thereof. Hegel assumes, in other words, that humans cannot win through to a teleological understanding of the various entities of the world unless they come to recognize that the world as a whole is ruled by a single, overriding *Telos*. And to say that the world is ruled by an overriding purpose is necessarily to argue that the World Spirit, or *Geist*, is ultimately responsible for the spiritual (re)integration between the human and nonhuman parts of nature that Absolute Knowledge entails. Since the transcendence of the opposition between objectivity and subjectivity in Absolute Knowledge is predicated on the existence of that Absolute Subject which is *Geist*, Absolute Knowledge necessarily includes the human awareness of *Geist*. And this awareness includes the recognition that both the initial separation of object and subject and their ultimate reconciliation are a work of *Geist*, and, as such, are inevitable. Put otherwise, Absolute Knowledge includes the awareness that it is but the ultimate stage in an unfolding of the self-knowledge of *Geist* that has included all the previous stages of human consciousness. All these stages and their respective transitions are thus understood to be necessary manifestations of a *Geist* that does its work through human intermediaries. Human history is but a vehicle for the development of a supra-human spirit.[69]

[69] For this summary of Hegel's notion of *Geist* I am indebted to Taylor, *Hegel*, Chs. 1, 3.

289

Thus Hegel mystifies the crucial problems of the origins and possible transformations of the different modes of symbolization. His notion of the inevitability of the transition from an Instrumental to a post-Instrumental mode of symbolization is of little comfort to those of us who presently suffer under the former and would aspire to contribute to the emergence of the latter: whether we interpret the assertion of ''inevitability'' to mean there is nothing for us to do or to mean that whatever we will do we must do, it tells us absolutely nothing about the practical imperatives of the struggle to transform the present mode of symbolization. And, insofar as the assertion of ''inevitability'' is a corollary to the notion of the World Spirit, it follows that this notion as well is at worst an obstacle to and at best a diversion from that struggle.

Moreover, the fact that thinkers after Hegel, such as Wilden and Marcuse, *have* articulated a vision of the integration of humans and nature that is not fundamentally different from that of Hegel (excluding the notion of the World Spirit) without having to take recourse to the assumption of the World Spirit, itself undermines Hegel's claim that the ability to articulate this vision is predicated on the recognition of the existence of a suprahuman subject. To put this another way: insofar as it is possible to conceptualize the whole as comprising a multiplicity of entities each possessing its own internal *telos* without giving in to the impulse to conceive these entities as emanations of a single, overriding *Telos* that underlies and guides the development of the whole, i.e., insofar as it is possible to repudiate a strictly teleological conception in favor of what Wilden calls a teleonomic conception of nature,[70] the notion of a World Spirit becomes superfluous. And, once we abandon the notion of a World Spirit, the transition from one mode of symbolizing nature to another can no longer be understood as inevitable.

The abandonment of Hegel's notion of the World Spirit re-opens the problem of clarifying, and thus contributing to, the possibility of the transformation from the Instrumental to a post-Instrumental mode of symbolization. Marx correctly abandons the notion of a World Spirit (although it can be argued that the notion covertly makes its way back into his thought in the form of the concept of the proletariat[71]), but incorrectly abandons as well the very real problem of a post-Instrumental mode of symbolization that Hegel simultaneously uncovers and obscures. In the process Marx throws out the proverbial baby with the bath water. The famous ''rational kernel'' that he attempts to separate from the infamous ''mystical shell'' in which it is wrapped is far larger than Marx imagines. As I have tried to demonstrate, the fact that

[70] Wilden, *System and Structure*, pp. xviii, 128.

[71] The notion that the proletariat will be historically compelled to overcome capitalist alienation and realize socialist dis-alienation implies that flesh-and-blood proletarians are but the vehicles for a suprahuman rationality that works its way through human history. See above, Chapter One.

Hegel mystifies the problem of the transition to a post-Instrumental mode of symbolization does not mean that there is anything mystical about the notion of a post-Instrumental mode of symbolization itself. Indeed, my claim is that this notion is the indispensable foundation of any adequate critical theory, any satisfactory analysis of human domination and the possibilities for human liberation.

Freed from the evolutionary assumptions with which Hegel burdens it, the vision of a post-Instrumental mode of symbolization enables us to avoid the ethnocentrism or cultural imperialism of Marxism or any other theory (such as the cognitive developmental psychology on which Habermas relies) that self-satisfiedly asserts the superiority of Western culture over the "primitive" cultures that preceded it. Measured against the standard of this vision, Western industrial societies are found to be every bit as far from a fully developed expression of human possibilities as the archaic societies they smugly denigrate as "undeveloped." Since it is a self-conscious synthesis of the modes of symbolization that predominate in these two radically antithetical forms of society, the vision of a post-Instrumental society asserts that the people of "modern" societies have as much to learn from the people of "primitive" societies as "they" have to learn from "us." Thus it refuses to legitimate but rather condemns outright any effort to impose "our" way of life on "them" in the name of historical progress or what Marx called "Mankind['s] . . . destiny." At the same time, however, it enables us to avoid the quagmire of a cultural relativism that would leave us utterly without any transcultural ground on which to stand. The notion of a post-Instrumental mode of symbolization implies that a society that realizes it would be a fuller, more complete expression of human possibilities than either of the two polar types that preceded it. It offers us a standard, in other words, in the light of which both primitive and modern societies are found wanting, and thus a means of transcending the debate between "primitivism" (or Romanticism) and "modernism" (or Rationalism) without giving in to a standardlessness that would preclude from the outset the possibility of a critical theory.

Thus the notion of a post-Instrumental mode of symbolization offers the possibility of a critical theory that simultaneously repudiates the either/or of ethnocentrism versus primitivism and the culturally relativistic and therefore inadequate response to this either/or, i.e., a critical theory that resolves the central dilemmas that have plagued this type of theory since it was initiated by Marx. Contrary to Marx, then, not the abandonment, but rather the material grounding of this notion is what is in order. Our task is to develop a non-Marxist but nevertheless materialist theory of the origins, persistence, and limits of the Instrumental mode of symbolization, the better to hasten its transformation into a post-Instrumental mode. This task, as we shall see, will oblige us to consider a synthesis of Hegel and Freud. The grounding of Hegel

291

by means of Freud will prove simultaneously to entail the historicization of Freud by means of Hegel.

NORMAN O. BROWN'S *Life Against Death*

In the preceding chapter we saw that Marcuse, following Freud, finds the source of the human domination of nature in the human instinct for death. The argument of the present chapter up to this point has established that (a) objectification necessarily entails the domination of nature and (b) objectification necessarily implies a cognitive totality that I have characterized as the Instrumental mode of symbolization. Thus it seems plausible to hypothesize that objectification and the Instrumental mode of symbolization of which it is an element are rooted in the death instinct. This hypothesis forms the starting point for a materialist grounding of Hegel that takes the form of a synthesis of Hegel and Freud.

Let us begin by recalling the limits of Marcuse's purported synthesis of Freud and Marx. According to his account of Freud, the destructive extroversion of the death instinct toward nature results from the sublimation of Eros demanded by (alienated) labor and the resulting weakening of Eros vis-à-vis its great adversary; once "unbound," the death instinct dons the mask of Thanatos, i.e., it assumes the form of destructive impulses toward nature. Since the domination of nature is linked in this way to alienated labor, it follows that an end to the domination of nature presupposes the elimination of alienated labor: unalienated labor makes possible a desublimation of Eros and thus a strengthening of the life instincts that "re-binds" the death instinct and thus precludes its destructive manifestation in the form of Thanatos. Insofar as the elimination of alienated labor is contingent on the overcoming of scarcity, Marcuse prescribes an advanced technological rationality as the necessary condition for the elimination of alienated labor and with it the technological domination of nature. His prescription, in other words, is more of the same, a remedy that is merely a continuation of the same disease.

Marcuse's purely quantitative solution to the problem of overcoming the domination of nature is prefigured in his purely quantitative account of its origins. He tries to explain a qualitative transformation of the death instinct—a change in form from an impulse to "return to the quiescence of the inorganic world"[72] to an impulse to annihilate nature—by referring to the growth in the strength of the death instinct relative to the strength of the life instincts. But why should a quantitative change, i.e., an increase in the power of the death instinct due to its release from the constraining power of the life instincts,

---

[72] Cited in Marcuse, *Eros and Civilization*, p. 23.

necessarily culminate in a qualitative change, i.e., the emergence of aggressive, violent impulses directed toward nature? To put this another way, we could conclude that this outcome was necessary only if it were the case that the tendency toward violence was already a tendency of the death instinct before its release from the constraining influence of Eros. But, if this is the case, then we have merely displaced (and left entirely unresolved) the problem of the qualitative transformation from "quiescence" to violence to an earlier stage. Marcuse's interpretation of Freud fails adequately to account for the origins of the domination of nature in the death instinct because it fails to explain the transformation of the latter into destructiveness. This failure, moreover, necessarily compromises his account of the end of the domination of nature: if the increase in the strength of the death instinct vis-à-vis the life instincts cannot explain why the former becomes violent, then a decrease in the strength of the death instinct relative to Eros cannot explain its "pacification." If, in other words, the death instinct is "aggressive" even before Eros loses control over it, then there is no reason to assume that it will cease to be "aggressive" when Eros regains control over it; its quality will have remained unchanged despite a change in its strength vis-à-vis Eros. In short, a quantitative relationship between the power of the death instinct and the power of the life instincts cannot account for the qualitative vicissitudes of the former and thus is unable to explain either the origins of or the end to the domination of nature.

There is another, related problem in Marcuse's Freudian explanation of the domination of nature. As we have seen, and despite his protestations to the contrary, Marcuse effectively makes "scarcity" the explanation of the alienated labor that is, in turn, responsible for the sublimation of Eros and its consequent weakening relative to the death instinct. His reliance on an advanced level of technological development as the condition for the overcoming of alienated labor rests on the assumption that this form of labor (along with its instinctual consequences) can only be overcome *via* the elimination of scarcity, i.e., on the assumption that scarcity is responsible for alienated labor and thus is the ultimate cause of the domination of nature. But, as I have suggested, scarcity cannot be understood as a primordial, "natural" condition but rather only as a culturally defined relation of ends to means in which the former outrun the latter;[73] as such, scarcity is properly grasped as the cultural assumption of a society based on an infinitely expanding technological dynamic, i.e., of a society based on the domination of nature or dominated by what I have called an Instrumental mode of symbolization. Thus Marcuse's explanation for the origins of the domination of nature really explains nothing at all, since it treats as a cause of this domination something (scarcity) that

[73] See above, Chapter Three.

293

is merely another name for this domination. And, since scarcity cannot possibly explain the emergence of the alienated, desexualized labor that is, according to Marcuse, ultimately responsible for the domination of nature, we are then left entirely in the dark as to why individuals would have ever submitted to the sexual repression that this form of labor entails. And, unless we know this, we will never understand the conditions for the undoing of this sexual repression and thus the conditions that make possible an end to the domination of nature.

Marcuse's Freudian explanation of the domination of nature leaves two large, unresolved problems: (a) the problem of why the death instinct assumes a destructive form vis-à-vis nature and (b) the problem of why individuals submit to sexual repression, the repression of their own bodies. The great merit of the work of Norman O. Brown is that he pursues both of these problems with unparalleled tenacity and with the insight that there is an intimate relationship between the two.

Let me begin with Brown's analysis of the second of these problems. The denial of the body, i.e., the sexual repression, that characterizes Western, indeed all, civilization up to the present time is rooted, according to Brown, in the equally universal denial of death. Not the death instinct per se, but rather its transmutation into the refusal to accept death, the fundamental fact of human mortality, inaugurates the refusal of bodily pleasure that culminates (in some, but, as we shall see, not all cultures) in the domination of nature. Our bodies, as the living reminder of our mortality, must be repressed, forgotten; the transformation of the polymorphous perversity of the infant into the narrow, genitally concentrated sexuality of the adult is the work not of the "outside" world but rather of the child who cannot tolerate death: the inability to die and sexual repression are the two unique and related "privileges" of the human animal. We rise above ourselves, in short, in order to rise above death; the result is the deadening of our bodies. A life in flight from death is ultimately, and ironically, a life dominated by death.[74] We impose sexual repression on ourselves; we suffer the deadening of our mortal bodies not because an external "reality principle" demands it but rather because *we* need it in order to be able to achieve immortality. The organization of the life (sexual) instincts thus takes shape from the very outset under the repressive auspices of a distorted death instinct, i.e., the refusal of the human organism to accept that "life is but a long detour to death."[75] Not scarcity, but the fear of death, demands that the body undergo the stunting and the maiming that transforms it into a potential instrument of objectification, of the domination of nature.

[74] Brown, *Life Against Death*, Ch. 9, and p. 284.
[75] Marcuse, *Eros and Civilization*, p. 25.

294

I have used the word "potential" advisedly. The universal sexual repression that the universal flight from death inaugurates must be grasped as the necessary, but not sufficient, condition for the destructive extroversion of the death instinct toward nature, since this extroversion is not, as we have seen, characteristic of primitive societies dominated by a pre-Instrumental mode of symbolization. We have been able to answer the second, but not yet the first question with which Marcuse left us; we have yet to explain why the flight from death and the sexual repression that it engenders culminate in the domination of nature in Instrumental but not pre-Instrumental cultures. Under what conditions, in short, is an internally aggressive death instinct transformed into an externally aggressive death instinct, under what conditions is the violence that it does to the human body directed outward to the "body" of nature?

In order to answer this question we must, according to Brown, probe more deeply into the human experience of death, an experience that begins with infancy.[76] Long before the individual is old enough consciously to grasp his or her mortality, he or she experiences unconsciously the psychic equivalent of death in the form of the mother's absence; the enforced and regular separations that the separate human being who is the mother necessarily imposes on the needy, helpless, and demanding infant dictate that the latter daily experiences death, i.e., the traumatic loss of the life on which its own life depends. And, if death means separation from the mother, then the human being's inability to accept death means, above all, the "human infant's incapacity to accept separation from the mother."[77] The adult's pathological stance toward death is thus rooted in the child's pathological stance toward its mother. It follows that the different (pre-Instrumental as compared to Instrumental) manifestations of this stance toward death are a function of different forms of this stance toward the mother.

There are, according to Brown, two different modes of denying death that correspond to two different modes of denying the separation from the mother. The first, or "primitive," mode symbolically annuls the possibility of death by effectively and unconsciously preventing the separation from the mother from ever permanently taking place. The "primitive" infant, like any other, resents the recurrent separations from the mother's breast and other loving, nurturing parts of her body that it is obliged to suffer; like the "modern" infant, then, its emotions necessarily involve a mixture of love and hatred for its mother. Unlike the "modern" child, however, the "primitive" child resolves this ambivalence through identification with the mother; its uncon-

[76] Or even with birth, according to Rank's theory of the birth trauma. But Brown generally follows Freud in emphasizing the significance of subsequent separations from the mother rather than the initial one.

[77] Brown, *Life Against Death*, pp. 115, 284.

scious guilt for hating the one whom it loves so much is expiated through the unconscious creation of a mother to whom one must give, to whom one is indebted. This psychic affirmation of dependence on the mother, in turn, is translated into the symbolization of nature as a loving, nuturing mother to whom one must give gifts, to whom sacrifices are to be made. The conscious relationship of dependence on nature that is characteristic of the pre-Instrumental mode of symbolization is thus rooted in the child's unconscious relationship of dependence on a "perfect" mother. This unconscious unity with the mother effectively eliminates the possibility of any permanently experienced separation from her; the "primitive" overcomes death through a psychic intimacy with the mother that is purchased, according to Brown, at the price of the loss of any possibility of the development of an autonomous self.

This affirmation of dependence on the mother is paralleled by the primitive's affirmation of dependence on tradition; the primitive tries to annul the passage of time and thus the separation from his or her ancestral origins just as he or she tries to cancel the separation from his or her mother. Citing Mercia Eliade's work on the difference between primitive and modern consciousness of time, Brown emphasizes the way in which primitive cultures function to negate history, to preclude the possibility of anything fundamentally new and different from ever occurring. "Archaic man," according to Eliade, "acknowledges no act which has not been previously posited and lived by someone else. . . . What he does has been done before. His life is the ceaseless repetition of gestures initiated by others." Potential threats to this "ceaseless repetition," moreover, such as a change in the calendar year, are typically accompanied by rituals that invoke the mythical origins of the primitive's tribe.[78] Thus every new year he or she is every bit as close to his or her ancestral origins as the previous year. Living in an eternal present, or what, from the perspective of "our" time consciousness would be described as living in the past, "archaic man conquers death by living the life of his dead ancestors."[79] Primitive societies are (in Levi-Strauss's phrase) "societies without history" because the denial of history—of the separation from origins in the form of a novel, creative event—is the way in which their members deny the existence of death.

The denial of death takes a radically different form in modern, Instrumental cultures. Like the primitive infant, the modern infant is unable to tolerate the enforced separations from the mother that it suffers and thus bitterly resents the very being on which it depends. Unlike its predecessor, however, the child of our culture resolves the guilt that accompanies hostility directed toward the loved mother by denying rather than affirming its dependence on

[78] *The Myth of the Eternal Return* (New York: Pantheon Books, 1954), p. 5 and Ch. 2.
[79] Brown, *Life Against Death*, p. 286.

296

her; not identification with the mother, but identification with the father, is the principal detour taken by the already perverted death instinct in modern, Instrumental cultures.[80] This detour enables the child unconsciously to deny that the mother matters; through identification with the adult who is of the opposite sex of the mother, the child develops a self whose autonomy is purchased at the price of the repression of any conscious feelings of dependence on the mother. If the primitive child expresses its incapacity to accept "deathly" separation from the mother through the denial that this separation has ever taken place, the modern child expresses its inability to tolerate this separation through the denial that this separation was painful. If the former resolves its mixture of love and hatred toward the mother in favor of love, the latter resolves its ambivalent feeling in favor of hate: "identification with the father involves a transformation of guilt into aggression."[81]

This aggression toward the mother, combined with the hostility that the modern individual (like the primitive) feels toward his or her mortal body, is the basis for the extroversion of the death instinct in the form of aggression toward nature. Whereas the primitive represses all hostility toward the mother, modern man sublimates this hostility, redirecting it toward the natural world in the form of a controlling, domineering, i.e., objectifying, stance toward this world. More precisely, according to Brown, the modern child unconsciously projects both his or her hated, stunted, "dead" body and his or her hated, dreaded mother onto nature; resentment toward the body and resentment toward the mother combine to produce resentment toward a nature that becomes the unconscious representative of the mother's body.[82] The child's unconscious denial of dependence on the mother is thus reproduced in the form of the adult's compulsion to overcome "embeddedness" in, or dependence on, the natural world; infantile rage in the face of the independent will of the mother culminates in the "adult" drive to annul the independence of, i.e., to dominate, nature. The mother that does not matter reappears in the form of a nature that is reduced to mere matter. Matter, moreover, that is the object of sadistic impulses that are merely the projection of the ma-

---

[80] *Ibid.*, p. 280.

[81] *Ibid.* Brown does not explain why the fear of separation from the mother takes the form of identification with the mother in one culture and identification with the father in the other. In order to do so, it would be necessary to examine the differences in mother-child interactions in primitive as compared to modern societies and the way these differences are conditioned by different family structures. I will examine this problem in the next chapter.

[82] Brown tends to place greater emphasis on hatred of the body than hatred of the mother in his account of the aggressive extroversion of the death instinct. This relative lack of emphasis on the latter cannot, however, be squared with his own understanding that unconscious antibody attitudes exist, but do not produce antinature attitudes, in primitive societies. My own formulation above, then, is already something of a correction and reformulation of Brown, one that anticipates the analysis of Dorothy Dinnerstein in the next chapter.

297

sochistic impulses of a human being burdened by guilt and hatred of his or her body. Objectification is thus a collective neurosis; an Instrumental culture is a sadomasochistic culture.

The time-consciousness of this culture is neurotic as well. The denial of dependence on the mother is paralleled by a denial of dependence on tradition, on the past. In contrast to the primitive who denies death through an identification with origins that effectively negates history, the modern human being denies death through a commitment to make history that is simultaneously a compulsion to obliterate his or her origins. Modern man, in short, is an historical being who constitutes himself through labor and thus denies his dependence on his predecessors. What do Marx's extraordinary claims that "labor is the basis of the whole sensuous world as it now exists" and that "the *entire . . . history of the world* is nothing but the begetting of man through human labor"[83] imply if not the unconscious denial of dependence on one's parents, (what Brown calls) the "child's project of becoming its own father,"[84] which should rather be called, to eliminate Brown's patriarchal lapse, the project of becoming one's own mother, i.e., the effort to become immortal, to become God? Does not the young Marx make this explicit when he defines Man as the "supreme divinity"?[85] Does not he, and the modern historical consciousness in general, attribute to human beings the very transcendent power that was formerly reserved for God alone?

The exercise of this power to transcend that which is, to surpass Being in favor of Becoming, demands a preoccupation with the future that necessarily denigrates the present. The objectifying individual, as we have seen, is the individual who elaborates a vision of a finished product, i.e., who imagines a future state, and then labors to bring it into existence. Unlike play (and remember that, according to Marx, labor cannot become play), labor demands that the individual transform the present into a mere means to the future. Quoting Keynes, Brown decries the time-consciousness of the " 'purposive' man [who] is always trying to secure a spurious and delusive immortality for his acts by pushing his interest in them forward into time."[86] The "progressive, continuous, irreversible" character of modern time, in short, is the time (consciousness) of the human being whose preoccupation with the future in the name of the (unconscious) drive to negate the past prevents him from living in, and enjoying, the present. "The war against death," Brown concludes, "takes the form of a preoccupation with the past and the future, and

[83] See above, n. 18 and Chapter One.
[84] Cited in Dorothy Dinnerstein, *The Mermaid and the Minotaur* (New York: Harper & Row, 1976), p. 137.
[85] Cited in Schmidt, *The Concept of Nature in Marx*, p. 39.
[86] Cited in Brown, *Life Against Death*, p. 107.

298

the present tense, the tense of life, is lost."[87] Thus does death exercise its dominion over the very life that wages war against it.

If Brown teaches us that an Instrumental mode of symbolization is rooted in a neurotic denial of death, his lesson is also that a post-Instrumental mode of symbolization can flower only in the soil of a healthy acceptance of death. Hegel was also aware of this, anticipating that in a post-Instrumental mode of symbolization the identification of the individual with a nature that outlives him or her would fundamentally alter this individual's consciousness of death so that he or she would come to understand, and accept, that "the nature of finite things as such is to have the seed of passing away as their essential being: the hour of their birth is the hour of their death."[88] Implied as well is a fundamentally different time-consciousness: it is not by accident that Hegel describes Absolute Knowledge as the end of history. But what Hegel was not, and could not be, aware of, since he lacked Freud's understanding of "the demands made upon the mind in consequence of its connection with the body,"[89] is that a transformation in the consciousness of death and time demands a transformation of an unconscious that is formed in a struggle between the demands of its mother and the demands of its body. Lacking any concept of the instinctual roots of the Instrumental mode of symbolization, Hegel likewise had no understanding of the instinctual transformation essential for the post-Instrumental mode of symbolization. Thus he was obliged to "spiritualize" the transition from one mode of symbolization to the other; he was convinced that individuals would only be able to accept death if they could accept the (notion of the) World Spirit. To put this another way, he saw no way that human subjects would be able to acknowledge the commonality they share with the other finite subjects of the world other than through the recognition that all finite subjects are vehicles for an infinite subject, because he could not envision a liberation of the human body that would enable human subjects to establish libidinal, eroticized relationships with the nonhuman subjects that surround them.

Brown, in contrast, recognizes that a transformed consciousness of death requires a transformed body and thus a transformed unconscious relationship with the mother. The individual who no longer denies death but comes to "see in the old adversary, a friend,"[90] can only be the individual strong enough to tolerate separation from the mother without having to resort either to an "over-dependent" identification with the mother or a "distancing" identification with the father. An end to the life-denying flight from death presupposes the elimination of the guilt that follows from resentment of the

[87] *Ibid.*, pp. 274, 284.
[88] Cited in Brown, *Life Against Death*, p. 104.
[89] Cited in *Ibid.*, p. 80.
[90] Brown, *Life Against Death*, p. 322.

299

mother and either the self-sacrificing (primitive) or the aggressive (modern) response that follows from this guilt. It demands as well the repudiation of hatred of the flesh, of one's own body, demands what Brown calls the "resurrection of the body." To embrace one's own mortality is to be able to affirm one's own flesh. A post-Instrumental relationship to death, and thus to nature, can only be based on a reversal of the genital organization with which "civilization" has stunted the sexuality of humanity and the emergence of an adult polymorphous perversity—the eroticization of the entire body— that has hitherto prevailed during infancy alone. Only the individual who truly loves his (and the other's) body can establish a loving but not self-abnegating, intimate yet autonomous, relationship with the body of nature.

The activity in which such a guilt-free, eroticized individual engages vis-à-vis nature "can only be called play."[91] Brown thereby implies, against Marx, that work *can* become play, that activity that has the consequence of sustaining the human being's "material" survival can become as spontaneous and joyful as the activity of *homo ludens*.[92] Thus the post-Instrumental individual will not be obliged to transform the present into a means to the future but will rather live fully in the present; unlike Marcuse, who holds on to the notion that, even in the ideal society, death will be "a necessity against which the unrepressed energy of mankind will . . . wage its greatest struggle"[93] and thereby fails to understand that the denial of death is incompatible with both "unrepressed energy" and an unrepressed time-consciousness, Brown grasps the inseparable connections among the acceptance of death, the celebration of the body, and the ability to live fully in the present.

These connections as well as the others established by Brown are summarized in Table 2, in which the relationship between humans and their mothers, their bodies, and their mortality is specified for the pre-Instrumental, Instrumental, and Post-Instrumental modes of symbolization. This specification of the unconscious, psychosexual bases of these three modes of symbolization complements Table 1's specification of the conscious relationship between humans and nature, their products and other human beings in these three modes. Taken together, the two tables conveniently summarize the distinctive logic of the totality of life in the pre-Instrumental, Instrumental, and post-Instrumental modes of symbolization.

[91] *Ibid.*, p. 307.

[92] I say "implies" because Brown is not entirely consistent on this point. His implicit support for the post-instrumental technology that Hegel anticipates is undermined by his tendency to define all sublimation as neurosis (p. 307) and all reason as repressive (p. 92), a tendency that would appear to establish the identity between human and non-human subjects at the cost of eliminating any difference between them. For a discussion of this problem see Dinnerstein, *The Mermaid and the Minotaur*, pp. 139-46.

[93] *Eros and Civilization*, p. 215.

TABLE 2

Mode of
Symbolization   *Object of Symbolization*

	Mother	Body	Death
Pre- *Instrumental*	Object of Identification	Repressed	Denied through Nullification of History
Instrumental	Object of Aggression	Repressed	Denied through Primacy of History
Post- *Instrumental*	?	"Resurrected"	Accepted

The great merit of the work of Norman O. Brown, then, is to have deepened dramatically our understanding of what is involved in the transformation from the Instrumental to the post-Instrumental mode of symbolization; this liberatory transformation, he teaches us, demands an acceptance of our mortality that presupposes, in turn, an ability to accept without guilt-producing resentment our early and inevitable separation from our mothers. The great weakness of Brown's analysis, however, is that he offers absolutely no insight into the conditions under which a toleration of this separation that is now apparently impossible will become possible and thus fails materially to ground his notion of a transformed, "accepting" stance toward death. He tells us that the cultural neurosis that is contemporary civilization "could [only] be abolished by an ego strong enough to die,"[94] but, in the absence of any discussion of the possibilities of a transformed relationship between mother and infant (thus the question mark in the relevant box in the table above), this appeal to a more courageous ego necessarily has the ring of a purely moral appeal that is likely to leave us wondering how this infant will ever be able to learn to tolerate a separation that is presently experienced as intolerable. At one point Brown argues that:

> [T]he acceptance of death, its reunification in consciousness with life, cannot be accomplished by the discipline of philosophy or the seduction of art, but only by the abolition of repression. . . . Only if Eros—the life instinct—can affirm the life of the body can the death instinct affirm death, and in affirming death magnify life.[95]

[94] Brown, *Life Against Death*, p. 113.
[95] *Ibid.*, p. 109.

But this reliance on the reversal of sexual repression as the condition for acceptance of death directly contradicts Brown's own argument that the denial of death is the cause of sexual repression in the first place. Thus he transforms into a cause of liberation what he earlier insists can only be the result of liberation; his argument moves in a circle, and at the end of it we are absolutely no closer than we were at the beginning to an answer to the question of the forces that militate in favor of the ability to face separation from the mother and thus to face death.

The logic of Brown's analysis points to the conclusion that this ability is contingent on a transformation of the mode of child rearing, but Brown fails to draw this conclusion and thus fails to explore this possibility. And the failure to explore this possibility yields a purely "idealist" overcoming of the Instrumental mode of symbolization. He moves us, even further than Hegel, in the direction of a transcendence of this mode of symbolization, but he does not and cannot take us all the way. The completion of this journey demands that we question, as Brown does not, the prevailing, gender-specific mode of child rearing that dictates that it is the mother who becomes *the* initial significant other of the child. The limits of Brown's vision, in short, are the limits of a thinker who calls everything into question but mother-monopolized child rearing. His silence on this question is the silence of someone who has thought his way beyond everything but patriarchy. The completion of our synthesis of Hegel and Freud, then, demands that we explode this limit and break this silence. Our Hegel-Freud synthesis, and thus our ability to think our way entirely beyond the Instrumental mode of symbolization, awaits its "feminization" at the hands of Dorothy Dinnerstein.

CHAPTER NINE

MOTHER-MONOPOLIZED CHILD REARING
AND THE INSTRUMENTAL MODE
OF SYMBOLIZATION

The preceding chapters have established the centrality of the mode of child rearing to the problem of domination. The character of the relationship between the adult self and its sexual, political, and "natural" others is decisively shaped by the character of the relationship established between the childhood self and its first and most salient, i.e., its parental, others. The structure of the struggle for recognition between the individual and his or her sexual, political, and "natural" partners, in other words, is anchored in and reproduced by the structure of the primordial, unconscious struggle for recognition that takes place between this individual and his or her parents. Thus psychoanalytic theory is essential for the comprehension of domination and its elimination. At the same time, however, we have seen that the emancipatory potential of psychoanalytic theory has been aborted by Freud's tendency to eternalize or universalize domination and thus by his failure even to envision a liberatory alternative. For Freud and those who follow him, patriarchy, the state, and the domination of nature are rooted in the structure of a childhood that is co-extensive with the very possibility of civilization itself. As we have also seen, it was precisely this assumption that led thinkers committed to human liberation to attempt to historicize Freud with the aid of Marx. Neo-Marxists have generally not questioned Freud's description of the childhood origins of sexual, political, and technological domination, but have instead assumed the accuracy of this description and merely attempted to establish its historical limits through a conceptual strategy that ultimately subordinates the problem of the form of childhood to the problem of the mode of production. But the argument of Part II demonstrated the failure of this strategy, and Chapter Eight revealed the historical limits to the assumption on which it is based. Our analysis to this point thus suggests that the solution to the problem of the construction of a satisfactory, critical psychoanalytic explanation of domination in its sexual, political, and technological dimensions demands a very different conceptual strategy.

I have, in fact, suggested at a number of points that the road to an adequate theory of the infantile origins of domination proceeds through a questioning of the accuracy, rather than a mere historicization, of Freud's description of these origins. At the end of Chapter Five I implied that a clearer illumination of the problem of patriarchy than the one that Freud and the Freudo-Marxists provide demands a psychoanalytic focus on the role of the mother in the struggle for recognition that is infantile and childhood development. Similarly, in Chapter Six I demonstrated that a coherent theory of political domination cannot be deduced from the assumption that the individual's acquiescence in or affirmation of authoritarian political structures merely reenacts the individual's early submission to the power of his or her father. Finally, in the last chapter I relied on Norman O. Brown in order to point to the connections between the problem of objectification, the domination of nature, and the problem of the inability to tolerate separation from the mother. In each of these cases I have intimated that Freud's virtually exclusive emphasis on the power of the father makes for a one-sided, inaccurate account of the initial struggle for recognition as well as the sexual, political, and technological struggles that follow it, and thus that this emphasis must, at the very least, be supplemented by an emphasis on the power of the mother. In this chapter I turn directly to this task, correcting Freud's patricentric account with the aid of those who have focused explicitly and centrally on the power of the mother over the formation of the self. This conceptual restoration of the salience of the mother in the earliest struggle for recognition, I shall demonstrate, makes possible a psychoanalytic explanation of domination in the adult struggles for sexual, political, and technological recognition that overcomes the limits of a psychoanalytic explanation that result from a neglect of her centrality. More specifically, I shall attempt to establish that what I have called the Instrumental mode of symbolization is rooted in a specific mode of mother-monopolized child rearing. This revision of the Freudian account of the childhood origins of domination, in turn, effectively uncovers what neither Freud nor the Freudo-Marxists could uncover, i.e., the way beyond domination. This way—the path to what I have called a post-Instrumental mode of symbolization—entails the elimination of *all* modes of mother-monopolized child rearing and the emergence of parenting that is shared equally between mother and father.

MOTHER-MONOPOLIZED CHILD REARING AND PATRIARCHY

In Chapter Five we saw that, for Freud, the domination of men over women is secured through the centrality of the father to the struggle over the formation of the identity of both male and female child. The formation of their identity is contingent on their submission to the Law of the Father; both male and female child are obliged unconsciously to acknowledge the privileged signifying function of the phallus and thus the woman comes to be recognized as the one who lacks what the man possesses, i.e., as the subordinate other of the man. Freud's theory of the childhood origins of patriarchy rests, then, on the assertion that the phallus must serve as the exclusive signifier of human power and thus that the father necessarily becomes *the* significant other of the child. But Freud is unable to buttress this assertion with anything other than remarkably unpersuasive appeals either to biology or mythology. Thus his theory of patriarchy ultimately stands or falls on an entirely unsubstantiated argument concerning the virtually exclusive salience of the father in the struggle for recognition of the identity of the child.

This argument flies in the face of an impressive array of evidence that establishes the centrality of the mother, rather than the father, to this struggle. Freud refuses to recognize this evidence; his exaggeration of the significance of the father is simultaneously a blindness to the overriding significance of the mother. The patricentric inflation of the power of the father is, in Freud, merely the other side of a coin whose face side is the denigration or even the denial of the power of the mother. Thus, although he is willing to acknowledge that the mother ''becomes [the child's] first love-object'' as well as ''its first protection against all the undefined and threatening dangers of the outer world . . . [its] first protection against anxiety,'' he nevertheless maintains that ''in this function [of protection] the mother is soon replaced by the stronger father, and this situation persists from now on over the whole of childhood.''[1] Similarly, despite his late appreciation of the significance of the ''preoedipal'' period—a discovery that he compares to the discovery of ''the Minoan-Mycenaen civilization behind the civilization of Greece''[2]—he continues to speak during the same period of his writing of ''the infant's helplessness and the longing for the father aroused by it'' and to insist that there is no need ''in childhood as strong as the need for a father's protection.''[3] Consequently he concentrates almost entirely on the power of the father and never even begins to develop a theory of the role of maternal power over children in the genesis of adult male domination over adult women. The result is not only an inadequate theory of patriarchy but also a patriarchal theory of patriarchy, one which participates in a celebration of male power that obscures the very maternal power that—as we shall see—gives rise to the need for this celebration in the first place.

[1] Sigmund Freud, *The Future of an Illusion* (New York: Livernight Publishing Corp., 1955), p. 41.

[2] Sigmund Freud, ''Female Sexuality,'' *Collected Papers*, Vol. V (London: Hogarth Press, 1950), p. 254.

[3] Cited in Long, Review of *Psychoanalysis and Feminism*, p. 186.

305

The insight that patriarchy or male domination over women is best grasped as a reaction-formation to the power exercised by the mother over the child has been developed by Dorothy Dinnerstein. Unlike Freud and his followers, Dinnerstein systematically explores the significance for adult relationships between the sexes of the fact that in all hitherto existing societies it is a woman rather than a man who is both the initial love-object and authority figure for the child, the being who simultaneously provides for and frustrates its emerging needs. It is, according to Dinnerstein, this universal dependence of children of both sexes on the mother that is ultimately responsible for the culturally universal male hatred of the female—what Freud considered "the normal male contempt for women"[4]—as well as the universality of the male-dominant practices that both reflect and reinforce this hatred. Woman becomes the subordinate other of man, in short, because a woman is the first and by far the most significant other on whom children of both sexes come to depend, and against whom they are obliged to struggle, for the formation of their selfhood.

But why should this be the case? Why should the consequence of mother-monopolized child rearing be the ideology and practice of male supremacy? Why should mother-raised men develop a profound stake in the subordination of women and mother-raised women develop an equally compelling need to acquiesce in this subordination? The answer to this question, according to Dinnerstein, lies in the differential way in which male as compared to female children experience and thus react to the "immense unilateral power" of the mother "during the period when [both children] need feeding, carrying, cleaning, shelter."[5] Both children, of course, are equally and critically dependent for their subsequent development on the relationship that they establish with their mother. On the one hand, it is their mother on whom they are dependent for the satisfaction of their imperious needs; it is she who feeds them when they are hungry, rocks them when they are cranky, caresses them when they need to be touched. It is the mother, in other words, who provides the early nurturance without which the helpless, demanding infant would be utterly unable to develop into a human being; "primary identification" with the nurturing mother is the absolutely indispensable first step toward the development of the human identity of the child.[6]

[4] Ruth Mack Brunswick, "The Preoedipal Phase of the Libido Development," in Robert Fliess, ed., *The Psychoanalytic Reader* (New York: International Universities Press, 1948), p. 246. This essay was the fruit of Brunswick's collaboration with Freud and is described by the editor as "an indirect although posthumous, statement of some of Freud's opinions on the subject" (p. 231).

[5] Dinnerstein, *The Mermaid and the Minotaur*, p. 242.

[6] For the significance of this nurturance to the "normal" development of the child, see, among others, Ashley Montagu, *Touching: The Human Significance of the Skin* (New York: Columbia University Press, 1971); René Spitz, *The First Year of Life* (New York: International Universities

On the other hand, it is also the mother who frustrates the needs of "his majesty the baby." The breast that is given is also the breast that can be, and is, taken away; the comforting presence of the one who cuddles and fondles can quickly give way to her dreaded absence. The person who protects the child from discomfort is also the person who wages war on the child's sphincters. The mother who encourages and nurtures the emerging will of the child is also, and necessarily, the mother who "is the will's first, overwhelming adversary."[7] Maternal frustration of the infant's needs is, in turn, as essential to its "humanization" as their satisfaction; "the infant achieves a differentiation of self only insofar as its expectations of primary love are frustrated."[8] The infant's capacity for individuation, in short, is contingent on his or her separation from the mother, and the perception of this separation is only enforced through the failure of the mother immediately and universally to respond to the beck and call of the infant. This means that the formation of the identity of the child is necessarily an extraordinarily painful process; the child becomes an "I" and, subsequently, a full-fledged self[9] only insofar as he or she discovers that the mother is "not-I," only insofar as he or she experiences repeated rejections at the hands of his or her primary love object, the very being whose attention and acceptance the infant most intensely and overwhelmingly desires. It follows that the dialectic of identification-separation-individuation that characterizes the mother-child relationship will generate intense resentment in the child toward the mother it wants to, but cannot, monopolize.

The "preoedipal" relationship between mother and infant of either sex, then, necessarily produces a child whose development will be accompanied by a profound emotional ambivalence vis-à-vis the mother. The identification with the mother that is essential to the first stage in the process of individual development must be at least partly suppressed if the individuation essential to the second stage of this process is to occur. And the suppression of this identification inevitably engenders hostility toward the agent of this suppression, namely the mother. Thus the mother who is loved is also the mother who is hated. As we shall see, this emotionally charged, intensely ambivalent relationship to the mother will continue to reverberate throughout the adult lives of the men and women who have experienced it.

The precise nature of this relationship, however, and thus of its subsequent reverberations, differs according to the sex of the child. Both the length and

---

Press, Inc., 1965); Margaret S. Mahler, *On Human Symbiosis and the Vicissitudes of Individuation* (New York: International Universities Press, Inc., 1968).

[7] Dinnerstein, *The Mermaid and the Minotaur*, p. 166.

[8] Chodorow, *The Reproduction of Mothering*, p. 69.

[9] For this distinction, see René Spitz, *No and Yes* (New York: International Universities Press, Inc., 1957), Ch. 12.

quality of the preoedipal dialectic of identification-separation-individuation are different for girls as compared to boys. More specifically, and as Chodorow emphasizes, the identification stage is likely to be longer, and the separation-individuation stage less clear-cut, for the "preoedipal" girl than the "preoedipal" boy.[10] On the one hand, mothers themselves "tend not to experience . . . infant daughters as separate from them in the same way as do mothers of infant sons"[11] and thus can be expected to prolong the period of symbiosis with their daughters beyond the point that it persists with their sons. Thus the hostility that the girl child necessarily comes to feel toward the mother is muted by a persistent, enduring primary attachment to her in a way that the hostility of the male child is not. For the male child, moreover, "masculinity and sexual difference ('oedipal' issues) become intertwined with separation-individuation ('preoedipal' issues) almost from the beginning";[12] whereas primary identification with the mother is the source of the female child's recognition that she, too, is a "woman," this identification with the mother is an obstacle that must be overcome if the male child is to become a "man."[13] The demands of "masculine" in contrast to "feminine" development thus dictate that the imperatives of individuation, of defining oneself in opposition to the mother, will be reinforced dramatically by the need of the male child to suppress the "female" within him. This means that the separation of the male child from his mother is likely to be both more extreme and more painful than that which the female child experiences. Consequently his fear and loathing of the mother will be more intense as well.

These differences between the male and female child's preoedipal relationship with the mother are reflected in the difference in the relationship they come to establish with the father during the oedipal stage of their development. The boy, having already achieved a large measure of individuation vis-à-vis the mother, seizes the opportunity of identification with the father in order to consolidate further his independence from her. Solidarity with one's own sex is the male child's vehicle for loosening whatever preoedipal ties remain that bind him to his mother; this solidarity, in turn, is the emotional basis for the "male bonding" in which he will later engage. Because the father is a distant, often-absent figure, the identification that the male child

---

[10] Chodorow, *The Reproduction of Mothering*, pp. 99-110, 166-67.

[11] *Ibid.*, p. 109.

[12] *Ibid.*, p. 106.

[13] For more on the preoedipal roots of femaleness as passive "being" and maleness as active "becoming," see Chodorow, "Being and Doing: A Cross-Cultural Examination of the Socialization of Males and Females," in Vivian Gornick and Barbara K. Moran, eds., *Women in Sexist Society: Studies in Power and Powerlessness* (New York: Basic Books, 1971), pp. 173-97.

establishes with him is "positional," rather than "personal";[14] the male child identifies only with the abstract role that the father fulfills in the world and thus does not transfer his preoedipal love from his mother to him. The result, as Dinnerstein emphasizes, is that the male child retains his ambivalent relationship to his mother and that, "if woman is to remain for him the central human object of the passions most deeply rooted in life's beginnings, his relation to her must embrace . . . *both* the worshipful and the derogatory, the grateful and the greedy, the affectionate and the hostile feeling toward the early mother."[15]

It is otherwise for the girl. She takes the occasion of identification with the father as an opportunity to begin to separate herself from the lengthy and intense preoedipal relationship she has established with her mother. Because this relationship is so overwhelming, she can only justify her rejection of her mother and her "turn" to her father by "shifting a substantial portion of the magical good [feelings toward the first parent] onto the second, so that her love for the opposite sex comes to be infused with the infant's grateful passion toward the mother while most of the hostile, derogatory attitudes remain attached to their original object."[16] Thus for the girl, as well as for the boy, identification with paternal authority is both a reaction to and a refuge from maternal authority; the Law of the Father is a welcome shelter from the power of the mother.[17] But the father to whose authority the girl, in contrast to the boy, submits is an over-idealized father who becomes the repository of all the magically good feelings that were previously directed to the mother. This means that the outcome of the girl's oedipal stage prepares her emotionally to idealize the men with whom she will subsequently be involved in sexual relationships; it leads her to establish a "worshipful, dependent stance"[18] toward the very beings who, as we shall see, have developed a profound emotional stake in her subordination. At the same time, moreover, the fact the girl's turn to the father, in contrast to that of the boy, entails a rupture of solidarity with the parent of the same sex encourages subsequent rivalry

[14] Philip E. Slater, "Toward a Dualistic Theory of Identification," *Merril-Palmer Quarterly of Behavior and Development* Vol. 7 (April, 1961), pp. 113-26.

[15] Dinnerstein, *The Mermaid and the Minotaur*, p. 69, emphasis in the original.

[16] *Ibid.*, p. 69; see also Chodorow, *The Reproduction of Mothering*, p. 123.

[17] This explanation goes a long way toward remedying the self-acknowledged deficiencies of Freud's account of this phenomenon. Whereas "identification with the aggressor" and "penis envy" are, respectively, dubious explanations for the turn of the boy and the girl toward the father, this turn becomes comprehensible when conceptualized as an escape from the power of the mother. Dinnerstein's theoretical restoration of the salience of the mother thus enables us to dispense with two of the more problematical concepts in the psychoanalytical arsenal. See above, Chapters Five and Six, as well as Chodorow, *The Reproduction of Mothering*, pp. 119-25.

[18] Dinnerstein, *The Mermaid and the Minotaur*, p. 53.

among adult women and militates against the possibility of "sisterly" collective resistance to their subordination.[19]

The different way in which male and female children experience mother-monopolized child rearing thus prepares the emotional ground for the domination of men over women. By the time that they are ready to engage in heterosexual relationships, both men and women are willing and able to play their complementary roles in an asymmetrical drama in which the woman becomes the subordinate other of the man. The man's adult relationship with his female partner evokes his relationship with his mother, and thus reproduces all the terror and hostility that the latter engendered. The woman represents for him the dreaded specter of the power of the mother, a power from which he has spent the better part of his emotional life trying to escape; the power of the woman must therefore be constrained—she must be kept in her place— lest she reestablish the maternal tyranny that the man experienced as an infant. To put this another way, the man is obliged to attempt to infantalize the woman—to treat her like a dependent child—in order to deal with his fears of infantilization at the hands of a powerful, autonomous woman. This infantilization of the woman is manifested in the culturally universal tendency to exclude women from political and technological arenas that are largely monopolized by men. At the same time, the male bonding that characterizes these disproportionately male preserves enables men both to minimize and mask their emotional dependence on women and to establish the "cool," distant relationships with them that allow men to be, or at least to feel, "in control."

The woman, in turn, and as I have already suggested, is psychologically prepared to acquiesce in her own domination. Having projected her "positive" dependency needs onto her father, she is ready to transfer these needs to the man who comes to take his symbolic place. Having learned from her prolonged preoedipal relationship with her mother to value interpersonal relationships rather than world-shaping enterprise,[20] the woman is emotionally inclined to accept her exclusion from the "public" world and to concentrate her energies on mothering both her biological child and her man-child, whose fear and loathing of infantilization at her hands does not entirely eliminate his need to be taken care of by a woman. Finally, the tendency toward interfemale hostility and competition engendered by the girl's turn from the mother precludes even the woman who does come to resent her dependency and chafe

---

[19] Insofar as the girl's profound preoedipal ties with the mother are never entirely severed, however, there remains a childhood basis for adult female solidarity. On the persistence of these ties throughout the girl's oedipal period, see Chodorow, *The Reproduction of Mothering*, pp. 125-29.

[20] Dinnerstein, *The Mermaid and the Minotaur*, pp. 211-14; Chodorow, *The Reproduction of Mothering*, pp. 169-70.

under male-imposed restrictions from easily experiencing that solidarity with her oppressed "sisters" which is the *sine qua non* of a collective rebellion against her domination.

Dinnerstein's psychoanalytic explanation of male domination is far more compelling than that of Freud, illuminating a critical aspect of this domination for which Freud could not account. According to Freud, the subordination of women is a function of their lack of what men possess; the male child perceives the female as castrated and therefore inferior. This explanation, however, cannot account for the universal hatred of women that permeates male-dominated culture: if women are merely weak, inferior beings we should not expect that men would have any reason to fear them. But, as we have seen, it is precisely the fear of women that generates the energy that men have so assiduously expended in an effort to secure their subordination.[21] Freud is never able to explain why men fear women and thus never able to clarify the emotional underpinnings of active, intentional efforts on the part of men to keep them in their place. What Freud obscures, Dinnerstein illuminates: the dread of women derives from the submission to and reaction against the power of the mother that necessarily characterizes the experience of all children under conditions of mother-monopolized child rearing.

At the same time, Dinnerstein's approach, in contrast to that of Freud, has the merit of conceptualizing male domination as a culturally determined and therefore transcendable phenomenon. Whereas Freud takes recourse to biological and mythological determinism in an effort to demonstrate that patriarchy is coeval with the possibility of civilization itself, Dinnerstein's derivation of patriarchy from mother-monopolized child rearing makes it possible to envision a nonpatriarchal civilization of the future. Although mother-monopolized child rearing *may* have originally followed "naturally" from the biological fact that the mother is the bearer of the child—repeated pregnancies and the virtually uninterrupted necessity of nursing one child after another may have made it impossible for the "primitive" women to participate in the hunting essential for the survival of their society—the division of labor that assigns child-rearing responsibilities exclusively or even disproportionately to women has long since ceased to be biologically determined.[22] Mother-monopolized child rearing, in short, is a culturally rather than physiologically imposed phenomenon, as is, therefore, the patriarchal relations between the sexes that is its inevitable consequence. It follows that the transcendence of mother-monopolized child rearing and the emergence of parenting that is shared equally between mother and father entails the elimination of the psy-

[21] Long, *Review of Psychoanalysis and Feminism*, p. 186.

[22] Dinnerstein, *The Mermaid and the Minotaur*, Ch. 2, and Chodorow, *The Reproduction of Mothering*, Ch. 2.

chological basis of male domination and the emergence of a psychological basis for genuinely egalitarian, reciprocal relations between the sexes.

More specifically, Dinnerstein suggests that when men and women come to participate equally in nurturance, in both meeting and frustrating the earliest demands of their infants, then women will no longer be the exclusive initial love-object of the infant and thus will no longer bear the brunt of the hostility it directs toward those who frustrate its primary needs. Under conditions of shared parenting, both mother and father will be primary love-objects of the child and both father and mother will be the recipients of the resentment it necessarily develops as a result of the inevitably painful process of separation-individuation that it must undergo. When mother and father are both equally loved and equally feared, then it will be possible for women "to stop serving as scapegoats . . . for human resentment of the human condition"[23]—and for men to cease serving as idealized refuges against maternal power—and for both women and men, for the first time to face up to, and accept, the inescapably painful character of this condition. Having truly grown up, men will no longer need to dominate women and women will no longer need to acquiesce in this domination.

The elimination of the asymmetries between the male and female child's preoedipal and oedipal experiences also entails the elimination of the psychological basis of the division of labor that has hitherto prevailed between women and men. Once the father joins the mother as an early caretaker of the male child, this child will now experience a primary identification with a parent of *his* sex; the formation of his masculine identity will therefore no longer demand the complete suppression of his primary identification and the assumption of an exclusively oppositional stance toward his first love-object. Under these conditions, boys can be expected to grow up far more "relationally-oriented" than they are under mother-monopolized child rearing. At the same time, once the mother is no longer the only original love-object of the female child, the girl's fusion with the mother will no longer be nearly so encompassing, and thus her predisposition to "lose herself" in interpersonal relationships is likely to give way to an enhanced sense of her own independence. The men and women who emerge from shared parenting, then, will be equally prepared emotionally for both the "public" world of "enterprise" and the "private" world of interpersonal relations and will therefore be able to establish relationships with each other in which intimacy and autonomy go hand in hand. Shared parenting thus holds the key to the liberation of the relations between the sexes.

If shared parenting is the basis for the liberatory transformation of the relationship between women and men, then a satisfactory theory of this trans-

---

[23] Dinnerstein, *The Mermaid and the Minotaur*, p. 234.

formation entails the clarification of the forces that militate in favor of shared parenting. At this point Dinnerstein's otherwise extraordinarily insightful analysis begins to falter. At the conclusion of this analysis she does attempt to locate the origins of the contemporary feminist movement of which her book is an expression and to which it is a contribution. She begins by arguing that there are "stresses" inherent in the patriarchal gender arrangements and that "these stresses . . . generate the tensions that move it to a new stage of development." The inadequacies of the very "solution" that male domination constitutes to the problem of early maternal power "force us into an effort . . . to outgrow it";[24] the "solution" ultimately leaves both men and women dissatisfied with their restrictive, partial roles and engenders pressure for their expansion and re-integration. But Dinnerstein ultimately fails to clarify the source of this dissatisfaction. At times she seems to assume the existence of a "growth process" inherent in the human species, but this assumption, however justifiable, in no way accounts for why dissatisfaction with existing gender arrangements has emerged now, rather than at some other time. Perhaps aware of this problem, Dinnerstein goes on to argue that these gender arrangements have become particularly untenable in the light of the contemporary ecological crisis for which, she argues (as we shall see below), they are ultimately responsible. She herself undermines the power of this explanation, however, when she acknowledges that "many of the people who are focally aware" of this crisis "fail to see that it has anything at all to do with our gender arrangements."[25]

Having failed thus far to explain the emergence of the contemporary feminist movement, Dinnerstein proceeds to locate its origins in the countercultural, New Left activism of the past two decades and the experiences of the disproportionately leftish parents who spawned this activist generation. Traumatized by the Holocaust and Hiroshima, these radical parents—mothers *and* fathers—retreated from the public, political arena into the private world of the family, diverting their considerable energies and sensibilities to the realm of interpersonal relations. Their male sons, not having experienced the depoliticizing traumas to which their parents were subjected, and thus anxious to assume their traditional place in the public world of "history making," were now in a position to project the "expressive," traditionally "feminine" concerns they had imbibed from their parents onto this public world. Thus "the personal is the political" became the watchword of this new generation of male leftists, a generation whose clothing, hairstyles, and mannerisms all symbolized their rejection of the traditional male, "instrumental" role. In short, New Left men began to politicize those needs that had traditionally

[24] *Ibid.*, pp. 251-52, 249.
[25] *Ibid.*, pp. 248, 255, 252-54.

been the central needs that women experienced and expressed within the confines of the family. At the same time, however, these men were unwilling and/or unable to give up their traditional male privilege, and expected that women would continue to play their subordinate and supportive role within a movement led by men that was rooted in sensibilities and dependent on talents that were disproportionately those of women! This combination of male usurpation of traditionally feminine themes and continued male domination of women, in turn, enraged women leftists, who sought collectively to deepen and transform the male-initiated assault on the sexual division of labor into a full-scale war against male privilege. Once the connections between male privilege and mother-monopolized child rearing began to be understood, this war came to include an attack on this latter institution and thus the demand for shared parenting. This demand, then, emerges as the final, and most essential element of a struggle undertaken by women who are no longer willing or able to acquiesce in their own subordination.[26]

There are two problems with this otherwise enlightening explanation. First, it neglects entirely, and thus fails to clarify, the problem of the specific changes in the mode of mother-monopolized child rearing that encouraged male children, who traditionally eschew "expressive" concerns, to embrace, and then politicize, these concerns as their own. Second, it likewise ignores the question of how—if at all—these changes have affected the willingness and/or ability of men to accede to the feminist demand for shared parenting. As Dinnerstein herself acknowledges, and Chodorow has demonstrated in far greater detail, mother-monopolized child rearing generally tends to produce women with "relational" capacities who are willing and able to "mother" and men whose "sense of self is separate"[27] and who therefore lack both the inclination and the ability to nurture another. In the absence, therefore, of an analysis of transformations in the form of child rearing that this generation of men have experienced, it is not at all clear whether even the best-intentioned of these men will have the emotional wherewithal to share the task that their sexual partners have urged them to undertake.[28] The two problems I have mentioned really boil down to one problem, namely the fact that Dinnerstein does not pose the problem of the specific form that mother-monopolized child rearing has assumed during the contemporary period and thus fails adequately to

[26] *Ibid.*, pp. 258-73 for the material on which this summary was based.

[27] Chodorow, *The Reproduction of Mothering*, p. 169 and *passim*.

[28] Nor is it clear whether women, notwithstanding their commitment to shared parenting, will be willing or able to tolerate equal male participation in a sphere of life which, after all, has been virtually the only sphere of life over which women have historically exercised more-or-less complete control, particularly in the light of a male incompetence in this sphere that will undoubtedly persist for some time to come. On this problem, see Diana Ehrensaft, "When Women and Men Mother," *Socialist Review*, No. 49 (January-February 1980), pp. 37-73.

illuminate the childhood origins of the contemporary struggle against patriarchy. I shall attempt to shed additional light on this question in the next, and final, chapter.

Dinnerstein's failure to pose the problem of the specific form of contemporary mother-monopolized child rearing is symptomatic of her more general tendency to eschew historical specificity in favor of an analysis of what is common to all forms of this heretofore culturally universal mode of child rearing. Her choice of this type of analysis, of course, accords perfectly well with her goal of explaining the common features of all hitherto existing patriarchal gender arrangements. But this type of analysis does not help us to comprehend what is unique about contemporary patriarchy and the child-rearing system that underlies and reproduces it, and thus it does not clarify the present possibilities for the elimination of patriarchy. This project demands, in contrast, that we develop at least the rudiments of a comparative, historical analysis of the varying modes of mother-monopolized child care and the differing forms of male domination that they engender.

We have seen that male domination is rooted in resentment toward the mother: the enforced separation from the primary love object that is essential for the child's individuation necessarily evokes the child's hatred of the very object with whom it so ardently wishes to, but cannot, remain united, and this hatred is subsequently directed against those who come to represent this object, i.e., all women. Insofar as hostility toward women results from the loss of the being with whom one has achieved identification, we should expect that the specific nature of this hostility will be a function both of the abruptness or completeness of that loss and the intensity and duration of this identification. A prolonged and intense identification with the mother followed by a radical more-or-less total break with her is likely to engender far more pain, and thus far more hostility, than an identification that is briefer or less profound and/or a separation which is less clear-cut or dramatic. It follows that cultures with modes of mother-monopolized child rearing that engender both intense identification with, and radical separation from, the mother should be more intensely misogynist than cultures whose mode of child-rearing produces either less extreme identification or less extreme separation, or both.

Factors Affecting the Intensity of Identification

Since the primary identification between infant and mother is a product of the gratification that the latter supplies to the former, the intensity of that identification should vary directly with the intensity of this gratification. The more indulgent the child-rearing practices of the mother, the more intense the identification between infant and mother should be: the identification of the child with a mother that consistently and warmly responds to its needs will

315

be deeper and more complete than the identification of the child with a mother who frustrates its needs by ignoring them and/or responding to them irregularly or inadequately. Thus cultures whose child-rearing practices encourage and sustain the oral, anal, and genital demands of the infant are likely to produce more intensely mother-identified children than cultures whose practices entail the suppression of the pleasures associated with these erotogenic zones. *Ceteris paribus*, breast feeding that is prolonged and/or "on demand" will engender closer identification than breast feeding that is abbreviated and/or "by schedule"; later and less severe toilet training will produce greater identification than training that begins earlier or is more severe; and tolerance of the infant's genital play will result in more intense identification than the repression thereof.[29] Similarly, child-rearing practices that satisfy the infant's generalized need for touching will foster more pronounced identification with the mother than those that fail to respond to the infant's demands for cutaneous contact.[30] Everything else being equal, we should expect that mothers who consistently carry, caress, and sleep in the same bed with their children will produce children who are more mother-identified than mothers who establish greater physical distance between themselves and their children. Finally, cultures with post-partum sexual taboos, separate residences for fathers, and other customs and institutions that discourage contact between the mother and her husband and between father and child are likely to encourage bonds of identification between mothers and children that are more intense than cultures that lack such institutions and customs.[31] The more the father is absent, the less we can expect that the "turn to the father" during the oedipal stage will attenuate the ties between mother and child that have developed during the preoedipal period.

All these considerations point to the conclusion that the identification between mothers and children is far more intense in most "primitive" and other "traditional" societies than in Western industrial societies. The available ethnographic evidence overwhelmingly indicates that child-rearing practices in primitive societies are generally far more indulgent than in ours; nursing lasts far longer (normally for two and sometimes even three or more years),

[29] Spitz, *The First Year of Life*; Montagu, *Touching*; John W. M. Whiting and Irvin L. Child, *Child Training and Personality* (New Haven, Conn.: Yale University Press, 1953); William N. Stephens, *The Family in Cross-Cultural Perspective* (New York: Holt, Rinehart and Winston, 1963).

[30] Spitz, *The First Year of Life*; Montagu, *Touching*.

[31] J.W.M. Whiting, R. Kluckhorn, and A. Anthony, "The Function of Male Initiation Ceremonies at Puberty," in Elanor E. Maccoby, T. M. Newcomb, and E. L. Hartley, eds., *Readings in Social Psychology* (New York: Holt, Rinehart and Winston, 1947); William N. Stephens, *The Oedipus Complex: Cross Cultural Evidence* (Glencoe, Ill.: The Free Press, 1962); Roger V. Burton and John W. Whiting, "The Absent Father and Cross-Sex Identity," *Merril-Palmer Quarterly of Behavior and Development*, Vol. 7 (April 1961), pp. 85-95.

316

toilet training is usually less harsh and begins later, and the child's genital play is normally far less repressed. Whereas Western child psychologists have long bemoaned the relative lack of cutaneous contact between Western mothers and their children, the primitive infant is rarely found who is not on the back, in the arms, or on the lap of his or her mother or mother-substitute. Finally, many primitive societies, particularly those with polygynous and/or matrilineal-matrilocal family structures, effectively exclude the father from any role whatsoever in early child rearing and generally minimize the contact between father and mother—and men and women generally—to a far greater extent than in Western industrial societies.[32] The inference which, as we saw in the last chapter, Norman O. Brown draws from his analysis of other aspects of primitive cultures, i.e., that these cultures are, by comparison with ours, characterized by a pronounced identification with the mother, is thus amply confirmed by ethnographies of their child-rearing practices.

On the other hand, the available evidence also suggests that the identification between mothers and children in advanced capitalist societies, although much less intense than in most primitive societies, is more pronounced than the identification characteristic of earlier "stages" of capitalist societies. Child-rearing practices in the United States, for example, have been far more indulgent since World War II than during the preceding half-century.[33] At the same time, although the father is by no means as isolated from child rearing and contact with the mother as the father in some rigidly sex-segregated primitive societies, growing geographical (and emotional) distance between workplace and home has undoubtedly contributed to the decline in his authority within the family and thus in his availability to serve as an object of

[32] Spitz, *The First Year of Life*; Montagu, *Touching*; Stephens, *The Family in Cross-Cultural Perspective*; Whiting and Child, *Child Training and Personality*; George Peter Murdock, *Social Structure* (New York: The Macmillan Co., 1949). For an exception to these generalizations, see Abram Kardiner, *The Psychological Frontiers of Society* (New York: Columbia University Press, 1945), Chs. 5-6.

[33] Spitz, *The First Year of Life*; Montagu, *Touching*. Even these relatively stricter, earlier capitalist child-rearing practices were, in certain respects, far more indulgent than practices that predominated in the precapitalist West. Under the old regime, urban mothers of all classes who could afford to do so regularly exiled their newborn infants to the care of wet-nurses for as long as two years. Many children never survived this exile; those that did returned home at two years of age to a mother with whom they had had absolutely no contact and from whom, therefore, they were utterly estranged. Under these circumstances we should expect that the identification between mothers and children was even lower than during the period of repressive child rearing under capitalism. For precapitalist child rearing in the West, see Stone, *The Family, Sex and Marriage in England, 1500-1800*; Poster, *Critical Theory of the Family*, Ch. 7; Lloyd DeMause, *The History of Childhood* (New York: The Psychohistory Press, 1974), Ch.1. There is no warrant, however, for Poster's claim that intense identification with parental figures is unique to the bourgeois nuclear family. This claim ignores entirely the evidence of even more intense mother-identification in primitive and other non-Western traditional societies.

317

identification that competes with the mother.[34] For both reasons, the theme of the seductive, "over-indulgent" mother has increasingly replaced that of the insufficiently nurturant mother as a common staple of contemporary cultural criticism.[35]

Factors Affecting the Radicalness of Separation

A number of different, although related, factors are likely to influence the abruptness or completeness with which the mother's attention is withdrawn from her mother-identified child and thus the intensity of the trauma that this enforced separation produces. Cultures in which women typically bear large numbers of children are more likely to be characterized by a radical separation between mother and any one of her children than cultures in which women's child-bearing responsibilities are more limited. Under the former circumstances, the arrival of each new child is likely to signal the onset of a dramatic diversion of the time and energy that the mother is willing and able to expend on the child who had previously monopolized her attention, whereas under the latter the mother is more likely to be able to effect a more gradual separation between herself and her child. Weaning is generally far more abrupt and thus far more traumatic in the former cultures than in the latter. The abrupt loss of the mother's breast in these societies, moreover, is often accompanied by an equally severe severance of other forms of physical contact with the mother. The birth of a new child often inaugurates a change in sleeping arrangements whereby the newborn infant usurps the place of the weaned child at the side of his or her mother. In those high-frequency childbearing societies in which "diffusion of nurturance" is high, i.e., where siblings and other kin are available to assume post-weaning child-care responsibilities, the loss of the mother's breast and bodily contact with her during the night is likely to be magnified by a dramatic decline in her physical presence during the day, far more dramatic than in those societies whose low diffusion of nurturance encourages or obliges the mother to assume the bulk of post-weaning child-care.[36] Thus, contrary to what one might expect, high diffusion of nurturance may well intensify the "separation anxiety" of the child by fostering a far more radical separation between the child and its special, irreplaceable other than would otherwise be possible.

[34] Max Horkheimer, "Authority and the Family," in *Critical Theory* (New York: Herder and Herder, 1972); Alexander Mitscherlich, *Society Without the Father* (New York: Schoken Books, 1970); Lasch, *The Culture of Narcissism*.

[35] Lasch, *The Culture of Narcissism*; Philip E. Slater, *The Pursuit of Loneliness* (Boston: Beacon Press, 1970), and *Earthwalk* (New York: Anchor Press, 1974).

[36] See Stephens, *The Family in Cross-Cultural Perspective*, and Yolanda Murphy and Robert Murphy, *Women of the Forest* (New York: Columbia University Press, 1974), pp. 168-70, for the ethnographic evidence on which this paragraph is based.

318

Low diffusion of nurturance is likely to be associated with a less radical separation for yet another important reason. Where the mother has virtually exclusive responsibility for raising the child, she can be expected to have a far greater "investment" in preserving and extending her symbiotic relationship to it than the mother whose intimate contact with any one child ends abruptly with the birth of another. This emotional investment is likely to discourage the mother from effecting a sharp separation from her child and may instead even encourage her to retard its individuation to the point where it lags well behind its "biologically predetermined maturation."[37] This tendency for "overinvested" mothers who cannot rely on substitute caretakers to prolong identification throughout the period of separation-individuation will be reinforced, of course, in those cultures where the number of children that any mother is likely to bear is low. Finally, the exclusion of mothers from "productive" labor can also be expected to foster maternal overinvestment and the attenuated separation that results from it, since it deprives mothers of any other creative outlets and encourages them to invest all their emotional energy in their child.

The foregoing discussion suggests that the separation of the child from the mother will generally be far less abrupt and far less radical in Western industrial than in primitive and other traditional societies. The increasing isolation of the contemporary nuclear family from any broader network of kinship relations engenders a diffusion of nurturance that is far more limited than that which exists in primitive and other preindustrial societies where siblings and other kin are typically enlisted for child-rearing duties. Sociologists from Parsons to Slater have underscored the "implosion" of the contemporary middle-class family, in which "no other adult woman has a role remotely similar to that of the mother" and the mother is thus likely to "overidentify" with her child.[38] This tendency toward overidentification is reinforced by birthrates that are low, by comparison to primitive and traditional societies, in contemporary industrial societies, and by the fact that child rearing and "housewifery" are the sole responsibilities for many women in the latter societies but never in the former. Thus the child's enforced separation from the body as well as from the generalized physical presence of the mother is far less radical and complete in Western industrial societies than in primitive cultures.[39]

If intense early identification with the mother and radical enforced sepa-

[37] Mahler, *On Human Symbiosis and the Vicissitudes of Individuation*, p. 235.

[38] Talcott Parsons, "The Kinship System of the Contemporary United States," in *Essays in Sociological Theory* (New York: The Free Press, 1958), p. 189; Slater, *The Pursuit of Loneliness* and *Earthwalk*. See also Stephens, *The Family in Cross-Cultural Perspective*, p. 366.

[39] Stephens, *The Family in Cross-Cultural Perspective*, Ch. 8; Beatrice B. Whiting, ed., *Six Cultures: Studies of Child Rearing* (New York: John Wiley and Sons, 1963).

319

ration from her combine to produce maximum hostility toward women, it follows that this hostility will be generally more evident and pronounced in primitive and traditional than in Western industrial societies. In the former societies the demands of "normal" masculine development dictate that the male child's rage provoked by his separation from his mother will be magnified dramatically by the imperative that he repress, at all costs, the considerable amount of femaleness that resides within him. The excruciatingly painful nature of this transition from female to male identification is evident in a variety of cultural practices designed to enforce it. Thus many primitive societies, especially those with long post-partum sex taboos and exclusive mother-child households, i.e., especially those in which the male child's mother-identification is likely to be most intense, oblige their adolescent boys to abandon their mother's household and take up residence elsewhere, either alone or in a "bachelor's hut."[40] Similarly, the cross-cultural frequency of primitive male initiation rites in which pubescent boys endure extreme forms of physical punishment in order to have their "manhood" affirmed, also varies directly with the frequency of mother-child households, post-partum sex taboos, and other institutions that encourage extreme forms of mother-identification on the part of the male child. As two students of male initiations suggest, these rites "serve psychologically to brainwash the primary feminine identity and to establish firmly the secondary male identity."[41] The precariousness of this task is reflected in the fact that primitive societies with exclusive mother-child households, extended post-partum sex-taboos, and male initiation rites are also likely to be characterized by extensive menstrual taboos and other restrictions on women that indicate the danger they are thought to pose to men.[42]

Margaret Mead also testifies to the relationship between child-rearing practices that foster the male child's identification with the mother, radical enforced separation from her, and the aggressiveness with which male dominance is asserted:

> What we find is that in those societies which have emphasized suckling, the most complementary relationship of all the bodily learning experience, there is the greatest symbolic preoccupation with the differentials between men and women. . . . When in addition male separateness from women has been developed into a strong institution, with a men's house

[40] Stephens, *The Oedipus Complex*, Ch. 9, and Whiting, *et al.*, "The Function of Male Initiation Ceremonies at Puberty."

[41] Burton and Whiting, "The Absent Father and Cross-Sex Identity," p. 90. See also Whiting, *et al.*, "The Function of Male Initiation Ceremonies at Puberty," and Stephens, *The Oedipus Complex*, Ch. 7.

[42] Stephens, *The Oedipus Complex*, Ch. 5; H. R. Hays, *The Dangerous Sex* (New York: G. P. Putnam's Sons, 1964), Ch. 4.

320

and male initiation ceremonies, then the whole system becomes an end-lessly reinforcing one, in which each generation of little boys grows up among women, identified with women, envying women, and then, to assert their endangered certainty of their manhood, isolate themselves from women. Their sons again grow up similarly focussed on women, similarly in need of over-compensatory ceremonial to rescue them-selves.[43]

This relationship between mother-identification, separation, and women-hat-ing is also confirmed by Slater's analysis of the Greek mother-son relationship during the Classical period. According to Slater, the extraordinarily misog-ynist nature of the Athenian culture of this period was a function of the overly intense identification formed between male children and their mothers in largely father-absent families and thus of the extraordinarily painful and pre-carious nature of the transition to male identification.[44]

The available evidence points convincingly to the conclusion, then, that woman-hating will be most virulent and culturally institutionalized in those societies in which intense identification with, is followed by extreme sepa-ration from, the mother. We should therefore not expect contemporary West-ern industrial societies to be as overtly and starkly misogynist as most primitive and traditional societies, since the former generally lack the intense mother-identification and/or radical separation from the mother that engenders max-imum fear and loathing of women. Having submitted neither to the intense and overextended dependence nor the extreme separation that characterizes the mother-son relationship in primitive cultures, men in contemporary in-dustrial societies will generally not need to express their independence from women in the extreme, segregated forms that this need assumes in those cultures. The masculinity of the modern man, like that of any other who has been exclusively woman-raised, derives from his unconscious need to deny his dependence on women. But it does not demand the extent of enforced separation from, and ritualized invocations of the inferiority of, women that the masculine development of his primitive counterpart demands, because his need to deny dependence on women is not as intense as the need of the more intensely mother-identified, more radically mother-separated, primitive. Rather this need will typically co-exist with a need for relationships—even friend-ships—with women, and will therefore tend to manifest itself in a pronounced tendency to maintain a controlling emotional distance within the context of ostensibly intimate heterosexual unions. Male domination under the Instru-

---

[43] *Male and Female* (New York: William Morrow & Co., 1949), p. 88. For another formulation of the same point, see Beatrice Whiting, "Sex Identity Conflict and Physical Violence: A Comparative Study," *American Anthropologist*, 67 (December 1965 Supp.), pp. 123-40.

[44] Philip E. Slater, *The Glory of Hera* (Boston: Beacon Press, 1968).

mental mode of symbolization, in short, is likely to be less overt and public, or, from another perspective, more devious and disguised, than it is under previous modes of symbolization. At the same time, however, the tendency of advanced capitalist, Instrumental modes of symbolization to adopt relatively more indulgent, as well as father-absent, modes of child rearing than those that prevailed during earlier capitalist periods may well mean that mother-identification has increased and that compensatory masculine denigration of women, while by no means as extreme as that which characterizes pre-Instrumental modes of symbolization, has likewise intensified. I shall return to a discussion of this transformation below.

MOTHER-MONOPOLIZED CHILD REARING AND POLITICAL DOMINATION

As we have seen, Freud's virtually exclusive preoccupation with the role of the father and his neglect of the centrality of the mother leads to a theory of political domination that is every bit as unsatisfactory as his theory of patriarchy. On the one hand, the assumption that support for authoritarian leaders and movements is but an expression of a longing for the father that is itself co-extensive with civilization transforms political domination into an immutable condition in the face of which resignation is the only realistic response. On the other hand, Freudo-Marxists like Reich, who were committed to rebellion rather than resignation but who also accepted Freud's assumption that acquiescence in political domination was, at bottom, rooted exclusively in a need for the domination of the father, were led to challenge Freud's equation of domination of the father and civilization in the name of the ultimately inadequate assumption that the structure of authority within the family is merely a function of the mode of production. At the same time, this unsuccessful Marxist effort to historicize Freud, since it did not embrace a challenge to his assumption that political domination is the domination of the father, entailed an uncritical acceptance of Freud's description of the dynamics of political domination that preserved all the ambiguities and inconsistencies of this description. Thus, for example, Reich's assumption that attachment to authoritarian leaders is a projection of a superego that is an introjection of the authority of the father could not, in the light of Freud's own arguments concerning the "undeveloped" feminine superego, account for the fact that the attachment of women to such leaders has often been equal to, or even greater than, that of men. Similarly, this assumption, we saw, is inconsistent with the persistence of political domination in advanced capitalist societies in which, there is good reason to believe, the authority of the father within the family has considerably decreased and thus the authoritarian personality with a highly developed superego is no longer likely to be the modal male personality type. In short, Reich's Freudian preoccupation with the power of the father leads him to develop a relatively powerless theory of political domination. Now that we, in contrast, have come to understand the power of the mother over childhood, we should be in a position to outline the essentials of a more powerful theory of the childhood origins of adult political domination.

Here, once again, Dinnerstein shows the way. As we have seen, it is the child's simultaneous (over)dependence on and resentment of the mother that is the decisive foundation for his or her subsequent development under conditions of mother-monopolized child rearing. Under these conditions, where need for oscillates with hatred of the mother, "male authority is bound to look like a reasonable refuge from female authority."[45] The turn to the "blameless"[46]—because uninvolved in the earliest frustrations imposed on the infant—father simultaneously enables both male and female child to repudiate the mother and thus gratify their hostile feelings toward her as well as to find a repository for their need for love and protection for which she was also initially responsible. "The father-image is a thin mask covering the image of the pre-oedipal mother";[47] paternal tyranny is both a continuation of, and a sanctuary from, the "tyranny" of the mother to which all mother-raised humans have originally been subjected.

If identification with the father is both the renewal and the rupture of the child's identification with the mother, then it follows that the identification with authoritarian political leaders and movements that is the exteriorization of this paternal identification must also be grasped as the inevitable consequence of the need for, and hatred of, the mother. On the one hand, the willingness, even longing, of adults to submit to authoritarian political protection is an expression of a continuing dependency on the mother that the turn to the father has displaced, permitted us to deny and thus prevented us from outgrowing.[48] On the other hand, support for (almost always male) political despotism continues that repudiation of the mother that began with the embrace of the despotism of the father. Thus the tendency to cede our sovereignty or subjectivity to a political subject (or subjects) in relation to whom we become objects is rooted in our profound, unconscious, and unreconciled ambivalence toward the first and most important subjectivity we experience in life, i.e., the subjectivity of the mother.

This restoration of the salience of the mother in the dynamics of political domination enables us to overcome the ambiguities and contradictions of the Freudian account of these dynamics that result from her neglect. To begin

---

[45] Dinnerstein, *The Mermaid and the Minotaur*, p. 175.

[46] *Ibid.*, p. 189.

[47] Cited in Norman O. Brown, *Love's Body* (New York: Random House, 1966), p. 77.

[48] Dinnerstein, *The Mermaid and the Minotaur*, pp. 188-89.

323

with, Dinnerstein's analysis enables us to understand, where Freud's and Reich's could not, the basis for women's, as well as men's, authoritarian political commitments. Whereas Freud's theory of the internalization of the authority of the father is predicated on the assumption of castration anxiety followed by identification with the (potential) aggressor, and thus leads to the conclusion that the (already castrated) girl-child's internalization of his authority will be far less pronounced or complete than that of the boy, Dinnerstein's theory of the internalization of paternal authority is based on the assumption of a need for and fear of maternal authority that is far more equal for both sexes and thus enables us to uncover, in contrast to Freud, the basis for both sexes' subsequent and generally equal authoritarian political commitments. Similarly, once we understand that it is the experience of maternal, rather than paternal, authority that is the ultimate source of acquiescence in and support for authoritarian politics, we no longer need to be perplexed by the fact that political domination persists in the face of a manifest decline in the authority of the father within the family. As long as mother-monopolized child rearing persists, Dinnerstein avers, the basis for an authoritarian reaction to the initial power of the mother will remain intact (even though, as we shall see below, the specific form of this reaction will be shaped by the changing nature and scope of the authority of the father).

Dinnerstein's analysis also overcomes the inadequacies of other psychoanalytically oriented theories of political domination that repudiate Reich's exclusive preoccupation with paternal authority but continue to ignore the role of the mother. For Marcuse, as we have seen, it is not the authority of the father but its decline that accounts for totalitarian political control: the absence of the father within the family precludes the child's formation of the strong ego-ideal, i.e., "positive" superego, that served as the basis for individual autonomy under early capitalism and leaves the individual directly exposed to the authoritarian socialization of the mass-media characteristic of late capitalism. But this account simultaneously obscures the basis for political authoritarianism in the nineteenth century and misjudges its contemporary origins. On the one hand, Marcuse's theory leads to the conclusion that there was no psychological basis for political domination prior to the emergence of contemporary capitalism and thus leaves us entirely in the dark as to why this domination did in fact exist. On the other hand, and in contrast to Reich, he correctly anticipates the persistence of political domination under late capitalism. But he can account for this persistence only by adopting the behavioristic thesis of direct societal socialization of the individual unmediated by any internalization of parental authority, a thesis which presumes that the "one-dimensional" tendencies he locates are already complete and thus pronounces as utopian the very protests he launches against them.[49]

---

[49] Herbert Marcuse, *One-Dimensional Man* (Boston: Beacon Press, 1964).

It is possible, however, to avoid this pessimistic, behavioristic conclusion once we understand, with the aid of Dinnerstein, that the conceptual either/or on which it is based—either socialization by the father or direct socialization by the society at large—is a Hobson's choice that obscures completely socialization by the mother and the political authoritarianism it engenders. If, in short, we want to conceptualize contemporary political domination in a manner that is both accurate and enables us to locate the sources of resistance to it, then we must transcend the patriarchal blindness to the early and overriding power of the mother that Marcuse shares with Freud and Reich and begin to illuminate the nature and political consequences of this power. Only then will we be able to avoid Marcuse's pure instinct theory of political liberation that is the other side of a coin whose face side is his purely behavioristic account of contemporary political domination. Having defined the social in such a way that it is exclusively a source of domination, Marcuse can only point to presocial instincts as the basis of liberation. But this reliance on the *deus ex machina* of "a biological foundation for socialism"[50] ignores the way in which what Freud called the "vicissitudes of the instincts" are socially formed, and formed through the infant's interactions with the mother in particular. Once we examine these interactions as the source of acquiescence in and resistance to political domination, we can avoid both the "instinctual" account of the origins of political liberation and the "one-dimensional" behavioristic theory of the origins of political domination to which it responds.[51] Thus we need not respond to the inadequacies of Marcuse's instinct-theory by abandoning—as does Erich Fromm—the analysis of the terrain of early parental fulfillment and frustration of infantile libidinal impulses as the foundation for an understanding of political domination and the possibilities for its supersession. To replace, as Fromm does, fear of the authority of the father with fear of freedom as the basis of authoritarian political commitments is to continue to fall victim to the patriarchal blind-spot of failing to acknowledge the power of the mother and thus to develop an utterly utopian analysis of the possibilities for political liberation. Political domination is not an escape from freedom anymore than it is merely a reaction to the power of the father; it is, rather, an escape from the "tyranny" of the mother. As such, political domination cannot be effectively combatted through characteristically Frommean appeals to increased courage and "faith in life and in truth, and in freedom" but rather only, in the last analysis, through an assault on mother-monopolized child rearing.[52] It is the failure of revolutionaries to launch this assault, then, that is ultimately responsible for the "element of self-defeat"

[50] Herbert Marcuse, *An Essay on Liberation* (Boston: Beacon Press, 1969), Ch. 1.

[51] After completing this chapter I discovered that a similar point is made by Morton Schoolman in his *The Imaginary Witness: The Critical Theory of Herbert Marcuse* (New York: The Free Press, 1980), Ch. 4, esp. pp. 185-86, and pp. 252-53.

[52] Erich Fromm, *Escape from Freedom* (New York: Avon Books, 1941), p. 303.

that, we saw in Chapter Six, Freud argues has been central to every "betrayed revolution."

Dinnerstein's theory has another decisive advantage over Marxist and Freudo-Marxist accounts of political domination: the focus on mother-monopolized child rearing as the source of political domination makes it possible to conceptualize this phenomenon as transcendable without having to take recourse to the conceptually inadequate and empirically unwarranted assumption that political domination is merely a function of particular modes of production. Chapter Three showed that Marx and Marxists are unable convincingly to link political domination directly to the mode of production, and in Chapter Six we observed that the Freudo-Marxist effort to link political domination indirectly to the mode of production through an analysis of the family that is ultimately subordinated to an analysis of the mode of production likewise proved abortive. Dinnerstein's analysis, in contrast, enables us to grasp political domination as a phenomenon that transcends particular modes of production precisely because it is rooted in a situation, namely mother-monopolized child rearing, that has been culturally universal.

Her analysis thus sustains the traditional anarchist critique of Marxism as an economistic, reductionist, and therefore politically dangerous theory of political domination, and complements the anarchist emphasis on the irreducibility of political relations to production relations and the consequent centrality of the struggle against authoritarian political relations within any genuinely revolutionary transformation. At the same time, Dinnerstein's focus on the unconscious basis of these relations in mother-monopolized child rearing overcomes the anarchists' self-acknowledged failure adequately to understand the psychological origins of these relations and the struggles against them. Lacking a psychoanalytically oriented account of politics, anarchists have typically oscillated between the crude assumption of an innate power-drive as an explanation for political domination and an equally crude, and contradictory, assumption of an impulse toward liberty as an explanation of the struggles to overcome it.[53] Having failed to uncover the concrete psychological bases of political domination, the anarchist analysis of the prospects for political liberation is typically every bit as abstract and utopian as the Marxist and Freudo-Marxist analyses we have already dismissed. The same is true for contemporary "libertarian socialist" or "revolutionary councilist" analyses, such as that of Albert and Hahnel, which insist on the relative autonomy of authority relations from (economically defined) class relations— which insist that they develop a "kind of force of their own"[54]—but are unable to specify the origins of this force and thus to clarify the conditions for its elimination.

[53] C. George Benello, "Anarchism and Marxism: A Confrontation of Traditions," in Howard J. Ehrlich, et al., *Reinventing Anarchy* (London: Routledge & Kegan Paul, 1979), pp. 156-71.
[54] Albert and Hahnel, *Unorthodox Marxism*, p. 185. See also p. 210.

326

What Dinnerstein makes clear, in contrast to the anarchists and libertarian socialists, is that political domination is rooted in mother-monopolized child rearing and the unconscious needs that develop therefrom, and that the struggle against political domination must therefore embrace a struggle against mother-monopolized child rearing. Shared parenting is the necessary condition for political liberation. Under conditions of shared parenting, the mother will no longer become the universal scapegoat for the inevitable pain of the human condition and the father will no longer be the "blameless" source of identification that enables the child simultaneously to renew its overdependence and to punish the mother. At the same time, since the mother would be no longer available as an exclusive target for hate and the father no longer available for idealized identification, the child would have to come to grips with the inevitably painful aspects of the process of separation-individuation and to do what the present system of gender-relations enables it to evade, namely to grow up, "to outgrow the wish to be taken care of" and "face the ultimate necessity to take care of ourselves."[55] Shared parenting will eliminate the twin bases for political domination—overdependence on and hatred of the mother—and establish the psychological foundations for liberatory political arrangements.

Since Dinnerstein's analysis of political domination is a by-product of her analysis of patriarchy, we should not be surprised to find that the former is as much lacking in historical specificity as the latter. Nowhere in her work does she discuss the way different forms of political domination are related to different forms of mother-monopolized child rearing. Our analysis of the form that political domination assumes under the Instrumental mode of symbolization demands that we attempt to sketch out at least the bare outline of the comparative, historical analysis from which she abstains.

If "all interpersonal relations have their first origin in the mother-child relation,"[56] then we should be able to link the differing forms of political domination to the changing nature of this primordial relation. More specifically, if the state at least partly originates in the need of the still childish adult both to reaffirm and to repudiate his or her mother-dependency, then the features of the state should be shaped in important ways by the extent of the child's dependency on, and hatred of, his or her mother. Our comparative analysis of political domination, however, immediately confronts the apparent paradox that the very societies in which this love-hate relationship is most intense are societies in which political domination, conventionally understood, is generally absent. It is precisely the earliest primitive societies, where identification with the mother is most extreme and the separation from her most dramatic and productive of resentment, that are least likely to be characterized

[55] Dinnerstein, *The Mermaid and the Minotaur*, p. 189.
[56] Spitz, *The First Year of Life*, p. 296.

327

by authoritarian political structures. Indeed, these societies are generally without separate political structures altogether; either they lack distinct, permanent leadership positions or the incumbents of these positions are typically unwilling and/or unable to command and are obliged to rely on persuasion that may or may not be successful.[57] In both cases these are "egalitarian" societies in which the monopoly of legitimate coercion within a given territory that is associated with the existence of the state is entirely lacking.[58] In short, the existence of societies in which mother-dependence/resentment is intense that are nevertheless "segmentary" or "stateless" in character would appear to constitute an anomaly for our theory of political domination.

This anomaly dissolves, however, once we appreciate the extent to which the kinship structures of these societies typically perform the functions undertaken by the state in other forms of society. In primitive societies, "the articulation of most interpersonal relations . . . is an aspect of the kinship system."[59] Thus either the society is coextensive with a "political unit [that] embraces people all of whom are united to one another by ties of kinship, so that political relations are coterminous with kinship relations and the political structure and kinship organization are completely fused," or else the (somewhat larger) society is organized into "political" units composed of family clans or lineages.[60] In either case the societies are sufficiently small and their division of labor sufficiently simple that their cohesion or integration can be secured through the kinship system and does not demand the existence of a structurally separate political system.

In primitive societies, moreover, the kinship structure not only performs integrative political functions but also undertakes those political functions necessitated by mother-monopolized child rearing that likewise fall to the state in other forms of society. The male-dominated network of consanguinous ties in which the conjugal family is enmeshed in stateless societies[61] provides "compensation" for the early experience of female power. This network supplements the compensation offered by the father in those communities in which he lives with the mother and child and is the only compensation

---

[57] Clastres, *Society Against the State*; John Middleton and David Tait, eds., *Tribes Without Rulers* (London: Routledge & Kegan Paul, 1958). For exceptions to these generalizations, see Napoleon A. Chagnon, *Studying the Yanomamo* (New York: Holt, Rinehart & Winston, 1974), Ch. 5, and David Maybury-Lewis, *The Savage and the Innocent* (Cleveland and New York: World Publishing Co., 1965), Ch. 11.

[58] Morton H. Fried, *The Evolution of Political Society* (New York: Random House, 1967). The term "egalitarian" properly applies, as we have seen, only to relations among the men of these societies.

[59] Fried, *The Evolution of Political Society*, p. 120.

[60] M. Fortes and E. E. Evans-Pritchard, *African Political Systems* (London: Oxford University Press, 1940), pp. 6-7. Middleton and Tait, *Tribes Without Rulers*; Fried, *The Evolution of Political Society*.

[61] Stephens, *The Family in Cross-Cultural Perspective*, pp. 117, 322, 407.

available in those communities characterized by mother-child households from which the father is generally absent. In both forms of primitive community, identification with the authority of the male head of either the husband's or the wife's kin group enables the conjugal pair and their offspring simultaneously to reject their mothers and to reaffirm the dependency needs that their prolonged and intense identification with them has engendered. Identification with the living male leader of the clan or lineage is reinforced, moreover, by identification with the male ancestor in relation to whom all the members of a lineage establish their connections. Thus Norman O. Brown was correct to suggest a connection between ancestor worship and identification with the mother in primitive societies: the inability to tolerate death, i.e., separation from the mother, engenders a domination of the dead over the living that, together with the domination of the male kin leader, effectively serves as a sanctuary from the early female authority to which the living are subjected.

This analysis of the role of kinship in primitive societies leads to a modification in the formulation of the relationship between political domination and mother-monopolized child rearing: specifically political structures will serve as a refuge from maternal authority to the extent that kinship structures are unable exclusively to perform this function. This proposition appears to be confirmed by the emergence of the first historical form of the state, i.e., by the rise of kingdoms. Political anthropologists differ markedly about the reasons for its emergence, but all agree that the growth of the state is coeval with the decline of kinship as a source of societal cohesion.[62] The historical correlation between the dissolution of kinship ties and the rise of the state as the overriding societal organizing force is so massive that one political anthropologist recently incorporated this opposition between state and kinship into his very definition of the state itself: "a state is . . . the complex of institutions by means of which the power of society is organized on a basis superior to kinship."[63] Another expresses this opposition, somewhat more formally, with the proposition that "there is an inverse relationship in any society between the political aspect of kinship roles and the level of political role differentiation."[64] Fried, Stanley Diamond and Habermas all emphasize that the state's monopoly of legitimate coercion came, and could only have come, at the expense of the claims of the ties of blood.[65]

Anthropologists and historians also agree that the rise of kingship was

[62] Fried, *The Evolution of Political Society*; Elman R. Service, *Origins of the State and Civilization* (New York: Norton, 1975); S. Lee Seaton and Henri M. Claessen, *Political Anthropology: The State of the Art* (The Hague: Mouton Publishers, 1979).

[63] Fried, *The Evolution of Political Society*, p. 229.

[64] Aidab Southall, "Typology of States and Political Systems," in *Political Systems and the Distribution of Power* A.S.A. Monographs 2 (London: Tavistock Publications; New York: Frederick A. Praeger, 1965).

[65] Diamond, *In Search of the Primitive* (New Brunswick, N.J.: Transaction Books, 1974). Habermas, *Communication and the Evolution of Society*, pp. 162-63.

329

associated with a profound increase in the power of the father within the nuclear, conjugal family. Stephens reports a remarkably high, positive correlation between deference to paternal authority within the family and autocratic political rule: "nearly all the cases with extreme son-to-father and wife-to-husband deference represent groups and communities which are, or were until recently, parts of kingdoms."[66] Lawrence Stone has emphasized the mutually reinforcing relationship between the increasing centralization of state power and the increasingly authoritarian presence of the father in sixteenth- and seventeenth-century England.[67] Both imply that childhood identification with an increasingly powerful father is the psychological basis for the adult's subsequent support for a monarch who—good psychologist that he is—typically acts to solidify paternal authority within the family.

That both the monarchical state and the patriarchal nuclear family are born with, and contribute to, the ruin of the extended kinship system suggests that these two structures come to assume the political functions formerly performed exclusively by this system. On the one hand, the structural separation of political system from familial system initiates the performance of integrative political functions on the part of both of these systems. On the other hand, this separation also redistributes the repressive, mother-related political functions formerly concentrated within the kinship system to both the kinship system and the political system. Both the father and the state come to fill the psychological void that would otherwise exist due to the dramatic decline in the power of the male head of kin and male ancestor, i.e., both serve as refuges from a maternal relationship which, although it may no longer be quite as intensely ambivalent as in a primitive society, nevertheless continues to engender a profound mixture of love and hate.[68]

We should not be surprised, then, to discover that the decline of unrestrained monarchical authority and the emergence of the representative-democratic state form is linked historically to the decline of the untrammeled power of the father within the family. This link receives its clearest philosophical expression in the famous political argument between Filmer and Locke. Whereas Filmer based his defense of unlimited authority of the king on the analogy of unlimited paternal authority within the family, Locke rested his case for a limited, representative monarchy at least in part on the argument

[66] *The Family in Cross-Cultural Perspective*, p. 333.

[67] *The Family, Sex and Marriage in England: 1500-1800*, Ch. 6.

[68] On the one hand, there is some evidence that child-rearing practices in kingdoms are somewhat less indulgent than in primitive societies (Stephens, *The Family in Cross-Cultural Perspective*, p. 371), and that mother-identification is therefore likely to be less extreme as well. On the other hand, the increased presence of the father within the household increases his availability for "compensatory" identification and thus probably eases somewhat the pain of separation from the mother. For both reasons, the love-hate relationship with the mother is likely to be somewhat less intense in kingdoms than in primitive societies.

330

that paternal authority is properly both limited and temporary.[69] It was Locke, of course, whose philosophical thesis was to be confirmed by the subsequent turn of both familial and political events. Thus Stephens finds that son-to-father and wife-to-husband deference is generally much lower in Western "democratic" states than in kingdoms, and political scientists typically emphasize the fit or congruence between democratic political and democratic family forms.[70]

But why should this be the case? What underlies this twofold decline in authoritarianism? If, as our theory suggests, the degree of authoritarianism is a function of the intensity of the child's love/hate relationship with its mother, then the dramatic reduction in arbitrary authority in both family and state should be associated with a marked decline in the intensity of this relationship. Indeed, there is good reason to believe that this was, in fact, the case. The Western representative-democratic state was born during a period—the end of the eighteenth through the beginning of twentieth centuries—characterized by a sharp increase in the severity of certain child-rearing practices. As I have earlier suggested, these practices in Western industrial societies are generally far less indulgent than in most primitive and traditional societies, with the mother frustrating the oral, anal, and genital drives of the child more frequently and earlier in the former than the latter. If this is the case, then we should expect that the child's identification with the mother will be generally less encompassing, and thus the pain of separation less intense, in Western industrial society than in its predecessors. And, if this is the case, we should also expect that the Western industrial society's child will need a correspondingly less severe, less boundlessly authoritarian political shelter from maternal authority. Our analysis points, in short, to the conclusion that a less devastatingly intense dialectic of identification-separation-individuation is the unconscious psychological basis for the fit between democratic political authority and democratic paternal authority that characterizes the early capitalist forms of the Instrumental mode of symbolization.

It is by now commonplace to argue that the transformation of the representative-democratic state into the contemporary bureaucratic or technocratic state follows inevitably from the massive expansion in the scope of state functions; a state that regularly and actively attempts to ensure the everyday welfare of its citizens is necessarily obliged to delegate effective decision-making power to administrative agencies and thus to undermine the rule of law in favor of rule by interest groups and/or technical experts.[71] Our analysis

[69] Stone, *The Family, Sex and Marriage in England: 1500-1800*, p. 239.

[70] Stephens, *The Family in Cross-Cultural Perspective*, pp. 333-34; Harry Eckstein, *A Theory of Stable Democracy* (Princeton: Center of International Studies, 1961).

[71] For one recent statement of this thesis, see Ike Balbus, "Politics as Sports: An Interpretation of the Political Ascendency of the Sports Metaphor in America," in Leon Lindberg, *et al.*,

331

in Chapter Three concluded that this extraordinary growth of the welfare state, in turn, cannot be attributed merely to the reproduction requirements of a specifically capitalist mode of production, and the analysis in this chapter suggests that a more complete comprehension of this growth demands an appreciation of the transformations in the form of child rearing that both underlie and are reinforced by it. What, then, are the unconscious psychodynamics of the transition to the bureaucratic state?

During the second half of the twentieth century child-rearing practices appear to have become considerably more indulgent than they were during the early capitalist period of the Instrumental mode of symbolization. Certainly in the United States, but probably elsewhere as well,[72] two generations of children have now been raised by more permissive methods: they have been fed on demand, rather than by schedule, been toilet-trained somewhat later, and probably less genitally repressed. It seems reasonable to speculate that this relatively more indulgent child rearing has intensified the child's early identification with an increasingly nurturant mother, and thus his or her love-hate relationship with her. At the same time, however, suburbanization has increased both the geographical and emotional distance between home and workplace and intensified the tendency toward father-absent families endemic to capitalist industrial societies. The result, as many have noted and Christopher Lasch has recently bemoaned,[73] is a further diminution of the father's authority within the family. This suggests that the father is increasingly less available to serve as a refuge from maternal authority precisely at that point in history when the child has come to have a more imperative, boundless need for such a refuge.

Into this breach steps the state. Now that compensatory authority functions can no longer be performed regularly or adequately within the family, these functions are increasingly monopolized by the state. The paternalism of the father is supplanted by the paternalism of the welfare state; what Lasch calls "paternalism without the father" enables the individual to fulfill his or her intensified dependency needs and his or her intensified need to reject "mommy" through identification with an ever more solicitous, even nurturant, state.[74]

Stress and Contradiction in Modern Capitalism (Lexington, Mass.: Lexington Books, 1975), pp. 321-36.

[72] Emmy Elisabeth Werner, *Cross-cultural Child Development* (Monterey, California: Brooks/Cole, 1979), Ch. 14.

[73] *The Culture of Narcissism*, Ch. 7.

[74] Lasch identifies only half of this dynamic, emphasizing exclusively the role of the bureaucratic state as a repository for intensified dependency needs and ignoring entirely its (expanded) role as a refuge from the power of the mother. Similarly, his indictment of the decline in the authority of the father is based exclusively on the assumption that identification with paternal authority is essential for overcoming maternally generated overdependence and the development of a strong, autonomous ego, and thus on the complete neglect of the role of paternal authority

These needs, in other words, are the unconscious emotional basis of support for a state that devotes itself to taking care of the individual, as the expression goes, "from cradle to grave." The increasingly encompassing scope of state authority, then, is rooted in the intensification of mother-related emotional needs that, with the increasing absence of the father, can no longer be even partly satisfied within the family. This is the psychological transformation that underlies the transformation of the individual from citizen of the limited state to client of the unlimited state;[75] therapeutic justice replaces the rule of law and the authority of the social worker supplants the authority of the judge because the state is obliged dramatically to expand its function of enabling the individual simultaneously to reaffirm, and repudiate, his or her dependence on the mother. Thus Marcuse was correct to locate a tendency toward totalitarian political domination in advanced industrial society, but incorrect to argue that the source of this tendency lies in an ever more direct subjection of the individual to a centralized, mass-media, and state-dominated process of socialization that entirely substitutes for socialization within the family. State socialization of the individual does not supplant, but instead builds upon, the mother's increasingly indulgent socialization of the individual within the family; the state does not merely impose needs on the individual but rather fulfills unconscious needs that have developed in the course of the individual's now-transformed relationship with his or her mother. In the process of fulfilling these dependency and mother-hating needs, of course, the state reinforces them and encourages their proliferation. Thus the contemporary welfare state is both a response to and a nurturer of the prevailing mode of mother-monopolized child rearing.

In Chapter Six, it will be recalled, I examined Habermas's analysis of the cognitive basis for unrepressive communication and thus for the emergence of a liberatory form of politics. His identification of a sequence of increasingly abstract, universalistic levels of collective cognitive development or "social integration" led to the conclusion that the modern age alone has reached a level of development such that the potential for ideal-speech—liberatory pol-

---

as a vehicle for the expression of mother-hatred and, later, of generalized hatred of women. Since he takes mother-monopolized child rearing for granted, and is oblivious to its patriarchal consequences, his critique of the existing family-state complex remains wholly within male-dominant horizons and even betrays a nostalgia for the authority of the nineteenth- early twentieth-century patriarch that he himself recognizes is misplaced. *The Culture of Narcissism*, Chs. 7, 10.

[75] *Ibid.* Thus the "cool" professionalism that claims superiority over "emotional," "irrational" methods of decision making is itself rooted in an unconscious, irrational fear of the mother in particular and all women in general. For an analysis of professionalism as a more conscious assault on the power of women, see Barbara Ehrenreich and Deirdre English, *For Her Own Good: 150 Years of the Experts' Advice to Women* (Garden City, New York: Anchor Press/Doubleday, 1978).

itics—supposedly inherent in human communication is realizable in practice. At the end of that chapter I took Habermas to task for failing to supplement this analysis of the cognitive basis of political liberation with an analysis of its psychosexual basis, and suggested that it was possible persuasively to argue that there are, in fact, profound psychosexual obstacles to unrepressive communication in the very modern age that Habermas upholds. Having completed our historical outline of the unconscious roots of political domination, it is now possible to elaborate further this argument. Our analysis suggests that the prevailing form of mother-monopolized child rearing engenders unconscious needs for political domination that militate powerfully against the possibility of the ideal-speech essential for political liberation. More generally, I have argued that any mode of mother-monopolized child rearing will generate an unconscious, internalized structure of communication with the mother that is neurotic at best and pathological at worst. Mother-monopolized child rearing perforce generates the unconscious basis for distorted, rather then emancipatory, communication among adults. Adults will inevitably be unable genuinely to recognize one another, and thus contribute to their mutual development, in political interactions, until they cease to see the other as either a mother whose authority is intolerable or a father whose domination is a welcome shelter from this authority. But this will not occur until mother-monopolized child rearing is eliminated and replaced by shared parenting. Only then will our internalized, unconscious patterns of communication with our first others provide a satisfactory libidinal foundation for conscious liberatory communication with the political others we encounter throughout our adult lives.

MOTHER-MONOPOLIZED CHILD REARING AND THE DOMINATION OF NATURE

In the preceding chapter we examined Norman O. Brown's analysis of the malignant drive to dominate nature that poisons the psychic life and the natural environment of Western industrial societies. This drive, according to Brown, is the expression of an adult inability to accept death, which, in turn, is rooted in the incapacity of the child to tolerate the first and most profound psychic equivalent to death, his or her separation from the mother. It follows that the transcendence of the instrumental relationship toward nature characteristic of Enlightenment societies in favor of an "erotic," post-instrumental relationship is predicated on a transformation of our death-denying, mother-defying unconscious psychic structure. Because Brown takes the existing mode of child rearing for granted, however, he fails to specify the changes in child rearing essential for the transformation of this psychic structure and is obliged to

334

"spiritualize," rather than materially ground, the transition from the Instrumental to a post-Instrumental mode of symbolization. At this point we must turn, once again, to Dorothy Dinnerstein, this time to help us overcome the limits of Brown's vision. Dinnerstein reveals, more clearly than Brown, the links between mother-monopolized child rearing and objectification and demonstrates in the process what Brown was unable to understand, namely that the emergence of a postobjectification relationship with nature demands the elimination of mother-monopolized child rearing and the inauguration of a mode of early nurturing that is shared equally by woman and man.

Dinnerstein establishes that the hitherto culturally universal tendency for nature to be symbolized as a woman[76] is umbilically tied to the equally universal fact that the child's first and most decisive encounter with the world is an encounter with a woman. It is, after all, a woman on whom every newborn infant depends for its survival; she is the one who feeds, shelters, and fondles it and who becomes, in the process, the world to which the infant is symbiotically related and from which it cannot, in its earliest months, distinguish itself. At the same time, it is a woman from whom the child must separate in order to become fully human; she is the other against whom the child must struggle in order to establish its selfhood. Thus it is that the adult symbolizes the natural world that is both the source of his or her being and the "other" in relation to which this being is defined as a woman: woman becomes the representative of nature because the child's relationship with its mother is paradigmatic of our subsequent relationship with the natural surround. The earth, in short, becomes "mother nature" because it is the mother who nurtures. If, as de Beauvoir argues, "nothing lies deeper in the hearts of men [and women] than this animism,"[77] this can only be because this animism is a projection of our earliest, most intense, and most significant relationship with the world—our relationship with our mother.

It follows that nature necessarily becomes a repository for our unconscious attitudes toward our mother. The intense ambivalence toward the mother that is the inevitable corollary of the dialectic of identification-separation-individuation will be projected onto nature: "she" is both the mother that we love and on whom we wish to remain dependent and the mother that we hate because this wish cannot be fulfilled. Thus our love-hate relationship with our mother becomes a love-hate relationship with nature; nature will be symbolized both as the loving woman to whom we owe our life and as the dreaded, hated woman who must be dominated or even destroyed. Dinnerstein ac-

[76] Hays, *The Dangerous Sex*; Mead, *Male and Female*; de Beauvoir, *The Second Sex*; Sherry B. Ortner, "Is Female to Male as Nature is to Culture?" in Rosaldo and Lamphere, *Woman, Culture and Society*, pp. 67-87; Carolyn Merchant, *The Death of Nature*, (New York: Harper & Row, 1980).

[77] Cited in Dinnerstein, *The Mermaid and the Minotaur*, p. 125.

knowledges that the balance between "respect, concern, awe" and "hostility and rapacity" varies "from culture to culture" and that "it need not always be tipped in the same direction for women and for nature"[78] but she (no more than Brown) does not attempt to account for the changing character of this balance. Rather she leaves us to conclude that an objectifying culture will be one in which the balance is tipped in the direction of destructive impulses toward the mother, and thus toward nature. In such cultures the unconscious desire to unite with mother-nature will be combined with an even more powerful, unconscious desire to defeat her. Objectification, in other words, is "union" with a nature (woman) that has been reduced to an object that can be controlled by a subject. The domination of nature is the domination of the mother: the symbolization of nature as an absolute, dangerous other which must be tamed lest it destroy us is rooted in the unconscious, childhood symbolization of the mother as an other who must be punished for having betrayed our love. Objectification is "getting back at mommy."

Dinnerstein is thus able to account for the peculiarly virulent, violent nature of the "unions" between human beings and nature in societies dominated by the Instrumental mode of symbolization: these unions are poisoned by the explosive mixture of love for, and hatred of, the mother that results from the form of mother-monopolized child rearing in these societies. The "rape" of nature that contemporary ecologists decry, then, is no mere metaphor, but accurately captures the unconscious, incestuous psychological underpinnings of the contemporary exploitation of the ecosystem.[79] Now we are in a position fully to understand what Marcuse intimated but could not adequately illuminate, namely the sense in which the "performance principle" is a "male principle" and the domination of nature is part and parcel of "patriarchal culture."[80] *Objectification is a patriarchal, or male principle because it both expresses and is rooted in the same condition that guarantees the domination of men over women, namely mother-monopolized child rearing.* It follows that both Marxism, for which objectification is the essential human activity,

[78] Dinnerstein, *The Mermaid and the Minotaur*, p. 101.

[79] After completing this chapter I discovered that these psychological underpinnings are explored not only by Dinnerstein but also by Annette Kolodny in *The Lay of the Land* (Chapel Hill: University of North Carolina Press, 1975). Like Dinnerstein, Kolodny argues that the symbolization of nature as woman is rooted in the child's relationship with the mother and that the symbolization of nature as a woman to be dominated grows out of the peculiar mixture of love and hatred for the mother that this relationship engenders. And, like Dinnerstein, Kolodny calls for an end to the symbolization of nature as a woman as an essential precondition for the elimination of the domination of nature. But this appeal for a new, nonmaternal metaphor appears abstract and utopian in light of the fact that Kolodny, unlike Dinnerstein, does not envision the elimination of the mother-monopolized child rearing that necessarily gives rise to the maternal metaphor (pp. 148-60).

[80] Marcuse, *Counter-Revolution and Revolt*, pp. 74-75.

336

and Neo-Marxism, for which objectification is an essential human activity, are inherently patriarchal modes of thought.

Without realizing it, Marx himself betrayed the patriarchal logic of his central category when, in *Capital*, he approvingly quotes William Petty's contention that "labour is its [use-value's] father and the earth its mother."[81] What Marx intended to convey with this analogy is that the process through which humans objectify nature in order to create a material product is as universal and as straightforward as the process through which men have intercourse with women in order to produce a child. Since Freud, however, we know that there is nothing straightforward about sexual intercourse, which, however much it is consciously connected to the goal of procreation, necessarily serves as an outlet for the libidinal impulses toward our parents that develop during our childhood. Since Dinnerstein, moreover, we know that these impulses include the desire to punish our mother. "Lacking the concept of . . . the unconscious,"[82] Marx did not and could not realize that sexual intercourse is an expression of profoundly complex, contradictory needs that develop in the course of mother-monopolized child rearing. For the same reason, he was unable to understand that the labor that is analogous to sexual intercourse likewise expresses unconscious, libidinal needs that derive from the fact that we are mother-raised. Since "Marx . . . is not free from the tacit assumption . . . that the concrete human needs and drives sustaining economic activity are just what they appear to be and fully in consciousness,"[83] he could not grasp that the human being who objectifies nature does so not merely to produce use-values but also to violate his or her mother. From this perspective, then, Marx's celebration of production as the distinctively human activity, and thus of the supremacy of the mode of production over the mode of child rearing, is an unconscious, characteristically male reaction to the power of the mother that simultaneously denies that this power was ever exercised to any determinative effect.

There is, according to Dinnerstein, yet another sense in which objectification is a patriarchal activity, namely that is normally an activity that is disproportionately undertaken by men. The closer preoedipal identification of the girl-child with her mother, she argues, results in this child's hostile, aggressive feelings toward the mother being more balanced by "reparative feelings" and "restitutive urges" than those of the boy-child. Thus nature, representative of the mother, is likely to be the repository of "solicitous impulses" of women and is therefore less likely to be attacked by them.[84] Dinnerstein's argument is confirmed by Chodorow, who argues, as we have

[81] Marx, *Capital*, Vol. I, p. 43.
[82] Brown, *Life Against Death*, p. 13.
[83] *Ibid.*, p. 17.
[84] Dinnerstein, *The Mermaid and the Minotaur*, p. 103.

337

seen, that the girl-child's longer preoedipal period and stronger primary identification with her mother lead girls "to experience themselves as less separate than boys . . . [and] to define themselves more in relation to others," in contrast to boys, whose need to define their masculinity in opposition to women leads them to develop a greater sense of their separation from the world.[85] It is also supported by other studies that have established that women in societies dominated by the Instrumental mode of symbolization have a greater sense of their connectedness to the world than men.[86]

It is men, then, whose childhood relationship to their mothers drives them to dominate a nature to which they feel unconnected, whereas women are impelled by their early relationship to their mothers to fulfill their richer relational needs through mothering their children and nurturing their men. Thus Dinnerstein's analysis corrects the patriarchal bias of Brown's account, which assumes that a psychic structure that is in fact disproportionately male is a human structure *tout court* and thus ignores entirely the distinctive psychic structure of women and the specific contribution of this structure to the reproduction of the domination of nature. According to Dinnerstein, this contribution is of capital importance. The prevailing psychic division of labor between men and women affords a mechanism that allows their mutual "misgivings" about the "death-denying," "life-rejecting" aspects of "enterprise" to be expressed, yet "sealed off" from the world of enterprise itself and thus rendered unthreatening to the existing structure of this world.[87] The existence of a "woman's" realm in which feelings and relationships count is a reminder to both men and women that the "male" realm of analytical, aggressive work is not the only realm, and there is, after all, a less burdensome, less repressive way of life. At the same time, the fact that these doubts are aired in a "private" domestic setting, emotionally and geographically separated from the setting in which enterprise is undertaken, means that they will not effectively infuse the manner of this enterprise and that it will therefore retain its pathological, nature-defying character. In this way, the exclusion of women from objectification, and thus from history, helps "keep History mad."[88]

Dinnerstein's analysis, finally, clarifies what Brown leaves unclear, namely the necessary conditions for the elimination of the domination of nature and the emergence of a playful or erotic form of human enterprise that respects, rather than violates, the integrity of nature. With the end to mother-monop-

[85] Chodorow, *The Reproduction of Mothering*, pp. 93, 104-10.

[86] David Bakan, *The Duality of Human Existence* (Chicago: Rand McNally & Co., 1966), Ch. 4, and Sarah Ruddick, "Maternal Thinking," *Feminist Studies*, 6 (Summer 1980), pp. 342-67.

[87] Dinnerstein, *The Mermaid and the Minotaur*, pp. 215, 227.

[88] *Ibid.*, p. 225.

olized child rearing and the inauguration of shared parenting, the infant's initial encounter with the world will be with both a woman and a man. Under these conditions we should expect that nature will no longer be symbolized exclusively as a woman but rather as both woman and man, or possibly androgynously. At the same time, and as we have seen, neither the woman nor the man, now that they share child-rearing responsibilities, will be the recipient of nearly as much resentment as the woman presently receives. Thus nature, as the representative of both parents, will no longer be symbolized as a parent that must be punished. Shared parenting, in other words, undermines the unconscious emotional basis of the domination of nature, tipping the balance for both sexes in favor of "solicitous impulses" toward nature. Now that the symbolization of nature is no longer poisoned by venomous hatred for the mother, our inevitably libidinal relationship with it can become a joyful, erotic rather than violent, rapacious relationship. And, as we come to embrace the nature outside of us, we come also to love the nature within us, i.e., to delight in, rather than repress, our bodies. Under these conditions, the split between work and play is overcome and enterprise is transformed into an intrinsically pleasurable activity as well as one that "can console us, though only in part, for the inexorable loss of our pure infant sense of omnipotent oneness with the world."[89] We will need, however, less consolation for this loss, both because we shall have come to accept the inevitable pain of a separate, mortal human existence and because neither men nor women will any longer feel as separate from, and opposed to, the world as men currently do. Nature will no longer be conceived as an absolute other, a pure object, but rather as an other from which we are distinguished yet with whom we are in communion. Shared parenting thus establishes the necessary psychological bases for what I have called the post-Instrumental mode of symbolization.[90]

Like her analysis of patriarchy and political domination, Dinnerstein's otherwise instructive account of the unconscious basis of the domination of nature lacks historical specificity. This lack is particularly glaring in light of the fact that this latter form of domination is a far more historically restricted phenomenon than the former two. As we have seen, the conceptualization of nature as a pure object to be controlled and manipulated by the subject only becomes hegemonic with the emergence and consolidation of Western "Enlightenment" societies from the seventeenth century onward. Prior to that time, nature was always symbolized as infused with purpose and subjectivity and was therefore not a target for the objectification that was subsequently

---

[89] *Ibid.*, p. 145.

[90] Necessary, but not sufficient: if the parenting of both the mother and the father is insufficiently nurturant, then it will not produce the strong primary identification with them in the child that is the essential unconscious basis for an empathic relationship between the child and nature.

339

imposed on it. Dinnerstein's analysis of the way in which mother-monopolized child rearing produces the unconscious and hostile emotional basis for objectification thus does not apply to the overwhelming bulk of human history but only to the past three or four hundred years. Her acknowledgment that the unconscious emotional balance between "respect" and "rapacity," and the extent to which this balance is tipped "in the same direction for women and for nature," is culturally variable undoubtedly signals her awareness of this fact. But, as I have already noted, nowhere does she attempt to account for it; she never undertakes to relate differences in this emotional balance to differences in the form of child care and thus fails to uncover the specific mode of mother-monopolized child rearing that underlies and helps reproduce the domination of nature. It is therefore necessary to complete her analysis by undertaking this effort.

Let me begin this task by recalling the child's unconscious relationship to the mother in societies not characterized by the domination of nature, and in primitive societies in particular. Primitive societies, we should remember, are societies in which nature is symbolized as a mother to whom it is necessary to give, to whom one owes a debt, i.e., societies in which the unconscious emotional stance toward nature is tipped overwhelmingly toward reparative rather than rapacious feelings. At the same time, these are societies in which the generally extremely indulgent and extended form of nurturance by the mother results in a primary identification with the mother that is far more intense and prolonged for children of both sexes than it is under contemporary modes of mother-monopolized child rearing, an identification so strong that "normal" masculine development for the boy can only be attained with the aid of cruel initiation rites and/or systematic segregation from women designed to overcome its effects. Since the child only develops a separate sense of self from frustrations that the mother imposes on its oral, anal, and genital drives, and these frustrations are imposed on the primitive child less frequently, harshly, and early than on the modern child, the former's sense of separateness from the mother will be correspondingly lower than the latter's. And, since the mother is the infant's "world" and thus becomes the unconscious referent for the symbolization of nature, it follows that the primitive child will likewise have a far less developed sense of separateness from his or her natural surround than the modern. The primitive child's intense, grateful dependence on the mother will be unconsciously, and very early on, translated into a worshipful dependence on nature that dictates that the "primitive . . . does not chop one tree or trace one furrow without 'appeasing the spirits' with a counter-gift or sacrifice."[91] This nature-worship persists notwithstanding the intensely hostile feelings that the child later develops toward the mother (and, at least for men,

[91] Baudrillard, *The Mirror of Production*, pp. 82-83.

toward women in general) as a result of his or her drastically abrupt and painful separation from her. Thus do we find the domination of men over women, but not the domination of nature, in primitive societies.

The thesis that intense primary identification with the mother resulting from a prolonged and indulgent preoedipal period produces an unconscious emotional structure that is incompatible with the domination of nature receives support from our analysis of the nature of woman's emotional structure in contemporary, objectifying societies. Both Dinnerstein and Chodorow argue that the relatively longer, perhaps more nurturant, preoedipal period of the girl and thus her relatively more intense and prolonged primary identification with her mother leaves her far less psychologically prepared to initiate objectifying assaults on nature than her brother: women generally lack the sense of separateness from the world that is the necessary psychic precondition for asserting one's will in opposition to this world. Contemporary women, in short, have an unconscious emotional structure that is, in certain respects, far closer to that of both primitive women and men than is the structure of contemporary men. The fact that a similar emotional structure results, in both cases, in similar, i.e., nonobjectifying, behavior, tends to confirm our thesis about the unconscious effects of this structure.

There is, as we have seen, some evidence that children in nonprimitive but nevertheless traditional, nonobjectifying societies experience a preoedipal period that is somewhat less indulgent, and thus develop an identification with the mother that is somewhat less intense, than primitive children.[92] But the socialization that children in all traditional, pre-Instrumental societies experience is generally far less repressive than that which children undergo in Instrumental societies, particularly during their early stages.[93] Western industrial mothers not only typically provide far less cutaneous contact for their children than their traditional counterparts but also impose far greater frustrations much more regularly and much earlier on their children. The Western (or Westernized) child has been nursed for a far shorter period,

---

[92] It would be important, and fascinating, to attempt to relate the differing child-rearing practices in the various types of traditional societies to the differences in their conceptions of nature. But this task is peripheral to mine, which is, once again, to uncover the emotional roots of the post-traditional conception of nature as an object of domination.

[93] Thus a review of some fifty cross-cultural studies concludes that "In spite of a great deal of cultural diversity, all of the infants drawn from pre-industrial communities shared certain experiences during the first year: membership in an extended family system with many caretakers, breast-feeding on demand, day and night; constant tactile stimulation by the body of the adult caretaker who carried the infant on her back or side, and slept with him . . . lack of set routines for feeding, sleeping, and toileting." Emmy E. Werner, "Infants Around the World: Cross-Cultural Studies of Psychomotor Development from Birth to Two Years," in Stella Chess and Alexander Thomas, *Annual Progress in Child Psychiatry and Child Development*, Vol. 6 (New York: Brunner/Mazel, 1973), pp. 84-112.

sometimes on schedule and not by demand, has been toilet-trained earlier and probably more severely, and has been genitally more repressed. He or she (especially he) is therefore likely to experience a much less intense primary identification with the mother, and thus a far greater sense of a self that is separate from her, than the traditional child. At the same time, the infantile and childhood resentments that inevitably accompany separation from the mother and the development of an individuated self will necessarily accumulate much sooner with the Western than the traditional child, since separations from her have likewise been imposed much earlier on the former than on the latter. Thus the Western child's symbolization of nature, in contrast to that of his or her traditional counterpart, will be established during a period of intensely ambivalent feelings toward the mother, with the mother serving as both an object of love and an object of hate. This balance, as we have seen, will lean more heavily toward hate in the case of the male child, whose normal masculine development demands that he define himself in active opposition to his mother. It follows that his masculinity also demands that he define himself in active opposition to the nature that is her representative, and that his emotional balance will therefore be tipped in the direction of "rapacious," rather than "reparative," unconscious feelings toward nature. The repeated frustrations of libidinal impulses that the male (as well as the female) child has experienced, moreover, have prepared him emotionally to tolerate the postponement of gratification that the labor that embodies these rapacious feelings demands. "Labour," Hegel has told us, "is desire restrained and checked, evanescence delayed and postponed,"[94] and the Western child is uniquely emotionally prepared to restrain his or her desire and delay his or her evanescence. Marx himself argued that, in order for labor to occur, "man . . . must conquer his relative existence, the power of desire and of mere nature in himself,"[95] but failed to understand that it is precisely for this reason that labor, strictly speaking, is performed only in Western industrial societies or contemporary Westernizing societies that are following in their footsteps: they are the only societies whose mode of mother-monopolized child rearing establishes its emotional prerequisites.[96]

[94] Hegel, *The Phenomenology of Mind*, p. 238.

[95] Cited in Schmidt, *The Concept of Nature in Marx*, p. 137.

[96] This psychoanalytic account of the roots of the domination of nature is more powerful, it seems to me, than those accounts that have emphasized the centrality of Christianity to our anthropocentric relation to the natural world. Although it is true, as Lynn White, Jr., has argued, that "especially in its Western form, Christianity is the most anthropocentric religion the world has seen" ("The Historical Roots of Our Ecological Crisis," in Shepard and McKinley, *The Subversive Science*, p. 347), it is also the case that the West endured 1500 years of Christianity without abandoning a teleological, nonobjectifying conception of nature. The Weberian argument, which attributes the growth and spread of instrumental rationality not to Christianity in general, but rather to its peculiarly ascetic, Protestant form is chronologically more plausible, but largely

The fact that developing or modernizing societies have progressively abandoned earlier, more extended forms of the family and increasingly adopted "some type of conjugal family . . . [characterized by] the relative exclusion of a wide range of affinal and blood relatives from its everyday affairs"[97] tends to confirm our thesis. If we assume that this worldwide trend to the modern form of the family is also accompanied by the adoption of modern mother-monopolized child-rearing practices, then the correlation between this transformation in family form and industrialization provides powerful support for the thesis that it is these child-rearing practices that create the emotional basis for the domination of nature that has thus far accompanied industrialization.

Additional support for our thesis comes, finally, from the contemporary "cultural contradictions of capitalism." Bell argues, along with others, that advanced consumption-oriented capitalist societies increasingly produce a hedonistic ideology of instant gratification that progressively supplants the ascetic achievement ethos, undermining the ideological support for the postponement of gratification that capitalist production demands.[98] Lasch, in turn, suggests that this economic and ideological transformation is nourished by a transformation in the modal personality type in advanced capitalist societies: according to psychoanalysts like Kernberg and Kohut, the "anal compulsive" type is increasingly replaced by the "narcissistic" type, whose "sense of selfhood [is] dependent on the *consumption* of images of the self."[99] Lasch links this psychological transformation to a decline in the authority of the father within the family, which both reflects and reproduces an increase in the intensity of the child's primary identification with its mother. We have already examined, and corrected, Lasch's analysis of the way in which this psychological transformation underlies and reinforces the progressive bureaucratization of the state by encouraging increasing dependence on "paternalism without the father."[100] As Lasch further emphasizes, "the same . . . development that turned the citizen into a client transformed the worker from a producer to a consumer":[101] the increasingly indulgent nurturance of the mother, unmitigated by "compensatory identification" with the (absent) father, results in a more intensely mother-identified child and thus one who is less able to postpone gratification than the child of the early capitalist

redundant, since it can be demonstrated that this form itself rests on repressive, anal instinctual foundations that are established by the early modern mode of mother-monopolized child rearing. See Brown, *Life Against Death*, Chs. 14-15.

[97] William J. Goode, *World Revolution and Family Patterns* (Glencoe, Ill.: The Free Press, 1963), pp. 25, 8.

[98] Bell, *The Cultural Contradictions of Capitalism*.

[99] Lasch, *The Culture of Narcissism*, p. 48, emphasis added.

[100] See note 74.

[101] Lasch, *The Culture of Narcissism*, p. 235.

mother. It is also likely that this more intensely mother-identified child is far more "relationally" oriented than his or her early modern predecessors.[102] For both reasons, the child of advanced capitalist societies is likely to be less emotionally attracted to objectification than his or her early modern counterpart. Hence the contemporary crisis in job satisfaction and productivity in many Western capitalist societies.[103] In short, the fact that a plausible argument can be constructed that links a lower tolerance for objectification to departures from the child-rearing practices of early capitalist conjugal families lends additional support to our thesis that these child-rearing practices produce the unconscious emotional foundation for the domination of nature.

SUMMARY: THE DOMINANCE OF THE MODE OF CHILD REARING WITHIN THE MODE OF SYMBOLIZATION

In the first and second parts of this book we saw that neither Marxism nor Neo-Marxism can account for contemporary sexual, political, and ecological domination. On the one hand, these structures of domination cannot be adequately comprehended as mere capitalist reproduction mechanisms; rather they display a relative autonomy from this mode of production. It is the awareness of this relative autonomy that justifies Neo-Marxism's claim to a certain superiority over Marxism. On the other hand, the awareness of Neo-Marxist theorists that the function of the three structures of domination as capitalist reproductive mechanisms does not establish the principle of unity that underlies them is never accompanied by a satisfactory specification of an alternative unifying principle: this awareness is either accompanied by the specification of a unifying principle that is logically incompatible with the Marxist principle of production with which they aspire to forge a synthesis or else unaccompanied by any specification of an alternative principle whatsoever.[104] In either case Neo-Marxism tends ncessarily to culminate in eclec-

---

[102] Lasch fails to emphasize this element of the new, narcissistic personality, and this is why his evaluation of this personality and the "human relations" movements to which it is attracted is so uniformly negative. A more balanced evaluation would necessarily result from an awareness of the way in which intensified mother-identification and the decline in the authority of the father engender not only less willingness to postpone gratification and thus less desire to produce and more to consume, but also a heightened, if still neurotic, need for relationships with other people. I shall return to this issue in the final chapter.

[103] *Work in America* (Cambridge, Mass.: M.I.T. Press, 1973). See also Kirkpatrick Sale, *Human Scale* (New York: Coward, McCann, and Geoghegan, 1980), pp. 340-41.

[104] Consider, for example the recent formulation of the authors of *Unorthodox Marxism*, that "we . . . live . . . in a society which has at its core a totality of entwined relations which manifest themselves in the forms of classism, racism, sexism, and authoritarianism" (p. 232), a formulation whose admirable recognition of the importance of structures of domination not

ticism, a culmination that is often masked by a covert reassertion of the primacy of the very principle of production that had earlier been denied. This oscillation between eclecticism and reductionism leaves no space for an adequate specification of the underlying unity of contemporary sexual, political, and ecological domination.

I have tried to demonstrate in the past two chapters that this hidden unity becomes visible once these three structures are reconceptualized as constituent elements of a specific mode of symbolization. Each of these structures embodies an identical, Instrumental mode of symbolizing the relationship between the self and the other, in which the other (whether sexual, political, or natural) is conceptualized as an object to be controlled and manipulated by an absolutely separate, sovereign subject. The coherence of the whole (or system), in other words, is established through each part's (or subsystem's) interiorization of a single, instrumental logic. The instrumental logic that pervades the adult's relationship to his or her sexual, political, and ecological others, moreover, first takes shape unconsciously in the course of the child's relationship to his or her mother: the form of his or her relationship to this most significant, simultaneously sexual, ruling, and natural other unconsciously establishes the pattern for his or her subsequent sexual, political, and technological relationships. Under contemporary conditions of mother-monopolized child rearing, the child's self-recognition can be achieved only at the price of the unconscious recognition of the mother as an object of domination, an unconscious structure of recognition that sets the stage for the adult's recognition of all subsequent others as objects of domination as well. Thus in this chapter I have tried to demonstrate the way in which the contemporary mode of mother-monopolized child rearing establishes the libidinal basis of the contemporary structures of sexual, political, and technological domination.

This emphasis on the determinative power of the relations of child rearing should not convey the impression, however, that causality within the (Instrumental) mode of symbolization is unidirectional and that the sexual, political, and technological relations that also constitute this mode have no determinative effect. On the one hand, these relations remain important media for recognition struggles in their own right; the personality and needs of the individual are by no means exhaustively determined by the struggle for recognition with his or her mother but, rather, continue to develop in the course of his or her later sexual, political, and technological relationships. On the other hand, the structure of these relationships powerfully reinforces the structure of child rearing. If it is true that mother-monopolized child rearing under

reducible to the mode of production is matched only by its complete failure even to attempt to specify the common logic embodied in these structures that allows them to be described as forming a coherent totality.

the Instrumental mode of symbolization engenders a sexual division of labor in which men typically display a controlling distance in their everyday, ostensibly intimate, relationships with women, it is also true that this distance is likely to encourage women to "invest" more heavily in their relationships with their children and thus to contribute to the reproduction of the prevailing mode of mother-monopolized child rearing. If this form of child rearing produces dependence on an authoritarian but nevertheless limited state, this state can be expected, in turn, to enforce legislative and ideological limitations on the authoritarian power of the father within the family. If the early capitalist form of the conjugal family prepares men emotionally to undertake objectification with abandon, the industrialization that unlimited objectification entails generates pressure for increased labor mobility that weakens the ties of extended kinship and thus reinforces the conjugal family. In short, sexual, political, and technological structures help support the very structure of child rearing of which they are an outgrowth. By the same token, although independent changes in the mode of child rearing can be expected to effect profound changes in sexual, political, and technological structures, we should not think that autonomous changes in these structures will have no effect on the mode of child rearing. A more complete treatment of the Instrumental mode of symbolization would examine in detail the complex chains of causality that determine the relationship among all the significant structures of the mode of symbolization. Such a treatment, however, would only supply additional, more concrete evidence of the reciprocal interaction among these structures that we have already, if briefly, established. On this point, at least, our analysis is consistent with that of Marx, and we can do no better than quote him: "Mutual interaction takes place between the different moments. This is the case with every organic whole."[105]

And yet this interaction is not entirely symmetrical. If I have overwhelmingly emphasized the effect of the relation of child rearing on sexual, political, and technological relations, rather than the reverse, this has not been accidental but rather a reflection of what I believe is a certain kind of causal primacy exercised by the former relation over the latter three. To make use, as we have, of psychoanalytic theory is to accept the proposition that what is learned earliest and therefore remains unconscious will have the most profound effects and be the hardest to alter. This proposition leads us to expect, in other words, that the unconscious, internalized relationship of the child to its mother will play a more significant determinative role over the sexual, political, and technological relationships of the adult than the latter will play over the former and thus that the mode of child rearing that engenders this unconscious re-

[105] *Grundrisse*, p. 100.

lationship to the mother should be considered the dominant structure within the organic whole which is the mode of symbolization.

In Chapter One we saw that Marx was groping toward a similar conception of causality but that his ontological commitment to production was inconsistent with this conception. Production cannot legitimately be considered a dominant function because the type of function it performs is not qualitatively different from the type of functions performed by those other structures (e.g., structures of distribution, exchange, and consumption) that are equally necessary for the reproduction of the organic whole that is a society. Structures of production, in other words, are no more dominant over the structures that fulfill these other organic functions than the brain is over the heart or the heart is over the liver: each of these structures is as essential as all the others to the reproduction of the organism—both social and physiological—at any given point in time. They are all structures of the same type, operating at the same logical level, and thus none can legitimately claim dominance over any other. Conversely, the only organic structures that might properly be said to be dominant are those whose functions are of different type or higher logical level than the functions of those structures over which they exercise causal primacy. Thus geneticists, for example, are entitled to claim a certain causal priority for the DNA molecule and the genetic program it contains because this structure performs a function—establishing a general plan that controls the overall development of the organism—that is of a different, higher logical level than the functions performed by those organs (e.g., the heart, brain, liver, etc.) that subsequently and "merely" serve to reproduce this general plan. This suggests that the thesis that the mode of child rearing is the dominant structure could only be sustained if it were possible to demonstrate that the *type of function performed by this structure differs from the type of functions performed by sexual, political, and technological structures in the same manner that the function performed by the genetic structure differs from those performed by the other structures of the physiological organism.* This is precisely what I shall attempt to demonstrate before I close this chapter.

Contemporary geneticists generally agree that the genetic inheritance of an organism dictates the "gross morphology" (general, overall structure) of the organism but that "environmental influences during epigenesis [the development of the embryo] play a very significant part in modulating the structure, especially in . . . the later stage . . . (in which learning processes become important)." In other words, both the genetic code of the organism and the environment to which it relates determine the ultimate, precise nature of the organism. Thus "the genetic information of an organism should not be looked upon as a blueprint for the organism but, rather, as a set of algorithms or instructions for assembling and maintaining the organism in conjunction with environmental impacts."[106] But this means that the determination exercised by the genetic code over the organism is more profound, more essential, than that exercised by the environment over the organism: the genetic instructions determine the form or pattern of the organism's interaction with its environment and thus establish the parameters or limits within which somatic changes that result from this interaction can occur.[107] "The individual organism adapts and develops" in response to environmental impacts but "only within narrow limits,"[108] limits established by the genetic program of the organism that is carried in its DNA molecules. In this sense, then, it is reasonable to argue that the genetic structure is the dominant structure within that whole that embraces the relationship of the organism to its environment.

This dominance is also expressed in the fact that evolutionary changes in the organism cannot occur in the absence of a change in its genetic program. This change, in turn, cannot be directly produced by the somatic changes that result from the organism's adaptation to its environment. These changes cannot be inherited by the individual offspring of this organism; reproduction transmits to the offspring the genes of its parent organism unmodified by whatever somatic changes the organism has experienced. "There is no direct Lamarkian inheritance."[109] But these individual somatic changes or learning experiences typically propose the possibility of genetic change at the level of the population as a whole. The "new forms of [organismic] behavior exert new [natural] selection pressures";[110] somatic changes "create a context for genetic change" by generating "better-adapted individuals on which selection can work." Whether this genetic change follows, i.e., whether an evolutionary transformation occurs, is "a separate question"[111]—one that depends in part on the random generation of genetic mutations—but *if* it occurs it will be because it was originally triggered by successful learning experiences on the part of individual organisms. Thus somatic changes can ultimately play an important, if indirect, role in the transformation of the very genetic structure that initially established the limits within which those changes could occur.

I want to suggest that there is a remarkable parallel between the nature of the causal relationship between the genetic structure of the organism and the development of the organism as a whole and the nature of the causal relationship between the unconscious structure of the individual produced by the

---

[106] Robin E. Monro, "Interpreting Molecular Biology," in John Lewis, ed., *Beyond Chance and Necessity* (London: Garnstone Press, 1974), p. 108.

[107] Gregory Bateson, *Mind and Nature: A Necessary Unity* (New York: E. P. Dutton, 1979), p. 178.

[108] Wilden, *System and Structure*, p. 368.

[109] Bateson, *Mind and Nature*, p. 160.

[110] Monro, "Interpreting Molecular Biology," p. 114.

[111] Bateson, *Mind and Nature*, pp. 181, 160.

mode of child rearing and the total development of the individual as an adult. This unconscious structure does not completely determine the development of the self any more than the genetic program exhaustively specifies the development of the organism. Just as the complete development of the organism is also influenced in important ways by its interaction with its environment, so the self whose "gross morphology" has been shaped unconsciously by the mode of child rearing continues to develop in the course of its relationship to its natural, sexual, and political environment. This conceptualization disposes of the charge of crude psychological reductionism and establishes the independent contribution of adult sexual, political, and technological relations to the development of the individual. But this contribution is not equal to that made by the mode of child rearing, any more than the contribution of organismic-environmental interactions to the development of the organism is equal to that of the genetic program. Just as the genetic program establishes the form of the organism's relationship to its environment and thus determines the limits within which somatic change resulting from this relationship can occur, so the mode of child rearing produces a set of unconscious instructions in the child to reproduce in his or her later, adult environmental interactions the structure of his or her interaction with the mother, establishing in the process strict limits to the learning that can take place within these later interactions. Thus the relations of child rearing are dominant over the adult sexual, political, and technological relations in precisely the same sense that the genetic structure of the organism is dominant over the interactions between the organism and its environment. The mode of child rearing is the social analogue of the DNA molecule: both determine the overall program or plan of development of the system of which they are a part, including the limits within which contributions to this development can be made by the other parts.

Just as the evolutionary transformation of organisms demands a transformation in the genetic program of the organism, so revolutionary social transformation—a transformation in the mode of symbolization—is impossible in the absence of a transformation in the mode of child rearing. And, just as the somatic changes that result from the organism's interactions with its environment can never directly, and may never even ultimately, engender genetic change, so the individual's learning experiences in the course of his or her sexual, political, and technological interactions will never in themselves produce a new mode of child rearing but will, at most, create a context for a possible, but never inevitable, change in this mode. What the individual learns in the course of his or her conscious sexual, political, and technological encounters is never sufficient to produce a transformation in the individual's unconscious mode of symbolization that was formed during his or her childhood. Since it is this unconscious mode of symbolization, in turn, that decisively determines the way this adult will relate to his or her children, it follows that the intergenerational reproduction of the mode of child rearing will be relatively impervious to these adult learning experiences. This is the social analogue of the absence of ''Lamarkian inheritance'': the barrier between the conscious and the unconscious parallels the barrier between the somatic and the genetic. Yet the former barrier is, over the long run, no more absolute than the latter. Conscious learning experiences can trigger a process of transformation of the unconscious mode of symbolization in much the same manner as somatic changes act as catalysts of genetic transformation.[112] Repeated frustrations of the individual's struggle for authentic recognition in his or her sexual, political and ''natural'' interactions may lead the individual to attempt to make conscious the unconscious, internalized structure of recognition that developed in the course of childhood interactions with his or her parents. (This of course is only possible in the context of a culture that has discovered the existence and the significance of the unconscious.) This analytical process, whether self-, group-, or professionally initiated, may well culminate in an effort on the part of this individual to rear his or her children in a mode that is fundamentally different from the one which he or she experienced as a child. Thus the reduction of the gap between the unconscious and the conscious can pave the way for an interruption in the intergenerational reproduction of the prevailing mode of child rearing and the emergence of a new mode of child rearing, and with it a new mode of symbolization.

I am not suggesting that this is the only way in which transformations in the mode of child rearing, and hence the mode of symbolization as a whole, can occur. Pressure to overcome the barrier between the unconscious and the conscious may not only emanate from the sexual, political, and technological interactions of the adult but may also be inherent in the parent-child interaction itself. Thus Lloyd DeMause claims that the child-rearing situation affords parents the opportunity ''to regress to the psychic age of their children and work through their anxieties of that age better the second time than in their own childhood.'' If they are able to do so, DeMause suggests, then they will be able to respond to the demands of their children with more empathy than their parents did to their demands. According to DeMause, this '' 'regression-progression' process,'' which he believes is culturally universal, ''is identical to that which produces change in psychotherapy'' in contemporary cultures:[113]

---

[112] But not *precisely* the same manner. There is no exact parallel in ''social evolution'' to the genetic mutations that result from ''errors in coding and transmission by DNA'' and that underlie the process of organic evolution. This means that social evolution is less affected by chance and thus more controllable by learning than organic evolution. Wilden, *System and Structure*, p. 367, and George Gaylord Simpson, ''Man's Place in Nature,'' in Ronald Munson, ed., *Man and Nature: Philosophical Issues in Biology* (New York: Delta Books, 1971), pp. 268-78.

[113] ''The Psychogenic Theory of History,'' *Journal of Psychohistory*, Vol. 4, (Winter 1977), p. 254.

350

both serve to overcome the barriers between the unconscious and the conscious and thus to initiate the possibility of a new mode of child rearing. There may, in fact, be additional mechanisms that initiate this possibility. I shall return to this large question in the next, and final chapter, in the course of my discussion of the contemporary origins of an embryonic post-Instrumental mode of symbolization. But it should already be clear that, just as evolutionary organic changes cannot occur in the absence of a change in the genetic program of the organism, there can be no transformation of the mode of symbolization as a whole without a transformation of the unconscious program of the individual and the mode of child rearing on which it depends and which, in turn, it serves to reproduce.

The parallel—perhaps even homology—that exists between the development of the organism and the development of the individual not only sustains the thesis of the dominance of the mode of child rearing within the mode of symbolization as a whole. It also lends powerful intellectual support to the struggle to develop a post-Instrumental mode of symbolizing the relationship between the human and the nonhuman parts of nature. The fact that the form of causality governing the relationship between the genetic program of the organism, the organism, and its interactions with its environment is virtually identical to the form of causality governing the relationship between the unconscious structure of the individual, the individual, and his or her interactions with sexual, political, and natural environments suggests that a common, unifying causality characterizes both natural and social processes. And, if both nonhuman organisms and the social organism are governed by the same developmental laws, then it is impossible to maintain an absolute, hard-and-fast distinction between the human and the nonhuman parts of nature: whatever difference exists between these parts exists within the context of a unity—or a community—that they share. Since both natural and social developmental laws are, as we have seen, teleonomic or goal-seeking in character, this community must be grasped, moreover, as a community pervaded by subjectivities or purposes rather than a mere mechanical or chemical identity. Thus we are back to Wilden's (and, at bottom, Hegel's) notion of the ecosystem as a vast network of information that is exchanged among all the communicative subsystems of this ecosystem. What distinguishes the human subsystem from nonhuman subsystems is not the fact that the human is capable of communication (and thus is a subject) while the nonhuman are incapable of communication (and thus are objects) but rather simply the level of complexity or degree of "semiotic freedom"[114] of the human and nonhuman communicative processes. The greater semiotic freedom of the social organism as compared to natural organisms is reflected in the fact, that, as we have seen, the evolution of the former depends less on chance and more on con-

[114] Wilden, *System and Structure*, p. 203.

351

scious learning processes than the evolution of the latter. By absolutizing this difference, the Instrumental mode of symbolization estranges humans from the rest of nature; by masking the common structure of human and natural development it precludes the possibility of human communion with the non-human and thus with the ecosystem as a whole. The parallel I have traced between the genetic development of the organism and the unconscious development of the individual is intended as a contribution to the restoration of this communion, which, as Wilden, Hegel, and Brown have all understood, is foreclosed by the Instrumental mode of symbolization.

What Wilden, Hegel, and even Brown have not understood, however, is that the Instrumental mode of symbolization is rooted in a specific mode of mother-monopolized child rearing and a specific unconscious character structure that this mode engenders. In this chapter I have explored these roots in order to uncover the unconscious obstacles to the postinstrumental relationship between humans and nonhuman nature that they envision. In this way I have, with the aid of Dinnerstein, attempted to extend the contribution that they have made to the contemporary struggle for a post-Instrumental mode of symbolization, the sexual, political, and ecological dimensions of which are the subject of the next, and final, chapter.

Chapter Ten

Feminism, Participatory Democracy, and Ecology: Toward a Post-Instrumental Mode of Symbolization

The thesis of this final chapter is that the sexual, ecological, and political liberation movements of the past two decades in Western industrial societies are the embryonic elements of a new, post-Instrumental mode of symbolization. As such, they are profoundly and directly revolutionary in character. The fulfillment of their liberatory potential does not depend on the subordination of these movements to or alignment with the class struggle that Marxists and Neo-Marxists, respectively, demand. Since sexual, political, and technological domination do not owe their existence to the mode of production, the efforts to eliminate them cannot properly be subsumed under the (class) struggle to transform the mode of production. Nor should the three liberation struggles be aligned with this latter struggle: a struggle whose commitment to transform the particular mode of objectification is coupled with, and rooted in, an even more fundamental commitment to objectification as the essential, immutable relationship betwen humans and their natural surroundings is necessarily inconsistent with the participatorily democratic, feminist, and alternative technological challenge to the domination of nature that objectification entails. The Marxian reliance on class struggle, in other words, is a reliance on a struggle for democratic control over the process and results of objectification on the part of those who engage in objectification, and thus on a struggle that remains wholly within the horizons of what I have called the Instrumental mode of symbolization. The proletariat, as Marxists and Neo-Marxists define it, cannot be understood as the or even a revolutionary agent within contemporary industrial societies; the Marxian claim that it is a universal class is immediately unmasked as ideological once we recognize that objectification is an historically contingent, rather than universal, human activity. (This does not mean, of course, that worker's struggles do not involve a liberatory component. Insofar as they challenge the authoritarian structure

353

of the workplace, they can be understood as one very important part of a broader struggle for participatory democracy, one whose success, however, ultimately depends, among other things, on the transcendence of their commitment to objectification.) The proletariat, then, is not the bearer of genuinely radical needs but rather the bearer of needs that merely reproduce the prevailing symbolic logic of the society of which it is an element. Thus proletarian class struggle is, in fact, a reactionary struggle that is incompatible with the genuinely revolutionary sexual, ecological, and political struggles for a new, post-Instrumental mode of symbolization. The contemporary Neo-Marxist call for these liberation struggles to align themselves with the "class struggle" threatens to undermine, rather than enhance, their revolutionary potential. The flowering of this potential thus demands the repudiation of this Neo-Marxist appeal.

The realization of this potential also demands that each of the three liberation movements come to embrace the others. There is a profound kinship among them: they all entail an effort to transcend an instrumental relationship between self and other in which the latter is symbolized as the means to the former in favor of a postinstrumental relationship in which self and other are symbolized as different but not opposed elements of a shared community. The feminist, participatory democratic, and alternative technology struggles are, at bottom, one struggle, the struggle to establish simultaneously intimate and autonomous relationships between ourselves and our world. I shall attempt to demonstrate that there is, moreover, an organic as well as symbolic basis for their unification: none of them can be won without the victory of the other two. A single movement embracing the objectives of feminism, participatory democracy, and ecology is, therefore, the organizational requisite for the attainment of any and all of these objectives. This movement will also have to include the struggle to replace mother-monopolized child rearing with forms of shared parenting that encourage, rather than inhibit, the formation of unconscious character structures that predispose individuals to strive for all of these organically related postinstrumental goals.

The existence of an organic basis for the organizational unification of the three liberation movements on which their ultimate success depends does not, of course, guarantee that this unification will be achieved. If it did, there would be no point to this chapter or, indeed, to this book, one of whose aims, after all, is to encourage this unification by persuading the participants and supporters of these movements of the existence of this basis. My entire theoretical enterprise, in other words, is predicated on the assumption of the inescapably open-ended nature of history and therefore on the recognition of the necessity of conceptual clarification of, and thus contribution to, the future possibilities to which one is committed. But this and other such contributions are by no means sufficient to engender these possibilities. As I suggested at

354

the end of the preceding chapter, the evolutionary impact of conscious learning experiences is ultimately contingent on transformations in the unconscious or "genetic" character structure of individuals and the mechanisms that produce this structure. This chapter will close, consequently, with a discussion of those changes in the contemporary mode of child rearing and associated character structure that have heretofore encouraged the emergence of the three liberation struggles and the incipient awareness of their inner unity; the discussion includes some speculation as to whether these changes are likely to continue and thus engender the expanding unconscious basis on which the increase in the strength and unity of these struggles depends.

FEMINISM, PARTICIPATORY DEMOCRACY, AND ECOLOGY AS POST-INSTRUMENTAL MOVEMENTS

The Feminist Movement

The feminist movement of the past two decades directly and profoundly challenges the instrumental nature of male-female relationships in contemporary industrial societies. On the one hand, women have insisted that they will no longer serve as the means through which men's ends are achieved. On the other hand, women have also repudiated the hierarchy of values that assigns superiority to men precisely by virtue of male propensities and capacities for instrumental action and have come to affirm as equally, or even more, authentically human the very female expressivity that has heretofore been considered a mark of women's inferiority. This twofold assault on male domination has been launched in the light of a vision of egalitarian, genuinely reciprocal interaction between men and women in which whatever difference remains between them is not transformed into hierarchical opposition but rather coexists fruitfully with their common human concerns and sensibilities.

Perhaps most obviously, the past two decades have been punctuated by persistent demands by women that they cease serving as the pure objects of male sexual appetite. This critique of male "objectification" of women has demonstrated the way in which heterosexual encounters from violent rape in the alley to gentle seduction in the bedroom are marked by woman's subservience to man's power and pleasure, and thus has uncovered the structural continuity beneath these ostensible extremes. At the same time, feminists have exhaustively described, and condemned, the way in which the family, the mass media, and other institutions of socialization contribute to the reproduction of this structure of sexual domination within which, in one way or another, woman are obliged to "put out and shut up."

If women are telling their male sexual partners that they will no longer be

355

their whores, they are also refusing any longer to be their mothers. Within the context of the Instrumental mode of male-female relationships, women serve not merely as the means to men's sexual ends but also as the vehicle through which their generalized needs for emotional support are fulfilled as well. As the "cheerleaders" for his projects, as the source of consolation when he falters or fails, women are expected to provide the nurturance without which their men would be unable effectively to perform in the harsh world outside the home. Much to the consternation of men, feminists over the past two decades have indicated in theory and in practice that they will no longer play this role of "earth mother"—a role that obliges women to suppress their own needs for nurturance every bit as much as the role of "whore" dictates that they subordinate their own claims to sexual satisfaction—nor support the panoply of institutions that enforce conformity to it. In short, women have announced that henceforth they will not serve as the objects of either the sexual or emotional subjectivity of men and have instead demanded male recognition of independent female subjectivity.

Women have also attempted to subvert the hierarchy of values that militates against this recognition. The Instrumental mode of male-female relationships prizes instrumentally rational over expressive personalities and thus embodies the contention that men who are presumed to monopolize the former are more fundamentally human than women who are saddled with the latter; male domination is rooted in and reproduced by the assumption that reason is superior to emotion and thus that reasonable men are superior to emotional women. This assumption, of course, not only legitimates the need of men to treat women as the means to their "higher" ends but also encourages the acquiescence of women to this instrumental treatment: if women view men as more capable and more important than themselves, they have little choice but to subordinate their "lesser" projects and desires to those of their men; in short, to live their lives through them. It is therefore not surprising that feminists who condemn this vicarious subordination have likewise repudiated the assumption that rationalizes it. The much-decried emotionalism of women, they have argued—in theoretical tracts as well as in the intimacy of everyday-life encounters with men—in fact signals a capacity fully to experience both the joy and the pain of human relationships that is lacking in men by virtue of their instrumental detachment from, and numbness to, the full range of human feelings. This feminist transvaluation simultaneously reasserts the worth of traditionally denigrated, characteristically female, personality traits and undermines the purported superiority of the male orientation toward the manipulation of objects: this orientation, feminists have claimed, is at worst inferior to, and at best must be supplemented by, the relational orientation that women have been able so well to develop within the expressive roles to

356

which the male-dominated division of labor has consigned them.[1] The man who fails to recognize the subjectivity of women and treats them instead as pure objects of his subjectivity is simultaneously the man whose own development has been, and remains, short-circuited. Dramatic reversal: it is men who are as limited as, perhaps even more limited than, women. In the realm of interpersonal relationships, at least, it is men who are the emotional cripples, the "second sex." This transvaluation not only legitimates the needs of women, undermining in the process the tendency of both women and men to subordinate these needs to those of men. It also demands that men actually learn from women, that men call into question their own needs and struggle against the instrumental rationality that inhibits their expressivity, that prevents them from being "in touch with their feelings." Thus is a presumed mark of superiority transformed into a sign of a *lack*, a lack which can only be overcome if men strive to become more like women. Through this effort men will be able to repair their flawed subjectivity and come to recognize and nourish the subjectivity of women as well.

The contemporary feminist movement, then, implies a postinstrumental vision of male-female relationships in which men as well as women affirm the centrality of these relationships to their personal development, and the orientations and capabilities essential for the conduct of these relationships are equally distributed across both sexes. These shared sensibilities will enable men and women to recognize one another as fully human, independent selves notwithstanding any differences between them that might persist. And, once the self is able to recognize the essential selfhood of its sexual other, it will be able to bask in the recognition that it receives from this other for the distinctive talents and sensibilities it displays. Under these conditions—when domination no longer perverts the struggle for recognition within the sexual dimension of human existence—intimate sexual relationships between men and women will foster, rather than inhibit, the development of the individual identity of each.

The Movement for Participatory Democracy

Just as the contemporary feminist movement has demonstrated that the prevailing sexual arrangements necessarily entail the domination of men over

---

[1] Lynda M. Glennon, *Women and Dualism* (New York: Longman, 1979). As Glennon points out, one tendency within the contemporary feminist movement, which she labels "Instrumentalism," has not participated in this transvaluation but has rather continued to assume the superiority of instrumental rationality and merely condemned the continued existence of cultural and institutional barriers to women's equal participation in roles that require it. This tendency remains entirely within the Instrumental mode of symbolizing male-female relationships and is thus reformist, rather than revolutionary, in character.

357

women, so the movement for participatory democracy has shown that representative and bureaucratic political forms perforce imply the domination of the representatives and the bureaucrats over the very people they are ostensibly obliged to serve. Moreover, just as feminists have undermined the ideology of male supremacy that legitimates the instrumental treatment of women on the part of men, so participatory democrats have called into question the ideologies that assert the inevitability of representative and bureaucratic forms and thus effectively "eternalize" the instrumental treatment of human beings that these forms necessarily embody. And, finally, this challenge to instrumental political forms and the ideologies on which they depend has been undertaken in the name of a vision of noninstrumental political interactions predicated on the understanding that the active participation of all is the condition for the maximum development of each, a vision that is the political counterpart of the one that informs the feminist movement.

The partisans of participatory democracy have convincingly made the case for the incompatibility of representative democracy and effective citizen control over the decisions that affect their lives. They have shown that the competitive electoral system does not, in fact, engender the accountability of the few to the many that this system is presumed to produce. On the one hand, electoral mandates, particularly in two-party electoral systems, are typically vague and ambiguous, and even the best-intentioned representative will find it difficult to interpret the will of the people or to apply this general mandate to specific decisions. On the other hand, representatives will inevitably develop interests of their own—above all the interest in maintaining and augmenting their power—that tend to compromise their commitment to represent the will of their constituents; the ambiguity of the latter, in turn, allows them to pursue their own interests with relative impunity. Moreover, participatory democrats have exhaustively described and analyzed the process through which effective decision-making responsibility within large-scale, centralized representative democratic polities has devolved out of the hands of elected representatives and into the hands of bureaucrats whose accountability to the electorate is far more tenuous even than that of their ostensible "superiors." Finally, the critics of representative democracy have detailed the way in which the political elite's manipulation of the mass media—to which it has unequal access—creates the very public opinion to which it is supposed to respond. For all these reasons, participatory democrats conclude that the overwhelming majority of individuals in representative "democratic" political systems lack the power to decide the issues that decisively shape their lives. They maintain, in other words, that the attenuated and much-maligned definition of democracy by Joseph Schumpeter—"that institutional arrangement for arriving at political decisions in which individuals acquire the power to decide by means of a competitive struggle for the people's

358

vote''[2]—is, in fact, a realistic rendering of the only kind of "democracy" that a representative system has to offer.

As such, representative democracy both implies and reproduces a division between the active few and the passive many in which the latter become dependent on the former. It demands the alienation of the average citizen's sovereignty or subjectivity that Rousseau—theoretical progenitor of contemporary participatory democrats—argued was the very defining mark of political domination: it transforms the political subject into an object of a political process over which he or she has no control and which he or she is obliged fatalistically to contemplate. Representative democracy thus necessarily engenders low levels of mass political interest and competence and, ultimately, an inability of individuals to perceive any connection between politics, i.e., collective decision making, and their personal development. It short-circuits the struggle for human recognition within the political arena, militating against or even precluding that development of the self which is predicated on the possibility of collective discourse and debate with its political others.

If representative democracy is a form of political domination, then the struggle against political domination demands a critique of the theory of the inevitability of representative democracy. Thus participatory democrats have sought in their theory and practice over the past two decades to undermine the prevailing ideological arguments for the inescapability of representative democracy and, correlatively, for the impossibility of participatory democracy. These arguments can be reduced to two main types. The first asserts a connection between size and representative democracy. If, it is argued, government is to provide solutions to the problems of a large-scale, highly interdependent contemporary society, then the unit on which government is based must be coextensive with the society itself, i.e., a large-scale political unit is inevitable. The inevitability of large-scale political units, in turn, signals the impossibility of participatory democracy, since "severe upper limits are set on effective participation in 'democratic' decisions by the sheer number of persons involved."[3] The conclusion is drawn that some form of representative democracy is the only practical alternative.

The second argument claims that representative democracy follows from inevitable differences in the level of citizen competence. Not all citizens are equally inclined to develop, or equally capable of developing, the competence demanded by informed political choice. Given these inherent differences in the level of political competence, "the fact that decisions on some matter

---

[2] Cited in Carole Pateman, *Participation and Democratic Theory* (Cambridge, Eng.: Cambridge University Press, 1970), p. 4. For another discussion of this definition, see Peter Bachrach, *The Theory of Democratic Elitism: A Critique* (Boston: Little, Brown & Co., 1967), Ch. 2.

[3] Robert A. Dahl, *After the Revolution?* (New Haven, Conn.: Yale University Press, 1970), p. 143.

affect your interests in a vital way does not mean that it is necessarily rational . . . to insist on participating. . . . For your own self-interest your participation ought to stop where significant differences in competence begin.''[4] Thus significant differences in competence preclude the possibility of informed participation by all those who are affected by decisions and demand instead that these decisions be made by those informed few who have the time, energy, and capacity to make them, i.e., by representatives and other political "specialists" in their employ. As we saw in Chapter Three, this traditional argument on behalf of the necessity of political expertise has recently been transformed into an argument against even representative democracy: the "technocracy thesis" maintains that, under contemporary post-industrial conditions, political issues are in fact, and increasingly, technical issues that merit an exclusively technical disposition. Common to both the traditional and the technocratic emphasis on the criterion of political competence, however, is the insistence that a participatory democratic system violates this criterion and must therefore be repudiated.

Participatory democrats have effectively challenged both the "size" and "competence" arguments on behalf of the inescapability of representative democracy. On the one hand, they have accepted the thesis of the incompatibility of large-scale communities and participatory democracy, and have transformed this thesis into a compelling case for small-scale communities. The presumption against participatory democracy evaporates, in other words, once we call into question the inevitability of huge communities and the "big is better" assumption that creates a presumption in their favor. Kirkpatrick Sale, in his recent, encyclopedic treatment of the problem of human scale, argues convincingly on behalf of both the desirability and the feasibility of the destruction of the megalopolis and the decentralization of the population of contemporary societies into small-scale communities whose limited population—from 5 to 10 thousand—would make direct, face-to-face democracy possible and whose approximate self-sufficiency and consequent lack of "spillover" effects would render this form of democracy generally consistent with the principle that all those who are affected by decisions should participate in their disposition.[5] Contrary to the conventional wisdom, large-scale political units are not inevitable, and neither therefore are the obstacles they present to participatory democracy. The same is true, argue the participatory democrats, of the unequal distribution of political competence that currently prevails in contemporary industrial societies. As we have seen, the generally low level of mass political interest and competence that the apologists for representative democracy take as a given can just as, or probably even more,

---

[4] *Ibid.*, p. 31.
[5] *Human Scale* (New York: Coward, McCann & Geoghegan, 1980), esp. Part Five.

plausibly be interpreted as a consequence of the political domination associated with representative democracy. The hypothesis that follows from this interpretation, of course, is that the elimination of representative democracy along with the domination that is its inevitable companion, and the creation of a participatory democracy, will eliminate the present obstacles to high levels of mass political interest and competence:

> Once the participatory system is established . . . it becomes self-sustaining because the very qualities that are required of individual citizens if the system is to work successfully are those that the process of participation itself develops and fosters; the more the individual citizen participates the better able he is to do so.[6]

Thus participatory democracy itself will engender the informed citizenry whose absence, we have seen, is one of the principal reasons cited for the necessity of representative democracy. In short, and contrary to orthodox "wisdom," there is no fatal contradiction between the criterion of competence and the commitment to the principle of an equal "individual share in those social decisions determining the quality and direction of his life."[7]

The struggles for workplace and neighborhood democracy of the past few decades are informed, then, by a vision of future communities within which political participation is an essential medium for the development of the human personality. Whereas a commitment to representative democracy presupposes the assumption that human needs are prepolitical in origin and thus that the function of politics is merely to re-present needs that already exist, allegiance to participatory democracy is founded on the recognition that human needs originate and evolve in the course of collective decision making itself, i.e., that politics is an authentic, irreducible realm of need creation and thus that an adequate politics cannot be merely representative in character. To put this another way, participatory democrats understand, while representative democrats do not, that collective decision making necessarily entails a struggle for human recognition in which the identity of the self is formed in and through its interactions with its political others. This understanding informs the participatory democrat's insistence on face-to-face political interactions: the only way in which humans can overcome the "otherness" of other humans, reciprocally to recognize each other and thus develop their respective identities, is actually to be present to one another. It also underlies his or her general preference for consensual, rather than, majoritarian decision making, i.e., for an organic or voluntary rather than artificial or arbitrary reconciliation of the will of the self and the will of others.

---

[6] Pateman, *Participation and Democratic Theory*, p. 25.

[7] From the Port Huron Statement, the founding manifesto of the Students for a Democratic Society, cited in Sale, *Human Scale*, p. 47.

The Ecology Movement

The ecology movement is the postinstrumental counterpart of feminism and participatory democracy. Like the participants in these movements, ecological enthusiasts have challenged a relationship in which the other serves as a pure means to the ends of an aggrandizing self. Like the partisans of feminism and participatory democracy, moreover, they have sought to undermine the paradigm within which this instrumental exploitation of the other is rationalized as the only possible form of the relationship between it and the self. And, finally, they too have done so in the name of an alternative, postinstrumental paradigm within which self and other are symbolized as complementary elements of a common whole.

Ecologists have struggled over the past two decades to persuade us that Western Enlightenment civilization imposes intolerable burdens on the ecosystem as a whole and thus ultimately on its human part. What we know of as technological progress, they demonstrate, is inextricably intertwined with a depletion and degradation of nonhuman nature that will, sooner or later, make it impossible for the latter to sustain human life. This progress, on the one hand, has been predicated on the unlimited plunder of natural resources. Having assumed that these resources are, for all practical purposes, inexhaustible, we have simply grabbed all that we are able to get. The "high entropy"[8] or energy-intensive economies of both contemporary capitalist and state socialist societies have purchased relative material abundance at the price of the maximum possible flow of energy. For the past several hundred years the availability of relatively abundant, and therefore relatively cheap, nonrenewable fuels such as coal, oil, and gas has made it possible to pay this price. But, as Rifkin, Ophuls, Commoner and many others have emphasized, we are rapidly reaching the point at which these sources will be exhausted and thus this price will become exorbitant.[9] Similarly, technological progress within industrial societies over the past several hundred years has been based on the unlimited exploitation of the mineral resources of the planet. The exponentially increasing demand for these resources since the onset of the industrial revolution now threatens their rapid depletion, even their complete exhaustion: according to one recent estimate, "just over half of [the] major minerals will be exhausted in less than 50 years at current growth rates."[10] We have, in short, reached the point where our present tendency to take everything from nonhuman nature as we see fit is undermining our future ability to take from it anything at all.

[8] Jeremy Rifkin, *Entropy: A New World View* (New York: Viking, 1980).

[9] Rifkin, *Entropy*, Part Three; Ophuls, *Ecology and the Politics of Scarcity*, Ch. 3; Barry Commoner, *The Poverty of Power* (New York: Bantam Books, 1977).

[10] Ophuls, *Ecology and the Politics of Scarcity*, pp. 65-66.

We are also rapidly reaching the point, ecological activists have informed us, where our predilection to do to nonhuman nature whatever we choose may well eliminate the possibility of ever doing anything with it again. It is by now commonplace to observe that Western civilization has, in two hundred short years, done far more damage to the natural surround than all other civilizations combined over the course of hundreds of thousands of years. The "benefits" of this civilization have been purchased at the price of unprecedented violations of the integrity of the ecosystem on which it depends. In order to survive, we have laid waste the land, despoiled our waters, and poisoned the atmosphere. The result is that much of our land is uninhabitable, our water undrinkable, and our air unbreathable, i.e., that our very survival is in question. The inherent tendency of large-scale, "high-technology" industry to engender life-threatening pollution has been accelerated since World War II, moreover, by the systematic displacement of products made from natural raw materials by products made from synthetics, a displacement engendered in part by the frenetic effort to overcome the dependence on minerals and other increasingly limited natural resources to which I have already alluded. This replacement of the organic by the synthetic results in the proliferation of products that are resistant to the natural process of biological degradation and intensifies the artificial oversimplification of the ecosystem that, since the onset of industrialization, makes it "vulnerable to stress and to final collapse."[11] Ecologists differ with respect to the imminence of this collapse, but none doubts that, in the absence of profound technological transformation, it is inevitable.

As we have seen, the apologists for the prevailing technological rationality are not blind to its presently disastrous environmental consequences. What they dispute, rather, is the contention that these consequences are the inevitable accompaniments of this rationality. In fact, they argue, it is the not-yet-fully-developed character of technological rationality that accounts for these consequences, and thus it is the extension of this rationality on which the elimination of these consequences depends. Better, more efficient large-scale technology can solve the problems associated with the technology that currently exists. Nuclear fission can eliminate our dependence on coal, oil, and gas and thus overcome the scarcity of energy that threatens our energy-intensive economies; if fission, in turn, turns out to be too dangerous, then there is always the possibility of fusion, the ultimate source of clean, safe energy. Better planning, moreover, can improve our ability to foresee the consequences of our technological interventions and thus reduce drastically if not eliminate entirely the unintended consequences that presently accom-

---

[11] Commoner, *The Closing Circle*, Chs. 2, 9; see also Ophuls, *Ecology and the Politics of Scarcity*, Ch. 1.

pany these interventions. Thus the solution to the pollution that accompanies modern industrial technology is not the wholesale abandonment of this technology but rather the development of an effective modern technology of pollution control. There is, in short, a technological solution to every technologically induced problem. Science will ultimately prevail over nature.

The proponents of the "technofix" demonstrate that the assumption that humans know best necessarily gives rise to an instrumental solution to the problem of the instrumental exploitation of nonhuman nature. As long as this anthropocentric assumption is maintained, the depletion and degradation of nature is likely to call forth an effort to extend, rather than to question, the very technology that accounts for this depletion and degradation in the first place. Ecologists have therefore sought to undermine the claim of human superiority that justifies the instrumental treatment of nonhuman nature. On the one hand, they have replaced the Enlightenment image of nature as a mute object whose "completion" awaits the intervention of an external human subject with the image of an intricate, extraordinarily complex network of reciprocally related processes that is complete in itself and on whose integrity the survival of the human subject ultimately depends. Each element of any given ecosystem is both cause and effect of all the others: in aquatic ecosystems, for example, "fish produce organic wastes; decaying microorganisms release nitrogen from organic forms and combine it with oxygen to form nitrate; this is reconverted to organic forms by algae; algal organic matter nourishes small aquatic animals; these in turn are eaten by fish."[12] Within this and every other natural system, "everything is connected to everything else": the survival of the fish depends on the survival of the algae, the survival of the algae depends on the production of nitrate, the production of nitrate depends on the production of organic wastes, and the production of organic wastes depends on the survival of the fish. Within this cycle, moreover, there is no waste: "in every natural system, what is excreted by one organism as waste is taken up by another as food."[13] Thus the ability of each element of the system to live off the others is ultimately contingent on the contribution it makes to the life of the others. The equilibrium of any natural system, in short, depends on the maintenance of a delicate balance of giving and taking among all its constituent elements.

Any disruption of this balance threatens the equilibrium of the system. A change in one of the elements of the system will produce far-reaching ramifications for the system as a whole. To return to the example of the aquatic ecosystem, a rapid growth of algae may result in the depletion of the oxygen content of the water, and thus ultimately threaten the survival of the ecosystem

[12] Commoner, *The Closing Circle*, p. 23.
[13] *Ibid.*, pp. 35-6.

364

as a whole. Under normal conditions, the other elements of this system will respond to the growth of algae in such a way as to minimize this threat. The "excess in algae increases the ease with which fish can feed on them; this reduces the algal population"[14] and forestalls the depletion of oxygen, thus restoring the equilibrium of the system. Natural systems, in other words, are homeostatic or self-correcting systems: they are "designed" to preserve their integrity in the face of external events that threaten to undermine them.

There are limits, however, to the homeostatic capacities of natural systems. A change in one of the elements of the system may simply be too great or too sudden for its compensatory mechanisms to handle. Suppose, for example, that the flow of industrial waste into a lake increases dramatically its algal population. If this increase is more rapid than the increased ease with which fish can feed off and thus reduce the algal population, then oxygen depletion will eventually result from the increased organic debris that itself results from the rapid death of algae at depths too low to receive the sunlight necessary for photosynthesis.[15] The ultimate result: the collapse of the entire aquatic ecosystem. A dead lake, a Lake Erie.

If the homeostatic capacities of natural ecosystems can be described as a form of "intelligence," the wanton disregard for, and violation of, these capacities that the human pretension to "master" nature entails can only be described as a form of gross stupidity. Humans are, in fact, the only living species that strives to dominate all the others, the only species foolish enough not to respect the laws of ecological balance on which the survival of all species, including the human, ultimately depend. Only humans regularly take more than they give to the global ecosystem, transforming a relationship that is properly one of the participation of one part within a whole into the exploitation by this part of all the other parts.[16] Thus only human life endangers the survival of other species and ultimately its own as well. If intelligence has something to do with long-range survival capability, can the human species fairly be described as more intelligent than any other? Is it not rather the case that the Western Enlightenment assumption of human superiority over non-human nature—the assumption that justifies the life-threatening exploitation of the global ecosystem—is the very height of folly itself? It would appear, then, that wisdom demands that the anthropocentric assumption that humans know best be replaced by the more modest, ecologically sound assumption that nature cannot be outwitted and that, in fact, "Nature knows best."[17]

Over the past two decades, ecological activists have struggled to work out the practical, technological implications of this non-anthropocentric, post-

14 *Ibid.*, p. 30.
15 *Ibid.*, p. 32.
16 *Ibid.*, p. 11.
17 *Ibid.*, p. 37.

instrumental theoretical assumption. Contrary to the contentions of the apologists of instrumental rationality, they have demonstrated that this assumption demands not the wholesale abandonment of technology—whatever that might mean—but rather the creation of an ecologically sound, alternative technology. This technology, in contrast to the one on which both contemporary capitalist and state socialist production are based, is consciously constructed to minimize its threat to the integrity of the various ecosystems of which it is a part. Thus, on the one hand, alternative technologies are designed to take as little from nature as possible; they make minimum use, in other words, of non-renewable resources. Renewable sources of energy—the sun, the wind, the water, and even human waste—are therefore greatly to be preferred over the nonrenewable sources on which our present industrial civilization is built. Much of the effort of alternative technologists over the past two decades, in fact, has been devoted to the demonstration of the practicality of solar power, wind power, tidal power, and methane gas as the energy sources of the future.[18] Additional effort has been expended to persuade us that nonrenewable resources must be carefully conserved and recycled. In sum, alternative technology is designed to ensure the minimum possible depletion of natural resources and thus implies a "steady-state" society that "has achieved a basic long-term balance between the demands of [the] population and the environment that supplies its wants."[19]

On the other hand, alternative technologies are designed to do as little damage to nature as possible. Diversified, organic farming is a substitute for monoculture and the dependence on ecologically destructive pesticides that it demands. Nonpolluting modes of transport such as the bicycle and the electric car are touted as replacements for the smog-producing internal-combustion automobile. The use of synthetic, nondegradable materials in the fabrication of the clothing we wear, the forms of shelter we inhabit, and the medicine we consume is to give way to reliance on natural materials on which degradative enzymes can work.[20] Sewage and garbage will be returned to the soil, as fertilizer, rather than dumped in lakes, rivers, and oceans as pollution. Alternative technologies, in short, "are closely adapted to natural cycles" and thus "cause as little interference with [these] cycles as possible."[21]

Alternative technologies, then, are embodiments of a cooperative, rather

---

[18] Bookchin, *Post-Scarcity Anarchism*; David Dickson, *The Politics of Alternative Technology* (Glasgow: William Collins & Co., Ltd., 1974); Stephen Lyons, ed., *Sun! A Handbook for the Solar Decade* (San Francisco, Friends of the Earth, 1978); Amory Lovins, *Soft Energy Paths* (Cambridge, Mass.: Ballinger, 1977).

[19] Ophuls, *Ecology and the Politics of Scarcity*, p. 13.

[20] Commoner, *The Closing Circle*, pp. 41, 282-83.

[21] Ophuls, *Ecology and the Politics of Scarcity*, p. 128; Dickson, *The Politics of Alternative Technology*, p. 98.

than exploitative relationship between the human and nonhuman parts of the natural whole. They are, to put it another way, the materialization of the understanding that the unimpeded development of the human self depends on the unhindered development of its "natural" other, that humans only learn about their own possibilities by learning about the possibilities of all the other beings with which they share a common destiny. As such, these technologies imply the very post-objectifying consciousness that Hegel envisioned a century and a half ago, a consciousness which, "while it stands in negative relation to things and assimilates them to itself, . . . equally finds individuality in them and does not encroach upon their independence, or interfere with their free self-determination."[22] They portend, in other words, that "*genuine* resolution of the conflict between man and nature" that Marx misleadingly identifies with the objectifying technologies they transcend.[23]

The Interdependence of Feminism, Participatory Democracy, and Ecology

The feminist, participatory democratic, and alternative technology movements, I have argued, all challenge an instrumental relationship between self and other in which the latter is but a means to the former in the name of a vision of a noninstrumental, reciprocal relationship between self and other in which the development of the latter is understood as the necessary condition for the development of the former. Since each movement equally defies the logic of the Instrumental mode of symbolization and anticipates the emergence of an alternative, post-Instrumental mode of symbolization, we should not be surprised to discover that each embodies elements of the other. This, indeed, is the case: the explicit commitment of each separate movement to the liberation it envisions is often accompanied by an implicit or partial commitment to the liberatory goals of its counterparts. This overlap of commitments signals an incipient awareness of participants in each of the liberation movements of the kinship among them.

Typically, the organizational forms within which feminist activity takes place are participatorily democratic. Consciousness-raising groups, which can perhaps be described as the organizational nucleus of the early stages of this contemporary movement—at least in the United States—normally involve the direct, face-to-face participation of no more than a dozen or so women. This organizational form encourages, even demands the involvement of all members in the discussions and is predicated on the assumption that the con-

---

[22] Miller, *Hegel's Philosophy of Nature*, p. 12.
[23] Marx, "Private Property and Communism," p. 70.

sciousness of each individual woman will develop—that each will become increasingly aware of the common, patriarchal root of her ostensibly "personal" problems as well as the common feminist solution—in the course of her interactions with her "sisters." This participatorily democratic commitment to the development of the self in and through intercourse with others is likewise evident in the internal structure of the impressive variety of feminist enterprises that have proliferated since the apparent decline in participation in consciousness-raising groups. Women's legal and medical clinics, restaurants, bookstores, presses, and university-study programs are characteristically managed by collectives that aspire to the elimination of hierarchical chains of command and the substitution of consensual for competitive forms of decision making. In short, feminists have recognized that participatory democratic forms are the most fertile political soil in which feminist consciousness and activity can flourish. Some feminists have even argued, in fact, that participatory democratic forms of decision making are specifically female political forms.[24]

The feminist commitment to participatory democratic governance of women's organizations is often accompanied by the insistence that these organizations avail themselves of alternative technologies. Women's restaurants, for example, typically offer vegetarian fare that has been "naturally" prepared, i.e., cooked without additives, refined sugar, etc. Partisans of the women's health movement have questioned the prevailing model of orthodox medical technology in the name of a "wholistic" model that legitimates an array of alternative techniques: herbal remedies (instead of synthetic drugs), acupuncture (instead of painkillers and "high-technology" operations), home birth and midwifery (instead of hospital birth and obstetricians). This challenge to orthodox medical technology is simultaneously a repudiation of the reliance on (predominantly male) professional expertise that has effectively robbed women of control over their bodies:[25] the alternative techniques emphasized in the women's health movement are designed to be administered by lay women and thus to enable them to reestablish this control. The woman's health movement, moreover, is only one example of a general repudiation of professionalism in favor of self-help within the contemporary feminist movement. Because male domination over women so often assumes the form of the dependence of women on male "experts," the feminist assault on male domination has come to embrace a challenge to the ideology of the inevitability of technocracy that functions to reproduce the prevailing form of technological domination. And so women have found it necessary to support the creation of technologies that are not only ecosystemically sound but also lend them-

[24] Nancy Hartsock, "Feminist Theory and the Development of Revolutionary Strategy," in Eisenstein, *Capitalist Patriarchy and the Case for Socialist Feminism*, pp. 56-77.
[25] Ehrenreich and English, *For Their Own Good*.

selves to popular control. In 1980, this emerging feminist commitment to alternative technologies crystallized in the form of a national conference on "Ecofeminism" in which American feminists explored the links between feminism and ecology and addressed, among other issues, the problem of the meaning of an authentically "feminist technology."[26]

If women with a primary commitment to feminism have lent their support to participatory democracy and alternative technology, activists who are primarily preoccupied with participatory democracy have likewise contributed to the development of alternative technologies and feminism. Community organizations have attracted the participation of large numbers of women who are able to assume public, political roles for the first time and thus to transcend the limits of the purely private, domestic roles to which they are normally confined. This participation often serves both to acclimate women to leadership positions and to oblige men who are uncomfortable with the exercise of female authority to come to terms with, and, perhaps, struggle to transcend, this discomfort. At the same time, the emphasis on the community or the neighborhood as an essential arena for participatorily democratic organizing activity politicizes traditionally female concerns such as housing and child care, removing them from the purely private, personal sphere and thus undermining in the process an important aspect of the contemporary patriarchal division of labor.

The participatorily democratic concerns of many community organization activists have also led them to explore the possibilities of alternative technologies and thus to call into question the large-scale, energy-intensive, highly centralized technologies on which their constituents are presently obliged to rely. Participants in "populist" campaigns against energy rate-hikes often couple their condemnation of the overbloated utilities with proclamations of the virtues of eventual reliance on the sun and other sources of energy that cannot easily be transformed into profitable commodities and that lend themselves to community control. Members of neighborhood food co-ops typically couple their commitment to community control over the distribution of food with a commitment to organic, small-scale farming. Local block clubs attempt to beautify their immediate surroundings by learning, and practicing, the techniques of neighborhood gardening. Reflecting and reinforcing the intersection of participatory democratic and alternative technological concerns, centers for "neighborhood technology" have sprung up over the past decade in our major metropolitan centers.[27] The intersection of these concerns is also

[26] See the agenda for this conference, in the files of the author. Two similar conferences took place in the United States during the first half of 1981. See Carolyn Merchant, "Earthcare: Women and the Environmental Movement," *Environment*, 23 (June 1981), pp. 6-13, 38-40.

[27] James Ridgeway, *Energy-Efficient Community Planning* (Emmaus, Penna.: The J. G. Press, n.d.).

evident in the fact that the 1980 annual meeting of the Conference on Alternative State and Local Politics—a nationwide coalition of organizations committed to participatory democracy—was devoted to the theme of alternative technology.

Finally, ecological activists have often embraced participatory democratic and feminist objectives. "Anti-nuke" movements in the United States and Western Europe are remarkably decentralized. In the United States, for example, the movement is dominated by local, state, or regional "alliances" whose constituent units are often "affinity groups" composed of a relative handful of participants. This internal structure reflects a profound distaste for centralized hierarchical chains of command as well as an equally intense commitment to face-to-face, consensual decision making. Similarly, the various ecology or "green" political parties that have recently begun to contest for national electoral power in the advanced capitalist societies generally emphasize that this national focus on the representative political arena is not intended to displace, but rather to enhance, "grass-roots" ecological activism. More generally, the partisans of alternative technology characteristically hammer home the point that the technologies to which they are committed, in contrast to the prevailing ones, are small in scale and relatively easy to understand, and thus compatible with a political commitment to decentralized, participatory democracy.

Many ecological enthusiasts are similarly hospitable to feminist concerns. Many American anti-nuke groups, for example, have a far higher proportion of female active members than the average American political group, perhaps because at least some women have grasped a connection between the degradation of nature and the degradation of women who are deemed to be "her" representatives, perhaps as well because women are traditionally more preoccupied with the fate of future generations, i.e., their children, than men. At the same time, many environmental activists have explicitly emphasized the disproportionate danger to women that radiation and a variety of industrial pollutants entail and have thus attempted to attract additional women to the movement. The relatively high participation of women within anti-nuke groups, in turn, demands that the male members of these groups at least pay lip service to the feminist critique of aggressive, characteristically male behavior within political groups. Anti-nuke women who find that this prohibition of male chauvinism in principle is not sufficiently enforced in practice have established explicitly feminist, women's anti-nuke groups. The link between ecology and feminism has recently, and vividly, been symbolized by the Citizens Party candidacy of feminist LaDonna Harris and ecologist Barry Commoner for the two highest political offices in the land.

The convergence of perspectives that I have detailed is not, however, complete. Although each liberation movement embraces elements of the others, each has nevertheless been reluctant fully and explicitly to endorse the goals of its counterparts. Activists in feminist organizations, notwithstanding the generally participatory character of these organizations, have generally not committed themselves to decentralized, participatory democracy as the appropriate mode of organization for the society as a whole, in part because they and their feminist constituents are not persuaded of the intrinsically repressive character of representative democracy and in part because they distrust the depth of the feminist commitment of many male community control activists who are. Militants in participatory democratic organizations, in turn, often refuse to endorse the full range of feminist demands, either because they fear the loss of members who are suspicious of "woman's lib" or because they fear that unity with feminists will dilute the intensity of their organization's overriding commitment to community control. Ecologists, finally, fear that an explicit identification with feminism will weaken their movement either by alienating male anti-nukers and alternative technologists who are not committed feminists or by introducing into their ranks feminists whose ecological commitments are suspect, or both. In short, significant elements of each movement fear that explicit identification with the aims of the other will dilute the strength of their movement and thus inhibit the fulfillment of its goals. Thus feminism, participatory democracy, and ecology remain, at present, three separate (although partially overlapping) movements.

This separation accurately reflects the present level of consciousness of the participants in all three movements: it is undeniably the case that many of the supporters of each are not fully in sympathy with the goals of the adherents of the others. Under these conditions, activists with a primary commitment to one movement who *are* committed to the goals of the other two are rightly apprehensive that the explicit identification of their movement with the other two might reduce its coherence or diffuse its focus. They are wrong, however, to take the existing level of consciousness, and the separation of movements that is both rooted in and helps to reproduce this consciousness, as a given and then to proceed from the assumption that their movement can be successful independent of the success of the others. It can in fact be demonstrated that none of the three liberation struggles of the past two decades can be won in the absence of the victory of the other two. Only when the participants of the feminist, participatory democratic, and alternative technology movements come to recognize that each movement is absolutely essential for the other will they strive for the ideological and organizational unification on which their mutual success ultimately depends. The following demonstration, then, is intended as a contribution to this recognition and thus to the eventual success of all three liberation struggles of which it is a precondition.

Let me begin with an analysis of the dependence of the movement for alternative technology on the movements for participatory democracy and

371

feminism. The conventional argument for the impracticality of alternative technologies makes it clear that their potential practicality is contingent on precisely those far-reaching political transformations that the participatory democrat has in mind. Alternative technologies, it is argued, are uniformly small in scale and thus incompatible with large-scale societies and the political-economic centralization that accompanies them. Thus, for example, the opponents of solar power and other "soft energy paths" are fond of pointing out that the energy resulting from these "alternative" sources will never be sufficient to meet the needs of the highly concentrated populations and industries of the American megalopolis. Thus we must resign ourselves to the use of those energy sources—coal, oil, and nuclear—which, whatever their degree of danger to the environment, allow for technologies that are sufficiently large-scale and centralized to meet these needs. As long as we take the prevailing demographic and industrial centralization as a given, this is a compelling argument. Even enthusiastic proponents of alternative energy sources, like Murray Bookchin, agree that

> these sources cannot supply man with the large blocks of energy needed to sustain densely concentrated populations and highly centralized industries. Solar devices, wind turbines and heat pumps will produce relatively small quantities of power . . . we cannot foresee a time when they will be able to furnish the electricity currently used by cities the size of New York, London, or Paris.[28]

It follows that it is only possible to make a persuasive case for the feasibility of ecologically sound technologies if this case is accompanied by a challenge to the prevailing demographic and political-economic centralization in the name of a vision of a fundamentally different, decentralized civilization:

> As in the case of agriculture . . . the application of ecological principles to energy resources presupposes a far-reaching decentralization of society . . . If urban communities are reduced in size and widely dispersed over the land, there is no reason why these devices [solar collectors and wind turbines] cannot be combined to provide us with all the amenities of an industrialized civilization. To use solar, wind and tidal power effectively, the megalopolis must be decentralized.[29]

And this decentralization, in turn, is precisely one of the central goals of the partisans of participatory democracy! As we have seen, the participatory democrat recognizes that direct face-to-face political participation presupposes

---

[28] Bookchin, *Post-Scarcity Anarchism*, pp. 128-29. See also Ophuls, *Ecology and the Politics of Scarcity*, p. 128; Dickson, *The Politics of Alternative Technology*, pp. 103-107; Sale, *Human Scale*, Part Three, Ch. 6.

[29] Bookchin, *Post-Scarcity Anarchism*, pp. 74-75.

decentralized small-scale communities and therefore commits him/herself to their proliferation. The movement for participatory democracy, then, is committed to a socio-political transformation without which the technological transformation envisioned by the ecologist would be an utter impossibility.

At the same time, the proponents of alternative technologies argue that the relative simplicity of the technologies will enable the average person to control them rather than be controlled by them. But human control over even these far less complex technologies presupposes a competent human being who is confident of his or her decision-making capabilities. Such a human being, however, is hardly likely to predominate in a society in which individuals have come to be passively dependent on the decisions of their political representatives and bureaucrats. The efficacious human being on whom the genuinely liberatory use of alternative technologies depends will only predominate in a society that regularly encourages the direct, active participation of all its citizens in the collective decision making of that society, i.e., a participatory democratic society.

For both reasons, Ivan Illich is correct to argue that "only participatory democracy creates the conditions for rational technology."[30] It follows that the struggle for rational, alternative technology cannot be won without the victory of the struggle for participatory democracy.

The movement for alternative technology is equally dependent on the feminist movement. As we have seen, the design and operation of ecologically sound technologies are predicated on a post-Instrumental symbolization of the human relationship to the natural surround. Generalized support for alternative technologies presupposes individuals who no longer strive to dominate nature and who seek instead to develop a more nurturant relationship with it. We have also seen, however, that the men of contemporary patriarchal society are typically oriented to the manipulation of objects—to an instrumental relationship with the world—and lack the expressive or relational orientation that women possess. A large part of the male population of contemporary industrial societies is undoubtedly emotionally unsuited for the postobjectifying technologies to which ecologists are committed! Thus the commitment to these technologies demands a commitment to a profound emotional transformation that would render men more expressive or relationally oriented. This, of course, is precisely one of the central emotional transformations to which the feminist movement aspires. The conclusion is inescapable, then, that support for alternative technology demands full-scale support for feminism.

This conclusion is inescapable for another reason as well. The proponents of alternative technologies generally agree that these technologies will be far

---

[30] Cited in Lyons, *Sun!*, p. 51.

more labor-intensive than the capital-intensive technologies that presently prevail.[31] Even if we assume that in the post-Instrumental society of the future the range of material needs will be far less extensive than that which currently exists, the volume of person-hours required to meet these needs through alternative technologies will be far greater than the volume demanded by today's large-scale, capital-intensive technologies. (Thus the post-Instrumental solution to the problem of "necessary" labor does not, in contrast to that of Marx, entail a progressive reduction through mechanization of the amount of time that humans labor to produce "necessities" that nevertheless presupposes that some such human production will always be necessary. It entails, rather, the elimination of "necessary" labor through the transcendence of objectification and the creation of a human relationship with nature in which the latter is no longer experienced as a means to human ends and thus labor that happens to *result* in survival is no longer undertaken *in order to* survive.) The operation of these technologies will require the significant participation of all the adult (if not younger) members of the society. These technologies are, therefore, incompatible with the prevailing sexual division of labor that, for example, assigns more than half of the adult female population of the United States to exclusively domestic tasks.[32] It follows that the operation of these technologies demands the elimination of this division of labor and the emergence of full and equal female participation in the public world of "enterprise." These demands, of course, are precisely the demands of the contemporary feminist movement. For this reason as well, the success of this movement is indispensable to the success of the movement for alternative technology.

Consider now the dependence of the movement for participatory democracy on the feminist and alternative technology movements. As we have seen, one standard argument against participatory democracy is that the decentralized, small-scale communities essential for direct, face-to-face democratic decision making are simply incompatible with the demands of the large-scale, highly centralized technologies of the modern age. Decisions concerning these technologies necessarily produce effects that cannot be contained within the boundaries of intimate, small-scale communities, effects which should properly become the object of decision making by constituencies that are coextensive with the extent of these effects and thus far larger than those that participatory democracy requires. Dahl, for example, concludes that direct democracy is generally inconsistent with what he calls the "principle of affected interests," i.e., the principle that all those who are affected by decisions have the right

[31] Dickson, *The Politics of Alternative Technology*, p. 103; Ophuls, *Ecology and the Politics of Scarcity*, p. 128.

[32] Kathleen McCourt, *Working-Class Women and Grass-Roots Politics* (Bloomington: Indiana University Press, 1977), p. 19.

374

to participate in these decisions.[33] The participatory democratic answer to this objection, as we have also seen, is that the largely self-sufficient, self-contained nature of the communities they envision will eliminate the bulk of the interdependencies that presently render the commitment to direct, face-to-face democracy inconsistent with the principle of affected interests.

The problem with this answer, however, is that local autonomy and self-sufficiency are, in fact, utterly incompatible with the prevailing reliance on large-scale, highly centralized technologies that dictates that communities do not produce the majority of goods and services they consume nor consume the majority of goods and services that they produce. Since self-sufficiency and the possibility of participatory democracy that depends on it are therefore incompatible with dominant technological realities, it follows that the commitment to participatory democracy demands a fundamental challenge to these technological realities. This is precisely the challenge of the movement for alternative technology. Its proponents argue persuasively that only the small-scale, "soft" technologies they envision are compatible with the preference for a modern society composed of large numbers of decentralized, largely self-sufficient, small-scale communities.[34] Whereas, for example, every small community can have its own complex of solar collectors and wind turbines, every small community obviously cannot have its own generators of nuclear power. Thus Illich correctly observes that "participatory democracy postulates low energy technology"[35] in particular and alternative technology in general. The struggle for the latter is therefore essential to the struggle for the former.

Participatory democracy is dependent on alternative technology in yet another sense. The critic of participatory democracy concludes that this form of democracy is incompatible with the criterion of competence, i.e., the principle that participation in decisions should vary in relation to variations in the level of competence of those affected by those decisions; the partisan of participatory democracy typically replies that participation itself will eliminate significant differences in the level of competence and thus that participatory democracy does not, in fact, violate this criterion. But, although participation is undoubtedly a necessary, it is not a sufficient, condition for competence. Competent decisions concerning the use of various technologies demand that the individuals making these decisions fully understand the design and operation of these technologies, and the design and operation of many of the "high-technologies" that presently predominate are undoubtedly beyond the ready understanding of even the most enthusiastic partisans of participatory democracy. Thus Harry Braverman correctly concludes his ency-

[33] Dahl, *After The Revolution?*, Ch. 2.

[34] Sale, *Human Scale*, Part Three, *passim*; Part Four, Ch. 10; Dickson, *The Politics of Alternative Technology*, Ch. 4.

[35] Cited in Lyons, *Sun!*, p. 51.

clopedic treatment of "labor and monopoly capital" with the observation that "worker's control," i.e., participatory democracy at the workplace, demands that workers assume "the scientific design, and operational prerogatives of modern engineering" and the "return of requisite technical knowledge to the mass of workers" but fails adequately to emphasize that the "demystifying of technology" that this transition entails necessitates as well a dramatic simplification of technology itself.[36] Technologies whose "operating modes [are] understandable by all,"[37] in other words, are the essential precondition for the competent political participation without which direct democracy cannot be effective. These are, of course, precisely the technologies to which contemporary ecological activists are committed.

For both reasons, then, participatory democracy is as dependent on alternative technology as alternative technology is dependent on participatory democracy. The struggle for one presupposes and reinforces the struggle for the other. Thus they are, at bottom, one struggle.

Consider now the dependency of participatory democracy on feminism. Genuine, nonrepressive direct democracy implies collective interactions in which each participant understands that recognition of others is the necessary condition for the self-recognition to which he or she aspires. Thus it is predicated on the participation of individuals who are psychologically prepared to enter into an authentic struggle for human recognition and to resist the temptation to short-circuit this struggle through manipulative, instrumental forms of behavior. To put this the other way around, participatory democracy is incompatible with the participation of individuals who have a psychological orientation toward political domination, who have (unconscious) needs to treat other individuals as the means to their own ends rather than as the beings on whose development their own development ultimately depends. But, as we have seen, instrumental, authoritarian psychological orientations tend to predominate, particularly among men, in contemporary industrial societies. A large part—probably even the better part—of the population of these societies is therefore emotionally unsuited for authentic participatory democracy. A commitment to the latter thus demands a corresponding commitment to a profound, far-reaching emotional transformation through which manipulative, objectifying needs are replaced with expressive or participatory needs.

It is just this transformation to which the feminist movement aspires. Its critique of aggressively male political styles is typically coupled with the insistence that men must learn—from women—to be more expressive and thus less apt to engage in the controlling forms of behavior that result from the repression of their feelings. At the same time, feminists have urged women

---

[36] Braverman, *Labor and Monopoly Capital*, p. 445. Ivan Illich, *Tools for Conviviality* (New York: Harper & Row, 1973).

[37] Dickson, *The Politics of Alternative Technology*, p. 103.

to refuse any longer to acquiesce in these forms of behavior and to become more self-assertive instead. Central to the feminist movement, then, is the struggle for precisely that psychological transformation of individual political actors without which genuine participatory democracy cannot exist. Solidarity with participatory democracy thus demands solidarity with feminism.

This is true for yet another reason. If participatory democracy means anything at all, it surely means the equal participation of all individuals in the decisions that affect their lives. Both the willingness and the ability of women actively and equally to participate in politics, then, are critical presuppositions for the operation of a participatory democracy that is something other than another form of male political rule. Under current conditions, however, both of these presuppositions remain largely unfulfilled. On the one hand, women who are expressive or relationally oriented are likely to be reluctant to enter a realm dominated by instrumentally oriented men and thus will eschew political participation in order to "let boys be boys."[38] On the other hand, the prevailing sexual division of labor that consigns women disproportionately or even exclusively to the private domestic functions of housework and child rearing prevents even those who would be willing from participating fully in active political life. Thus equal participation of women in politics—hence true participatory democracy—is contingent both on the psychological transformation of which I have already spoken and on the abolition of the existing sexual division of labor. And the feminist movement is as committed to this abolition as it is to this transformation. Once again the conclusion is inescapable that the feminist movement is an indispensable ally of the movement for participatory democracy.

Finally, let us examine the dependence of the feminist movement on the movements for alternative technology and participatory democracy. The feminist movement, we have seen, envisions a psychological transformation through which men become more expressive and less instrumental, more connected to the world around them and therefore less inclined to assume an objectifying stance toward this world. Opponents of this transformation have argued that the "feminization" it entails will leave men unable to identify with their work and thus unwilling to submit to the discipline on which modern technological development and economic growth depends.[39] They are undoubtedly correct: the "feminization" of men that the contemporary women's movement envisions pulls the emotional rug out from under the prevailing objectifying technologies and the obsession with growth with which they are associated. Precisely for this reason does a commitment to feminism demand a commitment to alternative, nonobjectifying technologies that enable human beings

[38] Dinnerstein, *The Mermaid and the Minotaur*, p. 157.

[39] Stephanie Engel, "Femininity as Tragedy: Re-examining the 'New Narcissism'," *Socialist Review*, No. 53 (September-October 1980), pp. 77-104.

to establish a reciprocal rather than exploitative relationship with nature and form the basis for a "steady-state" rather than growth-oriented economy.[40] Alternative technologies, in short, are the only technologies that can "materialize" the psychological orientation to the world that feminist liberation entails. Those who struggle for this liberation should therefore struggle for alternative technology as well.

Feminists should also struggle for alternative technology because this technology alone is compatible with the overcoming of the division between workplace and home, "male" realm of enterprise and "female" realm of domesticity, to which the feminist movement aspires. The emotional distance between these two realms that presently prevails will be eliminated in the sexually liberated society of the future in which men will assume an equal share of domestic tasks and women an equal share in enterprise. But the elimination of the emotional distance between these two worlds perforce implies the elimination as well of the geographic distance between them: just as the present emotional separation between workplace and home is rooted in and reinforced by the increasing physical distance between them, so the emotional reintegration of these worlds presupposes their spatial reunification.[41] Thus the small-scale community in which home and workplace are within easy—bicycling or even walking—distance of each other is the socio-geographical corollary of the feminist vision of the ultimate integration of the domestic and the productive realm. Only in such communities will it be possible, for example, for both men and women to alternate easily and equally between their child rearing and working responsibilities. We have seen, however, that such communities demand the decentralized, small-scale infrastructures that only alternative technologies provide. Alternative technologies are essential for the kind of communities without which the feminist vision of a reunification of home and work would be a hopelessly utopian vision.

Earlier we saw that the success of the movement for alternative technology depends decisively on the success of the feminist movement. Now we know that the reverse is equally true. Each movement implies, and nourishes, the other. Thus they, too, are ultimately but one movement.

To complete the picture: the feminist movement is as dependent on participatory democracy as it is on alternative technology. On the one hand, the demand for equal political power is a central feminist demand. On the other hand, and as I have already suggested, the prevailing hierarchical structures within which political power is exercised discourage the participation of women who have little or no tolerance for the aggressive, manipulative male political

---

[40] After completing this chapter I discovered that the same point is made by Sidney Oliver, "Feminism, Environmentalism and Appropriate Technology," *Quest: A Feminist Quarterly*, V (1980), pp. 70-80.

[41] Sale, *Human Scale*, pp. 257-58.

style that these structures demand. The existing bureaucratic and representative structures do not and cannot politically materialize the more expressive, relational orientation of women and are therefore incompatible with the demand of equal political power for women. It follows that this demand cannot be fulfilled in the absence of a profound political transformation that eliminates these structures in favor of ones that, in contrast, are hospitable to women's social-psychological orientations. This transformation, of course, is exactly what the partisans of participatory democracy have in mind.

Feminists should support participatory democracy for a second significant reason. Feminism is committed to the proposition that "the personal is the political": what goes on within the domestic realm is not purely private but is rather a legitimate subject for collective discussion and deliberation. The prevailing large-scale political units on which representative and bureaucratic structures are based, however, make it difficult if not impossible effectively to politicize the personal realm. Collective discourse and debate over domestic issues demands the elimination of these units and their associated structures in favor of political structures that are based on the intimate unit of the small-scale community. As we have seen, this is precisely what participatory democrats propose. In legitimatizing the community as a, if not the, central unit of decision making, participatory democracy politicizes domestic concerns such as child care and violence between spouses. In the short run, the likely consequence of participatory democracy is an increase in the political participation of women, whose place in the prevailing sexual division of labor obliges them to be disproportionately preoccupied with these concerns. In the long run, participatory democracy provides the appropriate political form for the collective expression of intimate community concerns by both women and men once this sexual division of labor has been overcome. Both the short-run and the long-run consequences of participatory democracy are essential for the ultimate success of the feminist movement. Once again, the implication is clear: devotion to the feminist movement demands devotion to the movement for participatory democracy.

Feminism as much depends on participatory democracy, then, as participatory democracy depends on feminism. These two movements are as symbiotically related to each other as each is to the movement for alternative technology. The demonstrated interdependence of all three movements confirms my contention that the victory of one requires the victory of the others and thus that their organizational unification is both possible and necessary. Possible, because all three movements are reciprocally interacting, mutually interdependent elements of an embryonic post-Instrumental mode of symbolization, of an entirely new civilization. Necessary, because in the absence of the nourishment and coordination that this unification would entail, this new mode of symbolization will not develop beyond its present embryonic

379

stage. Whether this unification and the development that is contingent on it will, in fact, occur, depends on whether the participants in the three movements come to recognize both its possibility and its necessity and thus to struggle to bring it about.

The recent formation of the Citizens Party in the United States is perhaps a sign of the emergence of this recognition and the struggle that follows from it. Whatever one thinks of the wisdom of the party's commitment to national electoral competition, it is undeniably the case that many of its activists are also committed to building a single organizational home for the feminist, participatory democratic, and ecology movements. It is my impression that many of the activists in the newly created "green" (ecology) parties in Western European industrial societies are similarly committed to all three movements and likewise conceive of their parties as the arena for their eventual unification.[42] The demonstration of the possibility and the necessity of this unification that I have undertaken is intended as a contribution to these and other similar organization efforts.

Although the organizational unification of the feminist, participatory democratic, and ecology movements is necessary, it is not sufficient for the maturation of the presently embryonic post-Instrumental mode of symbolization. The analysis in the preceding chapter demonstrated that a particular mode of symbolization implies a particular mode of child rearing; the structure of the relationship between the adult self and its sexual, political, and natural others is rooted in, and decisively dependent on, the structure of the relationship between the child and its parental others and the unconscious internalization of this relationship to which it gives rise. I suggested at a number of points, in fact, that a post-Instrumental mode of symbolization implies a post-mother-monopolized form of child rearing; the full flowering of liberatory relationships between the self and its sexual, political and natural others is possible only if these relationships are rooted in, and nourished by, the soil of shared parenting. If this is the case, then it follows that a post-Instrumental mode of symbolization will not be realized unless the struggles for feminism, participatory democracy, and alternative technology are complemented by the struggle for shared parenting, and the efforts to forge organizational unification are sufficiently encompassing to include this latter struggle as well. The ultimate success of the feminist, participatory democratic, and ecology movements is as dependent on the success of the movement for shared parenting as (we have seen) each of the first three movements is dependent on the other. It is also the case, as we shall see, that the fate of the movement for shared parenting is critically

[42] *In These Times* (September 3-9, 1980), p. 11.

380

dependent on the fate of these three movements. Thus the organizational unification of all four is essential.

Let us consider first the dependence of the three liberation movements on the movement for shared parenting. Although we may presume that the struggles of the activists in these movements for postinstrumental relationships are rooted in unconscious needs that developed in the course of the particular mode of mother-monopolized child rearing that they experienced, we also know that this mode of child rearing generates unconscious instrumental needs that limit their ability fully to achieve the postinstrumental relationships to which they aspire. Thus their conscious and unconscious struggle for liberation will be hampered by their unconscious needs for domination engendered by their earliest encounters with their parents. Feminists demand that men treat women more expressively and less instrumentally and that women no longer acquiesce in this instrumental treatment, but even the best-intentioned men and women who have been reared exclusively or even predominantly by their mothers will find it emotionally impossible entirely to fulfill these demands. The participatory democrat is committed to nonauthoritarian, nonhierarchical forms of politics, but even the most enthusiastic mother-raised supporters of these forms will be driven by unconscious needs for (paternal) authority that will inhibit their ability fully to create and perpetuate these forms. The ecologist argues in favor of a reciprocal, nonexploitative relationship with nature, but even the most ardent ecologist is not likely to be entirely free from the unconscious need to dominate nature that results from the form of mother-monopolized child rearing he or she experienced. In short, the behavior of this generation of mother-raised activists will necessarily fall short of the goals to which they are committed. Whether this will also be true—or as true—of the behavior of succeeding generations depends in important part on whether the present generation of activists abandons mother-monopolized child rearing and undertakes the shared parenting that can alone provide a satisfactory unconscious emotional foundation for the postinstrumental relationships to which they are committed.

There are indications that this task has, in fact, been taken up. *Ourselves and our Children*, the "Movement" successor to the widely read and extraordinarily influential *Our Bodies, Ourselves*, includes a chapter on "Sharing Parenthood" that both argues on its behalf and examines the obstacles—both psychological and social—that parents have encountered, and are likely to encounter in the future, to its implementation.[43] A more recent and extensive discussion of shared parenting appeared in *Socialist Review*, a decade-old American New Left journal with a current circulation of roughly 7,000.[44]

[43] (New York: Random House, 1978).
[44] Ehrensaft, "When Women and Men Mother," pp. 37-73.

381

Moreover, the fact that mother-monopolized child rearing has, as we have seen, become an object of serious critical theoretical analysis—in Dinnerstein's *The Mermaid and the Minotaur* and Chodorow's *The Reproduction of Mothering*—itself suggests that large numbers of people have found it to be increasingly problematical in practice and are attempting to replace it with forms of shared parenting. My own contact with the many couples I know who are committed to one or more of the three liberation movements to which this book is devoted leads me to observe that virtually all of them share child-rearing responsibilities to a far greater extent than did their parents. There is ample evidence, then, to support the conclusion that shared parenting has become the preferred mode of child rearing of the current generation of activists in the feminist, participatory democratic, and ecology movements.

Some evidence also suggests that the commitment to shared parenting extends beyond the rather narrow circles of the New Left. A couple of years ago a male-authored article appeared in *Ms.*, perhaps the only American feminist magazine with a large, "mainstream" constituency, touting the merits of the "Manly Art of Child Care."[45] Around the same time the San Francisco *Chronicle* detailed the trials and tribulations of a father who became a full-time "mother" for little more than two months.[46] The Academy Award-winning film of 1980, *Kramer vs. Kramer*, sympathetically depicts the efforts of a commercial artist working for a high-powered advertising agency to adjust to the responsibilities of caring for his young son after he has been "abandoned" by his mother. Among the recommendations of the recent White House Conference on the American Family was a proposal for flexible working hours which would, among other things, enable men to participate more readily in child care. In short, it is possible to point to a number of indications of the growing acceptability of the idea that men should be directly and intimately involved in the raising of their children. Thus it may even be the case that the support for the shared parenting on which the eventual success of the feminist, participatory democratic, and ecology movement depends is presently more extensive than the support for either one of these three movements.

The ultimate victory of the movement for shared parenting, however, is inseparably linked to the ultimate victory of the movements for feminism, participatory democracy, and alternative technology. Shared parenting is as dependent on these movements as these movements are dependent on shared parenting. This can be demonstrated through a brief analysis of the way in which the sexual, political, and technological domination challenged by these

---

[45] Kenneth Pitchford, *Ms.* (October 1978), pp. 96-99. After completing this chapter I discovered two magazines devoted to male parenting, one called *Nurturant Male* that was published during 1979 and another called *Co-Parent* that is still in existence.

[46] "A Father who Failed as a Mother," *San Francisco Chronicle*, September 6, 1978.

movements necessarily and drastically limits the extent to which parents of both sexes are able fully and equally to share the responsibilities—the burdens as well as the exhilaration—of child care.[47]

Consider first the man who is, in principle, committed to shared parenting. Given the prevailing patriarchal sexual division of labor, he is likely to be the primary breadwinner, either because he is the only full-time worker in his household or because his salary is probably far higher than that of his spouse. Under these circumstances, he may well feel that his work responsibilities outside the home are too onerous to leave him the time and energy fully to share in child care. Even where the man is not the primary bread-winner, or where he does not in fact believe that this status justifies his unequal participation within the home, he is unlikely to be willing and able equally to participate in what we now call "mothering." Having himself been socialized to be more instrumental than expressive, he is far less likely than his spouse to have developed the nurturing capacities on which successful mothering depends. He is therefore likely to discover that, whereas his spouse already knows how to mother, he does not: it is something that he must learn to do and that he can only learn to do with great difficulty. This difficulty, along with his own insecurities about being incompetent, gives even the most committed male proponent of shared parenting an incentive to backslide. This incentive, of course, is reinforced by the prevailing sexual division of labor of the society at large which encourages him to invest his ego in his work rather than in the home and thus enables him to compensate for his failures in child rearing by becoming more emotionally involved in his work. In all these ways, patriarchy functions to reduce drastically the likelihood that men who are committed to the principle of shared parenting will live up to this principle in practice.

Patriarchy discourages shared parenting in other ways as well. Even the most ardent female supporter of shared parenting is not likely to be entirely unambivalent about sharing child-care responsibilities with her male spouse. As Chodorow emphasizes, and as we saw in the last chapter, the female child's preoedipal relationship with her mother culminates in an unconscious relational orientation of which her own subsequent desire to mother a child is a conscious manifestation.[48] The woman, in contrast to her male mate, is emotionally equipped to mother and thus is likely to be far better at it. At the same time, since she lives in a patriarchal society whose structures drastically inhibit the exercise of her creativity outside the home, she is likely to feel that child rearing is the principal outlet for her creative energy, and, moreover, the only realm within which she is recognized as being more

[47] The following two paragraphs rely heavily on Ehrensaft, "When Women and Men Mother," pp. 37-73.

[48] The Reproduction of Mothering, passim.

competent than a man. Even if she is fortunate enough to be able to exercise competence outside child rearing, this latter activity is likely to be the only one in her life in which she exercises a certain measure of power. Thus she will be understandably reluctant to relinquish her traditional prerogatives in this realm and ambivalent about the invasion of this realm by her male spouse. Her participation in a patriarchal society, in short, inclines her to want to "mother" more than her mate and thus reinforces his desire to "mother" less. The net result is that genuinely shared parenting in practice is likely to be a rare exception to the general rule of disproportionate parenting by women even among the most dedicated contemporary supporters of this principle.

Since patriarchy so drastically limits the possibilities for authentically shared parenting, a commitment to shared parenting demands a commitment to an anti-patriarchal struggle. The absence of a sexual division of labor within the home presupposes the absence of the sexual division of labor throughout the society as a whole.[49] We already know, however, that the feminist struggle to eliminate this division of labor in the society at large cannot be won in the absence of the victory of the struggles for participatory democracy and alternative technology. It follows that the movement for shared parenting is as dependent on these two movements as it is on the feminist movement.

Earlier we saw that feminism, participatory democracy, and ecology are ultimately dependent on shared parenting. Now it should be clear that shared parenting is ultimately dependent on these three movements as well. The conclusion is inescapable, then, that all four movements are the reciprocally interacting, mutually interdependent elements of an emerging post-Instrumental mode of symbolization. The organizational unification of this new mode of symbolization must therefore embrace all four movements. The revolutionary organizations of the future will strive to coordinate, and thus to enhance, the struggles for feminism, participatory democracy, alternative technology, and shared parenting to which their members are all committed.

THE ORIGINS AND THE FUTURE OF THESE MOVEMENTS

There is no way to gauge with precision the present extent of support for these movements in contemporary Western industrial societies. But a good deal of admittedly impressionistic evidence suggests that it is substantial. I have already alluded to the indications of the increasing legitimacy of shared parenting in our society. The ecology movement has experienced a comparable development. After a decade of anti-nuclear power activism in the United States, it is now the case that a majority of the American population is opposed

[49] Ehrensaft, "When Women and Men Mother," p. 72.

384

to the construction of additional nuclear power plants in this country.[50] Although anti-nuke sentiment does not, of course, necessarily entail a commitment to alternative energy sources, it is nonetheless the case that popular enthusiasm for solar power in the United States has reached the point where a recent President would commit himself publicly to increased budgetary support for this alternative. There are other indications of a more generalized commitment to alternative technology. Kirkpatrick Sale estimates that the "several scores" of American magazines presently devoted to alternative technologies have "a combined circulation of . . . at least a million," and that there are now, worldwide, more than two thousand organizations involved in the production and distribution of these technologies.[51] Similarly, a 1975 survey by the Stanford Research Institute reported that some four to five million Americans are now living what the Institute rather quaintly refers to as a life of "voluntary simplicity," which it defines as a "life of frugal consumption, ecological awareness, individual reliance, and limited income."[52] It would appear, then, that a significant minority of the American population is already committed to a postinstrumental relationship between themselves and the natural surround.

There is also a good deal of evidence of a similarly widespread commitment to postinstrumental political relationships. On the one hand, intensified interest in participatory democracy within the workplace is reflected in the dramatic proliferation of "think tanks," conferences, and publications devoted to self-management across Western industrial societies over the past decade.[53] During this period of time, moreover, the governments of Sweden, Germany, Great Britain, and even the United States all enacted laws designed to facilitate workers' control and/or ownership of the firms in which they work. On the other hand, the commitment to participatory democracy within the community is, if anything, even more intense, at least in the United States. A recent study of the community control movement concludes that "In practically every sizeable state it is now possible to find statewide groups working for local control of health care, food-growing and marketing, housing, communications, alternative technology, energy development, education, and culture."[54] This nationwide development recently prompted the New York *Times* to proclaim, in a front-page story, that "Activist Neighborhood Groups are Becoming a New Political Force."[55] National coordination among such groups, moreover, is increasing: Massachusetts Fair Share, for example, is now allied

[50] Associated Press-NBC News Poll, reported in the *Chicago Sun-Times*, November 24, 1981.
[51] Sale, *Human Scale*, pp. 159-60.
[52] *Ibid.*, pp. 340-41.
[53] *Ibid.*, pp. 353-54.
[54] *Ibid.*, Part Four, Ch. 7, and p. 440.
[55] *Ibid.*, p. 439.

385

with seven other state-wide organizations, and ACORN has member groups in more than twenty states.[56]

The indications of popular support for the feminist movement are probably even more dramatic. The mass media of the United States and elsewhere have legitimated (and simultaneously exploited) the feminist challenge to the prevailing male-dominant sexual division of labor: the novels, movies, and television programs devoted to women's assault on "sex-typing" within and outside the home are by now so numerous that they may fairly be described as a staple of American popular culture. Organizational support for this assault is likewise substantial. The National Organization for Women, the mainstream yet increasingly leftish American women's organization, claims a current membership of roughly 100,000. A Harris survey of December 1975 revealed that a substantial majority of American women endorse the efforts of this and other, similar organizations.[57] Given the predominantly instrumental orientation of N.O.W., this overwhelming endorsement can by no means be taken as an indication of a comparable level of support for authentically postinstrumental male-female relationships. Yet even as early as 1970 almost one-third of the 3,000 women surveyed nationwide by Harris indicated that they would prefer their husbands to spend more time shopping, housecleaning, and taking care of children, and over 20 percent expressed agreement with the proposition that, "for the most part," women are an "oppressed group" in America.[58] This suggests—but does not, of course, demonstrate conclusively—sizable support for a postinstrumental solution to the problem of this oppression.

It would appear, then, that a postinstrumental sexual, political, and ecological consciousness has emerged among significant segments of the population of advanced industrial societies. This appearance is confirmed in a study by Ronald Inglehart of changing values in eleven Western capitalist societies. Inglehart finds that, depending on the particular country, from 7 to 14 percent of those surveyed embrace what he calls "post-Materialist" values—values that generally correspond to what I have called postinstrumental values—and that post-materialism is particularly pronounced "among the younger university-educated cohorts."[59] (Interestingly enough, Inglehart reports that the United States ranks second among all eleven nations in its proportion of post-

[56] Heather Booth, review of Harry C. Boyte, *The Backyard Revolution: Understanding the New Citizen Movement,* In These Times (November 19-25, 1980), p. 17.

[57] Cited in Sarah Evans, *Personal Politics: The Roots of Women's Liberation in the Civil Rights Movement and the New Left* (New York: Knopf, 1979), p. 221.

[58] *The Harris Yearbook of Public Opinion* (New York: Louis Harris and Associates, 1971), pp. 440, 444.

[59] Ronald Inglehart, *The Silent Revolution: Changing Values and Political Styles Among Western Publics* (Princeton, N.J.: Princeton University Press, 1977), pp. 38, 82.

materialists to materialists. This finding sheds important light on the classical thesis of American "exceptionalism," i.e., the thesis that revolutionary consciousness is peculiarly underdeveloped in America. Once this consciousness is redefined as a postinstrumental consciousness and many, if not most, adherents of traditional leftist parties and movements can therefore no longer be assumed to possess a revolutionary consciousness, American consciousness can no longer legitimately be interpreted as less revolutionary than elsewhere. Our post-Marxian theoretical transformation results, in other words, in a transformation in the meaning of American exceptionalism: the problem is now re-posed as the problem of accounting for the relatively underdeveloped nature of one form—namely Marxism—of nonrevolutionary, instrumental consciousness in America.) Indeed, Inglehart observes, among these cohorts "Post-Materialists are not far from constituting a majority"[60] in all eleven Western industrial societies. Thus the "greening of America" that Charles Reich celebrated a decade ago in his much-abused book by the same title is a "greening" of advanced capitalism as a whole: "Consciousness III"— Reich's term for a post-materialist, postinstrumental consciousness—was no mere short-lived fad peculiar to America but rather has become the permanent state of mind of a significant minority of the population of Western industrial societies.[61]

It nonetheless remains a minority consciousness. "Materialists," Inglehart concludes, "still outnumber Post-Materialists quite heavily in each of the countries surveyed."[62] Thus the "greening" of Western industrial societies has proceeded far less rapidly and uniformly than Reich anticipated ten years ago. It remains the case, in other words, that a substantial majority of the population of these societies thinks and acts within the framework of the Instrumental mode of symbolization and thus cannot be expected to support the postinstrumental movements for feminism, participatory democracy, and alternative technology. The future of these movements, then, depends not only on their organizational unification at current levels of popular support but also and critically on the possibility of a substantial, sustained increase in these levels of support. Intelligent speculation about the possibility of this increase in turn, demands a prior understanding of the origins of the support

[60] *Ibid.*, p. 83.

[61] Charles Reich, *The Greening of America* (New York: Random House, 1970). For recent evidence of the persistence of "post-materialist" values even in the face of the current capitalist economic slump, see Daniel Yankelovich "New Rules in American Life: Searching for Self-Fulfillment in a World Turned Upside Down," *Psychology Today* (April 1981), pp. 35-91, and Ronald Inglehart, "Post-Materialism in an Environment of Insecurity," *American Political Science Review*, 75 (December 1981), pp. 880-900. Inglehart concludes that "a decade's time series data indicate that Post-Materialism is a deep-rooted phenomenon with important political consequences" (p. 897).

[62] Inglehart, *The Silent Revolution*, p. 83.

that currently exists: we cannot know if a tree will grow to its full potential unless we know something about its roots.

The theory outlined in the preceding chapter locates the roots of the liberation movements with which we are preoccupied in the mode of child rearing their participants have experienced and in the unconscious character structures that result from this experience. As the dominant structure within the organic whole that is a mode of symbolization, the mode of child rearing establishes the limits within which adult learning can take place in the sexual, political, and technological dimensions of this whole. It follows that persistent lack of satisfaction with the experiences encountered in these dimensions will never in itself engender a transformation of the mode of symbolization, and will in fact contribute to this transformation only if it is accompanied by a transformation of the mode of child rearing. Thus, in the absence of this latter transformation, we should not expect that the frustration—however intense or frequent—that individuals encounter in the course of their instrumental relationships with their sexual, political, and natural others will produce anything other than further instrumental efforts to reduce these frustrations: the pollution engendered by instrumental exploitation of nature will give rise to yet another "technofix" solution, the failure of representatives effectively to represent their constituents will set in motion renewed efforts to make them truly accountable, and the exclusion of women from male-dominated instrumental roles will merely result in demands that they participate more equally in these same roles. A repudiation of instrumental in favor of postinstrumental solutions, on the other hand, presupposes that the unconscious foundation for the latter has been established in childhood; adult individuals will only be able to forge the elements of a new, post-Instrumental mode of symbolizing their relationship to their sexual, political, and natural others if their early relationship with their first significant other, i.e., their mother, has left them emotionally predisposed to do so.

Our theory thus leads to an examinaton of the specific form of mother-monopolized child rearing to which the present participants in the postinstrumental liberation movements were subjected. The expectation that such an examination will prove fruitful, moreover, seems particularly warranted in the light of the clearly generational character of these movements: all three of them are "youth" movements, the majority of whose participants have been born after World War II. We have already seen that, according to Inglehart, post-materialists are disproportionately found "among the younger university-educated cohorts." Inglehart notes that the educational background of individuals as well as the socioeconomic status of their fathers have an independent effect on their values, but he emphasizes that "when we have controlled for all these effects, a quite sizeable linkage persists between age cohort and value type." Indeed, he concludes that "the impact of a given generation unit's formative experience seems to be the most significant variable'' of them all. Inglehart speculates that "'child-rearing practices may be an important . . . variable'' in shaping this "formative experience,'' but he does not pursue this speculation.[63] This, in contrast, is precisely what our theory leads us to pursue: what distinctive mode of mother-monopolized child rearing did the post-World War II, post-materialist generation of supporters of the movements for feminism, participatory democracy, and alternative technology experience, and how did this experience prepare them psychologically to support these postinstrumental movements?

We have seen that women raised prior to World War II were far more likely than men to develop expressive rather than instrumental personalities. The more intense and extended preoedipal identification between female children and their mothers was the unconscious basis for a "solicitous,'' relational orientation to the world among women that differs dramatically from the aggressive, objectifying orientation among men who were raised by the same mothers.[64] Thus women in Western industrial societies have always been less emotionally prepared than men to relate instrumentally to the natural surround as well as to their fellow human beings. We should anticipate, then, that even in the absence of a transformation in the specific mode of mother-monopolized child rearing, many women would be unconsciously predisposed to favor reciprocal, noninstrumental relationships with their natural and social others and thus to support both the ecology movement and the movement for participatory democracy. Thus we need not look to a specific post-World War II transformation of child rearing to account for the psychological readiness of women to support these movements. (The willingness of previously "privatized'' women actively to *participate* in these "public'' movements, on the other hand, requires, and will receive, explanation.) For men it is different; in the absence of such a transformation, we should not expect that they will be emotionally prepared to support either ecology or participatory democracy. How then is it possible to account for their support for these movements?

In the last chapter I noted that child-rearing practices in the United States and other Western industrial societies since World War II have become far more indulgent and child-centered than they were in previous generations, and I suggested that this increase in nurturance, along with a decline in the availability of the father for "compensatory'' identification, has intensified and extended the period of primary identification between children and their mothers. Thus it is reasonable to hypothesize that post-World War II child-rearing practices have produced a generation of men whose unconscious mother-identification is far more pronounced than their male predecessors. I

[63] *Ibid.*, pp. 87, 96, 69.
[64] See above, Chapter Nine.

389

also suggested that the intensification of mother-identification has resulted in a diminution of the drive to engage in objectification: either nature is no longer symbolized as a mother against whom one must struggle or else individuals are no longer emotionally prepared to endure the postponement of gratification that this struggle demands, or both.[65] Given the increased salience of their preoedipal ties with their mothers, we should expect instead that increasing numbers of men will develop a more "connected," relational orientation to the world that approximates the one that women have traditionally developed and that leaves men, as well as women, with "solicitous impulses" toward nature. Thus post-World War II mother-raised men are likely to be far more emotionally hospitable than their fathers and grandfathers to nonobjectifying alternative technologies and to the more receptive, even playful, relationship with the natural surround that these technologies make possible. Male support for the ecology movement, in short, is rooted in a transformation of child-rearing practices that has decreased the psychological difference between women and men.

The same can be said of male support for participatory democracy. More relationally oriented men are far more likely than their predecessors to seek recognition from interpersonal relationships. And this concern for meaningful personal relationships is likely to lead traditionally publicly active men to be emotionally predisposed to favor participatory democracy, the one form of politics in which the personal and the political regularly and legitimately interpenetrate. It is plausible to hypothesize, then, that the preference of a post-World War II generation of men for less instrumental, more expressive forms of politics is rooted in their intensified and prolonged preoedipal relationships with their mothers and the more expressive, traditionally "feminine" unconscious orientations that result from this relationship. The emphasis on intimate participation, rather than distant representation, is an adult re-creation on the part of mother-identified men of their original unrepressed longing for oneness with their mothers; their search for political community is, at bottom, an effort to rediscover as adults the communion with her that they experienced as children.

This hypothesis receives support from a number of different sources. Con-

[65] This hypothesis receives support from a cross-cultural study that found "mother-child households," because they "favor the creation of mother-son dependency . . . are associated with low n-Achievement [achievement orientation]." It is also supported by a study of businessmen that discovered that "where the mother is strongly nurturant and overcompensating for the difficulties encountered in the relationship with the father, the degree of . . . self-confidence, and emotional independence achieved by these men would seem an unlikely outcome. Rather it would appear that the mother of the mobile man [successful businessman] is strict and severe in training practices, controlled and moderate in warmth and affection." Both studies are reported in David C. McClelland, *The Achieving Society* (Princeton, New Jersey: D. Van Nostrand, 1961), pp. 374, 404-405.

390

temporary psychoanalytic theorists confirm that the male personality transformation that I have outlined has indeed taken place. As we saw in the
preceding chapter, psychoanalysts like Kernberg and Kohut—as well as the
cultural critics, like Christopher Lasch, whom they have influenced—argue
that the "anal-compulsive" individual with an overly punitive superego is
no longer the dominant pathological type in American society; he is increasingly being replaced by the "narcissistic" individual with an underdeveloped
superego and an overdeveloped identification with his mother.[66] As Stephanie
Engel has recently pointed out, the thesis of the "new narcissism" amounts
to the claim that the modal male personality is becoming progressively more
"feminine":

> The augmented importance of emotional relatedness, embeddedness, and
> dependence, and the decline of radical emotional rupture and devastation
> (of castration threat) put the contemporary boy in an affective and de-
> velopmental position that looks much like that traditionally characteristic
> of little girls.[67]

Kernberg and Lasch's thesis that this transformation is entirely regressive, in
turn, must be interpreted as an expression of a "widespread fear of the
feminization of American society";[68] the assumption that the narcissistic
personality is wholly pathological participates in the characteristically male
psychoanalytic denigration of "female" psychology. The repudiation of this
patriarchal denigration of women and the re-assertion of the value of their
unconscious orientations lead, of course, to the very different conclusion that
the transformation to the narcissistic personality is an at least partly progressive, rather than wholly regressive, transformation.[69] Their patriarchal judgments notwithstanding, the theorists of the new narcissism demonstrate on
the basis of clinical evidence that there has, indeed, been a feminization of
the post-World War II generation of men and thus lend support to our thesis
that their disproportionate participation in the movements for alternative technology and participatory democracy derives precisely from such a transformation.

The fact that the participants in these movements seem to have been disproportionately recruited from upper-middle class, professional backgrounds
also lends support to our thesis. Both Richard Flacks and Kenneth Keniston

---

[66] Otto Kernberg, *Borderline Conditions and Pathological Narcissism* (New York: Jason Anderson, 1975); Heinz Kohut, *The Analysis of the Self* (New York: International Universities
Press, 1971).

[67] Engel, "Femininity as Tragedy," p. 97.

[68] *Ibid.*, p. 78.

[69] "Partly progressive," rather than wholly progressive, insofar as there are undoubtedly
pathological, as well as healthy, elements to the traditional modal female personality type.

found that activists in the university student movement from the mid to late 1960s were far more likely than nonactivists to have had professional parents.[70] If we assume that the participatory democrats and the ecologists of the 1970s were the student activists of the 1960s, then it follows that a disproportionate number of the participants in these two movements as well have been drawn from professional families. This conclusion is confirmed, moreover, by Inglehart's finding that post-materialist values are positively correlated with the educational level of the father of the respondents in all the Western capitalist societies for which these data exist.[71] The fact that many, if not most, participants in the ecology and participatory democratic movements have had highly educated, professional parents, in turn, bolsters our hypothesis that the transformation in child rearing that I have described engendered the unconscious emotional support for these movements. We learn from Lawrence Stone's massive history of the family in England from the sixteenth through the nineteenth centuries that major changes in child-rearing practices have typically been first undertaken by the professional classes,[72] and it is common knowledge that professional families in the United States were the first to adopt in widespread fashion the post-World War II, child-centered practices recommended by Dr. Spock. As the children of professional parents, then, the male supporters of ecology and participatory democracy were likely to have experienced precisely that form of child rearing that produces the intense and prolonged mother identification which, I have argued, is the unconscious basis for postinstrumental relationships between them and their natural and political others.

There is, finally, more direct evidence of this mother-identification among male New Leftists. Kenneth Keniston found that the maternal tie of the young radicals he interviewed at length "seems to have been particularly intense," and suggests that it is this tie that accounts for their "unusual *capacity for nurturant identification*" that he finds these participatory democrats to possess.[73] Flacks's interviews with University of Chicago activists also support the thesis that increased mother-identification is the unconscious foundation of student radicalism.[74] The fact that, at least in the United States, such an unusually high proportion of student radicals during the acme of this movement were Jewish men—men whose intense mother-identification has already

[70] Richard Flacks, "The Liberated Generation: An Exploration of the Roots of Student Protest," *The Journal of Social Issues*, 23 (July 1967), pp. 52-75; Kenneth Keniston, "The Sources of Student Dissent," *The Journal of Social Issues*, 23 (July 1967), pp. 103-37.

[71] Inglehart, *The Silent Revolution*, p. 80.

[72] Stone, *The Family, Sex and Marriage in England: 1500-1800*, pp. 449-50.

[73] *Young Radicals: Notes on Committed Youth* (New York: Harcourt, Brace & World, 1968), pp. 51-52, and "The Sources of Student Dissent," p. 120, emphasis in the original.

[74] Flacks, "The Liberated Generation."

become, thanks to Philip Roth and other Jewish-American writers, a staple of American literary folklore—lends further support to this thesis.[75]

If the intensified and prolonged preoedipal identification between men and their mothers leaves them emotionally prepared to support ecology and participatory democracy, it does not, however, leave them psychologically predisposed to support feminism. Indeed, if anything, exactly the opposite is the case. In the preceding chapter we saw that the peculiarly profound and persistent identification of primitive men with their mothers typically gives rise to a variety of particularly extreme misogynous practices that are designed to counteract this identification and thus to allow for the formation of a "normal" masculine identity. The intense mother-identification that unconsciously predisposes primitive man to nondominating relationships with nature and their male political partners simultaneously engenders a compensatory assertion of their masculinity that demands the radical subordination of the women with whom they interact. The extraordinarily painful separation from the mother that these men are obliged to undergo, in other words, produces an unconscious effort to deny their dependence on the mother that entails peculiarly extreme forms of domination over her symbolic representatives, i.e., over all women. If this is the case, then it follows that the closer, more extended preoedipal identification between post-World War II men and their mothers is likely to produce a fear and loathing of women that is, if anything, more intense than that to which pre-World War II mother-monopolized child rearing gave rise. We should not be surprised to discover, in other words, that male ecologists and participatory democrats have a particularly strong unconscious need to dominate women.

Nor should we be surprised to discover that this need will be expressed in the political relationships within the ostensibly participatory democratic organizations in which these men are involved. Faced with an unconscious conflict between his relational need for group participation and his misogynist need for domination, the male participatory democrat is likely to resolve this conflict by becoming a leader of the group and doing everything possible to discourage its women members from becoming the same. The male monopolization of positions of effective authority that is so characteristic of participatory democratic groups is rooted, in other words, in the particularly intense fear that the mother-identified men in these groups have of the authority of women. And this fear is also the basis of the willingness of men (as well as women) within these groups who are not leaders to acquiesce in the authority of the male "movement heavies" who are. This analysis of male authoritarianism within radical groups is confirmed by the finding of Stanley Rothman

[75] Stanley Rothman, "Group Fantasies and Jewish Radicalism: A Psychodynamic Interpretation," *The Journal of Psychohistory*, 6 (Fall 1978), pp. 211-40.

that the student activists to whom he administered TATs had "very high power drives."[76] Rothman is wrong, however, to conclude that this finding discredits the conclusions of Flacks, Keniston, and others concerning the expressive, nurturant capacities of these activists. Among post-World War II mother-raised men, these capacities and "high power drives" are not only not mutually exclusive but are, in fact, merely two sides of the same coin: both their emotional predisposition to intimate participation and their unconscious proclivity to dominate women are engendered by the intense and prolonged primary identification between their mothers and their selves that is formed in the course of post-World War II child rearing.

This brings us directly to the origins of the feminist movement. For it was the painful experience of women participants in the male-dominated participatory democratic movements of the 1960s that led them to inaugurate autonomous, radical feminist organizations in both the United States and Western Europe. The women who came to participate in these organizations, like the male members of participatory democratic and ecological organizations, were disproportionately recruited from upper-middle class professional backgrounds: "most of the women who identify with, or actively participate in, the women's liberation movement are white, upper-middle class, college-educated, and urban."[77] Like these men, moreover, "most feminists of the present era were born during the baby-boom years after World War II."[78] Thus we may presume that they experienced the same indulgent, child-centered mothering that male ecologists and participatory democrats experienced, and that their relational orientation was therefore, if anything, even more intense than that of past generations of mother-raised women. Unlike these women, however, the majority of contemporary feminists not only had nurturant mothers but also had highly educated mothers: as daughters of college-educated women who either worked outside the home (often in a professional capacity) or had worked during the war, they grew up with the expectation that they, too, would one day divide their time between their family and their career.[79] Why, then, did these "children of the 50s," in contrast to their mothers, come to challenge this division of labor?

I do not pretend to know the complete answer to this question. But I am certain that the experience of these women in the student movements of the mid- to late 1960s is an important part of this answer. These women, like their mothers, and their mothers before them, were obliged to confront the classical patriarchal double bind: to be equal you must be instrumental like

[76] Stanley Rothman, "Intellectuals and the Student Movement: A Post-Mortem," *The Journal of Psychohistory*, 5 (Spring 1978), p. 562.

[77] Glennon, *Women and Dualism*, p. 156. See also Evans, *Personal Politics*, Ch. 1.

[78] Glennon, *Women and Dualism*, p. 151.

[79] Evans, *Personal Politics*, Ch. 1.

a man, but if you are instrumental like a man you are no longer a woman. By all accounts, the response of their mothers to these contradictory imperatives was generally to resign themselves to their "inferior" status within the public world of work and to identify more wholeheartedly with the private world of the family for which they were chiefly responsible.[80] They did not, in other words, attempt to transcend the double bind entirely by repudiating the assumption of the supremacy of male instrumentalism on which it is based. But this is precisely what their militant daughters did after regularly experiencing this double bind in the male-dominated movements in which they participated. And regularly experience it they did. Marlene Dixon reports that a discussion of the "women's issue" at an SDS conference in December 1965 provoked "catcalls, storms of ridicule and verbal abuse, 'She just needs a good screw', or (the all-time favorite) 'She's a castrating female'." Women who demanded a plank on women's liberation at an SDS convention the following year "were pelted with tomatoes and thrown out of the convention." The effort of a woman to talk about the oppression of women at an antiwar demonstration in Washington, D.C., in January 1969 was met by male cries of "Take it off" and "Take her off the stage and fuck her!"[81] A woman who was protesting the failure of the male leadership of the 1967 National Conference for New Politics to consider a feminist resolution calling for 51 percent representation for women within the Conference received a condescending pat on the head by a male radical who told her: "Move on little girl; we have more important issues to talk about than women's liberation."[82]

The woman who received this by-now infamous pat on the head was Shulamith Firestone, author of the soon-to-be written radical feminist manifesto, *The Dialectic of Sex*. Firestone, as well as many other women who had been active in SDS and other male-dominated New Left organizations, left these organizations and went on to repudiate entirely the assumption of the supremacy of male instrumentalism underlying the double bind of which they were the victims.[83] Perhaps, as Dorothy Dinnerstein has suggested, the

[80] Mirra Komarovsky, "Cultural Contradictions and Sex Roles," in Robert F. Winch *et al.*, eds., *Selected Studies in Marriage and the Family* (New York: Holt, Rinehart & Winston, 1962), pp. 127-32.

[81] Both cited in Judith Hole and Ellen Levine, *Rebirth of Feminism* (New York: Quadrangle Books, 1971), pp. 112, 134.

[82] Cited in Evans, *Personal Politics*, pp. 198-99. American male New Leftists were by no means the only ones to indulge in miserably "macho" putdowns of their female comrades. Juliet Mitchell reports that European male leftists were often equally insulting. *Woman's Estate*, pp. 84-86.

[83] Thus Firestone conceptualizes the feminist cultural revolution as a transcendence of the (male) "technological mode" that will entail a synthesis between elements of that mode and the (female) "aesthetic mode" with which it has heretofore been inseparably linked. It is possible to argue, however, that this synthesis is far too heavily weighted on the side of the "technological

assertion of male superiority in the political realm became absolutely intolerable once this realm was being redefined as an expressive, participatory realm.[84] The subordination of women within this realm was bound to be experienced as especially infuriating since it was being enforced just at the point when this realm was becoming more emotionally attractive to, and dependent on the unique expressive capacities of these women. Men, in short, were telling women to "stay back or get out" of politics even as they worked for its "feminization." It is not surprising that women who received this advice proceeded to challenge the assumption of male supremacy in the name of "female" attributes and thus to find men wanting precisely because they lack these attributes. This reversal of values enabled feminists to de-legitimate their exclusion from politics and to argue that a properly feminized, authentically participatory political realm demands both that women play a leading role within this realm and that men learn from women how to be more "human" within it.

Our analysis of the psychological origins of the movements for feminism, participatory democracy, and alternative technology tells us that we should be neither overly pessimistic nor overly sanguine about the prospects for the success of these movements and thus of the post-Instrumental society they anticipate. On the one hand, the unconscious propensity to support these movements is rooted in child-rearing practices that are not likely to be abandoned by the more highly educated strata of the population who have relied on them now for two generations. Indeed, it may even be the case that these more indulgent, child-centered practices will spread to less educated strata of the population of Western industrial societies, although the economic circumstances of working parents in these strata may make it difficult for them to devote a great deal of attention to their newborn infants. It is, at any rate, very probable that the proportion of people who have experienced more nurturant forms of child rearing will increase progressively during the remaining years of this century. As Inglehart notes,

> the younger cohorts now entering [adulthood] are so much more highly educated than those dying off that the educational level . . . as a whole would continue to rise for at least a couple of decades even if the percentage receiving higher education were permanently frozen at its present level.[85]

mode"—as her notorious commitment to the "freeing of women from the tyranny of their reproductive biology by every means available" implies—and that, in the end, Firestone does not, in fact, make good on her claim to have repudiated the supremacy of "male" instrumentalism. *The Dialectic of Sex* (New York: Bantam, 1971), Ch. 9 and p. 206.

[84] See above, Chapter Nine.

[85] Inglehart, *The Silent Revolution*, p. 98.

Given the association between higher levels of education and child-centered child rearing, we can reasonably anticipate a progressive increase in the proportion of supporters of our three postinstrumental movements as well.

On the other hand, our analysis has revealed a profound obstacle to the unification of these three movements and thus to their eventual success. The more indulgent, child-centered mode of mother-monopolized child rearing simultaneously engenders unconscious male support for ecology and participatory democracy and unconscious male opposition to feminism. This mode of child rearing, then, is the basis for a significant psychological, and thus political, division between the adherents of the first two movements and the adherents of the last. Women are, and will continue to be, justifiably wary about undertaking joint efforts with the men of the ecological and participatory democratic movements as long as the lip service that they pay to feminist principles is regularly betrayed by their misogynist practices. As long as these practices, and the unconscious fear and loathing of women that they reflect persist, the prospects for the three movements eventually becoming one are dim indeed. And this unification, I have demonstrated, is a necessary precondition for the success of each and all of these movements.

In the short run, it is up to the male participants in ecology and participatory democracy who do pay lip service to feminist principles to do whatever they can to make their practice consistent with these principles. They must learn from the women with whom they relate exactly what this effort entails. At the same time, in their therapy sessions or their men's groups they must struggle to make conscious their unconscious hostility to women, the better to be able ultimately to reduce it. But there is, after all, only so much that they—that we—can do: we will never be able entirely to undo the misogynist effects of our mother-monopolized child rearing. The psychological barriers to the unification of all three movements will inevitably persist, if in attenuated form, among this generation of radical political people.

The extent to which these barriers will persist among future generations depends, in important part, on the extent to which the present generation is able to abandon mother-monopolized child rearing and create authentic forms of shared parenting. As we have seen, these forms are the only ones that will not culminate in unconscious hatred of women on the part of men and thus the only ones that can entirely eliminate the prevailing psychological obstacle to the unification of our three movements. The commitment to these movements thus demands a commitment on the part of their present male supporters to participate actively and equally in both the burdens and the joys of raising their children. The men of this generation are undoubtedly far more unconsciously predisposed to undertake this commitment than those of previous generations: their more expressive, relational orientation that results from their more intense, extended preoedipal tie with their mothers is likely to include an enhanced need to "mother" their children. But, as we have also seen, they, as well as the women with whom they share their lives, will inevitably also be fearful of, and resistant, to this undertaking. The success of this undertaking, then, is an entirely open question. All that can be said is that the ultimate fate of the movements for feminism, participatory democracy and alternative technology, and the post-Instrumental society of which these movements are the anticipation, is dependent on its outcome. Thus new meaning accrues to the words of the rock anthem of the Woodstock generation: "teach your children well."

BIBLIOGRAPHY

BOOKS

Adam, Barry D., *The Survival of Domination*. New York: Elsevier, 1978.

Agger, Ben, *Western Marxism: An Introduction*. Santa Monica, Calif.: Good-year, 1979.

Albert, Michael, and Robin Hannel, *Unorthodox Marxism*. Boston: South End Press, 1978.

Althusser, Louis, *Reading Capital*. London: New Left Books, 1970.

Arato, Andrew, and Eike Gebhardt, *The Essential Frankfurt School Reader*. New York, N.Y.: Urizen Books, 1978.

Arendt, Hannah, *The Human Condition*. Chicago: The University of Chicago Press, 1958.

Axelos, Kostas, *Alienation, Praxis, and Techne in the Thought of Karl Marx*. Austin: University of Texas Press, 1976.

Babb, Hugh W., ed., *Soviet Legal Philosophy*. Cambridge, Mass.: Harvard University Press, 1951.

Bachrach, Peter, *The Theory of Democratic Elitism*. Boston: Little, Brown & Co., 1967.

Bakan, David, *The Duality of Human Existence*. Chicago: Rand McNally & Co., 1966.

Balandier, Georges, *Political Anthropology*. New York: Pantheon Books, 1970.

Baran, Paul A., and Paul M. Sweezy, *Monopoly Capital*. New York: Monthly Review Press, 1966.

Bateson, Gregory, *Mind and Nature: A Necessary Unity*. New York: E. P. Dutton, 1979.

Baudrillard, Jean, *The Mirror of Production*. St. Louis, Mo.: Telos Press, 1975.

Bayer, Ronald, *Homosexuality and American Psychiatry: The Politics of Diagnosis*. New York: Basic Books, 1981.

Bell, Daniel, *The Coming of Post-Industrial Society*. New York: Basic Books, 1973.

———, *The Cultural Contradictions of Capitalism*. New York: Basic Books, 1976.

Bernstein, Richard J., *The Restructuring of Social and Political Theory*. Philadelphia: University of Pennsylvania Press, 1978.

Beyme, Klaus von, *German Political Studies*, Vol. I. Beverly Hills, Calif.: Sage Publications, 1974.

399

Birnbaum, Norman, ed., *Beyond the Crisis*. London: Oxford University Press, 1977.

Blackburn, Robin, ed., *Ideology in Social Science*. New York: Vintage Books, 1973.

Bookchin, Murray, *Post-Scarcity Anarchism*. Berkeley, Calif.: Ramparts Press, 1971.

Bottomore, T. B., ed., *Karl Marx: Selected Writings on Sociology and Social Philosophy*. New York: McGraw-Hill, 1964.

Braverman, Harry, *Labor and Monopoly Capital*. New York: Monthly Review Press, 1976.

Brown, Norman O., *Life Against Death*. New York: Vintage Books, 1959.

————, *Love's Body*. New York: Random House, 1966.

Carillo, Santiago, *"Eurocommunism" and the State*. London: Lawrence & Wishart, 1971.

Chagnon, Napoleon, *Studying the Yanomamo*. New York: Holt, Rinehart & Winston, 1974.

Chess, Stella, and Alexander Thomas, *Annual Progress in Child Psychiatry and Child Development*, Vol. 6. New York: Brunner/Mazel, 1973.

Chodorow, Nancy, *The Reproduction of Mothering*. Berkeley, Calif.: University of California Press, 1978.

Clastres, Pierre, *Society Against the State*. New York: Urizen Books, 1977.

Cockburn, Alexander, and James Ridgeway, eds., *Political Ecology*. New York: Times Books, 1979.

Cockburn, Alexander, and Robin Blackburn, eds., *Student Power*. Middlesex, England: Penguin Books, 1969.

Cohen, G. A., *Karl Marx's Theory of History: A Defence*. Princeton, N.J.: Princeton University Press, 1978.

Commoner, Barry, *The Closing Circle*. New York: Bantam Books, 1971.

————, *The Poverty of Power*. New York: Bantam Books, 1977.

Dahl, Robert A., *After the Revolution?* New Haven, Conn.: Yale University Press, 1970.

de Beauvoir, Simone, *The Second Sex*. London: Jonathan Cape, 1960.

DeMause, Lloyd, ed., *The History of Childhood*. New York: The Psychohistory Press, 1974.

Diamond, Stanley, *In Search of the Primitive*. New Brunswick, N.J.: Transaction Books, 1974.

Dickson, David, *The Politics of Alternative Technology*. Glasgow: William Collins & Co., Ltd., 1974.

Dinnerstein, Dorothy, *The Mermaid and the Minotaur*. New York: Harper & Row, 1976.

Domhoff, G. William, *Who Rules America?* Englewood Cliffs, N.J.: Prentice Hall, 1967.

Dreitzel, Hans Peter, ed., *Recent Sociology, no. 2*. New York: Macmillan, 1970.

Edwards, Richard, *Contested Terrain: The Transformation of the Workplace in the Twentieth Century*. New York: Basic Books, 1979.

Ehrenreich, Barbara, and Deirdre English, *For Her Own Good: 150 Years of the Experts' Advice to Women*. Garden City, N.Y.: Anchor Press/ Doubleday, 1978.

Ehrlich, Howard J. et al., *Reinventing Anarchy*. London: Routledge & Kegan Paul, 1979.

Eisenstein, Zeilah, *Capitalist Patriarchy and the Case for Socialist Feminism*. New York: Monthly Review Press, 1979.

Eliade, Mercia, *The Myth of the Eternal Return*. New York: Pantheon Books, 1954.

Ellul, Jacques, *The Technological Society*. New York: Vintage Books, 1964.

Evans, Sarah, *Personal Politics: The Roots of Women's Liberation in the Civil Rights Movement and the New Left*. New York: Knopf, 1979.

Figes, Eva, *Patriarchal Attitudes*. New York: Stein and Day, 1970.

Fleiss, Robert, ed., *The Psychoanalytic Reader*. New York: International University Press, 1948.

Fortes, M., and E. E. Evans-Pritchard, *African Political Systems*. London: Oxford University Press, 1940.

Freud, Sigmund, *An Outline of Psychoanalysis*. New York: Norton, 1949.

———, *Beyond the Pleasure Principle, SE*, Vol. XVIII. London: Hogarth Press and Institute of Psycho-Analysis, 1956.

———, *Civilization and its Discontents*. London: Hogarth Press, 1949.

———, *Group Psychology and the Analysis of the Ego*. London: Hogarth Press, 1949.

———, *Moses and Monotheism*, New York: Knopf, 1949.

———, *New Introductory Lectures on Psychoanalysis*. New York: Norton, 1965.

———, *The Ego and the Id, SE*, Vol. XIX. London: Hogarth Press and Institute of Psycho-Analysis, 1961.

Fried, Morton H., *The Evolution of Political Society*. New York: Random House, 1967.

Friedan, Betty, *The Feminine Mystique*. New York: Norton, 1963.

Fromm, Erich, *Escape from Freedom*. New York: Avon Books, 1941.

Giddens, Anthony, *The Class Structure of the Advanced Societies*. New York: Harper Torch Books, 1975.

Glennon, Lynda M., *Women and Dualism*. New York: Longman, 1979.

Goldfield, Michael, and Melvin Rothenberg, *The Myth of Capitalism Reborn*. San Francisco: Soviet Union Study Project, 1980.

Gombin, Richard, *The Radical Tradition*. New York: St. Martin Press, 1979.

Goode, William J., *World Revolution and Family Patterns*. Glencoe, Ill.: The Free Press, 1963.

Gornick, Vivian, and Barbara K. Moran, eds., *Women in Sexist Society: Studies in Power and Powerlessness*. New York: Basic Books, 1971.

Gouldner, Alvin W., *The Future of Intellectuals and the Rise of the New Class*. New York: Seabury, 1979.

————, *The Two Marxisms: Contradictions and Anomalies in the Development of Theory*. New York: Seabury, 1980.

Goux, Jean-Joseph, *Freud, Marx, Economie et Symbolique*. Paris: Editions du Seuil, 1973.

Grahl, Bart and Paul Piccone, *Towards a New Marxism*. St. Louis, Mo.: Telos Press, 1973.

Gramsci, Antonio, *Prison Notebooks*. New York: International Publishers, 1971.

Habermas, Jurgen, *Communication and the Evolution of Society*. Boston: Beacon Press, 1979.

————, *Knowledge and Human Interests*. Boston: Beacon Press, 1971.

————, *Legitimation Crisis*. Boston: Beacon Press, 1975.

————, *Theory and Practice*. Boston: Beacon Press, 1973.

————, *Toward a Rational Society*. Boston: Beacon Press, 1970.

Harrington, Michael, *The Twilight of Capitalism*. New York: Simon & Schuster, 1976.

The Harris Yearbook of Public Opinion. New York: Louis Harris and Associates, 1971.

Hays, H. R., *The Dangerous Sex*. New York: G. P. Putnam's Sons, 1964.

Hegel, G.W.F., *The Phenomenology of Mind*. J. B. Baillie, trans. New York: Harper & Row, 1967.

Heller, Agnes, *The Theory of Need in Marx*. New York: St. Martin's Press, 1976.

Hole, Judith, and Ellen Levine, *Rebirth of Feminism*. New York: Quadrangle Books, 1971.

Holloway, John, and Sol Picciotto, *State and Capital: A Marxist Debate*. Austin: University of Texas Press, 1978.

Horkheimer, Max, *Critical Theory*. New York: Herder and Herder, 1972.

Horkheimer, Max, and Theodor W. Adorno, *Dialectic of the Enlightenment*. New York: Herder and Herder, 1972.

Howard, Dick, *The Marxian Legacy*. New York: Urizen Books, 1977.

Howard, Dick, and Karl E. Klare, *The Unknown Dimension: European Marxism Since Lenin*. New York: Basic Books, 1972.

Hunt, Richard N., *The Political Ideas of Marx and Engels*. Pittsburgh: Pittsburgh University Press, 1974.

Illich, Ivan, *Tools for Conviviality*. New York: Harper & Row, 1973.

Inglehart, Ronald, *The Silent Revolution: Changing Values and Political Styles Among Western Publics*. Princeton: Princeton University Press, 1977.

Irigaray, Luce, *Speculum: De L'Autre Femme*. Paris: Les Editions de Minuit, 1974.

Janowitz, Morris, *The Last Half-Century: Societal Change and Politics in America*. Chicago: University of Chicago Press, 1978.

Kardiner, Abram, *The Psychological Frontiers of Society*. New York: Columbia University Press, 1945.

Keniston, Kenneth, *Young Radicals: Notes on Committed Youth*. New York: Harcourt, Brace & World, 1968.

Kernberg, Otto, *Borderline Conditions and Pathological Narcissism*. New York: Jason Anderson, 1975.

Kohut, Heinz, *The Analysis of the Self*. New York: International Universities Press, 1971.

Kolodny, Annette, *The Lay of the Land*. Chapel Hill: University of North Carolina Press, 1975.

Kosik, Karol, *Dialectics of the Concrete*. Holland, Boston: D. Reidel Pub. Co., 1976.

Lasch, Christopher, *Haven in a Heartless World*. New York: Basic Books, 1977.

————, *The Culture of Narcissism*. New York: Norton, 1978.

Latham, Earl, *The Group Basis of Politics*. Ithaca, N.Y.: Cornell University Press, 1952.

Leiss, William, *The Domination of Nature*. New York: George Braziller, 1972.

Lewis, John, ed., *Beyond Chance and Necessity*. London: Garnstone Press, 1974.

Lindberg, Leon N., Robert Alford, Colin Crouch, and Claus Offe, eds., *Stress and Contradiction in Modern Capitalism*. Lexington, Mass.: Lexington Books, 1975.

Lovins, Amory, *Soft Energy Paths*. Cambridge, Mass.: Ballinger, 1977.

Lukacs, Georg, *History and Class Consciousness*. Cambridge, Mass.: MIT Press, 1971.

Lyons, Stephen, ed., *Sun!: A Handbook for the Solar Decade*. San Francisco: Friends of the Earth, 1978.

Maccoby, Elanor E., T. M. Newcomb, and E. L. Hartley, eds., *Readings in Social Psychology*. New York: Holt, Rinehart & Winston, 1947.

McCourt, Kathleen, *Working-Class Women and Grass-Roots Politics*. Bloomington: Indiana University Press, 1977.

Mackinnon, Catherine A., *Sexual Harassment of Working Women*. New Haven, Conn.: Yale University Press, 1979.

403

Mahler, Margaret, *On Human Symbiosis and the Vicissitudes of Individuation.* New York: International Universities Press, 1968.

Mallet, Serge, *Essays on the New Working Class.* St. Louis, Mo.: Telos Press, 1976.

Mandel, Ernest, *Marxist Economic Theory*, Vol. II. New York: Monthly Review Press, 1968.

Marcuse, Herbert, *An Essay on Liberation.* Boston: Beacon Press, 1969.

————, *Counter-Revolution and Revolt.* Boston: Beacon Press, 1972.

————, *Eros and Civilization.* Boston: Beacon Press, 1955.

————, *Five Lectures.* Boston: Beacon Press, 1970.

————, *One-Dimensional Man.* Boston: Beacon Press, 1964.

————, *Studies in Critical Philosophy.* Boston: Beacon Press, 1973.

Marx, Karl, *Capital*, Vol. 1. New York: International Publishers, 1967.

————, *Grundrisse: Foundations of the Critique of Political Economy.* Middlesex, England: Penguin Books, 1973.

————, *Theories of Surplus Value*, Vol. II. London: Lawrence & Wishart, 1969.

————, *The Poverty of Philosophy.* New York: International Publishers, 1967.

K. Marx and F. Engels on Religion. Moscow: Foreign Languages Publishing House, 1957.

Marx, K., and F. Engels, *Selected Works.* New York: International Publishers, 1968.

Mauss, Marcel, *Sociologie et Anthropologie.* Paris: Press Universitaires de France, 1950.

Maybury-Lewis, David, *The Savage and the Innocent.* Cleveland and New York: World Publishing Co., 1965.

McCarthy, Thomas, *The Critical Theory of Jurgen Habermas.* Cambridge, Mass.: MIT Press, 1978.

McClelland, David C. *The Achieving Society.* Princeton, N.J.: D. Van Nostrand, 1961.

McLean, George F., ed., *Man and Nature.* Calcutta: Oxford University Press, 1978.

McLellan, David, *Karl Marx: Selected Writings.* Oxford: Oxford University Press, 1977.

————, *Marx Before Marxism.* London: Macmillan, 1970.

————, *The Thought of Karl Marx.* New York: Harper & Row, 1971.

Mead, Margaret, *Male and Female.* New York: William Morrow & Co., 1949.

Merchant, Carolyn, *The Death of Nature.* New York: Harper & Row, 1980.

Meszaros, Istvan, *Marx's Theory of Alienation.* London: Merlin Press, 1970.

Middleton, John, and David Tait, eds., *Tribes Without Rulers*. London: Routledge & Kegan Paul, 1958.

Miliband, Ralph, *Marxism and Politics*. Oxford: Oxford University Press, 1977.

————, *The State in Capitalist Society*. New York: Basic Books, 1969.

Miller, A. V., *Hegel's Philosophy of Nature*. Oxford: The Clarendon Press, 1970.

Mitchell, Juliet, *Psychoanalysis and Feminism*. New York: Vintage Books, 1974.

————, *Woman's Estate*. New York: Vintage Books, 1971.

Mitscherlich, Alexander, *Society Without the Father*. New York: Schocken Books, 1970.

Montagu, Ashley, *Touching: The Human Significance of the Skin*. New York: Columbia University Press, 1971.

Munson, Ronald, ed., *Man and Nature: Philosophical Issues in Biology*. New York: Delta Books, 1971.

Murdock, George Peter, *Social Structure*. New York: Macmillan Co., 1949.

Murphy, Yolanda, and Robert Murphy, *Women of the Forest*. New York: Columbia University Press, 1974.

Ollman, Bertell, *Alienation: Marx's Concept of Man in Capitalist Society*. Cambridge: Cambridge University Press, 1971.

O'Neill, John, ed., *On Critical Theory*. New York: The Seabury Press, 1976.

Ophuls, William, *Ecology and the Politics of Scarcity*. San Francisco: W. H. Freeman and Co., 1977.

Parsons, Talcott, *Essays in Sociological Theory*. New York: Free Press, 1954.

————, *Social Structure and Personality*. Glencoe, Ill.: The Free Press, 1964.

Parsons, Talcott, and Robert F. Bales, *Family, Socialization and Interaction Process*. Glencoe, Ill.: The Free Press, 1955.

Parsons, Talcott, and Edward A. Shills, eds., *Toward a General Theory of Action*. New York: Harper & Row, 1962.

Pateman, Carole, *Participation and Democratic Theory*. Cambridge, Eng.: Cambridge University Press, 1970.

Perez-Diaz, Victor M., *State, Bureaucracy and Civil Society*. London: Macmillan Press Ltd., 1978.

Piven, Frances Fox, and Richard A. Cloward, *Regulating the Poor*. New York: Vintage Books, 1972.

Polanyi, Karl, *The Great Transformation*. Boston: Beacon Press, 1957.

Political Systems and the Distribution of Power, A.S.A. Monographs 2. London: Tavistock Publications; New York: Frederick A. Praeger, 1965.

Polsby, Nelson, *Community Power and Political Theory*. New Haven, Conn.: Yale University Press, 1963.

Poster, Mark, *Critical Theory of the Family*. New York: Seabury, 1978.

Poulantzas, Nicos, *Pouvoir Politique et Classes Sociales*, Vol. I. Paris: Maspero, 1971.

———, *State, Power, Socialism*. London: New Left Books, 1978.

Rader, Melvin, *Marx's Interpretation of History*. New York: Oxford University Press, 1979.

Rawls, John, *A Theory of Justice*. Cambridge, Mass.: Harvard University Press, 1971.

Reich, Wilhelm, *The Mass Psychology of Fascism*. New York: Farrar, Straus & Giroux, 1970.

———, *Sex-Pol*. New York: Vintage Books, 1972.

———, *The Sexual Revolution*. New York: Farrar, Straus and Giroux, 1970.

Reiter, Rayna, ed., *Toward an Anthropology of Women*. New York: Monthly Review Press, 1975.

Rescher, Nicholas, *Distributive Justice*. New York: Bobbs-Merrill, 1966.

Ricoeur, Paul, *Freud and Philosophy*. New Haven, Conn.: Yale University Press, 1970.

Ridgeway, James, *Energy-Efficient Community Planning*. Emmaus, Pennsylvania: The J. G. Press, n.d.

Rifkin, Jeremy, *Entropy: A New World View*. New York: Viking, 1980.

Rosaldo, Michelle Zimbalist, and Louise Lamphere, *Women, Culture and Society*. Stanford, Calif.: Stanford University Press, 1974.

Rothman, Harry, *Murderous Providence*. London: Rupert Hart-Davis, 1972.

Rowbotham, Sheila, *Woman's Consciousness, Man's World*. Middlesex, England: Penguin Books, 1973.

Sale, Kirkpatrick, *Human Scale*. New York: Coward, McCann & Geoghegan, 1980.

Sahlins, Marshall, *Culture and Practical Reason*. Chicago: University of Chicago Press, 1976.

Sargent, Lydia, ed., *Women and Revolution*. Boston: South End Press, 1981.

Sartre, Jean-Paul, *Critique of Dialectical Reason*. London: New Left Books, 1976.

Schmidt, Alfred, *The Concept of Nature in Marx*. London: New Left Books, 1971.

Schoolman, Morton, *The Imaginary Witness: The Critical Theory of Herbert Marcuse*. New York: The Free Press, 1980.

Schram, Stuart R., *The Political Thought of Mao Tse-Tung*. New York: Praeger, 1963.

Schumacher, E. F., *Small is Beautiful*. New York: Harper & Row, 1973.

Seaton, S. Lee, and Henri M. Claessen, *Political Anthropology: The State of the Art*. The Hague: Mouton Publishers, 1979.

Sennet, Richard, *The Uses of Disorder*. New York: Vintage Books, 1971.

Service, Elman R., *Origins of the State and Civilization*. New York: Norton, 1975.

Shaw, William H., *Marx's Theory of History*. Stanford, Calif.: Stanford University Press, 1978.

Shepard, Paul, and Daniel McKinley, eds., *The Subversive Science: Essays Toward an Ecology of Man*. Boston: Houghton Mifflin Co., 1969.

Slater, Philip E., *Earthwalk*. New York: Anchor Press, 1974.

———, *The Glory of Hera*. Boston: Beacon Press, 1968.

———, *The Pursuit of Loneliness*. Boston: Beacon Press, 1970.

Spitz, Rene, *No and Yes*. New York: International Universities Press, Inc., 1957.

———, *The First Year of Life*. New York: International Universities Press, 1965.

Stephens, William N., *The Family in Cross-Cultural Perspective*. New York: Holt, Rinehart and Winston, 1963.

———, *The Oedipus Complex: Cross-Cultural Evidence*. Glencoe, Ill.: The Free Press, 1962.

Stone, Lawrence, *The Family, Sex and Marriage in England: 1500-1800*. New York: Harper & Row, 1977.

Tanner, Leslie, B., ed., *Voices From Women's Liberation*. New York: Mentor, 1970.

Taylor, Charles, *Hegel*. Cambridge, Eng.: Cambridge University Press, 1975.

Therborn, Goran, *Science, Class and Society*. London: New Left Books, 1976.

Tucker, Robert C., ed., *The Marx-Engels Reader*, first ed. New York: Norton, 1972.

Unger, Roberto, *Knowledge and Politics*. New York: The Free Press, 1975.

Weinbaum, Batya, *The Curious Courtship of Women's Liberation and Socialism*. Boston: South End Press, 1978.

Weinstein, James, *The Corporate Ideal in the Liberal State*. Boston: Beacon Press, 1968.

Weinstein, James, and David W. Eakins, eds., *For a New America*. New York: Vintage Books, 1970.

Wellmer, Albrecht, *Critical Theory of Society*. New York: Herder and Herder, 1971.

Werner, Emmy Elizabeth, *Cross-Cultural Child Development*. Monterey, Calif.: Brooks/Cole, 1979.

Whiting, Beatrice B., ed., *Six Cultures: Studies of Child Rearing*. New York: John Wiley & Sons, 1963.

Whiting, John W. M., and Irvin L. Child, *Child Training and Personality*. New Haven, Conn.: Yale University Press, 1953.

Wilden, Anthony, *System and Structure: Essays in Communication and Exchange*. London: Tavistock Publications, 1972.

Winch, Robert F., Robert McGinnis, and Herbert M. Barringer, eds., *Selected Studies in Marriage and the Family*. New York: Holt, Rinehart & Winston, 1962.

Wolfe, Alan, *The Limits of Legitimacy*. New York: The Free Press, 1977.

Women's Liberation and The Socialist Revolution. New York: Pathfinder Press, 1979.

Work in America. Cambridge, Mass.: MIT Press, 1973.

Wright, Erik Olin, *Class, Crisis and the State*. London: New Left Books, 1978.

PERIODICALS

Adamson, Walter L., review of G. A. Cohen, *Karl Marx's Theory of History: A Defence*; Melvin Rader, *Marx's Interpretation of History*; and William H. Shaw, *Marx's Theory of History* in *History and Theory*, 19 (February 1980), 186-204.

Balbus, Isaac, "Commodity Form and Legal Form: An Essay on the 'Relative Autonomy' of the Law," *Law & Society Review*, 11 (Winter 1977), 571-88.

———, "Ruling Elite Theory vs. Marxist Class Analysis," *Monthly Review*, 23 (May 1971), 36-46.

Best, Michael, H., and William E. Connolly, "Politics and Subjects: The Limits of Structural Marxism," *Socialist Review*, No. 48 (November-December 1979), 75-99.

Booth, Heather, review of Harry C. Boyte, *The Backyard Revolution: Understanding the New Citizen Movement, In These Times* (November 19-25, 1980), p. 17.

Burton, Roger V., and John W. Whiting, "The Absent Father and Cross-Sex Identity," *Merril-Palmer Quarterly of Behavior and Development*, 7, (April 1961), 85-95.

Cardan, Paul, "Marxisme et theorie revolutionnaire," *Socialisme ou barbarie*, No. 39 (March-April 1965), 16-66.

Castoriadis, Carlos, "From Marx to Aristotle . . . from Aristotle to Us," *Social Research*, No. 45 (Winter 1978), 667-738.

Clark, John, "Marx, Bakunin and the Problem of Social Transformation," *Telos*, No. 42 (Winter 1979-80), 80-97.

Dahl, Robert A., "A Critique of the Ruling Elite Model," *American Political Science Review*, 52 (June 1958), 463-69.

408

DeMause, Lloyd, "The Psychogenic Theory of History," *Journal of Psychohistory*, 4 (Winter 1977), 253-67.

DiNorcia, Vincent, "From Critical Theory to Critical Ecology," *Telos*, No. 22 (Winter 1974-75), 85-95.

Ehrensaft, Diane, "When Women and Men Mother," *Socialist Review*, No. 49 (January-February 1980), 37-73.

Emmanuel, Arghiri, "The State in the Transition Period," *New Left Review*, Nos. 113-114 (January-April 1979), 111-31.

Engel, Stephanie, "Femininity as Tragedy: Re-examining the 'New Narcissism'," *Socialist Review*, No. 53 (September-October 1980), 77-104.

Esping-Anderson, Gosta, et al., "Modes of Class Struggle and the Capitalist State," *Kapitalistate*, Nos. 4-5 (Summer 1976), 186-220.

Fay, Margaret, review of *State and Capital: A Marxist Debate*, in *Kapitalistate*, No. 7 (1978), 130-52.

Flacks, Richard, "The Liberated Generation: An Exploration of the Roots of Student Protest," *The Journal of Social Issues*, 23 (July 1967), 52-75.

Fyodorov, Yevgeny, "Against the Limits to Growth," *New Scientist*, 57 (February 22, 1973), 431-32.

Gilan, Garth Jackson, "Toward a Critical Conception of Semiotics," *Cultural Hermeneutics*, 3 (July 1976), 407-27.

Glucksmann, Andre, "A Ventriloquist Structuralism," *New Left Review*, No. 72 (March-April 1972), 68-92.

Godelier, Maurice, "Infrastructure, Societies and History," *New Left Review*, No. 112 (November-December 1978), 84-96.

Gold, David A., Clarence Y. Lo, and Erik Olin Wright, "Recent Developments in Marxist Theories of the Capitalist State," *Monthly Review*, 27 (October-November 1975), 29-43, 36-51.

Gorz, Andre, "Technical Intelligence and the Capitalist Division of Labor," *Telos*, No. 12 (Spring 1972), 27-41.

Gouldner, Alvin W., "Prologue to a Theory of Revolutionary Intellectuals," *Telos*, No. 26 (Winter 1975-76), 3-36.

Habbib, Seyla Ben, review of Thomas McCarthy, *The Critical Theory of Jurgen Habermas,* in *Telos*, No. 40 (Summer 1979), 177-87.

Habermas, Jurgen, "Ernst Bloch—A Marxist Romantic," *Salmagundi*, No. 10-11 (Fall-Winter 1969-70), 311-24.

Katznelson, Ira, "Considerations on Social Democracy in the United States," *Comparative Politics*, No. 11 (October 1978), 77-99.

Keniston, Kenneth, "The Sources of Student Dissent," *The Journal of Social Issues*, 23 (July 1967), 103-37.

Lichtman, Richard, "Marx and Freud," *Social Revolution*, No. 30 (October-December 1976), 3-55; No. 33 (May-June 1977), 59-84; No. 36 (November-December 1977), 37-78.

Long, Elizabeth, review of Juliet Mitchell, *Psychoanalysis and Feminism*, in *Telos*, No. 20 (Summer 1974), pp. 183-89.

Marglin, Stephen, "What do Bosses Do?" *Review of Radical Political Economics*, 6 (Summer 1974), 33-60.

Miliband, Ralph, "Poulantzas and the Capitalist State," *New Left Review*, No. 82 (November-December 1973).

Miller, James, review of Ralph Miliband, *Marxism and Politics*, in *Telos*, No. 36 (Summer 1978), 183-91.

Mishra, Ramesh, "Technology and Social Structure in Marx's Theory: An Exploratory Analysis," *Science & Society*, 43 (Summer 1979), 132-57.

Offe, Claus, "Political Authority and Class Structures—an Analysis of Late Capitalist Societies," *International Journal of Sociology*, 2 (Spring 1972), 73-108.

Oliver, Sidney, "Feminism, Environmentalism and Appropriate Technology," *Quest: A Feminist Quarterly*, 5 (1980), 70-80.

Poulantzas, Nicos, "The Capitalist State: A Reply to Miliband and Laclau," *New Left Review*, No. 95 (January-February 1976).

———, "The State and the Transition to Socialism," *Socialist Review*, No. 38 (March-April 1978), 9-39.

———, "Towards a Democratic Socialism," *New Left Review*, No. 109 (May-June 1978), 75-87.

Przeworski, Adam, "Proletariat into a Class: The Process of Class Formation from Karl Kautsky's *The Class Struggle* to Recent Controversies," *Politics and Society*, 7 (1977), 343-401.

Rothman, Stanley, "Group Fantasies and Jewish Radicalism: A Psychodynamic Interpretation," *The Journal of Psychohistory*, 6 (Fall 1978), 211-40.

———, "Intellectuals and the Student Movement; A Post-Mortem," *The Journal of Psychohistory*, 5 (Spring 1978), 551-66.

Ruddick, Sarah, "Maternal Thinking," *Feminist Studies*, 6 (Summer 1980), 342-67.

Sahlins, Marshall, "La Première société d'abondance," *Les Temps modernes*, 268 (October 1968), 641-80.

"A Father Who Failed as a Mother," *San Francisco Chronicle*, September 6, 1978.

Singer, Peter, "On Your Marx," *New York Review of Books* (December 20, 1979), 44-47.

Slater, Philip E., "Toward a Dualistic Theory of Identification," *Merril-Palmer Quarterly of Behavior and Development*, 7 (April 1961), 113-26.

Traub, Rainer, "Lenin and Taylor: The Fate of 'Scientific Management' in the (Early) Soviet Union," *Telos*, No. 37 (Fall 1978), 82-92.

Vajda, Mihaly, "The State and Socialism," *Social Research*, No. 45 (Winter 1978), 844-65.

Whitebook, Joel, "Pre-Market Economics: The Aristotelian Perspective," *Dialectical Anthropology*, 3 (August 1978), 197-220.

———, "The Problem of Nature in Habermas," *Telos*, No. 40 (Summer 1979), 41-69.

Whiting, Beatrice, "Sex Identity Conflict and Physical Violence: A Comparative Study," *American Anthropologist* 47 (December 1965 Supp.), 123-40.

Yankelovich, Daniel, "New Rules in American Life: Searching for Self-Fulfillment in a World Turned Upside Down," *Psychology Today* (April 1981), 35-91.

Zaretsky, Eli, "Capitalism, the Family, and Personal Life," *Socialist Revolution*, Nos. 13-14 (January-April 1973), 66-125, and No. 15 (May-June 1973), 19-70.

———, "Male Supremacy and the Unconscious," *Socialist Revolution*, Nos. 21-22 (January 1975), 7-55.

INDEX

accumulation, primitive, 141,

ACORN, 386

actually existing socialism, 62, 85

Adorno, T. W., 283

Agger, Ben, 276

Albert, Michael, 326

alienation, of the capitalist, 43; from nature, 42; from objects, 42-45; from people, 45-47

alternative technology, 366-67, 371-76

Althusser, Louis, 33-36, 186

anarchism, 326

Annenkov, P. V., 32

anthropocentrism, 158, 160, 273

Aristotle, 133

authoritarian character structure, 201-18

Axelos, Kostas, 275n

Bachofen, Johann Jacob, 80

Bacon, Sir Francis, 240-41, 272

Bakunin, Mikhail B., 110, 120n

Baran, Paul A., 69

base-superstructure, 22-24; in Habermas, 228-30; in Reich, 207

basic repression, 238

Bateson, Gregory, 258

Baudrillard, Jean, 34

Bell, Daniel, 343

Benston, Margaret, 68

Bloch, Ernst, 274n

Bookchin, Murray, 372

Braverman, Harry, 145, 148, 153n, 375

Brown, Norman O., 7, 264, 329, 338, 352; on the domination of nature, 292-302; on primitive societies, 295-96

Brunswick, Ruth Mack, 306n

bureaucratic state, 331-33

capitalist mode of production, 37-47, 75-76

Cardan, Paul (Cornelius Castoriadis), 34

Castro, Fidel, 155

character structure, 203

child rearing: determining power of, 345-51; unders the old regime, 317n; in primitive societies, 316-17, 320; in representative

democracies, 331; in western industrial societies, 316-17, 341-42. *See also* mother-monopolized child rearing

China, 74, 138

Chodorow, Nancy, 308, 314, 382; on female preoedipal stage, 337, 341, 383

Christianity, 342n

Citizens Party, 370, 380

class struggle theories, 104-108

Cloward, Richard A., 107

Cohen, G. A., 17n, 24n, 142n

commodity form, 37, 102

Commoner, Barry, 127, 138, 362, 370

communicative action, 219. *See also* symbolic interaction

communicative competence, 221-24

communism, 19, 42

concrete totality, 26-27

consciousness, false, 56, 203

Council Communism, 55n, 122-23, 202

DNA molecule, 347-49

Dahl, Robert A., 374

death instinct, 235-36, 292-95

de Beauvoir, Simone, 335

DeMause, Lloyd, 350

democracy, participatory, 84-86, 108-109, 357-61, 371-80; representative, 108-109, 330-31, 358-61

derivation theories, 101-104

Diamond, Stanley, 329

dictatorship of the proletariat, 74, 75n, 85, 112-13, 113n

Dinnerstein, Dorothy, 7, 265, 297n, 302, 341, 352, 382, 395; on domination of nature, 335-40; on patriarchy, 306-315; on political domination, 323-27

Domhoff, G. William, 87

domination, 3-4, 12

Durkheim, Emile, 184

East European state socialism, 138

ecofeminism, 369

ecology, 126-28, 362-67

Eisenstein, Zeilah, 77, 82n

413

414

Library of Congress Cataloging in Publication Data

Balbus, Isaac D.
  Marxism and domination.

  Bibliography: p.
  Includes index.
  1. Communist state.   2. Communism and psychology.
3. Communism and society.   4. Dominance (Psychology)
I. Title.
JC474.B336   335.4'1   82-47582
ISBN 0-691-07621-9   AACR2
ISBN 0-691-02210-0 (pbk.)